Fodor's

National Parks of the West

FOURTH EDITION

Fodor's Travel Publications, Inc.
New York • Toronto • London • Sydney • Auckland
www.fodors.com/

Fourth Edition

ISBN 0–679–03509–5

Fodor's National Parks of the West

Editors: Amy McConnell, Conrad Paulus

Contributors: Alex Aron, Jen Brewer, Clare Hertel, Bob Howells, Edie Jarolim, Bud Journey, Jonathan Leff, Kristina Malsberger, Chelsea Mauldin, Jane McConnell, Greg McNamee, Diana Lambdin Meyer, Candy Moulton, Donald Olson, Bill Sherwonit, Don Thacker, Kirby Warnock, Tom Wharton, Dick Willis

Editorial Production: Janet Foley

Maps: Maryland Cartographics, *cartographer;* Steven K. Amsterdam, Robert Blake, *map editors*

Design: Fabrizio La Rocca, *creative director;* Guido Caroti, *cover design*

Production/Manufacturing: Mike Costa

Cover Photographs: Raymond Gehman/ Corbis (landscape photo); Stephen Krasemann/Tony Stone Images (cactus photo)

CONTENTS

Wide-open spaces, sky-skimming mountains, giant sequoias, wilderness beaches—these images are indelibly etched in our national heritage. Every year millions of people pack up their outdoor gear and head for the outdoors—and they'll continue to do so for centuries to come. Today we are so accustomed to enjoying our national parks that it's hard to imagine what life would be like without them.

There was a time when the wide open land of the United States and Canada was a spectacle to be exploited and expended. The original leaders of the National Park Service knew such a time—which is precisely why they fought so hard for the protection and preservation of our land. Perhaps nothing expresses the valor of the National Park Service's mission as well as the following farewell statement of Horace M. Albright, the original Director of the National Park Service. Albright wrote this letter to the National Park Service personnel upon his resignation in 1933, but his words stand as a reminder to all of us—that we all act as guardians of our country's land.

In this letter, perhaps one of my last official statements to you, let me urge you to be aggressive and vigorous in the fulfillment of your administrative duties. The National Park Service, from its beginning, has been an outstanding organization because its leaders, both in Washington and out in the field, worked increasingly and with high public spirit to carry out the noble policies and maintain the lofty ideals of the service as expressed in law and executive pronouncement. Do not let the service become "just another Government bureau"; keep it youthful, vigorous, clean and strong. We are not here to simply protect what we have been given so far; we are here to try to be the future guardians of those areas as well as to sweep our protective arms around the vast lands which may well need us as man and his industrial world expand and encroach on the last bastions of wilderness. Today we are concerned about our natural areas being enjoyed for the people. But we must never forget that all the elements of nature, the rivers, forests, animals and all things co-existent with them must survive as well.

I hope that particular attention will be accorded always to that mandate in the National Park Service Act of 1916 and in many organic acts of the individual parks which enjoin us to keep our great parks in their natural condition. Oppose with all your strength and power all proposals to penetrate your wilderness regions with motorways and other symbols of modern mechanization. Keep large sections of primitive country free from the influence of destructive civilization. Keep these bits of primitive America for those who seek peace and rest in the silent places; keep them for the hardy climbers of the crags and peaks; keep them for the horseman and the pack train; keep them for the scientist and student of nature; keep them for all who would use their minds and hearts to know what God had created. Remember, once opened, they can never be wholly restored to primeval charm and grandeur.

I also urge you to be ever on the alert to detect and defeat attempts to exploit commercially the resources of the national parks. Often projects will be formulated and come to you "sugar-coated" with an alluring argument that the park will be benefitted by its adoption. We National Park Service men and women know that nature's work as expressed in the world-famous regions in our charge cannot be improved upon by man.

Park usefulness and popularity should not be measured in terms of mere numbers of visitors. Some precious park areas can easily be destroyed by the concentration of too many visitors. We should be interested in the quality of park patronage, not by the quantity. The parks, while theoretically for everyone to use and enjoy, should be so managed that only those numbers of visitors that can enjoy them while at the same time not overuse and harm them would be admitted at a given time. We must keep elements of our crowded civilization to a minimum in our parks. Certain comforts, such as safe roads, sanitary facilities, water, food and modest lodging, should be available. Also extra care must be taken for the children, the elderly and the incapacitated to enjoy the beauty of the parks.

We have been compared to the military forces because of our dedication and esprit de corps. In a sense this is true. We do act as guardians of our country's land. Our National Park Service uniform which we wear with pride does command the respect of our fellow citizens. We have the spirit of fighters, not as a destructive force but as a power for good. With this spirit each of us is an integral part of the preservation of the magnificent heritage we have been given, so that centuries from now people of our world, or perhaps of other worlds, may see and understand what is unique to our earth, never changing, eternal.

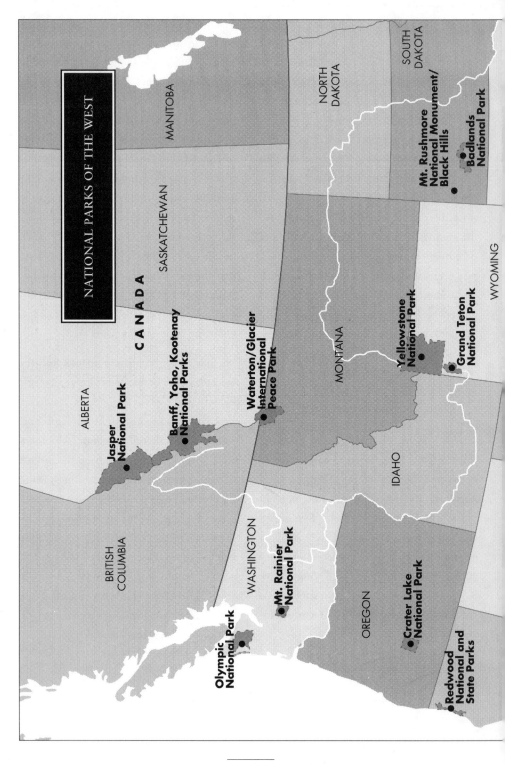

NATIONAL PARKS OF THE WEST

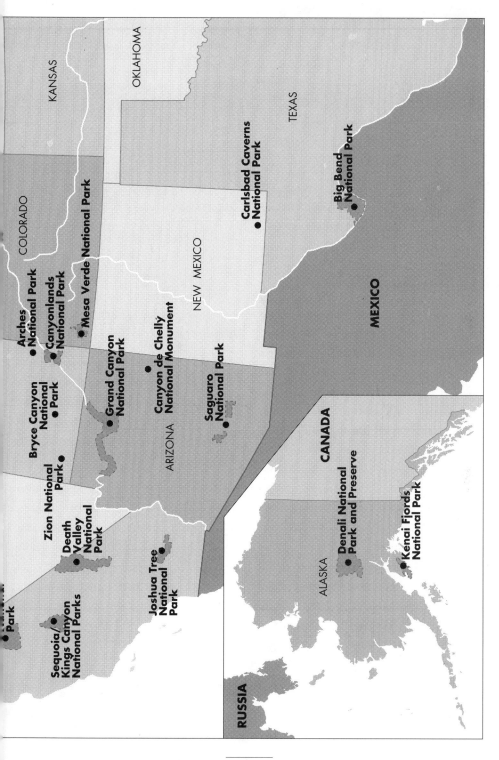

ACKNOWLEDGMENTS

We would like to thank those who helped ensure the accuracy of this book. Special thanks go to the following, who, unless stated otherwise, are employees of the U.S. National Park Service.

Arches: Diane Allen. **Badlands:** Chris Niewold. **Banff:** Bill Leonard. **Big Bend:** Valerie Naylor. **Black Hills:** Todd Phillipe. **Bryce Canyon:** Dave Mecham. **Canyon de Chelly:** Wilson Hunter. **Canyonlands:** Paul Henderson. **Carlsbad:** Bob Hoff. **Crater Lake:** Kent Taylor. **Death Valley:** Terry Baldino. **Denali:** Jane Tranel. **Glacier:** Amy Vanderbilt. **Grand Canyon:** Rod Torrez. **Grand Teton:** Bill Swift. **Jasper:** Gloria Keys-Brady. **Joshua Tree:** Erik Oberg. **Mesa Verde:** William R. Morris. **Mt. Rainier:** Karla Tanner. **Mt. Rushmore:** James Popovich. **Olympic:** Matt Graves. **Point Reyes:** John Dell'Osso. **Redwood:** Peter Keller. **Rocky Mountain:** Douglas Caldwell. **Sequoia and Kings Canyon:** Malinee Crapsey. **Waterton:** Karen Skorenky. **Yellowstone:** Marsha Kerle. **Yoho/Kootenay:** Pam Clark. **Yosemite:** Christine Cowles. **Zion:** Denny Davies.

While every care has been taken to ensure the accuracy of the information in this guide, the passage of time will always bring change, and consequently, Fodor's cannot accept responsibility for errors that may occur.

All prices and opening times quoted here are based on information supplied to us at press time. Hours and admission fees are likely to change, however; the prudent traveler will avoid inconvenience by calling ahead.

Fodor's wants to hear about your travel experiences, both pleasant and unpleasant. When a campground, hotel, or restaurant fails to live up to its billing, let us know and we will investigate the complaint and revise our entries where the facts warrant it. Write to Fodor's Travel Publications, 201 East 50th Street, New York, New York 10022.

Essential Information

Revised by Kristina Malsberger and Chelsea Mauldin

GENERAL VISITOR INFORMATION The National Park Service **Office of Public Inquiries** (Box 37127, Room 1013, Washington, DC 20013-7127, tel. 202/208–4747) provides general information and park brochures. Their Web site, at http://www.nps.gov, has up-to-date information on each of the national parks—everything from current admission and camping fees to historical essays spotlighting various parks. If you're looking for areas long on beauty and short on crowds, you can request a brochure called "Lesser Known Areas of the National Park System" (Superintendent of Documents, Consumer Information Center, Dept. 134b, Pueblo, CO 81009) for $1.50.

For online information, **National Park Service Parknet** is one of the best travel resources on the Web, with extensive historical, cultural, and environmental features in addition to comprehensive listings for all of the U.S. national parks. The **National Park Foundation** (1101 17th St. NW, Suite 1102, Washington, DC 20036-4704, tel. 202/785–4500), the private, non-profit arm of the park service, provides park information at http://www.nationalparks.org. **American Park Network,** a publisher of visitor guide magazines for the national parks, now broadcasts much of its information online, at http://www.americanparknetwork.com.

For information on the Canadian park system, contact **Parks Canada** (Calgary Service Center, 552 4th Ave. SE, Calgary, Alberta, Canada T2G 4X3, tel. 403/292–4401 or 800/748–7275, fax 403/292–6004). Their Web site is http://www.parkscanada.pch.gc.ca.

REGIONAL VISITOR INFORMATION The following regional offices of the U.S. National Park Service provide general information on the parks of the West. For detailed information on the individual parks (weather, special events, campsite availability), contact each park directly. When you arrive at a park, stop by one of the visitor centers and pick up a free map and literature. Some visitor centers have exhibits, slide presentations, and orientation films.

Alaska Area Field Office (2525 Gambell St., Room 107, Anchorage, AK 99503, tel. 907/257–2574).

Intermountain Field Office (12795 Alameda Pkwy., Denver, CO 80225, tel. 303/969–2500).

Pacific West Field Office (600 Harrison St., Suite 600, San Francisco, CA 94101, tel. 415/744–3888).

BOOKS AND MAPS *The Complete Guide to the National Parks,* published by the National Park Foundation and distributed by Fodor's, is the official guide to all 369 national parks.

National Parks Visitor Facilities & Services can be purchased for $4.50 from the **National Park Hospitality Association** (1331 Pennsylvania Ave. NW, Suite 724, Washington, DC 20004-1703, tel. 202/662–7097).

Many of the national parks have bookstores that sell field guides, maps, and other publications on local history, geology, plants, and wildlife. Peterson Field Guides publishes an indispensable reference series for identifying plant and animal life, including *Western Birds, Rocky Mountain Wildflowers, Pacific States Wildflowers, Pacific Coast Shells,* and *Western Butterflies.* Also look for the Audubon Society Field Guides, including *North American Birds, North American Trees,* and *North American Wildflowers.* Other good sources of information are *The Field Guide to Wildlife Habitats of the Western United States* (Simon & Schuster), by Janine Benyus; *Park Rangers Guide to Wildlife* (Stackpole Books), by Arthur P. Miller; *Wild Plants of America: A Select Guide for the Naturalist and Traveler* (John Wiley & Sons), by Richard M. Smith; and *The Traveling Birder* (Doubleday), by Clive Goodwin.

America's National Parks Electronic Bookstore, operated by **Eastern National** (1100 E. Hector St., Suite 105, Conshohocken, PA 19428, tel. 800/821–2903, fax 610/832–0898), is a comprehensive online catalog (www.NationalParkBooks.org) of books and other products—videos, stamps, tote bags, and the like—relating to the park system and the nation's natural heritage. A portion of each sale benefits the National Park System.

The most detailed topographical maps of the national parks are those published by the **United States Geological Survey** (Box 25286, Denver Federal Center, Denver, CO 80225, tel. 303/202–4700 or 800/435–7627, fax 303/202–4693). **Trails Illustrated** (Box 4357, Evergreen, CO 80437-1643, tel. 303/670–3457 or 800/962–1643) has an excellent line of national park topographical maps printed on plastic.

Free information kits for every national park can be ordered by calling the National Park Service at 800/365–2267. Kits include a map, information on accessibility, important phone numbers, and a list of facilities and activities.

TOUR OPERATORS Several associations lead tours that may involve hiking, biking, camping, and/or canoeing. Others have special educational programs, seminars, workshops, and field trips focusing on everything from kayaking to bird-watching and ecology. These tours can be rugged and ambitious or relaxed and luxurious.

American Wilderness Experience (Box 1486, Boulder, CO 80306, tel. 303/444–2622 or 800/444–0099, fax 303/444–3999) leads wilderness tours in the national parks, from backpacking through the Canyonlands to horseback riding in Yellowstone.

Backroads (801 Cedar St., Berkeley, CA 94710-1740, tel. 510/527–1555 or 800/245–3874, fax 510/527–1444) offers biking, hiking, river-rafting, heli-hiking, and cross-country skiing trips in a number of western national parks.

Bi Ways Cycle Tours (Box 43, Site 5, RR#1, Cochraine, Alberta, Canada T0L 0W0, tel. 403/932–7547 or 800/639–3812) is a Canadian company with multiday biking and hiking trips to Banff, Yoho, Kootenay, and Jasper.

Canyonlands Field Institute (Box 68, Moab, UT 84532, tel. 801/259–7750 or 800/860–5262, fax 801/259–2335) schedules seminars designed to educate people about the Colorado Plateau. These range from one-day field hikes to weeklong canoe and river-rafting trips, with an eight-person minimum for custom trips.

Earthwatch (680 Mount Auburn St., Watertown, MA 02272, tel. 617/926–8200) is a nonprofit organization that coordinates field research expeditions, many in national parks. Volunteers serve as short-term assistants to scientists on research expeditions that range from counting and photographing wildlife populations in the Shenandoah Valley to documenting dolphin behavior from boats off the eastern coast of Florida.

National Wildlife Federation (8925 Leesburg Pike, Vienna, VA 22184, tel. 703/790–4000 or 800/822–9919) runs weeklong seminars in the national parks, including nature hikes, classes, and workshops.

Outward Bound U.S.A. (Rte. 9D, R2 Box 280, Garrison, NY 10524, tel. 800/243–8520) conducts educational wilderness programs designed to foster self-esteem and self-reliance in individuals age 14 and up. Trips are 8, 14, or 22 days long; semester courses are also available.

Questers Worldwide Nature Tours (381 Park Ave. S, New York, NY 10016, tel. 212/251–0444 or 800/468–8668) pampers participants on its naturalist-led luxury tours to some of the western national parks.

Sierra Club (85 2nd St., 2nd floor, San Francisco, CA 94105, tel. 415/977–5500) runs a variety of outdoor tours, from river rafting in the Grand Canyon to backpacking in Canyon de Chelly. On their service trips, participants help with trail maintenance and revegetation projects.

Southern Utah Adventures (Box 21276, Oakland, CA 94620, tel. 510/654–5873 or 800/882–4238) leads backcountry hiking trips through the desertlands of Bryce, Zion, and Grand Canyon national parks.

Wild Horizons Expeditions (5663 West Fork Rd., Darby, MT 59829, tel. 406/821–3747), a guide and outfitter licensed by the National Park Service, runs customized wilderness trips every year within various national parks.

PARK ACCESS

FEES AND PASSES **Fees.** Many national parks have an entrance fee, ranging from $4 to $20 per vehicle, that provides access for one to seven consecutive days. In addition to entry fees, most parks charge fees for drive-in campgrounds, ranging from $6 to $16. Backcountry tent sites are typically free. Fees may also be assessed for hunting permits, tours and transportation, use of picnic areas, and other recreational services. Due to severe budget cuts, all park rates are expected to increase within the next few years.

Passes. Senior travelers, travelers with disabilities, and frequent park goers may want to take advantage of the Federal Recreation Passport Program, which includes a number of passes that waive entrance fees for the cardholder and an accompanying carload of passengers.

The **Golden Access Passport** is free and available to those with permanent disabilities. The passport is good for life and can be obtained at the entrance of any of the parks that charge an entrance fee; applicants must have a letter from their doctor stating their disability, plus proof of the federal benefits they receive as a result of their disability. Holders of this pass get in to the parks free and receive a 50% discount on all park facilities and services (excluding those run by private concessionaires). The U.S. park system has made a number of other efforts to be accessible to people with disabilities. Visitor centers provide information in braille, large-print, and tape-recorded formats. At some visitor centers and park museums, free wheelchairs are available, and ramps are strategically placed throughout the parks.

The **Golden Age Passport,** available to travelers 62 years and older, is good for life, and costs just $10, a one-time fee. Provided you have proof of your age and U.S. citizenship or permanent residency status (a drivers' license or birth certificate is fine), you can pick up your pass at any of the national parks that charge an entrance fee. In addition to free admission to the parks for the pass holder and everyone in his or her vehicle, the pass gives a 50% discount on park facilities and services (excluding those run by private concessionaires).

The **Golden Eagle Pass** costs $50 and entitles the cardholder and an accompanying party to free admission to all parks for the calendar year. It is neither refundable nor transferable and, unlike the Golden Age and Golden Access passes, does *not* cover additional park fees, such as those for camping and parking. The Golden Eagle Pass can be purchased in person or by mail by sending $50 to any of the National Park Service headquarters or regional offices.

A **Park Pass** is a good option for those planning to visit one specific park repeatedly. A single-park pass, available for $10 to $40 depending on the park, gives the pass holder and accompanying party free admission to that park for the calendar year. The pass can be purchased in person or by mail from the specific national park at which it will be honored. It is neither transferable nor refundable.

WHEN TO VISIT Early fall and late spring are ideal times to visit most of the national parks—the landscape is lovely and crowds are few. Summer is without question the busiest time of year, so be prepared to deal with full parking lots and traffic jams. (Desert parks are an exception, as the heat keeps the crowds away.) If you must travel during this time, go early or late in the season to avoid the midsummer peak.

During winter, some northern parks close certain roads because of heavy snowfall. Others are just as popular in winter as in summer: In Yosemite and Mount Rainier, for example, hiking paths become cross-country ski trails and rangers conduct snowshoe walks.

The parks and the areas around them host seasonal festivals and events. For information about goings-on and dates for a specific park, *see* Seasonal Events in the individual park chapters.

OPEN HOURS Natural areas of the parks are usually open 24 hours a day, 365 days a year, but fees are generally collected only during peak seasons and hours. If the fee station is closed you may enter the park free, but consider making a donation to help maintain the park.

The buildings within national parks, including visitor centers, are generally open daily from 9 to 5, but these times do vary from park to park and season to season. Most park buildings are open every day of the year except Christmas.

DINING AND LODGING OPTIONS

In addition to campgrounds in and near the national parks, you'll find everything from chain hotels and motels with modern appliances to rough and rugged wilderness camps with kerosene lamps instead of electricity. Cabins with housekeeping facilities are one of the most popular types of lodging. There are also small, family-owned bed-and-breakfasts and a handful of grand old established hotels and lodges with excellent restaurants.

DINING With very few exceptions—such as the dining rooms in historic park lodges—dress at national park restaurants is casual; jeans are allowed almost everywhere.

Prices for meals (per person, excluding drinks and taxes) at restaurants listed in this book are as follows: $$$, over $25; $$, $10 to $25; $, under $10.

LODGING If you're traveling during the high season—roughly between Memorial Day and Labor Day—it's advisable to make reservations three or four months in advance. At some of the most desirable hostelries, such as the Jenny Lake Lodge in Grand Teton National Park and El Tovar in Grand Canyon National Park, guests are known to make reservations for the next summer as they check out. Bear in mind that prices are higher in summer. In fact, they sometimes drop as much as 25% when the season comes to a close.

Prices for lodgings (for two people in a double room) listed in this book are as follows: $$$, over $70; $$, $40 to $70; $, under $40.

CAMPING Most automobile campsites in the national parks are available on a first-come, first-served basis. If you are traveling during peak summer months, be sure to arrive early or make reservations at a nearby public campground.

You can make campground reservations through **Destinet** (tel. 619/452–8787 or 800/365–2267) for some of the most popular parks, including Death Valley, Grand Canyon, Joshua Tree, Rocky Mountain, Sequoia and Kings Canyon, and Yosemite. Reservations are available up to five months in advance. Fees, ranging from $6 to $16, are payable by MasterCard, Visa, and Discover.

For some National Forest Service campgrounds, you can make reservations six months to a year in advance through the **U.S. Forest Reservation Center** (tel. 800/ 280–2267). Fees range from $8.25 to $16.50.

Essential camping equipment includes a ground cloth, tent, sleeping bag, sleeping pad, lantern, flashlight, first-aid kit, food, water, matches in a waterproof case or lighter, and extra clothes for cold nights; you may also choose to bring a stove, fuel, cooking utensils and dishes, and scouring pad.

RVING Driving an RV—short for recreation vehicle—is a convenient, relatively economical way to the visit the parks, especially for families. Depending on the size of the vehicle, daily rental rates run from $125 to $175 a day during high season and most rental companies have a minimum rental time, usually about three days. (Reserve far in advance.) Gas and campground fees are extra, and gas can be expensive, since large-sized RVs get only 8 to 9 mi to the gallon; campground fees are generally $6 to $16 a night when operated by

the National Park Service, $15 to $25 when operated by private concessions.

Most campgrounds in the national parks are equipped for RVs, although the majority have only the basic facilities. Electrical hookups, water pumps, and disposal stations are available only at a handful of stations. **Go Camping America** has a Web site (http://www.gocampingamerica.com) with detailed information on campgrounds that accommodate RVers.

First-time motor-home renters can call 888/ 467–8464 to receive a free video on "the RV lifestyle," including information on driving and renting RVs. To locate a rental agency, look under "Recreation Vehicles—Renting and Leasing" in the yellow pages for the dealer nearest you. You can also order a directory of RV-rental agencies called *Who's Who in RV Rentals,* published by **RV America** (tel. 703/591–7130). It costs $10, including first-class delivery. The largest nationwide RV-rental firm is **Cruise America** (tel. 800/327–7778).

HEALTH AND SAFETY

The three leading causes of death in the parks are, in order, motor-vehicle accidents, drownings, and falls. Use common sense: Keep your eyes on the road while driving, assess water temperature and currents before taking the plunge, and stay on trails to avoid falling from cliffs. If you find yourself in an emergency situation, call 911; there are telephone booths at the visitor centers and other locations throughout the parks. Some of the parks have their own emergency numbers as well.

Before you go, be sure to pack a first-aid kit, including a first-aid manual, aspirin, adhesive bandages, butterfly bandages, sterile gauze pads, 1-inch-wide adhesive tape, an elastic bandage, antibacterial ointment, antiseptic cream, antihistamines, razor blades, tweezers, a needle, scissors, insect repellent, Calamine lotion, moleskin for blisters, and sunscreen.

Keep in mind that even during summer the weather can change unexpectedly—especially in the mountainous parks. Temperatures can rise into the 90s during the day and drop into the teens or lower at night. Always have warm clothing and rain gear handy, no matter how promising the day.

ALTITUDE SICKNESS One of the most common problems for hikers is altitude sickness, which results when a hiker ascends to heights over 8,500 ft without being properly acclimated. To help prevent altitude sickness, spend a night or two at the higher elevation before attempting any strenuous physical activity, and if you have a history of heart or circulatory problems, talk to your doctor before planning a visit to areas at high altitudes.

Symptoms of altitude sickness include headache, nausea, vomiting, shortness of breath, weakness, and sleep disturbance. If any of these occur, it's important to *retreat to a lower altitude.* Altitude sickness can develop into high-altitude pulmonary edema (HAPE) and high-altitude cerebral edema (HACE), both of which can be permanently debilitating or fatal.

ANIMAL AND SNAKE BITES Some animals, especially rodents, carry dangerous diseases. If you are bitten by a wild animal, it's important to see a doctor as soon as possible. Many animal bites require a tetanus shot and, if the animal could be rabid, a rabies shot.

Snakes will do everything to avoid you, but if you are bitten, it's necessary to act quickly. If it's a harmless snake, ordinary first aid for puncture wounds should be given. If it is poisonous, the victim should remain as still as possible so as not to spread the venom through the body. He or she should lie down, keeping the wound area below the rest of the body, and another person should seek medical help immediately.

GIARDIA You can't see *Giardia,* but these tiny water-borne organisms can turn your stomach inside out. It is best to carry bottled water for day trips; drinking water is available at many campgrounds. If you're hiking into the backcountry you may not be able to carry enough water, so you will have to purify spring or stream water for drinking. Do this no matter how crystal clear the water looks.

The easiest way to purify water is to add a water-purification tablet to it. The most widely used brand is Potable Aqua, which is made by Wisconsin Pharmacal and sells for about $5.50 for 50 tablets (good for 50 quarts of water). However, iodine tablets can build up in the body and are not recommended for long-term trips; a better option is to filter your water through a water-purification pump, available at camping equipment stores. Boiling water is the least favorite method since it takes time and uses fuel, but, if it is the only method available, use it; bring the water to a boil for at least 10 minutes, longer at high altitudes.

HIKING PRECAUTIONS Three things should be taken into consideration when choosing hiking trails suitable to your physical condition and the amount of weight you plan to carry: How long is the trail? How steep is it and how quickly does the elevation increase? How acclimated are you to the altitude at the start and finish? Always be aware of the possibility of altitude sickness. All hikers, particularly solo hikers, should give their intended route, length of trip, and return date to a park ranger before setting out on multiday backcountry trips.

Proper hiking attire is essential, especially on more rigorous hikes. Hiking boots should be sturdy, with good traction and ankle support, and should be well broken in ahead of time; if you'll be hiking through snow or in wet conditions, waterproof boots are best. On less rigorous trails, some hikers prefer to wear athletic shoes instead. Wear thick wool socks, and always bring a second pair in case one gets wet. Rain gear is always a good idea, since the weather in most of the national parks can change drastically within moments. Always carry at least 2 quarts of water per person per day, even more if you are staying overnight or are hiking in hot weather.

HYPOTHERMIA AND FROSTBITE It does not have to be below freezing for you to get hypothermia: This potentially fatal decrease in body temperature occurs even in relatively mild weather. Symptoms are chilliness and fatigue, followed by shivering and mental confusion. The minute these signs are spotted, get the victim to shelter of some kind and wrap him or her in warm blankets or a sleeping bag. Ideally another member of the party should get in the sleeping bag with the victim for added warmth. If practical, it's best for both people to be unclothed, but if clothing remains on, it must be dry. High-energy food and hot drinks also aid recovery. To avoid hypothermia, always carry warm, dry clothing, avoid immersion or exposure to cold water or rain, and keep energy levels up by eating high-calorie foods such as trail mix.

Frostbite is caused by exposure to extreme cold for a prolonged period of time. Symptoms include the numbing of ears, nose, fingers, or toes; white or grayish yellow skin is a sure sign. Frostbite victims should be taken into a warm place as soon as possible, and wet clothing should be removed. The affected area should then be immersed in warm—not hot—water or wrapped in a warm blanket. *Do not* rub the frostbitten area, as this may cause permanent damage to the tissues. When the area begins to thaw, the victim should exercise it, to stimulate blood circulation. If bleeding or other complications develop, get to a doctor as soon as possible.

LYME DISEASE This potentially debilitating illness is caused by a virus carried by deer ticks, which thrive in dry, brush-covered areas. When walking in woods, brush, or through fields in areas where Lyme disease has been found, wear tick repellent and long pants tucked into socks. When you undress, search your body for deer ticks—which are no bigger than a pencil point—and remove them with rubbing alcohol and tweezers. Watch the area for several weeks. Some people develop a bull's-eye-like rash or flulike symptoms; if this happens, see your physician immediately.

Lyme disease can be treated with antibiotics if caught early enough.

PLANT POISONS If you touch poison ivy, poison oak, or poison sumac, wash the area immediately with soap and water. Ointments such as Calamine lotion and cortisone cream may relieve itching.

SUNBURN AND HEATSTROKE Take great care in protecting yourself from the sun—even when it's cloudy or there's snow on the ground. At higher altitudes, where the air is thinner, burning ultraviolet rays are stronger. Sun reflected off snow, sand, or water can be especially strong, even on overcast days. Liberally apply a sunscreen of SPF 15 or higher before you go out, and wear a wide-brimmed cap and sunglasses.

If you are exposed to extreme heat for a prolonged period, you run the risk of heatstroke (also known as sunstroke), a serious medical condition. It begins quite suddenly with a headache, dizziness, and fatigue but can quickly lead to convulsions and unconsciousness or even to death. If someone in your party develops any of the symptoms, have one person go for emergency help; meanwhile, move the victim to a shady place, wrap him or her in wet clothing or bedding, and try to cool him or her down with water or ice.

WILD ANIMAL ENCOUNTERS As human development shrinks wildlife habitats, animal encounters are increasingly common in national parks. To avoid attracting bears, raccoons, and other scavengers, all campers should animal-proof their food supplies. Animal-proof containers are available at most developed campsites, but backcountry campers must hang food in a bag or container at least 15 ft above ground and as far away from the trunk of the tree as possible.

Hikers should avoid walking at dawn or dusk, when encounters with mountain lions are most common. If you do see a mountain lion, back away slowly without turning your back to the animal or bending down. Bears and their cubs should be likewise avoided.

PARK PRESERVATION

More than ever, our national parks are being discovered and rediscovered by travelers who want to spend their vacations appreciating nature, watching wildlife, and taking adventure trips. But as the number of visitors to the parks increases, so does stress on wildlife and plant life. Tourism can drum up concern for the environment, but it can also cause great physical damage to parks. **Leave No Trace** (tel. 800/332–4100) an organization dedicated to the responsible use of wilderness areas, prints free brochures with information on protecting the environment; call for a copy.

FIRE PRECAUTIONS When it comes to fire, never take a chance. Don't build fires when you're alone. Build small fires. Always build campfires in a safe place (away from tinder of any kind). Use a fireplace or fire grate if one is available. Clear the ground around the fireplace so that wind cannot blow sparks into dry leaves or grass. Throw used matches into the fire. Never leave a fire unattended. Always have a pot of water or sand next to a campfire or stove. When finished, be sure the fire is out cold (meaning you can touch it with your bare hands). Never cook in your tent or a poorly ventilated space.

MINIMUM-IMPACT CAMPING AND HIKING Responsible park usage takes a little extra effort, but it's a small price to pay for the future of North America's natural beauty. Do not leave garbage on the trails or in campgrounds. If you hike into the backcountry, carry your trash out with you. Bury human waste at least 100 ft from any trail, campsite, or backcountry water source in a hole at least 8 inches deep. Some parks and many environmental organizations advocate packing out even human waste. Do not wash dishes or clothing in lakes and streams. If you must use soap, make sure it is biodegradable, and carry water in clean containers 100 ft away from its source before using it for cleaning.

RESPECTING WILDLIFE Have respect for the animals you encounter: Never sneak up on them, don't disturb nests and other habitats, don't touch animals or try to remove them from their habitat for the sake of a photograph, don't stand between animal parents and their young, and never surround an animal or group of animals. You can also help to protect endangered species by reporting any sightings. Information on endangered species in the national parks is available from the NPS **Wildlife and Vegetation Division** (National Park Service, Box 37127, Washington, DC 20013).

PETS IN THE PARKS Generally, pets are allowed only in developed areas of the national parks, including drive-in campgrounds and picnic areas, but they must be kept on a leash at all times. With the exception of guide dogs, pets are not allowed inside buildings, on most trails, on beaches, or in the backcountry. They also may be prohibited in areas controlled by concessionaires. Some of the parks have kennels, which charge about $6 a day, but before you decide to bring a pet to a national park, call to find out about specific restrictions.

VOLUNTEERING Air pollution, acid rain, wildlife poaching, understaffing of rangers, and encroaching development are among the threats to many national parks. These problems are being addressed by the National Park Service, but you can help by donating time or money. The National Park Service's Volunteers in the Parks program welcomes volunteers to do anything from paperwork to lecturing on environmental issues. To participate, contact the VIP coordinator at the park where you would like to work; an application will be sent to you.

To make financial contributions to the parks, contact the **National Park Service** (Budget Division, Box 37127, Washington, DC 20013) or the **National Parks Preservation Fund** (1101 17th St. NW, Suite 1102, Washington, DC 20036-4704. The latter is a nonprofit organization that supports the park service with supplementary assistance programs.

Arches and Canyonlands National Parks
Utah

By Tom Wharton

In his 1967 introduction to *Desert Solitaire,* Edward Abbey wrote of southern Utah's canyon country, "In the first place you can't see *anything* from a car; you've got to get out . . . and walk, better yet crawl, on hands and knees, over the sandstone and through the thornbush and cactus. When traces of blood begin to mark your trail you'll see something, maybe."

Although Abbey probably would be dismayed by today's development in southeastern Utah's national parks, to a large degree Arches and Canyonlands remain wild, inhospitable, and deeply beautiful lands that no humans can tame. With little in the way of amenities, they are certainly among the most undeveloped national parks. In fact, until 30 years ago, only a few hardy souls—Native Americans, cowboys, such notorious outlaws as Butch Cassidy, and, most recently, uranium prospectors—had penetrated the canyonlands.

Rushing waters carved out this desolate region of arches, box canyons, balanced rocks, and narrow sandstone canyons whose colors change with the season and with the time of day. In Arches National Park you will find nature's sculpture garden: here, the world's greatest concentration of natural arches combines with other intricate formations. In nearby Canyonlands National Park, the surging Colorado and Green rivers and the rugged canyon roads make up one of the United States' ultimate adventure terrains.

Of the two parks, Arches is unquestionably the easier to see. It is ideal for people who enjoy relatively effortless hikes of 1 to 5 mi starting from trailheads along the main park road. Canyonlands, on the other hand, demands more of its visitors. There are only two paved roads in the park, one leading into the Island in the Sky district, southwest of Moab, and the other to the Needles area, northwest of Monticello. The Maze district, on the west side of the Green and Colorado rivers, can only be reached on foot or with a four-wheel-drive vehicle. To get to the Colorado and Green rivers, you must take a long, difficult hike or a raft trip.

Adventure-sports enthusiasts flock to Canyonlands. The park's dirt roads are heaven for mountain bikers, and people with four-wheel-drive vehicles love to challenge their driving skills and the capabilities of their machines by tackling Elephant Hill or the Flint Trail. Rafters roar through the surging rapids of Cataract Canyon. In addition, there are commercial backcountry and airplane tours.

The small town of Moab serves as the hub for this region, and since you will find no food and lodging in the parks, Moab will come to look like civilization. But even with the advent of tourism, this old mining town has retained an authentic southern Utah gruffness.

Arches was made a national monument in 1929. Over the years its boundaries were adjusted, and in 1971 it was made into a national park. Canyonlands was proclaimed a national park in 1964.

ESSENTIAL INFORMATION

VISITOR INFORMATION For information on Arches, contact the Superintendent, **Arches National Park,** Box 907, Moab, UT 84532, tel. 435/259–8161, fax 435/259–8341, TTY 435/259–5279. For information on Canyonlands National Park, write to Superintendent, **Canyonlands National Park,** 2282 S. West Resource Blvd., Moab, UT 84532; or call 435/259–7164. The **Moab Information Center** (Main and Center Sts., Moab, UT 84532, tel. 800/635–6622) is staffed by five agencies—the National Park Service, the U.S. Forest Service, the Bureau of Land Management, the Grand County Travel Council, and the Canyonlands Natural History Association. The center is open daily from 9 to 12:30 and 1:30 to 5 from December through February, with extended hours the rest of the year; call for exact hours.

A permit is required if you plan on spending the night in the backcountry at either Arches or Canyonlands. This can be picked up at the Arches visitor center, the visitor centers near the entrances of the Island in the Sky and Needles districts of Canyonlands, or the Hans Flat Ranger Station near the Maze district of Canyonlands. Permits to some areas are limited and go fast; reservations for the White Rim Trail in Canyonlands are suggested at least six months in advance.

In Canyonlands, permits are also required for boating, rafting, canoeing, and kayaking on the Green and Colorado rivers. Only experienced boaters should attempt Cataract Canyon; if you plan to take a noncommercial river trip through Cataract Canyon, you must obtain a noncommercial boating permit by contacting the park well ahead of your trip. More detailed information on where and when to boat in the Canyonlands area may be found in the "Canyonland River Recreation" and "Calm Water Float Trips" brochures, which are available free from the **Grand County Travel Council** (tel. 435/259–8825 or 800/635–6622).

FEES The entrance fee is $10 per vehicle for a seven-day pass. Fees are charged at the Needles and Island in the Sky districts of Canyonlands and at Arches. Passes purchased at Arches cannot be used at Canyonlands or vice versa, but if you plan to visit often, consider purchasing a $25 annual pass, which is valid at both parks for the calendar year. A $5 individual fee is charged for bicyclists, motorcyclists, and walkers.

PUBLICATIONS The classic book on this area is Edward Abbey's *Desert Solitaire,* which ranks among the greatest philosophy/natural-history books ever written.

Books, maps, videos, river guides, posters, and slides on both Arches and Canyonlands national parks can be purchased at the visitor centers or obtained from the **Canyonlands Natural History Association** (3031 S. Hwy. 191 Moab, UT 84532, tel. 435/259–6003 or 800/840–8978). **Back of Beyond** (83 N. Main St., Moab, UT 84532, tel. 435/259–5154), a well-stocked bookstore, also sells many of the publications listed here.

Hikers should consider buying Sandra Hinchman's *Hiking the Southwest's Canyon Country,* published by the Mountaineers. *Canyon Country Hiking and Natural History,* by F. A. Barnes, is another good guide to trails in Arches and Canyonlands. Many of Barnes's other guidebooks are standard resources on canyonlands country, including *Canyon Country Exploring, Canyon Country Highway Touring, Canyon Country Arches and Bridges, Utah Canyon Country, Canyon Country Geology,* and *Canyon Country Off-Road Vehicle Trails* (three volumes).

Geologic maps of Arches ($6.50) and Canyonlands ($10) and the more detailed United States Geological Survey (USGS) maps are also available from the Canyonlands Natural History Association. **Trails Illustrated** (tel. 303/670–3457), based in Evergreen, Colorado, sells detailed maps of the area for $8.99 each.

GEOLOGY AND TERRAIN Deep beneath Arches and Canyonlands lies a thick bed of salt deposited more than 300 million years ago, when the sea that once flowed over southern Utah evaporated. This fragile and unsteady salt foundation has caused the land above it to fold, buckle, break, and bend into formations later to be refined by the artistry of water.

The more than 2,000 sandstone arches that crowd Arches National Park represent the greatest concentration of natural stone openings in the world. These arches are found in narrow walls of sandstone called fins, which are a result of the upthrusting and faulting of the earth. The arches are formed by water, which freezes and expands in cracks in the fins, putting pressure on the sandstone until a chunk of it falls out. Other formations resulting from this strenuous environmental wear and tear are spires and balanced rocks. Natural bridges differ from natural arches in that they are carved mainly by flowing water, not the freezing action of water. There are few natural bridges in Arches and Canyonlands; to see three outstanding examples you'll have to travel to Natural Bridges National Monument, west of Blanding and south of Canyonlands National Park.

Canyonlands, with 337,570 acres of land as compared to Arches' 73,379 acres, comprises an even wider selection of geological formations. The Colorado and Green rivers meet here, dividing the park neatly into three distinct districts: the Island in the Sky, a high-level mesa in the northern part of the park; the Needles, an assemblage of dramatically sculpted formations in the southeast, including arches, potholes, spires, and grabens; and the remote Maze, with its labyrinthine box canyons. Then there are the rivers themselves, carving out canyons and meanders and roaring with rapids—particularly in Cataract Canyon.

The reddish Kayenta, crumbly Chinle, and light-colored, erosion-resistant White Rim Sandstones in Canyonlands are slightly older than the Entrada and Navajo varieties found at Arches. (Navajo sandstone is also found at Canyonlands, on top of the Kayenta in the Island in the Sky district.) White Rim Sandstone forms benches and rims at the heads of canyons and can be seen on the eponymous White Rim Road in the Island in the Sky district. The red-and-white Cedar Mesa Sandstone prevalent in the Needles and Maze districts tends to be eroded into potholes and desert catch basins, where runoff and rainwater support desert wildlife. Slickrock (large expanses of sandstone where little or no vegetation can grow) is found throughout both parks.

Traveling on the entrance road to the Needles district, visitors will see the area's most prominent example of desert varnish, which looks like dark paint splashed over the rocks. In fact, desert varnish's color can range from red to black and is directly related to the amount of manganese and iron in its composition. Also composed of clay minerals, grains of sand, and other trace elements, rock varnish is cemented to rock surfaces by microorganisms living on the rock. These microorganisms take manganese out of the environment—from airborne dust and runoff—oxidize it, and imbed it in the rock. In the course of thousands of years, the 300- to 700-ft-high Wingate cliffs have been covered by a thin layer of the dark brown to black "varnish." Where sections of the cliff have chipped off, the difference in color is particularly dramatic.

For more information on geology, see *Canyonlands Country: Geology of Arches and Canyonlands National Parks,* by Donald L. Baars, or F. A. Barnes's *Canyon Country Geology.*

FLORA AND FAUNA The sparse rainfall and dry desert climate of Arches and Canyonlands limit the variety of plants and animals that can survive here. But from mid-April to mid-June, desert wildflowers bloom in the canyons and the meadows. Particularly after a year of heavier-than-usual rainfall, expect to see the brilliant blooms of prickly poppy, evening primrose, Indian paintbrush, jimsonweed (late summer), and rabbitbrush (fall). From April through October, the Arboretum of Utah provides a "wildflower hot line" (tel. 801/581–4747), which gives information about which flowers and plants are blooming; in September and October it has information on fall foliage.

"Pygmy forests" of piñon and juniper trees dominate the landscape (so called because of their short stature). Large, stately cottonwood trees grow in washes or near the few flowing streams and rivers. Exotic tamarisk chokes the sides of the banks of both the Green and Colorado rivers and some washes. Such common desert plants as the yucca, sagebrush, Mormon tea, prickly pear cactus, and buffaloberry can be viewed on most hikes. An easy self-guided nature trail near the entrance to the Arches visitor center introduces some common local plant species. Brochures on the park's plant life are available at the center.

The Canyonlands Natural History Association sells bird, plant, and reptile/amphibian lists (50¢–$1 each) covering the species found in the area.

When visiting Canyonlands or Arches, you will be reminded by rangers not to step on the cryptobiotic soil. A delicate, dark crust made up of various fungi, algae, lichens, and mosses, it covers untrammeled desert regions. This substance requires years to grow and is as fragile as it is necessary to the desert ecosystem. It acts as a natural shield, helping to prevent erosion and to keep in moisture needed for plants to grow. Stay on trails or walk on bare rock or in sandy washes.

Wildlife does not thrive in great numbers in the inhospitable climate of canyon country. Nonetheless, some mammals and reptiles can be viewed easily. Sightings of mule deer and jackrabbits around campgrounds are common. Lizards sun themselves on rocks along the trails. Resident birds include golden eagles, red-tailed hawks, turkey vultures, and piñon jays. Glimpses of coyotes, ringtail cats, foxes, and even cougars are rare, but memorable. If you are taking a river trip down Cataract Canyon, search the sides of canyons for rare desert bighorn sheep. In the winter, visitors might also spot an occasional bald eagle or peregrine falcon.

WHEN TO GO The best times to visit Arches and Canyonlands national parks are in the spring and fall, when temperatures are most conducive to hiking and mountain biking. During a warm spring rainstorm, hikers are delighted by the waterfalls that appear miraculously. River trips down the Colorado and Green rivers, however, are best in the summer, when rafters can beat the heat by plunging into the cool, muddy waters.

Crowds disappear from the parks in the winter months, and even the most popular trails and overlooks are left all but deserted. Imagine gazing out at the snowcapped peaks of the Henry, La Sal, and Abajo mountains on a January afternoon just after a flurry has dusted snow over the red rock canyons.

The climate in this area is dry year-round, with the humidity seldom climbing above 10%. Temperatures fluctuate quite a bit even in winter months. In January, record highs of 66°F and record lows of -18°F have been recorded at Arches, but the average high is 41°F and the average low, 18°F. In April and October, expect temperatures to reach into the 70s and drop to the low 40s at night. The hottest month of the year is July, when the maximum temperature hovers around 99°F in Arches and 92°F in Canyonlands, and the minimum is about 65°F in Arches and 62°F in Canyonlands. October is the rainiest month at Arches, and surprisingly, August, with its sudden, spectacular thunderstorms, is the second-wettest. In Canyonlands, July is the wettest month.

SEASONAL EVENTS Week before Easter: More than 1,000 Jeeps from all over the country and the world sign up for the **Moab**

Jeep Safari. Guides take groups of Jeepers, from beginner to expert, along four-wheel-drive roads on Bureau of Land Management land. For more information, call 800/635–6622. **First week in June: Butch Cassidy Days** (tel. 800/635–6622) in Moab include a professional rodeo, barbecue, shoot-outs, dances, and live entertainment. **Mid-October:** The **Fat Tire Festival** (tel. 800/635–6622) is a mountain-bike gala with bicycle polo, a bicycle rodeo, guided rides, dances, and entertainment; it concludes with a costume ball.

WHAT TO PACK Canyonlands and Arches are short on creature comforts: Drinking water, food, gasoline, stores, and lodgings are not available within the park (with the exception of a seasonal water supply at Squaw Flat Campground in the Needles district of Canyonlands and Devils Garden Campground in Arches); and heat can be extreme in the summer. Be sure to carry an adequate amount of water (a gallon per person per day), as well as sunscreen and a sun hat. If you go on a guided river trip, chances are your guide will provide you with waterproof bags and equipment, but be sure to ask—the rapids are a drenching experience.

GENERAL STORES There aren't any stores inside Canyonlands or Arches. Stopping for supplies in town—Moab, Green River, Monticello, or Blanding—is a must. All four towns have 24-hour service stations that can provide the basics. The **City Market** (425 S. Main St., tel. 435/259–5181) in Moab, at the southern end of town, is the largest full-service grocery and drugstore in the area. Open 24 hours a day, every day of the year except Christmas, it carries just about anything you might need. The small and expensive **Needles Outpost** (tel. 435/979–4007), near the Needles entrance to Canyonlands, sells some camping gear, gasoline, and food. It is open from early March to the end of October, from 7 to 9 daily.

ARRIVING AND DEPARTING The best way to get to Canyonlands and Arches is by automobile. Although some public transportation is available to Moab, getting around inside the parks requires a car. If you take a guided river, mountain bike, or four-wheel-drive trip, however, the outfitters will usually arrange for your transportation from Moab to the park.

By Bus. **Greyhound** buses stop at Crescent Junction, about 27 mi north of Moab. Arrange for shuttle service from the station with Thrifty Rent-a-Car (*see below*).

By Car and RV. The town of Moab, the main access point into Arches National Park and Canyonlands' Island in the Sky and Needles districts, lies between the two parks on Highway 191, which links I–70 in Utah to I–40 in Arizona. Plan on a driving time of just under five hours for the 236-mi trip between Salt Lake City and Moab. Traveling on I–70 from Denver to Arches, plan on a 380-mi trip taking just under seven hours. The North Rim of the Grand Canyon is 402 mi and eight hours away; Zion National Park, in the southwest corner of Utah, is a 325-mi, 6½-hour drive.

To reach Highway 191 from Salt Lake, travel south on I–15 to Spanish Fork. Take the Price–Manti exit to Highway 6. Stay on that road through the towns of Price and Wellington until reaching I–70. Go about 20 mi east on I–70 to Crescent Junction and turn off for Highway 191.

The only entrance to Arches is in the south of the park, just off Highway 191 and about 5 mi north of Moab. There are three entrances to Canyonlands but only two paved routes, both of which are accessible from Highway 191. One paved route is along Highway 313 to the Island in the Sky district, only 35 mi from Moab; the other follows Highway 211 into the Needles district, 80 mi from Moab and 50 mi northwest of the town of Monticello, where the nearest motels are located.

Entering Canyonlands through the Maze district is not recommended without a four-wheel-drive vehicle. To reach this entrance, take I–70 to Highway 24 and drive south 24 mi to the turnoff near Goblin Valley State Park, 20 mi north of Hanksville. Then plan on a long, dusty, and often rugged trip to the Maze along an 80-mi dirt road, which includes the challenging switchbacks of the Flint Trail Road. The small Horseshoe Canyon Unit of Canyonlands, which is separated from the main part of the park by Bureau of Land Management lands, is accessible by passenger car, but only in dry weather. To get to Horseshoe Canyon, follow the directions above, but after traveling 25 mi on the dirt road, turn left and continue 5 mi to the canyon rim.

By Plane. Alpine Air (tel. 435/373–1508 or 800/253–5678), a small commuter airline, provides daily service to Moab from Salt Lake City. Flights leave Salt Lake City at 8:10 AM and arrive at 9 AM. The Moab airport is 17 mi from downtown, so plan on using the local shuttle service. The closest major airport to Arches and Canyonlands is in Grand Junction, Colorado, 125 mi away. From there you can rent a car through **Avis** (tel. 800/331–1212), **Hertz** (tel. 800/654–3131), **Thrifty** (tel. 800/367–2277), or **Budget** (tel. 800/527–0700).

EXPLORING

Canyonlands. The difficulty of exploring Canyonlands is part of its charm. Most visitors drive through the park, taking short hikes off the main roads. Those roads, however, are limited, so if you want to penetrate the park, you should choose a longer hike or a rafting, mountain biking, or four-wheel-drive adventure in the backcountry. If you are a newcomer to the area, consider one of the guided tours (*see below*). Plan on spending at least one day each in the Island of the Sky and Needles districts; to understand what the park is all about, you'll have to take one more day to go rafting down one of the rivers that formed the canyons.

Of Canyonlands' three districts, Island in the Sky is the most accessible. A paved road leads to several dramatic viewpoints—Grand View Point, Green River Overlook, and the Upheaval Dome are the best—and to trailheads for some short hikes. Here you will also find mountain bikers' favorite route, the White Rim Road.

The Needles district to the south is more remote. A paved road leads to the entrance, but it runs only slightly more than 8 mi into the park. Elephant Hill, the consummate four-wheel-drive challenge, and the hikers' favorite, Joint Trail near Chesler Park, are both in Needles.

The third district of Canyonlands, the Maze, may be the least accessible national park area in the lower 48 states. There are no paved roads in the Maze, so you must either hike in (it takes a full day) or have a four-wheel-drive vehicle and at least two days to spare. Only the Horseshoe Canyon Unit of the Maze is even close to accessible by passenger car (*see* Arriving and Departing, *above*). It is also the most visited area in the Maze district.

Arches. In contrast to Canyonlands, Arches can be explored easily by car on a 22-mi paved road. You will not, however, want to stay in your car and miss two of the greatest hikes in Utah, Fiery Furnace and Delicate Arch. Mountain biking is restricted to the paved road, which is somewhat narrow, and a few dirt roads. You'll need at least one full day here.

THE BEST IN ONE DAY It is possible to see both Arches and the Island in the Sky district of Canyonlands in one day, but it wouldn't be much fun. This is a land of great expanses, and unless you want to spend the whole day driving, you would do best to visit just one park. First-time travelers to this region should opt for Arches.

Arches. Without the Fiery Furnace and the Delicate Arch hikes (*see* Longer Hikes, *below*), a visit to Arches would be incomplete. Rangers lead the strenuous jaunt around Fiery Furnace; sign up at the visitor center. (Since the required reservations can be made up to 48 hours in advance, you'll be lucky to get a spot.) Then, head out to the Wolfe Ranch (*see* Historic Buildings and Sites, *below*) and the trailhead for Del-

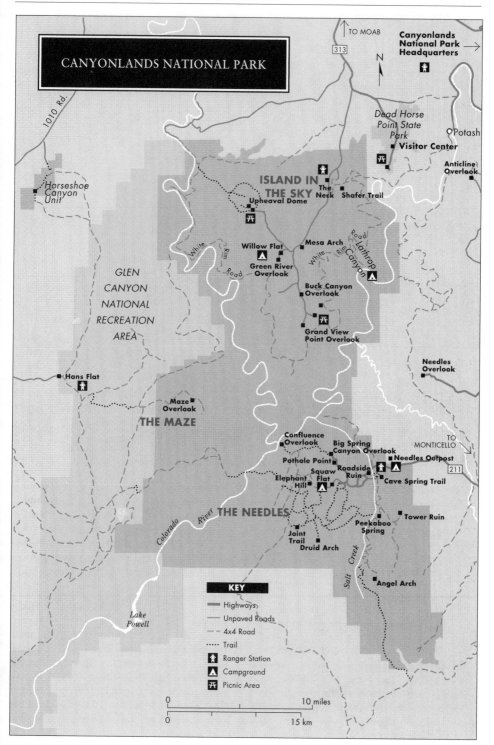

CANYONLANDS NATIONAL PARK

TO MOAB

313

Canyonlands National Park Headquarters

N

Dead Horse Point State Park

○Potash

■ **Visitor Center**

Anticline Overlook ■

1010 Rd.

Horseshoe Canyon Unit

ISLAND IN THE SKY **The Neck** **Shafer Trail**

Upheaval Dome

White Rim Road

Willow Flat ▲ **Mesa Arch**

Green River Overlook

Buck Canyon Overlook

Lathrop Canyon Road

GLEN CANYON NATIONAL RECREATION AREA

Grand View Point Overlook

Needles Overlook

■ **Hans Flat**

Maze Overlook ■

THE MAZE

Confluence Overlook

Big Spring Canyon Overlook

TO MONTICELLO

Pothole Point

■ **Needles Outpost**

Squaw Flat

Roadside Ruin

Elephant Hill

Cave Spring Trail

211

Colorado River

THE NEEDLES

Tower Ruin ■

Joint Trail

Peekaboo Spring

Druid Arch

Salt Creek

Angel Arch

Lake Powell

KEY
━━━ Highways
─── Unpaved Roads
─ ─ 4x4 Road
···· Trail
🚹 Ranger Station
▲ Campground
🍴 Picnic Area

0   10 miles

0   15 km

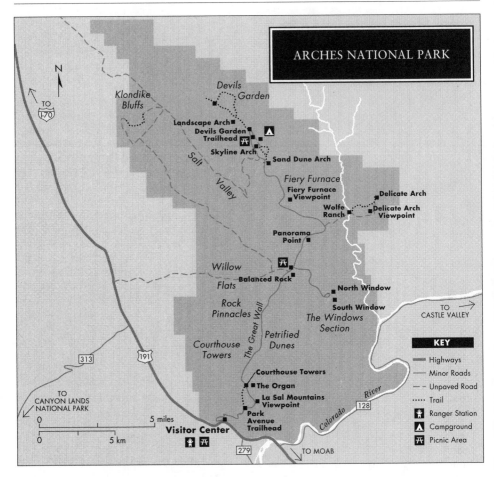

ARCHES NATIONAL PARK

N

TO
I-70

Klondike
Bluffs

Devils
Garden

Landscape Arch
Devils Garden
Trailhead

Skyline Arch

Salt

Valley

Sand Dune Arch

Fiery Furnace

Fiery Furnace
Viewpoint

Wolfe
Ranch

Delicate Arch

Delicate Arch
Viewpoint

Panorama
Point

Willow

Flats

Balanced Rock

North Window

Rock
Pinnacles

South Window

The Windows
Section

TO
CASTLE VALLEY

The Great Wall

Petrified
Dunes

Courthouse
Towers

KEY

Courthouse Towers

The Organ

La Sal Mountains
Viewpoint

Colorado River

128

TO
CANYON LANDS
NATIONAL PARK

313

191

Park
Avenue
Trailhead

Visitor Center

279

TO MOAB

0   5 miles

0   5 km

Highways

Minor Roads

Unpaved Road

Trail

Ranger Station

Campground

Picnic Area

icate Arch—perhaps one of the best hikes in the state. Since this trail is quite exposed, you will enjoy it much more in the cooler hours of the day.

Continue on to the meeting place for the Fiery Furnace hike. Despite its name, this is the best place to be in the heat of the day, because you will be walking in shade cast by sandstone fins. Note that there is a $6 entrance fee, which must be paid at the visitor center. When you've had enough walking, drive out to the Balanced Rock and the famed Windows section, where scenes from *Indiana Jones and the Last Crusade* were filmed (*see* Nature Trails and Short Walks, *below*). Take plenty of photos in the late afternoon light.

As you work your way back toward the visitor center and the entrance to the park, drop some members of your party off at the Courthouse Towers viewpoint. Here they can begin the 1-mi stroll up Park Avenue to see the sandstone skyscrapers that line this trail. Pick them up at the Park Avenue Trailhead and exit the park where you entered in the morning.

Canyonlands. A day's itinerary in Canyonlands will entail more driving than walking. Island in the Sky is the easiest part of Canyonlands to see in a short amount of time. Leaving Moab, take Route 313 to Dead Horse Point State Park for a vista over the Colorado River and the Island in the Sky district (*see* Scenic Drives and Views, below). You'll have to backtrack to reach the junction of Route 313 and the road that enters Canyonlands. Your first stop in the park should be the visitor center at the Neck. There you can ask questions and pick up a map and brochures. From the Neck, drive straight through to Grand View Point Overlook and walk the Grand View Trail (see Nature Trails and Short Walks, below). Driving back toward the Neck, stop first at the Buck Canyon Overlook, then continue on the main road going north; at the fork, turn left to reach the Green River and Upheaval Dome overlooks. Upheaval Dome is a mound of earth in the center of a large crater. You can't get to the dome without taking a long hike, but from the parking area a .5-mi trail leads to Crater View Overlook, from which you can see Upheaval Dome jutting out of the center of the crater.

Head back toward the Neck and stop to hike out to the Mesa Arch (see Nature Trails and Short Walks, below). The La Sal Mountains in the afternoon light provide great pictures. Before exiting the park, stop near the Shafer Trail to watch the antics of the four-wheel-drive and mountain bike enthusiasts on the treacherous switchbacks below.

Arches and Canyonlands. If you insist on seeing both Canyonlands and Arches in the same day, get an early start and head to the Island in the Sky district southwest of Moab, where you can easily spend four to five hours. Don't miss the views from Dead Horse Point State Park, Grand View Point, and Crater View Overlook/Upheaval Dome. Take the short hike to Mesa Arch. After breaking for a picnic lunch, head into Arches for a late afternoon drive and take a sunset hike to the Delicate Arch or to the Double Arch in the Windows section.

ORIENTATION PROGRAMS Visitor centers at the entrances to Arches and the Island in the Sky and Needles districts of Canyonlands sell books, maps, and posters; provide information about the geology and human history of the area; and coordinate interpretive activities and guided hikes. At

Arches, an interesting slide show is shown, and a short, self-guided nature walk at the front of the visitor center provides an introduction to the desert environment.

GUIDED TOURS Moab, with a population of less than 6,000, may offer more guided tours than any town its size in the country. You can sign up for river trips, horseback excursions, mountain bike tours, airplane flights, and four-wheel-drive expeditions through Canyonlands. Since the guide business in Moab is extremely competitive, most tour operators are known for excellent service. When you sign up with a Moab guide, high-quality meals, first-class equipment, and hair-raising campfire tales await you. Expect to pay about $100 to $125 per person per day for a guided trip, which can last anywhere from a half day to a week or more. Contact the **Utah Travel Council** (Council Hall/Capitol Hill, Salt Lake City, UT 84114, tel. 801/538–1030 or 800/200–1160) for a free brochure, "Utah Tour Guide," which lists all of the state's guide services. A list of tour operators licensed to operate in Arches and Canyonlands national parks is available through both parks (see Visitor Information, above).

Visitors who expect to tour the parks by bus may be disappointed. Because of the area's sparse population and dearth of large hotels, bus tours are not regularly scheduled.

Canyonlands Field Institute (Box 68, Moab, UT 84532, tel. 435/259–7750 or 800/860–5262) runs educational trips ranging from archaeological digs and biological field trips to writers' workshops.

SCENIC DRIVES AND VIEWS It's difficult to select a drive in the Canyonlands area that isn't scenic and doesn't lead to spectacular views, but a few are especially noteworthy.

The most scenic journey is the 50-mi drive first north from Moab along **Highway 191 to Route 313** and then generally south across the narrow mesa of the Canyonland's Island in the Sky district, with a detour into Dead Horse Point State Park. Plan on five hours to enjoy the views at

Dead Horse Point, the Grand View Point, and the Upheaval Dome. True to its name, the Grand View Point provides the best overall vista of Canyonlands National Park, including the Maze, the Needles, and the Henry, La Sal, and Abajo (known locally as Blue) mountain ranges looming in the distance like islands.

The popular 24-mi drive on the main road and two spur roads through **Arches National Park** leads to a half dozen short hikes (*see* Nature Trails and Short Walks, *below*), balanced rocks, and views of many arches. In the Windows area alone, visitors can see five large arches from their cars and take short, easy hikes (all less than a mile) to the bases of the formations.

A drive many visitors unwisely ignore originates about 30 mi south of Moab, just south of the Wilson Arch, on Highway 191. The road travels west off the highway and leads through Canyon Rims Recreation Area to the Bureau of Land Management's Windwhistle Campground and the **Needles Overlook.** Although the approximately 25-mi drive does not actually pass through the borders of Canyonlands National Park, it affords an impressive view of the Needles section of the park. The road is paved and on most days can be experienced in relative solitude.

HISTORIC BUILDINGS AND SITES Few humans have succeeded in leaving their mark on these rugged lands. Aside from some Native American ruins and restored pioneer buildings, few man-made artifacts exist in Arches and Canyonlands.

The **Wolfe Ranch** in Arches National Park was originally built in 1889 by Civil War veteran John Wesley Wolfe and later restored. Found at the trailhead to the Delicate Arch, this ranch gives visitors a glimpse of early pioneer life. A brochure available at the cabin describes what life was like here in the late 19th century.

In the Needles district of Canyonlands National Park, the Cave Spring Trail, which originates near the Salt Creek four-wheel-drive road, leads to an authentic **cowboy line camp** dating to the late 1800s. A short hike from the trailhead just past the Needles visitor center takes you to **Roadside Ruin,** an Anasazi granary once used to store corn, seeds, and nuts. **Tower Ruin** in the Needles' Horse Canyon is an example of an Anasazi cliff dwelling. Better-preserved Anasazi buildings can be seen at nearby Hovenweep National Monument, Edge of the Cedars State Park in Blanding, and Mesa Verde National Park in Colorado.

NATURE TRAILS AND SHORT WALKS Despite the rough terrain and size of Arches and Canyonlands, there are a number of short hikes in both parks.

Arches. First-time visitors will enjoy the short **Arches Desert Nature Trail,** which introduces the various indigenous plants. It begins near the visitor center. One of the most popular hikes for kids is the .25-mi walk through an extremely narrow canyon to **Sand Dune Arch,** a shaded rock formation guarding a sand dune. Kids love to play in the fine, pink sand. The parking area at the trailhead is found just before the entrance to the campground.

Another short hike in Arches leads around the **Balanced Rock** (.5-mi). In the nearby **Windows** section, you can stroll on one or more of the mostly flat trails to the North and South Windows, Turret Arch, and/or Double Arch, which was featured in *Indiana Jones and the Last Crusade.* Visible from your car, these formations are just short walks from the road.

Canyonlands. There are three relatively easy hikes with self-guiding trail brochures in the Needles district of Canyonlands. The short **Roadside Ruin** hike leads to a small Anasazi granary (*see* Historic Buildings and Sites, *above*). The .25-mi **Pothole Point** trail, off the road to Big Spring Canyon Overlook, leads to sandstone potholes, often filled with water, and fairy and tadpole shrimp. In fact, these tiny potholes harbor myriad creatures that form a fragile ecosystem. Hikers should not disturb them—not even by splashing in the water. The oils from your skin can change the pH of the water enough to kill or damage the desert dwellers. These potholes are also the only water source for wildlife, so use the water only in an emergency—and if you do, dip a clean cup or pot into the water, and be sure to boil or treat the water before drinking it. Finally, the **Cave Spring Trail,** a .5-mi loop, takes you into an authentic cowboy line camp and then under a giant alcove.

The best easy walk in the Island in the Sky district is the .25-mi trail through a piñon-juniper forest to **Mesa Arch.** Take along a camera with a wide-angle lens so you can frame the small arch and the La Sal Mountains in the distance. The brochure available on the .5-mi hike to the Crater View of **Upheaval Dome** raises questions about how this unusual dome was formed—one theory is that a meteor crashed to earth here. The flat 1.5-mi walk along the edge of **Grand View Point** provides some of the best views of the canyon country, as well as of three major mountain ranges: the Henrys, La Sals, and Abajos.

LONGER HIKES **Arches.** Do not leave Arches without making the 1.5-mi trek to the **Delicate Arch.** Though the 480-ft ascent can be grueling on a hot summer day, the reward of seeing this 45-ft-high, 33-ft-wide arch, one of nature's most fantastic creations, is well worth the work. The trail is designed so that the arch does not become visible until the last possible second. Take time to sit on the warm red rock of the natural amphitheater surrounding the arch to contemplate the forces that created it. Bring plenty of water.

Another exceptional hike in Arches is the strenuous 2-mi **Fiery Furnace** hike, which takes 2½–3 hours to complete. This labyrinth of narrow canyons, twisted passageways, and hidden arches is so disorienting that it's best to go through with a ranger. Reservations are required for this hike and must be made at the Arches Visitor Center in person, no more than 48 hours in advance. Rangers lead the hike twice daily, from March through October.

A pleasant day can be spent exploring the **Devils Garden** area, near the Arches Campground, at the north end of the park road. The Devils Garden trail leads up to seven arches—including the famous Landscape Arch, with its 306-ft span the longest in the park—and provides views of several more. The world seems to drop away beyond the Double O Arch. Allow at least three hours for this moderately strenuous 4-mi round-trip hike, but plan on more time if it's a hot day. Hikers can take side trips from here.

Canyonlands. One of the most rewarding hikes in Canyonlands is the 3.25-mi trek into the **Great Gallery,** in the Horseshoe Canyon Unit of the park. Since no drinking water is available there, bring plenty of your own. Reaching the trailhead often requires driving on rough dirt roads, but can be done in a two-wheel-drive vehicle depending on the weather. To reach the trailhead, drive north from Hanksville on Highway 24 until you see the turnoff to the Maze district, across and south of the road from the Goblin Valley State Park turnoff. Follow the signs for just over 30 mi to reach the trailhead. From there, you will descend about 800 ft into the bottom of the canyon, then walk upstream almost 2 mi more until you see a haunting, prehistoric, Native American rock art panel, the 100-ft Great Gallery, which includes the image of the Ghost King. Along the walk, watch for other examples of Native American petroglyphs and ruins.

Hiking into the **Maze,** while exciting, can also be frightening and potentially dangerous because of the many box canyons, which seem to lead to one dead end after another. The main drainages in this area are quite obvious, but once you are down inside one of the side canyons, finding your way back out can be difficult. Make sure to bring a map, compass, and guidebook to this seldom-visited area.

There are several fine, long hikes in the Needles district of the Canyonlands, and many of them are great for backpacking. One of the best, the 6-mi **Joint Trail,** in the

Chesler Park area, south of Elephant Hill, winds through narrow cracks or joints in the rock, past potholes, and up to points with sweeping vistas. Other hikes in the **Needles district** include the 5.4-mi hike to Druid Arch; the 5-mi hike from the Big Spring Canyon Overlook to the Confluence Overlook; the 5-mi trek to Peekaboo Spring; and the nearly 8.75-mi loop through Squaw and Lost canyons. Most of these hikes originate at Squaw Flat.

Longer hikes in the **Island in the Sky district** are more difficult; you must be prepared to hike back up after hiking down into the canyons. Rangers at the visitor center can give suggestions on routes through this area. Serious hikers should consider purchasing guides with more detailed descriptions of trails (*see* Publications, *above*).

OTHER ACTIVITIES Back-Road Driving. Some of the nation's premier four-wheel-drive roads are in Canyonlands National Park. People come from all over the world to tackle **Elephant Hill** in Needles District. At one point, the trail is so narrow that the driver has to back up to the edge of a steep cliff to make a turn. If you would like to view the towering canyons from a lower vantage point, try the less-dizzying route along the **Salt Creek** wash to **Angel Arch** in the Needles District. This trail has limited access and costs a nominal fee.

The greatest driving challenge in the Maze district is the **Flint Trail.** Four-wheel-drive and high clearance are required to make the steep, twisting trip up to the Maze Overlook. Bring plenty of water and extra gasoline on this journey as service stations and stores are miles away.

The trip to **Gemini Bridges,** east of Canyonlands National Park, and the **White Rim Road** in Canyonlands' Island in the Sky district provide beautiful views over the canyons.

Although less well known, the few Jeep trails in Arches National Park are enjoyable; try **Klondike Bluffs** or **Willow Flat.**

A good way to discover the best four-wheel-drive roads in the area is to join the annual **Moab Jeep Safari,** an event that takes place the week before Easter (*see* Seasonal Events, *above*) outside the parks.

Although not quite as popular as river trips, guided four-wheel-drive expeditions through Canyonlands present yet another adventure available in few U.S. national parks. One of the best four-wheel-drive tour operators into Canyonlands and Arches national parks is **Tag-A-Long Expeditions** (452 N. Main St., Moab, UT 84532, tel. 435/259–8946 or 800/453–3292). Another reputable operator is **Lin Ottinger Tours** (600 N. Main St., Moab, UT 84532, tel. 435/259–7312).

You can rent a four-wheel-drive vehicle from **Certified Ford-Mercury** (500 S. Main St., Moab, UT 84532, tel. 435/259–6107), **Farabee Rentals** (234 N. Main St., Moab, UT 84532, tel. 435/259–7494), or **Slickrock 4 by 4 Rentals** (284 N. Main St., Moab, UT 84532, tel. 435/259–5678).

Bird-Watching. Spring is the best time to go birding in Canyonlands and Arches national parks. During the summer heat, the prime bird-viewing times are before sunset and around sunrise. Concentrate your efforts on the river washes or around cottonwood trees. Canyonlands birds include flickers, scrub and piñon jays, grosbeaks, canyon wrens, swallows, hummingbirds, and many different types of raptors, such as red-tailed hawks and even peregrine falcons. A bird list published by the Canyonlands Natural History Association is available at the visitor centers at Arches and Canyonlands.

Boating and Rafting. If you want to challenge the wildest rapids this side of the Grand Canyon, take a river trip through **Cataract Canyon** on the Colorado River in Canyonlands. The rapids reach their raging peak in June and taper off through the summer. Plan to spend from three to six days on the river and from $400 to $800, depending on the type of trip you take. High-water trips must be booked six months in advance, but during August and September, when the waters run low, it is possible to make arrangements with just a week's notice.

For those who want a smaller taste of the waters, there are half-day trips on the Colorado near Moab for as little as $25. These can be arranged with one day's notice.

The best-known river guide companies are **Sheri Griffith River Expeditions** (Box 1324, Moab, UT 84532, tel. 800/332–2439), **Holiday River and Bike Expeditions** (544 E. 3900 S, Salt Lake City, UT 84107, tel. 800/624–6323), **Moki Mac River Expeditions** (Box 71242, Salt Lake City, UT 84171, tel. 800/284–7280), **Tag-A-Long Expeditions** (*see above*), **Western River Expeditions** (7258 Racquet Club Dr., Salt Lake City, UT 84121, tel. 800/453–7450), and **World Wide Expeditions** (153 E. 7200 S, Midvale, UT 84047, tel. 801/566–2662).

Some calm-water trips on both the Colorado and Green rivers can also be enjoyed. The best of them runs from the Ruby Ranch on the Green River to Mineral Canyon, just outside of Canyonlands National Park. This is especially good in canoes during the late summer months.

Private rafting trips are allowed through sometimes-dangerous Cataract Canyon, but you must have a permit in advance to run these rapids. The permits are $25, and to get one, you must convince the ranger in charge that you are an experienced rafter. For information on permits, write to the superintendent of Canyonlands National Park (*see* Essential Information, *above*). Free brochures on river recreation in the area are available through the Grand County Travel Council (805 N. Main St., Moab, UT 84532, tel. 800/635–6622).

Raft and canoe rentals are available from **Holiday River and Bike Expeditions** (*see above*), **Moki Mac River Expeditions** (*see above*), **Rental Rafts** (105 Thompson, Green River, UT 84525, tel. 801/564–3322), **Tag-A-Long Expeditions** (*see above*), and **Western River Expeditions** (*see above*). **Tex's Canyonland River Expeditions** (Box 67, Moab,

UT 84532, tel. 435/259–5101) provides both canoe outfitting and shuttle service for canoers and rafters.

Fishing. Anglers are out of luck at Arches; fishing within the park is nonexistent. And, while a few catfish may be caught in the Colorado and Green rivers, fishing within Canyonlands is generally poor and river access extremely limited. For trout fishing in the area, try Ken's Lake or the La Sal Mountain lakes near Moab. Warm-water fishing is best in Lake Powell. Licenses, available in Moab grocery and outdoors stores, cost $40 per season for nonresidents, $18 for residents; five-day licenses cost $15, and one-day licenses are $5.

Flight-Seeing. Flying over the canyonlands is an exhilarating and relatively inexpensive way to get a feel for the immensity of this landscape and an overview of its complex geology. Because flights can be as brief as half an hour, they're ideal for people in a hurry. Flights take off from Moab, Blanding, Price, and Monticello airports. An hour in the air costs about $60 to $90. Flying from the tiny airport at Hite Marina in the Glen Canyon National Recreation Area back to Moab after a Cataract Canyon river trip can be almost as much fun as the river trip itself. But be warned: The landing strip at Hite is one of the scariest around. The 500-ft cliff at the edge of the runway makes for very dramatic takeoffs.

Airplane operators offering tours over the canyonlands include **Lake Powell Air Service** (Box 1385–901 N. Sage Navajo, Page, AZ 86040, tel. 800/245–8668), **Needles Outpost** (Box 1107, Monticello, UT 84535, tel. 435/259–6568), **Redtail Aviation** (Box 515, Moab, UT 84532, tel. 435/259–7421), and **Scenic Aviation** (Box 67, Blanding, UT 84511, tel. 435/678–3222).

Mountain Biking. The most rugged way to see Canyonlands short of a major backpacking trip is on a mountain-bike tour along Jeep roads, such as the **White Rim Road,** which runs from the top of the Island in the Sky district to the White Rim, 1,200 ft below the top of the mesa. Several operators conduct mountain biking expeditions ranging from a half day to seven days.

White Rim is perhaps the most popular route, but Jeep trails through the Maze and Needles districts also make for great rides. Bikers must keep to the road and stay off the hiking trails. This is critical to protect the fragile makeup of the earth's crust, which helps hold the loose desert sands together.

Bicycle rentals are available from **Adrift Adventures** (378 N. Main St., Moab, UT 84532, tel. 801/259–8594 or 800/874–4483), **Poison Spider** (497 N. Main St., Moab, UT 84532, tel. 435/259–7882 or 800/635–1792), **Western Spirit Cycling** (478 Mill Creek Dr., Moab, UT 84532, tel. 435/259–8732 or 800/845–2453, fax 435/259–2736), **Tag-A-Long Expeditions** (*see above*), and **Rim Cyclery** (94 W. 100 N, Moab, UT 84532, tel. 435/259–5333).

Scenic Byways Bicycle Touring (153 E. 7200 S, Midvale, UT 84047, tel. 800/231–2769) leads mountain biking/hiking trips in the Maze area. Other good bicycle tour operators are **Slickrock Adventures** (Box 1400, Moab, UT 84532, tel. 435/259–6996) and **Western Spirit Cycling** (*see above*).

Rock Climbing. No climbing permits are required at Arches or Canyonlands national parks, but it's a good idea to pick up climbing guidelines from the visitor center. Both parks prohibit climbing in geological features named on the USGS map. A good book on rock climbing in the area is Eric Bjørnstad's *Desert Rock: Rock Climbs in the National Parks* (Chockstone Press, Box 3505, Evergreen, CO 80439, tel. 303/674–6888), which describes more than 100 climbs in the parks and surrounding areas.

Ski Touring. Warm weather restricts ski touring in Arches and Canyonlands, but during heavy snow years, it is not just possible—it's dazzling. The dry crystal snow sparkling on the bright orange rocks creates a striking tableau. If you're lucky, you might spot a coyote. The nearby La Sal Mountains provide the best ski touring in the area. Rentals are available through **Rim Cyclery** (94 W. 100 N, Moab, UT 84532, tel. 435/259–5333) and **Global Expeditions** (711 N. 500 W, Moab, UT 84532, tel. 435/259–6604, fax 435/259–8069). **Nichols Expeditions** (497 N. Main St., Moab, UT 84532, tel. 800/648–8488) lead guided trips of the White Rim Trail.

Swimming. The Colorado River, with its often fast and powerful currents, is not the safest place to swim. Lake Powell, southwest of Canyonlands park, is a popular alternative, but be careful when diving there—dangerous rock formations lie beneath the water. In Moab, swimming is limited to motel pools and a public pool, which is open in summer. Many backpackers use the showers at the Moab city pool.

CHILDREN'S PROGRAMS Both parks have a Junior Ranger program for children ages six to 12, with some hands-on nature activities and special interpretive hikes geared to children. The visitor centers at both parks sell publications for kids. Some river guide companies sponsor family raft trips on the Colorado. For baby-sitting services, check with the Grand County Travel Council (805 N. Main St., Moab, UT 84532, tel. 800/635–6622).

EVENING ACTIVITIES **Arches.** Arches offers a standard evening program each night just after sunset at an amphitheater in the Devils Garden Campground. Underneath Skyline Arch, this is one of the most dramatic theater settings in the National Park Service system. Evening programs usually begin before Easter weekend and run into October, depending on staff. Check at the visitor center for details.

Canyonlands. Evening programs are held at the Squaw Flat Campground in the Needles district and at the Willow Flat Campground in Island of the Sky Campground. From April through October these programs take place at least three times a week, but check with the park for a schedule.

DINING

Since there are no lodges in either Canyonlands or Arches, you will have to venture outside the park to find a restaurant. The towns of Green River and Monticello have a few restaurants, but Moab has the greatest selection of cuisines and particularly good Mexican fare. Authentic 1950s diners also abound in this area; they are great places to find inexpensive food, a powerful cup of coffee, and plenty of colorful local characters. Dress is always casual. If you expect to have a drink with your dinner, make sure the restaurant you choose serves alcoholic beverages; lots of restaurants in Utah do not.

Sunset Grill. Once the home of uranium magnate Charlie Steen, this restaurant is a Moab landmark. It was formerly called Mi Vida, which was the name he gave to his lifelong project: a patent for a uranium mine. Built high on a cliff overlooking town, the Sunset Grill serves fresh meat and seafood. *900 N. Hwy. 191, Moab, UT, tel. 435/259-7146. AE, DC, MC, V. $$$*

Buck's Grill House. Originally built for a movie set, Buck's Grill House looks like a fort from the outside. You'll be surprised, however, by the urbane setting inside, complete with linen tablecloths, chandeliers, paneling, and even stained-glass windows. The owner and chef, Tim Buckingham, serves up local specialties such as buffalo meat loaf and venison stew, as well as fresh fish, pasta, and vegetarian dishes. *Hwy. 191, Moab, UT, tel. 435/259-5201. AE, MC, V. No lunch. $$-$$$*

Grand Old Ranch House. This two-story brick building is listed on the National Register of Historic Places. Inside, the place brings back memories of grandma, with standard fare: German dishes, prime rib, seafood, and steaks. *N. Hwy. 191, Moab, UT, tel. 435/259-5753. AE, DC, V. Closed mid-Dec.–Feb. No lunch. $$-$$$*

Bar M Chuckwagon Suppers. An old cowboy camp may come to mind when you enter this open-air restaurant; there's even a small western theme park on the property with a log-cabin gift shop, a Native American tepee (somewhat out of place in a cowboy camp), and a shooting gallery. Barbecued beef and chicken, baked beans, sourdough biscuits, and peach cobbler are served to guests seated around picnic tables. Nightly entertainment can include such western favorites as clogging and cowboy singing. Inclusive dinner price is $16. Beer and wine coolers are served. *N. Hwy. 191, 8 mi north of Moab, UT, tel. 435/259-2276 or 800/214-2085. MC, V. Closed Oct.–Mar. No lunch. $$*

Center Cafe. In perhaps the most eclectic and imaginative of Moab's eateries, chefs Paul and Zee McCarroll prepare unusual culinary delights such as roasted eggplant, and lasagna made with polenta. Vegetarians will be more than happy here. *92 E. Center St., Moab, UT, tel. 435/259-4295. D, MC, V. No lunch. $$*

Eddie McStiff's Brew Pub & Restaurant. After a tough, dusty day of mountain biking, this pub is a great place to unwind. Sample one of the five types of ales brewed in McStiff's brewery, followed by a New York– or Chicago-style pizza, both specialties of the house. Also on the menu are pastas, sandwiches, salads, steaks, and charbroiled burgers. *57 S. Main St., Western Plaza, Moab, UT, tel. 435/259-2337. MC, V. $$*

Honest Ozzie's Café and Desert Oasis. A play on the Native American name Anasazi, Honest Ozzie's is a haven for vegetarians in this land of steak lovers. Natural foods and seafood are the specialties. Two popular dishes are the breakfast waffles and Ozzie's Oriental, a vegetable stir-fry. Outdoor seating is available in a shady, quiet garden. *100 West, Moab, UT, tel. 435/259-8442. Reservations not accepted. No credit cards. No dinner. $$*

La Hacienda. This Mexican restaurant adjacent to a motel feels like a franchise, but the large portions of fine food more than make up for any lack of ambience. La Hacienda serves delicious Mexican breakfasts, including *huevos rancheros*. Beer is the only alcohol served. *574 N. Main St., Moab, UT, tel. 435/259–6319. Reservations not accepted except for 6 or more. MC, V. $$*

Slick Rock Cafe. In the Historic Slick Rock Building on Main Street, you can sample vegetarian and southwestern fare. Reproductions of the state's famous petroglyph panels decorate the colorful café's walls. *5 N. Main St., Moab, UT, tel. 435/259–8004. DC, MC, V. $$*

Fat City Smokehouse. Historic photos and local art cover the walls of this old house a block off Center Street. There are generous portions of Texas-style barbecued beef, ribs, chicken, sausage, and pork, as well as vegetarian entrées. *36 S. 100 W, Moab, UT, tel. 435/259–4302. AE, MC, V. $–$$*

Milt's Stop and Eat. At this little drive-in with only about eight stools around its lunch counter, you'll get the same kind of good food this place served back in the 1950s, when it opened. Chili and chili-cheeseburgers are specialties. Milt's is an especially good place for breakfast. *356 Millcreek, Moab, UT, tel. 801/259–7424. No credit cards. Closed Sun. $*

PICNIC SPOTS Picnic areas are limited in both Arches and Canyonlands. Since there are no stores inside either park, make sure to bring your own supplies and plenty of water. In Arches, picnic areas with tables and fire grates are found at the **visitor center,** near **Devils Garden Campground,** and at the turnoff to **Balanced Rock.** In Canyonlands, the Island in the Sky district has picnic tables at **Upheaval Dome** and near the **Grand View Point Overlook.** There are also tables scattered throughout the Needles district.

LODGING

There are no overnight accommodations in Arches or Canyonlands national parks. Motels in the towns of Moab, Green River,

Hanksville, and Monticello are fairly standard. The best of the chain motels are **Best Western Canyonlands** (16 S. Main St., Moab, UT 84532, tel. 435/259–2300), **Best Western Greenwell** (1055 S. Main St., Moab, UT 84532, tel. 435/259–6151 or 800/528–1234), **Comfort Suites** (800 S. Main St., Moab, UT 84532, tel. 435/259–5252), **Ramada Inn** (182 S. Main St., Moab, UT 84532, tel. 435/259–7141 or 800/272–6232), and **Super 8** (889 N. Main St., Moab, UT 84532, tel. 435/259–8868 or 800/800–8000). If you can afford it, the nicest and most authentic place to stay in southeastern Utah is the Pack Creek Ranch (*see below*).

For a complete list of lodges and campgrounds in Moab and Green River, contact the Moab Visitor Center (Center and Main Sts., Moab, UT 84532, tel. 435/259–8825 or 800/635–6622). Make reservations well ahead of time if you plan to visit Moab between Easter weekend and the end of October. If you plan to bring your children with you to a bed-and-breakfast, consult with the proprietors in advance.

Castle Valley Inn. The best thing about this inn is the hot tub, with its great views of the red rock cliffs that rise 2,000 ft overhead. Castle Valley is a half hour northeast of Moab, by car, on a serene 11-acre property. Rooms are decorated in a Southwestern style with a collection of Navajo rugs from some of the finest weavers in the area. A full breakfast with fresh fruit and homemade breads is included in the price. To get here, follow the Colorado River to Fisher Towers and then follow the signs. *424 Amber La., Castle Valley, Moab, UT 84532, tel. 435/259–6012. Reservations: Castle Valley Star Route, Box 2602, Moab, UT 84532. 8 rooms. MC, V. Closed Jan. $$$*

Pack Creek Ranch. In the foothills of the La Sal Mountains, this dude ranch is a southern Utah institution and one of the best lodgings in the state. You won't find phones or televisions in the rooms, which are in individual cabins, but you will enjoy comfortable chairs, wood-burning fireplaces, well-stocked bookshelves, and breathtaking views over the Moab Rim and the La Sal Mountains. The cowboy-western feel of Pack Creek could not be more authentic; the life of Ken Sleight, the ranch's owner, was the inspiration for the polygamist river runner Seldom Seen Smith in Edward Abbey's book *The Monkey Wrench Gang*. The Pack Creek Ranch is 15 mi southeast of Moab, just off the La Sal Mountain Loop Road. Breakfast, lunch, and dinner are included with the room rate. *Box 1270, Moab, UT 84532, tel. 435/259–5505, fax 435/259–8879. 11 rooms. Facilities: restaurant. AE, MC, V. $$$*

Sunflower Hill. This B&B is in a 100-year-old farmhouse with adobe walls. The colorful barnyard signs and painted objects scattered around the rooms are the handiwork of the owner. A buffet breakfast is served every morning. *185 N. 300 E, Moab, UT 84532, tel. 801/259–2974. 11 rooms, 1 suite. MC, V. $$*

Lazy Lizard International Hostel. Popular with mountain bikers, this hostel is not fancy, but the $7 to $10 a night price range makes it almost as inexpensive as camping. Large groups are accommodated in two houses in town. The Lazy Lizard belongs to the American Association of International Hostels (AAIH), but you do not need a hostel card to stay here. Showers are available to nonguests for $2. There's also a picnic area on the grounds. *1213 S. Hwy. 191, Moab, UT 84532, tel. 435/259–6057. 5 dorm rooms (4–7 people), 8 cabins (4 people), 5 private rooms (1–2 people). Facilities: hot tub, kitchen, coin laundry. No credit cards. $*

CAMPING

Sites cannot be reserved at campgrounds in Arches and Canyonlands national parks, unless you are part of a large group. Opt for Dead Horse Point State Park or Bureau of Land Management campgrounds over the generally unattractive private campgrounds near Moab.

Though campers may be fined for pitching their tents within 10 mi of Moab, there are developed and primitive campsites along the Colorado River further up- and down-river from Moab. At the primitive sites, campers have no shower facilities and must use portable toilet stalls and existing fire rings. Check with the Bureau of Land Management (tel. 435/259–6111) for regulations.

INSIDE THE PARKS You will have to get up very early in the morning to get a campsite at **Devils Garden Campground,** the only one in Arches. It begins filling in early March and stays full until the end of October. Set against a backdrop of red slickrock and surrounded by the park's famous arches, it is justly popular. There are 54 sites here, for both RVs and tents, as well as two group sites accommodating up to 50 people. Vault toilets are used during the winter, and water is turned off from November through mid-March. Sites cost $8 per night, $5 when the water is off. Check at the entrance station or visitor center for information on availability.

There are 26 tent and RV sites in **Squaw Flat,** in the Needles section of Canyonlands. These are a good distance from one another and are nestled in little rock coves. The water is turned off from October through mid-March, but the campground remains open. Sites cost $8 from March through October; during the rest of the year you can camp free of charge.

Perched atop a mesa and accessible by a 1-mi dirt road from the main paved road is **Willow Flat,** a primitive camper's delight in the Island in the Sky district of Canyonlands. The 10 sites for tents and two for RVs are shaded by a few trees, but the ubiquitous gnats detract from the scenic grandeur throughout much of the summer. Sites are spaced 30 to 50 ft apart and will accommodate a 22-ft RV. There are vault toilets and fire grates here but no water, and year-round you can set up camp for up to seven days without paying a fee.

Canyonlands has a number of backcountry campsites in the Island in the Sky, Needles, and Maze districts. In Island in the Sky District these are along the popular White Rim

ARCHES AND CANYONLANDS CAMPGROUNDS

Campground	Total number of sites	Sites suitable for RVs	Number of hookups	Drive to sites	Hike to sites	Flush toilets	Pit/chemical toilets	Drinking water	Showers	Fire grates	Swimming	Boat access	Playground	Disposal station	Ranger station	Public telephone	Reservation possible	Daily fee per site	Dates open
INSIDE ARCHES																			
Devils Garden	54	54	0	•		•	•***	•		•								$5–$8	year-round
INSIDE CANYONLANDS																			
Squaw Flat	26	26	0	•			•***	•		•								$6*	year-round
Willow Flat	12	2	0	•			•			•								free	year-round
NEAR THE PARKS																			
Dead Horse Point State Park	21	21	0	•		•		•		•				•	•	•	•**	$9	late Mar.–late Oct.
Hatch Point (BLM)	10	10	0	•			•	•***		•								$6	year-round
Windwhistle (BLM)	19	19	0	•			•	•***		•								$6	year-round
Oowah Lake (National Forest)	6	6	0	•			•											free	June–late Sept.
Warner Lake (National Forest)	20	20	0	•			•	•		•								$7	mid-May–Oct.
Needles Outpost	46	20	0	•		•			•								•	$10	mid-Mar.–Oct.
Moab KOA	103	59	39	•		•		•	•	•	•		•	•		•	•	$16–$20.25	mid-Feb.–mid-Nov.
Slickrock Country	198	148	103	•		•		•	•		•					•	•	$14.50–$27	year-round
Up the Creek	20	0	0	•				•	•									$8	mid-Mar.–Oct.

*Fee charged only when water is available.   ** Reservation fee charged.   *** Water turned off in winter.

Road and can be reserved by mail or by fax (Canyonlands National Park Reservation Office, 2282 Southwest Resource Blvd., Moab UT 84532, tel. 435/259–4351, fax 435/259–4285) with MasterCard or Visa. Permits cost $10 and are required for all backcountry campsites; reserve far in advance.

Camping with any vehicle (bikes are considered vehicles) within the park boundaries requires a designated campsite. The Willow Flat and Squaw Flat campgrounds can accommodate passenger cars, but they are small and have very limited facilities. No reservations are taken, and the campgrounds often fill up by early morning from March through June and mid-September to October.

Backpacking is permitted in the backcountry at both Arches and Canyonlands, but in both parks you must obtain a backcountry permit from a visitor center or ranger station. Gathering firewood is not permitted in either park. Campers in front-country sites and designated four-wheel-drive sites can bring in their own wood or charcoal, but backpackers cannot have fires.

NEAR THE PARK If the Devils Garden Campground in Arches is full, the public camping area at **Dead Horse Point State Park** (Box 609, Moab, UT 84532, tel. 435/259–2614) near Canyonlands is a good second choice; it often fills a few hours later than Arches. Impressively set near the edge of a 2,000-ft cliff above the Colorado River, this facility has 21 RV and tent sites. Picnic tables are covered and have windbreaks. Although the rest rooms have no showers, they do have flush toilets and hot and cold running water. There is a disposal station here as well as a ranger station and a public phone. Sites cost $9 per night. Call 800/322–3770 to make reservations for a $5 fee. The campground is open year-round.

The Bureau of Land Management's (tel. 435/259–6111) two campgrounds along the eastern border of Canyonlands, **Hatch Point** and **Windwhistle,** are less crowded and more primitive than most of the campgrounds in this area. Both have drinking water, portable toilets, and fire grates. Hatch Point is near the Anticline Overlook and has 10 RV and tent sites; Windwhistle is on the road to the Needles Overlook and has 19 RV and tent sites. To get to these campgrounds from Moab, take Highway 191 south 32 mi and then go west 5 mi for Windwhistle, and west and north 25 mi for Hatch Point. These campgrounds are open year-round, but the water is on only from April through October. Sites cost $6 per night when there's water and are free when there's not.

High in the La Sal Mountains are two other public campgrounds, **Oowah Lake,** with six free, primitive sites, and **Warner Lake,** with 20 tent and RV sites ($7 each). Both have portable toilet stalls, but only Warner Lake has drinking water. Oowah is open from June through the end of September; Warner Lake, from mid-May to October. Call the U.S. Forest Service (tel. 435/259–7155) for more information.

The best private facility in the Canyonlands area is the **Needles Outpost** (Box 1107, Monticello, UT 84535, tel. 435/979–4007), at the entrance to the Needles district on Highway 211. A good alternative when the Squaw Flat campground inside the park is full, this facility has 26 sites for tents and 20 for RVs (no hookups), flush toilets, a snack bar, and the only showers within miles. Sites cost $10 per day. The campground is open from mid-March through October.

In the Moab area, there are eight private but less than outstanding campgrounds. The best of these is the **Moab KOA** (tel. 435/259–6682 or 800/562–0372), 4 mi south of Moab on Highway 191, which has a view of the Moab Rim, the cliffs surrounding town, and the farming area of Spanish Valley. This facility has 59 RV sites (39 with complete hookups), 44 tent sites, drinking water, flush toilets, showers, and a disposal station. In addition, it has a grocery store, snack bar, pay phone, swimming pool, and playground. Sites cost $16 to $20.25 per day. Overlooking the portal of the Colorado River at the other end of town, **Slickrock Country Campground** (1301½ N. Hwy. 191, Moab, UT 84532, tel. 435/259–7660) is another mediocre choice. It has 148 RV sites with full and partial hookups, 50 tent sites, and 14 cabins. Slickrock has flush toilets, showers, drinking water, swimming, three Jacuzzis, and fire grates and is open year-round. Two people can expect to pay $14.50 for tent sites, $19.75 for full hookups, $17.75 for water/electric, and $27 for cabins. The small **Up the Creek** campground (210 E. 300 S, Moab, UT 84532, tel. 435/259–6995), three blocks off Main Street in a residential neighborhood, is for tenters only, with just 20 sites that cost $8 per person. The campground has flush toilets, drinking water, and showers. It's open from mid-March through October.

Among Moab's private campgrounds, **Portal RV Park and Fishery** (1261 N. Hwy. 191, Moab, UT 84532, tel. 435/259–6108), is one of the newest, with 36 sites (25 with complete hookups), 11 sites with no hookups, 10 tent sites, a convenience store, a disposal site, flush toilets, showers, and laundry facilities. Trails from the park are adjacent to the Matheson Wetlands Pre-

serve. **Canyonlands Campark** (555 S. Main St., Moab, UT 84532, tel. 435/259–6848), is the most central, but also the busiest. It has 108 RV sites (60 have complete hookups), 70 tent sites, flush toilets, showers, drinking water, a swimming pool, a disposal station, and a public phone. **Holiday Haven RV Park** (400 N. 5th W, Moab, UT 84532, tel. 435/259–5834), in a quiet residential area, has 98 RV sites with complete hookups, flush toilets, showers, drinking water, fire grates, a playground, a swimming pool, and a public phone; it's open only from March through October. **Arch View Campground and Resort** (N. Hwy. 191 at 313, Moab, UT 84532, tel. 435/259–7854), a newer facility, has 44 RV sites and 33 tent sites, drinking water, flush toilets, showers, and laundry facilities. **Moab Valley RV and Campark** (1773 N. Hwy. 191, Moab, UT 84532, tel. 435/259–4469), a grassy, open field great for bird-watching, has 62 RV sites, 50 tent sites, six cabins, two shower houses, drinking water, flush toilets, a disposal station, and laundry facilities. **Spanish Trail RV Park and Campground** (2980 S. Hwy. 191, tel. 435/259–2411), has 60 RV sites and 13 tent sites, drinking water, flush toilets, showers, a picnic pavilion, and laundry facilities.

The Badlands, Mt. Rushmore, and the Black Hills

South Dakota

By Dick Hoyt Willis

he French Canadian trappers who visited what is now Badlands National Park in the 18th century declared these were "bad lands to travel across." They were right. The 244,000 acres of sheer cliffs and buttes are dramatic and eerie: The landscape is stark, almost lunar. Things have changed since the days of those grizzled mountain men, however, and visitors today will find easy driving, scenic overlooks, well-marked hiking trails, and the chance to safely experience the most desolate terrain of the Great Plains.

Adding to the attraction of the Badlands, but in sharp contrast to it, are Mt. Rushmore and the surrounding pine tree–blanketed hills, just two hours to the west. Set against the rugged natural beauty of the Black Hills, the carvings of George Washington, Thomas Jefferson, Theodore Roosevelt, and Abraham Lincoln on the granite face of Mt. Rushmore strike a curious note: one immense, man-made symbol carved into and surrounded by nature's spectacle. Work on this huge tribute to democracy, located 23 mi southwest of Rapid City, South Dakota, began in 1927 under the supervision of artist Gutzon Borglum. He employed jackhammers and dynamite to coax the presidents' images from the stone, and although the carving was completed 14 years later, in 1941, maintenance to protect the memorial from the ravages of the elements is an ongoing project. As the crown jewel of the Black Hills tourism industry, Mt. Rushmore National Memorial hosts 2.7 million visitors each year.

Most of these tourists pass through the area quickly, on their way to Yellowstone or the Tetons, leaving more thorough exploration to the hikers and naturalists. The well-traveled route between Rapid City and the memorial has become a home to roadside video arcades, giant water slides, and other capitalist ventures.

But since relatively few of these visitors stray off the beaten path into the forested backcountry, much of the Black Hills remains an unspoiled playground of secluded valleys thick with pine and aspen. It is only after you watch mountain goats graze in the forests of the Black Hills and feel the energy of an afternoon thunderstorm over the rocky cliffs of the Badlands that you can truly understand why many Sioux and Cheyenne consider these lands sacred.

The Badlands was designated a national monument in 1939, but did not become a national park until 1978.

ESSENTIAL INFORMATION

VISITOR INFORMATION If you are interested in visiting the Badlands, contact **Badlands National Park** or **Badlands Natural History Association** (Box 6, Interior, SD 57750, tel. 605/433–5361 for both). Rangers at the Badlands' **Ben Reifel Visitor Center** can answer many of your questions.

Several government offices and private organizations provide information on Mt. Rushmore and the Black Hills. Try **Mt.**

Rushmore National Memorial (Superintendent, Box 268, Keystone, SD 57751, tel. 605/574–2523), **Mt. Rushmore National Memorial Society** (Box 1524, Rapid City, SD 57709, tel. 605/341–8883), **Mt. Rushmore History Association** (Box 208, Keystone, SD 57751, tel. 605/574–2523), **Black Hills National Forest** (Supervisor's Office, R.R. 2, Box 200, Custer, SD 57730, tel. 605/673–2251), and **Black Hills Parks and Forest Association** (Rte. 1, Box 190–WCNP, Wind Cave National Park, Hot Springs, SD 57747, tel. 605/745–7020).

For information on Rapid City, contact the **Rapid City Convention and Visitors Bureau** (Box 747, 444 Mt. Rushmore Rd. N, Rapid City, SD 57709, tel. 605/343–1744), the **South Dakota Department of Tourism** (Capital Lake Plaza, Pierre, SD 57501, tel. 605/773–3301 or 800/732–5682), or the nearby **Custer State Park** (HC83, Box 70, Custer, SD 57730, tel. 605/255–4515).

A backcountry permit isn't required for hiking or camping in Badlands National Park, but it is a good idea to check in at park headquarters before setting out on a backcountry journey. Backpackers may set up camps anywhere except within a half mile of roads or trails. At Mt. Rushmore, visitors must stay on developed trails in the area of the memorial. No permits are needed to hike or camp in nearby Black Hills National Forest and Black Elk Wilderness.

FEES Entrance to Mt. Rushmore is free, but from April through November Badlands National Park charges $10 per car and $5 per person on a motorcycle or on foot. Bus rates are $30 for one to six passengers, $45 for seven to 25 passengers, and $100 for buses with more than 26 passengers.

Mt. Rushmore charges a nominal parking fee for a year-round pass for the main parking lot. (There's also a free side parking lot about .25 mi from the visitor center.)

PUBLICATIONS **Mt. Rushmore and the Black Hills.** One excellent book on the area is *America's Shrine of Democracy: A Pictorial History,* available from the Mt. Rush-

more History Association (*see* Visitor Information, *above*). The association also sells *Mount Rushmore: The Shrine,* a 20-minute videotape showing historic footage of the construction of the memorial. The most comprehensive map of the Black Hills is the "Black Hills National Forest Visitors Map," available from the Black Hills National Forest (*see* Visitor Information, *above*). The Sierra Club's "Hiking Map of the Norbeck Wildlife Preserve" includes the Black Elk Wilderness and gives more detail on these areas than the national forest's recreation map. It, too, is available from the Mt. Rushmore History Association.

The **Geology Department, South Dakota School of Mines and Technology** (Room 307, Mineral Industries Bldg., Rapid City, SD 57701, tel. 605/394–2461) sells USGS maps and publications, as well as a limited number of books. *An Introduction to Custer State Park,* a basic, inexpensive guide to the region's flora and fauna, is available from the Black Hills Parks and Forest Association (*see* Visitor Information, *above*).

The Badlands. *Badlands: Its Life and Landscape* can be purchased from the Badlands Natural History Association (*see* Visitor Information, *above*). The same association publishes *A Curious Country: Badlands National Park,* which is a good introduction to the plants, animals, geology, and history of the Badlands. The association's 18-minute video, *Buried Fossils, Living Prairie,* is also for sale, as is its Badlands topographic map, which is useful for hiking.

GEOLOGY AND TERRAIN The unique terrain at both Mt. Rushmore and the Badlands is the result of 60 million years of geologic activity. The Black Hills began as a mountainous landscape covered with limestone and shale sedimentary rock, but this covering gradually eroded away, exposing a granite face. Much of the sedimentary rock that eroded from the Black Hills was deposited in the Badlands, along with ash from the volcanoes in the Yellowstone area. Water flowed over the landscape and carved out the huge buttes and cliffs—a process that continues to this day. The gradual erosion also exposed fossils of a host of extinct animals, including ancient horses, camels, rodents, turtles, alligators, giant pigs, and saber-toothed cats. One of the Badlands' most unusual finds is the *brontothere,* a large beast with horns on its face. The Sioux called them thunder-horses, claiming they fell from the sky during rainstorms. While many of the Badlands fossils are now on display at museums around the world, you'll find a good number of them at the Ben Reifel Visitor Center, along the Fossil Exhibit Trail in the park, and at the Museum of Geology at the South Dakota School of Mines and Technology (501 E. St. Joseph St., Rapid City, tel. 605/394–2467).

FLORA AND FAUNA The lunar landscape of the Badlands seems barren at first, with its light color buttes and cliffs and sparse greenery. But closer inspection will prove your first impressions wrong: The prairie grass supports pronghorn antelope, mule deer, and white-tailed deer, which seek shelter under small clumps of juniper trees. Some 400 buffalo roam the park, and one of the country's largest populations of Rocky Mountain bighorn sheep occupies the steep buttes and cliffs. The bighorns are often spotted in the Pinnacles and Cedar Pass areas, and during winter they sometimes even walk on Highway 240.

Prairie rattlesnakes thrive in the rocky terrain of the Badlands, blending in well with the pale soil. The rattlers spend their winters underground in large dens, but during the summer they become very active, feeding on insects, mice, and eggs.

Meadowlarks, sharptail grouse, and mountain bluebirds are seen regularly, and visitors can often spot golden eagles, hawks, and turkey vultures soaring high above the park in the warm air currents. These birds eat prairie dogs, which are a common sight in the Badlands. In fact, there are so many prairie dogs in and around the park that this is one of the first spots in the world where the endangered, prairie-dog-eating, black-footed ferret has been reintroduced.

The green mountainsides of the Black Hills are quite different from the Badlands. The hills around Mt. Rushmore are dotted with ponderosa pine trees, while in the cooler, higher elevations spruce thrive. Stands of aspen and birch grow near the many streams, particularly in the northern part of the Black Hills.

Nature lovers will find that it's easy to spot mountain goats around Mt. Rushmore, especially in the big rock formations on Highway 244. Mule deer and white-tailed deer are also common in the area surrounding the memorial, and observers with sharp eyes should be able to spot porcupines, red squirrels, wild turkeys, and elk in the forest. Around the park concession are a number of chipmunks that are very accustomed to the presence of human beings.

WHEN TO GO Both Mt. Rushmore and the Badlands are open year-round, but the peak tourist season falls between Memorial Day and Labor Day, when daytime temperatures around Mt. Rushmore hover in the 80s and are even higher in the Badlands. Relief from the heat can be found at higher elevations in the Black Hills. About 20,000 people pass through Mt. Rushmore on a typical summer day, but the biggest crowds arrive during early August for the Sturgis Motorcycle Classic, when thousands of bikers roar through the Black Hills on Harley-Davidsons. The autumn weather is sunny and warm, with temperatures usually in the 60s or 70s, although by October the thermometer may fall below freezing and there may be some snow. Many consider fall the best time to visit, as temperatures cool and the crowds thin out. Spring is often wet, cold, and unpredictable, with surprise snowstorms as late as April.

SEASONAL EVENTS **Easter:** A nondenominational **Easter sunrise service** takes place at Mt. Rushmore's amphitheater (tel. 605/574–2523). **July 4: Independence Day** is always a big event at Mt. Rushmore. For a schedule of events contact the visitor center. **June to August:** Throughout summer, bands and choruses from across the country perform free concerts at the Mt. Rushmore amphitheater. Contact the visitor center for a schedule of related events. **Mid-September:** On **POW/ MIA Day** patriotic speeches and a band help to commemorate imprisoned and missing wartime servicemen and women.

WHAT TO PACK Hikers and campers should be prepared for abrupt changes in weather at any time of the year in the Black Hills. Bring rain gear and, in summer, sunscreen.

GENERAL STORES The **Rushmore Mall** (Exit 58 or 59 off I–90, Rapid City, tel. 605/348–3378) has 120 stores selling virtually everything but groceries. It's open weekdays 10–9, Saturday 10–7, and Sunday 11:30–5:30. **Krull's Market** (Hwy. 16/ 385, Hill City, tel. 605/574–2717), 1 mi east of Hill City's town center, sells groceries and general camping accessories, such as gloves, caps, and camp-stove fuel. It's open daily from 7:30 AM–9 PM. **Badlands Grocery** (Main St., Interior, tel. 605/433–5445) is 2 mi south of the Ben Reifel Visitor Center and is open daily 8–8 in the summer and Monday–Saturday 8–6 in the winter. **AMFAC Parks and Resorts** (Mt. Rushmore, tel. 605/574–2515), at the memorial, has a snack bar, dining room, and gift shop. Daily summer hours are 7 AM–10:30 PM; winter hours are 8–6. **Wall Drug** (510 Main St., Wall, tel. 605/ 279–2175) has a restaurant and carries a huge assortment of gift items, but since 1931, its claim to fame has been free ice water and a 5¢ cup of coffee. Wall Drug is open daily in summer from 6 AM to 10 PM and in winter from 6:30 to 5. **Cedar Pass Lodge** (Cedar Pass, tel. 605/433– 5460), near Ben Reifel Visitor Center in Badlands National Park, sells gift items and has a restaurant. It's open daily from 7 AM to 9 PM in summer, from 8 to 6 in fall, and is closed from November until mid-March.

ARRIVING AND DEPARTING The most practical way to reach Mt. Rushmore or the Badlands is by car. There is a bus station in Rapid City, as well as an airport outside the city, but unless you are planning to make a day-trip with a bus tour, you'll have to drive yourself. It is more than 23 mi from the memorial to Rapid City and another 50 mi or so from Rapid City to the Pinnacles entrance of the Badlands.

By Bus. The **bus station** (333 6th St., tel. 605/348–3300) in downtown Rapid City serves Jackrabbit and Powder River regional bus lines. Both make connections with Greyhound Lines elsewhere but neither goes to the parks. Bus service into the parks is available from several of the tour companies in the area throughout the summer (*see* Guided Tours, *below*), but if you are planning to stay in the parks for longer than a day, you'll have to negotiate prices with the company. **Budget** (Holiday Inn, 505 N. 5th St., tel. 605/343–8499) has a car-rental office within walking distance of the bus station.

By Car and RV. I–90 is the most direct route into the Badlands and Mt. Rushmore by car. Free state highway maps are available from the South Dakota Department of Tourism (*see* Visitor Information, *above*), and free maps for the Badlands are available from Badlands National Park (*see* Visitor Information, *above*).

To reach the Badlands, drive from Rapid City east on I–90 for 50 mi. You can pick up scenic Highway 240 to go through the park via the Pinnacles entrance (take exit 110 at Wall) or travel another 20 mi on I–90 to the other end of Highway 240 and enter the park at the northeast entrance (take exit 131 at Cactus Flat). Exit 110 is closer to the Badlands Wilderness Area; exit 131 is only a few miles from the Ben Reifel Visitor Center.

To reach Mt. Rushmore National Memorial from Rapid City, follow Mt. Rushmore Road (Highway 16) southwest for 23 mi. If coming in from I–90, take exit 57 to Mt. Rushmore Road and continue to the memorial. Yellowstone is a nine-hour, 440-mi drive west of Rapid City. Grand Teton National Park is another hour south of Yellowstone.

By Plane. Rapid City Regional Airport (tel. 605/394–4195) lies 10 mi southeast of Rapid City, off Highway 44. Two airport shuttles meet every flight at the airport baggage counter. Both provide shuttle service to any residence or business in Rapid City for $9 per person, $13 per couple, or $5 per person if the party is more than two people. The fare to go to any Rapid City motel is $7 per person, or $11 per couple. You can also opt for an airport limousine service, which costs about $1 per mile; try **ALSI Airport Shuttle** (2017 East Hwy. 44, Rapid City, tel. 605/343–5358 or 800/826–5358) or **Airport Express Shuttle** (428 Quincy St., Rapid City, tel. 605/399–9999 or 800/357–9998).

You can rent a car at the airport from **Avis** (tel. 605/393–0740), **Budget** (tel. 605/393–0488), **Hertz** (tel. 605/393–0160), **National** (tel. 605/393–2664), or **Thrifty** (tel. 605/393–0663).

By Train. The nearest train stations are in Williston, North Dakota, and Denver, Colorado—both more than seven hours from the park. There are no bus or plane connections from Williston to the Badlands, and it is neither cost-effective nor quick to take a plane or bus from Denver's train station.

EXPLORING

Mt. Rushmore National Memorial, to the southwest of Rapid City, and Badlands National Park, to the southeast, are only a two-hour drive from each other. Travelers with limited time can see both in one day, but to really appreciate the natural beauty of the area visitors should set aside at least three or four days to make a few side trips into the wilderness. The best way to explore the area is in your own car.

Mt. Rushmore is a must-see, naturally. Try to visit in the early morning, when the natural lighting is most dramatic, or at sunset, to see the nightly lighting ceremony. Other highlights are Custer State Park, with its herd of 1,400 buffalo, and the spelunkers' two favorites, Wind Cave and Jewel Cave.

For a good overview of the Badlands follow Highway 240 through the park, stopping at the 13 scenic overlooks along the way. The Ben Reifel Visitor Center provides informative brochures on the park's many hiking trails. Visitors who remain in their cars can see the most popular Badlands sights in about four hours, but if you're going to do any hiking, allow a full day.

THE BEST IN ONE DAY The 100-mi trip between Badlands National Park headquarters and Mt. Rushmore National Memorial can be driven in two hours, so you can visit both places in one day if you start out early and make a quick tour through each one. Coming from the east on I–90, take exit 131 at Cactus Flat in the Badlands, and head south on Highway 240 for 30 minutes until you reach the Ben Reifel Visitor Center. You can also take a short stroll along one of the hiking trails near the visitor center.

When you leave Cedar Pass follow Badlands National Park Highway 240 west, stopping at the scenic overlooks along the way. Shortly after the Pinnacles Overlook head north to I–90 to leave the park. Take I–90 through Rapid City, and then exit 57 to Mt. Rushmore Road (Highway 16). Follow that south, straight to the memorial. This route is lined with diversions: a water slide; reptile gardens; an aquarium; and Bear Country U.S.A., a wildlife park (*see* Children's Programs, *below*).

When you reach the memorial boundary, continue past it heading south on the Iron Mountain Road (*see* Scenic Drives and Views, *below*). You can double back to the memorial later in the day, in time to see the lighting ceremony. Iron Mountain Road connects Mt. Rushmore with Custer State Park in the southern hills. The park's Wildlife Loop Road takes about an hour to drive.

If time permits, leave the Wildlife Loop Road at Route 6 and continue south into Wind Cave National Park (Hot Springs, tel. 605/745–4600), which contains the fifth-longest cave in the country (*see* Other Activities, *below*).

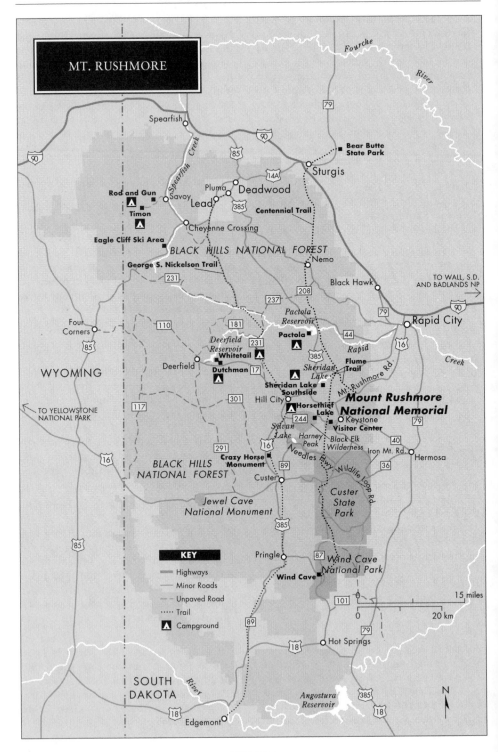

Later follow Highway 87 north out of Wind Cave National Park, into Custer State Park; continue on the Needles Highway through the Needles rock formations to Sylvan Lake. Keep going north past the lake on Highway 87 until you reach Highway 385/16. Follow this 100 yards to Highway 244, then head east toward Mt. Rushmore.

Mt. Rushmore National Memorial, the centerpiece, can be explored on foot in just an hour or so. At the visitor center you can watch a short video outlining the history of the memorial. During the summer you might be able to catch one of the many concerts held in the amphitheater below the huge carvings. The nightly lighting ceremony is preceded by a patriotic speech by one of the park rangers and a short film about the memorial. The time of the ceremony varies with the sunset in spring and fall, but it is at 9 PM during the summer. There is no ceremony in winter, but the mountain is illuminated for several hours beginning at sunset.

ORIENTATION PROGRAMS Scheduled to open in June 1998, a Mt. Rushmore museum will have 21 exhibits on how and why the memorial was carved, as well as a 125-seat theater. The memorial's **Information Center** (tel. 605/574–4104) has information about Mt. Rushmore and the surrounding Black Hills, with a four-minute video running continuously. It is open from 8 AM to 10 PM during summer, 8 to 5 during the off-season. The **Sculptor's Studio** (*see* Historic Buildings and Sites, *below*) has lectures about how the mountain was carved and displays of the equipment that was used, including a pneumatic hammer and a chair that carvers sat in while being hoisted up and down the faces.

At the **Ben Reifel Visitor Center** (tel. 605/433–5361) in Badlands National Park, an 18-minute video about Badlands geology and wildlife runs every half hour during summer. Exhibits about fossils, geology, wildlife, and the Sioux give visitors a basic understanding of the park.

GUIDED TOURS Gray Line of the Black Hills (1600 E. St. Patrick St., Rapid City, SD 57701, tel. 605/342–4461 or 800/456–4461) offers bus tours from Rapid City to Mt. Rushmore, Black Hills National Forest, Custer State Park, and Crazy Horse Monument, ranging in price from $16 to $32. **Stagecoach West** (Box 264, Rapid City, SD 57709, tel. 605/343–3113) and **Golden Circle Tours** (40 5th St. N, Custer, SD 57730, tel. 605/673–4349) lead similar tours in the same price range, but Golden Circle Tours also has a $25 tour out of Custer to more remote spots in the Black Hills, including visits to abandoned gold mines and a stop at Spring Creek, where guests can pan for gold and garnets. Stagecoach West has a full day tour, with an all-you-can-eat breakfast, Chuckwagon Dinner, and Cowboy Music Show for $42.

Gray Line of the Black Hills runs a tour to the Black Hills Passion Play in Spearfish every Tuesday and Sunday from June through August. The bus trip with a ticket to this reenactment of the last days of Christ costs $25. Golden Circle has an all-day mountain-bike tour that can be tailored to the ability of the participants. Bikes, helmets, and a picnic lunch are included, and a shuttle van joins the group at various points along the route to pick up tired bikers. The cost varies depending on time and distance.

ALSI Airport Shuttle (tel. 605/343–5358) provides a four-hour round-trip tour of the Badlands from Rapid City. The price starts at $85 for one person, with each additional person paying up to $10. A two-hour trip to Mt. Rushmore, including a half-hour stay at the monument, costs $40 for one person and up to $10 for each additional person. A full hour stay at the monument is $50.

SCENIC DRIVES AND VIEWS There are 13 scenic overlooks along the 27 mi of **Highway 240** (Badlands Loop Road) in Badlands National Park. You can easily take two hours or more driving this route, stopping at overlooks along the way to admire the splendid landscapes. The **Sage Creek Rim Road**, in the northwest part of the Badlands, is gravel, but it is safe for all kinds of

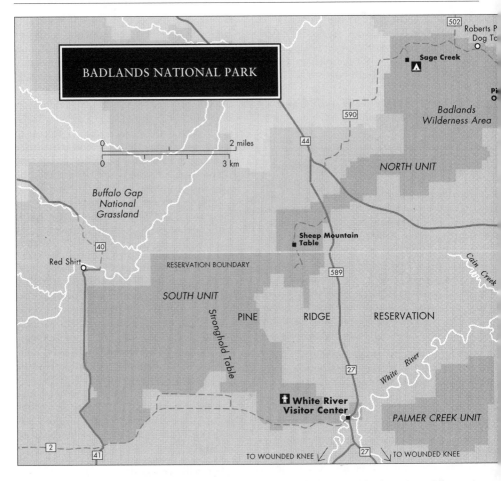

vehicles. To the south of this road lies the rugged Badlands Wilderness. A hike of even 50 yards or so into this rocky area will reward you with a more genuine appreciation of the Badlands. Explore the Roberts Prairie Dog Town on the north side of Sage Creek Rim Road, where you're likely to see some of these furry animals scampering about, constantly wary of the golden eagles that swoop down and snatch them in their powerful talons.

One span of **Mt. Rushmore Road** (Highway 16), the route most used from Rapid City to the memorial, is plastered with commercial billboards, but once it enters the Black Hills National Forest, nature takes the lead with pine forests and clear mountain lakes.

Mt. Rushmore Road meets **Iron Mountain Road** (Highway 16A), and the latter winds through some of the most rugged and dramatic sections of the Black Hills. Part of the **Peter Norbeck Scenic Byway,** this road was specially designed for sightseeing: As you follow it through mountain passes and over old wooden bridges, notice how tunnels along the route provide glimpses of Mt. Rushmore in the distance. The 17-mi drive from near the memorial to near the game lodge in Custer State Park takes more than half an hour.

Iron Mountain Road continues south into Custer State Park. A few buffalo can be spotted munching the prairie grass near the park's eastern entrance on Highway 36, and

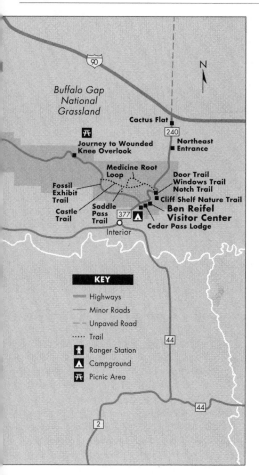

Buffalo Gap National Grassland

90

N

Cactus Flat

240

Journey to Wounded Knee Overlook

Northeast Entrance

Medicine Root Loop

Door Trail
Windows Trail
Notch Trail

Fossil Exhibit Trail

Cliff Shelf Nature Trail

Castle Trail

Saddle Pass Trail

377

Ben Reifel Visitor Center

Cedar Pass Lodge

Interior

KEY

— Highways
— Minor Roads
-- Unpaved Road
···· Trail
🏠 Ranger Station
⛺ Campground
🏕 Picnic Area

44

44

2

along the **Wildlife Loop Road** in Custer State Park, you'll often see them grazing at the side of the road or standing on the road itself. Don't attempt to shoo them away: These unpredictable animals can be extremely dangerous. Antelope, mule deer, coyotes, and eagles can also be spotted on the Wildlife Loop Road, particularly in the early morning and evening. The Loop takes an hour to drive if few stops are made.

From the northern stretch of the Wildlife Loop in Custer State Park, take **Highway 87** (Needles Highway), which is also part of the scenic byway, through the Needles rock formations. These impressive rock spires are popular with rock climbers. There are several tunnels along this section of road, and

RVs have been known to lose their side mirrors and pieces of their aluminum siding as they try to squeeze through. Cars, however, will have no trouble. Farther along Highway 87 you'll find Sylvan Lake, the highest lake in the Black Hills. Several parking areas along the roadside make it easy to pull over and take in the view. Across the lake is the spot where hikers begin the uphill trek to the top of Harney Peak, the highest point between the Wyoming and Colorado Rockies and the Swiss Alps.

Continue north past Sylvan Lake to Hill City, and take **Deerfield Road** (Highway 17) past little Newton Lake up to Deerfield Reservoir in the Black Hills high country. From Deerfield, venture off onto any one of the many gravel and dirt roads leading into the wild and remote country in the northern and western Black Hills. Some of these roads are good gravel; others are old logging roads that now barely qualify as trails. The best way to navigate this country is with a "Black Hills National Forest Visitors Map" (*see* Publications, *above*): Without it you stand an excellent chance of getting lost.

From Hill City you might also opt to take the **Black Hills Parkway** (U.S. 385) north through the scenic central hills up to Lead and Deadwood. Deadwood is an old mining town that has legalized gambling, with slot machines and poker, and a deliberate, commercialized Old West atmosphere. The huge underground Homestake gold mine sprawls under the town of Lead. A giant open pit gold mine can also be seen in the town. The road to Lead–Deadwood winds past the campground at Roubaix Lake (tel. 605/578–2744), a 10-acre lake stocked with trout; Custer Crossing Picnic Ground; and Strawberry Hill (tel. 605/578–2744), which has excellent access for people with disabilities. The 37-mi route north from Hill City through the central hills takes about 45 minutes with no stops.

If you're visiting during the fall you may want to continue past Lead–Deadwood up to **Spearfish Canyon** in the northern hills. Here, along another scenic byway, the trees lining the banks of the creek put on a breathtakingly colorful show as their leaves change color. To reach Spearfish, follow U.S. 85 southwest from Lead–Deadwood to Cheyenne Crossing and take U.S. 14A north past Savoy to the canyon. At Savoy, visit the Latchstring Village Center (tel. 605/584–2070), whose exhibits cover railroad and mining history as well as local geology and wildlife.

HISTORIC BUILDINGS AND SITES The creation of the **Mt. Rushmore National Memorial** began in 1927 under the supervision of artist Gutzon Borglum. Borglum died in 1941 after 14 years of work on the memorial, and his son Lincoln continued the project until funds ran out later that year. The faces of presidents Washington, Jefferson, Roosevelt, and Lincoln represent, respectively, independence, representation in government, leadership in world affairs, and equality and a strong union.

While at Mt. Rushmore, visit the **Sculptor's Studio,** which was built in 1939. It houses the working models of the memorial, as well as tools used for its construction. The studio is open to the public from mid-May through September. You can visit on your own or take a free tour, conducted daily from 9 to 5.

In the southern end of Badlands National Park is 3-mi-long **Stronghold Table,** a mesa that can be reached only by crossing one narrow land bridge just wide enough to let a wagon pass. It is on this mesa that one faction of the Sioux tribe gathered to perform the Ghost Dance, a ritual in which the Sioux wore white shirts that they believed would protect them from bullets. Some 600 Sioux danced here in 1890, praying for a future paradise where white men were gone and Native Americans once again dominated the Plains.

In December of 1890 the last Sioux left Stronghold Table to join Chief Big Foot and 350 other Sioux from the north in a trek to Pine Ridge, the headquarters of the Sioux reservation. They were planning to give up their fight for independence and submit to the U.S. government's authority, but when they reached Wounded Knee, they met with the U.S. 7th Cavalry in what was to be the last major military encounter between the Sioux and the United States Army. It is estimated that some 200 Sioux men, women, and children and 30 cavalry troopers died. Part of the route taken by the Sioux can be seen at **Journey to Wounded Knee Overlook** along Highway 240 in the park.

NATURE TRAILS AND SHORT WALKS Nature trails ranging in length from .25 mi to 12 mi wind through Badlands National Park near the Ben Reifel Visitor Center. All are well marked, so there is no danger of getting lost. You can buy trail guides to the Door, Fossil, and Cliff Shelf trails for 50¢ each, or borrow them at the trailheads and return them afterwards.

Notch Trail goes 1.5 mi round-trip over moderately difficult terrain and includes a climb up a ladder. Winds at the notch can be fierce, but the view of the White River Valley and the Pine Ridge Indian Reservation are worth the effort. Fossils are displayed under glass along the .25-mi loop of the **Fossil Exhibit Trail,** which is a good choice for those in wheelchairs. Walking the .75-mi round-trip course of **Door Trail** will give you a sense of what the Badlands country is all about; fossil soils, ash layers, and erosion are evident. **Cliff Shelf Nature Trail** is an easy .5-mi loop that runs past a pond bordered by cattails. Red-winged blackbirds live in this wet environment. **Castle Trail** stretches for 5.5 mi one-way from the Fossil Exhibit Trailhead on Highway 240 to the parking area for the Door and Windows trails; if you choose to use the **Medicine Root Loop,** which detours off the Castle Trail, you'll add .5 mi to the trek. This is an easy hike, but since you'll be walking for two hours you should bring drinking water with you. **Saddle Pass Trail,** which connects Highway 240 to the middle of Castle Trail and the beginning of the Medicine Root Loop, is a steep .5-mi climb up the side of "The Wall," an impressive rock formation.

LONGER HIKES You can cut out across the wild range of the Badlands' 64,144-acre **Badlands Wilderness** and walk for miles and miles, but bring along a topographical map (*see* Publications, *above*) to help you find your way—there are no marked trails.

Even more remote is the **South Unit** area: Again, there are no marked trails, and primitive conditions mean that hikers should bring their own water. Beware of parking along Highway 40 near Red Shirt Table, on the west side of the South Unit; vandals have been known to break into cars there. Stop at White River Visitor Center to ask about inconspicuous parking places.

Some of the finest hiking near Mt. Rushmore can be found just to the west, in the **Norbeck Wildlife Preserve** and the **Black Elk Wilderness**—both part of the Black Hills National Forest. The nearest trailhead (unmarked) starts just across Highway 244 from the Mt. Rushmore Memorial parking lot; it is a good place to start out on day hikes, but no overnight parking is permitted.

A trailhead that's easy to find is near **Horsethief Lake.** Go west of the memorial 2 mi on Highway 244 and make a left on the first gravel road, just before Horsethief Lake. The well-marked trailhead is a quarter-mile down the road. The trail wanders between rough boulders, and farther along, large rock formations jut up into the sky. Farther still, a network of trails crosses through the Black Elk Wilderness. The Sierra Club "Hiking Map of the Norbeck Wildlife Preserve" (*see* Publications, *above*) is a handy companion for full-day trips.

There's another good access point 3.5 mi farther west on Highway 244. Take the Palmer Gulch turnoff, which skirts some huge aspen stands. The strenuous **Lost Cabin Trail** goes uphill more than a mile before entering the Black Elk Wilderness and continuing to Sylvan Lake or Harney Peak. The summit at Harney Peak is a difficult two-hour climb from the lake. From the Sylvan Lake Dam, the relatively easy **Sunday Gulch Trail** winds 1.5 mi through lush bottomland forest along a tiny, sparkling mountain stream.

The very level and easily hiked 15-mi round-trip **Flume Trail** runs along an old mining flume from Sheridan Lake to Coon Hollow. Pick up the trail at either end.

Ten miles northeast of I–90 is **Bear Butte State Park** (Box 688, Sturgis, SD 57785, tel. 605/347–5240), which rises up out of the Plains east of Sturgis. The Cheyenne, Sioux, and other Native Americans hold this mountain sacred and make pilgrimages to it. Hiking trails lead through the pines to the top, where you can see five states on clear days. A 6.2-mi seasonal "volksmarch" (organized walk) takes place every day from May until mid-September. Admission is $2.

Other popular routes are the 111-mi **Centennial Trail,** which leads from Wind Cave National Park to Bear Butte State Park, running along the eastern edge of the Black Hills and through Custer State Park, Black Hills National Forest, and Fort Meade Recreation Area; and the 110-mi **George S. Mickelson Trail,** which follows a historic railroad grade past logging and mining camps.

OTHER ACTIVITIES Back-Road Driving. Driving off roads isn't allowed in Badlands National Park or Mt. Rushmore National Memorial. You can, however, drive on the many logging roads that wind through the Black Hills National Forest. To find those roads pick up a copy of the "Black Hills National Forest Visitors Map" (*see* Publications, *above*).

Bird-Watching. From high points in the Badlands during the summer, hawks and golden eagles floating along on the warm air currents are a common sight. In the Black Hills, some of the more interesting mountain birds include the Clark's nutcracker, dark-eyed junco, pine siskin, and various grosbeaks. Even if you're not a serious bird-watcher, bring along binoculars.

Fishing. In the Black Hills, Rapid Creek and Spearfish Creek are both popular spots to angle for wild brown trout, and all the headwater streams, including Grizzly Bear Creek near Mt. Rushmore, have brook trout. Horsethief Lake, also near Mt. Rushmore, is stocked with rainbow trout, as are other lakes in the Black Hills. Try Deerfield, Pactola, and Sheridan lakes in the Black Hills National Forest, and Center and Stockade lakes in Custer State Park. Non-resident fishing licenses are available at any sporting-goods store and many convenience stores; they cost $9 for one day, $29 for five days, and $49 annually.

Horseback Riding. Western horse-packing trips in Badlands National Park and the Black Hills are run by **Gunsel Horse Adventures** (Box 1575, Rapid City, SD 57709, tel. 605/343–7608) for about $160 a day. A six-day excursion covers some of the most secluded and scenic areas of the Badlands, and a 10-day trip treks 101 mi on the Centennial Trail, through pine forests and mountain meadows from Custer State Park, past Mt. Rushmore, to Bear Butte. There are also five-day pack trips from Rapid City to Deadwood, ending with an overnight stay in the historic Franklin Hotel.

Mountain Biking. Old logging roads in the Black Hills National Forest are just the right terrain for mountain biking. Few of these roads are marked on the Black Hills National Forest map, but if you follow any gravel road into the forest, such as Deerfield Road west of Hill City, you'll be able to connect with a logging road into the woods. You can rent mountain bikes in Rapid City from **Mountain Mania Bicycles** (4242 Canyon Lake Dr., tel. 605/343–6596) for $20 to $40 per day, or from **Two Wheeler Dealer Cycle & Fitness** (100 E. Blvd. N, tel. 605/343–0524) for $17.50 to $29. Mountain Mania also leads guided mountain biking trips in the Black Hills.

Rock Climbing. Rock climbing is becoming popular at Mt. Rushmore, where climbs vary in difficulty. Novice climbers should be especially cautious, and all climbers should register at park headquarters before starting out. Climbing the memorial is prohibited. Information on particular climbs, climbing courses, and guided climbing is available through **Sylvan Rock Climbing School and Guide Service** (tel. 605/574–

2425), which is based at Granite Sports in Hill City. Mountain Mania (*see above*) rents rock climbing equipment.

Skiing. The most popular cross-country ski areas are Eagle Cliff Ski Area, near O'Neil Pass, and Big Hill Ski Area, near Spearfish—both in the Black Hills National Forest. Passing beneath thick stands of pine and aspen, skiers sometimes see deer, bald eagles, elk, and porcupines. Eagle Cliff is the larger area, and it has consistently better snow. Equipment can be rented from **Ski Cross Country** (701 3rd St., Spearfish, tel. 605/642–3851). There are two downhill ski resorts in the northern hills—**Terry Peak Ski Area** (tel. 605/584–2165) and **Deer Mountain Ski Area** (tel. 605/584–3230). Equipment rentals are available at both.

Snowmobiling. More than 300 mi of groomed snowmobile trails link the Black Hills in South Dakota and Wyoming. The most extensive trails with the best snow run through the northern hills. Snowmobile maps are available free from the South Dakota Department of Tourism (*see* Visitor Information, *above*).

Spelunking. There are numerous caves throughout the limestone rock formations on the edge of the hills. The biggest and best known are Wind Cave National Park and Jewel Cave National Monument, both in the southern hills. Caves are usually 53°F, so a sweater is recommended. Also wear good walking shoes with nonslip soles to negotiate the uneven walkways, which are sometimes wet.

The fifth-longest in the country, **Wind Cave** (Hot Springs, tel. 605/745–4600) has 80 mi of mapped routes and is known for its boxwork formations. The visitor center is open from 8 to 7 in summer and from 8 to 5 in winter. There is no fee to enter the park, but you must take a ranger-guided tour to enter the cave. These are given year-round, from 8:30 to 6 in summer and at varying times in winter. Tours last from 1 to 1¾ hours and cost $4 to $6. Two longer tours are in summer; in the dead of winter, tours are offered half price.

With more than 108 mi of mapped passages, **Jewel Cave National Monument** (R.R. 1, Box 60AA, Custer, tel. 605/673–2288), west of Custer, is the second-longest cave in the country and is best known for the calcite crystals in many of its rooms. There is no entrance fee for the park, which is open year-round, but cave tours cost $6. Generally, tours are given from 8:30 to 6 in midsummer; the limited winter schedule varies.

Swimming. The best beaches in the Black Hills are near Hot Springs, at Angostura Reservoir, which is rimmed with miles of white sand. There are two small, often crowded beaches along Sheridan Lake in the Black Hills National Forest. Both beach areas charge a $2 daily use fee and have changing rooms, picnic tables, and barbecues; Angostura also has a snack bar. Neither lake has lifeguards on duty. Center Lake in Custer State Park has good beaches, too.

CHILDREN'S PROGRAMS Children ages five to 12 can take part in the free, two-day **Junior Ranger Program,** in which they learn about nature and Badlands National Park through the use of puzzles and games. Sign up at the desk at Ben Reifel Visitor Center (tel. 605/433–5361).

On Highway 16 leading to Mt. Rushmore, **Reptile Gardens** (tel. 605/342–5873) will delight children with animal shows and hundreds of reptiles and birds on display. It's open daily from 7 AM to 8 PM during the summer, with shorter hours in the off-season. Admission is $8.75.

Bears, elk, mountain lions, wolves, and other animals are displayed in the parklike setting of **Bear Country U.S.A.** (tel. 605/343–2290), which is also on Highway 16. This drive-through park is open only from Memorial Day to mid-October, daily from 8 to 6:30. Admission is $8.50. The maximum charge is $30 per family vehicle.

Another Highway 16 attraction that your kids will enjoy is the **Marine Life Aquarium** (tel. 605/343–7400), where dolphins and other aquatic creatures can be viewed

in tanks and in water shows. Open daily from 8 to 7, the aquarium charges $8.50.

EVENING ACTIVITIES **Badlands.** Nightly education programs and slide presentations take place in the amphitheater on summer evenings, covering such topics as fossils, geology, homesteading, and park birds. Check at the vistor center for times.

Black Hills. In Wind Cave National Park, the **Night Prowl** is a free, ranger-led talk about subjects such as cave exploration, wildlife, and astronomy. These evening lectures take place from early June through September; in September, the topic is usually elk-bugling in the park.

Mt. Rushmore. The 45-minute **Lighting Ceremony,** held between Memorial Day and Labor Day, includes a talk by rangers and a movie, as well as the dramatic illumination of the monument.

DINING

The specialty in these parts is buffalo, which is raised on a number of western South Dakota ranches. It tastes similar to beef but contains less fat and cholesterol. Most restaurants are found in the towns surrounding the Badlands National Park and Mt. Rushmore, and visitors should note that many of them close during winter.

INSIDE THE PARKS **Cedar Pass Lodge Restaurant.** Native American crafts decorate this family restaurant in Badlands National Park, near the Ben Reifel Visitor Center. It's the only full-service restaurant in the park; Native American tacos and quarter-pound buffalo burgers are the bill of fare. *Cedar Pass, tel. 605/433–5460. AE, D, DC, MC, V. Closed mid-Mar.–Oct. $*

Mt. Rushmore Dining Room and Snack Bar. Managed by AMFAC Parks and Resorts, this cafeteria-style eatery serves breakfast, lunch, and dinner from Memorial Day until Labor Day; only breakfast and lunch are served throughout the remainder of the year. The restaurant can seat 300 people, and the tables are set up so that everyone gets a view of the memorial. Breakfast, served from 7 to 11, includes your choice of four entrées, or à la carte items such as hash browns and fresh sweet rolls. At lunchtime (11–5) or dinnertime (5–8), entrées might include New England pot roast or baked chicken, plus a salad, potato or vegetable, and a beverage with dinner. Desserts, served from 8:30 to 10, are made on the premises. A snack bar next door serves hot dogs, hamburgers, and more June through August, daily from 10 to 10. *Mt. Rushmore National Memorial, tel. 605/574–2515. AE, D, MC, V. $*

NEAR THE PARKS **Casa Del Rey.** The Mexican food at this restaurant, on the main drag leading to Mt. Rushmore, is mild enough for almost any gringo's taste. Beige plaster walls and greenery create the right atmosphere for corn chips and salsa, chilies rellenos, and chimichangas. *1902 Mt. Rushmore Rd., Rapid City, tel. 605/348–5679. Reservations not accepted. AE, MC, V. $$*

Colonial House. This traditional American restaurant is conveniently located along Mt. Rushmore Road in Rapid City. Locals come for breakfast. Later in the day, the main draw is turkey steak. If you like cigars, the adjoining pub has Cigar Night on Thursday evenings. *2501 Mt. Rushmore Rd., Rapid City, tel. 605/342–4640. AE, D, MC, V. $$*

Harold's Prime Rib & Steak House. Harold's specializes in fine steak and prime rib, but also has good chicken and fish dishes. *318 East Blvd., Rapid City, tel. 605/343–1927. AE, D, DC, MC, V. $$*

La Costa. Twenty-four excellent dishes from the Jalisco area of Mexico make this pink-and-brick restaurant a hit. Service is excellent, and the location couldn't be more convenient: It's just off I-90 (take exit 58). *2125 N. Haines Ave., Rapid City, tel. 605/388–8780. MC, V. $$*

Alpine Inn. With a European atmosphere enhanced by opera music, the Alpine Inn serves a Continental lunch, but steak is the only entrée at dinner. Prices for the 6- and 9-ounce steaks are so reasonable that it's no wonder people drive 50 mi to the rustic logging town of Hill City to wait half an hour for a table. The stained-glass windows and rich wood interior create an unexpected touch of class. *Harney Peak Hotel, Main St., Hill City, tel. 605/574–2749. No credit cards. Closed Sun. $–$$*

Firehouse Brewing Co. This brewpub-restaurant is in the old Rapid City Fire Station. Microbrew beer such as Smokejumper Stout is served along with burgers, pasta, and fish. An outdoor beer garden is open in summer, with live entertainment on weekends. *610 Main St., Rapid City, tel. 605/348–1915. AE, D, DC, MC, V. $–$$*

Floridino's. In an old freight depot that's on the National Historic Register, Floridino's has live entertainment every weekend. There's a wide range of Italian food on the menu, as well as summer salads. *Omaha and 7th Sts., Rapid City, tel. 605/243–2454. D, MC, V. $*

Hearthstone. This quaint restaurant is located in an old Victorian house. A popular specialty is homemade soup served in a bread bowl. For a touch of Victorian England, try the Saturday afternoon English Tea. *807 Columbus St., Rapid City, tel. 605/341–4529. MC, V. $*

Meadowood Restaurant. At Meadowood you can go bowling before or after your meal; an alley adjoins the restaurant. You'll find daily luncheon specials here, as well as weekend all-you-can eat specials featuring traditional American food. *3809 Sturgis Rd., Rapid City, tel. 605/348–1564. No credit cards. $*

Parkway. The 1950s decor and rock music go well with the traditional American food selections. Malts and shakes are a hit. *312 E. North St., Rapid City, tel. 605/342–9640. MC, V. $*

PICNIC SPOTS There are great views from two picnic spots along Highway 240 in Badlands National Park: **Bigfoot Picnic Area** is near Journey to Wounded Knee

Overlook, just a few miles northwest of Cedar Pass, and **Conata Picnic Area** is about 10 mi past that. Picnic supplies can be purchased at grocery stores along I–90 in Wall or Kadoka, or at Badlands Grocery at Interior (*see* General Stores, *above*).

A half mile from Mt. Rushmore, you'll find the **Grizzly Bear Picnic Ground** turnoff, down Iron Mountain Road. From there a trail goes up Grizzly Creek to a series of small waterfalls, and beyond into the Black Elk Wilderness. Along Iron Mountain Road, not far from the Norbeck Memorial Overlook, lies **Iron Mountain Picnic Ground.** One mile west of Horsethief Lake on Highway 244 is **Elkhorn Picnic Ground,** and 2 mi farther west on Highway 244 is **Willow Creek Horse Camp,** where visitors can pull off the road and spread picnic blankets on the forest floor. All picnic grounds are free. Supplies can be picked up at the Safeway along Mt. Rushmore Road in Rapid City or at Mighty Mart, just east of Hill City.

LODGING

Hotel rates are highest in summer, but often are reduced by half or more after the peak season. To find the best value, choose a hotel far from I–90, the main tourist route into the Black Hills. Good deals for motels in mountain surroundings can also be found in the smaller Black Hills towns of Hill City, Custer, and Hot Springs, and in the outlying areas. Be sure to make your reservations well in advance, since motels are often booked solid during the summer. No campgrounds or hotels are available at Mt. Rushmore National Memorial, so most visitors to the memorial stay in Rapid City, Hill City, or in motels and campgrounds along the route. Visitors to Badlands National Park can find lodging in the Cedar Pass Lodge Cabins, located inside the park, or in the nearby towns of Interior, Wall, and Kadoka.

INSIDE THE PARKS **Cedar Pass Lodge Cabins.** The jutting peaks of Badlands National Park are visible from the windows of these park cabins, and Ben Reifel Visitor Center is within walking distance. Built in the 1930s, the clean, carpeted cabins were remodeled in 1987, but the knotty-pine walls remain. The cabins are air-conditioned but not equipped with TVs, and there is a restaurant nearby. Reservations are recommended. *Box 5, Interior, SD 57750, tel. 605/433–5460, fax 605/433–5560. 24 cabins. AE, D, DC, MC, V. Closed Nov.–mid-Apr. $*

NEAR THE PARKS **Hotel Alex Johnson.** This 11-story Rapid City landmark was built in 1928 and is a favorite with business visitors and tour groups. Rooms are small, but guests will enjoy the alpine woodwork and Native American artistry. Upper-story rooms have sweeping views of Rapid City, and those on the west side offer glimpses of the Black Hills. The decor in the public spaces has a Native American motif. The fact that five U.S. presidents have stayed here attests to the hotel's good standing. *523 6th St., Rapid City, SD 57701, tel. 605/342–1210 or 800/888–2539, fax 605/342–1210. 142 rooms. Facilities: room service. AE, D, DC, MC, V. $$$*

Edelweiss Mountain Lodging. The 20 vacation homes and cabins sit among pines on a gravel road 3 mi off Highway 385. Each is unique, and the prices range accordingly. Large groups might like the Waite cabin, which has four bedrooms on three carpeted floors, as well as a pool table. *12780 Black Forest Rd., Rapid City, SD 57702, tel. 605/574–2430. 20 houses, 10 cabins. MC, V. $$–$$$*

Budget Host Inn. Prices more than double in summer at this motel on the busiest strip in Rapid City. The location is convenient to all the sights, but it can be noisy, particularly in rooms facing the front of the building. Guest rooms have clean bathrooms and firm queen-size beds, but lack the charm of more secluded Black Hills lodgings. *2101 Mt. Rushmore Rd., Rapid City, SD 57701, tel. 605/343–5126 or 800/283–4678. 30 rooms. Facilities: pool. AE, D, MC, V. $$*

Castle Inn. The Castle Inn is comfortable, easy to reach, and typical of what is available in Rapid City in the mid-price range. Rooms are spacious enough for families. Since it is in town it can be a bit noisy and lacks the woodsy charm of some other, more rustic, accommodations. *15 E. North St., Rapid City, SD 57701, tel. 605/348–4120 or 800/658–5464. 60 rooms. Facilities: pool. AE, D, DC, MC, V. $$*

Plains Motel. Originally built in the '60s, the motel is just one block from I–90 in downtown Wall, making it an easy base for exploring Badlands National Park. The clean, comfortable rooms are large enough for families, and kids will appreciate the game room with video machines. Ask for one of the newer rooms and be sure to book in advance. *712 Glenn St., Box 393, Wall, SD 57790, tel. 605/279–2145 or 800/528–1234, fax 605/279–2977. 74 rooms. Facilities: pool, recreation room. AE, D, DC, MC, V. $$*

Lewis Park Cabins and Hotel. These cabins are tucked away among mountain ridges and aspen trees on the back streets of Hill City. Built in the 1930s, the cabins come with full kitchens and furniture that dates from the 1950s. There are lawn chairs on the small covered porches, and the buildings are painted a shockingly bright green. The motel-style rooms don't have the old-fashioned character of the cabins. Prices here swing wildly, ranging from $15 in the dead of winter to more than $65 in summer. *110 Park Ave., Box 382, Hill City, SD 57745, tel. 605/574–2565 or 800/317–2565. 5 rooms, 4 cabins. D, MC, V. $*

Spring Creek Inn. This friendly 1950s-era motel earns top honors as one of the best deals in the Black Hills during summer. New cedar siding with clean, spacious, knotty-pine rooms fit in well with the mountain setting. Just 1 mi north of Hill City on Highway 16/385, the place is especially popular with hunters and fishermen. (Don't be surprised to see deer hanging from poles in the front yard during the November hunting season.) In summer, volleyball and croquet games are set up on the grassy lawn, and fishermen angle for trout in nearby Spring Creek. *HCR 87, Box 55, Hill City, SD 57745, tel. 605/574–2591. 12 rooms, 5 cabins, 3 chalets, 1 cottage house. D, MC, V. $*

CAMPING

Primitive camping—with no facilities and lots of privacy—is easily found in this part of the United States. You can set up camp in the backcountry of Badlands National Park or off a secluded dirt road in the Black Hills. You can also choose a drive-in campsite at a national forest campground, with the luxury of flush or pit toilets, running water, and fire grates. There is no camping in Mt. Rushmore National Memorial.

The most elaborate camping facilities, with water, showers, electricity, and sewage disposal, are in commercial campgrounds scattered across the Black Hills and outlying parts of the Badlands. Most of these have spaces for RVs as well as tents. For a fairly complete listing, check the *South Dakota Campground Guide,* available free from the South Dakota Department of Tourism (*see* Visitor Information, *above*).

INSIDE THE PARKS Within the boundaries of **Badlands National Park** there are two campgrounds, and both assign sites on a first-come, first-served basis. You can also camp in the backcountry of the Badlands, if you're willing to hike in. Fires are not allowed anywhere in the Badlands.

At campgrounds in the **Black Hills National Forest** (tel. 605/673–2251) you'll find picnic tables, fire grates, flush or vault toilets, and drinking water, but little more. The lush forest setting is a big draw, however, and it helps that sites at 17 of the campgrounds may be reserved; call **U.S. Forest Reservations** (tel. 800/280–2267) well in advance of your arrival date. Reservations cost $8.25 each, in addition to the camp fee. You can usually find an open site without a reservation at most national forest campgrounds in the Black Hills, except

BADLANDS, MT. RUSHMORE, AND THE BLACK HILLS

	Total number of sites	Sites suitable for RVs	Number of hookups	Drive to sites	Hike to sites	Flush toilets	Pit/chemical toilets	Drinking water	Showers	Fire grates	Swimming	Boat access	Playground	Disposal station	Ranger station	Public telephone	Reservation possible	Daily fee per site	Dates open
BADLANDS																			
Cedar Pass	96	96	0	•		•	•	•		•				•	•	•	•*	$10***	year-round
Sage Creek	8	8	0	•			•											free	year-round
BLACK HILLS																			
Horsethief Lake	36	36	0	•		•		•		•	•					•	•*	$14–$16	Memorial Day–Labor Day
Sheridan Lake Southside	129	129	0	•		•	•	•	•**	•	•	•					•*	$13	Memorial Day–Labor Day
Whitetail	17	17	0	•		•	•	•	•	•	•					•	•*	$8	Memorial Day–Labor Day
Dutchman	45	45	0	•			•	•		•		•					•*	$8	Memorial Day–Labor Day
Pactola	80	80	0	•			•	•		•		•					•*	$12	year-round
Rod and Gun/Timon	14	14	0	•				•		•							•*	$5–$8	Memorial Day–Labor Day
NEAR THE PARKS																			
Berry Patch	130	116	113	•		•		•	•	•	•		•	•		•	•	$17.75–$24.50	year-round
Happy Holiday	210	150	150	•		•		•	•	•	•		•	•		•	•	$18.50–$24	
Mt. Rushmore KOA	500	355	355	•		•		•	•	•	•		•	•		•	•	$21.95–$29.95	May–early Oct.
Badlands KOA	144	82	82	•		•		•	•	•	•		•	•		•	•	$17–$24	May–mid-Oct.
Arrow Camp	100	100	72	•		•		•	•	•	•		•	•		•	•	$10.50–$16	May–mid-Oct.

*Reservation fee charged.   **Cold water only.   ***Free when water is turned off.

for the one at busy Horsethief Lake. The easiest way to find these campgrounds is by buying a "Black Hills National Forest Visitors Map" (see Publications, above) or requesting a free list of the campgrounds from the forest service.

A short stroll from the Ben Reifel Visitor Center in Badlands National Park, **Cedar Pass Campground** (tel. 605/433–5361) has 96 sites for tents or RVs, with flush and pit toilets, drinking water, disposal station, ranger station, and public phone. The campground is open year-round; sites cost $10 per night in season, and a bit less in winter, when the water is shut off. Cedar Pass often has space available.

The word to remember at **Sage Creek Primitive Campground** (tel. 605/433–5361) is *primitive:* there's no water, and pit toilets are the only facility. There are no set camp sites: Just park anywhere in the area. It's just south of the Sage Creek Rim Road, near the Badlands Wilderness Area. The campground is free, and open year-round.

Horsethief Lake Campground is the closest forest-service campground to Mt. Rushmore National Memorial and, as a result, the most crowded. Just 1 mi west of Mt. Rushmore off Highway 244, it's close to the Black Elk Wilderness, Norbeck Wildlife Preserve, and the Centennial Trail. The 36 sites are open from Memorial Day to Labor Day. There are flush chemical toilets. Sites cost $14 to $16 per night.

Also in the national forest, the 129 sites at the **Sheridan Lake Southside Campground** are near a beach, boat ramp, and the Centennial Trail. The best spots are closest to the shoreline. This campground is open from Memorial Day to Labor Day, except for the Rocky Loop, which is open year-round. Sheridan Lake has flush toilets as well as portable toilet stalls. There are cold showers at the lake. Sites cost $13. (Sheridan Lake North Cove Campground has 58 sites for groups only.)

Whitetail Campground, above Deerfield Reservoir, offers peaceful solitude and good fishing. There are 17 sites, which cost $8 per night and are open year-round.

At an elevation of 6,100 ft, **Dutchman Campground** is one of the coolest spots in the Black Hills, allowing campers to escape the summer heat, even in July. The 45 sites are open from Memorial Day to Labor Day and cost $8 per night.

Pactola Campground is large, with a boat ramp and 80 sites near Pactola Reservoir. There are flush toilets and a public phone here; hot showers are at a marina, .25 mi away. The campground is open from Memorial Day to Labor Day; sites cost $12 per night.

Rod and Gun Campground and **Timon Campground** both offer secluded camping along Little Spearfish Creek, not far from Roughlock Falls. Open all year, each has seven sites. Rod and Gun costs $5 and Timon costs $8 per night.

If you really want to rough it, try camping in the Black Hills backcountry. There are no facilities here, but it's free, it's legal, and campers have complete privacy. The many logging and gravel forest-service roads give access to all parts of the national forest. (Camping is prohibited in recreation areas, at administrative sites, and in the Black Hills Experimental Forest.) Remember, fires are not allowed in the Black Hills backcountry; if you want to have a campfire you'll have to use the campground fire grates. You can, however, bring a stove.

NEAR MT. RUSHMORE **Berry Patch** (tel. 605/ 341–5588), at exit 60 on I–90 in Rapid City, has 14 tent sites and 116 RV sites (113 hookups) on level lots with easy access. There are flush toilets, hot showers, drinking water, fire grates, a playground, swimming, a disposal station, and a public phone. Open from April 1 to November 1, Berry Patch charges $17.75 to $24.50

Happy Holiday (tel. 605/342-7365), across from Reptile Gardens on Mt. Rushmore Road, is conveniently located. It has 150 RV sites with hookups, as well as 60 tent sites with flush toilets, hot showers, drinking water, fire grates, playground, swimming, disposal station, and public phone. Open year-round, the campground charges $18.50 to $24 per night.

Mt. Rushmore KOA (tel. 605/574–2525) is a large commercial campground 5 mi west of Mt. Rushmore on Highway 244, with shuttle service to the Mt. Rushmore Lighting Ceremony, bus tours, restaurant, and car rentals. It has 355 RV sites and 145 tent sites, with flush toilets, hot showers, drinking water, fire grates, playground, swimming, disposal station, and public phone. The KOA is open from May 1 to October 1, and sites cost $21.95 to $29.95 per night.

NEAR BADLANDS The **Badlands KOA** (tel. 605/433–5337), 4 mi southeast of Interior on Highway 44, has 144 sites (82 hookups), with flush toilets, hot showers, drinking water, fire grates, a playground, a swimming pool, a disposal station, and a public phone. It's open from May 1 to October 7, and sites cost $17 to $24 per night.

The **Arrow Camp** (tel. 605/279–2112), in Wall, has 100 RV sites (72 hookups) as well as motel units. Here you'll find flush toilets, hot showers, drinking water, fire grates, cable TV, a playground, a swimming pool, a disposal station, and a public phone. The Arrow Camp is open from May 1 to October 15 and costs $10.50 to $16 per night.

Banff National Park with Yoho and Kootenay National Parks
Alberta and British Columbia

Updated by Don Thacker

 anff is to Canadians what Yellowstone is to Americans: their country's first and foremost national park. It's one of Canada's largest parks, with 6,641 square km (2,565 square mi) of rugged alpine terrain—twice the land mass of Yellowstone. Banff and Jasper, Kootenay, and Yoho national parks, along with three adjacent provincial parks, form the Canadian Rocky Mountain Parks World Heritage Site, some 23,300 square km (9,000 square mi) of massive mountains of rock, ice, snow, and thick evergreen forest.

In fact, the creators of Banff National Park conceived it not as a nature preserve, but rather an island of civilization among a sea of wilderness. Set aside in 1885 after the discovery of hot springs—the Cave and Basin Hot Springs in the area—the park first became widely accessible after the Canadian Pacific Railroad (CPR) completed its east–west route. Looking to fill his Canadian train cars, CPR general manager W. C. Van Horne reportedly declared: "If we can't export the scenery, we'll import the tourists!"—and the railroad entrepreneurs did just that. CPR built its first hostelry, the Banff Springs Hotel, in 1888; Lake Louise Chalet, which became Chateau Lake Louise, followed two years later.

Proprietors other than CPR have since surged into the town of Banff; today it has the most diverse lodging, dining, and shopping options in the Canadian Rockies. This is hardly surprising: Banff has a breathtaking location, just a short drive from untouched expanses of mountains and

such natural wonders as Moraine Lake and the Valley of the Ten Peaks—whose images decorated the Canadian $20 bill for many years—and Lake Louise, with the majestic Victoria Glacier as its backdrop. With all these assets, Banff attracts more than 4 million visitors annually.

In the face of constant development pressure, Banff National Park keeps a delicate balance between commercial development and Parks Canada's mandate for wilderness first, people second. Pro-development forces clamor for new hotels, shops, housing, and highway construction; environmentalists warn of threatened wildlife habitats.

In response to these conflicting goals, Parks Canada has developed the 1997 Banff Park Management Plan to guide the park for the next 15 years. More than 500 recommendations have been evaluated and brought to public consultation. The likely outcome will be strict controls on development (meaning accommodation prices for visitors will almost certainly continue to escalate), and trail quotas for some of the more popular backcountry hiking trails. The town of Banff has recently been granted most municipal functions, with Parks Canada maintaining final authority over major land-use decisions.

Regardless of decisions affecting its future, Banff National Park will always amaze visitors with its hulking snowcapped peaks, pale blue glaciers and ice fields, and deep-green forests and multicolored wildflowers. Even though peak elevations here are 600 to

900 meters (2,000 to 3,000 ft) lower than in the Colorado Rockies, the tree line is also lower—by about 1,000 meters (3,000 ft), exposing more craggy, rugged, high-alpine terrain. The massive walls of rock, ice, and snow rising high above evergreen forests make this area appear breathtakingly tall.

For an ideal summer vacation, spend at least several days in Banff town, and visit Lake Louise on a day trip or for a night or two. Take a trip along the Icefields Parkway (Highway 93), and walk a few of the nearly 2,000 km (1,120 mi) of well-maintained trails in the three parks; or come in the winter for some of the best skiing in Canada. The park's three lift-serviced areas—Mt. Norquay, Lake Louise, and Sunshine Village—keep Banff National Park busy well after Yoho and Kootenay have slowed down.

ESSENTIAL INFORMATION

VISITOR INFORMATION Keep in mind when seeking information that Banff National Park is within Alberta, while Yoho and Kootenay parks are in British Columbia, east and west, respectively, of the Continental Divide. Principal sources of information are **Parks Canada** (Canadian Heritage–Parks Canada, 220 4th Ave. SE, Room 552, Calgary, AB T2G 4X3, tel. 403/292–4401 or 800/651–7959, fax 403/292–6004), **Banff National Park Information Centre** (Box 900, 224 Banff Ave., Banff, AB T0L 0C0, tel. 403/762–1550), **Yoho National Park Visitor Centre** (Box 99, Field, BC V0A 1G0, tel. 250/343–6783), **Travel Alberta** (Commerce Pl., 10155 102 St., 3rd floor, Edmonton, AB T5J 4G8, tel. 800/661–8888), and **Tourism British Columbia** (Parliament Bldgs., Victoria, BC V8V 1X4, tel. 800/663–6000). Local information, specifically regarding lodging, dining, and shopping, is available from the **Banff–Lake Louise Tourism Bureau** (Box 1298, 224 Banff Ave., Banff, AB T0L 0C0, tel. 403/762–8421). For specific information (e.g., current weather conditions, camping availability) about **Kootenay** (tel. 250/347–9615) and **Lake Louise** (tel. 403/522–3833),

contact them directly. You can also call the visitor centers in **Kootenay** (tel. 250/347–9505 in summer, 250/347–9551 in winter) and **Yoho** (tel. 250/343–6783).

Backcountry campers should ask for a copy of the information pamphlet "Backcountry Visitors' Guide." *The Canadian Rockies Trail Guide* (*see* Publications, *below*) is also a valuable resource. Permits, required for all campers, cost $6 per person per night (to a maximum of $30 per person per trip or $42 annually) and may be obtained at the nearest park visitor center.

FEES Parks Canada has recently changed the per-vehicle entrance fee to a per-person entrance fee for visitors to the national parks. A National Parks Day Pass costs $10 and is valid for entry into Banff, Jasper, Yoho, and Kootenay parks. An annual pass, covering 11 national parks in western Canada, is $70. Travelers in nonstop transit through the parks are not charged.

PUBLICATIONS Travel Alberta, Tourism British Columbia, and Parks Canada (*see* Visitor Information, *above*) all publish visitor information packages. An excellent guidebook for hikers in all three parks is *The Canadian Rockies Trail Guide,* by Brian Patton and Bart Robinson. Wildflower lovers should look for *Wildflowers of the Canadian Rockies,* by George Scotter and Halle Flygare. Both are available in bookstores and gift shops in Banff.

GEOLOGY AND TERRAIN Formed between 50 and 120 million years ago, the Canadian Rockies are relative youngsters among mountains. Tectonic activity (the shifting of rock layers through faulting, folding, and upthrust) and erosion have conspired to give these young mountains their rugged configurations.

Glaciers have been the main erosive force, gnawing with their infinitely slow appetite at a rock surface composed largely of limestone, sandstone, and shale. Most glaciers in the region are receding—getting smaller by shedding their melted ice into the major rivers of western Canada and the northwestern United States. That leaves no shortage of ice, however. The Columbia Icefield alone, at 325 square km (125 square mi), covers about the same surface area as Yellowstone Lake in Yellowstone National Park and is estimated to be more than 300 meters (1,000 ft) thick in places.

Glacial erosion and recession have left a sprawling mountain sculpture cataloged in an arcane alpine terminology. Among the notable land features are cirques (rock amphitheaters), moraines (dikelike deposits of silt and rock), eskers (narrow, glacially deposited ridges of rock and sand), and arêtes (sharp mountain ridges).

Climate, latitude, and glacial activity have set the tree line at 2,100 meters (7,000 ft). The elevation of the town of Banff, in the Bow River valley, is 1,400 meters (4,582 ft), and the highest peaks top off well above 3,400 meters (11,000 ft).

FLORA AND FAUNA Coniferous trees—including spruce, fir, and pine—are predominant along mountain slopes, with a few hardwoods, trembling aspens in particular, mixing in at lower elevations. One of the spectacles of fall is the changing color of the larch trees, deciduous members of the conifer family, which turn a brilliant gold before shedding their needles.

In the valley bottoms, flower season runs from late May to August. Roadsides are scattered with columbine and gaillardia, and May and June witness calypso and lady-slipper orchids blooming in moist pine woods. Alas, the "flower-pickers" have depleted these orchids in the immediate vicinity of the town of Banff.

Above the tree line lay a world of tundra meadows. In summer, wildflowers flourish between 2,000 and 2,600 meters (6,500 and 8,500 ft). Alpine wildflowers include anemone, saxifrage, and forget-me-nots, with summer being the showiest bloom time.

Wildlife sightings in Banff, Kootenay, and Yoho are virtually assured. Bighorn sheep (Banff and Kootenay only) and elk tend to graze and wander along highway shoulders, not to mention the highway itself, attracted by roadside grasses and residual winter road salt. Be alert for animals on the road as well as for cars and humans stopped in unexpected places to photograph them; pull well off onto shoulders, and drive within the speed limit—for your own and the animals' safety. In springtime, be wary of mother elks protecting their calves—not only in the wilds, but perhaps more commonly on golf courses around Banff as well as right in town.

At higher elevations, marmots and pikas are common, burrowing beneath and between rocks. Much less common are the elusive cougar, bobcat, and mountain goat. At Kootenay in late spring or early summer, goats are commonly seen along the road in the salt beds at the base of Mt. Wardle.

Vermilion Lakes Drive, just off the West Banff exit from Highway 1, attracts elk, muskrat, and coyote. Near the east Banff exit from Highway 1 is the buffalo paddock, the place to see buffalo during the summer months.

Bear sightings and encounters are not frequent, but they do occur. Anyone hiking, biking, or camping in the backcountry should take all the proper precautions: suspending food above a bear's reach, and cooking and eating away from tent sites (*see* Wild Animal Encounters *in* Essential Information). Bear information is provided at the entrance to the park and should be read carefully.

WHEN TO GO All three parks are open to visitors year-round, although the relatively few visitor services within Kootenay and Yoho parks are cut back more in winter than those in Banff. The high season has been lengthening gradually as people try to avoid the mid-summer crush, and now runs from about the start of June to the end of September. Lodging prices during this period are typically 50%–100% higher than at other times of year. The Christmas and New Year's period is also considered high-season.

People who live in or visit the area often say their favorite time of year is September into early October. Crowds thin out and prices drop. Better yet, the first lasting snows have usually arrived at higher elevations, providing a backdrop for the radiant fall foliage, which usually peaks in late September. Be prepared at this time of year, however, for cooler, though generally pleasant, temperatures and the closing of some campgrounds, lodges, cabins, and a few restaurants. By mid-October, most campgrounds will be closed (one stays open through the winter in each of the parks), and many of the unheated cabins and lodges will have closed for the season. Most of the hotels and restaurants in the towns of Banff and Lake Louise remain open throughout the year.

With three major ski areas within Banff National Park and several others nearby, winter is also an active season. The scenic drives along Highway 1A and Highway 93 (the Icefields Parkway) and many of the groomed cross-country ski trails around Banff and Lake Louise townsites remain open and well maintained in winter, though snow closes many backcountry trails. Avalanches can pose serious danger during winter—a much greater danger than attacks from bears or other wildlife. Ask park officials about avalanche conditions before venturing out.

Daytime temperatures in summer typically range from the high teens to high 20s°C (60–80°F), and midwinter daytime highs range between –10 and –5°C (mid-teens to low-20s°F). But mountain weather is hard to predict—snowstorms can occur even in summer above the tree line. And in the valley bottoms, winter temperatures can range from the bone-chilling –30s°C (–20s°F) to a springlike 10°C (50°F). The saying "If you don't like the weather just wait 10 minutes" is not much of an exaggeration in the mountains.

SEASONAL EVENTS **June to August:** The **Banff Centre** (St. Julien Rd., Banff, AB T0L 0C0, tel. 403/762–6300), the cultural epi-center of the parks, hosts the Festival of the Arts, which includes classical music, jazz, ballet, opera, and other performing arts. **Late January:** At the Banff Winter Festival (Box 1298, Banff, AB T0L 0C0, tel. 403/762–8421) 10 days of lighthearted and die-hard competitions—from tugs-of-war and bar golf (golf holes set up in seven local bars) to serious cross-country ski races—are mixed with a parade, dances, ice sculptures, pancake breakfasts, and a town party.

WHAT TO PACK Weather in Banff is changeable, especially in the high country. Even in summer, pack a warm wool sweater or synthetic-fleece jacket, warm socks, light gloves, and a sturdy windbreaker (preferably of waterproof, breathable material).

GENERAL STORES Virtually anything you'd ever want or need in the parks, from crampons to crayons, can be found in one of Banff's many stores. What you won't find are bargains, Banff being not only a resort town but also one with a virtual monopoly on park commerce. If you're looking to save money on more costly items such as camping gear, shop in Calgary or even Canmore, 26 km (16 mi) east of Banff.

Samson Mall, in Lake Louise, and **Radium Hot Springs,** just outside the Kootenay Park boundary, are other places to stock up on food and equipment. The pickings are slim at grocery and convenience stores in Castle Mountain Village (between Banff and Lake Louise on Highway 1A), Field (Yoho National Park), and the Crossing (on the Icefields Parkway).

ARRIVING AND DEPARTING **By Bus. Greyhound Lines** (tel. 800/661–8747 in Canada, 800/231–2222 in the U.S.) provides regular service to Calgary and Vancouver. **Brewster Transportation and Tours** (tel. 800/661–1152) offers service between Calgary International Airport and Banff, Lake Louise, and Jasper.

By Car and RV. Highway 1, the Trans-Canada Highway, is the principal east–west route through the region. Banff is 128 km (80 mi) west of Calgary on Highway 1 and 858 km (532 mi) east of Vancouver. The principal highways from the south are: in Alberta, Highway 2, which runs directly north to Calgary from the Montana border; and, in British Columbia, Highway 93, which runs from Kalispell, Montana, through Radium Hot Springs, British Columbia, and into the southern end of Kootenay National Park. Note: The speed limit within the park is reduced to 90 kph (55 mph).

By Plane. Calgary International Airport is the most common gateway for travelers arriving by plane. Most major airlines provide regular service to Calgary.

By Train. Apart from a touring train service that makes a stop at Banff (*see* Guided Tours, *below*), there is no rail service to the park. You can, however, take a train to Jasper and the bus from Jasper to Banff.

EXPLORING

Most people arrive in **Banff** from the east, from Calgary via Highway 1. For almost all—casual tourists as well as avid outdoorspeople—the town of Banff is a kind of base camp. The reason is simple: Banff is the only town of size or substance in the three parks. Banff is neither architecturally nor atmospherically an exemplary town. Except for the oft-photographed Banff Springs Hotel, its architecture is modern, functional, and undistinguished.

Aside from the hotel, the other major point of reference in Banff is Banff Avenue, the main drag of a town core tightly crammed with shops and restaurants. The shop mix consists of "galleries" selling various art and quasi-art items, touristy gift shops, clothing stores (with an emphasis on sports and ski wear), and photo stores. If it all seems like shopping overload, remember that, except for a few boutiques at Chateau Lake Louise and Samson Mall, this is about all the shopping there is in the parks. Heading south, Banff Avenue bridges the Bow River, ending at a T in front of the Parks Administration Office.

Lake Louise is 54 km (35 mi) northwest of Banff on Highway 1. The actual village of Lake Louise is a crossroads barely noticed by most travelers on their way (another 5 km, or 3 mi) to Chateau Lake Louise. At the edge of the blue-green lake, and with the Victoria Glacier as a backdrop, the château runs head-to-head with the Banff Springs Hotel for the title of most-photographed building in the Canadian Rockies. Nearby Moraine Lake, in the Valley of the Ten Peaks, is another top-rated scenic attraction.

Kootenay National Park may be the least-visited of the three parks, but this is not indicative of an intrinsic lack of appeal. Far from it: From rugged, glacier-clad peaks in the north to dry, cactus-bearing slopes in the south, the park has many landscapes, all of which unfold along the scenic Banff/Windermere Highway (Highway 93) that bisects the park from north to south.

What Kootenay lacks, except in Radium Hot Springs at its southern extreme, is services. There are fewer campgrounds in Kootenay than in any of the other Canadian mountain parks, and there is only a single gas station, open from May to October, at Vermilion Crossing. Most travelers simply use Kootenay as a scenic driving route between Banff and Radium Hot Springs. This is a boon to backpackers, who have the park to themselves.

Yoho is reached by heading west along Highway 1 from Lake Louise. The park name, Yoho, is a Native American (Cree) word that means just what you'd think from the sound of it: "Wow!" The park indeed is a world of breathtaking scenery—lakes, glaciers, rock walls, ice fields, waterfalls, and more. In short, Yoho has compressed into its relatively small land area a little bit of everything that is the essence of the Canadian Rockies' allure.

The Yoho River valley is the main feature of the park's northern half, which has some of the finest backpacking and climbing in the parks. **Lake O'Hara** is the physical and spiritual epicenter of the park's southern half. For backcountry enthusiasts, Lake

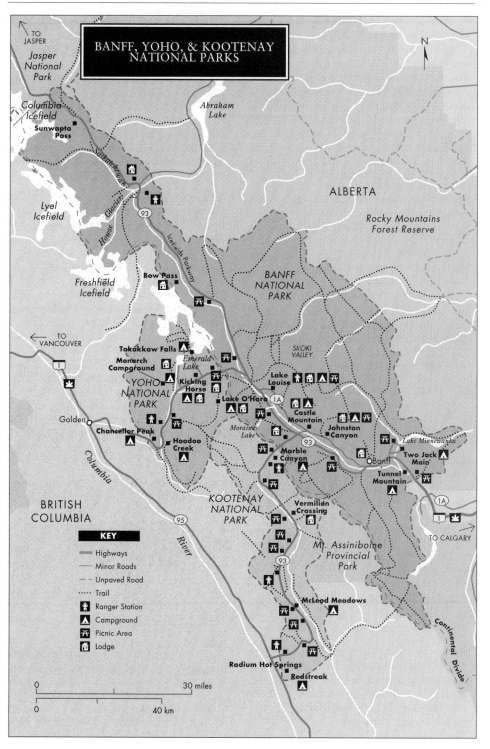

BANFF, YOHO, & KOOTENAY NATIONAL PARKS

TO JASPER

Jasper National Park

Columbia Icefield

Sunwapta Pass

Lyel Icefield

Freshfield Icefield

Abraham Lake

ALBERTA

Rocky Mountains Forest Reserve

93

Bow Pass

Saskatchewan

Glacier

Howse

Icefields Parkway

BANFF NATIONAL PARK

TO VANCOUVER

1

150

Golden

Takakkaw Falls

Monarch Campground

Emerald Lake

Kicking Horse

YOHO NATIONAL PARK

Chancellor Peak

Hoodoo Creek

SKOKI VALLEY

Lake Louise

Lake O'Hara

1A

Moraine Lake

Castle Mountain

Johnston Canyon

Marble Canyon

Lake Minnewanka

Two Jack Main

Banff

Tunnel Mountain

93

Columbia

River

95

KOOTENAY NATIONAL PARK

Vermilion Crossing

Mt. Assiniboine Provincial Park

1A

1

TO CALGARY

BRITISH COLUMBIA

93

McLeod Meadows

Radium Hot Springs

Redstreak

Continental Divide

KEY

- ▬▬ Highways
- —— Minor Roads
- – – Unpaved Road
- ···· Trail
- 🏠 Ranger Station
- ▲ Campground
- 🪧 Picnic Area
- 🏠 Lodge

0 _____ 30 miles

0 _____ 40 km

N

O'Hara is one of the best spots in the Canadian Rockies. Lake O'Hara Lodge (see Lodging, below) is usually fully booked many months in advance in summer; there are also alpine huts and a campground. Besides hiking in, the only way to get to Lake O'Hara is by taking a lodge-run shuttle bus (reservations are required and often hard to come by) on an 11-km (7-mi) fire road from Highway 1. Contact the Yoho National Park Visitor Centre (see Visitor Information, above) for details.

Rock-buttressed mountains and high-alpine lakes—more than two dozen within a few kilometers of Lake O'Hara itself—are all part of this area's appeal. The lodge is at 2,035 meters (6,700 ft), which gives it an alpine ruggedness not found at the valley-bottom hotels and motels. More elegant than most alpine lodges, it appeals to people who aren't keen on roughing it but still want a taste of the backcountry. The many climbers, hikers, and lodge guests who congregate here in summer don't mind sharing the splendor of the backcountry with others.

THE BEST IN ONE DAY If you want to see the best of the parks in one day, plan to spend as few hours as possible in the town of Banff. Weather permitting, the best option is to drive between the town and the Icefield Centre, just north of the Banff/Jasper park boundary. This is a four hour round-trip straight-out, but add two hours for scenic stops en route, or longer if you choose to explore the Athabasca Glacier. Leave time for an afternoon hike, perhaps at the Lake Louise/Moraine Lake area, justly famed for its scenery, although hardly undiscovered. If possible, work in time for afternoon tea at Chateau Lake Louise. The town of Banff has the largest concentration of restaurants; the Post Hotel (see Dining, below) in Lake Louise has perhaps the premier restaurant in the Canadian Rockies.

A more relaxed schedule for a one-day tour is a drive to Lake Louise and Moraine Lake, where you can soak in the views, wander through the Chateau Lake Louise, rent a canoe, or stroll along one of the many trails.

Those who prefer more leisurely excursions from Banff should consider a trip up the Sulphur Mountain Gondola onto an alpine ridge with expansive views, or a relaxing soak in the Upper Hot Springs pool. Short drives that capture the best of Banff's scenery include the Vermilion Lakes drive (10 km, or 6 mi, return), the Mount Norquay drive (12 km, or 7.5 mi, return), the Tunnel Mountain drive (20 km, or 12 mi, return), or the drive to Lake Minnewanka (16 km, or 10 mi, return).

ORIENTATION PROGRAMS The **Cave and Basin National Historic Site** (Cave Ave., Banff, tel. 403/762–1557) and **Lake Louise Visitor Centre** (next to Samson Mall, tel. 403/522–3833) feature a mix of exhibits and multimedia shows that explain the history and geology of the area. The **Banff Park Museum** (93 Banff Ave., tel. 403/762–1558) has wildlife displays, wildlife art, a library on the natural history of the region, and a discovery room for children. Admission is $2.25. It's open year-round. The **Whyte Museum** (111 Bear St., tel. 403/762–2291) gives a thorough historical perspective of the region through art, photography, artifacts, and rotating exhibits on life in the Canadian Rockies. Admission is $3. It's open from 10 to 6 May to mid-October, with somewhat abbreviated hours the rest of the year.

GUIDED TOURS **Brewster Transportation and Tours** (Box 1140, Banff, AB T0L 0C0, tel. 403/762–6700 in Banff, 403/522–3544 in Lake Louise, 403/221–8242 in Calgary, or 800/661–1152) offers half-day and full-day sightseeing bus tours of the parks, the most popular being the Icefields Parkway tours. **Tauck Tours** (Box 5027, 276 Post Rd. W, Westport, CT 06880, tel. 800/468–2825) arranges multiday bus tours and heli-hiking options in nearby mountains.

Minnewanka Boat Tours (Box 2189, Banff, AB T0L 0C0, tel. 403/762–3473) has 1½-hour summer boat cruises on Lake Minnewanka, near Banff, for $22.

Audiocassette tapes for self-guided auto tours of the parks are produced by **Auto**

Tape Tours and **Rocky Mountain Tape Tours.** Tapes can be rented or purchased at newsstands or gift shops in Banff and Lake Louise. **Canadian Wilderness Videos** (1010 Larch Pl., Canmore, AB T1W 1S7, tel. 403/678–3795) produces a series of videotapes illustrating highlights along specific routes. Tapes cost $29.95 plus $6 shipping, and are available in nine languages.

Challenge Enterprises (Box 8127, Canmore, AB T1W 2T8, tel. 403/678–2628) conducts winter snowmobile tours near the parks, from two-hour day trips to multiday trips with accommodation.

Mountain Fly Fishers (909 Railway Ave., Canmore, AB T1W 1P3, tel. 403/678–9522 in-season, 403/678–2915 off-season) offers fly-fishing instruction, guide services, and equipment rentals, and float-fishing tours on the Bow River.

Banff Alpine Guides (Box 1025, Banff, AB T0L 0C0, tel. 403/678–6091), the **Canadian School of Mountaineering** (629 10th St., Canmore, AB T1W 2E5, tel. 403/678–4134), and **Yamnuska Mountain Adventures** (1316 Railway Ave., Canmore, AB T1W 1P6, tel. 403/678–4164) conduct hiking, mountaineering, and backcountry ski tours.

Rocky Mountaineer RailTours (1150 Station St., Suite 130, Vancouver, BC V6A 2X7, tel. 800/665–7245 or 604/606–7200, fax 604/606–7201) operates two-day train trips from Vancouver to Banff or Calgary, via Kamloops, and other tours of up to two weeks, from mid-May to early October, starting at around $500. Its deluxe coach service caters to people accustomed to five-star hotels and luxury resorts. The Rail-Tours coaches travel through the Rockies during daylight only.

SCENIC DRIVES AND VIEWS A good alternative to the busy Highway 1 from Banff to Lake Louise is Highway 1A (the Bow Valley Parkway). The pavement is good and the views just as rewarding, but the pace is much more relaxed.

Hikers can use the Lake Louise trail network to reach **Moraine Lake** in the Valley of the Ten Peaks, but less energetic travelers can get to the lake by car or bus, 14 km (8.5 mi) from the Lake Louise crossroads. The lake's mountainous surroundings and remarkable blue-green color make it a match for scenic spots around the world—but be prepared to deal with tour-bus crowds.

Heading west from Lake Louise on Highway 1 and connecting with **Highway 93** (the Icefields Parkway), you'll find progressively higher, more glaciated and more spectacular country. The road reaches a high point at Bow Pass, which at 2,068 meters (6,787 ft) may be covered with snow as late as May and as early as September. Two lakes, Bow and Peyto, flank the pass; surrounded by rock, snow, and ice, they represent the epitome of Canadian Rockies scenery. This is a premier area for hiking, climbing, and backcountry skiing, offering easy access to a high, rugged, alpine world.

The highway descends gradually from Bow Pass to **Saskatchewan River Crossing,** a utility stop. Almost all travelers on this route stop here for gas, food, or both, but the cafeteria food presents a compelling reason to pack a picnic lunch if you're planning a day trip from Banff.

The road then descends into a valley where three rivers—the Saskatchewan, Howse, and Mistaya—diverge and where glaciers reaching from the giant ice fields ahead can be seen. As the road climbs again toward **Sunwapta Pass** (elevation 2,035 meters, or 6,675 ft) and the juncture of Banff and Jasper parks, keep an eye out on the left for the Parker Ridge Trail, 4 km (2.5 mi) before the pass summit. The short, moderate walk provides unusually quick access to high-alpine tundra, with a spectacular view of the 12-km- (7.5-mi-) long Saskatchewan Glacier from the top of the ridge. If you are lucky, you might spot some of the shy mountain goats that frequent the area around Sunwapta Pass. From here, the road continues on to the Icefield Centre in Jasper National Park.

You can reach Kootenay National Park by heading south on **Highway 93** (the

Banff/Windermere Highway), which splits from Highway 1 about 26 km (16 mi) west of Banff. Of all the major routes through the parks, Highway 93 through Kootenay probably gets the least travel, but the views are consistently stunning. The highway climbs steeply to **Vermilion Pass** (1,640 meters, or 5,416 ft), which is both the juncture of Banff and Kootenay parks and the summit of the Continental Divide. Lightning sparked a forest fire here that charred 6,000 acres in 1968, but the forest is regenerating. Amid the burnt tree skeletons left by the fire, new growth of lodgepole pine has turned the hillsides green once again; a series of interpretive exhibits along a 1-km (.5-mi) loop explain the regenerative process.

As the road descends from the pass, look for the **Stanley Glacier trailhead,** the start of an excellent day hike, a moderate 4-km (2.5-mi) climb to a large glacial cirque. Continuing south along Highway 93, keep an eye out for the trailhead to **Floe Lake,** one of the park's highlights and the start of a long (21-km, 13-mi, round-trip) day hike. Dark limestone walls rising 1,000 meters (3,300 ft) above the lake create a stunning backdrop to the lake and the small blue-white glacier that feeds it with ice floes and gives it its name.

Near narrow **Sinclair Canyon,** Highway 93 reaches the baths of Radium Hot Springs. This is certainly the most populated nook of the park, and the large, hot spring pool on the left side of the road can be packed with people during the summer (*see* Other Activities, *below*). For travelers wanting to make a day of it, lunch and dinner are served at the resort across the road.

To reach Yoho National Park, go west from Lake Louise on **Highway 1** over Kicking Horse Pass. The first point of interest is the viewing pull-off for the **Spiral Tunnels.** Drilled into the mountain by the Canadian Pacific Railroad in 1909, these two tunnels aid trains in negotiating the steep grade of the mountain. If you're lucky enough to show up when a long train is traversing the pass, you might see the front of the train emerging from the upper tunnel while the tail section is still entering the lower tunnel directly below.

To get just a taste of Yoho, many travelers make the 13-km (8-mi) excursion to **Takakkaw Falls,** a slender, 380-meter (1,248-ft) cascade. The Takakkaw Falls parking lot is also the base of a trail network that leads to Twin Falls and the Little Yoho River valley, both ranked highly among backpacking destinations. The road to the falls is open mid-June to early October, as snow permits, but because of a series of tight switchbacks, it's not accessible to trailers or large RVs.

Farther along Highway 1, the **Burgess Shale exhibit** contains the fossilized remains of 120 marine species dating back 530 million years. The actual site of the shale—which was designated a World Heritage Site in 1980—is accessible only by taking a difficult guided hike of approximately 20 km (12 mi). There is a shorter, steeper hike to the Mt. Stevens trilobite fossil beds. Guided hikes are also offered to extensions of the Burgess Shale fossils in Kootenay and Banff national parks. Allow a full day for any of the hikes, which are conducted from July through mid-September. They cost $35–$45 per person and are popular, so it's best to reserve well in advance. Contact **Canadian Wilderness Tours** (1010 Larch Pl., Canmore, AB T1W 1S7, tel. 403/678–3795) or the **Yoho-Burgess Shale Research Foundation** (Box 148, Field, BC V0A 1G0, tel. 800/343–3006).

Continue on to **Emerald Lake,** an 8-km (5-mi) side trip off Highway 1. Stroll around the vivid green lake, rent a canoe, have a cup of tea at the teahouse, or, if one day isn't enough, spend a night in the fine lodge (*see* Lodging, *below*). Although some tour buses do stop here, Emerald Lake rarely sees crowds comparable to those at stops nearer Banff.

HISTORIC BUILDINGS AND SITES These parks have few historic sites, the presence of settlers in this part of the world being a relatively new phenomenon. The most familiar landmark in the parks is the Banff Springs

Hotel, worth a visit just to experience the nonstop activity it embraces.

Cave and Basin Centennial Centre, a historic building, was the first site in Banff park to be given national-park protection (in 1885) after the discovery of hot springs by prospectors in 1883. (Native people knew of the springs long before this.) The springs are no longer in use at this site, but the facilities can be toured for a small fee.

NATURE TRAILS AND SHORT WALKS The twin trails at the **Cave and Basin Centennial Centre** are easy strolls, with signs along the way giving information about regional geology, flora, and fauna. The annotated nature trail encircling **Emerald Lake** is particularly interesting due to the considerably different climate zones and the vegetation on the eastern and western sides of the lake. Twenty-two kilometers (13.5 miles) east of Emerald Lake is the **Lake O'Hara** area, accessible by shuttle bus (contact the Yoho National Park Visitor Centre for details), and featuring several relatively easy trails in the 3-km (2-mi) range among rock-walled mountains and two dozen high-alpine lakes.

The short (3.4 km, 2.1 mi) but somewhat steep hike to the **Lake Agnes teahouse,** which seems to hang at the edge of a tiny, mountain-ringed lake, is among the most popular near Lake Louise, as is the somewhat longer (5.3-km, 3.3-mi) hike to the teahouse at the **Plain of Six Glaciers.** The Lake Agnes hike is a jaunt through the woods; the Six Glaciers hike leads out of the woods onto open glacial moraine. Expect plenty of company on both hikes.

The 2.4-km (1.5-mi) **Parker Ridge trail,** the trailhead just a few kilometers south of the Icefield Centre on Highway 93, consists of high-mountain terrain with exceptional glacier and ice-field views—and since it begins just a short distance below the tree line, it's one of the shortest climbs into alpine country. The trail is somewhat less traveled than those mentioned around Lake Louise, perhaps because most visitors rush on to the Icefield Centre or Jasper.

LONGER HIKES There are over 1,900 km (1,100 mi) of maintained hiking trails in the three parks, plus limitless opportunities for hiking backcountry. The hiking season runs from May to October, though it's shorter on higher trails that are snow-covered for most of the year.

The suggestions here are merely a sampler. Anyone interested in hiking or backpacking in the parks should get a copy of *The Canadian Rockies Trail Guide,* by Brian Patton and Bart Robinson, widely available in bookshops and gift shops in the area. Maps and compasses are unnecessary for hikers who stick to the trails, since most of them are well maintained and well marked.

For day hikers, the **Lake Louise/Moraine Lake** area is full of exceptional though well-traveled trails. The trail network connecting the two lakes, with a few fairly steep ups and downs, passes through aptly named Paradise Valley. Day hikers seeking more solitude in Banff National Park are more likely to find it farther north, between **Bow Pass** and the Banff-Jasper boundary. Two worthwhile hikes are the 7.2-km (4.5-mi) trip to **Nigel Pass,** of moderate difficulty, and the 8.1-km (5.1-mi) trip to **Sunset Pass,** which is grindingly steep in places. Yoho and Kootenay trails are better for escaping the crowds, though some, such as those in the Little Yoho River valley, are quite popular. In Kootenay, the longish round-trip (21 km, or 13 mi) to **Floe Lake** from Highway 93 is one of the parks' most rewarding.

Backpackers must pick up backcountry-use permits from the nearest visitor center. Among the best known (and most populated) backpacking areas are the aforementioned Paradise Valley, the **Skoki Valley** beyond the Lake Louise ski area, and the **Egypt Lake** area beyond Sunshine Village, a lake-dotted high-alpine zone not unlike the Lake O'Hara area. The fact that the Sunshine gondola, which gave less-energetic hikers a quick lift on their way to Egypt Lake, no longer runs in summer might discourage a few backpackers, but don't count on it.

Perhaps the most classic multiday backpacking hike in the area is the rugged **Rockwall Trail** in Kootenay, running from the Floe Lake trailhead to the Ochre Creek (Paint Pots) trailhead. The total trip is 55 km (34 mi) of considerable ups and downs.

OTHER ACTIVITIES **Back-Road Driving.** Virtually the only way to get off the main highways, Highways 1 and 93, is on foot, horseback, bike, or skis. Nevertheless, if you tire of the big roads and the traffic they attract, there are a few options. Highway 1A (Bow Valley Parkway), running roughly parallel to Highway 1, is a slower-paced way to travel between Banff and Lake Louise. Tunnel Mountain Drive offers a quick respite from the bustle of Banff, with various pull-offs for views and photos. In Yoho, many travelers turn off the road at the Takakkaw Falls Road to see the highest waterfalls in Canada, but just a bit farther west on Highway 1 is the 8-km (5-mi) road to Emerald Lake, a prettier side trip.

Biking. The three parks are not especially inspiring for bike touring, which is mostly a matter of cycling on the shoulders of the major highways. Still, the Icefields Parkway, with its mostly paved shoulders, is a fairly popular bicycle route. In recent years, mountain bikers have taken to the trails. Predictably, this has led to disputes among bikers and backpackers. Park officials have been trying to keep the peace by publishing a list of trails (available from the visitor centers) on which biking is permitted. Current trail information is posted in the visitor centers. Bikes can be rented from **Park and Pedal Bike Shop** (229 Wolf St., tel. 403/762–3190) in Banff.

Several operators lead guided bike tours. **Rocky Mountain Cycle Tours** (333 Baker St., Nelson, BC V1L 4H6, tel. 800/661–2453 or 250/354–1241) runs one- to seven-day tours in the Banff area and in British Columbia.

Bird-Watching. The more than 200 species of birds in the park make sightings common. You don't have to leave the roadways to spot the many opportunistic scavenger birds, such as jays, magpies, and ravens. Vermilion Lakes are a pit stop for migratory fowl such as Canada geese. The region is also classic terrain for birds of prey, including hawks, eagles, and owls; many do their preying along open scree (erosion-debris) slopes, feeding on the rodents that nest in the rocks.

Boating. Many rivers, lakes, and streams within the parks are great for canoeing. Lake Minnewanka, just 11.5 km (7 mi) from Banff allows motorized boating as well. In addition to tours, **Minnewanka Boat Tours** (Box 2189, Banff, AB T0L 0C0, tel. 403/762–3473) has boat and canoe rentals. Boats and canoes can also be rented at Emerald Lake in Yoho, and canoes are available at Lake Louise and Moraine Lake.

Fishing. Various trout species are the principal game fish in the lakes, rivers, and streams of the Canadian Rockies. Grayling, pike, and whitefish can also be caught. Keep in mind that higher, glacier-fed lakes, rich in glacial silt, usually don't provide very good fishing. The Bow, Kicking Horse, and Kootenay rivers tend to see a lot of action. Information on fishing regulations is available at the visitor centers. A basic, seven-day fishing license is $6; an annual license is $13. These licenses are valid only in the national parks. Provincial licenses are required to fish outside the parks.

Horseback Riding. A few outfitters offer trail riding inside the parks. In its *Accommodation and Visitors' Guide,* Travel Alberta lists several reputable outfitters in the area. Other information can be obtained from the **Guide-Outfitters Association** (Box 94675, Richmond, BC V64 4A4, tel. 250/278–2688).

For daily rides and riding instruction, arrangements can be made at the front desks of Banff Springs Hotel, Chateau Lake Louise, and Emerald Lake Lodge (*see* Lodging, *below*). Arrangements can also be made through **Sundance Stables** (Box 2280, Banff, AB T0L 0C0, tel. 403/762–2832).

Rafting. Trips on the Bow River in Banff, one to three hours in length, are leisurely, scenic floats, while trips on the Kicking Horse River in Yoho, especially in June when the river is swollen with snowmelt, tend to be more rollicking. For Bow River trips, contact **Rocky Mountain Raft Tours** (Box 1771, Banff, AB T0L 0C0, tel. 403/762–3632); for Kicking Horse River trips, contact **Alpine Rafting Company** (Box 2246, Golden, BC V0A 1H0, tel. 888/666–9494 or 250/344–5016).

Rock Climbing. Great climbs in the park are far too numerous to mention, although the highest peaks—for example, Mt. Temple, 3,554 meters (11,624 ft)—are considered the classics. Routes can be chosen to include rock climbing, ice climbing, glacier travel, scrambling, or any combination thereof. It is this variety that has lured many Alpine mountaineers to settle in the region.

Many of the Alpine transplants now ply a trade as mountain guides, so there is no shortage of experienced excursion leaders. Prospective climbers, especially those not familiar with glacier travel, should hook up with a guide service. Whether on independent or guided trips, all climbing parties must have permits, available at visitor centers. Mountaineering is a year-round activity in the Canadian Rockies.

The **Canadian School of Mountaineering** (629 10th St., Canmore, AB T1W 2E5, tel. 403/678–4134) and **Banff Alpine Guides** (Box 1025, Banff, AB T0L 0C0, tel. 403/678–6091)· conduct trips in the parks for climbers of all ability levels. Membership in the **Alpine Club of Canada** (Box 8040, Indian Flats Rd., Canmore, AB T1W 2T8, tel. 403/678–3200) is also worth considering. The club maintains several backcountry huts in and around the parks.

Skiing. There are three lift-serviced ski areas in Banff National Park: **Lake Louise** (across Hwy. 1 from the village of Lake Louise, tel. 403/522–3555); **Mt. Norquay** (on Mt. Norquay Rd., across Hwy. 1 from the town of Banff, tel. 403/762–4421); and **Sunshine Village** (on Sunshine Village Rd., 8 km [5 mi] west of Banff on Hwy. 1, tel.

403/762–6500 or 800/661–1363). Lake Louise has the largest variety of terrain and is generally regarded as one of Canada's premier slopes; Sunshine features moderately pitched, open-bowl skiing; and Mt. Norquay, known for its steepness, also has a good deal of intermediate terrain.

Ski Touring. From track skiing to ski mountaineering, the opportunities are limitless. For track skiers, December through March tends to be the best time; after that the snow on the lower-elevation flats starts deteriorating. Backcountry touring is usually better later in the season (February through April).

Although it's not actually in the parks, the **Canmore Nordic Centre** (1988 Olympic Way, Suite 100, Canmore, AB T0L 0M0, tel. 403/678–2400), 30 km (18 mi) east of Banff, must be noted. Site of the 1988 Olympic cross-country events, the center is among the best anywhere in North America. Approximately 70 km (44 mi) of groomed trails link with an extensive ungroomed network. Some trails are lit for night skiing. Groomed tracks (and rental equipment) can also be found near the Banff Springs Hotel and Chateau Lake Louise.

One of the most popular backcountry tours is to Skoki Lodge, 12 km (7.5 mi) from the base of the Lake Louise ski area. The skiing is over generally moderate terrain, with consistently good views. Mt. Assiniboine Lodge, which is in Mt. Assiniboine Provincial Park, and Lake O'Hara Lodge are other good ski-touring centers (*see* Lodging, *below*). The high country near Bow Pass also has a number of local adherents.

Anyone who ventures into the backcountry should keep in mind that avalanche hazards are considerable. (Information on avalanche conditions for Banff, Kootenay, and Yoho national parks is available at visitor centers and warden offices or by calling 403/762–1460.) One way to lessen the risk is to sign on with a local guide service. The **Canadian School of Mountaineering** and **Banff Alpine Guides** (*see* Rock Climbing, *above*) both lead backcountry tours in the area. The best place in Banff to rent such equipment as cross-country skis, mountaineering skis, and climbing gear is **Mountain Magic** (224 Bear St., tel. 403/762–2591).

Snowmobiling. Recreational snowmobiling is prohibited in the parks.

Swimming. Cold is the word here. The glacial sources of most lakes and rivers make for chilly dipping. The obvious exceptions are the hot spring–fed pools, though these are intended more for soaking than swimming. The largest of these is the **Radium Hot Springs Pools** in Kootenay (tel. 800/767–1611 or 250/347–9485). **Upper Hot Springs Pool** (tel. 403/762–1515) is the most popular in Banff. Suits, towels, and lockers are for rent, and hours vary with the seasons.

CHILDREN'S PROGRAMS With so much hiking, biking, boating, horseback riding, canoeing, and so on, the three parks are a giant camp for children. In addition to the **Banff Park Museum** and **Lake Louise Visitor Centre** (*see* Orientation Programs, *above*), the **Luxton Museum** (1 Birch Ave., Banff, tel. 403/762–2388) is worth a visit with young children. The museum has exhibits on natural history and Native American history in the region.

Outside the national-parks boundaries, **Fort Steele Heritage Town** (16 km [10 mi] northeast of Cranbrook on Hwy. 93/95, tel. 250/426–7532), open mid-June to early September, is well worth a visit. The authentically reconstructed pioneer town is a step back into the 1890s and the glory days of silver and lead mining.

EVENING ACTIVITIES From July through August, on every night but Sunday, Parks Canada gives interpretive talks on Banff's flora, fauna, history, and hiking trails, as well as musical theater programs, at several campgrounds in the parks. Programs begin at 8 or 9 PM. Check at the visitor center counters or campground kiosks for a schedule. For those more interested in cultural life, **Banff Centre** (tel. 403/762–6300) is the place in the parks to go for music (classical

to pop), dance, and drama. During summer, the center hosts the three-month Banff Festival of the Arts.

In Kootenay, mid-evening interpretive talks are given at Redstreak campground several nights a week in July and August. At the Marble Canyon campground, there are interpretive talks at 8 PM on Tuesday and Friday. There's also a nature walk at Redstreak campground every Sunday at 7 PM in July and August.

In Yoho, look for campfire talks, musical programs, and guided evening hikes throughout July and August. Check at the visitor centers or campground kiosks for current schedules.

DINING

With its vast tourist industry, the town of Banff caters to all tastes with everything from casual cafeterias to elegant restaurants. Though casual, basic, Western-style food is the norm, you'll find an international mix of Italian, Chinese, Greek, Continental, and Japanese (steadily increasing in numbers) restaurants. In addition, most backcountry lodges scattered around Banff, Yoho, and Kootenay parks have traditional lodge-style restaurants; Chateau Lake Louise has six restaurants under its roof.

BANFF **Le Beaujolais.** In casual Banff, this is the place to find big-city elegance. It can come across as a bit stuffy, but that does nothing to diminish its popularity. Tapestries give the restaurant a hint of baronial splendor, and the richness of the food is a match for the setting. Traditional French preparations of beef, veal, lamb, and fish are always on the menu. *212 Buffalo St., at Banff Ave., tel. 403/762–2712. Reservations essential. AE, MC, V. No lunch. $$$*

Giorgio's Trattoria. This split-level eatery serves high-quality Italian food and is immensely popular, so you might have to wait for a table during busy hours. Philippine mahogany tables and bar, Tuscan-style sponged walls, and a high beamed ceiling create a lovely setting for pizza, the house specialty; there's also a wide selection of pastas, as well as chicken and meat entrées. The homemade fruit sherbets are a must for dessert. *219 Banff Ave., tel. 403/762–5114. AE, MC, V. No lunch. $$*

Balkan Restaurant. A Mediterranean mood is highlighted with blue-and-white decor, cane-back chairs, and ample indoor vegetation. You can sample such classic Greek dishes as moussaka and souvlakia, as well as creative ethnic mixes such as Greek stir-fry (rice and vegetables with feta cheese). *120 Banff Ave., tel. 403/762–3454. MC, V. $–$$*

Barbary Coast. This sports-theme restaurant with neo-California cuisine has fast become a local favorite. The plant-filled, skylighted dining room is filled with sports paraphernalia—signed race bibs from skiers, hockey skates, old bikes, and more. New York steak is a house specialty, pizzas with pesto sauce are popular, and the menu also includes a variety of pastas. Live blues bands play in the bar daily after 10 PM. *119 Banff Ave., upstairs, tel. 403/762–4616. AE, DC, MC, V. $–$$*

Joe Btfsplk's Diner. It's either fun, camp, or overbearing, depending on your taste. A re-created '50s-style diner, it has red-vinyl banquettes and chrome-trimmed tables. The menu is right out of the true-American cookbook: bacon and eggs for breakfast; burgers, meat loaf, mashed potatoes, and apple pie for lunch or dinner. Fresh-baked cookies and muffins are available for take-out. *221 Banff Ave., tel. 403/762–5529. Reservations not accepted. AE, DC, MC, V. $*

LAKE LOUISE **Post Hotel.** This hotel restaurant is cited in almost every guide and magazine article as one of the true epicurean experiences in the Canadian Rockies. The atmosphere is both rustic (exposed beams, stone hearth) and elegant (tables adorned with fanned white linen napkins). Traditional European dishes such as veal and venison are prepared with light California influences; the house specialty is Alberta rack of lamb. Homemade pastries cap off

the meal and are also served in the hotel lobby throughout the afternoon. By Canadian Rockies standards, the service can be overly formal. *200 Pipestone Rd., tel. 403/522–3989. Reservations essential. AE, MC, V. $$$*

Chateau Lake Louise. The six restaurants here will satisfy your every whim, from light snacking to full-blown, night-on-the-town elegance. The château is perhaps best known—and recommended—for its meal between meals: afternoon tea in the Lakeside Lounge (open from early June to early September). The more formal restaurants require jackets at dinner. *Lake Louise Dr., tel. 403/522–3511. Reservations essential (at most restaurants) in summer. AE, D, DC, MC, V. $$–$$$*

Laggan's Mountain Bakery and Deli. This small deli-bakery at the Samson Mall is the place where park wardens, mountain guides, and local work crews congregate for morning coffee. As such, it's a nice place to pick up not only fresh-baked goods (muffins and poppy-seed bread) but a little inside information on what's up in the parks as well. This is a good place to buy picnic sandwiches for a hike around Lake Louise or for the drive north along the Icefields Parkway. *Samson Mall, tel. 403/522–2017. No credit cards. $*

YOHO **Emerald Lake Lodge.** The dining room is a glass-enclosed terrace with views of the lake through tall stands of evergreens. The furnishings are eclectic—some tables have upholstered chairs, some have straight-backs—evoking a funky-old-lodge atmosphere. Also eclectic is the menu, which combines familiar Canadian and American fare—steaks, game, fish—with such esoteric flavors as ginger-tangerine glaze. More often than not, the combinations are effective. Salads, quiches, and baked cheeses are served in the dining room and in the lounge area around a giant stone hearth. The lodge also serves an excellent breakfast and lunch. *8 km (5 mi) north of Field, tel. 250/343–6321 or 800/663–6336. AE, DC, MC, V. $$–$$$*

PICNIC SPOTS A hike of a mile or less gives you a choice of thousands of secluded, scenic picnic spots. If you're not eager to hike, though, picnic sites with tables are numerous along the major roadways. Some of the prettier spots are near Hector Lake, just south of Bow Pass; along the Emerald River beyond Field in Yoho; and between Vermilion Pass and Vermilion Crossing and at Olive Lake in Kootenay.

LODGING

Finding a place to stay in Banff and Lake Louise can be a tall order in the summer, even though there are more than 40 hotels, inns, and lodges in and around the park, not including bed-and-breakfasts. Reservations are a must. Finding reasonably priced lodging is even harder. Travelers on a budget should consider the more moderately priced lodging in Canmore, a 25-minute drive east of Banff. Budget-minded travelers should also avoid the June-through-September peak period, when room rates are typically 50%–100% higher than during the rest of the year. For basic lodging information, both Travel Alberta and Tourism British Columbia (*see* Visitor Information, *above*) publish excellent accommodations guides.

Bed-and-breakfast accommodations are plentiful in and around the national parks, but don't expect the quaint-old-home atmosphere you might find elsewhere in North America. Most B&Bs in this part of the world are simply ordinary rooms in ordinary homes, the main attraction being price rather than atmosphere. Two agencies handle bookings in the area: **Alberta's Gem B&B Reservation Agency** (11216 48th Ave., Edmonton, AB T6H 0C7, tel. 403/434–6098, fax 403/434–6098); and the **Bed and Breakfast Agency of Alberta** (410 19th Ave NE, Calgary, AB T2E 1P3, tel. 800/425–8160 or 403/277–8486, fax 403/237–5433). The former agency covers all licensed bed-and-breakfasts and charges a booking fee, but does not personally inspect establish-ments. The latter agency handles only about 50 bed-and-breakfasts, but personally inspects each property and does not charge a booking fee. Individual establishments are listed in Travel Alberta's *Alberta Accommodation and Visitors' Guide.*

There are many **guest ranches** near the national parks. Information on guest ranches is included in Travel Alberta's *Alberta Accommodation and Visitors' Guide.* Publications listing guest ranches are also available from Tourism British Columbia and the **Guide-Outfitters Association** (Box 94675, Richmond, BC V64 4A4, tel. 205/278–2688). There is also a hostel network in the parks; for information contact **Hostelling International Canada** (Southern Alberta Region, No. 203, 1414 Kensington Rd. NW, Calgary, AB T2N 3P9, tel. 403/283–5551, fax 403/283–6503).

BANFF **Banff Springs Hotel.** Built in 1888, this luxury hotel is the place that established Banff as a tourist destination. The massive, stone-wall hotel is a world of its own, a seemingly endless maze of hall-ways, stairwells, huge sitting areas, and banquet rooms, with stone, dark wood, and chandeliers abounding. The layout is both fun and wearying: The orienteering skills of even the most adept adventurer will be challenged; and getting lost, at some point, is a given for all guests. Old-hotel details, such as high ceilings, antique furniture, and rattling windows, give the establishment its charm, while a lavish spa lends a note of modern luxury. The hotel is a perpetual 20-ring circus, anything but a getaway mountain retreat. Be forewarned that rooms are not very soundproof, and over-booking can be a problem in peak season. *Spray Ave., Box 960, Banff, AB T0L 0C0, tel. 403/762–2211 or 800/441–1414, fax 403/762–5755. 804 rooms, 80 suites. Facilities: 12 restaurants, 3 bars, room service, indoor pool, outdoor hot tub, sauna, spa, 27-hole golf course, miniature golf, 5 tennis courts, bowling, health club, horseback riding, shops, convention center. AE, D, DC, MC, V. $$$*

Buffalo Mountain Lodge. Though it's newer than the Banff Springs Hotel, Buffalo Mountain is steeped in old-lodge ambience: The lobby is full of polished pine and exposed, rough-hewn beams, and the trademark stone hearth has a buffalo head over the mantel. In addition to the main lodge, a group of chalet buildings were remodeled in 1996 to provide comfortable modern accommodation in 42 suites, and there's also a modern hotel-condo cluster. Rooms are dressed in pastel shades and have small fireplaces, willow chairs, and pine cabinetry. Although the lodge sits off a high road on the outskirts of Banff, few rooms have views. *Tunnel Mountain Rd., Box 1326, Banff AB T0L 0C0, tel. 403/762–2400 or 800/661–1367, fax 403/762–4495. 40 rooms, 42 suites, 20 condos. Facilities: restaurant, bar, hot tub, steam room. AE, DC, MC, V. $$$*

Mt. Assiniboine Lodge. This is another of the original backcountry lodges of the Canadian Rockies. Built in 1928, the lodge remains deep in the backcountry today. Guests must hike in or ski (rentals are available) the 20 to 30 km (12 to 18 mi), although a helicopter can be hired from Canmore for those looking to save their energy, if not their money. The lodge is in Mt. Assiniboine Provincial Park, southwest of Banff, in a spectacular setting—across Lake Magog from Mt. Assiniboine. Accommodation is in a central lodge or individual cabins, with sturdy wood beds covered by down comforters. The lodge has some electricity and running water, but guests should be prepared to use outhouses. Opportunities abound for terrific hikes and ski tours, with the lodge offering rentals and a guide service. *Box 8128, Canmore, AB T1W 2T8, tel. 403/678–2883, fax 403/678–4877. Accommodations for 28 in 6 lodge rooms and 6 cabins, with propane heat and lights. 3 meals daily and guide service included. Facilities: sauna, skiing. MC, V. Closed Oct.–mid-Feb. and mid-Apr.–late June. $$$*

Red Carpet Inn. This is one of the few moderately priced lodging options in downtown Banff. The lobby consists of little more than a desk, an office, and a postcard stand. The motel-style rooms are small, but by Banff standards, so are the prices. Rooms in back, away from Banff Avenue traffic noise, are preferable. *425 Banff Ave., Box 1800, Banff, AB T0L 0C0, tel. 403/762–4184; 800/563–4609 in Canada; fax 403/762–4894. 52 rooms. Facilities: hot tub. AE, MC, V. $$$*

Skoki Lodge. You might think an 11-km (7-mi) hike (or ski) to a lodge without electricity or running water wouldn't be most people's cup of tea. Yet reservations for this basic lodge often must be made months in advance, especially for weekends. One of the original Canadian Rockies lodges, this was built of chiseled logs in 1931. There have been additions since, largely in the form of outlying cabins, but the log-cabin motif makes everything seem of the same age: Fill an exposed-log living room with a large stone fireplace, piano, books, and kerosene lamps, and you have just about all that a backcountry lodge is supposed to be. One shortcoming: The lodge has no hiking or ski-touring guide service. *Box 5, Lake Louise, AB T0L 1E0, tel. 403/522–3555, fax 403/522–2095. Reservations essential. Accommodations for 22 in 4 lodge rooms and 3 cabins. 3 meals a day and afternoon tea included. AE, MC, V. Closed Easter–late June and late Sept.–Dec. 21. $$–$$$*

Storm Mountain Lodge. Built as a backcountry lodge in 1922, Storm Mountain is hardly "backcountry" today. Highway 93 South now passes the lodge's doorstep on its way through Vermilion Pass. Once you're inside, though, the lodge's roots in tradition are evident in the sitting area, dominated by a large fireplace and the head of a bighorn sheep. The dining area embodies the elegance of simplicity: straight-back wood chairs and white tablecloths on an enclosed porch overlooking the pass. Bedrooms, in separate cabins tucked in the woods, are small but cozy, with fireplaces, old lamps, and down comforters. The lodge is open from mid-May to late September. *Rte. 93 S, 5 km (3 mi) west of the Hwy. 1 interchange, Box 670, Banff, AB T0L 0C0, tel. and fax 403/762–4155. 12 cabins. Facilities: restaurant, lounge. AE, MC, V. $$–$$$*

LAKE LOUISE **Chateau Lake Louise.** Terraces and lawns spread down to the famous aquamarine lake, with the Victoria Glacier as a backdrop. Large, horseshoe-shape windows make the dramatic exterior seem almost a part of the interior. Burgundy and brass and neo-Colonial furnishings lend an appropriately grand-hotel atmosphere, and some guest rooms have hand-painted floral designs on the doors and cabinetry. In terms of high-quality accommodations, the château, built in 1923, is hard to beat in the Canadian Rockies. On the downside, the château and lake, a major stop for tour buses and sightseers, are anything but quiet; overbooking can be a problem; and the rooms lack soundproofing. *Lake Louise Dr., Lake Louise, AB T0L 1E0, tel. 403/522–3511 or 800/441–1414, fax 403/522–3834. 511 rooms and suites. Facilities: 6 restaurants, 2 lounges, indoor pool, steam room, exercise room, horseback riding, boating, shops. AE, D, DC, MC, V. $$$*

Lake Louise Inn. This five-building complex has motel rooms and two-bedroom condo units, some with a balcony, fireplace, and/or a kitchenette. For economy-minded travelers, the Pinery, a separate 56-room building, offers few frills but comfortable accommodations. In winter, there is a shuttle service to the nearby slopes. *210 Village Rd., Box 209, Lake Louise, AB T0L 1E0, tel. 800/661–9237 or 403/522–3791, fax 403/522–2018. 222 rooms and condo units. Facilities: restaurant, pub, indoor pool, sauna, exercise room, ice-skating. AE, DC, MC, V. $$$*

Post Hotel. There's nothing especially remarkable about the Post's location, but the hotel makes up for this in other ways. Amber-color wood and gold siding and trim provide an ambience of elegance. Rooms come in 15 configurations, from standard doubles to units with sleeping lofts, kitchens, balconies, and fireplaces. Bathrooms are large, and most are equipped with whirlpool tubs. Seven new deluxe, two-level suites come with king-size beds and large living rooms with river-stone fireplaces. Rooms facing away from the highway have good views of Mt. Temple. Two streamside log cabins make for a more private getaway. The restaurant (*see* Dining, *above*) is regularly rated as one of the best in the Canadian Rockies. *Box 69, Lake Louise, AB T0L 1E0, tel. 800/661–1586 or 403/522–3989, fax 403/522–3966. 98 units, some sleeping 6 people. Facilities: restaurant, lounge, pub, indoor pool. AE, MC, V. Closed late Oct.–early Dec. $$$*

CANMORE **Rocky Mountain Ski Lodge.** In terms of facilities and price, several motels in Canmore are interchangeable as lower-price alternatives to Banff accommodations. A notch above the rest, Rocky Mountain Ski Lodge comprises three neighboring lodging establishments under one management. The newer of the two motel properties has the better accommodations; slanting, exposed-beam ceilings give a chaletlike feeling to the otherwise simple motel rooms. Rooms in the older units have kitchenettes. Condo units are also available. *Rte. 1A, Box 8070, Canmore, AB T1W 2T8, tel. 403/678–5445; 800/665–6111 in Canada; fax 403/678–6484. 82 units. Facilities: hot tub, sauna, playground. AE, MC, V. $$$*

KOOTENAY **Kootenay Park Lodge.** In the center of the park, at Vermilion Crossing, this group of cabins is set in a spruce and fir forest, 45 minutes southwest of Banff, 45 minutes southeast of Lake Louise, and 40 minutes north of Radium Hot Springs. Most cabins have a queen or two double beds along with a hot plate and small refrigerator, many have fireplaces, and all have showers. On rainy days, curl up beside the fireplace in the main lodge with a book from their library. A new interpretive center, including many displays from Parks Canada, opened in 1997. Like the cabins, the interpretive center, gas station, general store, and restaurant close during the off-season. There's a stream nearby for fishing (permits are sold at the store), and there are numerous hiking trails in the area. *Rte. 93 in center of Kootenay, Box 1390, Banff, AB T0L 0C0, tel. 403/762–9196, fax 403/762–5028. 10 cabins. Facilities: restaurant, library, laundry. MC, V. Closed late Sept.–mid-May. $$$*

YOHO **Emerald Lake Lodge.** A cross between hotel and mountain lodge, this enchanted spot is a 20-minute drive from Lake Louise, and a half hour from Banff. Cottages surround the log-cabin main lodge, set at the edge of a secluded, glacier-fed lake. A sitting area in the lodge has overstuffed chairs and small tables for light meals around a large stone hearth. There is also a full bar and an excellent restaurant (*see* Dining, *above*) on a glass-enclosed porch; and a teahouse with an outdoor deck is open in the summer. All rooms have fireplaces and balconies. *8 km (5 mi) north of Field, BC; Box 10, Field, BC V0A 1G0, tel. 250/343–6321 or 800/663–6336, fax 250/343–6724. 85 units in 2- and 4-room cottages. Facilities: 2 restaurants, bar, outdoor hot tub, sauna, exercise room, horseback riding, boating, recreation room. AE, DC, MC, V. $$$*

Lake O'Hara Lodge. Most of the rooms and cabins have private baths, and the dining room features à la carte dining (not the one-sitting, family-style dining common to backcountry lodges), with such items on its dinner menu as duck in cherry sauce and chocolate mousse. The lodge, due west from Lake Louise, is in one of the most scenic and popular hiking and climbing areas in the Canadian Rockies, meaning it gets very active in the summer. (Reservations for midsummer should be booked at least several months in advance.) Lodge guests are ferried in by bus along an 11-km (7-mi) fire road between Highway 1 and the lodge (other vehicles aren't permitted). In winter, guests must ski to the lodge. *Off Rte. 1 in Yoho National Park, Box 55, Lake Louise, AB T0L 1E0, tel. 250/343–6418; 403/678–4110 during off-season. 23 units in lodge and cabins. Facilities: dining room, hiking, boating, skiing. No credit cards. Closed Sept.–mid-Feb. and mid-Apr.–mid-June. $$$*

CAMPING

There are more than 20 drive-in campgrounds and 72 designated backcountry campgrounds in the three parks.

In Banff National Park, Tunnel Mountain has three drive-in campgrounds at the edge of Banff: **Trailer Court** (322 tent and RV sites; $24 per night), **Village 1** (622 tent and RV sites; $17 per night), and **Village 2** (189 RV sites, 35 tent sites; $21 per night). Convenience is the big asset here; you're just a few minutes from downtown. Similarly, **Lake Louise Campground** has access to the sites and scenery of Lake Louise, even if the setting itself is not especially scenic. The 409 tent and RV sites range from $14 to $18.

For more woodsy privacy, try the 140 tent and RV sites ($17 per night) at **Johnston Canyon,** on Highway 1A between Banff and Lake Louise. There are no hookups here, but there are showers.

Two Jack Main, relatively close to the town of Banff, is southwest of Lake Minnewanka. The 381 tent and RV sites are a bargain at $13 per night. There are flush toilets and drinking water but no showers.

Kootenay National Park is a good choice for campers who want to be removed from the settlements of Banff, Lake Louise, and Radium Hot Springs but who don't want to be far from the action. The **Marble Canyon** campground, closer to Banff, sits alongside the Vermilion River, with mountain ranges rising steeply on either side. Its 61 tent and RV sites cost $13 per night. **McLeod Meadows,** which is closer to Radium Hot Springs, is in the more open valley of the Kootenay River. It has 98 tent and RV sites that also cost $13 per night. Neither campground has hookups. For those, you'll have to stay at **Redstreak,** where 242 sites (88 with hookups) are set in a wooded area near Radium Hot Springs. The fee here ranges from $17 to $22 per night.

More removed from the main park action are **Kicking Horse** (89 sites; $17 per night) and **Monarch** (46 sites; $13 per night) in Yoho. Set alongside the broad, alluvial deposits of the Kicking Horse River, the campgrounds both have good views of the Yoho mountain ranges, and Lake Louise is less than a half-hour drive away. If those

SELECTED BANFF, YOHO, AND KOOTENAY CAMPGROUNDS

Columns grouped as: **INSIDE BANFF** — Tunnel Mountain Trailer Court, Tunnel Mountain Village 1, Tunnel Mountain Village 2, Lake Louise, Johnston Canyon, Two Jack Main; **INSIDE YOHO** — Hoodoo Creek, Chancellor Peak, Kicking Horse, Lake O'Hara; **INSIDE KOOTENAY** — Redstreak, Marble Canyon, McLeod Meadows.

	Tunnel Mtn Trailer Court	Tunnel Mtn Village 1	Tunnel Mtn Village 2	Lake Louise	Johnston Canyon	Two Jack Main	Hoodoo Creek	Chancellor Peak	Kicking Horse	Lake O'Hara	Redstreak	Marble Canyon	McLeod Meadows
Total number of sites	322	622	224	409	140	381	106	64	89	30	242	61	98
Sites suitable for RVs	322	622	189	409	140	381	106	64	86	0	242	61	98
Number of hookups	322	0	189	189	0	0	0	0	0	0	88	0	0
Drive to sites	•	•	•	•	•	•	•	•	•		•	•	•
Hike to sites										•			
Flush toilets	•	•	•	•	•	•	•		•		•	•	•
Pit/chemical toilets								•		•			
Drinking water	•	•	•	•	•	•	•	•	•		•	•	•
Showers	•	•	•	•					•		•		
Fire grates		•	•			•	•	•	•	•	•	•	•
Swimming													
Boat access													
Playground							•		•		•		
Disposal station	•*	•	•	•	•	•	•		•		•	•	•
Ranger station										•			
Public telephone	•	•	•	•	•	•					•		
Reservation possible										•**	•		•
Daily fee per site	$22	$16	$19	$14–$18[3]	$16	$13	$14	$12	$17	$10.50	$16–$21	$13	$13
Dates open	mid-May–late Sept.	year-round	mid-May–late-Sept.	mid-May–late-Sept.[3]	mid-May–mid-Sept.	mid-May–early Sept.	late June–early Sept.	late Apr.–mid-Oct.	mid-May–mid-Oct.	mid-June–late Sept.	mid-May–late Sept.	mid-June–early Sept.	mid-May–mid-Sept.

*Tunnel Mountain Trailer Court and Village 2 share a disposal station.   **By reservation only (tel. 403/343–6433).

campgrounds are full and you don't feel like hiking, try Yoho's **Hoodoo Creek** (106 sites; $14 per night) or **Chancellor Peak** (64 sites; $13 per night). Neither of these has hookups or showers, but Hoodoo Creek does have flush toilets and a disposal station.

Lake O'Hara has a lodge and a daily bus to carry lodgers and campers along the 11-km (7-mi) fire road connecting the lake and the Trans-Canada Highway. The 30 tent sites cost $10.50 each; all have access to short day hikes. Reservations are required for the campground and for the alpine huts in the area; they are accepted up to three months in advance.

Aside from the $6 permit (*see* Visitor Information, *above*), backcountry camping is free. Two of the prettiest and most popular backcountry campgrounds are **Paradise Valley** (10 sites) and **Egypt lakes** (15 sites). Paradise Valley is just around the corner (a few kilometers, that is) from Lake Louise; the Upper Meadows campground is a fairly easy 8-km (5-mi) hike from the Paradise Creek parking lot. Egypt Lake is just one of a half dozen small lakes reached by hiking from the Sunshine Village ski area parking lot. The lake-and-tundra setting is the essence of high-alpine Banff, but if you like your scenery in solitude, avoid the area on summer weekends.

It's hard to imagine a more spectacular campground setting than **Floe Lake** (18 sites) a small lake lying hard against a 3,000-ft rock wall in Kootenay. From here you can reach the equally spectacular, though rugged, Rockwall trail, where there are three other backcountry campgrounds.

On the other side of the Trans-Canada Highway in Yoho are **Twin Falls** (8 sites) and **Little Yoho Valley** (10 sites). A small chalet built in the 1920s near Twin Falls gives that area a slightly more civilized feeling than Little Yoho Valley. The falls are indeed quite a sight, and a day excursion from the campground to the Yoho Glacier is a must. The Little Yoho Valley campground is more secluded than Twin Falls, lying on a small meadow near the base of the President Glacier.

Big Bend National Park
Texas

By Kirby F. Warnock

he Wild West may be no more than a page in history books, but in Big Bend National Park you are reminded that it wasn't so long ago that outlaws and Native Americans roamed the countryside along the Rio Grande. The park remains rugged and remote, preserving a frontier spirit inherited from the Native Americans, cavalrymen, smugglers, cowboys, and Mexican revolutionaries who once called this patch of southwest Texas home.

The Comanches passed through this area each September before swooping across the Rio Grande for their annual raid on Mexican villages and *rancherias* (Mexican herdsman's huts). In the 1800s Big Bend received some more permanent tenants: A handful of hardy ranching families settled here and proceeded to carve out a life in the unforgiving countryside. Between 1914 and 1917 General John J. "Blackjack" Pershing's attempts to catch the notorious Mexican revolutionary Pancho Villa were centered here, and later, during Prohibition, the border along the Rio Grande became a favorite route for bootleggers smuggling mescal and tequila into the country. Between 1933 and 1944 Texas acquired the land that was to become Big Bend and donated it to the federal government. Big Bend National Park was established on June 12, 1944.

Named for the bend in the Rio Grande where the park is located, Big Bend spreads over 1,252 rugged square mi. It is more than 230 mi from the nearest airport and more than 100 mi from a town of any considerable size. You cannot fly into the park or arrive by bus or train—the only way to get here is by car, bicycle, or on foot. The terrain in Big Bend is surprisingly diverse: High mountain forests give way abruptly to harsh desert plains and lush river bottomland, all within a day's travel. Visitors can float lazily down a calm stretch of river or hang on for dear life through white-water rapids, ride horseback to the edge of the mountains and down through desert arroyos, and camp in the backcountry. And, like the adventurers who came in the frontier days, you can hike along mountain trails deep into a wilderness that is still so remote that it's easy to travel for a day or more without seeing any other people.

Big Bend is the kind of territory that inspired Hollywood's western soundstages: mountains; endless vistas of sky; rugged, mile-high peaks; steep-walled canyons; and broad desert plains punctuated by innumerable species of cactus. And while paved roads will carry you to all the main facilities, there are hundreds of miles of primitive dirt roads that lead to desert springs, river crossings, and abandoned mines and ranches. Big Bend is untamed and free, and, in this day and age, it may be the closest you'll get to a true frontier experience.

To the locals, the term "Big Bend" does not refer to the Park proper, but the entire region west of the Pecos River and north of the Rio Grande, including the communities of Fort Stockton, Alpine, Marathon, Marfa, Pecos, and Fort Davis. On your way into and out of the park you will pass through these small towns that look as if they are frozen in the 1950s.

Cross the muddy waters of the Rio Grande and you're in Mexico. But the Mexico found here is very different from the Mexico of the crowded, commercialized border towns of Tijuana and Nuevo Laredo. These Mexican villages—San Carlos, Boquillas, and Santa Elena—are comprised of little more than a few adobe houses, a cantina, and a church. Just as Big Bend gives you a no-frills glimpse into America's frontier past, the small villages all around the park invite you to witness the kind of small-town life that's hard to come by these days.

ESSENTIAL INFORMATION

VISITOR INFORMATION The **Panther Junction Visitor Center** (Big Bend National Park, Big Bend, TX 79834, tel. 915/477–2251) at the center of the park is the main source for maps, guidebooks, and visitor information. The smaller **Rio Grande Village Visitor Center** (tel. 915/477–2271), on the Rio Grande along the southeast border of the park, is open only from mid-November through April. **Persimmon Gap** (tel. 915/477–2393) is run by volunteers six days a week and by a ranger one day; it may be closed on occasion if staff is not available. **Chisos Basin** (tel. 915/477–2264) is generally open year-round.

A backcountry permit is required if you plan to do any overnight backpacking or primitive camping in the park. These are free at the Panther Junction Visitor Center.

FEES Entrance fees, good for one week, are $10 per vehicle or $5 per person entering on bicycle, motorcycle, or foot. If you plan to visit often, you might want to purchase the $20 Big Bend Park Pass, which is valid for one year from the date of purchase.

PUBLICATIONS *Big Bend Paisano,* the park newspaper, includes a park map and is available from the visitor centers or the Park Superintendent (Big Bend National Park, Big Bend, TX 79834). Several other publications are available from the **Big**

Bend Natural History Association (Box 68, Big Bend National Park, TX 79834, tel. 915/ 477–2236). For hikers and backpackers, two essential publications are the *Hiker's Guide* and *Chisos Mountain Trails.* Both outline a number of hikes and backpacking trips, providing length, degree of difficulty, and tips on what to see along the trail. For canoeing or river rafting on the Rio Grande, choose from three available guidebooks, *River Guides I, II,* and *III,* which detail three different stretches of the river.

Four-wheel-drive enthusiasts will appreciate the *Road Guide to Backcountry Dirt Roads,* while pavement-bound drivers should turn to the popular *Road Guide to Paved Roads.* Both contain maps, photos, and descriptions of the roads in the park.

GEOLOGY AND TERRAIN Covering 800,000 acres, Big Bend National Park is *big*—even by Texas standards. It is marked by rugged mountains, the tallest of which is Emory Peak (7,825 ft above sea level) in the Chisos Mountain Range. The Chisos Mountains, blanketed in evergreens, are as serene and cool as the surrounding desert is arid and harsh. The cactus-strewn Chihuahuan Desert, stretching from northern Mexico up into Texas, is the largest in North America. The difference between these two areas is striking: Within an hour's drive from the flatlands near the border up into the Chisos Mountains Basin, a bowl-like canyon at the top of a mountain, the temperature can drop 15 degrees. A third terrain parallels the Rio Grande, where the bottomland is populated with river reeds, salt cedars, and cottonwood trees, and the banks along some stretches of the Rio Grande, worn by centuries of white water, have formed impressive canyons framed by 1,500-ft cliffs.

Nearly 600 million years ago, the Big Bend area was covered by water. As the sea receded, layers of sediment were left behind and eventually hardened to rock. These layers are clearly visible along the Rio Grande in the Santa Elena Canyon. Heavy volcanic activity followed, including lava flows and upthrusts that formed lava domes and mountains. Dinosaurs and crocodiles roamed the Big Bend; in 1975 the remains of the largest flying creature known to man was discovered in the park. Ancient Native American groups lived in caves in the region, leaving pictographs on cave walls. The actual big bend of the Rio Grande was formed over millions of years as the river wore away at the layers of limestone, sandstone, and volcanic rock.

FLORA AND FAUNA Big Bend is a Biosphere Reserve, a unique area of plant and animal life where you will find several species that exist nowhere else on earth. Common in Big Bend but unique to the Chihuahuan Desert is the lechuguilla, a dagger-tipped plant that grows in clusters. The lechuguilla is an important food source for the javelina (pronounced have-ah-*leen*-ah), or collared peccary, a curious, piglike animal that can be found throughout the park. A nocturnal animal, the javelina has poor eyesight but a keen sense of smell.

Also common here is the ocotillo, a 10- to 15-ft plant with slender, thorny stems and a brilliant, red-orange flower. The century plant, a member of the Agave family, has a large stalk growing from the center of its spiny base that produces a bright yellow bloom. Contrary to popular folklore, it does not take the century plant a century to bloom, but it does take many years. And once the plant blooms, it dies.

Aside from the javelina, the park's most common animals include the desert mule deer and a subspecies of white-tailed deer called the Carmen Mountains whitetail. There are also mountain lions in the Big Bend, although sightings are rare: They are extremely wary of humans and are primarily nocturnal. Among the other animals are jackrabbits, roadrunners, ground squirrels, black bears, and the gray fox and coyote, seen around the Rio Grande Village campgrounds.

Bird species in the area include the golden eagle, Mexican jay, roadrunner, pyrrhuloxia, white-winged dove, western bluebird, scaled quail, and endangered peregrine falcon, which nests on the cliffs along the Rio Grande and the peaks in the Chisos Mountains from February through July. These birds may be spotted throughout the park, but are most likely to be seen along the Rio Grande and in the Chisos Basin.

Free programs on the park's flora and fauna are given most nights in the amphitheaters at the Chisos Basin or Rio Grande Village (*see* Evening Activities, *below*). For more in-depth looks at the plant and wildlife, you may take part in seminars hosted by the Big Bend Natural History Association (*see* Publications, *above*). The seminars are held outdoors, and include hikes and lectures by park rangers and noted area authorities.

WHEN TO GO Big Bend is busiest in March and April, when the desert is in full bloom. If you don't mind fighting the crowds you will be rewarded by the sight of colorful blooming cacti, the giant Big Bend bluebonnets (which stand nearly 2 ft tall), and the cascading blossoms of the yucca plants. The weather is usually very temperate during this season, ranging from the 50s through the 80s, with warm days and cool nights. Since most people visit in spring, campsites are usually full and the in-park lodgings are booked solid, but you can still get away from the crowds if you don't mind roughing it on backcountry trails and at backcountry campsites. It's best to avoid Big Bend altogether during spring break, when students from high schools and colleges in Texas descend en masse, and even the backcountry campsites fill up.

Many visitors opt to visit during the fall, particularly in October, when the crowds are gone and the weather is optimal. Temperatures hover in the high 70s, and the Rio Grande runs at its highest, providing peak white water for rafting or canoeing. Summertime can be unbearably hot along the Rio Grande, where the thermometer regularly rises above 100°F, though it is usually 10 to 20 degrees cooler up in the Chisos Basin. The rainy season falls between late July and October, when sudden cloudbursts can cause flash floods that sometimes impede travel. In winter, temperatures range between 36°F and 62°F throughout the park, snow is rare, and campers are few. Bird-watchers will enjoy visiting at this time, as many migratory birds can be seen on their way south.

SEASONAL EVENTS **February:** The Chihuahuan Desert Mountain Bike Club hosts the **Chihuahan Desert Challenge Mountain Bike Festival** (Box 448, Terlingua, TX 79852, tel. 915/371–2727) on President's Day weekend in Lajitas. Mountain-bike riders from around the nation gather near the Rio Grande to race through the Chihuahuan Desert during this three-day festival. Events include a cross-country mountain-bike race; a circuit race; the Log Pull, in which contestants see how far they can drag a log tied onto their bikes; and the Chainless Race, a downhill race that allows no pedaling (contestants must remove their bike chains before racing). **Big Bend Pioneer Reunion** (tel. 915/477–2236) is also hosted in early February, with several pioneers and old-timers as well as authors showing up to exchange tales of life in the Big Bend before it became a national park. The reunion usually takes place at the Panther Junction headquarters; phone ahead for details. **March:** On the first weekend in March, the **Texas Cowboy Poetry Gathering** (tel. 915/837–8191) is held in Alpine. Cowboy poets and storytellers are on hand to make the old west come alive with three days of folklore, music, and poetry of the American cowboy. There are evening chuck-wagon sessions, a team roping competition, and a cowboy church service on Sunday morning. **October:** On the third Saturday of the month, Big Bend National Park hosts its **International Good Neighbor Day,** held in cooperation with local Mexican communities. The festival takes place at Rio Grande Village Campground and includes traditional Mexican dancing, arts, crafts, and food. Contact the visitor center for more details. **November:** The area's biggest and craziest festival is the **Annual International Championship Chili Cookoff**

(tel. 512/629–4275 or 713/523–2362), held the first weekend of the month in Terlingua, a ghost town just 20 mi outside of the park. Chili cooks from around the world descend upon this normally empty town to cook chili, dance, and enjoy a huge party in the middle of the desert. Close to 10,000 people come to the area for this weekend, so be sure to reserve lodging in advance.

WHAT TO PACK This is rough country, so wear clothes that you don't mind roughing up a bit. Always pack a light jacket or sweater—nights are cool, even in summer: Nighttime temperatures can drop into the 50s in the middle of July. For winter trips bring plenty of warm clothing, including a hat and gloves. A rugged windbreaker is essential for those fierce west Texas winds. A hat or cap is highly recommended, since the sun shines brightly year-round.

GENERAL STORES The nearest full-service grocery stores are in Alpine and Fort Stockton, approximately 100 and 126 mi from the park, respectively. **Furr's Supermarket** (104 N. 2nd, tel. 915/837–3295) and **Baeza's Thriftway** (101 E. Sul Ross Ave., tel. 915/837–7307) are in Alpine. Furr's is open daily from 8 AM to 9 PM. Baeza's Thriftway is open Monday through Saturday from 8 AM to midnight and Sunday from 8 AM to 10 PM. In Fort Stockton, **Furr's Grocery** (1300 W. Dickinson St., tel. 915/336–3341) is open daily from 7 AM to 10 PM. You can also buy food at **Lowe's** (108 W. 10th St., tel. 915/336–3919), open Monday to Saturday from 8 AM to 10 PM and Sunday from 8 AM to 9 PM. The town's **Wal-Mart** (1700 W. Dickinson St., tel. 915/336–3389) is a good place to stock up on any other supplies you might need. It's open from 7 AM to 9 PM Monday through Saturday and from 9 AM to 7 PM Sunday. There are drive-through windows at **First National Bank** in Fort Stockton (1000 W. Dickinson St.), **Quicksilver Bank** in Terlingua (intersection of Hwys. 118 and 170), and **First National Bank** in Alpine (101 E. Avenue E).

Smaller general stores selling gas, ice, beer, and some staples are inside the park at the

Rio Grande Village Campground (tel. 915/ 477–2293) and the **Chisos Basin** (tel. 915/ 477–2291). Outside the park you can find a few basic items at the **Lajitas Trading Post** (tel. 915/424–3234) in Lajitas (40 mi west on Hwy. 170), at the **Study Butte Store** (tel. 915/371–2231) in Study Butte (26 mi west on Hwy. 118), and at the **Stillwell Store** (tel. 915/376–2244), just north of the park on Route 2627, 6 mi off Highway 385. The Lajitas Trading Post is open daily from 8 to 7; the Study Butte Store is open daily from 8 to 8; and the Stillwell Store is open daily from 7 AM to 8 PM, 365 days a year.

ARRIVING AND DEPARTING Big Bend is in a remote corner of Texas, hours away from any sizable city. The park is vast, and although public transportation can deliver you to some of the nearby towns, there is no way to travel through the park itself except in a car. Gas stations are few and far between, so always fill your tank whenever you have a chance.

By Bus. Greyhound Lines (tel. 800/231– 2222) and **Kerrville Bus Company** (tel. 915/336–5151) can bring you into Alpine, where you can rent a car (*see* By Train, *below*).

By Car and RV. I–10 is the major artery that cuts across this part of Texas, nearly 140 mi north of the park. You can reach I–10 from several directions, including I–20 from Dallas/Fort Worth. At Fort Stockton leave I–10 and pick up Highway 385 south to Panther Junction in the park. If you are coming from El Paso in the west, you may follow I–10 to Van Horn, pick up Highway 90 south to Alpine, then take Highway 118 to Study Butte at the park's western border. Be prepared to drive distances of 70 mi or more between gas stations, phones, and food.

By Plane. The nearest airport—really just an airstrip—is **Alpine Airport** (tel. 915/ 837–3009), 100 mi away. It's served by private and charter aircraft. Larger but farther away are **Midland International Airport** (tel. 915/563–1460), 238 mi away, and **El Paso International Airport** (tel. 915/772– 4271), 325 mi away. Private planes can land on dirt airstrips in Lajitas and at the Terlingua Ranch (several miles north of Lajitas), at Alpine Airport, and on paved landing strips in Marfa and at the Heath Canyon Ranch (20 mi south of the Stillwell store).

By Train. Amtrak (tel. 800/872–7245) has stations in Sanderson and Alpine and makes regular stops at both depots. There are no car-rental agencies in Sanderson, but in Alpine you can rent a car at the **Big Bend Aero Auto Rental** (Alpine Airport, tel. 915/ 837–2744).

EXPLORING

While hikes and bicycle trips are useful for experiencing small sections of the park up close, Big Bend's vast acreage can be thoroughly explored only by car. A drive-and-hike combination is the best strategy. It is possible to see all the major sites from your car in a day; if you'd like to stop to take a closer look at the sites, allow yourself three days. But if you want to take in all the sites, do some hiking, go river rafting, explore by horseback, and enjoy the evening programs held in the amphitheaters, give yourself at least five days. You could spend three days exploring the Chisos Basin alone and another three days just paddling on a raft trip down the Rio Grande.

THE BEST IN ONE DAY Stow a picnic lunch in the car and drive up to the Chisos Mountain Lodge Restaurant at daybreak for breakfast and some beautiful views of the Chisos Basin, the bowl-shape canyon at the top of the mountain. Early morning is the best time to spot wildlife, and along this drive you are likely to find javelinas and deer; if you are very lucky, you might even see a black bear. Enjoy breakfast as you watch the sun rise over the mountains, then head to the Window Trail for a moderate, 5.25-mi round-trip hike that takes you down through a dry creek bed and along a narrow canyon. You'll end up at a scenic overlook where you can look out through a "window" formed by the canyon walls at the desert below.

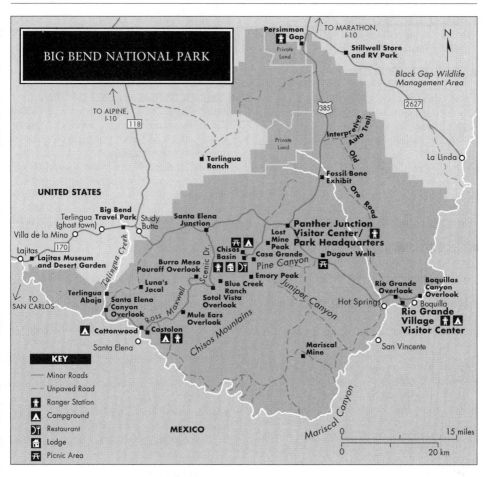

BIG BEND NATIONAL PARK

Persimmon Gap — Private Land — TO MARATHON, I-10 — Stillwell Store and RV Park — Black Gap Wildlife Management Area — N

TO ALPINE, I-10 — 118 — 385 — 2627 — Interpretive Auto Trail — La Linda

Private Land — Old Ore Road — Fossil Bone Exhibit

UNITED STATES

Terlingua Ranch

Big Bend Travel Park — Study Butte — Santa Elena Junction — Panther Junction — Lost Visitor Center/ Park Headquarters — Mine Peak

Terlingua (ghost town) — Villa de la Mina — Lajitas — Lajitas Museum and Desert Garden — 170 — Terlingua Creek

Chisos Basin — Casa Grande — Dugout Wells

Burro Mesa Pouraff Overlook — Pine Canyon — Emory Peak

Luna's Jacal — Blue Creek Ranch — Rio Grande Overlook — Boquillas Canyon Overlook

Terlingua Abaja — Santa Elena Canyon Overlook — Sotol Vista Overlook — Juniper Canyon — Hot Springs — Boquilla — Rio Grande Village Visitor Center

Ross Maxwell Scenic Dr. — Mule Ears Overlook — Chisos Mountains

TO SAN CARLOS

Cottonwood — Castolon — Santa Elena — Mariscal Mine — San Vincente

KEY

— Minor Roads
-- Unpaved Road
Ranger Station
Campground
Restaurant
Lodge
Picnic Area

MEXICO — Mariscal Canyon

0 — 15 miles
0 — 20 km

Return to your car and head down the Basin drive toward Panther Junction. Go past park headquarters, continue west, and turn south onto Ross Maxwell Scenic Drive, named after Big Bend's first park superintendent. Winding between the Chisos Mountains and Burro Mesa, this 30-mi road climbs up along the western edge of the Chisos to the Sotol Vista Overlook and then heads southward past Mule Ears Peaks into Castolon, the old outpost for the U.S. Cavalry's pursuit of Pancho Villa. From here, follow signs toward the Cotton-wood Campground, and find a picnic table beneath the grove of cottonwood trees, right on the Rio Grande. As you eat lunch, watch for rafters drifting by and Mexicans crossing over to the village of Santa Elena, which lies just over the river.

After lunch, get back in your car and drive to the Santa Elena Canyon overlook, where an observation point gives you a view of the tail end of Santa Elena Canyon, carved over the centuries by the Rio Grande. You might see a few rafters coming out of the canyon. (The northward turn of the Rio Grande is the origin of the name Big Bend).

No visit to Big Bend would be complete without seeing the three distinct geo-graphic regions that make up this country. By this time, you will have experienced all three: the mountains, the desert, and the river. Return to your campsite by backtracking along the Ross Maxwell Scenic Drive, which will be an uphill pull on most of the return.

ORIENTATION PROGRAMS There are a number of daily activities held throughout the park, designed as informative introductions to area attractions. At least one nature walk is organized most days, and there are various workshops and lectures. At the Persimmon Gap and Rio Grande Village visitor centers you will find a Big Bend orientation video, which can be viewed on request. Check with any of the visitor centers for a schedule of events occurring during your visit.

GUIDED TOURS The **Big Bend Natural History Association** (*see* Publications, *above*) holds seminars on topics such as birds, nature photography, and wildflowers. The seminars are led either by park rangers, professors from nearby Sul Ross State University, or other knowledgeable professionals, and cost between $40 and $300.

An increasing number of private outfitters conduct a variety of combination car-and-hike tours. **Desert Sports** (*see* Other Activities, *below*) leads trips that combine hiking and rafting or canoeing; the **Big Bend Touring Society** (Box 609, Terlingua, TX 79852, tel. 915/371–2548) provides private tour guides.

SCENIC DRIVES AND VIEWS The **Ross Maxwell Scenic Drive** (*see* The Best in One Day, *above*) makes a great tour of the scenery inside the park. Paved side roads lead to the Sotol Vista Overlook, Burro Mesa Pouroff, and Mule Ears Overlook, all worthy detours. Note: The steep climb may overtax the cooling systems of RVs over 24 ft and vehicles towing trailers over 20 ft.

The drive to the **Chisos Basin** is a steep uphill climb through canyon country. Although it is only 7 mi long, the sharp curves and steep grade make it a challenging drive, to be taken slowly; it is not recommended for trailers over 20 ft or RVs over 24 ft. Once you reach the basin you'll find several hiking trails, including the Window Trail, the Lost Mine Trail, and the challenging 14-mi South Rim hike. A copy of the *Chisos Mountain Trails* map (available at Panther Junction) is useful in choosing a trail.

HISTORIC BUILDINGS AND SITES There are many structures of historic interest in Big Bend, including ranches, cavalry outposts, and vestiges of farming and mining communities, some listed on the National Register of Historic Places. One special site is the **Hot Springs Hotel and Post Office.** The geothermal mineral spring at this site was used for medicinal purposes by Native Americans, and around the turn of the century J. O. Langford built a resort here. The stone buildings may be abandoned and crumbling, but the springs are still flowing. After a long day of driving and hiking, nothing beats a soak in these hot mineral springs alongside the Rio Grande.

Although the park service tore down many of the buildings on the area's various ranches in the park's early days, some do remain. One is off Ross Maxwell Scenic Drive, between Santa Elena Junction and the Sotol Vista Overlook. It was part of the **Blue Creek Ranch,** which was owned by Homer Wilson, a successful rancher in the Big Bend area. The structure was the ranch-foreman's house.

On the Old Maverick Road, south of Chimneys West primitive campsite, is **Luna's Jacal,** an old earthen, wood, and thatch structure built by Gilberto Luna, whose family farmed the floodplains of Alamo Creek from the mid-1800s until the National Park Service bought his land in the 1940s. With a succession of wives, Luna raised dozens of children in the barren desert and lived to the age of 108. If you follow the dirt road south toward Santa Elena you will find the ruins of **Terlingua Abaja,** the farming community just west of the Terlingua Abaja primitive campsite.

The largest historic structure in the park is the **Mariscal Mine,** an abandoned mercury mine that was in operation until about 1944. It is off the four-wheel-drive dirt road that runs by Mariscal Mountain. Here you'll find several shacks that once housed the Mexican miners who crossed the river to work here. The old, open retorts, where mercury ore was extracted, are still partially intact: These contraptions are believed to have contributed to the deaths of dozens of Mexican laborers who breathed the mercury fumes during the smelting process.

There are literally hundreds of ruins in the abandoned mining village of **Terlingua,** about 12 mi outside the park's border on Highway 170 to Lajitas. Old mine shafts and miners' houses stand as testimony to what was once a bustling village—there is even a converted theater and an old cemetery.

NATURE TRAILS AND SHORT WALKS The **Rio Grande Village Nature Trail** is a 1.25-mi loop that runs along the Rio Grande and has several markers noting area plant and animal life.

At Dugout Wells is the **Chihuahuan Desert Nature Trail,** an easy .25-mi round-trip that serves as an excellent introduction to the vast shrub-desert habitat.

The **Fossil Bone Exhibit,** 9 mi north of park headquarters, displays re-created fossilized bones of 50-million-year-old mammals. Part of the exhibit compares the area in prehistoric times to the current vista.

The **Santa Elena Canyon Trail** is a 1.75-mi round-trip walk right down the canyon walls to the Rio Grande. Concrete steps and handrails have been added, making this hike more accessible to frailer visitors and children.

Boquillas Canyon, another of the spectacular sights in Big Bend, is accessible via a 1.5-mi round-trip hike, which starts at the end of the Boquillas Canyon Road, near Rio Grande Village.

The 5.25-mi round-trip **Window Trail** (*see* The Best in One Day, *above*) is another favorite hike.

LONGER HIKES Longer hikes out here can mean anything from a 14-mi all-day stroll to a multiday backpacking excursion into lands that are accessible only by foot. The most popular and scenic of the longer hikes goes to the **South Rim** by way of a network of trails called the High Chisos trails. This challenging 14-mi round-trip trek up from the Chisos Basin runs through the mountains to an overlook at the south rim of the Chisos Mountain Range. The view from this point over the mountains and the desert below is breathtaking. Many people take two days or more to make this trip, camping overnight at one of the backcountry campsites along the way (you'll need a permit). Bring water and ready-to-eat meals; wood fires are not allowed.

The **Lost Mine Trail** is another of the more popular hikes in the Chisos Mountains. Nearly 5 mi round-trip, the trail passes Casa Grande, rounds the head of Juniper Canyon, and ends overlooking Pine Canyon, going from an elevation of 5,600 ft to 6,850 ft. The hike is not too strenuous but can be tough if you are out of shape.

To reach **Boot Canyon** you can start out on the Pinnacles Trail from the Chisos Basin Trailhead. You'll pass the cowboy boot–shape landmark that gives the canyon its name on this 9-mi round-trip hike. Boot Springs, just off the trail, is a popular (although unreliable) freshwater spring used by high-country hikers. Any water used for drinking that comes from this spring should be treated or filtered first.

The **Strawhouse–Telephone Canyon Trail** is a 24-mi one-way path that weaves through a labyrinth of dense brush and mesquite and takes at least two days to complete. There is no water available along the entire route, and summer temperatures can top 100°F, so be sure to carry plenty of water and have lots of protection against the sun.

For a complete, descriptive list of trails, get a copy of the *Hiker's Guide* (*see* Publications, *above*).

OTHER ACTIVITIES **Back-Road Driving.** No off-road driving is permitted inside the park, but there are several primitive roads where you will need a four-wheel-drive vehicle, or at least one with a high clearance, spare tire, jack, and plenty of water. If you should break down, stay with your car. Do not attempt to walk for help. A disabled vehicle is much easier to spot from the air than a solitary figure walking across the desert. It is very important that you carry at least a gallon of water per person per day on any back-road trip, no matter how short it may be. Check with a ranger before you head out.

Biking. Cycling is permitted on all designated roads but not on any hiking paths or off-road. **Desert Sports** (Box 448, Terlingua, TX 79852, tel. 915/371–2727 or 888/989–6900) leads guided mountain bike tours and also rents mountain bikes.

Bird-Watching. Bird-watching is excellent throughout the park. Varieties and species vary with the seasons and the migration patterns (*see* Flora and Fauna, *above*). The best spots to watch are the Chisos Basin and the Rio Grande. Check with the rangers to find out which species are in the area during your visit. The **Big Bend Touring Society** (Box 609, Terlingua, TX 79852, tel. 915/371–2548) leads bird-watching tours.

Fishing. Fishing is permitted in the Rio Grande, and the catch is primarily catfish. No fishing license is necessary. Trot lines may not extend across the river, and jug fishing is not allowed.

Horseback Riding. Rental horses are no longer available inside the park. You may bring your own horse, provided you obtain a free horse permit and bring your own feed.

Outside the park, try **Lajitas Stables** (Star Rte. 70, Box 380, Terlingua, TX 79852, tel. 915/424–3238), in nearby Lajitas, and **Big Bend Stables** (Box 178, Terlingua, TX 79852, tel. 800/887–4331) in Study Butte. Both operations take riders on guided trips on private land and property not inside Big Bend National Park. Rides range from one-hour tours to multiday trips and can be combined with river-rafting trips. Reservations are suggested.

Rafting. Rafting is permitted on the Rio Grande with a free float permit obtained at Panther Junction. Because of the fickle nature of the river, which switches quickly from slow and lazy to roaring white water, it is wise to travel with one of the outfitters in the region. Should you go without a guide, be sure to ask the park rangers to recommend the best stretch of river to suit your abilities. You should also consult one of the books in the *River Guide* series (*see* Publications, *above*).

Rafts are available for rent from **Rio Grande River Outfitters** (tel. 915/371–2424), based in the old Lajitas Trading Post in Lajitas; canoes may be rented from **Desert Sports** (tel. 915/371–2727 or 888/989–6900). Some of the more popular trips include those through the Mariscal Canyon and Colorado Canyon, but the best one-day raft trip, strictly for experienced rafters, is the Santa Elena Canyon tour, which passes through a stretch of canyon known as the Rock Slide. Huge rocks, some as large as houses, have fallen off the canyon walls over the centuries, creating an obstacle course of narrow channels through the rocks.

The river-running outfitters in the area all offer one-day trips, which cost from $80 to $100. They will handle all the work and even supply a buffet lunch. Some of the local river guides and outfitters are **Far Flung Adventures** (Box 377, Terlingua, TX 79852, tel. 915/371–2489 or 800/359–4138), **Big Bend River Tours** (Box 317, Lajitas, TX 79852, tel. 915/424–3219 or 800/545–4240), and **Texas River Expeditions** (Box 583, Terlingua, TX 79852, tel. 800/839–7238).

The only barrier between the United States and Mexico is the Rio Grande, so if you raft or canoe you can easily leave the country just by beaching your craft on the opposite shore. The U.S. Customs Service recently issued a directive asking visitors to cease crossing at Boquillas, Lajitas, and Santa Elena, and to use the official port of entry at Presidio (nearly 50 mi away). Although Customs declares that violators may be fined, the order is almost universally ignored. For people who still choose to cross at Lajitas, Boquillas, or Santa Elena, passports are not needed and there is no customs office along the river: People still come and go as they wish here, as they have for centuries. The only place that you may be stopped and asked to produce proof of citizenship will be at a border-patrol roadblock on Highway 118 or Highway 385, 50 to 75 mi north of the park. No exchange of currency is necessary, despite what some natives will tell you.

Rock Climbing. Climbing is discouraged because the rock in Big Bend is very unstable and fragmented. Some rappelling is done in the Chisos Basin, but check with the rangers beforehand; some peaks are off limits during certain wildlife-breeding seasons.

Swimming. Swimming in the Rio Grande is allowed, but because of currents, drop-offs, and submerged hazards it is not encouraged. However, one spot where people do swim regularly is at the hot springs just upriver from Rio Grande Village. Bathers can alternate between the warm, soothing waters of the springs and the cold Rio Grande running alongside. You can also come down to the hot springs at night and soak while you watch the stars above you. Bring a lantern: There is no lighting along the narrow footpath leading to the springs. Overnight use of the hot-springs area is not allowed.

CHILDREN'S PROGRAMS Educational workshops and puppet shows geared specifically to children are conducted on topics such as Native American life in Big Bend, predator-and-prey relationships, reptiles and amphibians, and dinosaurs. Programs are usually held at the Panther Junction Auditorium. These programs are held year-round. Call 915/477–2251 for a detailed schedule of events.

EVENING ACTIVITIES Free interpretive programs are held on most nights in the amphitheaters at the Rio Grande Village or Chisos Basin campgrounds. The programs rotate, and a different topic is addressed each night, covering everything from bats

to Columbus and the Comanches. Schedules are available at the ranger stations. The hour-long, ranger-led shows, accompanied by slides, usually begin shortly after dark. Bring a flashlight and a jacket, and arrive early for the best seats.

DINING

The rough-and-ready frontier atmosphere of Big Bend is reflected in the area's informal restaurants, which vary from rustic adobe huts to classic southwestern ranch buildings, complete with antique furniture and candles. Although low-fat, nouvelle cuisine is inching its way into the repertoire here, the focus in Big Bend is on simple, inexpensive, hearty fare enjoyed by cowboys and oil tycoons: Tex-Mex, steaks and burgers, and barbecue, all in healthy portions that are meant to stick to your ribs. Be prepared to drive some distance between restaurants: Alpine, the nearest town of any size, is over 100 mi from the park.

INSIDE THE PARK **Chisos Mountain Lodge.** The National Park Concessions runs the only restaurant within Big Bend National Park. The main attraction here is the view: Large picture windows on three sides of the restaurant allow diners to soak in the beauty of the Chisos Basin; juniper and piñon trees and steep, red-rock cliffs encircle the restaurant. Chicken-fried steak, chicken, and burgers make up the bulk of the menu. The quality of the food can be inconsistent; the best time to come is early morning, when you can sip a cup of coffee and watch the sun rise over the mountainside. *Chisos Basin, tel. 915/477–2291. Reservations not accepted. AE, DC, MC, V. $$*

NEAR THE PARK **Starlight Theatre.** This restaurant in Terlingua was built in 1937 by Howard E. Perry as a movie house for his workers in the Terlingua Mining Company. The old adobe building has been completely remodeled and now has a southwestern look, with pink-adobe walls, green door frames, mesquite-wood chairs, dark-green tablecloths, and a noteworthy handmade mesquite bar. Local musicians frequently perform here before a largely local audience. Order a large T-bone, or try one of the authentic Mexican dishes such as home-style tamales. *Off Hwy. 170, Terlingua, tel. 915/371–2326. MC, V. $$*

Reata Cowboy Café. Named after the ranch in the movie *Giant* (which was filmed in nearby Marfa), this restaurant serves Old-West-meets-nouvelle cuisine. Grilled fish and specialty salads satisfy health-conscious eaters, while three-quarter-pound burgers and steaks appeal to heartier palates. Look for the daily specials. *203 N. 5th, Alpine, tel. 915/837–9232. MC, V. No lunch. $–$$*

Big Bend Motor Inn Café. This small café, next to the Big Bend Motor Inn at the intersection of Highways 170 and 118, serves basic truck-stop fare: burgers, chicken-fried steak, and sandwiches. The atmosphere is unpretentious and down-home. *Hwys. 170 and 118, Terlingua, tel. 915/371–2218. AE, D, DC, MC, V. $*

Cafe Cenizo. In the small town of Marathon, 70 mi north of Big Bend National Park, the Gage Hotel's full-service restaurant is the last place where you can get a full-course meal before driving down into the park. Local ranchers stop by for their morning coffee when they come into town. (The other morning special is homemade oatmeal with plump raisins and cinnamon.) The restaurant also serves Tex-Mex, steaks, chicken, and fish. Stuffed animal heads, Native American artifacts, saddles, and wood tables and chairs create an authentic southwestern mood. *Gage Hotel, Hwy. 90W, Marathon, tel. 915/386–4205. D, MC, V. $*

La Kiva. An entryway modeled after a Navajo kiva, or underground ceremonial chamber, makes La Kiva feel like a desert oasis. A cavelike passageway leads to a lower-level bar, and there is a large patio out back. The menu emphasizes barbecue—beef, ribs, and chicken—but also includes filet mignon. *Hwy. 170W, Terlingua Creek, tel. 915/371–2250. AE, MC, V. No lunch. $*

Sarah's Café. The last word on authentic Tex-Mex for Big Bend, Sarah's has been operated by the Castelo family for more than 60 years. The lunch crowd that packs this place includes local politicians, oil tycoons, and ranchers, while dinner sees more families. The tangy dishes are all prepared from scratch with ingredients that are made fresh daily. Try the enchiladas, chilies rellenos, or Sarah's Special, a huge sampler platter with a little of everything. This place is quite a drive from the park, but if you're passing through Fort Stockton, don't miss it. *106 S. Nelson, Fort Stockton, tel. 915/336–7124. MC, V. Closed Sun. $*

PICNIC SPOTS If you'd like to picnic in the shade, head to the **Dugout Wells** picnic tables, in the middle of the desert off the main road from Panther Junction to Rio Grande Village. Tables are tucked inside the long and leafy branches of some giant cottonwood trees growing in the moist ground over a nearby seep. For a close-up view of the Rio Grande, try the picnic table underneath a desert palm tree just down the path from the old **Hot Springs Post Office;** you'll have a good view of the river rafters and the bathers hiking to the hot springs a few hundred yards downriver. A premium place for the picnicking crowd is the **Chisos Basin,** although it can be a bit chilly to eat outside here in the winter months.

LODGING

Most of the accommodations in and around Big Bend National Park are very basic, moderately priced motels in rustic settings. Most of the motels in the region do not have telephones or televisions in every room, and some of them require that you share a bathroom, but you'll find that the staff will usually go out of their way to try to make you comfortable.

The park's one motel is very popular, and during the peak spring season you are unlikely to find a room there unless you book as much as a year in advance or stumble across a cancellation. The park is so large, however, that visitors who stay in surrounding towns often drive no farther than those staying inside the park to visit certain sights.

INSIDE THE PARK **Chisos Mountain Lodge.** The park's only lodge is in Chisos Basin and adjacent to the more popular hiking trails. It's decorated in basic motel style— nothing fancy, but it's clean. There are no phones or televisions in any of the rooms. The newest addition is the Casa Grande Lodge, with private balconies and a second story, but the most sought-after accommodations are the six stone cottages. Book your reservations well in advance of your trip. *Big Bend National Park, Big Bend, TX 79834, tel. 915/477–2291, fax 915/477–2352. 72 rooms, 6 cabins. Facilities: restaurant. AE, DC, MC, V. $$*

NEAR THE PARK **Cibolo Creek Ranch.** The region's only luxury accommodation, 24 mi south of Marfa, is a 25,000-acre guest ranch with 10 guest rooms and one cottage, all furnished with antiques, goose-down pillows, and bathrobes. Horseback riding, sporting clays, and swimming are available to guests, and there's a private landing strip on the grounds. All meals and beverages are included in the fee. *Box 44, Shafter, TX 79850, tel. 915/358–4696 or 800/525–4800. 10 rooms, 1 cottage. Facilities: restaurant, pool, health club, horseback riding. AE, MC, V. $$$*

Badlands Hotel/Cavalry Post Motel. Both of these lodgings are part of a resort complex in Lajitas that incorporates numerous shops, tour outfitters, restaurants, stables, and even a museum. Although the complex was built in the 1970s, it was carefully constructed to look like an old western town, complete with wood sidewalks and a saloon. The two-story Badlands Hotel is in the center of town, and the Cavalry, about 200 yards away, was built on the foundations of the original cavalry headquarters that stood here at the turn of the century. Both have simple rooms decorated in generic motel style. The hotel and motel are popular with river

rafters, golfers, and people planning day trips into the nearby Mexican village of San Carlos. *Rte. 170, Terlingua, TX 79852, tel. 915/424–3471 or 800/527–4078, fax 915/424–3277. 82 rooms, 27 condominium units. Facilities: restaurant, bar, lobby lounge, pool, 9-hole golf course, 2 tennis courts, horseback riding. AE, DC, MC, V. $$–$$$*

Big Bend Motor Inn. This small motel is just 3 mi from the park's western border at the intersection of Highways 118 and 170. The friendly staff and convenient location make up for the basic, somewhat spartan motel rooms. There is a large RV park behind the motel. *Box 336, Terlingua, TX 79852, tel. 915/371–2218 or 800/848–2363. 82 rooms, 10 with kitchenettes. Facilities: restaurant, pool. AE, D, DC, MC, V. $$*

Captain Shepherd's Inn. This restored, two-story home was once the residence of Captain Shepherd, the founder of Marathon. (Upon coming to the country in the 1800s, he remarked that it reminded him of the plains around Marathon, Greece.) The house is now a bed-and-breakfast inn with an outdoor hot tub and a television room. There's a carriage house in the back of the main house, with two bedrooms, one bath, and a kitchenette and fireplace. *Ave. D and 2nd St., Box 46, Marathon, TX 79842, tel. 800/884–4243. 7 rooms, 3 with bath; 1 carriage house. MC, V. $$*

Gage Hotel. Without a doubt, this is the most romantic place to stay near Big Bend. Built in 1928 by wealthy rancher Alfred Gage as a place to lodge his numerous friends and business contacts, the restored building is a registered Texas Historic Landmark, complete with a front porch with rocking chairs. Each room is unique, furnished with handmade, antique ranch furniture in wood and leather. Walls are covered with southwestern artifacts and paintings, and the lobby is filled with stuffed animal heads, saddles, and cowboy gear. There are no phones or televisions, and, while some rooms come with a private bath, most guests must share a community bathroom. The new Los Portales addition across the road has 20 rooms, all with private baths (but no TVs or phones) and all decorated in Old West–style, including viga-beam ceilings and cowboy paraphernalia on the walls. *Box 46, Marathon, TX 79842, tel. 915/386–4205, fax 915/386–4510. 40 rooms, 27 with bath. Facilities: restaurant, pool. D, MC, V. $$*

Mission Lodge. This standard motel is owned and operated by the same folks who own the Big Bend Motor Inn across the road. The sparsely decorated rooms all have queen-size beds. *Box 169, Terlingua, TX 79852, tel. 915/371–2555. 24 rooms. AE, D, DC, MC, V. $$*

Chisos Mining Company/Easter Egg Valley. These no-frills motel rooms and cabins in Study Butte all have kitchenettes, but no rooms have phones, and only some have televisions. There are five RV sites on the property. *Box 229, Terlingua, TX 79852, tel. 915/371–2254. 28 rooms, 8 cabins with kitchenettes. AE, D, MC, V. $*

Heath Canyon Ranch. If you're looking for rustic and remote, this is it. At the end of Highway 2627, the complex was built for employees of the Du Pont family, which operated a fluorspar mine just across the Rio Grande in the Mexican village of La Linda. Today, the mine is closed and La Linda is a ghost town, but the Heath Canyon Ranch remains, having been bought by Andy Kurie, a former Du Pont employee, in 1991. Guests stay in a six-person bunkhouse or a four-person trailer; nearby is the Open Sky Café. Surrounded by about 650 acres of rugged canyon country, this is an ideal area for hiking, climbing, birding, and rafting on the nearby Rio Grande. *Box 386, Marathon, TX 79846, tel. 915/376–2235. 6-room bunkhouse, 4-room trailer. Facilities: café. $*

Terlingua Lodge. Remote solitude awaits you here. The lodge can be reached only by driving 18 mi down a dirt road off Highway 118. It stands on the property of the Terlingua Ranch at the base of the Christmas Mountains, almost 60 mi from Panther Junction. This is a very quiet spot, with big skies, mountainous landscapes, and starry nights. Rooms have no phones or televisions. *HC 675, Box 220, Alpine, TX 79830, tel. 915/371–2416. 32 rooms. Facilities: restaurant, pool, private airstrip. MC, V. $*

CAMPING

Camping is extremely popular in Big Bend, where you can choose from isolated primitive sites and three major campgrounds with toilets and grills. Only one campground has RV hookups. Sites at the park's campgrounds are assigned on a first-come, first-served basis, and a single stay is limited to 14 days. The nightly fee is $7 at developed campgrounds; primitive backcountry camping is free. All campgrounds are open year-round.

All major campgrounds are usually filled to capacity during Easter, spring break, Thanksgiving, and Christmas holidays—particularly the popular Chisos Basin Campground. Primitive backcountry campsites are usually available, except at spring break; but some of these are accessible only with a high-clearance vehicle.

INSIDE THE PARK The 63-site **Chisos Basin** remains the most popular campground because of its scenery, wildlife, and easy access to several hiking trails. It is also near a store and a restaurant, and rest rooms are close by. The campsites are fairly close to each other, and many hikers pass through the campground on their way to the trails; nevertheless, it is surprisingly quiet.

You can get more isolation down at the 35-site **Cottonwood Campground,** just next to the Rio Grande, where the only people you will see are other campers and the occasional river rafter. There are pit toilets, grills, picnic tables, and water.

The campgrounds with the most amenities are at **Rio Grande Village.** The park-service campground here has 100 sites, with picnic tables, grills, and nearby rest rooms. A park concessionaire runs 25 RV sites with full hookups and disposal stations near the

BIG BEND CAMPGROUNDS

	INSIDE THE PARK			NEAR THE PARK					
	Chisos Basin	Cottonwood	Rio Grande Village	Primitive campsites	Big Bend Motor Inn	Big Bend Travel Park	Lajitas RV Park	Terlingua Ranch	Stillwell RV Park
Total number of sites	63	31	125	114	106	95	94	24	8
Sites suitable for RVs	0	0	125	0	106	45	77	24	80
Number of hookups	0	0	25	0	106	45	77	24	80
Drive to sites	•	•	•	•	•	•	•	•	•
Hike to sites				•					
Flush toilets	•		•		•	•	•		•
Pit/chemical toilets	•	•							•
Drinking water	•	•	•		•	•	•	•	•
Showers			•		•	•	•	•	•
Fire grates	•	•	•		•	•			•
Swimming					•		•	•	
Boat access			•						
Playground								•	
Disposal station	•		•			•		•	•
Ranger station	•	•	•						
Public telephone	•	•	•		•	•	•	•	•
Reservation possible					•	•	•	•	•
Daily fee per site	$7	$7	$7–$11	free	$7.50–$14.50	$12	$9–$15	$8–$9	$4–$13
Dates open	year-round	year-round	year-round	year-round	year-round	year-round	year-round	year-round	year-round

fairly well-stocked general store. There are also laundry facilities, showers, and a service station at the store. Rio Grande Village is close to the hot springs, where you can go for a relaxing natural Jacuzzi, and the village of Boquillas, should you want to make a quick trip across the border into Mexico.

If you really want to get away from it all, try a primitive, backcountry roadside campsite. There are 114 of them along the dirt roads in the park, some of which can be reached only by four-wheel-drive vehicle or on foot. There are no facilities at these spots. One of the most remote and peaceful is the **Fresno primitive campsite,** a short walk from the abandoned Mariscal Mine. It is too hot to camp here during the summer, but in fall and winter the solitude is inspirational.

NEAR THE PARK Since there is only one campground with full RV hookups in the park, many RVers head to the RV parks in Study Butte, Lajitas, Terlingua, and at the Stillwell Store.

The **Big Bend Motor Inn** (Box 336, Terlingua, TX 79852, tel. 915/371–2218), at the intersection of Highways 170 and 118 in Study Butte, has a swimming pool and a restaurant, as well as picnic tables, grills, water, electrical hookups, and fuel. There are 106 tent and RV sites here. Tent camping costs $14.50 per night; RVing costs $7.50.

Big Bend Travel Park (Box 146, Terlingua, TX 79852, tel. 915/371–2250) is next to La Kiva restaurant, on Highway 170 in Study Butte. The 45 RV sites cost $12 each per night, including full hookups. Facilities include a restaurant, showers, flush toilets, and a laundry facility. Fifty tent sites are also available.

Next to the Lajitas Resort on Highway 170, the **Lajitas RV Park** (HC70, Box 400, Terlingua, TX 79852, tel. 915/424–3471) has 77 full hookup sites, 58 with cable television, for $15 each per night. The park also has a nine-hole golf course, two tennis courts, and a pool. The 17 tent sites cost $9 per night.

The 24 sites at **Terlingua Ranch** (Box 220, Highway Contract 65, Alpine, TX 79830, tel. 915/371–2416) are 26 mi north of the park off Highway 118. Facilities include water, sewer, electrical hookups, and gravel pads; the fee ranges from $8 to $9.

Stillwell RV Park (Box 430, Alpine, TX 79830, tel. 915/376–2244), off Highway 2627 30 mi north of the park on a large west Texas ranch, is a gem of a camgpround, with 80 RV sites and unlimited tent sites, a well-stocked general store, and a museum. Four-wheel-drive tours to view ancient Native American campsite pictographs are available, and films about the region are shown nightly. Water, gravel pads, and electricity are available; there are also laundry facilities and showers. Sites cost between $4 and $13 per night.

Bryce Canyon National Park
Utah

By Tom Wharton

he first view of Bryce Canyon's iridescent colors defies belief. It is almost impossible to imagine such brilliant hues of red, buff, and tan existing in nature. And then there are the shapes—fantastic shapes resembling spires, cathedrals, goblins, and the tops of fairy-tale castles. For years people have tried with little success to describe this brightly colored land.

One of the most heartfelt descriptions allegedly came from Ebenezer Bryce, the Mormon settler who came here in 1875 and gave his name to the park. Folklore has it that Bryce exclaimed "This is a hell of a place to lose a cow!" Others gave the trails and major formations such names as Fairyland Point, the Queen's Garden, Peekaboo Loop, the Silent City, and the Chinese Wall. Nearly 50 years after Ebenezer Bryce built his homestead at the mouth of the canyon, the area was set aside as Bryce Canyon National Monument under the Forest Service. In 1928 Bryce Canyon National Park was officially established.

In fact, Bryce Canyon is really not a canyon; it's a series of natural amphitheaters carved from the encircling cliffs by rain, snow, and ice. Its colors change with the season, the time of day, and the weather, but walk through it in the early morning or late afternoon, and you'll see them at their deepest—colors that almost seem to glow.

Except during the height of the summer travel season, when the lodge is full and finding a motel room near the park can be difficult, Bryce is a relatively quiet place, easily seen from the 18 mi of main road and four major spur roads that lead to the park's many scenic overlooks. Simply sitting on a bench at Sunrise or Sunset Point and contemplating the vista is enough for many; those who want a more complete experience will need to hike down into the amphitheaters.

ESSENTIAL INFORMATION

VISITOR INFORMATION Write to **Bryce Canyon National Park,** Box 17001, Bryce Canyon, UT 84717; or call 435/834–5322. A permit available from the visitor center is required for overnight backcountry trips, which are allowed only on the Under-the-Rim Trail and the Rigg's Spring Loop, both south of Bryce Point.

FEES The entrance fee is $10 per vehicle for a seven-day pass; $5 for pedestrians or bicyclists; rates vary for entry by bus. An annual park pass, good for one year from the date of purchase, costs $20.

PUBLICATIONS Useful maps and publications can be purchased from the **Bryce Canyon Natural History Association** (Bryce Canyon, UT 84717, tel. 435/834–4602), at the park's visitor center. *Bryce Canyon National Park,* by Fred Hirschmann, is the best of the color photo books. Tully Stoud's 44-page *Bryce Canyon Auto and Hiking Guide* includes information on the geology and history of the area. The "Bryce Canyon Hiking Guide," with an amphitheater hiking map and aerial photo, supplements the free map given to park visitors at the entrance. The "Kid's Guide to Bryce Canyon" introduces the region to children five to 10 years old.

GEOLOGY AND TERRAIN In Bryce Canyon National Park, more than 90 million years of geologic history can be studied through oddly shaped and colored limestones, sandstones, redstones, and shale. (The park's name is something of a misnomer since it is essentially a huge amphitheater and not a canyon.) The park comprises 35,835 acres. Its main geological feature is the Pink Cliffs, which sit atop another large set of cliffs; together, these are referred to as the Grand Staircase. This begins at the bottom of Arizona's Grand Canyon and gradually ascends, both in elevation and in geological time, to a height of more than 9,100 ft at Bryce. The park stands at a higher elevation (and therefore enjoys lower temperatures) than the other national parks in Utah—Arches, Canyonlands, Capitol Reef, and Zion. Stands of piñon-juniper in the lower parts of Bryce give way to communities of huge, majestic ponderosa pines and then, near Rainbow Point, to forests of spruce, aspen, and fir.

Unlike many of the parks in the Colorado Plateau region, where sandstone is the dominant rock, Bryce is filled with brightly colored, almost glowing limestones, and the forces of flowing water, rain, snow, and ice have eroded them into exotic shapes.

Approximately 60 million years ago the Bryce area was covered by vast lakes, and the sediments that eventually formed the red rocks were deposited under water. Continents moved, climates changed, and the lakes disappeared—but large sediment loads remained. About 15 million years ago, the pressures associated with plate tectonics that created the coastal mountains also raised much of the western half of North America as high as 2 mi above sea level. The major faults of western North America began to form during this period of uplift, and the activity and movements of these faults, along with climactic changes, set in motion the erosional forces that continue to carve Bryce Canyon.

FLORA AND FAUNA Spotted on rare occasions browsing in the meadows in the early morning or late evening, the elk is the largest mammal you're likely to see in Bryce. Porcupines, mule deer, skunks, gray foxes, coyotes, and a number of small rodents, such as chipmunks, marmots, pine squirrels, and prairie dogs, also inhabit the park.

Birders have identified 172 bird species in the park, including the common nighthawk, three kinds of hummingbirds, the northern flicker, Steller's jay, pygmy nuthatch, meadowlark, bluebird, robin, swift, and swallow, as well as the occasional owl. A checklist is available at the visitor center.

Bryce's often long and snowy winters are a prelude to colorful displays of wildflowers throughout the spring and summer and early fall, with sego lilies, penstemons, asters, clematis, evening primrose, skyrocket gilias, Indian paintbrush, and wild iris. Rabbitbrush and goldenrod bloom in the early fall.

WHEN TO GO At a higher elevation than other Utah parks and with cooler summer temperatures (daytime highs in the low 80s, evenings in the mid-40s), Bryce would be an ideal summer vacation area if only no one else knew about it. Some 75% of Bryce's visitors come in the summer months—June, July, and August—and the crowds can pack trails, local motels, and campgrounds to capacity. Although thunderstorms may dampen a summer trip, the resulting rainbows and the play of the thunderclouds and sunlight on the red rocks more than make up for the inconvenience. The lodge is open from April through October, during which time horseback riding and many interpretive activities are available.

By contrast, when the snow begins to cover the formations, Bryce is nearly deserted. Although the major road into the park is almost always open and local motels offer winter specials and discounted rates, only a few lucky visitors have discovered the benefits of a winter trip to this area. Conditions are usually good for snowshoeing and cross-country skiing from late December into March—taking a lonely snowshoe trip on a clear, blue January morning ranks among the most pleasurable experiences to be had in any Utah park. Skiing along the rim of the amphitheaters and out to several of the major overlooks allows you to see a face of the park enjoyed by few. Daytime temperatures can be as low as 30°F, but since humidity is also low, the climate is generally pleasant. In January the average high is 39°F and the average low 9°F.

Fall may be the best season to see Bryce. The weather is usually quite clear; temperatures rise into the 60s during the day and dip into the 30s at night; the aspens begin to turn gold and, seen against the park's evergreens, create a spectacular sight.

The weather is less predictable in the spring, often bringing rain and snow. Trails, though passable, can be muddy, and average lows remain below freezing well into May. But on a clear spring day when the leaves just begin to peek out and the first warm sun hits the amphitheater, such inconveniences are soon forgotten.

SEASONAL EVENTS Except for the nearby town celebrations honoring Mormon pioneers, the following events are hosted by Ruby's Inn (tel. 801/834–5341).

President's Day Weekend: The **Winter Festival** features a 10-km cross-country ski race, a dance, Nordic tours, and ski clinics. **Memorial Day to Labor Day:** Step into the Wild West six nights a week at the **Bryce Canyon Rodeo,** held in an arena across the highway from Ruby's Inn. **First weekend in June:** Take rides in the area surrounding Bryce Canyon during the **Mountain Bike Festival,** and learn what your bike and you can do. **Saturday closest to July 24:** Towns near Bryce Canyon, including Tropic, Panguitch, Cannonville, and Hatch, hold local celebrations to honor the day the **Mormon pioneers** first came to the Salt Lake Valley.

WHAT TO PACK You won't need any special equipment in Bryce, except for sturdy hiking boots with good tread and ankle support. In spring, when the hiking trails tend to be muddy, an extra pair of shoes can come in handy, and since nights can be cool, even in the middle of the summer, bring a warm jacket or light parka. Because the sun is usually out, in both summer and winter, a good sunscreen, sunglasses, long sleeves, and a hat are recommended. And don't forget to bring an adequate supply of water bottles—especially if you plan to be out on the trails in June, July, or August. (A gallon per person per day is the rule of thumb.)

GENERAL STORES The **General Store at Bryce Canyon** (tel. 435/834–5361), near Sunrise Point, sells film, souvenirs, groceries, and fast food from the end of April through October. It is open daily from 7 AM to 9 PM.

Ruby's Inn (tel. 435/834–5341), north of the park boundary on Highway 63, has a large facility with a good selection of groceries, souvenirs, and camping equipment. Ruby's is open daily year-round from 7 AM to 10:30 PM.

Four miles northwest of the park, **Fosters** (tel. 435/834–5227) has a general store, which is open daily in spring, summer, and fall, from 7 AM to 8 PM. Fosters's 24-hour towing and car-repair operates year-round.

Doug's (tel. 435/679–8633), a small general grocery store in Tropic, is usually open daily in summer from 7 AM to 11 PM. Winter hours vary at the owner's discretion.

ARRIVING AND DEPARTING As is the case for many national parks, the easiest way to get to Bryce Canyon is by car, driving from Las Vegas (237 mi) or Salt Lake City (256 mi). The nearest small city from which you can rent a car or board a tour bus is Cedar City, 78 mi west of the park, but you can also rent a car in St. George, 126 mi southwest of Bryce.

By Bus. Greyhound Lines (tel. 801/355–9589) serves St. George and Cedar City.

From either city you can rent a car, take a taxi, or take a tour bus to the park (*see* Guided Tours, *below*).

By Car and RV. The drive from either Salt Lake City or Las Vegas to Bryce Canyon takes about five hours. Many people combine a trip to Bryce with visits to Zion National Park (an 84-mi, two-hour drive) and, during summer, the North Rim of the Grand Canyon (a 152-mi, three-hour drive).

There are three ways to approach Bryce. The only entrance is in the northwest of the park and can be approached from the south on U.S. 89 via Kanab and Hatch or from the north on U.S. 89 via Panguitch. You will have to turn east onto Route 12 and then south onto Highway 63, which leads directly to the park entrance. The drive from U.S. 89 to the Bryce entrance is about 17 mi. An alternate route, making a loop toward Capitol Reef National Park, will take you along what is perhaps the most scenic road in the state. From Salt Lake City, take I–15 to the Scipio exit. Pick up U.S. 50 to I–70 and then at the Sigurd exit take Route 24 to Route 12. You will drive near Capitol Reef, through the Dixie National Forest, and past the Anasazi Indian Village and Escalante Petrified Forest state parks to enter Bryce after passing through the town of Tropic. The section of road between the towns of Grover and Boulder on Route 12 is particularly beautiful. When you reach the junction of Highways 12 and 63, turn left onto Highway 63 and drive 3.5 mi to the park entrance.

Because the road running south into the park is narrow and twisting, trailers cannot be taken beyond the Sunset campground near the park's entrance; they can be left at your campsite, the parking lot at Ruby's Inn, or the visitor-center parking area. RVs longer than 25 ft are not allowed at Paria View Point.

By Plane. Bryce Canyon airport is 4 mi from the entrance to the park. It is larger than other southern Utah airports because it is used for emergency landings. **Bryce Air Service** (tel. 435/834–5208) has rental cars ($30 half day, $45 full day) and rental vans ($55 half day, $80 full day, for up to 15 passengers); it also shuttles visitors from the airport to Bryce Lodge or Ruby's Inn for $6 one-way. **Air Nevada Airlines** (tel. 800/ 634–6377) flies Monday, Wednesday, and Saturday year-round from Las Vegas to Bryce and the Grand Canyon as long as there are at least four people flying. It costs $319 per person to fly round-trip.

If you fly into Las Vegas, Salt Lake City, Cedar City, or St. George, you can rent a car or limousine from these airports and drive to the park. It generally costs just under $40 per day to rent a compact car, but you can get a better deal by calling in advance.

Cedar City car rentals include **Avis** (Sky West, tel. 435/586–3033) and **National Car Rental** (tel. 435/586–7059). You can rent a car in St. George from **Avis** (St. George Municipal Airport, tel. 435/673–3451), **Budget** (1275 N. Highland Dr., tel. 435/673– 6825), **Dollar Rent-A-Car** (1175 S. 150 E, tel. 435/628–6549), and **National** (St. George Municipal Airport, tel. 435/673–5098).

To rent a car in Salt Lake City or Las Vegas, call **Avis** (tel. 800/831—2847), **Budget** (tel. 800/527–0700), **Hertz** (tel. 800/654–3131), or **Thrifty** (tel. 800/367–2277).

EXPLORING

Bryce Canyon is a relatively easy park to visit, largely because so much of it can be viewed from the major overlooks, which are connected by an 18-mi paved rim road. In a single day you can drive the rim, go for a short hike, take a horseback ride into the canyon, and come away with a decent sense of the park.

If you have extra time, consider either taking an all-day hike into one of the amphitheaters or driving to nearby Kodachrome Basin State Park, Anasazi Indian Village, Escalante Petrified Forest State Park, or Dixie National Forest (tel. 435/865–3700) to enjoy the area's varied and unusual scenery. (For information about any Utah state park, call 801/538–7221.)

Regardless of how much time you have, be sure to explore the park in the very early morning or in the late afternoon, when the sun sets the rocks ablaze with color. You should also set aside 30 minutes or more to descend, if only briefly, into the amphitheater.

THE BEST IN ONE DAY If you're short on time, get up before sunrise and grab a quick breakfast at either Ruby's Inn or Bryce Canyon Lodge (see Dining, below) before heading to any of the scenic overlooks to watch the sun come up.

Consider hiking into the Queen's Garden (see Nature Trails and Short Walks, below) and, depending on how much energy you have, perhaps tackling the 1.5-mi Navajo Loop Trail (see Longer Hikes, below). It takes about three hours to hike both trails; you'll end up back on the rim at Sunset Point, a .5-mi walk from Sunrise Point, just in time for a picnic lunch.

After lunch, you have several options: You could wander back to the visitor center to browse through books and watch the slide show, tag along on an interpretive hike with a ranger, saddle up a horse for a half-day trot, or head for the helipad at Ruby's Inn, where you'll be airlifted over the canyon.

The best way to see the overlooks is to stop your car and take brief walks along the rim trail. If it isn't too hot, a good choice of hikes is the 1.5-mi Bristlecone Loop trail from Rainbow Point, which takes you past ancient bristlecone pines.

Make sure you end the day at sunset, at Inspiration Point, camera in hand.

ORIENTATION PROGRAMS The 10-minute introductory slide show at the visitor center is worth viewing. It runs every 30 minutes during peak season, and on request during off-season. The rangers also offer a number of interpretive programs and guided hikes during the summer months. Check at the visitor center for times and topics.

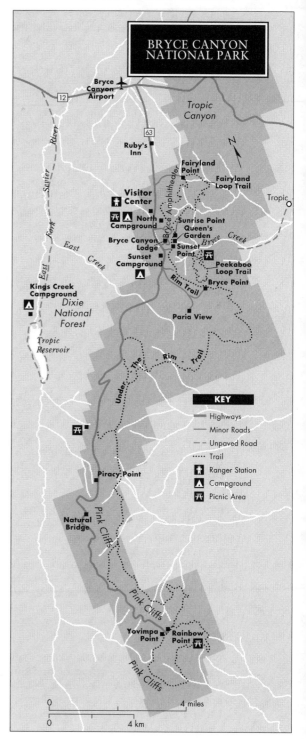

BRYCE CANYON NATIONAL PARK

KEY

Highways
Minor Roads
Unpaved Road
Trail
Ranger Station
Campground
Picnic Area

GUIDED TOURS Several operators run tours of Bryce Canyon, often combined with trips to other national parks and monuments in the area, including the North Rim of the Grand Canyon and Zion National Park. **Passage to Utah** tours (Box 520883, Salt Lake City, UT 84152, tel. 801/281–4523) runs one- to three-day tours to Bryce and Zion. **Utah Escapades** (Box 2690, Park City, UT 84060, tel. 800/268–8824, fax 801/649–9948), conducts customized tours to Bryce and Zion National Parks. While concentrating more on Capitol Reef National Park, **Wild Hare Expeditions** (Box 750194, Torrey, UT 84775, tel. 888/304–4273, fax 435/425–3999) will customize trips to Bryce or to the nearby Grand Staircase Escalante National Monument.

You can spend from 10 minutes to three hours in the skies above Bryce Canyon with **Bryce Canyon Helicopters** (Box 41, Ruby's Inn, Bryce Canyon, UT 84764, tel. 435/834–5341). The price is $90 per person.

For information about bicycle and horseback tours, *see* Other Activities, *below.*

SCENIC DRIVES AND VIEWS The only road that passes through Bryce Canyon National Park is a section of **Highway 12,** which runs more or less east–west through the northern end. **Highway 63** branches south off Highway 12 to enter the park and become the **Park Road,** winding southwest for most of its length to dead-end 18 mi from the entrance, at **Rainbow Point,** where there is a superb 270-degree view of the surrounding canyon country. The road is open year-round, but after a heavy snowfall it may be closed for a few hours while crews clear the way. The park's most famous formations are best viewed just after sunrise or just before sunset from Fairyland, Sunrise, Sunset, Inspiration, and Bryce points, as well as from Paria View.

Both walkers and wheelchair-bound visitors enjoy the paved portion of the Rim Trail, which runs for .5 mi from Sunset Point to Sunrise Point. The entire Rim Trail is 5.5 mi long (one-way). Major overlooks

are rarely more than a few minutes' walk from the parking areas.

HISTORIC BUILDINGS AND SITES Designed by Stanley Gilbert Underwood for the Union Pacific Railroad and built in the mid-1920s, the **Bryce Canyon Lodge** is one of the few park lodges that hasn't fallen victim to fire. (The Union Pacific also constructed lodges at Zion and at the North Rim of the Grand Canyon, but both of these later burned.) A National Historic Landmark, it has been faithfully restored, right down to the reproduced hickory furniture, which was built by the same company that produced the originals.

Outside the park entrance stands **Ruby's Inn,** an area landmark that has been operated by the Syrett family since 1919. Unfortunately, the original building has been the victim of several fires, and although parts of the inn retain a rustic look, the facility is relatively new.

NATURE TRAILS AND SHORT WALKS Those who prefer their exercise in short, slow doses will find any stretch of the 11-mi **Rim Trail** suitable for strolling, especially the paved area between Sunrise and Sunset points. If it's a long, relaxed stroll you want, consider trading keys with another driver so that you can walk along the entire rim of the Bryce Amphitheater and have a car on the other end to take you back.

There are few short easy walks into the canyon, largely because the sloping nature of the amphitheater forces hikers to descend quickly. If you are willing to put a little work into your walk, try the moderately strenuous .75-mi trek to the **Queen's Garden.** This is the easiest hike into the canyon itself, with a descent—and subsequent ascent—of 320 ft. Another short hike is the **Bristlecone Loop,** a 1.5-mi jaunt beside a bristlecone forest.

LONGER HIKES You can get down into the Bryce Amphitheater, but be warned: All the trails that bring you closer to the forces that shape the canyon involve some steep descents and ascents. These trails are demanding, especially in the hot summer months. Be prepared with hat, sunscreen, sunglasses, and plenty of water.

The longest trail in the park, and one of the only two along which overnight stays are allowed (with the requisite permit), is the **Under-the-Rim Trail**, which begins at Bryce Point and runs for more than 22.5 mi to Rainbow Point on the far southern end. The park's other backcountry trail is the 9-mi **Riggs Spring Loop Trail** (*see* Camping, *below*).

Perhaps the best and most popular average-length hike is one that combines **Queen's Garden** and the **Navajo Loop Trail**. This covers 3 mi, with a 521-ft ascent, and leads through the most dramatic parts of the amphitheater. The trail is open year-round, except when ice makes it impassable. The least strenuous way to hike this route is to begin at Sunset Point, descending the switchbacks of the Navajo Loop first. The section of the trail near the Queen's Garden is not as steep, so it will be less work to ascend there. You will end up at Sunrise Point; the walk along the rim back to Sunset Point adds .5 mi.

The 5.5- to 7.5-mi trek on the **Peekaboo Loop** will take you three to four hours, and you'll have to work a little harder than on the Navajo Trail. You can start at Sunrise, Sunset, or Bryce points, and depending on which you choose, you will have to climb 500 to 800 ft. Along the way you'll happen upon some terrific formations: the Cathedral, the Three Wisemen, and the Wall of Windows. This trail is intended for those on horseback; if you cover it on foot, be sure to give way to horses.

OTHER ACTIVITIES **Biking.** Bicycles are permitted only on the park's paved roads. The 18-mi main road that passes through Bryce can provide an enjoyable half-day to day-long bicycle trip, but it can also be dangerous. The road has only two lanes, and there is no shoulder, so cyclists must always be on the lookout for cars, especially during the summer. The Old Brycetown bike store at Ruby's Inn (tel. 435/834–5341), near the park's northwest entrance, rents bicycles for $4 an hour, $12 for four hours, and $20 for 24 hours. Bike racks are few in the park, so if you want to leave your bike unattended, you may have trouble finding a place to lock it up.

Mountain bikers should head for **Dixie National Forest** (tel. 435/865–3700), where backcountry roads and mountain biking trails abound.

Backcountry Bicycle Tours (Box 4029, Bozeman, MT 59772, tel. 406/586–3556) operates relatively easy, fully supported, and catered six-day bike trips to Bryce and Zion. **Backroads Bicycle Touring, Inc.** (801 Cedar St., Berkeley, CA 94710, tel. 510/527–1555 or 800/245–3874, fax 510/527–1444) leads a nine-day trip to Bryce, the Grand Canyon, and Zion.

Bird-Watching. More than 170 bird species have been spotted at Bryce. The best time to see them is from May through July, during the migration season. A checklist is available at the visitor center.

Boating and Fishing. There's no boating or fishing inside the park, but you can do both at nearby Otter Creek Reservoir in **Otter Creek State Park** (tel. 435/624–3268), at the **Escalante Petrified Forest State Park** (tel. 435/826–4466), and at **Tropic Reservoir, Pine Lake,** and **Panguitch Lake** in Dixie National Forest (tel. 435/865–3700).

Horseback Riding. Bryce–Zion–Grand Canyon Trail Rides (Box 128, Tropic, UT 84736, tel. 435/679–8665 or 435/834–5500) leads two-hour ($25) and half-day ($35) rides into Bryce Canyon on the Peekaboo Loop trail, from early April through early October. Reservations are suggested.

Ski Touring. Unlike Utah's four other national parks, Bryce Canyon usually receives plenty of snow, making it an ideal and increasingly popular cross-country ski area. You can rent skis from **Ruby's Inn** (tel. 435/834–5341), which grooms a 31-mi trail that connects with an ungroomed trail in the park. The 2.5-mi Fairyland ski loop is marked, as is the 5-mi Paria loop, which runs through ponderosa forests into long, open meadows.

Snowshoeing. The National Park Service lends out snowshoes, free of charge, at the Bryce visitor center. Just leave your driver's license or a major credit card with a ranger for as many pairs of snowshoes as your group needs. Snowshoes can be taken on the rim trails but the Park Service discourages their use below the rim. Check at the visitor center for information.

Swimming. There is no place to swim in the park. However, **Escalante Petrified Forest State Park** (tel. 435/826–4466), about 40 mi east of Bryce, has an attractive swimming beach at Wide Hollow Reservoir, which is next to a campground.

CHILDREN'S PROGRAMS The Junior Ranger program runs from Memorial Day to Labor Day; children ages six to 12 can sign up at the park visitor center. In addition, some interpretive programs and hikes are geared especially for kids. To prepare your children for the trip, consider ordering the 32-page "Kid's Guide to Bryce Canyon," for children 5 to 10 (*see* Publications, *above*).

EVENING ACTIVITIES Bryce Canyon and the surrounding area have little in the way of formal nightlife. In summer, the National Park Service has campfire programs nightly near the campgrounds. Check at the visitor center for details. A popular nighttime activity is the Bryce Canyon Rodeo, which runs every night but Sunday from Memorial Day to Labor Day. Tickets cost $7; they may be purchased the day of the show at Old Bryce Town, across the street from Ruby's Inn (tel. 435/834–5341), which hosts the event. Ruby's also hosts a chuckwagon dinner, hayride, country music, and dancing during the summer months.

DINING

Restaurants in the area surrounding Bryce lack pretension: They serve filling, Western-style foods in simple but pleasant settings. Steak is the food of choice, so

vegetarians will have to make do with salad bars. Prices in this part of Utah are low; for instance, the most expensive entrée on the dinner menu at Bryce Canyon Lodge is $15.25. Most restaurants are clustered outside the main park entrance, and none of these require reservations.

INSIDE THE PARK Bryce Canyon Lodge. Nestled among towering pines, this rustic old stone and wood lodge is the only place to dine within the park. Meals here are probably the best in the park, although the lunch menu is rather standard. Vegetarians will appreciate a vegetarian menu, something that can be difficult to find in the Bryce area. The Santa Fe chicken is also good. For dinner, try the roast pork or barbecued chicken. *Bryce Canyon, UT, tel. 435/834–5361. Reservations essential. AE, DC, MC, V. Closed late Oct.–Mar. $$*

NEAR THE PARK Bryce Canyon Pines Restaurant. If you have hungry kids, head for this small restaurant where kids menu prices run low. For adults there are consistently good six-course dinners, with steaks and burgers as the main theme. Other specialties are homemade soup, chili, and banana-blueberry pie. *Hwy. 12 (7 mi from park entrance), tel. 435/834–5441. D, DC, MC, V. Closed Dec.–Feb. $$*

Doug's Place. In the tiny hamlet of Tropic, east of Bryce, Doug's Place specializes in steak dishes, including breaded *Milanesa* (with tomato sauce), and a *Milanesa à la Neopolitonia* (with ham and Swiss cheese). Also on the menu are inexpensive taco salads, hamburgers, soft flour tacos, and homemade pies and sweet rolls. On Friday and Saturday nights Doug's serves a great prime-rib dinner with salad bar. *141 N. Main St., Tropic, UT, tel. 435/679–8633. AE, D, DC, MC, V. $$*

Fosters Family Steakhouse. With its stone fireplace and picture windows, Fosters is a clean, relatively quiet, modern steak house, and one of the most pleasant restaurants in the area. The menu features prime rib, steaks, and basic chicken and seafood dishes. Only wine and beer are served. It is

2 mi west of the junction of Highways 12 and 63. *Hwy. 12, tel. 435/834–5227. AE, D, MC, V. Closed Mon.–Thurs. in Jan. $$*

Hungry Coyote. Decorated with antiques and pictures from the area, this Bryce Valley restaurant has outside dining and specializes in Mexican food. Don't miss the Number One Burrito—seasoned chicken or beef on a 12-inch tortilla covered with salsa and cheese. *Bryce Valley Inn, 200 N. Main St., Tropic, UT, tel. 435/679–8822. AE, MC, V. $$*

Ruby's Inn. This historic motel, store, and dining complex has been owned by the Syrett family since 1919. Due to several fires, Ruby's has been remodeled many times over the years, but it continues to attract hordes of Bryce visitors. Two restaurants serve diners: a fast food restaurant with hamburgers and the like, and a dining room with a cowboy buffet for breakfast, lunch, and dinner. The cowboy buffet features traditional Western fare. *Hwy. 63 (1 mi north of park entrance), tel. 435/834–5341. AE, D, DC, MC, V. $$*

Harold's Place. About 15 mi west of Bryce, on Highway 12 at the entrance to Red Canyon, stands Harold's, designed to resemble a log cabin. On the eclectic international menu are Philly burgers (⅓-pound burger with green peppers, onions, mushrooms, and melted Swiss cheese), Italian meatball sandwiches, fajitas, and Mexican-style pizza. Harold's has a beer license only. *3066 Hwy. 12, tel. 435/676–2350. MC, V. Closed Nov.–Mar. $–$$*

PICNIC SPOTS There are three picnic areas inside the park. The one near **Rainbow Point,** at the southern end of the park, and the one near the **North Campground** are the most developed. The Rainbow Point picnic area is the more scenic of the two. Another smaller facility is halfway between the entrance and Rainbow Point, just north of a place locals call Piracy Point. Picnic supplies are available inside the park from the general store near Sunrise Point.

LODGING

New properties are springing up in the towns surrounding Bryce Canyon, although they can be quite a distance from the park. Panguitch, the nearest town of any significance, is 24 mi from the park entrance. With the exception of the Bryce Canyon Lodge, don't expect much more than roadside motels in the park's vicinity. The facilities listed below are clustered within an 11-mi radius of the main entrance, in the northwest corner of the park. Advance reservations are a must in summer. At the very least, arrive early in the day.

INSIDE THE PARK **Bryce Canyon Lodge.** Many of the materials from the original Bryce Canyon Lodge were used in the stone and timber building's 1989 reconstruction, so that the lodge and its western-style cabins retain the rustic feel of an authentic 1920s retreat. Weary hikers rest on replica bark-covered hickory chairs while warming their hands before the lobby's grand limestone fireplace. The main lobby of this National Historic Landmark is lighted by a log and wrought-iron chandelier. There are four suites on the second floor, and 15 lodgepole-pine cabins on one side of the lodge. These sleep up to four people, and most have 12-ft cathedral ceilings and gas fireplaces. There are also two motel-style buildings with 70 additional rooms that have either ground-floor porches or upstairs balconies. Reservations are hard to come by: Call several months ahead, or, if you're feeling lucky, call the day before your arrival—cancellations occasionally make last-minute bookings possible. *Bryce Canyon, tel. 303/297–2757; 435/834–5361 in season. 114 rooms. Facilities: restaurant. AE, DC, MC, V. Closed Nov.–Mar. $$–$$$*

NEAR THE PARK **Bryce Canyon Pines Motel and Restaurant.** This quiet, relatively modern motel complex is nestled in the woods 6 mi from the park entrance. Most of the rooms have excellent mountain views. Two housekeeping cottages and three cabin-suites are available. A campground and RV park are nearby. *Hwy. 12, Box 43, Bryce, UT 84764, tel. 435/834–5441, fax 435/834–5330. 51 rooms. Facilities: restaurant, indoor pool. D, DC, MC, V. $$–$$$*

Bryce Valley Inn. With wood inside and out this facility in the tiny community of Tropic is more like a motel than an inn. A shuttle service takes hikers and bicyclists to the park, and a gift shop sells Native American crafts. *200 N. Main St., Box A, Tropic, UT 84776, tel. 435/679–8811, fax 435/679–8846. 63 rooms. Facilities: restaurant, coin laundry. AE, MC, V. $$*

Doug's Country Inn. With rustic, wood-beamed rooms and homemade quilts on the beds, this inn is small and intimate. *141 N. Main St., Tropic, UT 84776, tel. 801/679–8633. 28 rooms. Facilities: restaurant, hot tub. AE, D, DC, MC, V. $$*

Pink Cliffs Bryce Village Inn. At the junction of Highway 12 and 63, the Pine Cliffs has bunkhouse-style cabins that evoke the Old West. On the grounds are a trading post, a convenience store, a deli, and a service station. *Hwys. 12 and 63, Box 64006, Bryce Canyon, UT 84764, tel. 800/834–0043, fax 435/834–5256. 53 rooms, 14 cabins (seasonal). Facilities: restaurant, café, pool, coin laundry. AE, DC, MC, V. $$*

Ruby's Inn. Ruby's is the largest and longest-operating facility in the area. It is also the most complete, with two restaurants, two pools, a convention center, a gas station, a shopping complex, a western art gallery, nightly rodeo in summer, helicopters, an RV park, horseback riding, ski and bicycle rentals, and even a U.S. post office. Fifty-one rooms have whirlpool tubs. Reserve several months in advance, especially for summer stays. *Hwy. 63 (1 mi north of park entrance), Box 1, Bryce, UT 84764, tel. 435/834–5341 or 800/528–1234, fax 435/834–5265. 365 rooms. Facilities: 2 restaurants, 2 indoor pools, 2 hot tubs, barbershop, beauty salon, shops, convention center. AE, D, DC, MC, V. $$*

CAMPING

INSIDE THE PARK There are two large public campgrounds in Bryce National Park: the **North Campground** and **Sunset Campground,** which provide a total of 218 sites for both tents and RVs. No reservations are accepted, and the campgrounds generally fill every night from May through September. It is best to arrive by 2 PM. To find out in advance if sites are available, call the visitor center (tel. 435/834–5322). The fee is $10 per night. Before planning a winter camping trip, check with park headquarters: Though the park is open year-round, budget cuts may cause the campgrounds to close in winter.

There are some designated RV sites at these campgrounds, and tenters may have an RV in the site next to them. Hookups are not available at either campground. There is one sewage dump station near North Campground, but it's shut down during freezing weather.

Set amid pine trees, all the sites in these campgrounds are similar; each has a fire grate and picnic table. Rest rooms scattered throughout the areas have flush toilets and cold running water. During the summer, campers can enjoy evening programs at both facilities.

Near Sunrise Point, just a short distance from either campground, are a store, pay showers ($2 for seven–nine minutes), and laundry facilities ($1.25 to wash and dry one load). These are open from early May through mid-October.

Hikers who choose to overnight on the Under-the-Rim Trail must camp at designated backcountry sites and must have a free backcountry permit, available at the visitor center. There are seven of these sites along the trail—at Yellow Creek, Sheep Creek, Swamp Canyon, Natural Bridge, and Iron Spring. The 9-mi Riggs Spring Loop below Rainbow and Yovimpa Points has three additional backcountry sites at Yovimpa Pass, Riggs Spring, and Corral

BRYCE CANYON CAMPGROUNDS

	INSIDE THE PARK		NEAR THE PARK									
	North	Sunset	Red Canyon (National Forest)	White Bridge (National Forest)	Kings Creek (National Forest)	Kodachrome Basin State Park	Escalante Petrified Forest State Park	Ruby's Inn	Bryce Canyon Pines	Bryce/Zion KOA	Red Canyon RV Park	Riverside
Total number of sites	107	111	40	28	40	26	22	160	40	81	45	77
Sites suitable for RVs	47	49	40	28	25	26	22	110	25	59	45	47
Number of hookups	0	0	36	0	0	0	0	43	25	19	45	47
Drive to sites	•	•	•	•	•	•	•	•	•	•	•	•
Hike to sites												
Flush toilets	•	•			•	•	•	•	•	•	•	•
Pit/chemical toilets			•	•	•							
Drinking water	•	•	•	•	•	•	•	•	•	•	•	•
Showers		•			•	•	•	•	•	•	•	•
Fire grates	•	•	•	•	•	•	•	•	•	•	•	•
Swimming						•			•	•		•
Boat access				•		•						
Playground									•	•	•	•
Disposal station	•	•**		•	•	•	•	•	•	•		•
Ranger station	•						•					
Public telephone	•	•			•	•	•	•	•	•	•	•
Reservation possible		•*	•*			•*	•*	•	•	•	•	•
Daily fee per site	$10	$9	$10–$13	$9	$6	$9–$10	$9–$10	$13–$22	$10–$17	$15–$18.50	$8–13.50	$11–$17
Dates open	year-round	early May–mid-Oct.	Apr.–Oct.	June–Oct.	June–mid-Sept.	year-round	year-round	Apr.–Oct.	Apr.–Nov.	early May–mid-Oct.	Apr.–Oct.	May–Oct.

*Reservation fee charged. ** Closed during freezing weather.

Hollow. All of these sites are simply cleared areas for tents. Only six people may camp in each site; if your party consists of seven to 10 people you must obtain a special permit for one of the group sites at Yellow Creek or Riggs Spring. Open campfires are not allowed, so if you plan to cook, bring a portable stove.

NEAR THE PARK There are two relatively primitive but spectacular U.S. Forest Service camping areas in the Dixie National Forest near Bryce Canyon. The appropriately named **Red Canyon** (tel. 435/676–8815), on Highway 12 about 8 mi from the entrance to Bryce, has 40 sites for tents or RVs, surrounded by pine trees, in a brilliant red rock canyon not unlike the Bryce amphitheater. The fee ranges from $10 to $13 per night. **White Bridge** (tel. 435/865–3700), on Highway 143, about 30 mi from Bryce, has 28 sites for tents or RVs in a quiet meadow. Sites cost $9 per night. Both areas have fire grates and drinking water. They are open from May or June through October.

Tenters will enjoy the alpine setting of **Kings Creek Campground** (tel. 435/676–8815), also in Dixie National Forest. It is about 11 mi from Bryce, just west of the park boundary and near Tropic Reservoir; to get there, turn off Highway 12 west of the junction with Highway 63 and drive south for 7 mi down a dirt road. King's Creek has 40 individual sites for tents or RVs and one group site. The campground is open from mid-May to mid-September. Sites cost $6 per night.

Two of the best public campgrounds east of the park are found at **Kodachrome Basin State Park** and at **Escalante Petrified Forest State Park.** Kodachrome Basin is 9 mi southeast of the town of Cannonville and about 23 mi east of Bryce. Its unusual monolithic rock formations make it an attraction in its own right, and the 26-site campground there ranks among the best in Utah. Escalante Petrified Forest, about 45 mi east of Bryce on Highway 12, has 22 sites for tents and RVs. Both campgrounds

have showers, flush toilets, drinking water, fire grates, and a disposal station. Both charge $10 per night. Campsites at any Utah state park can be reserved for $5 (on your credit card) by calling 800/322–3770; call 801/538–7221 for general information.

Several private campgrounds are near the park. One of the closest is **Ruby's Inn** (tel. 435/834–5301), which has 110 RV and tent sites with 43 hookups, most set in shaded areas. Ruby's has everything a camper could ask for—flush toilets, showers, drinking water, fire grates, disposal station, public phone, laundry room, heated pool, and game room. It is open from April to November; sites cost $12 to $19.

Shady, quiet sites in a wooded setting can be found at **Bryce Canyon Pines** (tel. 435/834–5441), 6 mi from the park entrance on Highway 12. This smaller campground has 40 sites for tents and RVs (25 hookups), with flush toilets, hot showers, drinking water, fire grates, playground, disposal station, and public phones. Campers can enjoy horseback riding, a game room, and a swimming pool. There is also a convenience store, laundromat, and gas station. Sites cost $10 to $17 per day. The campground is open from April to November.

If you are heading to Zion, you might break up your trip by staying at the **Bryce/Zion KOA,** on Highway 89, about 50 mi from both Bryce and Zion and 90 minutes from the Grand Canyon. The campground is set amid juniper and oak trees at the base of majestic pink cliffs. It has 59 RV (19 water/electric and 22 full hookups) and 20 tent sites as well as two large group sites accommodating up to 40 people. There are flush toilets, hot showers, drinking water, fire grates, a disposal station, and a public phone here. Laundry facilities and a general store are convenient additions, and the playground, swimming pool, hiking trails, and guided horse tours will keep campers busy. The KOA is open from May 1 to October 15. Sites cost $15 to $18.50 and should be reserved in advance. Contact Glendale KOA, Box 186, Glendale, UT 84729, tel. 801/648–2490.

The **Red Canyon RV Park** (tel. 435/676–2690) is 16 mi from Bryce; it's near Red Canyon on Highway 12, 1 mi east of U.S. 89. The 45 RV sites all have full hookups, and visitors can choose to stay in either a tepee that sleeps up to five or one of four log cabins. A desert campground where sagebrush and mountain views are plentiful, Red Canyon has a shower and rest room facility, as well as fire grates, a playground, and a public phone. There is a covered picnic spot out in the open, right off the highway. Tenters can use the sites for $8 per site per night; RVers pay $13.50 per site, and kids under 10 stay free. Cabins start at $17. This campground is open from April until October.

The **Riverside Campground** (tel. 435/735–4223 or 800/824–5651) is .5 mi north of Hatch on the Sevier River, on U.S. 89. Its 124 sites (47 with full hookups) are nestled together well off the road. Open year-round, Riverside has flush toilets, drinking water, showers, fire grates, river swimming, a playground, a disposal station, and a public phone, as well as eight motel units. Campsites cost $11 to $17.

Canyon de Chelly National Monument

Arizona

Updated by Gregory McNamee

When Spanish conquistadors first approached the Dinetah, the land of the Navajo, in the 16th century, they heard reports of a place they called Canyon de Chelly (pronounced de-*shay*)— a remote vastness they assumed to have been named after a leader or tribe they had yet to encounter. The conquistadors, however, had simply misunderstood what was being said. The Navajo word *tsegi* means "within the rocks," and the name is certainly appropriate. Here stone reigns supreme; within the boundaries of this masterpiece of geology and history, walls of rock rise hundreds of feet above the canyon floor, like sentinels guarding the desert's history. Tall monoliths point toward the heavens, and massive red sandstone buttes and mesas dot the landscape. Gracious cottonwoods and tilled fields on the canyon floor, however, reveal a softer, more hospitable side of this imposing land.

In the northeast corner of Arizona, Canyon de Chelly occupies 131 square mi of Navajoland, the largest Native American reservation in North America. It was officially declared a reservation in 1868, but the Navajo, now numbering more than 200,000, have occupied this land for almost 400 years. Their 25,000-square-mi reservation, spreading across Arizona, New Mexico, and Utah, is near such famous American landmarks as Monument Valley, the Petrified Forest, the Painted Desert, and Glen Canyon. But the most impressive and dramatic of the area's destinations is certainly Canyon de Chelly National Monument, which encompasses three of the most magnificent canyons in the Southwest: Canyon de Chelly, Canyon del Muerto, and Monument Canyon.

Beautiful though it may be, Canyon de Chelly National Monument amounts to much more than just another pretty rock face: The landscape here serves as the backdrop for centuries of Native American history. The land was long occupied by early Pueblo Indians, widely known by the Navajo name *Anasazi* ("enemy ancestors") and more than 100 of the former village sites dating back as far as the 4th century are here. All types of dwellings are found, from simple pit houses to many-storied pueblos, history's first apartment houses. Canyon del Muerto's famous Mummy Cave, with its three-story tower, is where two mummies preserved by the desert's dryness were found. Other prize archaeological finds include Antelope House, named for the Navajo antelope drawings found on its walls, and White House, which has a whitewashed top.

The Navajo who farm Canyon de Chelly's bottomland today moved in some 300 years after the original ancestral Puebloan tenants had migrated late in the 13th century. It was from here in 1864 that Kit Carson and his troops forced the Navajo to make the infamous 300-mi Long March to the Bosque Redondo in eastern New Mexico. Of the 9,000 Navajos taken captive, 3,000 to 4,000 died, many stricken by smallpox once they arrived in New Mexico. The Navajo resettled Canyon de Chelly in 1868, and today they continue to farm and raise sheep here in the tradition of their ancestors. The area became a national monument in 1931.

Visitors to this park should remember to respect the privacy and customs of the Navajo people. Approach homes only when invited, and do not wander across residential areas or disturb property. Obtain permission before taking photographs of Navajo people; a small gratuity may be expected.

ESSENTIAL INFORMATION

VISITOR INFORMATION For specific information about Canyon de Chelly contact the superintendent's office at **Canyon de Chelly National Monument** (Box 588, Chinle, AZ 86503, tel. 520/674–5500, fax 520/674–5507). The **Arizona Office of Tourism** (1100 W. Washington St., Phoenix, AZ 85007, tel. 602/542–8687 or 800/842–8257) provides a variety of informative printed material. For information and help with hotel reservations, contact the **Native American Travel and Tourism Center** (4130 N. Goldwater Blvd., Scottsdale, AZ 85251, tel. 602/945–0771), and for additional information regarding Navajo country, contact the **Navajoland Tourism Department** (Box 663, Window Rock, AZ 86515, tel. 800/806–2825 or 520/871–6436).

The visitor center opens at 8 AM year-round and closes at 6 PM from April 30 through September 30 and at 5 PM the rest of the year. If you need to contact a park ranger outside those hours, call 520/674–5523.

Note: The Navajo nation observes Daylight Savings Time, while the rest of Arizona and the Hopi Reservation (located virtually in the center of the Navajo Reservation) do not. Plan accordingly.

FEES Admission to Canyon de Chelly and its visitor center is free; this includes the North and South rim drives and the self-guided tour to White House Ruin. Some ranger-led hikes are also gratis; check the visitor center for a current schedule.

All other tours of Canyon de Chelly and its tributaries, made either on foot, horse, or in four-wheel-drive vehicles, must be made in the company of authorized Navajo guides, who are available for hire at the visitor center. The beautiful rock formations seen here are not without their hazards. Loose rocks, quicksand, and flash floods are common in these canyons: Guides are necessary to ensure the safety of visitors. Guided tours on horseback and in four-wheel drive vehicles are run by concessionaires (*see* Guided Tours, *below*). You must have a permit, available free at the visitor center, to participate in any tour.

PUBLICATIONS Indispensable for a visit to the national monument is the *Canyon Overlook Guide.* Available at the Canyon de Chelly Visitor Center and all area hotels, this guide lists current schedules for ranger-led activities and talks and provides detailed information about local concessionaires. Also recommended are the inexpensive motoring guides to the North and South Rim and the trail guide to the White House Ruin, all sold at the visitor center.

In addition, the visitor center carries a good selection of books about both the canyon and Native American country. Some that provide a nice background to the park are *Canyon de Chelly: Its People and Rock Art,* by Campbell Grant; Donald J. Hagerty's *Canyon de Chelly: 100 Years of Painting and Photography;* David Grant Noble's *Houses Beneath the Rock: The Anasazi of Canyon de Chelly and Navajo National Monument;* and the inexpensive *Canyon de Chelly Handbook,* which gives practical tips for exploring and enjoying the spectacular canyon.

The Book of the Navajo, by Raymond Friday Locke, is perhaps the most comprehensive survey of the history and legends of the Navajo people. Other books worth reading while you're on the reservation include *The Main Stalk: A Synthesis of Navajo Philosophy,* by John R. Farella; *Diné Bahane: The Navajo Creation Story,* by Paul G. Zolbrod; *Sa'anii Dahataat: The Women are*

Singing, by Luci Tapahonso; *Navajo Rugs: How to Find, Evaluate, Buy and Care for Them,* by Don Dedera; and *Navajo Pottery Traditions and Innovations,* by Russell P. Hartman and Jan Musial.

Because of Navajoland's sheer expanse, you'll find a good road map indispensable. An excellent map containing lists of area attractions is available free from the Navajoland Tourism Department (*see* Visitor Information, *above*).

GEOLOGY AND TERRAIN Sheer sandstone cliffs, though heavily eroded over time, still rise as high as 1,000 ft within the Canyon de Chelly. Their evolution began about 50 to 60 million years ago, when a group of rock formations nearly 50 mi wide and 100 mi long began to uplift along what is now the northern border of Arizona and New Mexico. Over the millennia this piece of land, known geologically as the Defiance Uplift, underwent upheaval that wrenched and twisted the layers of colored rock. Meanwhile, raging rivers from the nearby Chuska Mountains cut deeply at the foundations, forming the canyons. Over the years, a persistent wind, still experienced by those who visit today, has carved swirling striations into the sheer cliff walls, and manganese deposits from rain and river runoff, combined with ancient bacteria and other microorganisms, have painted a black wash on the red rocks—a striking phenomenon known as desert varnish.

Today, area streams are often dry, although they do run fast in the spring, when filled with runoff from the mountain snows, and throughout the summer rainy season. The main canyons, Canyon de Chelly and Canyon del Muerto, both about 26 mi long, continue to stand over yesterday's ruins and today's fields, pastures, and traditional Navajo hogans (dwellings made of logs and mud), despite the harsh treatment of centuries of wind and water.

FLORA AND FAUNA The 24,347 square mi that make up the Navajo reservation are mostly arid or semiarid, with coniferous vegetation at the higher levels. While various forms of cactus, such as the prickly pear, and other desert plants can be found on the Canyon de Chelly plateau, it is the common reed and the sacred datura that are most often associated with the area. Douglas and Canadian fir trees grow along the upper reaches where snow lingers longest. Juniper trees and piñon pines, whose small edible nuts are prized, can be found along the canyon rim. At the lower altitudes are cottonwood trees, coyote willow, tamarisk, and fragrant Russian olive, the latter brought from western Asia in the 1800s to help stop water erosion in the area. Wildflowers such as beeplant and desert paintbrush cover the canyon floor during the spring and summer.

Animal life consists primarily of desert rodents: squirrels, chipmunks, skunks, and raccoons, all especially pesky from August through September, during the corn harvesting season. Hawks and eagles soar gracefully overhead, and canyon wrens, ravens, swallows, and piñon jays are also at home here.

WHEN TO GO Canyon de Chelly is open to visitors year-round, but during the cold winter months most travelers steer clear of the area's snow and hazardous road and trail conditions. A better time to visit is between May and October, when the weather is more hospitable and all of the ranger-led activities, canyon hikes, and other programs are in full swing. Daytime temperatures from April through November range from 60°F to 98°F, but it can cool down considerably after sunset. Winter daytime temperatures fall between 30°F and 65°F but can quickly drop to below zero; also, the wind at the canyon's higher altitudes can be fierce. KTNN radio (AM 660), broadcasting from Window Rock, gives periodic weather updates in English and Navajo.

SEASONAL EVENTS July 1 to 4: The Navajo nation hosts more Native American rodeos than any other Native American reservation in the United States or Canada, and the **Fourth of July Rodeo,** held 65 mi south of

Canyon de Chelly in Window Rock, capital of the Navajo nation, is by far the most spectacular. Included is the Navajo Nation Powwow, a large Native American fair. **Late August/early September:** Two similar events, both involving lots of food, dances, and arts and crafts, take place in late summer on the reservation—first the smaller **Central Navajo Fair** held in Chinle, then the **Annual Navajo Nation Fair** in Window Rock. For information about these festivities and others on the reservation, contact the Navajoland Tourism Department (see Visitor Information, above).

WHAT TO PACK If you're planning to hike into the canyons, you'll need all the standard hiking essentials, including plenty of water, plus a small towel (be prepared to walk through water). If you're going to be out after sunset be sure to bring a sweater or jacket; the temperature can drop dramatically. Winter temperatures can hover around 0°F, so if you're planning an off-season visit, dress warmly.

GENERAL STORES The tiny town of Chinle (Navajo for "where the water flows out") is roughly 2 mi west of Canyon de Chelly. You can find most of what you need at **Tseyi' Shopping Center** on Highway 191. It has a large **Bashas** supermarket (tel. 520/674–3464 or 520/674–3465), open daily year-round, from 8 AM to 10 PM Monday through Saturday and from 8 to 8 Sunday. Next door, **the General Store** (tel. 520/674–5486) carries a selection of basic goods, including clothing, camping gear, and cooking supplies. It is open year-round, from 9 to 9 Monday through Saturday and from 10 to 5 Sunday and holidays. In addition, there are some small grocery stores, gas stations, laundromats, and a half dozen fast-food outlets in Chinle.

You'll find a fairly good selection of Navajo crafts in town; the gift shops at the Holiday Inn and Thunderbird Lodge are particularly worth browsing. But if you have the time, head south on U.S. 191 for about 45 minutes to visit the famous **Hubbell Trading Post** (Rte. 264, 1 mi west of Ganado, tel.

520/755–3475), a museum and general trading post that is listed on the National Register of Historic Sites and operates much as it did over a century ago (see Historic Buildings and Sites, below). There you'll find one of the best selections of Navajo rugs in the state. Prices are generally expensive, but there are some on-the-spot bargains and clearance sales. The post is open June to September, daily from 8 to 6, and October to May, daily from 8 to 5.

ARRIVING AND DEPARTING Although public transportation serves several towns on the outskirts of the reservation, there is no major air, train, or bus service to Navajoland itself: Cars are essential here.

By Bus. Greyhound Lines (tel. 800/231–2222) provides bus service to numerous Arizona destinations, including Page and Flagstaff, where car rentals are available. You can also take a Greyhound bus to Gallup, New Mexico (tel. 505/863–3761 bus depot), and make a connection with a Navajo Nation Transit bus, which will take you to Fort Defiance; from there you can transfer to a bus bound for Chinle. Call Navajo Transit (tel. 520/729–4002) for information, or pick up a schedule at the Gallup Greyhound station.

By Car and RV. To reach Canyon de Chelly National Monument from Flagstaff, take I–40 east to Chambers, then U.S. 191 north to Ganado, where the road jogs west for 6 mi, and continue on U.S. 191 for another 47 mi north to Chinle. If you're driving from Page, take Route 98 southeast to Highway 160, then go north to Highway 59. Follow Highway 59 southeast to Many Farms, then pick up U.S. 191 south to Chinle. The monument is approximately 2 mi east of Chinle on Indian Route 7.

Drivers should remain alert for animals on the roads, especially after dark. The Navajo reservation has an open range policy; livestock are not fenced in and frequently wander onto roadways.

By Plane. The closest commuter air connections are in Gallup, New Mexico (tel.

505/722–4896 airport) on Old Highway 66 in western New Mexico, about 100 mi from the park. Other options are the airport in Flagstaff (tel. 520/556–1234), located off I–17, 216 mi from the park, just outside the southwestern corner of the Navajo reservation, or in Page (tel. 520/645–4160), on U.S. 89 near Lake Powell and Arizona's northern border, 180 mi from the park. Arizona's major air hub for these areas is **Sky Harbor International Airport** (tel. 602/273–3300) in Phoenix, served by nearly all major U.S. airlines. **America West** (tel. 800/235–9292) has daily flights from Phoenix to Gallup and Flagstaff. The town of Page is served every day from Phoenix by Delta's **SkyWest** commuter service (tel. 800/453–9417).

At the airport in Gallup, the car-rental agents are **Avis** (tel. 505/863–9309 or 800/331–1212) and **National Interrent** (tel. 505/863–6578 or 800/227–7368). At Flagstaff Pullium Airport, you can rent a car from **Avis** (tel. 520/774–8421), **Budget** (tel. 520/779–0306 or 800/527–0700), or **Hertz** (tel. 520/774–4452 or 800/654–3131). At Page Airport, try **Avis** (tel. 520/645–2024) or **Budget** (tel. 520/645–3977), but note that it's considerably less expensive to rent a car in Flagstaff than it is to rent one in Page.

By Train. Amtrak (tel. 800/872–7245) provides daily service into Arizona from east and west, making scheduled stops in Gallup and Flagstaff from both directions. The Gallup station is at 201 East Highway 66, and car rentals are available at the airport (*see* By Plane, *above*), 2.5 mi away. The station in Flagstaff is downtown (1 E. Rte. 66), within walking distance of **Budget** (100 N. Humphreys St., tel. 520/774–2763) and **Triple A** (602 W. Rte. 66, tel. 520/774–7394) car-rental offices.

EXPLORING

For excellent views of the canyon and ruins, there are two spectacular rim drives: the South Rim Drive, covering 36 mi round-trip and leading to eight dramatic overlooks, and the North Rim Drive, which is 34 mi round-trip and leads to four overlooks (*see* Scenic Drives, *below*). The White House Ruins trail, beginning at White House Trail Overlook, about 6 mi southeast of the visitor center, can be hiked independently; arrangements for the Navajo guides required for the many other spectacular hikes into the canyon can be made at the visitor center. You will need a permit (ask at the visitor center) and a guide to take a four-wheel-drive or horseback tour into the canyon (*see* Guided Tours, *below*). Be aware that canyon roads and trails are often impassable in winter and during and after heavy rains. Visitors are not allowed to enter any of the ruins.

THE BEST IN ONE DAY The visitor center opens at 8 AM, and this is the best place and time to begin your visit. Throughout the summer, special programs, hikes, and performances are scheduled on short notice and this is the place to find out about them. Here you can browse through the center's bookstore and museum and pick up literature and maps. In the busy summer season, ranger talks are given daily, but the schedule varies, so check for times.

If you're in good shape, sign up at the visitor center for a Navajo-led hike into the canyon. These treks are rather strenuous, so don't join the intrepid bands of adventurers unless you're completely comfortable with your physical condition. A horseback ride is a less difficult way to enter into the canyon, and a four-wheel drive truck ride is the easiest of all; *see* Guided Tours, *below,* for details on all these tour options.

If you take a morning tour, you'll be back in time for lunch; in the afternoon you might catch a ranger talk and demonstration at the visitor center. Those who spent the morning on a horse or truck might want to take the short unguided White House Trail hike (*see* Nature Trails and Short Walks, *below*). Later in the afternoon, when the sun casts dramatic shadows on the canyon walls, you might drive along the North and South rims for an overall view of everything you've just seen up close (*see* Scenic

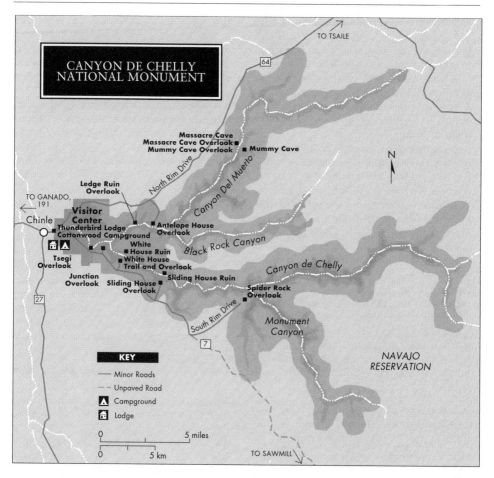

CANYON DE CHELLY
NATIONAL MONUMENT

TO TSAILE

64

Massacre Cave
Massacre Cave Overlook ■
Mummy Cave Overlook ■ ■ Mummy Cave

North Rim Drive

Canyon Del Muerto

N

Ledge Ruin
Overlook

TO GANADO,
191

Chinle

Visitor
Center
■ Thunderbird Lodge ■ Antelope House
■ Cottonwood Campground Overlook
White
■ House Ruin   Black Rock Canyon

Tsegi
Overlook

■ White House
Trail and Overlook

Canyon de Chelly

Junction
Overlook   Sliding House ■ ■ Sliding House Ruin

27   Sliding House
Overlook

Spider Rock
■ Overlook

South Rim Drive

Monument
Canyon

7

NAVAJO
RESERVATION

KEY

—— Minor Roads
-- -- Unpaved Road
▲ Campground
🏠 Lodge

0   5 miles

0   5 km

TO SAWMILL

Drives and Views, *below*). On the hottest summer days, it's a good idea to rearrange this schedule and do the long hike when the sun is least intense.

ORIENTATION PROGRAMS The helpful ranger staff at Canyon de Chelly National Monument gives demonstrations and talks on such topics as the history of the park and the Navajo people, Native American crafts, and Navajo mythology. For a full schedule of programs, consult the visitor center (tel. 520/674–5500). The visitor-center museum has displays providing background on the Anasazi cliff dwellers who lived in Canyon de Chelly from about AD 300 to AD 1300 and on the Navajo people who followed.

GUIDED TOURS Visitors are free to explore the rim of the canyon or hike the well-marked trail to the White House Ruin unescorted, but no one may explore the bottom of the canyon without a permit and a guide. You can almost always book a guided hike, even during off-season, but in summer, there are sometimes free ranger-led tours. Since the number of people allowed on these walks is limited, you must sign up at the visitor center no earlier than 48 hours in advance.

To hire one of the canyon's knowledgeable, authorized guides, almost always resident Navajo, stop by the visitor center. These guides are available for four-hour tours for walking parties of up to 15 people; the cost is $10 per person (minimum $50 for four persons or less). As many as three hikes take place each day during the busy season (April through October or November): generally, a morning hike, from 9 AM to 1 PM; an afternoon hike from 1 to 5; and a trek from 4 to 8. The hikes, which go into either the Canyon de Chelly or the Canyon del Muerto, are approximately 4 mi round-trip. Note: Although a descent into the canyon is an extremely rewarding experience, trails are not graded and routes may involve steep ascents. Those with health problems and those who are out of shape or afraid of heights should question the guide carefully about the difficulty of the hike they're considering. Guides for smaller groups or individuals may also be hired for $10 per hour. In high season, Ernest Jones, an authorized Navajo guide, leads two-hour-long night walks into the canyon ($12 per person), departing half an hour before sunset; at Petroglyph Rock, he talks about the canyon's cultural and archaeological history. Look for his sign announcing the hike .25 mi north of Thunderbird Lodge, or write Jones at Box 2832, Chinle, AZ 86503.

Visitors who plan on driving their own four-wheel-drive, high-clearance trucks through the canyon can hire one guide for groups of as many as five vehicles for $10 per hour for a single vehicle; add on another $5 per hour for each additional vehicle. Free permits are required for anyone hiking or driving into the canyon; they can be obtained at the visitor-center information desk seven days a week.

The Thunderbird Lodge (*see* Lodging, *below*) offers motorized tours of the canyon, led by Navajo guides and conducted in flatbed trucks refitted as buses, almost every day of the year. The half-day tours take canyon goers halfway up Canyon del Muerto and Canyon de Chelly. The cost is $35.34. Full-day tours going deeper into the canyons, with lunch included, cost $56.79 per person. Call for reservations in high season.

Three authorized operators lead guided tours on horseback: **Justin's Horse Rental** (Box 881, Chinle, AZ 86503, tel. 520/674–5678), which is beside the park entrance on South Rim Drive; **Twin Trail Tours** (Box 1706, Window Rock, AZ 86515, tel. 520/674–8425 summer only), on North Rim Drive, 9 mi north of the visitor center, just past Antelope House turnoff; and, the newest, **Tohtsoni Ranch** (Box 434, Chinle, AZ 86503, tel. 520/755–6209), on the South Rim Drive, 1.3 mi east of the Spider Rock turnoff toward Sawmill. Extended and overnight trips by horseback are also available.

A package photo tour of Canyon de Chelly National Monument is offered to photography buffs by the **Friends of Arizona Highways** (tel. 602/271–5904) in the autumn. The package includes instruction by professional photographers, transportation from Phoenix, Navajo guides, three nights' lodging at the Thunderbird Lodge, meals and snacks, slide shows, and photo tips. The cost is $1,150 per person, double occupancy.

SCENIC DRIVES AND VIEWS The **South Rim Drive** covers 36 mi round-trip and includes seven important overlooks, so it can take about two hours to make the trip. The first stop is **Tsegi Overlook,** from which you'll get a breath-stopping glimpse down the sheer canyon face to tranquil Navajo farming fields below. The hogan (octagonal Navajo dwelling) that you see on the farm is occupied during the warm weather. At the next stop, **Junction Overlook,** canyon walls come together, forming a tall, circular peninsula where Canyon del Muerto meets Canyon de Chelly. Two Anasazi cliff dwellings can be glimpsed from this vantage point. **White House Overlook** provides access, via a 2.5-mi round-trip trail, to the best-known Anasazi cliff dwelling, White House, named after a long wall in the upper part of the ruin covered with white plaster (*see* Historic Buildings and Sites, *below*). Farther down South Rim Drive (another 3 mi) is **Sliding House Overlook,** from which you will see an ancient abode perched so precariously along a narrow ledge that it appears about to topple into the canyon far below. **Face Rock Overlook** gives you a bird's-eye view of canyon dwellings high in an opposite wall. **Spider Rock Overlook,** at the end of the route, is best saved for last. Here the walls drop more than 1,000 ft, and the slender, 800-ft-high Spider Rock monolith rises majestically from the canyon floor. Spider Rock was named by the Navajos as the home of the Spider Woman of Navajo legend; she is believed to have brought weaving to the tribe.

The **North Rim Drive,** along Canyon del Muerto, covers 34 mi round-trip and leads to four important overlooks; it, too, can be a two-hour ride. **Ledge Ruin Overlook** is the first stop. From here you'll see some of the Anasazi ruins and get sweeping views up and down the canyon. Four miles up the road are the two overlooks at **Antelope House,** both at the point where Canyon del Muerto and Black Rock Canyon join (*see* Historic Buildings and Sites, *below*). Skillful paintings of antelopes, attributed to a Navajo artist who lived here in the 1830s, are drawn on the canyon wall to the left of the ruin. The towering Navajo Fortress, once an important refuge from enemy raiders, can be seen across the canyon. The next turnoff, 8 mi up the highway on the right, brings you to two vista points for Canyon del Muerto. **Mummy Cave Overlook** is a remarkably unspoiled pueblo dwelling so named because corpses were found inside, preserved by the dryness of the cave. From nearby **Massacre Cave Overlook,** you can glimpse the ledge where more than 100 men, women, and children were slaughtered by Spanish soldiers in 1805. The North Rim Drive turns into Highway 64, which runs northeast to Tsaile, home of the Navajo Community College.

HISTORIC BUILDINGS AND SITES Canyon de Chelly National Monument contains more than 800 archaeological sites. White House, Antelope House, and the other well-preserved dwellings at Canyon de Chelly are among the best examples of multistory Anasazi pueblos to be found anywhere in the Southwest. People are not allowed to enter any of the ruins.

A 2.5-mi round-trip trail leads to **White House,** the best-known Anasazi cliff dwelling. In the upper part, there is a long wall that's covered with white plaster, which gives the ruin its name. It is believed that the construction of the White House, set into the cliffs "between heaven and earth," was begun around 1060. The two-level structure may have originally contained as many as 80 rooms, but today there are only 60 of them, along with four kivas (ceremonial structures), some of which could be reached only by ladders. Historians believe that once safely inside, the occupants withdrew the ladders so that intruders could not enter. White House, which could accommodate 50 or 60 people, was inhabited from the 11th to the 13th centuries. Near this pueblo are some of the unique, foot-size steps that Anasazi throughout the Southwest chipped into steep canyon walls to facilitate the climb to their dwellings high in the cliffs. The trail to White House is the only area in Canyon de Chelly that may be visited without a guide.

Antelope House, an ancient Anasazi dwelling, is named for its colorful antelope drawings, made by a Navajo artist more than 150 years ago. A pit house under this impressive ruin dates from AD 693, and the site was probably occupied from then until the middle of the 13th century. The circular pits found here held kivas, and 91 rooms—some used for storage, some for living quarters, and some for religious purposes—are still intact. From the overlook here, visitors can see the juncture of Canyon del Muerto and Black Rock Canyon.

The **Hubbell Trading Post** (*see* General Stores, *above*), a museum and historic shop, is listed on the National Register of Historic Sites. Navajo men and women give frequent demonstrations of jewelry making and other traditional crafts. The trading post, now operated by the National Park Service, was founded in 1878 by John Lorenzo Hubbell, who was not only a merchant, but also a friend, teacher, and frequently a doctor to the Navajo people; during the smallpox epidemic Hubbell's home was transformed into a hospital. Hubbell, who died in 1930, is buried not far from the trading post.

The **Thunderbird Lodge** (*see* Lodging, *below*) in Chinle also began as a trading post, built in 1902 by trader Sam Day. Like other trading posts on the reservation, it served not only as a store but also as a bank, post office, community meeting place, and courtroom (with Day serving as sheriff, judge, and jury). On occasion, the lodge was even used as a makeshift hotel and hospital. The original trading-post building, which has changed owners many times over the years, is now part of a much larger facility incorporating a hotel and cafeteria.

Although not a historic building, the **Ned Hatathli Museum** (tel. 520/724–3311), at the Navajo Community College in Tsaile, has an extensive collection of historic Navajo and other Native American arts, crafts, and artifacts. Many of the artwork and handicraft items are for sale. There's also a cafeteria, open to the public. The museum is free and is usually open weekdays from 8 to 5, but call ahead to check the times.

NATURE TRAILS AND SHORT WALKS The only inner canyon trail at Canyon de Chelly that visitors may explore without a guide is the well-maintained, 2.5-mi round-trip **White House Trail** from the White House Overlook to the White House Ruin. The moderately difficult trail descends to the canyon floor 600 ft below. Hikers should be prepared to wade across Chinle Wash. Rangers and Navajo guides are emphatic about protecting the canyons: Visitors are cautioned not to pick up or remove any objects and not to sit on the walls of canyons or ruins. Be sure to carry water.

There is a .5-mi round-trip walk to the overlook at **Spider Rock**, at the end of the South Rim Drive, with many scenic vantage points. Hikers may do this without a guide. The hike takes about 10 minutes. Brochures are available at the visitor center.

LONGER HIKES Hikers interested in making longer treks into Canyon de Chelly's backcountry must do so with a hired guide (*see* Guided Tours, *above*). There are no consistently marked trails in the park—only undesignated treks through the stark yet stunning, high-desert canyon country.

CHILDREN'S PROGRAMS All activities and programs at Canyon de Chelly are family oriented. Check the bulletin board at the visitor center (tel. 520/674–5500 or 520/674–5501) for specially scheduled children's activities. A Junior Ranger activity sheet is available for children, who may check off the plants, animals, and overlooks they see during the day, then turn in the completed sheet at the visitor center to get a certificate confirming their accomplishment.

EVENING ACTIVITIES The nightly 9 PM campfire program at the Campground Amphitheater is devoted to a different subject each night; topics include Navajo history, rock painting, and Anasazi culture. Check at the visitor center, the Thunderbird Lodge, or on the campground bulletin board for schedules.

DINING

There is very little of what might be considered fine dining in Canyon de Chelly country. The best restaurant in the region is also the newest: Garcia's, in the lobby of the Holiday Inn Canyon de Chelly (*see* Lodging, *below*), is low-key by big-city standards, but serves well-prepared versions of Native American dishes and good fish, pasta, and meat entrées. The restaurants in the town's other two motels (*see* Lodging, *below*) serve hearty, basic American-style cuisine and some Native American specialties such as fry bread and Navajo stew. Otherwise, only fast-food establishments are available. These include **Taco Bell** (tel. 520/674–5376) and **Burger King** (tel. 520/674–3700), both in the Tseyi' Shopping Center on Highway 191 in Chinle. **Bashas** supermarket (tel. 520/674–3464 or 520/674–3465), in the same complex, has a deli section; sandwiches, salads, fried chicken, and other dishes may be carried to a small upstairs lounge with booths and tables.

Note: The possession and consumption of alcoholic beverages is illegal at Canyon de Chelly and everywhere else on the reservation.

LODGING

There is only one lodging inside the park. Outside the park there are only two other motels, and one smaller, traditional Navajo lodging.

INSIDE THE PARK **Thunderbird Lodge.** Ideally located at the mouth of Canyon de Chelly, in a grove of cottonwood trees .5 mi southwest of the visitor center, this National Park Service–authorized hotel and restaurant traces its history to the turn of the century; its stone and adobe units match the architecture of the site's original trading-post building, now part of the Thunderbird's cafeteria. The large air-conditioned guest rooms have ceilings of exposed, hand-hewn beams, rustic wood furniture, and Native American decor throughout. Southwestern and Native American motifs are also found in the smoke-free cafeteria, where inexpensive American fare—from soups and salads to complete chicken and steak meals—are served along with such Native American dishes as heaping Navajo tacos. *Box 548, Chinle, AZ 86503, tel. 520/674–5841, 520/ 674–5842, 520/674–5843, or 800/679–2473; fax 520/674–5844. 72 rooms. Facilities: cafeteria. AE, D, DC, MC, V. $$$*

NEAR THE PARK **Best Western Canyon de Chelly Inn.** This low-slung Spanish-tile-roof motel has attractive rooms decorated in shades of turquoise and terra-cotta, with solid oak furnishings and Navajo art prints and patterns on drapes and bedspreads. All have air-conditioning, cable TV, clocks, and coffeemakers. Plain but tasty versions of American, Navajo, and Mexican dishes share the menu at the motel's casual, inexpensive Junction Café, frequented by Chinle locals. *Hwy. 64, .25 mi east of U.S.*

191, Box 295, Chinle, AZ 86503, tel. 520/ 674–5875 or 800/327–0354, fax 520/674-3715. 102 rooms. Facilities: restaurant, indoor pool. AE, D, DC, MC, V. $$$

Coyote Pass Hospitality. This unusual lodging, a roving bed-and-breakfast run by the Coyote Pass clan of the Navajo Nation in Tsaile, isn't for everyone: Guests sleep on bedding on the dirt floor of a hogan (the location depends on the season, but most are near the Canyon de Chelly), use an outhouse, and eat a Navajo-style breakfast— blue corn pancakes and herbal tea, for instance—prepared on a wood-burning stove. But for those who don't mind roughing it a bit, this is a rare opportunity to be immersed in a Native American culture in beautiful surroundings. Guided hikes, nature programs, and other meals are optional. Rates for lodging are $85 for the first person, $10 for each additional person (maximum group size 15). *Contact Will Tsosie Jr., Box 91B, Tsaile, AZ 86556, tel. 520/724–3383 or 520/724–3258. 12 hogans for up to 15 people. No credit cards. $$$*

Holiday Inn Canyon de Chelly. Opened in late 1992, the newest lodging near Canyon de Chelly is less generic than one might expect: This territorial-style, Navajo-staffed complex is built on the site of a former trading post and incorporates part of the historic structure. Rooms, on the other hand, are predictably pastel-toned and contemporary. Service is a bit erratic in the attractive lobby restaurant, but the food more than compensates. The lobby gift shop sells some outstanding Navajo crafts. Native American dance and music shows take place here when weather permits. *BIA Rte. 7, Box 1889, Chinle, AZ 86503, tel. 520/ 674–5000 or 800/234–6835, fax 520/674-8264. 108 rooms. Facilities: restaurant, pool. AE, D, DC, MC, V. $$$*

CAMPING

There are two camping facilities in Canyon de Chelly National Park, which, remember, is part of the Navajo Reservation. Because of the rough, rugged terrain and the fact that visitors are not permitted to wander without a seasoned guide, camping in the backcountry is both illegal and foolhardy.

Near the visitor center is **Cottonwood Campground** (tel. 520/674–5500), which has 95 RV and tent sites, all free. The campground is open year-round, but running water is available only from April through October. Each site has a fire grate and picnic table, and a disposal station is open from April through October. Campground hosts are on duty in summer only.

Campsites at Cottonwood are available on a first-come, first-served basis; during the busy summer months you should try to arrive by early afternoon to be assured of a space, particularly if you have an RV. There is a five-day maximum stay for campers. Group sites, in which RVs are not allowed, can be reserved 90 days in advance for a maximum of three days. Campers are advised to bring their own fuel. Fires are permitted only in the available grills; no open-ground fires are permitted in the campground.

The relatively new **Spider Rock Park & Camping Too** (tel. 520/674–8261) is on the South Rim Drive near the Spider Rock overlook, about 10 mi east of Chinle (you'll see a sign for it on the road). The setting—a wooded area, is more scenic than that of Cottonwood. As the campground develops, the owner expects to put in 50 RV hookups with water and electricity and a dump station; a cable connector with satellite and a convenience store are possibilities, too. There are currently 45 tent sites with fire pits and picnic tables; another 10 to 15 will likely be added. Rates run about $9 to $12 for tent sites, $19 to $28 for RV sites. Reservations are accepted.

Carlsbad Caverns National Park
New Mexico

Updated by Clare Hertel

he huge subterranean chambers, fantastic rock formations, and delicate mineral sculptures of Carlsbad Caverns National Park draw about three-quarters of a million people each year to a remote corner of southeast New Mexico. Although the park is in the Chihuahuan Desert foothills, near the rugged canyons and peaks of the Guadalupe mountain range and the piñon and ponderosa pines of Lincoln National Forest, the most spectacular sights are all below the earth's surface, with such evocative names as the Green Lake Roo, the King's Palace, the Devil's Den, the Monarch Room, the China Wall, and Iceberg Rock. Here are delicate aragonite crystals, and massive stalactites and stalagmites; the deeper you go, the more your mind soars.

This cave system, millions of years in the making, is one of the world's largest and most impressive, but it was rediscovered only in the last century. Pictographs near the cave entrance tell us that Native Americans took shelter in Carlsbad Cavern more than 1,000 years ago, but archaeologists doubt they ventured in very far: Access to the depths was limited, and the tribe may have believed that the dwellings of the dead lay below.

It wasn't until the 1880s that nearby settlers, curious about the huge numbers of bats they saw in the area, rediscovered the caves. In the early 20th century, the caves were mined for bat guano (dung), which was used as fertilizer. It was one of the guano miners, Jim White, who explored the caves and began telling people about this amazing underground universe.

White brought a photographer, Ray Davis, to bear witness to his extravagant claims for the place. Displayed in the nearby town of Carlsbad in 1915, Davis's black-and-white pictures astounded people and heightened interest in the caverns. White became a tour operator, taking people down 170 ft in a bat-guano bucket, lighting their way with kerosene lamps.

In the early 1920s, the folks in Washington became convinced that this natural wonder should be checked out, and in 1923 inspector Robert Holley was dispatched by the U.S. Department of the Interior to investigate. His report was instrumental in getting Carlsbad Caverns declared a national monument later that year by President Calvin Coolidge. The area was designated a national park in 1930.

Carlsbad Caverns National Park was much in the news early in 1991 when Emily Davis Mobley, an expert caver, broke her left leg some 1,000 ft underground while mapping what is now known as Lechuguilla Cave. It took rescuers four days to carry, lift, and pull her over gaping pits and narrow passageways to safety, while the world held its breath. Of course, unless you're an expert on an approved expedition, you won't be allowed to explore the same route or even anything like it. Of the 85 caves in the park, only three—Carlsbad Cavern, Spider Cave, and Slaughter Canyon Cave (formerly called New Cave)—are open to the public.

ESSENTIAL INFORMATION

VISITOR INFORMATION Contact the **Carlsbad Caverns National Park** (3225 National Parks Hwy., Carlsbad, NM 88220, tel. 505/785–2232). Other sources of information on the area surrounding Carlsbad are **Guadalupe Mountains National Park** (HC 60, Box 400, Salt Flat, TX 79847, tel. 915/828–3251), **Lincoln National Forest** (Guadalupe Ranger District, Federal Bldg., Room 159, Carlsbad, NM 88220, tel. 505/885–4181), **Living Desert State Park** (Box 100, Carlsbad, NM 88220, tel. 505/887–5516), **Brantley Lake State Park** (Box 2288, Carlsbad, NM 88220, tel. 505/457–2384), and **Carlsbad Chamber of Commerce** (302 S. Canal St., Carlsbad, NM 88220, tel. 505/887–6516).

All hikers are advised to stop at the visitor-center information desk for current information about trails; those planning overnight hikes must get a free backcountry permit. Trails are poorly defined but can be followed with a topographic map.

FEES There is no fee to enter the above-ground portion of the park, but to descend into Carlsbad Cavern or lantern-lit Slaughter Canyon Cave costs $6. Interpretive headsets for self-guided tours (*see* Orientation Programs, *below*) cost an additional $3. The fees for scheduled, guided trips into other undeveloped cave areas range from $4 to $12 a person; reservations are required.

PUBLICATIONS The **Carlsbad Caverns–Guadalupe Mountains Association** (Box 1417, Carlsbad, NM 88221-1417, tel. 505/785–2232, ext. 483), a nonprofit, educational organization, sells a number of books, maps, posters, and booklets. The association is open to public membership ($25 annual dues); members receive a 15% discount on all purchases, special discounts on seminars, and a quarterly newsletter.

Visitors planning a trip to Carlsbad Caverns should find the following books of particular interest: *Bats of Carlsbad Caverns* (30 pages, with color photos), by noted bat researchers Dr. Scott Altenbach and Dr.

Ken Geluso, along with cave expert Ronal Kerbo, examines the bat phenomenon of the area, shedding light in dark places; *Carlsbad Caverns: Silent Chambers of Timeless Beauty* (32 pages, with color photos), by former park naturalist John Barnett, covers the history, geology, and surface features, as well as the underground features, of Carlsbad Caverns National Park; *Stories from Stone* (42 pages, with color photos), by geologist David Jaganow and writer Rebecca Jaganow, tells about the geography of the Guadalupe Mountains and Carlsbad Caverns; *Caves Beyond* (238 pages, with black-and-white photos), by Joe Lawrence, Jr., and Roger W. Brucker, takes a look at famous caves throughout the United States; *Speleology* (150 pages, with black-and-white photos), by George W. Moore and G. Nicholas Sullivan, is a general guide to cave exploring. If bats hold your interest and you want a simple introductory souvenir of your visit to Carlsbad Caverns, the first two books listed should fill the bill. Readers seeking a more detailed examination of caves and cave exploring will find the latter books compelling.

The association also publishes *Captain Reef,* a 12-page quarterly covering Carlsbad Caverns as well as nearby recreational areas, and produces "The Spirit of Exploration," a 52-minute video, as well as a CD-ROM called "The Caverns." The video and CD-ROM cost $19.95 each; contact the association (*see above*) for copies.

GEOLOGY AND TERRAIN The vast cave system that comprises Carlsbad Caverns National Park owes its existence as much to slow drips and accretions as to cataclysmic events. Its origins go back some 250 million years, when 400-mi-long Capitan Reef formed around the edge of the warm, shallow sea that once covered this region. After its connection to the ocean to the southwest was cut off, the sea evaporated and the reef was buried until a few million years ago, when it was slowly pushed above the surface to form a part of the Guadalupe Mountains. Over the millennia, huge cavities formed when acidic groundwater slowly dissolved the soft limestone and dolomite of which the reef was made. The dissolved limestone, in turn, was deposited on the ceilings of these vast rooms as carbon dioxide in the mineral-laden drops of water escaped into the cave air. These limestone deposits grew into great hanging stalactites, and, over time, massive stalagmites and other more delicate formations—cave pearls, draperies, popcorn, and lily pads—also formed.

FLORA AND FAUNA Occasionally, raccoons or ringtail cats may wander into the caverns, but, below ground, Mexican free-tail bats rule the roost. They share their spacious home with other species but not ones that most visitors would want to contemplate—generally, arthropods and crawling insects. (The bats, who dine out every evening, prefer the flying kind.) Human misconceptions about bats, along with the use of pesticides, have helped cause some species—there are more than 900—to become endangered, but the fact is, few of these flying mammals are rabid and their unique echolocation system enables them to avoid people. Scientists have not yet figured out how a bat hanging upside down in a dark cave knows when to fly out.

Some algae grows around the entrance to the caves and around the electric lights, but most plants need more light and moisture than caves provide. It is the inanimate, intricately shaped, and often beautifully colored mineral formations that are the natural attractions in this subterranean world.

Above ground, the park's terrain varies with its many elevation levels, so vegetation is diverse. Texas black walnut, oak, desert willow, and hackberry proliferate along the canyon bottoms. Desert plants, such as yucca, agave, sotol, sticklike branches of ocotillo, and clusters of sparse desert grass, grow within the ridges and walls of the canyons. Plants—even clumps of grass—stand far apart in the desert so that their roots will not compete for water. Higher up, piñon pine, juniper, ponderosa pine, and Douglas fir dominate.

Animals that scamper about or roam the area at a more leisurely pace include raccoon, skunk, rabbit, fox, gopher, mice, porcupine, mule deer, coyote, and the ever-elusive badger, bobcat, and mountain lion. There are plenty of snakes in the region, including western diamondback rattlers and banded-rock rattlers, but since they are both nocturnal and shy, visitors rarely see them. Snakes generally appear in summer; if you see one, give it a wide berth. More than 330 species of bird come and go at Carlsbad, including the magnificent golden eagle.

WHEN TO GO For most people, weather is not a major factor in deciding when to visit the park. The caves are a constant temperature year-round: 56°F in Carlsbad Cavern and 62°F in Slaughter Canyon Cave. Above ground, the climate of the park is semiarid, with hot summers and mild winters. The sun shines most of the time, and humidity is generally low.

If you're interested in hiking the backcountry, summer days may be too hot, with high temperatures from mid-May through mid-September almost always exceeding 90°F and frequently climbing over 100°F. Even during the hottest periods, however, nights are comfortably cool.

Winters are dry and sunny, with January, the coldest month, averaging daylight shade temperatures of 58°F.

You'll avoid the crowds if you come between late September and early May, except during the Christmas, New Year, and Easter holiday periods. Hiking will be the most comfortable during those months, but you may miss the bats, which winter in Mexico. Their nightly (around sunset) forays and dawn returns en masse begin in May and usually continue through October. The nightly ranger bat flight program at the cave entrance is one of the highlights of a visit to Carlsbad Caverns.

SEASONAL EVENTS August: It's not exactly the swallows returning to Capistrano, but usually on the second Thursday of August each year, early risers gather at 5 AM for a

Bat Flight Breakfast at the entrance to Carlsbad Cavern. More than 400 bat fanciers may show up to watch tens of thousands of bats return from a night out feeding on insects and fly back into a black hole that descends steeply into the ground. Park rangers are on hand for a talk and to answer questions. The bats' homecoming may be viewed each morning (although there is no formal program) from mid-May through October, but the breakfast is a once-a-year affair. For additional information, contact Superintendent, Carlsbad Caverns National Park (*see* Visitor Information, *above*).

WHAT TO PACK The temperature inside Carlsbad Cavern remains at a constant 56°F, but it's damp, so a sweater or flannel shirt and slacks rather than shorts are recommended. Comfortable, nonskid shoes are essential. Because of the moisture, the underground walkways are slippery. Slaughter Canyon Cave is a bit warmer (a constant 62°F) but even more rugged: If you're planning to do some serious caving, take strong-grip hiking shoes. In addition, anyone wishing to visit Slaughter Canyon Cave must bring along a flashlight and water.

GENERAL STORES In 1927 Charlie L. White (no relation to explorer Jim White) established White's Cavern Camp 7 mi from the entrance to Carlsbad Cavern as a convenience to the ever-growing number of tourists who were coming to the area to see the spectacular cave. Now known as White's City, this is the best place to find lodging, food, and shopping facilities near the park. The small **White's City Grocery Store** (tel. 505/785–2291) sells camping supplies as well as groceries and sundries and is open daily year-round, from 7 AM to 8 PM, and from 7 to 10 during summer.

You'll have a better selection, however, if you head 20 mi north to the city of Carlsbad, which has a large variety of supermarkets and general stores. Among them are **Albertson's** (808 N. Canal St., tel. 505/885–2161), which is open daily from 6 AM to 11 PM; **Furr's** (809 W. Pierce, tel. 505/887–3333), open daily from 7 AM to 10 PM; **Thriftway** (1301 S. Canal St., tel. 505/887–5514), open from 7 AM to 10 PM; and **IGA Foodliner** (609 S. Canal St., tel. 505/887–3074), open Monday through Saturday from 8 to 8 and Sunday from 9 to 6.

ARRIVING AND DEPARTING The one entrance to Carlsbad Caverns National Park is 27 mi southwest of Carlsbad, New Mexico, on U.S. 62–180, in the southeastern part of the state. The park is 35 mi north of Guadalupe Mountains National Park, about 250 mi from Big Bend National Park, and 210 mi from Pecos National Historical Park.

By Bus and Van. TNM&O (tel. 505/887–1108) provides bus service to the town of Carlsbad, but not to the park. **Silver Stage** (tel. 800/522–0162) runs buses into the park from El Paso and Midland Texas Airports, via the town of Carlsbad; reservations are required. No bus service is available to the park.

By Car and RV. There are two major routes from Albuquerque to Carlsbad Caverns. For the 5½-hour scenic route, drive south on I–25 for about 77 mi, exit onto U.S. 380 East, and continue for 165 mi to Roswell. There switch to U.S. 285 and go south directly to the town of Carlsbad, about 75 mi from Roswell (a total of 320 mi from Albuquerque). The last part of the drive is monotonous, with miles of uninterrupted flat, scrubby brush as far as the eye can see, but the U.S. 380 leg through the Valley of Fire lava flows and the hilly Lincoln National Forest offers some dramatic scenery. You can stop in the historic towns of Capitan (home of Smoky Bear State Park) and Lincoln, where the Lincoln County War was centered.

For a shorter but less scenic route, take I–40 east of Albuquerque to Clines Corners, then U.S. 285 south to Carlsbad. Watch for pronghorn antelope grazing near the highway. A third option is to detour to El Paso, Texas, then continue through the Guadalupe Mountains another 147 mi on U.S. 180 to Carlsbad Caverns. Eighty-four miles northwest of Pecos, Texas, Carlsbad can also be reached via U.S. 285.

By Plane. Albuquerque International Airport, 380 mi north of Carlsbad, is the gateway to New Mexico and is served by most major airlines. Air shuttle service via **Mesa Airlines** (tel. 505/885–0245 or 800/637–2247) connects to Cavern City Air Terminal in Carlsbad. There are five flights daily Monday through Friday, two flights on Saturday, and two on Sunday. Flying time aboard the 19-passenger Beechcraft 1900s is about 60 minutes. The highest fares are $159 one way, $310 round-trip, but discount fares are available on advance ticket purchases.

Carlsbad car-rental agencies include **Hertz** (tel. 505/887–1500) at Cavern City Air Terminal and **Enterprise Rent-a-Car** (tel. 505/887–3039). Taxi transfers from the Carlsbad airport are also available via **Carlsbad Transit** (tel. 505/887–2121) and **Cavern City Cab Company** (tel. 505/887–0994).

By Train. The closest city to Carlsbad served by **Amtrak** (tel. 800/872–7245) is El Paso, Texas, 147 mi away. Car rentals are available at the airport, which is roughly 20 minutes from the train station. Try **Alamo** (tel. 800/327–9633), **Hertz** (tel. 800/654–3131), or **Budget** (tel. 800/527–0700).

EXPLORING

Without a car you'll be limited in what you can do in the park. Hikers have lots of scenic—if rugged—backcountry trails to choose from, but those who wish to get to Slaughter Canyon Cave from Carlsbad Cavern without a car or bicycle are out of luck: It's a 25-mi trek across flat, unshaded terrain.

You can easily see what most people come to see, Carlsbad Cavern, in one day, but it would be a pity not to explore other sites in this unique area. Plan to spend a couple of days hiking the park trails or visiting one of the nearby natural attractions: Guadalupe Mountains National Park, Lincoln National Forest, Living Desert State Park, or Brantley Lake State Park (*see* Visitor Information, *above*).

THE BEST IN ONE DAY Your schedule for the park will be determined largely by the amount of time you want to spend below ground: Caving enthusiasts will be interested in exploring the Slaughter Canyon Cave as well as Carlsbad Cavern, while those who prefer open space have a number of outdoor options.

The trip through **Carlsbad Cavern** is an experience like none other. Whether you take the Natural Entrance Tour, the Big Room Tour, or other guided options, the treks are long, and you may find yourself getting a bit disoriented. The sheer vastness of the interiors are overwhelming, and the proportions seem to shrink and expand. Although you may be tempted to touch the cave's walls and jutting rock formations, heed the ranger's warning against doing so. Oil from the human hand forms a type of waterproofing that inhibits the natural water seepage, and some of the formations are easily broken. Visitors are also warned not to leave the guided pathways. They're not always told, however, that if they wander astray, alarms may quickly summon park rangers. The interior of Carlsbad Cavern is well lighted, but many people seem more concerned about where they're stepping than what's ahead and make much of the trip looking down at their feet. Walk cautiously, but take time to stop and look around.

There are two self-guided tours through parts of Carlsbad Cavern and one guided tour. Each covers about 1.25 mi. The self-guided Natural Entrance Tour leads from the cave entrance along the paved walkway that winds down the Main Corridor of the cavern, passing through a series of underground rooms, including Devil's Den and the Boneyard, and past 200,000-ton Iceberg Rock. The trail can be slick in places, and the grades are fairly steep as you descend to a depth of about 750 ft. The Main Corridor is distinguished by its size: It's more than 1.25 mi long, and parts of its ceiling are 200 ft high. The Natural Entrance Tour ends at

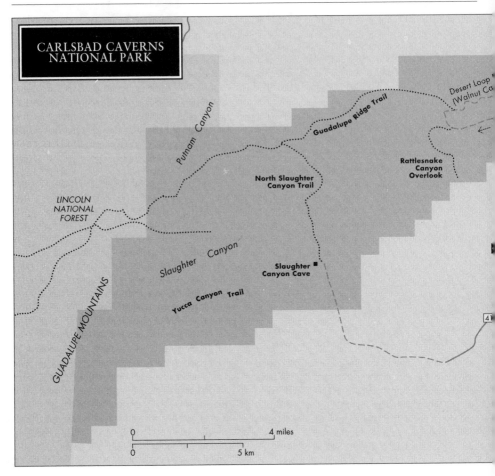

CARLSBAD CAVERNS
NATIONAL PARK

the base of the high-speed elevator, which is where the self-guided Big Room Tour and the guided King's Palace Tour (*see below*) begin (you can take the elevator down from the visitor center to start here).

On the Big Room Tour, you walk around the T-shape Big Room, which has a floor area equal to that of 14 football fields. The ceiling is as high as 255 ft; the White House could fit in one corner. The room has many cave formations—stalagmites, stalactites, columns, draperies, and flowstone—and such natural phenomena as Mirror Lake and the Bottomless Pit. This is a circular tour.

The King's Palace Tour, which leaves from (and returns to) the underground lunch room, is a 90-minute guided walk through four rooms with beautiful formations: the Green Lake Room, the King's Palace, the Queen's Chamber, and the Papoose Room. These tours generally leave daily at 9, 11, 1, and 3, but there are sometimes as many as six tours per day during the busy summer season. Be sure to call ahead at least a month in advance to reserve a spot on any of the guided tours.

No matter which tour or tours you choose, you should be able to stop at the gift shop and exhibit displays by late morning. In the afternoon, take a picnic lunch to **Rattlesnake Springs** (don't let the name scare you—rattlesnakes are rarely seen there). To

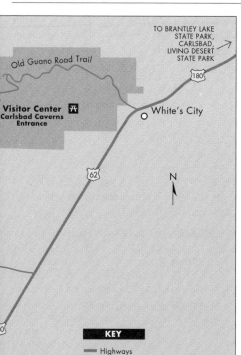

TO BRANTLEY LAKE
STATE PARK,
CARLSBAD,
LIVING DESERT
STATE PARK

Old Guano Road Trail

180

Visitor Center
Carlsbad Caverns
Entrance

White's City

62

N

80

KEY

— Highways
— Minor Roads
– – Unpaved Road
····· Trail
🏠 Ranger Station
🏕 Picnic Area

Canyon Cave after lunch (you must make a reservation several weeks in advance). This rugged cave is 23 mi from Carlsbad Cavern and much less accessible: You'll have to provide your own transportation to get there. The last few miles of the roadway that leads to the cave are gravel, and the mouth of the cave is a .5-mi climb up a 550-ft rise. It takes about 45 minutes to walk to the entrance from the parking area. Tours begin at the cave entrance and not the parking area, so plan your time accordingly. Reservations are required for the two-hour ranger-led tour (tel. 505/785–2232, ext. 429); children under six are not permitted. You'll need to bring along your own flashlight, hiking boots or good walking shoes with rubber soles (sneakers are not recommended), and drinking water. Tours take place daily in summer but only on weekends during the winter season.

Slaughter Canyon Cave, in remote Slaughter Canyon, was not discovered until 1937, when Tom Tucker, a local goatherd, came across it. Because it was discovered later than Carlsbad Cavern, it was for many years called New Cave at Slaughter Canyon. The name was eventually shortened to New Cave, but in 1992 the park service began calling it Slaughter Canyon Cave to avoid confusion with such other "new"—that is, unexplored—caves as Lechuguilla Cave.

Slaughter Canyon Cave consists primarily of a single corridor, 1,140 ft long, with numerous side passages. The lowest point is 250 ft below the surface. Outstanding formations are Christmas Tree, the Monarch Room, Klansman, Tear Drop, and the China Wall. Photographs are permitted, but no tripod setups are allowed since the group moves along at a relatively brisk pace, and you *really* wouldn't want to be left behind (the cave is so dark that the flick of a cigarette lighter has been known to cause temporary blindness). Unless you're in good physical shape, with a long attention span, Slaughter Canyon Cave may be more cave-peeping than you bargained for.

get there take Highway 62–180 from White's City 5 mi south and turn onto Route 418, traveling 3 mi west. It's about 25 minutes by car from the visitor center. Rattlesnake Springs has a pleasant picnic area with shade trees, grass, tables, water, and grills. Close to the Black River, this spring was a source of water for Native Americans hundreds of years ago. Army troops exploring the area used it as well, and it was also the site of a Civilian Conservation Corps camp. Today it's the main water source for all the park facilities, and a favorite spot for bird-watchers.

If you have an appetite for more underground adventure, head for **Slaughter**

If you'd like to stay above ground, you can get a bit of exercise after lunch by taking the self-guided .5-mi **Desert Nature Walk** (*see* Nature Trails and Short Walks, *below*). Afterward, if you don't want to venture too far afield, take the 9.5-mi **Walnut Canyon Desert Drive** (*see* Scenic Drives and Views, *below*), which starts near the visitor center. Another good option for the afternoon is the nearby **Living Desert State Park** (*see* Visitor Information, *above*), atop Ocotillo Hills, about 1.5 mi northwest of the town of Carlsbad (off U.S. 285; look for the signs). Here many plants and animals native to the Chihuahuan Desert live in natural surroundings; among them are mountain lions, deer, elk, Mexican wolves, buffalo, rattlesnakes, and other indigenous species. The park's Desert Greenhouse has hundreds of exotic cacti and succulents from around the world. Admission is $3. It's open daily from 8 to 8 (last entrance at 6:30) between Memorial Day and Labor Day and from 9 to 5 (last entrance at 3:30) throughout the rest of the year.

Whatever you do during the daylight hours, if you visit the park from late May through mid-October, be sure to come back to Carlsbad Cavern to view the **nightly bat flight.** Each evening at about sunset, bats by the tens of thousands go out from the natural entrance of the cave and scout about the countryside for flying insects. They consume them in flight, collectively more than three tons of bugs per night. Because bats, albeit less lovable than furry kittens, are among the most maligned and misunderstood of creatures, park rangers give informative talks about them each evening prior to the mass exodus, sometime around sunset. The time of the bat flights varies over the course of the season, so ranger lectures are flexible as well; the time is usually posted, but if not, check at the visitor center. Lectures are suspended during the winter months, when the bats leave for Mexico.

ORIENTATION PROGRAMS At the visitor center you can rent interpretive headsets ($3) that explain what you'll see on the Entrance and Big Room tours. An exhibit area at the visitor center (tel. 505/785–2232, ext. 446)

features a model of Carlsbad Cavern as well as displays detailing the archaeology, geology, and history of the area. Photos from the guano mining days are fascinating. In addition, a short film on bat flight is shown. This is especially worthwhile if you visit in the winter, when the bats are away, or if you don't plan to be around in the evening to see them for yourself.

Before you embark on your underground adventure, a park ranger gives an orientation talk. And from late May to mid-October, the rangers give nightly interpretive talks on bats (*see* The Best in One Day, *above*).

GUIDED TOURS The King's Palace Tour (*see* The Best in One Day, *above*) is the only guided tour through the developed part of Carlsbad Cavern. It covers four of the cavern's decorated rooms in one hour. In addition, rangers lead a two-hour guided tour of Slaughter Canyon Cave (*see* The Best in One Day, *above*). For the self-guided Natural Entrance and Big Room tours, you can rent interpretive headsets at the visitor center.

Off-trail guided tours of Carlsbad Cavern are offered daily by pre-paid reservation. The tour to Left Hand Tunnel leaves at 9 AM seven days a week; Monday through Friday at 1 it is to Lower Cave, and on Saturday at 1 it is to the Hall of the White Giant. On Sunday at 1 there's a trip to nearby Spider Cave; call the visitor center (*see* Orientation Programs, *above*) for more information and for reservations.

Monthly interpretative explorations of the Chihuahuan Desert organized by the nearby **Living Desert State Park** (tel. 505/ 887–5516) sometimes venture into the Guadalupe Mountains. Near the time you're thinking of visiting, call to find out what special tours are being run.

The Carlsbad Caverns–Guadalupe Mountains Association (*see* Publications, *above*) sponsors a year-round seminar program featuring one- to five-day, in-depth programs on caving, geology, nature photography, bird-watching, and history. Write or call for a free catalog.

SCENIC DRIVES AND VIEWS **Walnut Canyon Desert Drive,** also known as the Scenic Loop Drive, is a 9.5-mi loop that begins .5 mi from the visitor center and travels along the top of the Guadalupe Ridge to the edge of Rattlesnake Canyon, then back down through upper Walnut Canyon to the main entrance road. The trip, along a twisting one-way gravel road, takes about an hour to an hour and a half for a leisurely drive. It's perfect for late afternoon or early morning, when you can enjoy the full spectrum of the desert's changing light and dancing colors. A pamphlet describing this drive is available at the visitor center bookstore.

NATURE TRAILS AND SHORT WALKS Try taking the .5-mi self-guided **Desert Nature Walk** that begins off the cavern entrance trail, 200 yards east of the visitor center, while waiting for the nightly bat flight program to begin. The tagged and identified flowers and plants make this a good place to get acquainted with much of the local desert flora. Take the short (.25-mi) **Rattlesnake Canyon Overlook Trail,** off Walnut Canyon Desert Drive, for superlative views of Rattlesnake Canyon.

LONGER HIKES Backcountry hiking in Carlsbad Caverns National Park can be exhilarating—the desert terrain is stark and awesome—but few trails are as clearly marked as those in other national parks and there is no water, so you'll need to bring plenty: Rangers recommend that you carry from two quarts to one gallon per person for each day hike. Topographic maps, available at the visitor center, are essential on all but the most well-marked trails. Permits aren't required, except for overnight backpacking trips, but all hikers are requested to register at the information desk at the visitor center. If you don't register and you get lost, it's likely that you won't be found for a long time in this little-trafficked area. No pets or guns are permitted. Following is a sampling of some of the most interesting and most easily accessible trails.

Old Guano Road Trail, an abandoned road that runs a little more than 3.5 mi one way, was originally the truck and wagon route that miners used to transport bat dung (a fertilizer) from Carlsbad Cavern to Carlsbad. The first visitors to Carlsbad Cavern also took this route, which follows the escarpment ridge south of the entrance road. Starting at the Bat Flight Amphitheater, the trail affords good views of the eastern escarpment of the Guadalupe Mountains. The terrain is mostly flat but drops sharply down to the White's City campground at the end. Because the trail follows a more direct route, it covers about half the distance of the highway to White's City. Give yourself two to three hours to complete the walk.

The 6-mi round-trip **Rattlesnake Canyon Trail** descends from 4,570 to 3,900 ft as it winds down into the canyon. This trail, which is defined and marked with rock cairns, starts at marker number 9 on Walnut Canyon Desert Drive. Allow three to four hours to trek down into the canyon and make the somewhat strenuous climb out.

The **North Slaughter Canyon Trail** begins at the Slaughter Canyon parking lot and traverses a heavily vegetated canyon bottom into a remote part of the park. As you begin hiking, look off to the east (to your right) to see the magnificent Elephant Back formation, the first of many dramatic limestone formations visible from the trail. The route travels 5.5 mi one way, with the last 3 mi steeply climbing onto a limestone ridge escarpment. Allow six to eight hours round-trip.

Yucca Canyon Trail, about 6 mi round-trip, begins at the mouth of Yucca Canyon, which you'll reach by taking the Slaughter Canyon Cave road to the park boundary, then turning west along the boundary fence line to the trailhead. The trail climbs up to the top of the escarpment, where there are sweeping views of the Guadalupe Mountains and El Capitan. Most people turn around at this point; the hearty can continue along a poorly maintained route that follows the top of the ridge, ascending to elevations that range between 4,300 and 6,150 ft. Along much of the trail you'll see oak, piñon, and juniper, with a sprinkling of ponderosa pine. The first part of the hike takes about four hours round-trip; if you continue on, add another four hours.

OTHER ACTIVITIES For the most part, unless you bring along your own horse, boat, fishing gear, or bicycle, you'll be somewhat restricted in terms of recreational activities in the park.

Back-Road Driving. The 9.5-mi Walnut Canyon Desert Drive (*see* Scenic Drives and Views, *above*) is the only unpaved road recommended by the rangers; a number of people who have taken the Guadalupe Ridge Trail, which heads west along the north edge of the designated wilderness area, have found themselves stranded.

Biking. The park is not a favorite with bicyclists. The entrance road is too narrow and congested for bicycles, and the unpaved Walnut Canyon Desert Drive and Slaughter Canyon Cave roads are narrow and dusty and not conducive to safe and enjoyable riding. Mountain bikers will do no better here: Bikes are not allowed on park trails, and cross-country travel is prohibited.

Bird-Watching. Some 330 bird species have been identified in Carlsbad Caverns National Park. The best place to go birding in the park, if not the entire state, is Rattlesnake Springs, a desert oasis on Route 418, 3 mi off Highway 180–62 and 5 mi south of White's City; the best times of year are spring and early summer. Ask for a checklist at the visitor center, and then start checking: red-tailed hawk, red-winged blackbird, white-throated swift, northern flicker, pygmy nuthatches, yellow-billed cuckoo, roadrunner, mallard, American coot, and green- and blue-winged teals, among others. Another good bird-watching spot is at Oak Springs, west of the visitor center. Ask about the occasional ranger-led bird-watching walks.

Boating. There are no water activities in Carlsbad Caverns National Park, but the Pecos River, which runs through Carlsbad, has been dammed up to form a long, narrow lake in the middle of the town. The upper lake attracts water-skiers and boaters, but no equipment rentals are available.

If you're hauling a boat trailer, you can set your vessel afloat at the upper lake or 12 mi north in **Brantley Lake State Park** (tel. 505/457–2384), where the views are especially dreamy. On late summertime afternoons, dark storm clouds form in the distance over Brantley Lake, and shafts of golden sunlight streak through vivid green trees. The state park has a well-developed campground, boat ramps, a day-use area with a playground, and good fishing most of the year.

Caving. Only three of Carlsbad's 81 caves are open to the public, but 10 backcountry caves may be explored by serious cavers under the park's Cave Management Plan and permit system. Those who have training from one of the chapters (called Grottos) of the National Speleological Society, headquartered in Huntsville, Alabama, should contact the **Cave Resources Office** (tel. 505/785–2232, ext. 363) for more information. Nonaffiliated amateur cavers may catch the weekly ranger-guided trip to Spider Cave or occasionally to an undeveloped area of Carlsbad Cavern; however, these trips are limited in size, so you'll need to call ahead for reservations or check at the visitor center when you arrive.

Fishing. There is no fishing in the park, but Carlsbad's lower municipal lake is popular with anglers, who know that it is stocked with trout in winter. Bass and catfish nibble the lines at **Carlsbad Municipal Beach Park** (no phone) which covers the shores of the river from where it is crossed by the Hobbs Highway Bridge in the south up through the North Canal Street Bridge. Cast off from the fishing dock at **Brantley Lake State Park** (*see above*) for black bass, white bass, walleye, channel catfish, and bluegill. Anyone over 12 must have a New Mexico fishing license, which can be obtained from a local sporting goods store, or any store that carries fishing or hunting equipment. A one-day license costs $8, and a five-day license costs $16. For more information, call the **New Mexico Department of Game and Fish** (tel. 505/841–8881).

Horseback Riding. It's too hot much of the year to make renting horses a worthwhile proposition for area residents. Horseback riding is permitted in Carlsbad Caverns National Park, but there are only limited corral facilities to accommodate those traveling with horse trailers, and the trails are not particularly good for riding. A better place to bring a horse is **Guadalupe Mountains National Park** (tel. 505/828–3251), 55 mi from Carlsbad, which has two visitor corrals, one at Pine Springs, the other at Dog Canyon. Reservations are required. Horseback riding is permitted on approximately 80% of the park's 80 mi of mountain trails, most of which are moderately difficult. For a view of the high country conifer forest, the Tejas Trail is particularly recommended. The El Capitan–Williams Ranch Trail also makes for an excellent ride, with sweeping views of the salt flats and Patterson Hills from the base of El Capitan's sheer cliff face.

Swimming. From early May to Labor Day, lifeguards are on duty at the **Carlsbad Municipal Beach Park** (*see above*). Across the river, at **Pecos River Village** (no phone), there's unsupervised swimming at the lake from Memorial Day to Labor Day. If you don't mind taking an unsupervised plunge, the water at **Brantley Lake State Park** (*see above*) is fine.

CHILDREN'S PROGRAMS A Junior Ranger program is geared toward children ages 4–13. Call the visitor center (tel. 505/785–2232) for information about additional special tours for kids.

The long trek through the cavern is a bit much for little children, and baby strollers are not permitted on the narrow cave trails due to safety considerations. The park no longer has a nursery, but there are baby-sitting services in Carlsbad. Ask your hotel for recommendations.

EVENING ACTIVITIES Aside from the bat flight program at the entrance of Carlsbad

Caverns at sunset (*see* The Best in One Day, *above*), there are no regularly scheduled evening activities in the park. Interpretive programs are given only when a special event, such as a meteor shower or lunar eclipse, occurs.

At **Guadalupe Mountains National Park** (tel. 915/828–3251), ranger programs addressing both the natural and the cultural histories of the Guadalupe Mountains take place nightly from late May through late August, and three or four times a week in the fall and spring.

DINING

Box lunches and other simple fare are available in the underground lunchroom, which is open daily from 8:30 to 5 in summer, and from 8:30 to 3:30 throughout the rest of the year. The park has a full-service restaurant above ground with a similar selection—eggs, pancakes, Mexican dishes, chicken, steak, soups, hot dogs, and burgers, at moderate prices; it's open daily from 8:30 to 6:30, and until 5 in the winter. Nearby White's City and Carlsbad have a good number of eateries, but don't expect haute cuisine; in this part of the country, your best bet is always Mexican.

NEAR THE PARK **Ventanas.** Tour groups frequent this classy but comfortable restaurant inside the Holiday Inn Carlsbad. A semi-exposed kitchen allows diners to watch the chefs as they prepare grilled fresh salmon, filet mignon, and other classics. Or you may sit by the enormous picture windows that look out onto a quiet courtyard where there's patio dining in summer. This is some of the most sophisticated cuisine you'll find in Carlsbad—and the wine list is extensive. *601 S. Canal St., Carlsbad, tel. 505/885–8500. AE, D, DC, MC, V. $$–$$$*

Lucy's. There's not much in the way of atmosphere at this popular, family-owned Mexican restaurant. A large-screen TV blares accompaniment to meals, which are served in the adjoining lounge when the restaurant gets crowded. But the food is fresh, the service is friendly, and it's one of the few places in town that has a liquor license. All the New Mexican standards are available, many of them in low-fat variations. *701 S. Canal St., Carlsbad, tel. 505/ 887–7714. AE, D, MC, V. $$*

Velvet Garter Restaurant and Saloon/Fast Jack's. You can take your pick of these two adjoining White's City restaurants in a pueblo-style building: While Fast Jack's is a casual diner, Velvet Garter offers full service and a more comprehensive menu, including steak, chicken, catfish, shrimp, and Mexican food. True to its name, the Velvet Garter conjures up images of Mae West, with bawdy paintings on the wall, the Carlsbad Cavern in stained glass, and a bar with specialty "Garter" drinks. At Fast Jack's next door, you can enjoy good burgers, 32 flavors of ice cream, and fresh baked pies at either a counter or a booth. Jack White, whose grandfather founded White's City and who owns almost everything in this tiny tourist town, is a Stanford graduate with an electrical engineering degree. He makes sure his restaurant's bank of video games and souvenir slot machines are all in working order. *26 Carlsbad Caverns Hwy., White's City, tel. 505/785–2291. AE, D, DC, MC, V. $–$$*

Cortez. This charming family-owned Mexican restaurant, with an all-brick interior and photo murals of Old Mexico, has been in business for more than half a century. Nothing on the menu costs more than $8. Try the combination plate, fajitas (tortillas stuffed with beef or pork), or sour-cream enchiladas. *506 S. Canal St., Carlsbad, tel. 505/885–4747. No credit cards. $*

LODGING

Although there's a wide choice of motels and other services in Carlsbad, few provide much in the way of charm or individuality. Most are strung out along the highway that leads to the caverns, appropriately called

National Parks Highway. At the turnoff from the highway to the caverns, White's City has three motels, a tent and RV campground, restaurants, a post office, souvenir shops, a museum, and a saloon.

NEAR THE PARK **Holiday Inn Carlsbad.** This Spanish Colonial–style link in the Holiday Inn chain has a pink stucco exterior, red-tile roofs, and portal-style balconies. Rooms are attractively decorated in deep tones from the southwest, with misty blue-and-maroon pattern bedspreads and curtains, light oak furniture, and Native American prints. Those seeking amenities not widely available in the area—key-card security, no-smoking and fully accessible rooms, fitness center, free guest laundry, and spa—might find the slightly higher rates here worthwhile. *601 S. Canal St., Carlsbad, NM 88220, tel. 505/885–8500 or 800/742–9586; 800/465–4329 for reservations. 100 rooms. Facilities: 2 restaurants, pool, playground, meeting rooms. AE, D, DC, MC, V. $$$*

Quality Inn. This two-story, stone-facade property encloses a landscaped patio with a pool and sundeck about as large as an aircraft hangar. Rooms are comfortable, with undistinguished modern furnishings and a king-size or two double beds with bright Native American–design bedspreads. The Cafe in the Park serves breakfast, and the Chaparral Grill Room, a more formal dining room, is open for dinner. The hotel provides free airport shuttle service. *3706 National Parks Hwy., Carlsbad, NM 88220, tel. 505/ 887–2861 or 800/321–2861; 800/221–2222 for reservations. 124 rooms. Facilities: 2 restaurants, bar, sports bar, pool, hot tub, recreation room. AE, D, DC, MC, V. $$$*

Best Western Cavern Inn. A two-story motor inn with southwestern-style rooms, this Best Western is the closest accommodation to Carlsbad Caverns, and is an immediate neighbor of the popular Velvet Garter Restaurant (*see* Dining, *above*). It's a pleasant, friendly place, determined to help you have a good time. Tour groups and families stay here often. *17 Carlsbad Cav-*

erns Hwy., White's City, NM 88266, tel. 505/ 785–2291; 800/528–1234 for reservations. 63 rooms. Facilities: restaurant, bar, café, no-smoking rooms, pool, 2 hot tubs, tennis, playground. AE, DC, MC, V. $$

Best Western Stevens Inn. This is a reliable old favorite, both with tour groups and locals. The brightly colored guest rooms have mirrored vanities and modern furnishings. Some have kitchenettes, some have private patios, and some have both. Buildings are scattered over a landscaped area covering more than a city block. The motel's Flume Room, an elegant local-favorite dining spot, serves steaks and prime ribs. There's also a coffee shop with regional and Mexican specialties, and the Silver Spur Bar and Lounge, where locals go to hear country-western music. The hotel is owned by Carlsbad's former mayor, Bob Forrest, but even knowing him won't get you a table in the Silver Spur on a Saturday night when the Country Heat band is playing. 1829 S. Canal St., Box 580, Carlsbad, NM 88220, tel. 505/887–2851; 800/ 730-2851 for reservations. 202 rooms. Facilities: restaurant, bar, café, pool, playground, laundry. AE, D, DC, MC, V. $$

Carlsbad Travelodge South. Two miles from the airport and one block from the Convention Center in Carlsbad, this three-story motel has rooms decorated in bright desert colors, although the furnishings are generic. Breakfast is free for up to two adults sharing a room and for children under six, and there's a $2 fee for each additional person in the room. There is no restaurant on the premises, but Jerry's restaurant, in the immediate vicinity, serves standard coffee-shop fare 24 hours a day. 3817 National Parks Hwy., Carlsbad, NM 88220, tel. 505/887–8888; 800/578–7878 for reservations. 60 rooms. Facilities: pool, hot tub. AE, D, DC, MC, V. $

Continental Inn. The Continental Inn has simple rooms with matching curtains and bedspreads in colorful southwestern patterns. All rooms have coffeemakers and cable TV. The small grounds are beautifully landscaped and well kept, and rates are about as low as they come in town. The inn is south of Carlsbad on National Parks Highway, 30 minutes from Carlsbad Caverns. 3820 National Parks Hwy., Carlsbad, NM 88220, tel. 505/887–0341. 60 rooms. Facilities: pool. AE, D, DC, MC, V. $

Stagecoach Inn. A shaded playground and picnic area make this motor inn a good choice for people with children. Rooms are generically furnished, but it's close to many of the major Carlsbad attractions and rates are affordable. 1819 S. Canal St., Carlsbad, NM 88220, tel. 505/887–1148. 56 rooms. Facilities: restaurant, pool, wading pool, hot tub, laundry. AE, D, DC, MC, V. $

CAMPING

You will have to hike into the backcountry to set up a campsite within the confines of Carlsbad Caverns National Park, and your site must be far enough from established roadways so as not to be seen or heard.

If you want an RV hookup or a drive-in campsite, you will have to camp outside the park. Public campgrounds include those in nearby Guadalupe Mountains National Park, Brantley Lake State Park, and Lincoln National Forest. In addition, a number of commercial sites are available at White's City.

INSIDE THE PARK You will need a free backcountry permit to camp in Carlsbad Caverns National Park, which has no designated campsites. Permits can be obtained at the visitor center, where you can also pick up a map of areas closed to camping. Campfires are illegal in Carlsbad, but you may use a camp stove. There is no water in the backcountry, so be sure to bring an adequate supply (at least one gallon per person per day).

Use of the backcountry here is presently very light, so you need not worry about crowds. The rugged beauty of Slaughter Canyon, the ridge above Yucca Canyon, and the far western part of the park near Putman Patrol Cabin are attractive destinations for those who have the stamina to reach them.

NEAR THE PARK Twelve miles north of Carlsbad via Highway 285, and another 4.5 mi east via Capitan Reef Road, **Brantley Lake State Park** campground (Box 2288, Carlsbad, NM 88221, tel. 505/457–2384) has 51 sites, all with water and electric hookups. It also has a primitive camping area, where there are no designated sites (just pull off the dirt road wherever you please). The established campground has flush toilets, drinking water, fire grates, showers, a disposal station, a ranger station, and a public phone. The primitive camping area has only chemical toilets. You can swim in the lake at your own risk. Boating is allowed, but rentals are not available. The campground is open year-round; sites cost $11 per night with hookups, $7 per night in developed campground, $6 per night in primitive area. Reservations are not accepted.

You can camp for free almost anywhere you like in **Lincoln National Forest** (tel. 505/434–7200), which abuts the southwest corner of Carlsbad Caverns National Park. At Sitting Bull Falls picnic area (day-use only), you'll find tables, grills, and toilets; this is also the starting point of five hiking trails, including a 2.2 mi round-trip hike to the falls themselves. There are a number of places for dispersed camping in the forest, but none have facilities, so bring water and proper clothing for backcountry camping. Watch your campfire very carefully and make sure it is out before you leave.

In the heart of White's City, the popular **AAA White's City RV Park** (31 Carlsbad Caverns Hwy., Box 128, White's City, NM 88268, tel. 505/785–2291; 800/228–3767 for reservations) has 50 full hookups and 22 water and electric hookups, as well as an open area that can accommodate 40 to 50 tents. There are flush toilets, hot showers, drinking water, barbecue grills, and shaded picnic tables. Guests have access to two pools and two Jacuzzis at nearby motels. Sites cost $16 per night.

The shaded, full-service **Carlsbad RV Park and Campground** (4301 National Parks Hwy., Carlsbad, NM 88220, tel. 505/885–6333) has 95 level gravel sites—85 with full hookups and 10 with water and electric hookups only. For tents there are 41 additional grass sites. The campground has canopied picnic tables, a seasonal indoor swimming pool, laundry, public phone and phone hookups, hot showers, flush toilets, a kitchen, a grocery store, grills, and sewage disposal. There's a professional RV service station next door. Open year-round, this campground charges $19.75 for a site with full RV hookups, $18.75 for one with water and electricity only, and $14.50 for tents.

Windmill RV Park (3624 National Parks Hwy., Carlsbad, NM 88220, tel. 505/885–9761) has 61 RV sites, all with hookups. There are laundry facilities, hot showers, and flush toilets here. In summer, guests use the outdoor pool. Windmill charges $11 per site per night, $1.50 extra for cable TV hookups. It's open year-round.

Run by the town of Carlsbad, the **Lake Carlsbad Campground** (Greene St., Box 1569, Carlsbad, NM 88220, tel. 505/885–4435) is on the Pecos River, about a mile from downtown Carlsbad. There are no designated sites, but half of the camping area is gravel and half is grass. The campground has flush toilets, hot showers, drinking water, picnic tables, and grills. Each car or camper is charged $4.45 per night.

Crater Lake National Park
Oregon

Updated by Donald Olson

f old Mt. Mazama had held its powder some 7,700 years ago, this area in Oregon's southern Cascades might never have rated a national park. Geologists say it was a big mountain, perhaps the highest in the state, but otherwise unremarkable.

As it happens, the great eruption of Mt. Mazama would have made the 1980 eruption of its northern cousin Mt. St. Helens look like a cherry bomb. Mazama spewed out so much debris that, when it was all over, the mountain collapsed. The result is a unique body of crystal-clear water encased in a goblet of a mountain. The park, at 183,224 acres among the smallest in the West, is sometimes derided as having little to it other than the lake, beautiful though it may be. But if Crater Lake lacks the three-ring circus lineup of Yellowstone and Yosemite, it also lacks anything resembling the crowds. About 500,000 visitors annually drink in the sights at Crater Lake, compared to the millions that throng the other parks.

Crater Lake remains an undiscovered gem among national parks, in part because the region is so remote—the nearest major metropolitan area, Portland, is 250 mi away—and in part because the high mountain environment is so unforgiving that little development has taken place. Only on the caldera's south rim is there any development of consequence. But even there, at 7,100 ft, 50-ft snowdrifts have taken their toll. Crater Lake Lodge, built from 1909 to 1915, is one of the most spectacular lodging destinations in the national parks system.

The main attraction in this park is the lake, mesmerizing with its pure blue color and dizzying setting. The first look at its placid, clear waters will take your breath away. The lake is about 6 mi across and 1,000 or more ft below the rim, which ranges from 6,600 to 8,000 ft in elevation. This makes a little shortness of breath only natural. The winds on the rim can be bracing, if not brisk, and the vertiginous heights and sheer cliffs make everyone feel exposed—if you have trouble with heights, think twice before coming here.

Once you descend to the surface of the lake, however, the mood changes. The protective cliffs cradle the lake, and in calm weather its mirrorlike surface is sometimes hauntingly still. At 1,932 ft it's the deepest lake in the United States, and the seventh-deepest in the world.

At times this huge body of water appears to be a giant mirage, as it probably did to the European Americans who first saw the lake in 1853. Out of food at the headwaters of the Rogue River, near what is now the northwestern corner of the park, a party of prospectors set off in search of game. Two of them came up a long slope that simply broke off into space. Beneath them hung this huge, incredibly blue lake. The men continued their search for food, encountering some Native Americans nearby who vehemently denied the existence of any such lake. To them, the lake was sacred, and they believed that anyone with the temerity to gaze into its depths would be struck dead.

Crater Lake lay undisturbed by European Americans for another decade. In fact, the shore of the lake was not reached until 1865. The lake wasn't photographed until 1874, when pioneer photographer Peter Britt's images of the still-unexplored splendors of the West captivated the nation. A 16-year-old Kansas schoolboy named William Gladstone Steel saw an article about Crater Lake in a local newspaper and decided he would journey there and row out to the strange cinder cone now called Wizard Island. In 1885 he did just that, and then he dedicated himself to making Crater Lake a national park.

Bills to preserve Crater Lake were introduced in each Congress and routinely dismissed after lobbying by ranchers, land speculators, and timber tycoons. The battle went on for 17 years. But Steel persevered, and in 1902 he won the conservation-minded President Theodore Roosevelt over to his cause. Crater Lake became the nation's sixth national park.

ESSENTIAL INFORMATION

VISITOR INFORMATION Write to **Crater Lake National Park** (Box 7, Crater Lake, OR 97604) or call 541/594–2211, ext. 402. Free backcountry permits are required for overnight stays in the backcountry. These are available at any information center within the park.

FEES The entrance fee is $10, from May to October; there is no fee for off-season entrance. Hikers walking in and bicyclists without cars pay $5. Note: Oregon Highway 62 passes through the southwest corner of the park, and no fee is charged unless the visitor turns north at the Annie Spring Entrance Station toward the lake.

PUBLICATIONS A handy mail-order catalog of books and maps about the park is available from the **Crater Lake Natural History Association** (Box 157, Crater Lake, OR 97604), as are the following books:

Ron Warfield's *A Guide to Crater Lake National Park—the Mountain That Used to Be* gives a useful and lushly illustrated overview of Crater Lake's history and physical features. The National Park Service uses Stephen Harris's *Fire Mountains of the West* in its ranger training; the detailed handbook covers Cascade Range geology. *Wildflowers of the Olympics and Cascades,* by Charles Stewart, is an easy-to-use guide to the flora and fauna of the Northwest's mountainous areas. For information on the park's natural history, geology, plants, and wildlife, use Jeffrey P. Schaffer's *Crater Lake National Park and Vicinity,* a readable guide with excellent topographic trail maps, or KC Publications' *Crater Lake, the Story Behind the Scenery.*

GEOLOGY AND TERRAIN Crater Lake National Park encompasses about 400 square mi of high alpine meadows, the lunar-looking Pumice Desert, deep canyons, snowy peaks, virgin forests, and, of course, the natural wonder that gives the park its name.

The park straddles the southern Cascade Range and is part of a network of high mountain wilderness areas that stretch from North Cascades National Park in northern Washington to California's Sequoia National Park. The northern third of Crater Lake National Park contains a small, broad plain of volcanic dust called the Pumice Desert. At a 5,000-ft elevation, this very dry and fragile area supports only small ground-hugging vegetation.

Toward the northwest end of the park, on the moister Pacific side of the Cascades, the dry pumice gradually gives way to lush alpine meadows and forests. Here the famous Rogue River begins its 150-mi journey to the sea in a series of springs embedded in a high cliff. Streams such as Crater Creek, Bybee Creek, and Castle Creek in the western section of the park carve deep canyons through pumice and layer upon layer of lava flows. The most dramatic is Castle Creek Canyon, which is filled with mammoth pumice spires 100 ft high. Highway 62 enters the park from the west and passes by Castle Creek on its way toward the rim. On the western edge of the park, south of Castle Creek and Highway 62, Union Creek erupts from a hillside at Thousand Springs.

Union Peak, a 7,709-ft hunk of stone that is actually a volcanic plug, holds sway over the southern part of the park, giving way to a smaller volcanic area known as Pumice Flat and the canyon of Annie Creek, which heads southeast toward upper Klamath Lake. Farther east are the high, wild slopes of Crater Peak and the park's other notable geologic oddity: the Pinnacles.

The Pinnacles are created from fused remnants of ancient fumaroles (holes from which gases can escape). Mt. Mazama's climactic eruption filled the canyons of Annie Creek, Sun Creek, Wheeler Creek, and Sand Creek with hundreds of feet of ash. As hot gases bubbled to the surface, fumaroles were formed, and the material around the holes fused into hardened "pipes" as the superheated gas escaped. Over time, streams caused the erosion of the softer ash material, leaving pillars of heat-tempered ash behind. Now the pillars dot the canyons of the park's southeastern section.

The relatively narrow eastern part of the park is high, wild, and completely undeveloped. Mt. Scott, at 8,929 ft the highest point in the park, is the main landmark in this 45-square-mi section of meadows and pine forests.

In the middle of the park is the lake itself, surrounded by cliffs that range from 500 ft to almost 2,000 ft above the water's surface. South of the rim, you'll see U-shape valleys carved by glaciers that once existed on the ancestral Mt. Mazama.

Other geologic features of note are within the lake itself. Near the western shore is Wizard Island, a 700-ft-high cinder cone that is the product of eruptions that occurred after Mazama's cataclysmic collapse. In the southeast portion of the lake is the Phantom Ship, a tattered, eerie island of basalt that, in certain lights, resembles the Flying Dutchman of maritime legend.

FLORA AND FAUNA An excellent cross section of Cascade Range vegetation and wildlife can be found in Crater Lake National Park. In the higher elevations, the dominant trees are Shasta red fir and mountain hemlock. Lower down are white fir, ponderosa pine, and lodgepole pine, which grows everywhere except in the austere precincts of the Pumice Desert. Around the rim, where harsh winterlike conditions may occur any time of the year, look for whitebark pines, the mainstay of the Cascade and Rocky mountains.

In the high country, growing seasons are very short, but the park is awash in wildflowers. Glacier lilies are the first to appear, breaking through the snowbanks in spring. Western pasqueflowers, which evolve into the white-bearded "old men of the mountain," also flourish by the vanishing snowbanks. Newberry knotweed, lupines, penstemon, phlox, pussy paws, monkey flowers, Jacob's ladders, spreading phlox, forget-me-nots, and bleeding hearts all grow in fissures, bogs, and meadows of the park.

Crater Lake's larger wildlife are a shy lot. Roosevelt elk roam in the southern portion of the park and near Union Peak, and black bears inhabit much of the park. Neither species is often seen by visitors, because the animals tend to stay away from roads and buildings. The Sky Lakes Wilderness, due south of the park, stretches about 40 mi before hitting a road. The Union Creek and Red Blanket Creek canyons are also remote and provide a good haven for the animals. Deer, both mule and black-tailed, are common, as are yellow-bellied marmots and the rabbitlike pika.

Birds also thrive in the park. The most common year-round birds—Clark's nutcracker, Steller's and gray jays, and ravens—are often seen gliding above the rim. Great horned owls, water ouzels, hairy woodpeckers, red-breasted nuthatches, mountain chickadees, golden-crowned kinglets, red crossbills, and dark-eyed juncos are regularly sighted. Hawks—red-tailed, marsh, and goshawks—are found near Mt. Scott, where occasional sightings of bald eagles also occur.

Fish were introduced to Crater Lake in 1888 by William Steel. Stocking continued until 1941. Only two species, rainbow trout and kokanee salmon, remain.

WHEN TO GO Summer here—above 7,000 ft in the Cascades—is a relative thing. Midsummer snowstorms on the rim of Crater Lake are not uncommon. Nor, of course, is the bright, clear December day in the 50°F range.

High season for the park is July and August. From October through July, virtually the entire park closes due to heavy snowfall and freezing temperatures. Although the barometer in the surrounding lower valleys often reaches 110°F in summer, in the higher elevation of the park it is usually a breezy 75°F to 80°F, even during the hottest months. Warm, clear days are the rule for July and August, but because of the elevation, at night the temperature can fall below freezing, even after a day when it has been in the 70s.

The average yearly precipitation at park headquarters is 69 inches. Most of the precipitation comes in winter, spring, and fall and quickly turns to snow, which is the park's main source of moisture. Outside of Mt. Rainier, no other national park receives as much annual snowfall as Crater Lake. In the steeply sloped area, drifts of up to 50 ft are common. A year without at least 10 ft (120 inches) of snow at Rim Village is considered abnormal.

During winter, temperatures range from 20°F to 40°F and rarely fall below zero. The lake seldom freezes. The last hard freeze of Crater Lake occurred in 1949.

WHAT TO PACK As in other high mountain areas, the weather is highly changeable. Always be prepared for sudden storms; pack rain gear, and wear layered clothing. For sightseeing above or on the lake, binoculars are a must.

GENERAL STORES Inside the park, there is only one store, **Camper's Service Store** (tel.

541/594–2255), at Mazama Village, near Highway 62. The store is small, but carries food supplies and such camping necessities as stove fuel and lantern mantels. It is open daily, weather permitting, from June through mid-October. The hours are from 7 AM to 10 PM between July and September and from 8 to 8 in June and October.

There are no other stores within 20 mi of the park. **Diamond Lake Resort** (tel. 541/793–3333 or 800/733–7593), 25 mi north on Highway 138, has basic food supplies and fishing tackle. Daily summer hours are from 7 AM to 10 PM, and winter hours are from 8 to 6. About 25 mi southwest of the park on Highway 62 is **Union Creek Resort** (tel. 541/560–3565), which also stocks staples and fishing gear. The store is open daily year-round. Summer hours are from 8 to 8; winter hours vary month to month.

ARRIVING AND DEPARTING There are three entrances to Crater Lake—the north entrance on Highway 138 and the west and south entrances on Highway 62. The most popular route is Highway 62, which visitors take northeast from Medford or northwest from Klamath Falls. This is also the only road to the park kept open during fall, winter, and spring.

By Bus. There are **Greyhound** (tel. 800/231–2222) bus depots in Roseburg, Chemult, Bend, Klamath Falls, Medford, and Grants Pass, but there is no public transportation to the park from any of those locations. Car rentals are available in Roseburg from **Chrysler Rental Service** (tel. 541/672–6555), in Bend from **Hertz** (tel. 541/388–1535), in Klamath Falls from **Avis** (tel. 541/882–7232), and in Medford from **Hertz** (tel. 541/773–4293) or **National** (tel. 541/779–4863).

By Car and RV. The drive from Medford, Oregon (population 55,000), to the park runs on Highway 62 northeast along the Rogue River, gradually gaining elevation through thick forests. The trip is about 80 mi and takes about two hours. This route provides the quickest access to Rim Village.

To get to the park from Klamath Falls (population 17,000), travel north on U.S. 97 for 30 mi and then pick up Highway 62 traveling northwest for another 25 mi to the park entrance.

The park is about a 2½-hour drive from Bend, Oregon (population 30,000), south along U.S. 97 and west on Highway 138. Those arriving from Willamette Valley to the west or central Oregon to the east can also enter the park via Highway 138. From Roseburg (population 15,000) to the west, this road twists up the canyon of the North Umpqua River skirting the northern edge of the park. A hundred miles (2½ hours) from Roseburg it reaches the north entrance and then continues east to U.S. 97.

From Portland—about 250 mi away—the park is a five-hour drive by one of several routes, most involving one or two mountain passes. The fastest, with the least amount of climbing, is I–5 to Eugene, about 100 mi south of Portland, then east on Highway 58, south on U.S. 97, and west on Highway 138. Crater Lake is about 400 mi, via Portland, from Mt. Rainier National Park. Lassen Volcanic Park is about 300 mi to the southeast, traveling along Highway 62 to Medford and then taking I–5 to Redding, California, and Route 44 east.

By Plane. The closest airport of any size is the **Rogue Valley International Airport** in Medford, 75 mi southwest of the park. Medford has daily service on United and Horizon airlines from Portland, the Bay Area, and points beyond. There is no public transportation to Crater Lake. Car rentals are available at the airport from **Avis** (tel. 541/773–3003), **Budget** (tel. 541/773–7023), **Hertz** (tel. 541/773–4293), and **National** (tel. 541/779–4863).

By Train. The nearest **Amtrak** station (tel. 800/872–7245) is in the town of Chemult (population 250), 43 mi northeast and about 40 minutes away by car. Chemult has no car rentals, however, and no public transportation to the park. Klamath Falls, 57 mi south of the park, has an Amtrak station and car rentals (call Avis, tel. 541/882–

7232) but no public transportation to the park.

EXPLORING

A car and a pair of reliable hiking shoes can get you around Crater Lake quite nicely. The 33-mi Rim Drive encircles the lake, providing access to more than a dozen vistas, some of which are right on the road and others that are less than a mile from the road. Keep in mind, however, that the Rim Drive is usually open only from mid-June until mid-September.

A thorough job of rounding the lake can take up an entire day, although most visitors find a half day more than adequate. Biking the Rim Drive provides more time to observe, but only able bicyclists should make the journey. The road is on average at an elevation of 7,000 ft, and some portions are steep and narrow. The Pacific Crest Trail (which leads from Canada to Mexico) runs along the west rim of Crater Lake. The lake itself can be reached only on foot, and it can be explored only aboard one of the park concession's motor launches. Touring the lake properly is also a full day's job, although many do it in half that time.

THE BEST IN ONE DAY About 90% of the people who visit Crater Lake never actually stick a finger in the lake itself. Why? The main reason is that the lake is only accessible by one very steep, 2-mi round-trip trail: Getting down isn't so difficult, but the climb back up is a deterrent. If you really want to understand the power and scope of the lake, however, make the effort to get down to the water.

To reach the boats, head north from Rim Village along Rim Drive. The road has several excellent views of the lake, with numerous turnouts for picture taking. If you get up very early you should be able to get in one good hike before you reach the boat launch, and that hike should be the almost .75-mi uphill trek to the Watchman, an 8,035-ft precipice with a fire tower at the top. Park in the large parking area at the Watchman

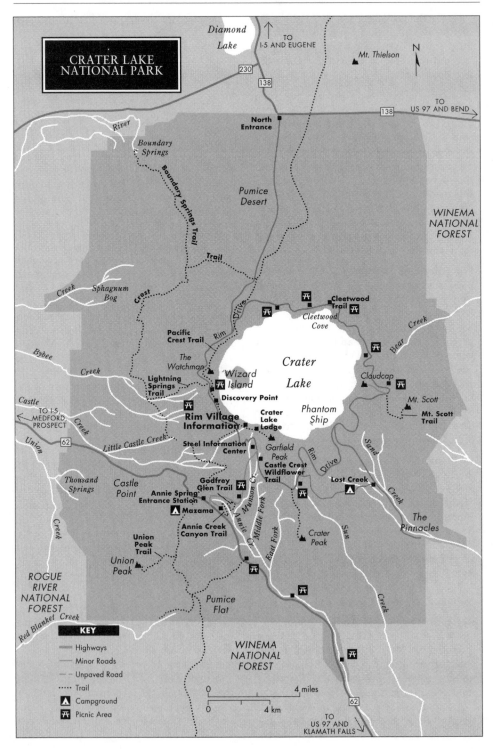

CRATER LAKE
NATIONAL PARK

Diamond
Lake

TO
I-5 AND EUGENE

Mt. Thielson

N

230

138

TO
US 97 AND BEND

138

River

Boundary
Springs

North
Entrance

Pumice
Desert

WINEMA
NATIONAL
FOREST

Boundary Springs Trail

Creek

Sphagnum
Bog

Crest

Trail

Cleetwood
Trail

Cleetwood
Cove

Creek

Bear

Pacific
Crest Trail

Rim

Drive

Bybee

The
Watchman

Crater
Lake

Cloudcap

Creek

Lightning
Springs
Trail

Wizard
Island

Mt. Scott

Discovery Point

Phantom
Ship

Mt. Scott
Trail

Castle

TO I-5,
MEDFORD,
PROSPECT

Rim Village
Information

Crater
Lake
Lodge

Union

62

Little Castle Creek

Steel Information
Center

Garfield
Peak

Rim

Drive

Sand

Creek

Thousand
Springs

Castle
Point

Castle Crest
Wildflower
Trail

Lost Creek

Godfrey
Glen Trail

Creek

Sun

Annie Spring
Entrance Station

The
Pinnacles

Creek

Mazama

Annie Creek
Canyon Trail

Middle Fork

East Fork

Crater
Peak

Union
Peak
Trail

Annie Creek

Union
Peak

ROGUE
RIVER
NATIONAL
FOREST

Red Blanket Creek

Pumice
Flat

WINEMA
NATIONAL
FOREST

62

KEY

Highways

Minor Roads

Unpaved Road

Trail

Campground

Picnic Area

0   4 miles

0   4 km

TO
US 97 AND
KLAMATH FALLS

overlook and look for signs to the Watch-man Trail. From here you can look down 2,000 ft into the lagoon of Wizard Island, where the boat will soon be taking you.

After the hike, continue along Rim Drive, which pulls away from the lake for a few miles, affording views of spirelike Mt. Thielsen, lying just north of the park. The road returns to hug the rim just east of Llao Rock, one of the park's most distinctive features. Picnic areas along here are good for brief stops.

It's an 11-mi, 30-minute drive from Rim Village to Cleetwood Trail, which you must descend to reach the boats. It takes about 25 minutes to walk down the 1-mi trail. Give yourself enough time, and try to catch the first boat, which usually leaves at 10 AM (tour times vary according to the weather and time of year). The boat ride takes about an hour and 45 minutes. You can get off at Wizard Island and spend most of the day hiking, climbing, fishing, and picnicking; the truly intrepid even swim in the incredibly clear, cold, 45°F to 55°F water. If you have the time, it's worthwhile spending at least some time on the island, but remember the last launch leaves at about 4:30 PM. Boat hours are posted, and overnight stays are prohibited.

When you return to the mainland, give yourself at least an hour for the hike out—unless you're in extremely good shape. If you chose not to stay on Wizard Island, it will be early afternoon when you disembark, and you'll have the rest of the day to make it around Rim Drive. From Cleetwood Trail, continue clockwise around the lake.

If you're interested in observing the park from another dramatic perspective, save time for a stop at Cloudcap, a lookout that you can reach via a mile-long spur road at the far eastern end of the lake. From here, Wizard Island and all the postcard views of the lake are several miles away.

Circling back west, you'll reach the 7-mi spur road that leads to the Pinnacles, an area of eerie-looking ash-and-pumice spires. Because the road dead-ends, you'll have to drive the same stretch twice. But hang in there. The Pinnacles and the canyons leading up to them are spectacular, and although many travelers pass them by, you should not. Unfortunately, there are no trails out here.

After viewing the Pinnacles, you'll have to backtrack to Rim Drive and continue west. The road veers away from the lake, climbing behind Garfield Peak just east of Rim Village, at the lake's southern edge. If you have any energy left, trek the 1.75 mi from the old lodge to the top of Garfield Peak, where you'll be rewarded with good views of the entire lake.

ORIENTATION PROGRAMS Ranger-led talks (10 to 15 minutes) on the origins of Crater Lake are presented at the Sinnott Memorial Overlook in Rim Village. A scale model of the lake helps visitors understand the forces at work even today at Crater Lake. Rangers are well prepared to answer questions.

At Steel Information Center (tel. 541/594–2211, ext. 402), adjoining the park headquarters, an 18-minute video shown every half hour introduces visitors to the park. There's some decent footage, but the small screen does little to capture the grandeur of the setting; you may want to avoid it, unless you're unlucky enough to arrive on one of the park's snowy or foggy days.

GUIDED TOURS The most extensively used guided tours in Crater Lake are aboard the lake boats. Run by the park's concessionaire, the launches carry 60 passengers on a one-hour, 45-minute tour accompanied by a ranger. No private boats are allowed on the water, so this is your only opportunity to get a close-up look at the lake.

Depending upon the weather and on how well the boats survived the winter, boat tours usually begin by July 1 and end in mid-September. The first of 10 tours leaves the dock at 10 AM; the last departs at 4:30 PM. The fee is $12.50.

SCENIC DRIVES AND VIEWS The 33-mi **Rim Drive** is the main scenic route, affording views of the lake and its cliffs from every conceivable angle. The drive alone takes over an hour. Frequent stops at viewpoints and short hikes stretch this to half a day. The Rim Drive is often closed because of heavy snowfall from mid-September to early July.

All along Rim Drive are scenic turnouts and picnic areas. Two of the best spots are on the north side of the lake, between Llao Rock and Cleetwood Cove, where the cliffs are nearly vertical.

If you want to walk for your views, the best short hike is to the Watchman. While the hike is less than a mile each way, the trail climbs more than 400 ft—not counting the steps up to the actual lookout.

The only other scenic drive is the 7-mi trip to the Pinnacles, to the southeast, off Rim Drive. The road scoots along the Sand Creek Canyon with its weird volcanic landscape and ends up at the **Pinnacles,** a canyon full of strange-looking spires composed of hardened ash deposits.

NATURE TRAILS·AND SHORT WALKS The three best nature hikes are in the Munson Valley, near the Steel Information Center park headquarters. The .25-mi loop of **Castle Crest Wildflower Trail** is in the upper part of Munson Valley. Park your car at Steel Center, cross the street, and look for the sign pointing the way to the trailhead. The creek-side walk is easy going, and in July the wildflowers are in full bloom. Drive 2 mi farther down the Munson Valley, and you will reach the parking area for **Godfrey Glen Trail.** This 2-mi loop takes you through an excellent example of what geologists term a hanging valley—the place where one valley hangs over a lower valley, with a cliff and a waterfall between them. Deer are frequently seen here, and the flowers are plentiful. The **Annie Creek Canyon Trail,** which sets off from Mazama Campground, is more strenuous but still easy compared to some of the steep rim hikes, such as that of the Cleetwood Trail. The 2-mi loop threads through the Annie Creek Canyon, giving views of the narrow cleft,

scarred by volcanism and carpeted with lichen. This is another good spot to look for flowers and deer.

LONGER HIKES The 2.75-mi **Mt. Scott Trail** takes you to the park's highest point, the top of Mt. Scott, at 8,929 ft. It will take the average hiker 60 to 90 minutes to make the steep uphill trek and about 45 minutes to get down. The trail starts at an elevation of about 7,800 ft, so the climb is not extreme but does get steep in spots. The view of the lake is wonderful, and views to the east and south of the broad Klamath Basin are equally spectacular. Mt. Scott is the oldest volcanic cone of Mt. Mazama.

The **Pacific Crest Trail** extends from Mexico to Canada and winds for more than 30 mi through the park, entering it about a mile east of the north entrance road and shadowing the road along the rim of Crater Lake for about 6 mi. Often called the prime backcountry experience of the park, the trail follows the west side of the rim for about 6 mi, then descends down Dutton Creek to the Mazama Village area. After crossing Highway 62 near Mazama Village, the trail enters the wildest area of the park. It gets steeper as it passes by Union Peak and skirts the wide expanse of Pumice Flat before leaving the park and entering the 40-mi-long Sky Lakes Wilderness Area.

If you're up for a challenge, consider a trip to **Boundary Springs.** The 8-mi one-way trail begins at the Pacific Crest Trail parking lot, just off the North entrance road. There is parking on the road, but you must watch closely for the signs. From here, the trail eases down the gradually sloping northwestern shoulders of the old Mt. Mazama. To the east you'll see the barren Desert Cone and the Pumice Desert. To the west the thick forests begin. The trail angles toward them, ending up at Boundary Springs, one of the sources of the Rogue River. To avoid a long walk back, many hikers arrange to be picked up at Lake West, a small campground outside the park, easily accessible via Highway 230 from the Diamond Lake area.

Beginning at the Pacific Crest Trail about 4 mi south of Highway 62, the poorly maintained **Union Peak Trail** scales 7,709-ft Union Peak in the far southeast corner of the park. Elk herds roam the area, and bears are occasionally sighted. There is no view of the lake from the top, but the vistas west and south to the Union Creek, Red Blanket Creek, and Rogue River canyons are excellent.

OTHER ACTIVITIES Within the park, there is no off-road driving or bicycling because of the fragile alpine and volcanic soils. No private craft are allowed on the lake, no boat rentals are available, and rock climbing is not permitted within the caldera.

Biking. The 33-mi Rim Drive is popular with bicyclists, although no designated bike route exists. The road is steep and narrow in places, and the shoulder is dangerously small, so use extreme caution. No bike rentals are available in the park.

Bird-Watching. Clark's nutcracker and Steller's and gray jays are found throughout the park, and ravens strut and croak near virtually all rim viewpoints. Hawks and bald eagles are sighted on occasion.

Fishing. Fishing is allowed in the lake, but many find it more impractical than pleasurable. A state fishing license is not required. Those who do fish try the area near the boat launch or take poles on the boat tour and fish off Wizard Island. Rainbow trout and kokanee salmon lurk in Crater Lake's aquamarine depths, some growing to monster lunker size. The problem is finding them—or, rather, getting them to find you.

Horseback Riding. Few people ride in the park. There are no stables, and only three trails are open to horses, mules, and llamas: the Pacific Crest Trail, the Lightning Springs Trail, and the Bald Crater Loop. Only pellet-shape feed is allowed; riders must carry enough for their entire stay. A free brochure on park regulations is available at visitor centers.

Ski Touring. Equipment rentals are not available at the park, so visitors must bring their own cross-country skis or rent them from Diamond Lake Resort (tel. 541/793–3333 or 800/733–7593) for $12 a day. There are no maintained trails. Most cross-country skiers follow a portion of Rim Drive as best they can. The road is plowed to Rim Village, but it may be closed temporarily by severe storms.

Snowmobiling. Snowmobiling is allowed only on the north entrance road up to its junction with Rim Drive. Tours are offered by Diamond Lake Resort (tel. 541/793–3333 or 800/733–7593), 25 mi northwest, for $65–$120 per person. You can also rent snowmobiles at the Diamond Lake Resort for $40 per hour, $120 for a half day, or $225 for a full day; a $300 credit card deposit is required. Some adventurous cross-country skiers ride snowmobiles to the remote north rim to ski that area or the large, flat Pumice Desert.

Snowshoeing. Rentals are available at Diamond Lake Resort (*see above*) for $3 a day. Snowshoeing can be difficult in the deep, drifting snow around the rim, but this is still the most popular area in the park for the sport.

Swimming. Swimming is allowed in the lake, but not usually advised. Made up entirely of snowmelt, Crater Lake is very cold—about 45°F to 55°F during summer. The swimming that does take place is in a lagoon on Wizard Island, but even then it's only appealing when the air temperature rises above 80°F.

CHILDREN'S PROGRAMS From late June to Labor Day, Crater Lake offers a Junior Ranger program. Contact the Steel Information Center (tel. 541/594–2211, ext. 402) for details.

EVENING ACTIVITIES During the summer, the park service conducts slide shows at an outdoor amphitheater near Mazama Campground. The shows focus on natural and cultural history and are well attended by overnight visitors.

DINING

If you can't survive without espresso and duck à l'orange, Crater Lake is not the place for you—unless you eat every meal in Crater Lake Lodge's fine dining room. Aside from lodge fare, fast food and picnic supplies are the only sustenance available within the park itself. The park is so isolated that few other dining options exist nearby.

INSIDE THE PARK **Crater Lake Lodge.** With its unsurpassed lake views, the lodge's dining room provides one of the most scenic and romantic dining experiences north of San Francisco. An original fireplace of rustic stone, beamed ceilings, wood floors, and bark-trimmed windows create a timeless ambience. Savor Chinook salmon oven-roasted in olive oil and white wine, filet mignon topped with artichoke hearts, or pork medallions in a brandy cream sauce. The short wine list represents only Northwest wines; local beers are available too. *Rim Village, tel. 541/594–2255. Dinner reservations essential. MC, V. Closed mid-Oct.–mid-May. $$–$$$*

The Watchman. Although it can't compete with Crater Lake Lodge, this full-service dining room is known for good, simple food in large quantities, priced for family consumption. In addition to steak and seafood choices, the Watchman makes a great Lake Majesty (vegetarian patty with sprouts and avocados) and a Mount Mazama Burger (with cheese and mushrooms). For dinner, try the broiled salmon or shrimp stir-fry. *Rim Village, tel. 541/594–2255. MC, V. Closed Sept.–May. $$*

Llao Rock Cafeteria. It's family-style dining at this barnlike cafeteria, where hamburgers and simple sandwiches constitute the bulk of the menu. *Rim Village, tel. 541/594–2255. MC, V. $*

NEAR THE PARK **Prospect Hotel Restaurant.** The dining room of this beautiful old hotel serves hearty food in surprisingly civilized surroundings. Dinners are six courses, with such entrées as rack of lamb and fresh seafood. From 8 to noon on weekends, there's also a champagne brunch where you can customize your omelet. *391 Millcreek, Prospect, tel. 541/560–3664. MC, V. $$*

Diamond Lake Resort. The resort has three restaurants, ranging from a snack bar to an informal dining room. The small, casual ground floor café is a great place for hearty breakfasts and lunches. On the south side of the lake is a standard pizza parlor. Upstairs at the lodge is the rustic Dinner House, where specialties include prime rib and chicken cordon bleu. *25 mi from Crater Lake on Hwy. 138, Diamond Lake, tel. 541/793–3333 or 800/733–7593. D, MC, V. $–$$*

Beckies Café. Beckies is a local institution, serving home-cooked meals to hungry hunters, fishermen, loggers, and park rangers since the 1930s. The trout is excellent, and the tiny café is famous for its succulent huckleberry pie. *23 mi south of park on Hwy. 62, Union Creek Resort, Prospect, tel. 541/560–3563. MC, V. $*

NOT SO NEAR THE PARK The Ashland area, about 80 mi south of the park on Highway 62, has southern Oregon's best dining options, centered around Ashland's Tony Award–winning Oregon Shakespeare Festival. Standouts include: **Chateaulin** (50 E. Main St., Ashland, tel. 541/482–2264), a classic French restaurant with an elegant, romantic, ivy-wall ambience; **Gen Kai** (180 Lithia Way, Ashland, tel. 541/482–9632), the best in Japanese dining; **Thai Pepper** (84 N. Main St., Ashland, tel. 541/482–8058), where fiery and satisfying (if not scrupulously authentic) Thai food is served in a soothing creek-side setting; and **Winchester Country Inn** (35 S. 2nd St., Ashland, tel. 541/488–1113 or 800/972–4991), another classic French restaurant that competes with Chateaulin as Ashland's best, and usually scores higher for imaginative dishes.

PICNIC SPOTS Rim Drive has perhaps a half dozen picnic-area turnouts. While all have good views, they can get very windy. If something a little less spectacular and more peaceful appeals, try some of the spots off the rim proper. The Vidae Falls picnic area on the upper reaches of Sun Creek has an alpine setting, as does a small picnic area between Mazama Village and park headquarters, near the Godfrey Glen trailhead.

LODGING

Accommodations are limited in or near the park. There are fewer than 230 units of any kind within a 25-mi radius of Crater Lake. The good news is that prices are low, especially during the winter.

INSIDE THE PARK **Crater Lake Lodge.** With gleaming woodwork, Craftsman-style furnishings, and geometrically patterned rugs, this 71-room guest lodge is clearly your best bet if you plan an overnight stay. Be sure to request a room on the lake side of the lodge, but don't expect miracles during the busy midsummer season. *Rim Village, Crater Lake 97604, tel. 541/830–8700. 71 rooms. MC, V. Closed mid-Oct.–mid-May. $$$*

Mazama Motor Inn. Near Highway 62, these low-slung four-plexes were built to weather the winter. Rooms are basic with few frills. *Box 128, Crater Lake 97604, tel. 541/830–8700. 40 rooms. MC, V. Closed mid-Oct.–May. $$$*

NEAR THE PARK **Diamond Lake Resort.** Near a mountain lake 25 mi northwest of Crater Lake, this large resort has 40 motel rooms and 10 housekeeping units. The housekeeping units are simple and rustic, while the motel rooms are modern and plain. *Diamond Lake 97731-9708, tel. 541/793–3333 or 800/733–7593. 40 rooms, 10 housekeeping units. Facilities: 3 restaurants, bar, boating, fishing. D, MC, V. $$$*

Prospect Hotel & Motel. This lovely old roadhouse hotel, built in 1889, was brought back from the dead in 1990. Looking like a set from a John Ford movie, it lies 38 mi from the park's west entrance. There are eight smallish (but nice) rooms in the main hotel, where the tariff includes Continental breakfast. The 14 motel rooms out back are

larger and better for people with children. *391 Millcreek, Prospect 97536, tel. 541/560–3664 or 800/944–6490, fax 541/560–3825. 23 rooms. Facilities: restaurant, bar. D, MC, V. $$*

Union Creek Resort. This resort is 3,000 ft lower than Rim Village, and although it gets plenty of snow, the climate is much warmer. The lodge and adjacent cabins were built during the 1930s, and the entire settlement is listed on the National Register of Historic Places. The bulk of the accommodations are in 14 individual cabins strung out behind the lodge. These vary from very small sleeping cabins to larger units with kitchenettes. The nine lodge rooms, paneled in knotty pine, are more colorful, but cramped and sometimes noisy. *Prospect 97536, tel. 541/560–3565 or 541/560–3339. 9 rooms and 14 cabins. MC, V. $–$$*

CAMPING

Crater Lake has two camping areas: the large, 198-site **Mazama Campground,** with flush toilets, hot water, drinking water, showers, laundry facilities, fire grates, disposal station, and public phone; and the smaller, more remote, 16-site **Lost Creek Campground,** with chemical flush toilets, drinking water, and fire grates. Mazama is open from mid-June through mid-October, and sites cost $13 per night. You can camp at Lost Creek from mid-July through mid-September for $10 per night. Reservations are not accepted, but sites are usually available on a daily basis. During July and August arrive early to secure a spot. Call the Crater Lake Lodge Company (tel. 541/594–2255) to check on space availability.

Lost Creek is for tent campers only; RVs must stay at Mazama. About half the spaces at Mazama are pull-throughs, but no hookups are available. The best tent spots are on some of the outer loops above Annie Creek Canyon.

Death Valley National Park
California

Updated by Jennifer Brewer

There is a general misconception that Death Valley National Park consists of mile upon endless mile of flat desert sands, scattered cacti, and an occasional cow skull. Many people don't realize that across the valley floor from Badwater—the lowest point in the Western Hemisphere—Telescope Peak towers 11,049 ft tall. In fact, Death Valley is surrounded by rugged, seemingly impassable mountain ranges. At the park's western entrance, motorists drive from sea level to nearly 5,000 ft in a space of 20 mi.

So dynamic is the Death Valley area that in October 1994, Congress approved the landmark Desert Protection Act, which gave the national monument national park status as well as 1.3 million additional acres of land. The entire valley is now within park boundaries, making Death Valley the largest national park outside Alaska, at just under 3.4 million acres. The new acreage adds waterfalls, a Joshua tree forest, canyons, mountains, and springs that provide a critical habitat for bighorn sheep.

Botanists say there are 900 species of plants here (21 of which exist nowhere else in the world), but at times that's hard to believe. Many plants lie dormant for all but a few days of the year, when spring rains trigger a bloom. The rest are congregated around limited sources of water. Part of the attraction of Death Valley is observing how plants, animals, and humans survive in this extremely harsh environment, one that can quickly become life-threatening.

The air-conditioned auto may have eliminated many of the rigors of a trip through the area, but Death Valley National Park is still a harsh place in an isolated location, and, outside of Furnace Creek, there are very limited facilities. This area has the hottest, driest climate in North America; nights are marked by star-filled skies and howling coyotes.

But in the middle of the desert is the oasis at Furnace Creek, a well-known resort where people come to play golf and tennis, swim, and dine. The atmosphere here is low-key, and many visitors are content to stroll among the palms, relax poolside after a day of exploring, or browse in the souvenir shop at the general store. Warm, dry winters attract a large contingent of senior citizens, who drive their motor homes or pull their trailers to Furnace Creek for stays of up to a month.

Long before the creation of RVs, Furnace Creek was home to four successive American Indian cultures. Last to arrive were the Shoshone, who settled here around 1,000 years ago. In 1849 emigrants looking for the California gold fields accidentally stumbled into the valley, and eventually prospectors came looking for gold and silver. In 1873 borax, the so-called white gold of the desert, was discovered in Death Valley, and its harvesting and mining soon followed. Twenty-mule teams operated from 1883 to 1889, carrying the borax out of the valley, over passes in the Panamint Mountains, and through the desert to the railroad station at Mojave.

In 1882 Bellerin Tex Bennett founded the Greenland Ranch, and in 1888 he sold the property to the Pacific Coast Borax Company, which renamed it the Furnace Creek Ranch. In 1927, in response to growing interest in the area, the company opened the Furnace Creek Inn to provide more luxurious accommodations to travelers. The Fred Harvey Company assumed operation of the inn in 1956 and purchased the property in 1969.

It was officials of the Pacific Coast Borax Company who brought the beauty of Death Valley to the attention of the National Park Service. On February 11, 1933, President Hoover signed a bill creating Death Valley National Monument, and 61 years later, Congress made it a national park.

ESSENTIAL INFORMATION

VISITOR INFORMATION Contact the Superintendent, **Death Valley National Park,** Box 579, Death Valley, CA 92328, tel. 760/786–2331; 760/786–3225 TDD.

Though a permit is not required, those planning to visit the backcountry are encouraged to complete a registration form at the **Furnace Creek Visitor Center,** open daily 8–5. Backcountry camping is allowed in areas that are at least 5 mi from maintained campgrounds, 2 mi from the main paved or unpaved roads, and .25 mi from water sources. Most abandoned mining areas are restricted to day use.

FEES The entrance fee is $10 per vehicle and $5 for those entering on foot, bus, bike, or motorcycle; it covers seven days. Annual park passes, valid only at Death Valley, are $20.

PUBLICATIONS The **Death Valley Natural History Association** (Box 188, Death Valley, CA 92328, tel. 760/786–3285) publishes pamphlets outlining self-guided tours; these cost 50¢ and are available from the association or the bookstore at the visitor center (tel. 760/786–2331). The association also puts out a waterproof, tear-proof topo-

graphical map of the entire park, ideal for backcountry exploration and hiking, for $9.

The bookstore carries other useful publications. One of the most comprehensive guides to the park, with information on its natural and cultural history, is Richard Lingenfelter's *Death Valley and the Amargosa— A Land of Illusion.* The 600-page book covers the valley's evolution from precivilization to the present and includes old maps and pictures of the area. Robert and Barbara Decker's *Road Guide to Death Valley* lists the best vehicle-access areas for sightseeing and picture-taking. The 88-page *Exploring Death Valley,* by longtime resident Ruth Kirk, includes an introduction to the area's geology, accounts of the prospectors' arrival in 1849, and the life of the Shoshone; it also gives information on where to go and what to see. Chuck Gebhardt's *Inside Death Valley* is a comprehensive guide to backroad driving and hiking destinations, with information on the area's geology and history. Gebhardt also wrote *Backpacking in Death Valley,* which has ideas for day hikes and overnight hikes in the valley, with trail descriptions and a discussion of necessary precautions for surviving in the desert. Those interested in the area's natural history should check out Michael Collier's *An Introduction to the Geology of Death Valley,* which provides a detailed account of the area's natural evolution to date in a style that is easily understood.

GEOLOGY AND TERRAIN Part of the Mojave Desert, Death Valley National Park, which covers 3.3 million acres, ranges from 6 to 60 mi wide and measures 140 mi north to south. Elevation within the park ranges from the lowest point in the Western Hemisphere, 282 ft below sea level, near Badwater, up to 11,049 ft, at Telescope Peak. The highest point reached by auto is at the Charcoal Kilns, an elevation of approximately 7,000 ft. Within the park, the Panamint Range parallels Death Valley to the west, the Amargosa Range to the east. Minerals and ores in the rugged, barren mountains turn them a variety of shades, from green to yellow to brown to white to black. Scores of alluvial fans spread across the valley floor, which is composed of alkali flats and sand dunes. Relief from the desert environment can be found around the oasis at Furnace Creek, where warm-water springs support a variety of vegetation, including cottonwoods and palms.

Death Valley is in a vast area geologists call the basin-and-range province. Block faulting and tectonic forces caused part of the land to uplift to form mountain ranges, while adjacent areas dropped to form valley floors. Today, lava and cinder cones are evidence of occasional volcanic activity. The major forces of erosion here are wind and rain, which carve away the soft spots in rocks, creating unusual formations such as Artists Palette and Zabriskie Point (*see* The Best in One Day, *below*).

FLORA AND FAUNA A majority of the plant and animal life in Death Valley is found near the limited sources of water. One seldom-seen mammal here is the bighorn sheep, which spends most of its time in the secluded upper reaches of the park's rugged mountain ranges, finding toeholds and perches on rock faces where there seemingly are none. Other four-footed park inhabitants include bobcats, coyotes, and rodents. The coyotes can often be seen lazing in the shade next to the golf course and have been known to run onto the fairways to steal a golf ball.

The only fish in the park is the pupfish, which grows to slightly longer than 1 inch. During winter, when the water is cold, the fish lie dormant in the bottom mud, becoming active again in the spring. Because they are wary of large moving shapes, you must stand quietly over a pool at Salt Creek to see them. Pickerelweed and salt grass are found in the Salt Creek marsh, and ravens, killdeer, and great blue herons may be sighted near spring sources in some of the canyons.

Between 60 and 100 feral burros, descendants of the miners' stock, still wander the park. Because these burros were overgrazing on the bighorn sheep's habitat, more

than 6,000 of them were removed in recent years. You might also see a kit fox or a desert banded gecko here. The gecko is 3 to 4 inches long and is colored bright yellow and pink with white banding. There are more than 250 bird species in Death Valley, including yellow warblers, kingfishers, hawks, peregrine falcons, Canada geese, and an occasional golden eagle. The best areas to bird-watch are Scotty's Castle and Salt Creek.

Because the park receives an average of less than 2 inches of rainfall per year, most of the low-elevation vegetation is concentrated around the oases at Furnace Creek and Scotty's Castle, where magnolias, palms, and cottonwoods grow. At the higher elevations, visitors will find piñon, juniper, and bristlecone pines. A majority of the park's wildflowers are seen for just a few days each spring, with rainfall and temperature largely determining when they bloom. Several publications help visitors locate various plants and animals within the park. These are available at the visitor center or from the Death Valley Natural History Association (*see* Publications, *above*).

WHEN TO GO Amazingly, an increasing number of visitors come to the park each year during the summer. Death Valley is the hottest place in North America, and they want to see the place at its fiery best.

Some are disappointed if they don't arrive on the hottest day of the year. (In 1972 the Park Service recorded a ground temperature of 201°F.) From May through September, daytime highs are 99.5°F to 116°F. It is not unusual for summertime temperatures, including the overnight low, to remain above 100°F for a week. In December, January, and February, daytime highs are 65°F to 73°F, while overnight lows are 40°F to 50°F.

However, most of the park's 1.25 million annual visitors still come between late fall and early spring, taking advantage of moderate temperatures and the lack of rainfall. Although during these cooler months you will need to book a room in advance, the park never feels crowded.

During the winter, the tops of the mountain ranges surrounding the park are often dusted with snow. Although precipitation in the park averages less than 2 inches annually, rainfall here can be a dramatic occurrence. Because there is little vegetation and the ground is too hard to soak up the rain, flash floods are common; sections of roadway can be flooded or washed away. The wettest month of the year is February, when the park receives an average of .33 inch of rain.

Generally, the air in the park is dry year-round, except during an infrequent storm. The dry air can wick moisture from the body without causing a sweat, so visitors should remember to drink plenty of water. In several places within the park it is possible to drive to an elevation higher than 5,000 ft, where the air temperature is generally 15 to 20 degrees cooler than on the valley floor. Winds are not uncommon, especially at higher elevations at sunrise and sunset. Most facilities within the park remain open year-round.

SEASONAL EVENTS **Early November:** The **Death Valley 49er Encampment Days,** which began as a centennial celebration held in 1949 to honor the area's first European settlers, annually draws thousands of visitors from around the world. The week-long celebration includes art shows, organized seminars and walks, demonstrations, and dances. For information, call the park at 760/786–2331.

WHAT TO PACK The weather here can be extremely hot and dry. Bring a gallon of water per person if you plan to be out all day; and wear plenty of sunscreen. Make sure you have enough cash: There are no banks in Death Valley. In winter months, a sweater or sweatshirt and long pants are often necessary. And although it seldom rains, when the skies open up here, you'll be glad you brought a waterproof jacket.

GENERAL STORES There are two general stores in Death Valley: The one in **Furnace Creek** (tel. 760/786–2345) is open year-round, from 7 AM to 10 PM, and the one in **Stovepipe Wells Village** (tel. 760/786–2387) is open year-round, from 7 AM to 9 PM. Both carry food, sundry items, souvenirs, camping supplies, and film. Prices in these stores are 20% to 50% higher than those in grocery stores in most urban areas.

ARRIVING AND DEPARTING Because transportation is limited within Death Valley, driving is the best way to get around. No trains or public bus routes service the area, although motorized tours are available within the park. Because the park's sights are so distant from each other, having a car is essential. Motorists should bear in mind that gas is available only at Stovepipe Wells, Furnace Creek, Scotty's Castle, and Panamint Springs. Fill up whenever possible. Diesel fuel is available in the park at Furnace Creek; you can also get it in Beatty, Amargosa, Baker, Lone Pine, Olancha, and Pahrump. Entering the park from the north allows visitors to see Scotty's Castle and Ubehebe Crater, the two major draws at the park's northern end, more than 50 mi from Furnace Creek.

By Car and RV. Death Valley is not easily reached by car. When choosing a route, keep in mind that the drive to the park can be part of the Death Valley and Mojave Desert experience. Be aware of possible winter closures or driving restrictions due to snow. Call the California State Department of Transportation hot line (tel. 800/427–7623) for updates on road conditions.

It is 140 to 155 mi from Las Vegas to Death Valley, about a three-hour drive; 260 to 315 mi from Los Angeles, a 6½-hour haul; and about 645 mi from San Francisco, which will take you 9½ to 12 hours to travel by car. The nearest national parks are Sequoia and Kings Canyon, from which you can reach Death Valley in about eight or nine hours traveling about 430 mi, and Yosemite, which is about 530 mi (10½ hours) away.

There are three major routes to Death Valley out of **Las Vegas.** The first follows U.S. 95 north for 86 mi to Amargosa Valley and the town of Lathrop Wells, where you'll turn south to take Nevada Highway 373 (which turns into Highway 127) to Death Valley Junction. From Death Valley Junction, take California Highway 190 west for 29 mi to Furnace Creek.

The shortest route (120 mi) is via Highway 160 to the north end of Pahrump. There, turn left on Bella Vista Road, which leads to Death Valley Junction.

You can also take U.S. 95 all the way to Beatty (an additional 29 mi from Lathrop Wells), where there are several casinos and motels, then turn onto Nevada Highway 374 (which turns into California Highway 190) west for the approximately 30-mi trip into the park. This road passes the ghost town of Rhyolite.

The most scenic route out of Las Vegas is on Nevada Highway 160 west. Follow the highway for 42 mi, then take the Old Spanish Trail, on your left. This road runs for 35 mi to Tecopa, California, and the public mineral baths in Hot Springs, the adjacent town. Tecopa has an RV park, restaurant, stores, and a post office. Hot Springs has several RV parks. From Tecopa, continue west on the Old Spanish Trail for 4 mi to California Highway 127, which you'll take north for 8 mi to Shoshone—a dusty wide spot in the road with a motel and service station. From Shoshone you can enter the park by traveling 77 mi on the scenic Highway 178 west to Furnace Creek, past Badwater and other attractions. A less scenic but more direct route is via Highway 127: Go north 28 mi to Death Valley Junction, then continue into the park on Highway 190. Along this route you will pass Zabriskie Point (*see* Longer Hikes, *below*).

You also have the option of taking Highway 160 all the way to Pahrump, Nevada (54 mi), where there is casino gambling, golf, and bowling. From Pahrump, travel on Nevada Highway 372 west to the California–Nevada state line, and then on California Highway 178 for a total of 26 mi to Shoshone, from which you can follow the directions above.

From **Los Angeles,** there are several routes. You can take I–5 to San Fernando, then travel east on Highway 14 for 129 mi to U.S. 395; or take I–15 to reach U.S. 395, which leads north to Red Mountain, where you'll pick up Highway 178 heading east into the park at Towne Pass. Alternatively, turn onto Highway 178 at Red Mountain and drive east through Ridgecrest and Trona to the park's Wildrose entrance. This is an unpaved road and not advisable unless you have a four-wheel-drive vehicle. Inside the park, signs point to Stovepipe Wells. You can also continue on U.S. 395 to Lone Pine and pick up Highway 190 east into the park. Highway 190 enters the park via Towne Pass, then passes Stovepipe Wells and the sand dunes.

The southeastern route passing through the eastern Mojave Desert from Los Angeles is the most scenic. Take I–15 through Barstow and Baker, then go north on Highway 127 at Baker to Shoshone. At Shoshone, you have the option of turning west on Highway 178 and driving through the park to Furnace Creek (gas up: there are no service stations for 77 mi from Shoshone to Furnace Creek), or continuing north on Highway 127 to Death Valley Junction, where you must take Highway 190 into the park.

From **San Francisco** take I–80 over the Oakland Bridge to I–580 east, which will bring you to I–5. Travel south on I–5 for 204 mi toward Bakersfield. At Highway 58, go east 92 mi to Highway 14 (watch for the cutoff sign as you approach Mojave) and follow the directions for routes out of Los Angeles, *above.*

By Plane. The nearest major airport is **McCarron International Airport** (tel. 702/261–5743) in Las Vegas, over 140 mi away. About a dozen car-rental agencies serve the airport. Within Death Valley, there are public airstrips near Furnace Creek and Stovepipe Wells Village.

EXPLORING

The distances between the major attractions in Death Valley make it necessary to travel by vehicle. Much of the park can be toured on a variety of regularly scheduled bus tours, but these often don't allow time for hikes to sites not seen from the road, such as Salt Creek, Golden Canyon, and Natural Bridge. The best option is to drive to a number of the sites, get out of the car, and walk.

Two full days of driving and hiking will give you a feeling for the park, but if you have five or six days you won't run out of activities.

THE BEST IN ONE DAY What you can see and do in one day at Death Valley depends a lot on where you plan to enter and exit the park. If you begin the day in Furnace Creek, you can see many different sights without doing much driving. Get up early and drive the 20 mi on Highway 178 (*see* Scenic Drives and Views, *below*) to Badwater, which looks out on the lowest point in the Western Hemisphere and is a fine place to watch the sunrise. Returning north, stop at Natural Bridge, a medium-size limestone rock formation that has been hollowed at its base to form a span across two rocks, and then at the Devil's Golf Course, so named because of the large balls of salt present here. These balls, which are about a foot in diameter, formed when an ancient lake that covered the area evaporated. Detour to the right onto Artists Drive, a 9-mi route that passes Artists Palette. The reds, yellows, oranges, and greens here are evidence of the minerals in the rocks and the earth. Four miles north of Artists Drive you will come to the Golden Canyon Interpretive Trail, a 2-mi round-trip that winds through a canyon with colorful rock walls. Just before Furnace Creek, take a short side trip on Highway 190 east 3 mi to Zabriskie Point (another good place to watch the sunrise) and the Twenty Mule Team Canyon (*see* Scenic Drives and Views, *below*). By this time you will be ready to return to Fur-

nace Creek, where you can have lunch and visit the Death Valley Museum. Here you'll find photographs and artifacts, some with accompanying push-button audio presentations outlining the natural and cultural history of the valley. There are slide presentations and movies in the museum's theater, and a three-dimensional model illustrates the topography of the area.

Heading north from Furnace Creek, pull off the highway and take a look at the Harmony Borax Works (*see* Nature Trails and Short Walks, *below*). Twenty miles up the road are the sand dunes, a good place to be at sunset.

A major consideration for those who have only one day is whether to make the one-hour drive to the park's north end for a tour of Scotty's Castle, with its unique construction and living-history program (*see* Historic Buildings and Sites, *below*), and the nearby Ubehebe Crater—a volcanic crater well worth a visit. The in-season wait at Scotty's can be from one to two hours (reservations are available for organized tour groups), but you can time it so that you take your lunch break while you wait. If you get up and catch the sunrise at Badwater, you can hit all these sights and visit Scotty's Castle, with enough time left to be back at the dunes to watch the sunset.

ORIENTATION PROGRAMS Year-round, the **Death Valley Museum** (tel. 760/786–2331) in Furnace Creek has orientation programs every half hour. Special programs are presented every evening in the fall, winter, and spring (check visitor center for times). Subjects include birds of the park, characters of Death Valley during the 1800s, desert sheep, the area's geology, and the mining of borax. These high-quality, informative presentations are led by park rangers and are free.

GUIDED TOURS Guided tours in passenger vans are operated year-round by the **Fred Harvey Company** (tel. 760/786–2345, ext. 222), which holds the concession rights in Furnace Creek and Stovepipe Wells. Tours leave from Furnace Creek, generally cost

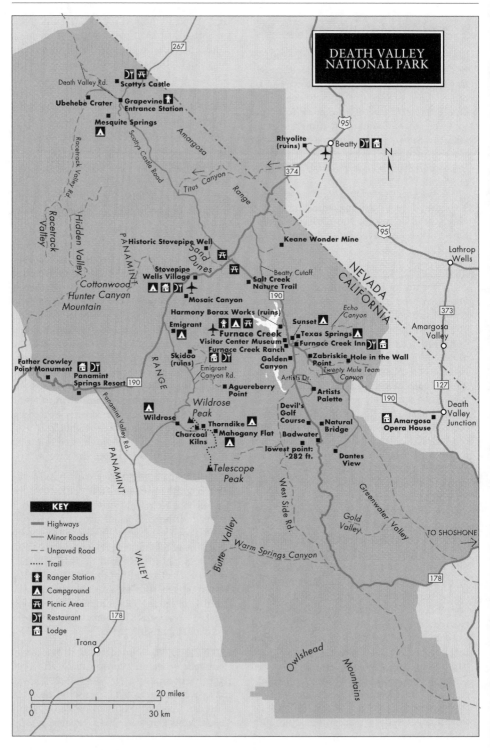

DEATH VALLEY
NATIONAL PARK

267

Death Valley Rd. Scottys Castle

Ubehebe Crater Grapevine
Entrance Station

Mesquite Springs

95

Rhyolite
(ruins) Beatty

N

374

Racetrack Valley Rd.

Scottys Castle Road

Amargosa

Titus Canyon

Range

Racetrack
Valley

Hidden Valley

PANAMINT

Historic Stovepipe Well

Sand

Dunes

Keane Wonder Mine

NEVADA
CALIFORNIA

Lathrop
Wells

95

Cottonwood
Hunter Canyon
Mountain

Stovepipe
Wells Village

Beatty Cutoff

Salt Creek
Nature Trail

Mosaic Canyon

190

Echo
Canyon

373

Amargosa
Valley

Harmony Borax Works (ruins)

Emigrant Furnace Creek
Visitor Center Museum
Furnace Creek Ranch

Sunset

Texas Springs

Furnace Creek Inn

Father Crowley
Point Monument Panamint
Springs Resort 190

RANGE

Skidoo
(ruins)

Emigrant
Canyon Rd.

Golden
Canyon

Zabriskie
Point Hole in the Wall

Twenty Mule Team
Canyon

127

Panamint Valley Rd.

Aguereberry
Point

Artists Dr.

Artists
Palette

190

Death
Valley
Junction

PANAMINT

Wildrose
Peak

Wildrose

Thorndike

Charcoal Mahogany Flat
Kilns

Devil's
Golf
Course

Badwater

lowest point:
-282 ft.

Natural
Bridge

Amargosa
Opera House

Telescope
Peak

Dantes
View

West Side Rd.

TO SHOSHONE

KEY

Highways
Minor Roads
Unpaved Road
Trail
Ranger Station
Campground
Picnic Area
Restaurant
Lodge

Butte Valley

Warm Springs Canyon

Gold
Valley

Greenwater Valley

178

178

VALLEY

Trona

0   20 miles
0   30 km

Owlshead

Mountains

$20–$30, and require a minimum of four adults. Most popular is the **Lower Valley Tour,** which stops at such natural wonders as Mushroom Rock, the Devil's Golf Course, Badwater, and Mustard Canyon, as well as at the Harmony Borax Works. Other excursions go to **Titus Canyon,** with a visit to the Rhyolite ghost town and an optional stop for a short hike; to the **Charcoal Kilns and Aguereberry Point**; to **Dante's View** and the Twenty Mule Team Canyon; and there's an evening at Death Valley Junction's **Amargosa Opera,** where the renowned Marta Beckett performs dance-mime. A half-day trip to **Scotty's Castle,** with a ranger-led tour of the mansion and stops at Ubehebe Crater, the original Stovepipe Well, and the sand dunes, requires a minimum of six adults.

Fred Harvey (*see above*) also offers special **casino/gaming** trips to Beatty or Pahrump, Nevada, which must be arranged 24 hours in advance and have a four-person minimum. Call for prices. Additionally, "taxi service" to any of the park's trailheads costs $50 for one to six adults. The company has one van equipped with a rack that can accommodate up to four bicycles.

The **National Park Service** runs 50-minute walking tours of **Scotty's Castle,** led by park rangers. These tours are offered year-round, hourly from 9 to 5. During the summer season, tours are held periodically throughout the day. Call the visitor center (tel. 760/786–2331) or Scotty's Castle (tel. 760/786–2392) for tour times. Tickets are sold the day of the tour on a first-come, first-served basis and cost $8. Tours are limited to 19 people.

SCENIC DRIVES AND VIEWS **Titus Canyon,** named for a young mining engineer who perished there, is a box canyon where limestone walls tower several hundred feet above the floor. From Furnace Creek, you can reach the beginning of the one-way road that passes through the canyon by taking Highway 190 west to the Beatty Cutoff Road, then following that north and picking up Highway 374 east. The entrance to the canyon will be on your left, about 13 mi from the point where you join Highway 374, or a total of 35 mi from Furnace Creek. A steep, occasionally rough gravel road makes the 26-mi descent through the canyon. The lighting is best at midday, when the sunshine creeps down the steep canyon walls. You will exit the canyon onto Scotty's Castle Road, which you can take southeast for 33 mi to reach Furnace Creek. Allow six hours for the trip. Titus Canyon Road is closed in summer.

Another interesting drive from Furnace Creek is the 24-mi, 40-minute trip to **Dante's View.** Drive east on Highway 190 for 11 mi, stopping at **Zabriskie Point** (the best time to come here is sunrise) and detouring on the **Twenty Mule Team Canyon drive,** a graded dirt road that passes through mudstone hills formed in an ancient lake that has since evaporated. Turn right onto the Dante's Point spur; it's 13 mi to the end. From this 5,475-ft vantage point, it is nearly a sheer drop down to Badwater, at 282 ft below sea level. You can see much of Death Valley and, across the valley, the Panamint Range and 11,049-ft Telescope Peak. No buses or trailers are allowed on the Twenty Mule Team Canyon drive or on the last few miles of the road to Dante's View.

The lowest point in the Western Hemisphere (282 ft below sea level) can be seen from **Badwater,** 17 mi south of Furnace Creek on **Highway 178** east. If you make this a predawn drive, you can watch the sunrise here. Along the drive back to Furnace Creek there are several sights worth stopping for, but you will have to hike a short distance to reach them. Just 3.5 mi north of Badwater is a right-hand turnoff for **Natural Bridge,** which spans a colorful canyon. The road to the trailhead is a rough 1.5 mi, but it's an easy .25-mi walk to the arch. Returning to Highway 178, drive 2 mi to the left-hand turnoff for the **Devil's Golf Course,** the vast beds of golf ball–shape salt crystals, which pioneers crossed in covered wagons in 1849. A bumpy 1.5-mi gravel road puts you at the edge of the area. The entrance to the one-way **Artists Drive** is 2 mi farther up Highway 178. The 9-mi drive winds through country that attracts painters because of its colorful rocks. Yet another spur road brings you to the trailhead for the moderate 2-mi trek to **Golden Canyon,** where the rocks range from deep purple to gold. Look for Mushroom Rock along the side of Highway 178.

At the western entrance to the park, on Highway 190, **Father Crowley Point** affords eastbound visitors their first sweeping views of Death Valley. The best view is from the edge of Rainbow Canyon, from which you can take a short hike into Darwin Falls, 10 mi southeast of Father Crowley Point. Look for the turnoff 7 mi east of Father Crowley Point Monument on Highway 190.

HISTORIC BUILDINGS AND SITES In the northern end of Death Valley, **Scotty's Castle** is a Mediterranean-style hacienda that was built over a couple of decades as a winter retreat for the wealthy Albert Johnson and his wife, Bessie. The castle is named for their friend Walter Scott, a local prospector and raconteur also known as Death Valley Scotty, who was financed by the Johnsons, visited them often during their stays at the castle, and spent the final six years of his life there after Albert Johnson died in 1948. Death Valley Scotty, who was seldom known to work, became notorious for his long-winded, creative tales of his adventures. Scotty's Castle has elaborate Spanish tiling, a clock tower, and sits amid an oasis created by springs bubbling from the mountainside. Rooms are decorated with original furniture, bedding, and rugs from Majorca. Costumed guides lead living-history tours, recounting tales of Scotty, the Johnsons, and the valley (*see* Guided Tours, *above*).

The **Furnace Creek Inn** (*see* Lodging, *below*) is situated on the spring-fed oasis at Furnace Creek. It was built in 1927 by the Pacific Coast Borax Company in answer to what company officials recognized as a growing tourist interest in Death Valley.

The inn is similar in architecture to Scotty's Castle.

Travel 37 mi northeast from Furnace Creek toward Beatty, Nevada to see the genuine ghost town of **Rhyolite,** once the largest town in the Death Valley area. In the gold boom of the early 1900s, Rhyolite supported from 2,000 to 10,000 people and was called the Queen City of Death Valley. Today, visitors can see the old train depot, as well as the Bottle House, the jailhouse, and the remains of a few three-story stone buildings.

NATURE TRAILS AND SHORT WALKS To explore the park's massive, rolling **sand dunes,** either begin from the turnoff on Highway 190, 2.5 mi east of Stovepipe Wells, or from the sand-dunes picnic area, 21 mi north of Furnace Creek. There are no trails here; hikers are free to roam where they please. Watch for animal tracks and interesting sand formations. Remember where you parked your car: It is easy to become disoriented in this ocean of sand. If you lose your bearings, simply climb to the top of a dune and scan the horizon for the parking lot.

Take a close look at Salt Creek, with its vegetation, birds, and desert pupfish, on the .5-mi **Salt Creek Nature Trail,** a boardwalk circuit that loops through a spring-fed wash. The small nearby hills are brown and gray, but the floor of the creek's wash is alive with aquatic plants such as pickerel-weed and salt grass. Look closely and you may find the tracks of nocturnal visitors such as lizards, bobcats, coyotes, ravens, and snakes. The tiny pupfish is the only surviving fish in Death Valley. Stand still and you may see one of these shy, inch-long fish moving in the shadows of overhanging vegetation. The trailhead is 1 mi down a gravel road off Highway 190, 14 mi north of Furnace Creek.

For a close encounter with some of Death Valley's more recent history, stroll down the .25-mi **Harmony Borax Works Interpretive Trail,** 2 mi north of Furnace Creek. The hard-surface trail leads to adobe ruins, borax-mining equipment, and a 20-mule-team wagon from the 1880s.

Late afternoon is the best time to hike the 2-mi round-trip **Golden Canyon Interpretive Trail,** when diffused sunlight accentuates the rock colors. After following this gradual uphill trail through rock canyons, you can continue from here to Zabriskie Point (see Longer Hikes, below) or the Red Cathedral. The trailhead is on Badwater Road, 3 mi south of Furnace Creek.

The trailhead for the .5-mi round-trip through **Natural Bridge Canyon** begins 2 mi off Badwater Road, 15 mi south of Furnace Creek. Although the access road can be rough, the uphill walk is gradual, with interesting geological features beyond the natural bridge.

Thirty-seven miles south of Stovepipe Wells you will come to the **Charcoal Kilns.** Charcoal produced in these beehive-shape kilns was transported to ore smelters in the Argus Range. Take Highway 190 to Emigrant Canyon Road and continue 8.5 mi past Wildrose Campground.

There are several short walks at **Scotty's Castle.** A .5-mi loop explores the grounds at the castle and signs explain the construction of the building. The .75-mi **Windy Point Trail** climbs 160 ft to a view of Scotty's grave and an overview of the Death Valley Ranch, on which Scotty's Castle sits. The **Tie Canyon Trail** is an easy .75-mi walk through a canyon once used to store building materials for the castle.

LONGER HIKES A moderately strenuous, unmaintained trail from **Golden Canyon** to **Zabriskie Point** climbs over ridges in Golden Canyon. Rock formations tinted red, green, yellow, orange, and purple rise on both sides of the trail; at Zabriskie Point you get a view of Death Valley. From there you can retrace your steps or extend the hike by looking for the drainage ditch that leads back to Highway 190, which you can follow back to your starting point. The trailhead is 3 mi south of Furnace Creek on Badwater Road, and the hike is 5 mi round-trip. This trail can be a little tricky to follow; be sure to obtain a free trail map at the visitor center.

The western entrance to deep and shadowy **Titus Canyon** is a 2-mi, two-way dirt road, 33 mi northwest of Furnace Creek on Scotty's Castle Road. From there, a one-way road (closed to vehicles during summer) continues 24 mi east and eventually connects with Highway 374 (see Scenic Drives and Views, above). The narrow canyon floor is hard-packed gravel and dirt, and it's a constant, moderate uphill walk for hikers. Klare Spring and some petroglyphs are 5.5 mi from the mouth of the canyon, but you can get a feeling for the area on a shorter walk. The views here are vertical: canyon walls rising 40 to 60 ft and the rugged, rocky ridges above them. The canyon's steep walls and deep shadows give it an eerie, desolate feel.

Allow two hours for the 2-mi round-trip trail that follows a historic aerial tramway to the **Keane Wonder Mine.** The way is very steep, but the views of the valley make it worth the extra effort. Do not enter the tunnels or hike beyond the top of the tramway—it's dangerous. Look for the access road 17.5 mi north of Furnace Creek, on the Beatty Cutoff Road; it's 3 unpaved and bumpy miles to the trailhead.

A gradual uphill trail (2 mi one way) winds through the smoothly polished walls of narrow **Mosaic Canyon.** There are dry falls to climb at the upper end of the canyon. The trailhead is off Highway 190, just west of Stovepipe Wells Village, via a 2-mi dirt road that is rough in places but accessible to most vehicles.

The 8.25-mi round-trip **Wildrose Peak Trail** starts at the Charcoal Kilns and passes through piñon- and juniper-pine country. Moderately steep, it offers sweeping views of the valley and is best hiked in the afternoon, when the sinking sun adds color and dimension to the Funeral Range, east across the valley.

The 14-mi round-trip **Telescope Peak Trail** begins at Mahogany Flat Campground, about 9 mi east of Wildrose Campground. The steep trail winds through piñon, juniper, and bristlecone pines, with excellent views of Death Valley and Panamint Valley. Ice axes and crampons may be necessary in the winter—check at the visitor center. It takes a minimum of eight hours to hike to the top of the 11,049-ft peak and then return.

OTHER ACTIVITIES **Back-Road Driving.** With 150 mi of roads covering 3 million acres of backcountry, Death Valley is a popular destination among four-wheel-drive enthusiasts. Driving off established roads is strictly prohibited in the park. Overnight camping is permitted, but you must be at least 5 mi from a maintained campground, 1 mi from major paved and unpaved roads, and .25 mi from any water source. Topographic maps covering select areas of the park are available for $5 each at the visitor center or from the Death Valley Natural History Association (*see* Publications, *above*).

The more popular back-road destinations include Butte Valley, Hunter Mountain, and Echo Canyon. Butte Valley is a 21-mi trail (via Warm Spring Canyon) that climbs from 200 ft below sea level to an elevation of 4,000 ft. The geological formations along this drive reveal the development of Death Valley. Hunter Mountain (from Teakettle Junction to the Park Boundary) is 20 mi long and climbs from 4,100 ft to 7,200 ft, winding through a piñon-and-juniper forest. This route may be closed or muddy in winter and spring. Echo Canyon (beginning at Highway 190) is 30 mi long, climbing 4,400 ft and topping out at 4,800 ft. Camping is not permitted along the first 4 mi of this trail.

Biking. There are no bike rentals in the park, but mountain biking is permitted on any of the back roads open to the public. These roads receive very little traffic. A free flier with suggested bike routes is available at the visitor center. Easy routes include Mustard Canyon (1.5 mi) and Twenty Mule Team Canyon (3 mi). Among the moderate routes are Hole-in-the-Wall (6 mi) and Skidoo (8 mi). Racetrack Valley (30 mi), Hidden Valley (30–35 mi), Cottonwood Canyon (20 mi), Greenwater Valley (30 mi), West Side Road (40 mi), and Artists Drive (9 mi, paved) are more difficult to negotiate.

On-road bicycling is becoming increasingly popular along the paved roads of Death Valley, particularly in the cooler months from late fall through early spring. But be aware that there are no shoulders on these roads and that drivers are often distracted by the surrounding scenery.

Bird-Watching. Approximately 250 bird species have been identified in Death Valley. The best place for bird-watching is along the Salt Creek Nature Trail, where you might see ravens, common snipes, spotted sandpipers, killdeer, and great blue herons. At the golf course at Furnace Creek (stay off the greens) look for kingfishers, peregrine falcons, hawks, Canada geese, yellow warblers, and an occasional golden eagle.

Golf. The **Furnace Creek Golf Club** (tel. 760/786–2301) is open year-round. Greens fees for guests of Furnace Creek Ranch and Furnace Creek Inn are $20 for 18 holes, $10 for nine holes; for nonguests the rate is $30 for 18 holes, $15 for nine holes. Cart rentals are $20 for 18 holes and $10 for nine holes. Club rental is $10 for nine holes and $15 for 18 holes. Special rates for two to 20 weeks of play are available. Golfers should make reservations for winter mornings.

Horseback and Carriage Riding. Guided horseback and carriage rides are available at **Furnace Creek Ranch** (tel. 760/786–2345) from October through May. Horseback rides cost $20 per person for one hour, $35 for two hours. Moonlight rides are $30. Hour-long, morning wagon rides depart from the general store and cost $5 per person. Evening carriage rides take passengers around the golf course and Furnace Creek Ranch for $10 per person. Cocktail rides, with champagne, margaritas, and hot spiced wine, are available for $50 per couple; reservations are required.

Swimming. There are pools at the Furnace Creek Inn, Furnace Creek Ranch, and Stovepipe Wells Village. The pools at Furnace Creek Ranch and Stovepipe Wells are open to the public (nonguests pay $2). Both pools at Furnace Creek are spring-fed, with no filters, and remain just over 80°F. All pools are open year-round.

Tennis. There are four lighted tennis courts, for guests only, at Furnace Creek Inn (tel. 760/786–2361) and two lighted courts at Furnace Creek Ranch (tel. 760/786–2345), where the public is welcome. There is no fee to play tennis at the ranch.

CHILDREN'S PROGRAMS A Junior Ranger program, available sporadically, lets children go on special hikes. They can also earn badges by completing workbooks geared to individual age groups. Call the Furnace Creek Visitor Center (tel. 760/786–2331) to find out if any junior-ranger activities will take place during your visit.

EVENING ACTIVITIES During the fall, winter, and spring months, evening programs are held nightly at the visitor center, beginning at 7 PM. Subjects include birds of Death Valley, characters from the early 1900s, borax mining, desert sheep, types of deserts, and Death Valley's geology. For more information, contact the visitor center (tel. 760/786–2331).

DINING

There aren't a lot of dining options in Death Valley, and it's 40 mi to the nearest town. Fortunately for the park's visitors, the few restaurants in the area have good food and a wide price range.

INSIDE THE PARK **Inn Dining Room.** Located in the Furnace Creek Inn, which was built in 1927, this restaurant provides silver service in a grand-hotel setting, with lace table linens, crystal, and candlelight. Painted ceiling beams enhance the building's adobe walls; and there are two fireplaces as well as views of the valley. Breakfast, lunch, and five-course dinners

are served; standout entrées are the southwestern chicken Caesar salad and the pepper-crusted salmon with mango-papaya salsa. A large selection of California premium wines ranges from $22 to $70. Nonguests are welcome. For dinner, reservations are strongly recommended and a jacket is suggested. *Furnace Creek Inn, CA, tel. 760/786–2361. AE, D, DC, MC, V. $$–$$$*

Furnace Creek Ranch. Two family-style restaurants are housed in one complex at the ranch: the Wrangler Steak House and the 49er Coffee Shop. Both serve good food in a simple setting. The coffee shop serves typical American fare for breakfast, lunch, and dinner. The steak house offers buffet breakfast and lunch, and dinner favorites such as filet mignon, lobster tails, and barbecue pork ribs. The steak house is slightly more formal than the coffee shop, and patrons pay slightly higher prices for more attentive service. Dinner reservations are advisable for the steak house. *Furnace Creek Ranch, CA, tel. 760/786–2345. AE, D, DC, MC, V. $–$$*

Toll Road Restaurant. There are wagon wheels in the yard and Old West artifacts on the interior walls at this restaurant in Stovepipe Wells Village. A stone fireplace heats the dining room. A full menu, with steaks, chicken, fish, and pasta, is served October through mid-May; breakfast and dinner buffets are laid out during summer. *Stovepipe Wells Village, CA, tel. 760/786–2604. AE, D, DC, MC, V. $–$$*

19th Hole. This open-air lunch spot at the Furnace Creek Golf Club is designed with the active golfer in mind. The menu includes hot dogs, chicken sandwiches, and the special Mulligan Burger, which has twice the beef, twice the cheese, and twice the bun of a regular burger. It is served with potato chips and iced tea. *Furnace Creek, CA, tel. 760/786–2345. AE, D, DC, MC, V. $*

NEAR THE PARK The closest restaurants outside the park are in Beatty, Nevada, 40 mi from Furnace Creek. Beatty sees many travelers on the Reno–Las Vegas run and many heading to or from Death Valley, so the restaurants draw an eclectic crowd.

There is also a popular café in Shoshone, 89 mi from Furnace Creek.

Burro Inn. This restaurant is part of a casino/inn complex in Beatty, Nevada, but the seven booths, six tables, and 11 counter seats fill up with visitors of all types, including families. Breakfast, lunch, and dinner are served around the clock, with such American basics as eggs, pancakes, hamburgers, and hot and cold sandwiches. There are daily dinner specials after 11 AM; the prime rib, on Friday and Saturday, comes with appetizers, salad, or soup, and a potato (baked, mashed, or french-fried). *U.S. 95 and 3rd St., Beatty, NV, tel. 702/ 553–2225. AE, MC, V. $*

Exchange Club Motel. Also part of a casino/motel complex in Beatty and also open 24 hours a day, the Exchange Club seats 133 people at booths, tables, and a small counter. Many a traveler stops here while passing through, but the atmosphere is relatively quiet and kids can choose from their own menu. Breakfasts include eggs, pancakes, or waffles; lunch is cold or hot sandwiches or burgers. Prime rib is served Friday and Saturday; it usually sells out. For vegetarians, there are garden burgers and chef salads. Try the lemon meringue or blueberry pie—it's homemade. *614 Main St., Beatty, NV, tel. 702/553–2368. AE, MC, V. $*

Red Buggy Café. For over 60 years this café in the old mining town of Shoshone has shared the same wood building with an adjacent saloon. Inside are a half dozen wood tables with red-and-white tablecloths, red curtains, and a counter that seats 11 people. Photographs of the town in its mining heyday hang on the walls. The menu comes in the form of a newspaper (yes, you can keep it), with Mexican and American selections that fill two pages. All the food is homemade. *Hwy. 127, Shoshone, CA, tel. 760/852–9908. AE, D, MC, V. $*

Stagecoach Hotel. Remodeled in 1991, the brick-walled Stagecoach has light-color booths surrounding a center fountain. It seats 100 and has a no-smoking section in the back. Breakfast standards are eggs, pancakes, and waffles; sandwiches and burgers are served for lunch. Pizza, meat loaf, and chicken-fried steak are among the dinner specials; calorie counters can order a dieter's plate or a chef's salad. *U.S. 95, Beatty, NV, tel. 702/553–2419. AE, D, MC, V. $*

PICNIC SPOTS If you're looking for a shady spot to spread out a blanket, your choices are limited to the oasis at **Furnace Creek** or **Scotty's Castle,** where many visitors opt to eat lunch while waiting the hour or two for a tour. A luncheon stand at Scotty's Castle sells hot dogs and hamburgers. There are picnic tables—but no shade—at the **Salt Creek** trailhead, which is at the end of a 1-mi bumpy road and gets less traffic than other areas; the self-guided tour around the creek's marsh provides an easy after-meal stroll. There are also several picnic tables by the date grove in the Furnace Creek area, and at the sand dunes parking area east of Stovepipe Wells Village (the turnoff is at the intersection of Highway 190 with Scotty's Castle Road). Supplies can be purchased at the general store at Furnace Creek or Stovepipe Wells Village.

LODGING

In addition to campgrounds, there are four places to lay your head within Death Valley National Park: Furnace Creek Inn, Furnace Creek Ranch, Stovepipe Wells Village, and Panamint Springs Resort. Furnace Creek is at the center of the park, adjacent to the visitor center, the museum, and many of the park's natural attractions. A golf course is shared by guests of the two Furnace Creek hotels and is open to the public, as are the tennis courts at the Furnace Creek Ranch. Stovepipe Wells Village is 26 mi northwest of Furnace Creek, and Panamint Springs Resort is at the park's western entrance. During the busy season, from November through March, reservations should be made at least one month in advance.

There are a number of moderately priced motels (with casinos) in Beatty, Nevada, 40 mi northeast of Furnace Creek. Many visitors stay in Shoshone, 60 mi southeast of Furnace Creek, but there is only one hotel there; reservations are strongly advised.

INSIDE THE PARK **Furnace Creek Inn.** This stone-and-adobe Spanish-villa inn was built on a hill above Furnace Creek in 1927 and is a designated U.S. Historic Landmark. It is now operated by the Fred Harvey Company. Some rooms have superb views of the valley, while others overlook a lush, spring-fed garden, planted with desert grasses, magnolia trees, and stately 50-ft palms. Each room has a king-size or twin beds, as well as Spanish-tile floors, antique ceiling fans, and pedestal sinks; some have balconies and spa bathtubs. Amenities include refrigerators, hair dryers, bathrobes, alarm clocks, and irons. Reservations for spring weekends should be made one to two months in advance. Rooms are substantially discounted from mid-May to mid-October. *Box 1, Death Valley, CA 92328, tel. 760/786–2361 or 800/ 236–7916, fax 760/786–2514. 66 rooms. Facilities: restaurant, bar, pool, massage, golf course, 4 tennis courts, exercise room. AE, D, DC, MC, V. $$$*

Furnace Creek Ranch. Also operated by the Fred Harvey Company, the ranch provides fewer luxuries than the Furnace Creek Inn, but it is also less expensive. A clean, quiet, family-oriented motel with one- and two-story buildings, it has a pool, tennis courts, and golf course on the grounds and is within walking distance of the visitor center and museum, post office, general store, and two restaurants. Many of the rooms overlook the golf course or landscaped pool area. Each room has two double beds, air-conditioning, TV, and telephone. *Box 1, Death Valley, CA 92328, tel. 760/786–2345 or 800/236–7916, fax 760/786–2514. 224 rooms. Facilities: 2 restaurants, pool, golf course, 2 tennis courts. AE, D, DC, MC, V. $$$*

Stovepipe Wells Village. This motel, operated by the Fred Harvey Company, is a scaled-down version of Furnace Creek Ranch. It, too, has pleasant landscaping and a refreshingly cool swimming pool. Buildings are modern but tastefully decorated to a western theme. The 83 rooms are clean, comfortable, and spare, with no TVs or telephones. Water in some rooms is unsuitable for drinking. There are also 15 RV hookups on the grounds. *Stovepipe Wells Village, Death Valley, CA 92328, tel. 760/786–2387, fax 760/786–2389. 83 rooms. Facilities: restaurant, bar, grocery, pool. AE, D, MC, V. $$–$$$*

Panamint Springs Resort. This 40-acre property lies on a quiet stretch of Highway 190, 28 mi west of Stovepipe Wells, near the park's western boundary. It's a modest mom-and-pop-style operation with a wraparound porch and a rustic, country atmosphere. In addition to 14 motel rooms, there are 12 RV sites surrounded by cottonwood trees. One room has a king-size bed, and two of the rooms accommodate up to six people. A pay phone, a gas pump, and a grocery store are on the premises; there are also 12 RV sites. *Hwy. 190, 48 mi east of Lone Pine, Ridgecrest, CA 93556, tel. 702/ 482–7680, fax 702/482–7682. 14 rooms. Facilities: restaurant, bar. $$*

NEAR THE PARK **Exchange Club Motel.** Many guests at this modern motel would give it three stars. It's clean and quiet, and each carpeted room has a refrigerator and a cable TV with remote control. Some rooms have king- or queen-size beds, and one is equipped with a Jacuzzi. Two rooms are accessible to people using wheelchairs. *614 Main St., Box 97, Beatty, NV 89003, tel. 702/ 553–2333. 44 rooms. Facilities: restaurant, bar, casino, coin laundry. AE, MC, V. $$*

Shoshone Inn. The dusty town of Shoshone is only a wide spot in the highway, and the rustic Shoshone Inn, with its hodgepodge of architectural styles, is the only hotel in town. Accommodations here are adequate, and each room has a private bath. Advance reservations are advisable year-round. *Hwy. 127, Box 67, Shoshone, CA 92384, tel. 760/852–4335. 16 rooms. Facilities: pool. AE, D, MC, V. $$*

Amargosa Hotel. The Pacific Coast Borax Company built the Amargosa in 1923 to serve railroad passengers stopping in Death Valley Junction, then a borax-mining town. The adobe building, neighbor to the Amargosa Opera House, was renovated and reopened in 1991. Its rooms have one or two double beds but no phones or TVs. Reservations should be made at least one to two months in advance during winter. *Box 608, Death Valley Junction, CA 92328, tel. 760/852–4441. 14 rooms. AE, MC, V. $–$$*

Burro Inn. This two-story wood structure is 15 years old. Each room has queen-size beds and a private bath; there is one suite with a queen-size murphy bed, couches, and kitchenette. Guests include senior citizens, families, and Europeans. *U.S. 95 and 3rd St., Box 7, Beatty, NV 89003, tel. 702/553–2225. 62 rooms. Facilities: restaurant, casino. AE, MC, V. $–$$*

Stagecoach Hotel. Each of the 32 Western-style rooms in this hotel has a refrigerator and cable TV with remote control. The price makes it appealing, but the curt, unfriendly staff makes it decidedly less so. *U.S. 95, Box 836, Beatty, NV 89003, tel. 702/553–2419 or 800/424–4946. 32 rooms. Facilities: restaurant, casino. AE, D, MC, V. $*

CAMPING

There are 1,500 campsites at nine campgrounds in Death Valley National Park, although not all of them are open year-round. Furnace Creek, Mesquite Springs, and Wildrose campgrounds are open throughout the year; Texas Spring, Sunset, and Stovepipe Wells are open from October to April; Emigrant is open from April to October; Thorndike and Mahogany Flat are open from March to November. Reservations for individuals are available only at Furnace Creek; make them through Destinet (tel. 800/365–2267). Holidays that fall from October through March are busy times in Death Valley, but the only time it may be difficult to find a site is during the 49er Encampment Days, which are held in early November.

There are two group campsites for 40 people each at Texas Spring campground. They cost $50 per night, per group, and are available on a first-come, first-served basis.

Fires are allowed in fire grates at all campgrounds except Sunset and Emigrant, and may be restricted during certain seasons at Thorndike, Mahogany Flat, and Wildrose (check with rangers about current conditions). Wood-gathering is prohibited at all campgrounds. A limited supply of firewood is available at general stores in Furnace Creek and Stovepipe Wells, but campers are better off bringing their own.

The **Sunset** campground, 1 mi north of the Furnace Creek Visitor Center, is a gravel-and-asphalt RV mecca with 1,000 sites. It also serves as an overflow site for tents. It has flush and pit toilets, drinking water, playground, disposal station, ranger station, and public phone. Hookups are not available, but campers can walk across the street for pay showers, laundry facilities, and a swimming pool at the Furnace Creek Ranch. Many of the campers here are senior citizens who migrate to Death Valley each winter to play golf and tennis or just to enjoy the mild, dry climate. Sites cost $10 per night per vehicle. Pull-throughs (for RVs) are available here and at Stovepipe Wells. The Sunset is closed May through September.

With 200 sites, **Stovepipe Wells** is the second-largest campground in the park. Like Sunset, this area is little more than a giant parking lot, but it has flush and pit toilets, drinking water, disposal station, and a public phone. Pay showers and laundry facilities are available at the Stovepipe Wells motel. Sites cost $10 per vehicle per night. Stovepipe Wells is closed between May and September.

The most popular low-elevation campgrounds are **Furnace Creek,** with 136 sites, flush and pit toilets, drinking water, fire grates, disposal station, ranger station, and public phone; **Texas Spring,** with 92 sites, flush and pit toilets, drinking water, fire grates, and disposal station (no generators are allowed), closed from May through September; and **Mesquite Springs,** with 30 sites, flush toilets, drinking water, and disposal station. Each of these areas has a few mesquite trees and creosote bushes, but not enough to provide shade; for the most part, the campsites sit among dry, dusty, rock-strewn terrain. Furnace Creek and Texas Spring, however, are near the hub of valley civilization, and so they draw a wide variety of campers, from senior citizens to foreigners to families. Mesquite Springs, on the other hand, is more removed, the only campground in the north end of the park, and so it is frequented by a younger group intent on getting away from the crowds. Sites cost $10 per vehicle per night at Mesquite Springs and Texas Spring, and $16 per vehicle per night at Furnace Creek.

In summer, some campers prefer the higher-elevation campsites of **Wildrose** (4,100 ft), **Thorndike** (7,500 ft), and **Mahogany Flat** (8,200 ft), where the temperature is generally 15 to 20 degrees cooler than it is on the valley floor. The road into Thorndike and Mahogany Flat is not suitable for trailers, campers, or motor homes, and at times it is necessary to have a high-clearance or four-wheel-drive vehicle to get through. Mahogany Flat, with 10 sites, pit toilets, and fire grates, is the most scenic campground, set among piñon pines and junipers, with a view of the valley.

Thorndike has eight sites, pit toilets, and fire grates. Since it is on a paved road at a lower elevation, Wildrose, with 30 sites, pit toilets, and fire grates, is less likely to be closed because of snow in the winter. The view here is not as spectacular as that from Thorndike or Mahogany Flat, but it does overlook the northern end of the valley. Although there is much more vegetation at these three campgrounds than at any of those in the valley, you still won't be camping under the shade of a large tree; the harsh climate here tends to result in dwarfed vegetation. No fee is charged at these campgrounds.

The free, 10-site campground at **Emigrant,** with flush toilets and drinking water, near the western entrance to the park, is one of the least scenic campgrounds. The surrounding rock formations here are less dramatic than those at other campgrounds in the valley. Still, Emigrant is free and has potable water, which makes it an acceptable spot when no others are available.

Backcountry camping is allowed in areas that are at least 5 mi from maintained campgrounds, 2 mi from the main paved or unpaved roads, and .25 mi from water sources. For your own safety, fill out a voluntary backcountry registration form so the rangers will know where to find you.

Denali National Park and Preserve
Alaska

Updated by Bill Sherwonit

vast wilderness of taiga, tundra, and ice-capped peaks, with blue glacial pools and seamless snowfields, Denali National Park and Preserve is, and has always been, best known as the home of the highest mountain in North America—the 20,320-ft Mt. McKinley. In fact, the park is named for the mountain, which Native Americans called *denali* (the high one).

Climbers from all over the world come to scale the rugged Alaska Range, and dramatic Mt. McKinley offers the greatest challenge. The first successful ascent occurred in 1913, but is was not until 1967 that a team of climbers actually reached the apex in the middle of winter. Today, climbing parties assemble at the village of Talkeetna, south of the park on a spur road that branches from the George Parks Highway at about mile 99. On any spring day, you will find a group at the airstrip preparing for their ascent.

These mountains were not always so accessible. In 1917 the area was established as a game refuge to protect moose, sheep, and caribou from exploitation by market hunters from Fairbanks and the Alaska Railroad construction camps. At that time, it was called Mount McKinley National Park (the name was changed in 1980—the year that the park was expanded from 1.9 to 6 million acres). It was not until 1923, when the railroad was completed, that the first commercial tours of the area began to trickle in.

You need not climb Mt. McKinley to appreciate Denali; the park is both a hiker's and wildlife-watcher's paradise. The one 88-mi road into the heart of the park is unpaved after the first 14.8 mi, and summer visitors now travel it on shuttle buses, from which they watch for grizzly bears, wolves, caribou, and moose. The bulk of the parkland, however, is accessible only on foot in summer or by dog team or cross-country skis in winter.

Most of the park lies above the tree line and in summer it gets 16 to 20 hours of daylight—which means you'll have plenty of time to enjoy the expansive views of unspoiled landscape and to catch a few glimpses of Alaskan wildlife in the open spaces. (Bring binoculars and a camera, as Denali is one of the country's premier outdoor photography locations). Just outside the park, there's also horseback riding on wilderness trails, boating and white-water rafting on the Nenana River, and helicopter or fixed-wing flight-seeing in the skies above Mt. McKinley.

ESSENTIAL INFORMATION

VISITOR INFORMATION Visitors can obtain information about the park by writing to the Superintendent, **Denali National Park and Preserve** (Box 9, Denali National Park, AK 99755, tel. 907/683–2294). Information is also available at the **Alaska Public Lands Information Center** (605 W. 4th Ave., Anchorage, AK 99501, tel. 907/271–2737; 250 Cushman St., Suite 1A, Fairbanks, AK 99701, tel. 907/456–0527).

Backcountry permits are required for all overnight trips in the park and can be obtained a day in advance at the **visitor center** near the park entrance. Since there are no maintained trails in the backcountry, hikers should be skilled in reading topographic maps, which are available at the park visitor centers. Most private cars are banned from the 88-mi park road beyond the Savage River Bridge (mile 14.8).

FEES Admission to the park (beyond Savage River) is $5 per person or $10 per family for up to seven days. You may opt for an annual $20 pass, which entitles visitors to unlimited entry for the calendar year.

PUBLICATIONS Read the park's annual newspaper, the *Denali Alpenglow,* as well as the park brochure, which are both available at the visitor center. While you're there, pick up a guide describing the local birds and mammals. You can also purchase the *Denali Road Guide,* which gives a mile-by-mile description of the geological history, terrain, and wildlife visible from the park road.

The **Alaska Natural History Association** (Box 230, Denali National Park, AK 99755, tel. 907/683–1272, fax 907/683–1408; 401 W. 1st St., Anchorage, AK 99501, tel. 907/274–8440, fax 907/271–2744) will send you its latest brochure, which contains an extensive listing of helpful books on natural history, wildlife, and mountaineering in Alaska. *Denali,* published by the **Alaska Geographic Society** (Box 93370, Anchorage, AK 99509, tel. 907/562–0164, fax 907/562–0479), describes the history, geology, flora, and fauna of the park, utilizing numerous color plates of the mountain and the surrounding preserve. **Trails Illustrated** (tel. 800/962–1643), based in Evergreen, Colorado, sells detailed maps of the area.

GEOLOGY AND TERRAIN Denali National Park and Preserve spans 6 million acres of taiga, tundra, and high mountain peaks— it's actually larger than the state of Massachusetts. The park entrance is in the taiga (a Russian term for boreal or northern forest), a coniferous forest lying in the lower river valleys, where there is more moisture and the microclimate is a little warmer.

Taiga within the park reaches elevations up to 2,700 ft.

The tundra begins at the tree line. Covering more of the slopes and sitting at higher elevations, this ecosystem of small shrubs and miniature wildflowers has a short, cool three-month growing season. Tundra may be moist, with swampy fields of tussocks, or it may be dry and brittle, on high, rocky ground.

The most prominent geological feature of the park is the Alaska Range, a 600-mi-long crescent of summits that separates south-central Alaska from its vast interior. These peaks are all immense, but the truly towering ones are Mt. Hunter (14,573 ft), Mt. Foraker (17,400 ft), and Mt. McKinley (20,320 ft). These mountains are the result of tectonic plate activity along the Denali Fault, North America's largest crustal break, and earthquakes are still common in the park. In fact, a major quake hit in the spring of 1992, terrifying climbers and resulting in the avalanches that pummeled the Ruth Amphitheater.

Mt. McKinley rises from 2,000-ft lowlands at Wonder Lake, and when measured from base to peak it is one of the tallest mountains in the world. Because it reaches so far above every other feature around it, the mountain creates its own weather systems. Climbers often fail to reach McKinley's peak because of its powerful storms, which obscure the mountain, create fierce winds, and drive temperatures down. During the first successful winter ascent in 1967, climbers calculated that the temperature, adjusted for windchill, dropped as low as –168°F during one storm high on the peak.

Mt. McKinley's granite heart is covered with glacial ice, which is hundreds of feet thick in places. Glaciers, in fact, are abundant along the entire Alaska Range, and a few are visible from the park road. Muldrow Glacier is only 5 mi from the park road, near mile 67.

Glaciers are largely responsible for forming and feeding the rivers of the park. Note that most glacial rivers are murky: This is caused by the glacier, which grinds rocks and dirt in its path into a fine silt that does not clear in the water. This is why a glacial river can be especially dangerous to cross on foot: The bottom is not visible, and its water level can rise and fall dramatically during the day as the sun warms and melts the glacier that feeds it.

FLORA AND FAUNA The taiga is abundant in small spruce, interspersed with aspens, birch, and balsam poplar. Ground cover in the taiga forest includes such shrubs as dwarf birch, blueberry, and willows. From the road the taiga looks open, with wide views and very few trees, but the dense bushes make it difficult for inexperienced hikers.

Tundra is a fascinating miniature forest. Get down to ground level to examine the variety of miniature plants; you may have seen their full-size counterparts elsewhere in the park. Fireweed, the ubiquitous pinkish-purple stalk of flowers that bloom along Alaska roads in late summer, has a tundra version—a tiny beauty sometimes less than 6 inches high. Berries are a common tundra food source for people as well as animals; low-bush cranberries, blueberries, and crowberries are all prized by Alaskans. In the wide pass south of the park near Cantwell, late August finds families picking blueberries on the tundra. At the same time, the tundra flora generates brilliant color: Bearberry leaves turn bright red, boasting their shiny dark-blue berries; the mountain slopes turn deep gold and orange; and the fragrant bouquet of wine permeates the tundra as fruit ferments on the bush.

Although Denali's unique landscape and sensational wildflower displays deserve high accolades, the animals are the reason most people visit. You might see grizzly bears, caribou, moose, and Dall sheep, as well as smaller mammals and birds.

Grizzlies appear routinely in the park, but black bears are seldom sighted (although they do appear along the wooded rivers to the north and east). Don't expect to identify a bear by its color; grizzlies can range from very light gold to chocolate to black. What distinguishes a grizzly from a black bear is the large hump across its shoulders and its broad, flat face. With a heavier-set stature than a black bear, a male grizzly typically weighs 450 pounds, a female 260.

Be aware that bears can be dangerous, especially if surprised. Although most charges are bluffs, bears that feel threatened may choose either the flight or fight response; it's wise to heed the park administration's guidelines on how to avoid problems. Make noise when hiking, leave dogs in the camper or car, and keep food smells off yourself and your clothes. If you see a bear, make noise, alter your route, and back off. If a bear approaches, speak calmly, hold up your arms, and back away. If the grizzly charges, do not run away. If contact is imminent experts advise falling to the ground, tucking into a fetal position to better take the blow, and playing dead. You can't outdistance a grizzly, which can run 40 mi per hour.

The Denali caribou herd has diminished over the years from between 15,000 and 20,000 during the 1940s to some 2,000 animals today. Male caribou in particular have large antlers and big, round hooves that provide good support in snow and on the tundra. They forage for green sprouts, lichens, willow, and sedge grasses. Flies and mosquitoes are a special nuisance to the caribou; flies lay eggs on their coats and the larvae penetrate the body. A caribou can commonly be seen holding its nose close to the wet ground for relief from the nostril flies that enter it. Hot, calm days encourage the flies; the herd will look for high breezy ground to forage.

Moose don't travel in herds; they are commonly seen in small groups or wandering alone in Denali. Bulls may weigh as much as 1,500 pounds and have 70-inch antlers. Both sexes are potentially dangerous, females especially so when it comes to protecting their calves; equipped with strong legs, they manage a powerful kick. As herbivores, moose look for tender tips of willow and birch in winter; in summer they eat grasses from lake bottoms, often emerging from the water with grass trailing out of their mouths and water pouring off their antlers. Look for evidence of winter browsing along roads and trails; moose like the easy access to bushes. Willows are often eaten back to the thicker branches.

Dall sheep roam the higher elevations of the park during the summer season and are commonly seen on slopes along the park road. These bright white animals travel in bands of about 60. Males flaunt big, curling horns; females have little spikes. Eager shuttle-bus passengers scan the rocky hillsides for this Denali favorite. Look for them grazing on grasses and at natural salt licks. The Igloo Creek area is a good place to find them.

Though not seen as often as the four species above, Denali's wolves are sometimes spotted from the park road and, more rarely, lope along the road itself.

Smaller mammals commonly spotted in the park are arctic ground squirrels (whose quick whistle and prairie dog–like stance are easily recognized on tundra slopes), hoary marmots, red foxes, lynx, wolverines, martens, mink, and weasels. Beavers inhabit the park's lakes and rivers. In all, 37 species of mammals reside in the preserve.

There are also 159 bird species in the park. Among the most common are ravens—big, bossy black birds that would happily frequent hotel dumpsters and garbage cans were the containers not bear- and raven-proof. Also look for the willow ptarmigan, Alaska's state bird, a type of grouse with feathered feet. These birds are brown-and-white speckled in summer and will freeze when approached. Golden eagles can sometimes be spotted soaring in wide arcs in the sky.

WHEN TO GO Summer is the most popular season to visit the park. Most campgrounds open Memorial Day weekend and close in mid-September. From June through August,

temperatures generally range from around 40°F to 65°F, though they may occasionally reach into the 70s. In early summer, trails may be muddy and all the trees won't be fully leafed out, but young animals may be more readily visible. High runoff may limit rafting activities on the Nenana River. Late in summer, the tundra colors brighten up; berry picking, a traditional Alaska activity for both bears and people, is allowed in Denali. Rain is common throughout summer. During this time, waiting periods for a shuttle-bus (see Guided Tours, below) pass can be as long as two or three days—and for campsites, even longer.

Fall comes and goes quickly. Autumn colors peak the third week in August and disappear by September. Snow automatically closes western portions of the park road any time after mid-September, and they do not open again until after the first week in June. If you're fortunate enough to be in the park during an early snowfall—before the tourism season is over and the hotels have closed—you'll experience a taste of the Denali winter. Those braving the winter climate find good cross-country skiing, dogsled touring, and solitude; the drawback is limited guest facilities. Although Riley Creek campground is open all year, all bathroom facilities within the park are shut down, and winter snow and cold discourage all but the hardiest. The January low temperature averages −7°F but can drop as low as −50°F.

SEASONAL EVENTS June 21: Alaskans celebrate the **summer solstice** with all-night softball games, barbecues, and footraces at midnight. Though this does not occur inside the park, you can check with park visitor centers, concessionaires, and local restaurants and hotels for locations.

WHAT TO PACK Wildlife viewing is the park's main attraction for most visitors, so binoculars and specialized camera equipment are important (see Other Activities, below).

Mosquitoes can be a great nuisance, especially from late June through mid-August.

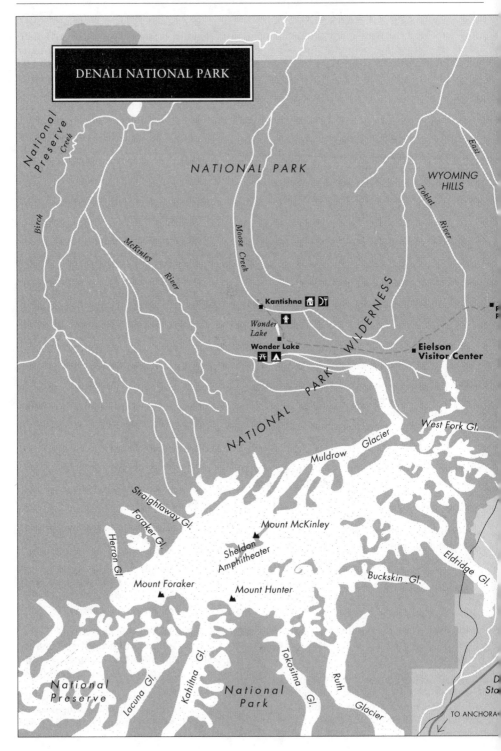

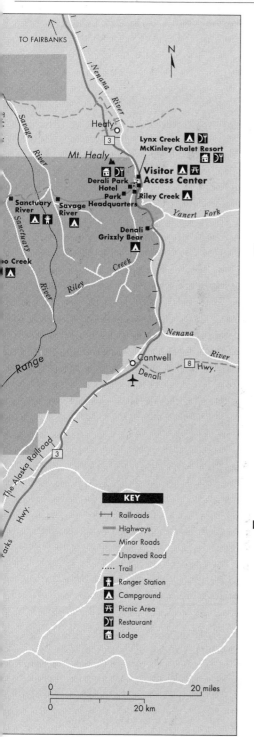

Alaskans carry insect repellent everywhere. If you're hiking overnight into the backcountry, you might even want to bring a head net. Some people have trouble sleeping in the long daylight of Alaska summers, so a great many hotels have black-out drapes. In campgrounds eyeshades are a good idea.

There is no food available west of the Denali National Park Hotel; shuttle-bus riders should pack a lunch or have their hotel supply one. A thermos of hot coffee can make a long, wet day on the bus more pleasant. The only stop for water is at the Eielson Visitor Center (mile 66 on the park road).

GENERAL STORES McKinley Mercantile (tel. 907/683–2215), at mile 1.4 on the park road, carries groceries and camping supplies, including propane. There are showers ($3) in back of the building. It's open daily from 7 AM to 10 PM during peak summer season and from 8 AM to 9 PM in spring and fall. The **Lynx Creek Campground general store** (tel. 907/683–2548) is at mile 238.6 on the George Parks Highway, 1.5 mi north of the park entrance on the river side of the road. Here you'll find a good selection of staples, prepared foods, liquor, gas, ice, and camping supplies such as sleeping bags and mattresses, camp stoves, fuel containers, and dehydrated foods. It's open daily 24 hours between June and August and from dawn to dusk in May and September.

ARRIVING AND DEPARTING Denali is accessible by road and railroad from Anchorage and Fairbanks; the scenery between the cities and the park is nearly as lovely as the park itself. Though the railroad generally stays close to the road, occasionally it detours into more remote country.

By Bus. Gray Line of Alaska (*see* By Train, *below*) provides round-trip bus transportation from Anchorage for $150.

By Car and RV. The park is 237 mi north of Anchorage and 121 mi south of Fairbanks on the George Parks Highway (Highway 3). Roadhouses, which sell food and gas, appear every 50 mi or so along more remote sections of the highway. In winter, the roads are often snow-packed; you should always travel with emergency supplies, including a warm sleeping bag and a change of clothing. Studded tires and chains are a good idea. Also note that from September through May there may be a span of 200 mi without an open gas station, especially at night. Gas up whenever you can.

Count on a five-hour drive to the park from Anchorage and a 2½-hour drive from Fairbanks. The country along the George Parks Highway north of Willow (mile 70) is mostly wilderness with broad views to the mountains. Streams along the way provide fine fishing opportunities. Byers Lake, 147 mi north of Anchorage in Denali State Park, has picnic tables and is a good spot for a picnic lunch en route.

RV rentals are available in Anchorage. Typically, a four-person motor home rents for between $125 and $150 per day. Try **Murphy's RV** (Box 202063, Anchorage, AK 99520-2063, tel. 907/276–0688), **ABC Motorhome Rentals** (2360 Commercial Dr., Anchorage, AK 99501, tel. 907/279–2000) or **Clippership Motorhome Rentals** (5401 Old Seward Hwy., Anchorage, AK 99518, tel. 907/562–7051).

By Plane. There is no scheduled service to the park, but you can charter a flight from Anchorage or Fairbanks, the nearest major airports.

By Train. The **Alaska Railroad** (Box 107500, Anchorage, AK 99510-7500, tel. 907/265–2494 or 800/544–0552 in Anchorage; 907/456–4155 or 800/895–7245 in Fairbanks) runs daily trains from Anchorage and Fairbanks to the park. Hotels outside the park entrance provide transportation to and from the train depot, which is right across the street from the Denali National Park Hotel, inside the park entrance. The northbound train leaves Anchorage at 8:15 AM, arriving at the park at 3:45 PM. The southbound train leaves Fairbanks at 8:15 AM, arriving at noon. The round-trip fare from Anchorage is $198 and from Fairbanks

$106. The Alaska Railroad has a vista dome car on each train, and passengers can sit on top. Locals bring a picnic lunch, but in summer there's a full-service dining car on board.

Private tour companies hook up plush touring cars to the train. **Princess Tours'** Midnight Sun Express (519 W. 4th Ave., Suite 200, Anchorage, AK 99501, tel. 907/276–7711; 3045 Davis Rd., Fairbanks, AK 99709, tel. 907/479–9660) and **Gray Line of Alaska**'s McKinley Explorer (745 W. 4th Ave, Anchorage, AK 99501, tel. 907/277–5581; 1980 S. Cushman Ave., Fairbanks, AK 99701, tel. 907/456–7741) charge $250 round-trip from Anchorage and $130 round-trip from Fairbanks.

EXPLORING

Since cars are largely prohibited beyond mile 14.8 on the park road, most visitors to Denali Park ride the park service shuttle buses. The park hotel also runs narrated bus tours (*see* Guided Tours, *below*).

Bicycles are currently allowed on the park road. The Alaska Railroad transports bikes on the baggage car if space is available. The road is suitable only for mountain bikes.

The real wilderness experience in Denali is reserved for those who get off the buses and walk. There are excellent day hikes near the entrance, and overnight options are unlimited, since there are no formal trails. Many hikers follow riverbeds or ridges. To avoid potentially dangerous encounters with wildlife, follow the advice of park rangers about routes and safety.

THE BEST IN ONE DAY Because 250 to 300 million visitors descend on Denali each year, shuttle-bus coupons can be as rare and valuable as a gold nugget in the Kantishna Hills; you may need to wait a day or two to secure a coupon, unless you reserve seats in advance. Day-trippers unable to wait this long can explore the area near the park entrance. Here they will find hiking trails—the only marked paths in the park—

and dogsled demonstrations at the kennels near park headquarters.

At the Denali National Park Hotel, try catching some of the films and educational activities planned in the hotel auditorium. Programs run throughout the day; check park bulletin boards or the park newspaper for schedules. The half-hour *Denali Wilderness* is particularly good.

Since the days in Denali are long, those who are so inclined will still have time to experience firsthand the rapids of the Nenana River. A two-hour trip costs $45 per person (*see* Guided Tours, *below*). Then, after dinner, stretch your legs with a 1-mi hike down to Horseshoe Lake, a little jewel surrounded by spruce and aspen forest.

ORIENTATION PROGRAMS You can catch a 15-minute orientation to the park throughout the day at the **visitor center** (tel. 907/ 683–1266). Ranger-naturalist-led activities take place near the park entrance daily. Sled dog demonstrations at the dog kennels on the park road are scheduled three times daily; free bus transportation from the visitor center and the park hotel is provided. Slides and films about the park are shown nightly in the park hotel auditorium.

GUIDED TOURS Rangers lead free daily walks at Eielson Visitor Center, at mile 66 on the park road. Staff members also lead off-road discovery hikes exploring ridges, tundra, and river valleys in the park. Registration for these off-road hikes is required at the visitor center.

Guided bus tours depart from the **Denali National Park Hotel** (241 W. Ship Creek Ave., Anchorage, AK 99501 year-round, tel. 907/276–7234 or 800/276–7234; Box 87, Denali Park, AK 99755 in summer, tel. 907/683–2215) daily between 6 AM and 3 PM. These buses are more comfortable than the park service's buses, and they provide lunch. The wildlife tour lasts six to eight hours and costs $58. Shorter (three- to four-hour) natural history tours cost $34. You can book these private tours well in advance of your arrival. Those who wish to

go through the park on their own may take a shuttle-bus ride. Reservations (tel. 907/ 272–7275 or 800/622–7275) are available for $12 to $30 per person, depending on destination. They can be made beginning in mid- to late February.

Denali Air (Box 82, Denali National Park, AK 99755, tel. 907/683–2261) gives 70-minute small-plane tours of the park, departing from mile 229 of the George Parks Highway; price is $135 per person. **K2 Aviation** (Box 545, Talkeetna, AK 99676, tel. 907/733–2291 or 800/764–2291) and **Doug Geeting Aviation** (Box 42, Talkeetna, AK 99676, tel. 907/733–2366 or 800/770–2366) are air taxi services that fly out of Talkeetna on a spur road off mile 99 on the George Parks Highway; both conduct flight-seeing tours of the mountain and glacier landings. Prices range from $75 to $165 per person, depending on the operator, number of persons, length of the flight, and inclusion of a glacier landing. **ERA Helicopters** (6160 Carl Brady Dr., Anchorage, AK 99502, tel. 907/266–8351 or 800/843–1947 year-round, 907/683–2574 in summer) operates 50-minute tours for $179 per person from its helipad 5 mi north of the park entrance.

Raft trips down the icy, class-four white-water Nenana River attract both visitors and locals. Operators provide waterproof gear, and some tours include a shore lunch with a campfire. The river is run in two stretches. The part south of the park entrance is tamer and more suitable for children. The rapids are in the northern section. **Denali Raft Adventures** (Box 190, Denali Park, AK 99755, tel. 907/683–2234) leads four different river excursions ranging from an overnight trip ($375 per person) to an all-day outing ($130 per person) to two-hour canyon rapids or scenic float trips (both $45 per person). These latter two-hour trips may be combined. **Nenana Raft Adventures** (Box 500, Healy, AK 99743, tel. 907/683–2628) leads several trips daily, with prices ranging from $45 to $58. **McKinley Raft Tours** (Box 138, Denali Park, AK 99755, tel. 907/683–2392) has a two-hour white-water canyon run or a two-hour scenic tour for $45, plus a combination of both for $58. **Denali Outdoors Center** (Box 1171, Denali Park, AK 99755, tel. 907/683–1925) has both kayaking and raft tours; prices start at $45.

Kantishna Wilderness Trails (Box 81670, Fairbanks, AK 99708, tel. 907/479–2436 or 800/942–7420, fax 907/479–2611) provides private bus transportation to Kantishna Roadhouse, at the end of the park road; tours cost $99, plus the park entrance fee. Have lunch at the log lodge, then spend the day hiking and panning for gold.

SCENIC DRIVES AND VIEWS Visitors can disembark at any shuttle-bus stop in the park for hiking and sightseeing, then catch the next bus in either direction to continue the trip. Buses generally run every half hour. **Polychrome Pass,** at mile 46 of the park road, is a popular place to disembark, walk around, and take in the wide views of the stream valleys and tundra below.

Wonder Lake, at the end of the road, is a good spot to picnic, hike, and enjoy the tundra before the long ride back to the park entrance at Riley Creek. There are good views here of the north face of Mt. McKinley.

HISTORIC BUILDINGS AND SITES In the early days of the park, horse-drawn carriages brought visitors to the **Savage Road Camp** just south of the present Savage River campground. Campers stayed overnight on cots in canvas tents. The stage route fell out of use in the early 1940s. A few yards south of the campground, indentations from the old camp can still be seen in the fragile tundra.

The old **Kantishna Roadhouse** at the end of the park road, beyond Wonder Lake, was part of the old townsite of Kantishna. The gold rush in the Kantishna Hills at the turn of the century attracted more than 2,500 people to the area. A new, modern roadhouse is now one of four private wilderness lodges in the old gold-mining district (*see* Lodging, *below*).

NATURE TRAILS AND SHORT WALKS All developed trails are near the park entrance at Riley Creek. The **Taiga Trail Loop,** a 1.3-mi easy walk through dense spruce forest near the campground, has enticing views of a rushing creek. It starts and ends at the Denali National Park Hotel and takes an hour at most to complete. The **Horseshoe Lake Trail** is a 1-mi hike, also beginning near the park hotel, to small Horseshoe Lake at the bottom of a canyon.

LONGER HIKES The only relatively long, marked trail for hiking in the park, **Mt. Healy Overlook Trail** gains 1,700 ft in 2.5 mi and takes about four hours round-trip, with outstanding views of the Nenana River below and the Alaska Range above. Carry water.

Mt. Healy Overlook Trail is a great jumping-off point for overnight backcountry hiking. Wise and careful planning is necessary to undertake any overnight or even daylong trek through Denali's rugged and often unpredictable wilderness. At the very least, consult with park rangers at the visitor center well before departing. Though you cannot make advance reservations for backcountry camping, you can ask the rangers for practical advice on where best to take advantage of Denali's vast resources—and where bears have been sighted recently.

The day before your hike, you will have to stop in at the visitor center (open in summer from 7 AM to 8 PM) to pick up your free backcountry permit if you plan to camp overnight. On the map, Denali is divided into three sections: Denali National Park Wilderness (through which the park road passes), Denali National Park, and Denali National Preserve. Different regulations apply to the three regions: Campfires, firearms, and pets are prohibited in the Wilderness backcountry. Fishing is allowed with a license in the park and preserve, and without a license in the Wilderness backcountry.

Learn to use a topographic map; some areas in the park are extremely dense with brush, and in these regions it's very easy to become lost. It's safest to hike along ridge tops and alongside gravel riverbeds, away from the brush. The park is replete with glacial rivers, many of them dangerous to cross. Ask rangers about techniques for crossing these rivers. Never attempt to cross a river barefoot, and always choose a route that allows you the option of returning to the shoreline. If in a group, spread out when crossing tundra to minimize the tendency to imprint your own trail on the delicate landscape. Because of Denali's fierce subarctic climate, the earth beneath you is easily damaged and repairs itself slowly. It is important to realize that the number of visitors to the park—which has risen steadily in recent years—poses a great threat to both the precious wildlife and the fragile terrain. A study done in the 1980s showed that the increase in visitor numbers had begun to disturb the park's ecosystem and reduce the number of wildlife sightings. It is your responsibility to leave the park exactly as you found it.

Remember also that private dwellings are scattered throughout Denali National Park and Preserve. No camping is allowed within sight of lodges or private property, or within .5 mi of the park road, and you must not hike through private property. Hiking in the backcountry is carefully monitored by backcountry rangers and, depending on the crowds, you may not be permitted to hike in certain regions of the park. Again, the key to successful and enjoyable hiking is researching your trip prudently and checking with the appropriate authorities.

OTHER ACTIVITIES All-terrain vehicles and bicycles are not permitted to leave the park road. In winter, you can travel wherever you wish on a dogsled, snowshoes, or cross-country skis; however, as with hiking, you should plan ahead and consult rangers before setting off. Commonly used routes make travel easier than breaking new trails.

Biking. Bicycling in Denali has caught on in recent years. Given the restricted use of the park road, however, cyclists should pick up a copy of the park brochure "Rules of the Road" before departing. A travel permit is not required, but bicycles are not allowed off the roadways. Also, if you're planning an overnight trip, you must register with the visitor center, just as if you were planning an overnight hike (*see* Longer Hikes, *above*). Inside the park, **Denali Mountain Bike** (tel. 907/457–2453) rents mountain bikes for $25 per day or $7 per hour. The **Denali Princess Lodge** (tel. 907/683–2283 or 800/426–0500), outside the park entrance, has mountain bikes for rent for customers of the lodge only.

Bird-Watching. Denali is an excellent place to find several species of bird. The ubiquitous song of the tundra, the falling notes of "Three Blind Mice," is sung by the white-crowned sparrow, common throughout Alaska. There are also golden eagles, falcons, ducks, and loons.

Boating. Denali Wilderness Safaris (Box 181, Cantwell, AK 99729, tel. 907/768–2660) provides narrated trips down the Nenana River aboard covered, heated tour boats that lead to an operating prospector's camp. Tours last 3½ hours and cost $75.

Fishing. There's good fishing throughout Interior Alaska. A number of local rivers and lakes are full of grayling and pike. Though fishing licenses are required in the more remote areas of Denali (Denali National Park and Denali National Preserve), a license is not required for fishing within the limits of Denali Wilderness; check with the visitor center to learn Wilderness boundaries. A three-day, nonresident license costs $15 and is available at most general stores and gas stations.

Flight-Seeing. The vastness of the park takes on new dimensions when you view it from the air. Several companies offer helicopter and small-plane rides (*see* Guided Tours, *above*).

Horseback Riding. You can't ride a horse inside the park unless you're a guest at Kantishna Roadhouse (*see* Lodging, *below*). **Denali Wilderness Lodge** (tel. 907/683–1287 or 800/541–9779), 30 mi east of the park, offers horseback riding, as well as daily fly-in packages to its grounds; the property is a former bush camp, homestead, and hunting lodge, first settled after the turn of the century. **Wolf Point Ranch** (tel. 907/768–2620) has guided horseback rides just south of the park in Cantwell.

Photography. Denali is renowned among outdoor photographers. Big skies, big mammals, and the biggest mountain in North America provide plenty of subject matter. The shot of a moose wading in Wonder Lake, water cascading from its antlers, is a classic. Bring a generous supply of film— long summer days allow for plenty of photo opportunities.

Rafting. Rafters should not attempt the portion of the Nenana River north of the park entrance unless they have run the rapids with a commercial operator as guide (*see* Guided Tours, *above*) and have skills to navigate class-four or higher white water. Many fatal accidents have taken place on this river.

Ski Touring. Opportunities for wintertime cross-country skiing are unlimited in the backcountry. Cross-country skis and camping gear can be rented in Anchorage at **REI** (1200 W. Northern Lights Blvd., Anchorage, AK 99503, tel. 907/272–4565).

CHILDREN'S PROGRAMS During the summer, park rangers have a free **Junior Ranger program** in which children earn badges by completing certain activities. Call the visitor center for details.

EVENING ACTIVITIES The Alaska Cabin Nite dinner theater at the **McKinley Chalet Resort** (tel. 907/683–2215) has seatings twice nightly from mid-May through mid-September, for $35. Waiters and waitresses perform musical skits recalling the gold rush days in Alaska. Reservations are recommended.

Riley Creek, Savage, Teklanika, and **Wonder Lake campgrounds** have free evening programs led by ranger-naturalists. Check the bulletin boards for times and topics.

Ranger's talks, movies, and slide shows take place nightly in the Denali National Park Hotel auditorium. The topics presented vary from year to year.

DINING

One drawback of a road trip in Alaska or the Yukon is the limited choices of restaurants you'll encounter along the way. Denali National Park and Preserve is no exception. Alaska hotels and roadhouses generally serve good hamburgers and seafood. In Denali, basic is usually better.

NEAR THE PARK **Alaska Cabin Nite at McKinley Chalet Resort.** This family-style establishment serves barbecued ribs and salmon at its dinner and show. Nearly two hours of gold rush–era skits and a barbecue feast for $35 per person make this a good value. *George Parks Hwy., 1.5 mi north of park entrance, tel. 800/276–2234 year-round, 907/683–2215 in summer. AE, D, MC, V. Closed winter. $$$*

Summit Restaurant. In the Denali Princess Lodge, the Summit Restaurant has a predictable menu of steak, salmon, and pasta. Since local salmon become mushy after their long journey up the interior rivers, the fish here come from south-central ports; ask for them grilled. A wood-paneled dining room overlooks the Nenana River, so be sure to request a window table. *George Parks Hwy., 1 mi north of park entrance, Denali, tel. 907/683–2283. AE, DC, MC, V. Closed winter. $$$*

Lynx Creek Campground Pizza & Pub. This modest, low-frame building beside the gas station is plain-looking outside and in, but it's popular with young park and hotel workers as well as tourists. The jukebox usually blaring rock music, and the friendly customers mingle at the common tables. Order reindeer-sausage pizza, and wash it down with locally brewed Alaskan beer. *George Parks Hwy., 1.5 mi north of park entrance, tel. 907/683–2548. No credit cards. Closed winter. $–$$*

Totem Inn Restaurant. Affordable prices, a casual ambience, and round-the-clock service draw many locals to this restaurant in Healy, just a few minutes drive from the park. Burgers and steaks are the specialty; it also has one of the only salad bars in the area. *George Parks Hwy., 12 mi north of park entrance, Healy, tel. 907/683–2420. MC, V. $–$$*

PICNIC SPOTS You can picnic anywhere along the park road. Tundra is soft and smells like medicinal potpourri, and napping here is pleasant after lunch on a sunny day. Ask the shuttle-bus driver where bears have been spotted that day and avoid those areas. Horseshoe Lake is an easy short walk (*see* Nature Trails and Short Walks, *above*) for lunch near the park hotel.

LODGING

There is only one hotel inside the park entrance, but plenty of lodges in the Kantishna gold-mining district provide a true wilderness experience without sacrificing the modern comforts of hot showers and queen-size beds. These properties are very expensive, averaging $250 or more per person, per night, and some require a minimum two- or three-night stay. Most hotels close during winter. There are several large hotels and cabin compounds near the park. Reservations for all accommodations should be made a full season in advance.

INSIDE THE PARK Denali National Park Hotel. Built in 1973, this practical hotel consists of modular buildings. Its only advantage over others in the area is its proximity to the railroad station and shuttle buses. Free ranger talks are given nightly in the hotel's 300-seat auditorium. *ARA Mark Denali Park Hotel, Box 87, Denali Park, AK 99755 in summer, tel. 907/ 683–2215; 241 W. Ship Creek Ave., Anchorage, AK 99501 year-round, tel. 907/276– 7234 or 800/276–7234. 100 rooms. Facilities: restaurant, cafeteria. AE, D, MC, V. Closed winter. $$$*

Kantishna Roadhouse. This roadhouse at the end of the park road takes as long as five to six hours to reach by bus from the park entrance. Surrounding the historic roadhouse are 27 log cabins and a hand-hewn log lodge. Activities include gold panning, mountain-bike riding, guided hikes, horse-wagon rides, and sightseeing by plane. Three daily meals are included in the rather pricey rates; the chef will accommodate dietary restrictions. Prepayment in full by check or money order is required 45 days prior to your stay. *Box 81670, Fairbanks, AK 99708, tel. 907/479–2436 or 800/ 942–7420, fax 907/479–2611. 27 cabins. Facilities: bar, dining room, sauna, library. Closed Sept.–May. $$$*

The Kantishna district's other wilderness lodges are **Camp Denali** and **North Face Lodge** (Box 67, Denali Park, AK 99755, tel. 907/683–2290, fax 907/683–1568, $$$) and **Denali Backcountry Lodge** (Box 189, Denali Park, AK 99755, tel. 907/683–2594, fax 907/683–1341, $$$).

NEAR THE PARK Denali Princess Lodge. This grand, wood-sided hotel prides itself on being the most luxurious in the Denali area. Since its opening in 1987, the property has been expanded twice and now houses 280 rooms. Big wood decks off the back of the hotel overlook the Nenana River, and suites all have Jacuzzis. The interior has a log-cabin feel but is also sophisticated, with fine carpets and fabrics in jewel tones. A free shuttle takes guests to the park. *George Parks Hwy., 1 mi north of park entrance, Box 110, Denali Park, AK 99755, tel. 907/683–2283 in summer. Reservations: 2815 2nd Ave., Suite 400, Seattle, WA 98121-1299, tel. 800/426–0500. 280 rooms. Facilities: 2 restaurants, outdoor hot tubs, meeting rooms. AE, DC, MC, V. Closed winter. $$$*

McKinley Chalet Resort. This sprawling complex of chalet-style cedar lodges on the George Parks Highway occupies a bluff overlooking the Nenana River; the log buildings house a number of river-view rooms. The majority of the 300 rooms are two-bedroom suites. The dinner theater is where Alaska Cabin Nite takes place (*see* Dining, *above*). You can arrange for the kitchen to pack you a box lunch for trips into the park. *George Parks Hwy., 1.5 mi north of park entrance, Milepost 238, Box 87, Denali Park, AK 99755, tel. 907/683–2215 in summer. Reservations: Denali Park Resort, 241 W. Ship Creek Ave., Anchorage, AK 99501, tel. 907/276–7234 or 800/276–7234. 300 rooms. Facilities: restaurant, pool, hot tub, exercise room. AE, D, MC, V. Closed winter. $$$*

Other lodge-type options near the park are **Denali Cabins** (200 W. 34th Ave., Suite 362, Anchorage, AK 99503 in winter, tel. 907/258–0134; Box 229, Denali Park, AK 99755 in summer, tel. 907/683–2643: $$$), **Denali Crow's Nest Log Cabins** (Box 70, Denali Park, AK 99755, tel. 907/683–2723, $$$), and **Denali Grizzly Bear Cabins and Campground** (Box 7, Denali Park, AK 99755, tel. 907/683–2696, $$–$$$). The **Denali Hostel** (Box 801, Denali Park, AK 99755, tel. 907/683–1295, $) is 10 mi north of the park entrance, near Healy, and provides bus service back and forth to the park. All of these lodgings are open in summer only; the actual dates vary depending on the weather. Always call or write ahead. For those age 55 and older, **Denali Foundation Elderhostel** (Box 212, Denali Park, AK 99755, tel. 907/683–2597) has a seven-day educational program including day hikes, classes on wildlife photography, and slide presentations. The week includes two trips into the park. Trips are available only from mid-May until mid-September.

CAMPING

INSIDE THE PARK There are seven campgrounds in the park. The dates of opening and closing depend on snow conditions, but most years the campgrounds are closed from late September to late May. Riley Creek is open year-round, but there is no water in winter.

Patience and planning are the keys to obtaining one of Denali's 231 sites (not including spaces for backpackers at Morino). Each site is assigned at the visitor center. Usually you will find that campgrounds are full; if so, your best bet may be to come to Denali, register at the visitor center (registration is not permitted more than a day or two in advance), and spend your one- or two-day wait at a nearby private campground. A number of these private establishments, in addition to the one described below, are listed on the visitor center bulletin board. Be aware that stays in the park are limited to 14 days during the summer (30 during winter), and nonrefundable payment is due upon registration. Only Riley Creek, Savage River, and Teklanika campgrounds accept RVs. The campgrounds at Sanctuary River and Igloo Creek have no water supplies.

Note that Wonder Lake is closed, due to snow, for a longer period of the year than the others; check the visitor center for exact dates and a number of additional rules and regulations that apply to each campground. Fire is never allowed outside of established pits, and pets must be on a leash at all times. Bears are a potential problem at all of Denali's campgrounds. Always keep food, fragrant toiletries, and food-soiled clothing out of your tent; food-storage lockers have been placed at several campsites. Clean up after meals and store food in your car or in the locker. Backcountry camping is allowed by permit anywhere in the park, unless restricted for safety or wildlife-preservation reasons. Restricted areas change from time to time, so check with a ranger before setting out. Apply for a permit at the visitor center (*see* Longer Hikes, *above*).

Riley Creek is .25 mi west of the George Parks Highway, along the park road. It has 100 RV and tent sites, with flush toilets, piped water, a disposal station (except during winter), and a pay phone. Sites cost $12 per night. **Morino Backpacker Campground** is at mile 1.9 and has room for 60 backpackers. There is piped water here, as well as chemical toilets and a pay phone at the nearby hotel. Sites cost $3 per night. **Savage River,** with 33 RV and tent sites and three group sites that accommodate between nine and 20 persons each, is at mile 13. It has piped water and flush toilets. Sites cost $12 per night and $40 per group site. **Sanctuary River,** at mile 23, has seven tent sites ($6 each), with chemical toilets. **Teklanika River** is at mile 29. It has 53 RV and tent sites, piped water, and chemical toilets. Sites cost $12 per night. **Igloo Creek,** on mile 34, has seven tent sites ($6 each), and pit toilets. **Wonder Lake** is at mile 85. It has 28 tent sites, piped water, and flush toilets. Sites cost $12 per night.

NEAR THE PARK Outside the park, several campgrounds have full-service campsites for tents and RVs. One of the best:

Denali Grizzly Bear Cabins and Campground. An Alaskan family has owned and operated this campground since 1958. A number of authentically restored trapper's cabins here date back to 1904. Campsites cost $16 per night plus $5 for an electrical hookup and $1 for a water hookup. The five walled tents are the bargain of the area: only $23 a night for three if you bring your own linens. The campground is 6 mi south of the park entrance. Reservations are recommended. *Box 7, Denali Park, AK 99755, tel. 907/683–2696. 72 campsites, 21 cabins, 5 walled tents. D, MC, V.*

Grand Canyon National Park
Arizona

Updated by Edie Jarolim

he Grand Canyon is often called the Temple of the World because of the reverence it instills in virtually all who view it for the first time. Naturalist John Muir, more than a century ago, said of the canyon, "It will seem as novel to you, as unearthly in the color and grandeur and quantity of its architecture, as if you had found it after death, on some other star."

Creation of the canyon began more than 80 million years ago when a great upheaval of the earth's crust began forming what is now the huge domelike Colorado Plateau in northern Arizona. Nearly 6 million years ago the force of the Colorado River began carving an erratic path through the uplifted region, sculpting a gorge that is, today, 277 mi long, as much as 17 mi wide, and nearly 6,000 ft deep in some places.

Although the great buttes and erosion-blasted gorges of the canyon have been in place for millions of years, the canyon is an ever-changing spectacle. Clouds, shadows, and the moving sun constantly repaint what the viewer sees. The sharply defined colors of the rock merge and soften as sunlight shifts. Clouds float by and purple shadows creep into the depths. During the gentle fall of rain, a haze tints and softens the landscape. As the sun flames in the west, some of the canyon walls turn almost blood red. Then, as night falls, the depths become obscured, and the purples get deeper, until finally all is cloaked in darkness. Next day, the show begins anew.

There are clearly plenty of reasons why the Grand Canyon is such a thrilling destination for those who like visual adventure. And the regions immediately surrounding the canyon offer similarly stunning views: North and west of the canyon's North Rim are the wonders of Zion and Bryce Canyon national parks, both in southwestern Utah. The magnificent emerald waters of Lake Powell and thousands of square miles of the Glen Canyon National Recreation Area lie north and east of the Grand Canyon. Directly to the east is the sprawling 25,000-square-mi Navajo Indian Reservation, a land of red dunes and soaring buttes. It's no wonder that more than 5 million visitors come to Grand Canyon country each year.

There are great differences between the North and South rims of the Grand Canyon: The South Rim is more accessible, more developed, and more crowded. (From Flagstaff it's 81 mi to the South Rim and 210 mi to the North Rim.) There are more services, attractions, and amenities at the South Rim, but the North Rim is set in a lush forest where you can find sylvan solitude only a few yards from motel and campground areas. The long drive to the North Rim is through lonely but scenic country.

ESSENTIAL INFORMATION

VISITOR INFORMATION For detailed information about the park, contact **Grand Canyon National Park** (Box 129, Grand Canyon, AZ 86023, tel. 520/638–7888); request the complimentary *Trip Planner,* updated regularly by the National Park Service (the park also publishes a free *Accessibility Guide*). If you have questions about lodging, touring, and recreation within the park, contact **Amfac Parks and Resorts** (14001 E. Iliff, Suite 600, Aurora, CO 80013, tel. 303/297–2757). For same-day reservations on the South Rim, call 520/638–2631; on the North Rim, it's 520/638–2611. The **Grand Canyon Chamber of Commerce** (Hwy. 64 in IMAX Theater, Tusayan 86023, tel. 520/638–2901) can help with accommodations just outside the South Rim, and with various commercial activities inside the park. The **Kane County Travel Council** (78 S. 100 E, Kanab, UT 84731, tel. 800/ 733–5263) has a similar function relative to the North Rim, though the office is considerably farther from the park.

Hikers descending into the canyon (via any of the numerous trails) for an overnight stay need a backcountry permit, which costs $20 (plus $4 per person per night) and must be obtained in person or by contacting the **Backcountry Office** (Box 129, Grand Canyon, AZ 86023, tel. 520/638– 7888). The office's free *Backcountry Trip Planner* can help answer your hiking questions. Permits are limited, so make your reservation at least several months in advance. Day hikes into the canyon or anywhere else in the national park do not require a permit; overnight stays at Phantom Ranch require reservations but no permits. Before attempting a descent to the bottom of the canyon, discuss your plans with a park ranger, and acquaint yourself with all the required safety precautions. Unless you have a backcountry permit, overnight camping in the national park is restricted to designated campgrounds.

FEES The National Park Service charges visitors $20 to enter Grand Canyon National Park by motorized vehicle, regardless of the number of passengers. Individuals arriving by bicycle or foot pay $10. The entrance gates are open 24 hours a day. If you arrive when a gate is unpatrolled, you may enter legally without paying the fee.

PUBLICATIONS Visitors at either rim are given *The Guide,* a free newspaper, as they enter the park. It contains a detailed area map, a complete schedule of free programs, and other useful information. It's also available at the visitor centers and lodges. Maps are available at the visitor centers and at many of the lodges and stores. Books on various aspects of the canyon—geology, history, and photography—are on sale in the visitor centers, various gift shops, and museums at both rims.

The **Grand Canyon Association** (Box 399, Grand Canyon, AZ 86023, tel. 520/638– 2481 or 800/858–2808, fax 520/638–2484) has a listing of informative publications on Northern Arizona, including *Along the Rim,* by Nancy Loving, a short but helpful guide to the flora and fauna you'll encounter on both rims; *Introduction to Grand Canyon Geology,* by Michael Collier, which gives a concise and easy-to-follow overview of the park's geology; *In the House of Stone and Light,* by J. Donald Hughes, a careful and revealing history of the canyon; and the *Official Guide to Hiking the Grand Canyon,* by Scott Thybony, with detailed descriptions of 19 trails. These books and many others can be ordered by fax, mail, or phone.

GEOLOGY AND TERRAIN Grand Canyon National Park consists of more than 1,900 square mi, and both rims are surrounded by the vast Kaibab National Forest. The inner canyon reflects a geologic profile of much of the earth's history. At the very bottom of the canyon is a layer of rock called Vishnu Schist, which is close to 2 billion years old.

The terrain at the North Rim of the canyon is a part of the Kaibab Plateau, a heavily forested region as high as 9,000 ft. The South Rim, part of the Coconino Plateau, lies in an area that is essentially flat, at an elevation of about 7,000 ft, where highland trees are abundant.

FLORA AND FAUNA The South Rim is forested primarily by stands of ponderosa pine, piñon pine, and Utah juniper. Shrubs include cliffrose, mountain mahogany, and fernbush. In the Kaibab Plateau on the North Rim, ponderosa pine, spruce, fir, and quaking aspen thrive.

Animal life abounds in the park on both rims. Eighty-eight different species of mammal, 24 types of lizard, 24 kinds of snake, and more than 300 species of bird inhabit the park. Two species are unique to the Grand Canyon: The rare Kaibab squirrel with its white tail and tufted ears is found only on the North Rim, and the pink Grand Canyon rattlesnake stays at lower elevations in the canyon, the only place it is found. Mule deer are often seen in the park—frequently crossing the roads—so drive carefully. Coyotes are seldom seen but often heard as they howl and yip at night. Hawks and ravens are regularly observed riding on the updrafts over the canyon. It is illegal and unsafe to feed the animals: Their health can be maintained only on a natural diet, and visitors have been bitten while feeding.

WHEN TO GO The high and low seasons at Grand Canyon are not sharply defined. Changes in activities, prices, and the availability of services are often based on demand, funding, and weather. For example, the number of months that the free shuttles run at Grand Canyon Village (South Rim) may depend in part on the availability of National Park Service funding. When the number of visitors remains high, retail stores continue their longer summer hours well into the fall. Although crowds start arriving around Easter and stay until November, and warm weather can last from May to September, for practical purposes, consider the term "summer season" to mean roughly the months of June, July, and August. The term "colder months" means roughly all the others.

The South Rim, lower in elevation than the North Rim, is open year-round. There, summers normally consist of shirtsleeve days and crisp evenings with short but somewhat frequent afternoon thundershowers. Spring and fall are moderate: Temperatures generally stay above 32°F and often climb into the 70s. In winter, days typically range from about 20°F to 50°F, although subzero temperatures are not uncommon in mid-

winter. Snowfall is common during winter months, but it enhances the beauty of the canyon, and the roads are kept open. The North Rim, which is for the most part higher than 8,000 ft, is generally open from mid-May through late October, but unexpected snowfall, which blocks access roads, may change these dates. As at the South Rim, late summer afternoon rains are common here.

Summer crowds at the South Rim can be a major irritation. Around 5 million people come to the canyon each year, and 90% of them arrive at the South Rim. If you choose to visit in spring, fall, or winter, there are fewer people—and thus fewer parking problems. However, since spring and fall are far better for inner-canyon hiking than summer, backcountry permits can be just as hard to get. Lodging prices within the park, in nearby Tusayan, and in such northwestern Arizona communities as Valle, Flagstaff, and Williams, generally drop during colder months.

SEASONAL EVENTS **Mid-May to early June:** Coconino Center for the Arts (2300 N. Fort Valley Rd., tel. 520/779–6921) sponsors the **Trappings of the American West,** a celebration of cowboy art, including everything from paintings and sculpture to cowboy poetry readings. **Late May to early September: Celebration of Native American Art,** featuring exhibits of work by Zuni, Hopi, and Navajo artists, is held at the Museum of Northern Arizona (3101 N. Fort Valley Rd., tel. 520/774–5211). **July and August:** Coconino Center for the Arts (2300 N. Fort Valley Rd., tel. 520/779–6921) hosts a **Festival of Native American Arts. August: Flagstaff SummerFest** (Fort Tuthill Coconino County Park, S. Hwy. 89A, tel. 520/774–5130) features an arts-and-crafts fair on the first weekend of the month. **Flagstaff Festival of the Arts** (Box 22402, Flagstaff 86002, tel. 520/774–7750 or 800/266–7740) fills the air with the sounds of classical music and pops, much of it performed by world-renowned artists. **September:** Flagstaff's observatories help make the **Festival**

of Science (tel. 800/842–7293 for information) a stellar attraction.

WHAT TO PACK Good hiking gear and plenty of water are essential. In summer, bring lightweight upper-body wear for warm sunny days and heavier clothes for chilly evenings, including light jackets and sweaters. In colder months, bring heavy jackets, scarves, warm headgear, and gloves.

GENERAL STORES Both rims of the Grand Canyon have convenience stores. On the South Rim, **Babbitts General Store** has locations in Grand Canyon Village (tel. 520/638–2262), Tusayan (5 mi south of Grand Canyon Village on U.S. 180, tel. 520/638–2854), and Desert View (near east entrance to South Rim on Rte. 64, tel. 520/638–2393). All three locations are well stocked, but the main store in Grand Canyon Village has the widest range of goods: groceries; deli food; clothing; camping, hiking, and cross-country skiing equipment (including rentals); and RV supplies. Hours vary from store to store but are generally from 8 to 8 in summer and from 9 to 6 in winter; all Babbitt's stores are open daily year-round. The nearby village of Tusayan also has several other convenience stops and service stations.

On the North Rim, groceries, traveler's supplies, and some clothing can be found at the **North Rim General Store** (2 mi north of Grand Canyon Lodge off Rte. 67, tel. 520/638–2611, ext. 370).

Automotive service on the South Rim is available year-round, daily from 8 to 5, at the **Fred Harvey Public Garage** (tel. 520/638–2631) in Grand Canyon Village. There's a gas station at **Desert View** (tel. 520/638–2365), just inside the east entrance to the South Rim, and there are other places to get gas in the nearby village of Tusayan. On the North Rim, the **Chevron Service Station** (tel. 520/638–2611, ext. 290) repairs cars daily from 8 to 7; it is inside the park on the access road leading to the North Rim Campground.

ARRIVING AND DEPARTING The most convenient way to visit the Grand Canyon is by car. The South Rim is more accessible than the North Rim, since it is less than 100 mi from Flagstaff, while the North Rim is 235 mi from the South Rim and far from major towns or cities. The South Rim is roughly 250 mi from Phoenix and 260 mi from Las Vegas. It's also within a 300-mi radius of Bryce, Canyon de Chelly, Mesa Verde, and Zion national parks. Once you arrive at Grand Canyon Village on the South Rim, you can either walk or catch a park shuttle (summer only), commercial shuttle, or taxi to get around.

By Bus. Greyhound Lines (tel. 800/231–2222) provides bus service from all over the United States to either Flagstaff or Williams. From either town, continue to the South Rim with **Nava-Hopi Tours** and on to the North Rim on the **Trans Canyon Shuttle** (*see below,* for both).

By Car and RV. If you're traveling from the east or south, the best access to the Grand Canyon's South Rim is from Flagstaff or Williams, both on I–40. There are two routes out of Flagstaff: One, U.S. 180, heads 81 mi northwest to Grand Canyon Village; the other runs north on U.S. 89 and then turns west on Route 64—a total of 107 mi to Grand Canyon Village. The latter route is generally considered the more scenic but can be dangerous or impassable during winter.

If you're crossing Arizona on I–40 from the west, the most direct route to the South Rim is on Route 64 from Williams to Grand Canyon Village, a distance of 58 mi.

To reach the North Rim from Flagstaff, proceed north on U.S. 89 to Bitter Springs, then take U.S. 89A to Route 67, and head south to the North Rim, a total of 210 mi.

By Plane. Sky Harbor International Airport (tel. 602/273–3300), in Phoenix, and **McCarran International Airport** (tel. 702/261–5743), in Las Vegas, both served by all major airlines, are the most accessible airports. From both you can catch a connecting flight to the South Rim's **Grand Canyon National Park Airport** (tel. 520/638–2446), about 6 mi south of Grand Canyon Village. There is no commercial airline service to the North Rim of the Grand Canyon, but air travelers can take the **Trans Canyon Shuttle** (tel. 520/638–2820) 235 mi from the Bright Angel Lodge in Grand Canyon Village to the North Rim. The shuttle bus, the only public transportation to the North Rim, leaves daily at 1 PM from May 15 to the end of October, takes 4½ hours, and costs $60 one-way, or $100 round-trip. Reservations should be made two weeks in advance. You can also rent a car at Grand Canyon Airport from **Budget** (tel. 520/638–9360 or 800/527–0700).

Most visitors who arrive at the South Rim's Grand Canyon Airport have lodging reservations either in the village of Tusayan, 6 mi south of Grand Canyon National Park, or in Grand Canyon Village on the South Rim. Transportation to either location is provided by the **Tusayan/Canyon Airport Shuttle** (tel. 520/638–0821) for all arriving flights. The all-day fare is $7. **Fred Harvey Transportation Company** (tel. 520/638–2822 or 520/638–2631) runs a 24-hour taxi service from the airport to Tusayan, Grand Canyon Village, and other points in the area.

By Train. Amtrak (tel. 800/872–7245) provides daily service into Arizona from both east and west. The stop for the Grand Canyon is Flagstaff. From here bus connections can be made to Grand Canyon Village through **Nava-Hopi Tours** (tel. 520/774–5003 or 800/892–8687). To continue on to the North Rim, take the **Trans Canyon Shuttle** (*see above*).

In 1989 train service was reinstated between Williams (63 mi away) and the South Rim's Santa Fe Railway Station. The handsome 1923 passenger cars, which chug along behind near-turn-of-the-century engines, transport visitors year-round (limited schedule between early October and late March). For reservations and schedule information, contact the **Grand Canyon Railway** (tel. 800/843–8724). The cost of this 4¼-hour round-trip (same-day) treat is $60, including the park entrance fee.

EXPLORING

Most scenic areas, museums, hotels, and restaurants are within easy walking distance of both Grand Canyon Village, on the South Rim, and Grand Canyon Lodge, on the North Rim. Those sights that require more than a short walk are usually accessible by shuttle or taxi, and you can always opt to take a bus tour of either rim.

From October through May, traveling by car will increase your flexibility and allow you to take scenic drives in and around the national park. If you're going to the South Rim during the summer months, however, a private vehicle may be more trouble than it's worth, as parking is extremely limited. Roads in Grand Canyon Village can also be very congested during high season, as can those on the North Rim.

THE BEST IN ONE DAY Although Grand Canyon National Park covers more than 1,900 square mi, you can see all the primary sights at either rim in one full day—but you will most likely enjoy the experience more if you plan two days. If you do not arrive the night before, a one-day visit to the North Rim is difficult, since it takes several hours just to get there. At the South Rim, you can drive all of the suggested roads (*see* Scenic Drives and Views, *below*) if you start early and move briskly, or get out of your car and take the Rim Trail (*see* Nature Trails and Short Walks, *below*). It covers a small area and short distances, but it does give you a view of the canyon from various perspectives.

ORIENTATION PROGRAMS The National Park Service conducts orientation activities daily at both the North and South rims. These include lectures on nearly every aspect of the canyon—from geology, plants, and wildlife to history and ancient inhabitants. Guided tours and hikes are also available. The free *Grand Canyon Guide* contains a daily schedule of such activities, which continue into the evening. For a daz-zling introduction to the Grand Canyon, head to the **IMAX Theater** (tel. 520/638–2203) in nearby Tusayan. *Grand Canyon, The Hidden Secrets* is shown here on a 70-ft-high screen that draws the viewer right into the picture. Tickets are $7.50. In high season, the theater is open daily 8:30 to 8:30 with shows starting on the half hour.

A quick tour of the South Rim Visitor Center will enhance your stay in the park. The cen-ter can orient you to many facets of the Grand Canyon, and it's also an excellent source of trip information on lodging, din-ing, transportation, and recreation within the park. Exhibits, short movies, and slide programs present an intriguing profile of the canyon's natural history and a chronicle of pre-Columbian human life in the region. A bookstore has publications, videotapes, and slides, and park rangers can answer ques-tions and help you plan your excursions.

GUIDED TOURS From April through Octo-ber, the **Grand Canyon Field Institute** (Box 399, Grand Canyon 86023, tel. 520/638–2485, fax 520/638–2484) leads guided hikes around the canyon. Tour topics include everything from archaeology and back-country medicine to photography and land-scape painting. Contact GCFI for a current schedule and price list.

Though small-plane and helicopter flights over the Grand Canyon have been restricted, a number of Tusayan-based com-panies still offer these tours, including **Air Grand Canyon** (tel. 520/638–2686 or 800/ 247–4726) and **Kenai Helicopters** (tel. 520/ 638–2412 or 800/541–4537). Helicopters usually hold up to six passengers, planes between five and 20. Flights typically last 30 to 90 minutes and cost about $90 to $165 per person, depending on the aircraft and the length of the trip. A 50-minute flight allows excellent coverage of both rims as well as the inner canyon. No flights are available from the North Rim.

The **Fred Harvey Transportation Company** (Grand Canyon Village, South Rim, tel. 520/ 638–2822, 520/638–2631, or 303/297–2757)

conducts motor-coach sightseeing trips along the South Rim and as far away as Monument Valley on the Navajo Reserva-tion. Prices range from $12 for short excur-sions to $80 for all-day tours. On the North Rim, **Amfac** (tel. 303/297–2757) runs a three-hour van tour of Cape Royale, Angels Window, and other scenic viewpoints for $20. On-site reservations and information are available at the registration desk of the Grand Canyon Lodge (tel. 520/638–2611).

Mule rides into the canyon from the South Rim are justly renowned. Riders must be at least 4′ 7 ″ tall, weigh less than 200 pounds, and understand English. Children under 15 must be accompanied by an adult. Riders must be in fairly good physical condition, and pregnant women are advised not to take these trips. All-day trips, which include lunch, cost $100, and overnights to Phantom Ranch at the bottom of the canyon cost $251.75 per person or $447.50 per cou-ple; rates include lodging and meals. Make reservations far in advance—as much as 11 months if you're planning to visit in sum-mer—by contacting **Amfac** (14001 E. Iliff, Suite 600, Aurora, CO 80013, tel. 303/297–2757, fax 303/297–3175).

White-water trips down the Colorado River and through the Grand Canyon are said by most rafting aficionados to be the adventure of a lifetime. These trips can also be quite expensive, and reservations need to be made sometimes as much as one year in advance; however, it is possible to book some shorter and less spectacular trips—particularly dur-ing the off-season—as few as three or four days in advance. Some trips cover more than 200 mi; those that terminate at Phantom Ranch, at the bottom of the canyon, are about 100 mi. More than 15 companies offer raft trips on the Colorado. Among them are **Canyoneers, Inc.** (tel. 520/526–0924; 800/ 525–0924 outside AZ), **Diamond River Adventures** (tel. 520/645–8866 or 800/343–3121), and **Expeditions Inc.** (tel. 520/774–8176). Companies that specialize in smooth-water rafting include **Fred Harvey Trans-portation Company** (tel. 520/638–2822, 502/638–2631, or 303/297–2757) and **Wil-**

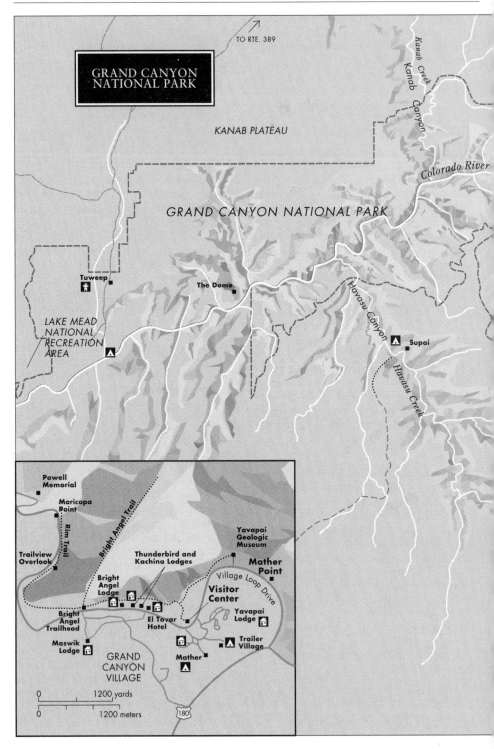

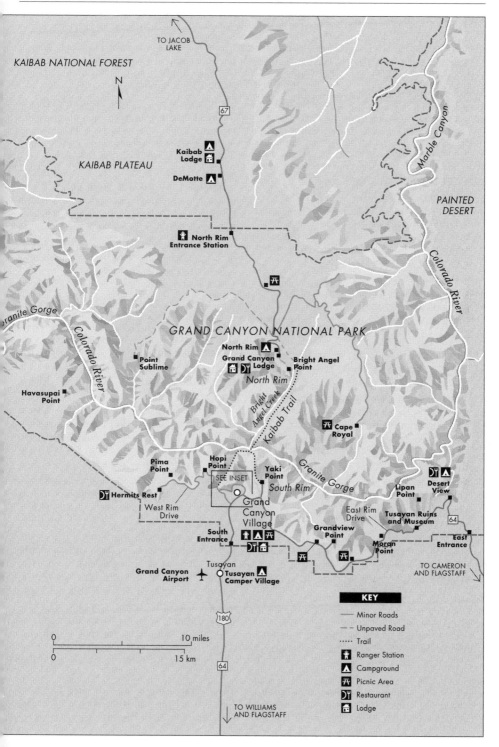

TO JACOB
LAKE

KAIBAB NATIONAL FOREST

N

67

KAIBAB PLATEAU

Kaibab
Lodge

DeMotte

North Rim
Entrance Station

GRAND CANYON NATIONAL PARK

Point
Sublime

North Rim
Grand Canyon Lodge

Bright Angel
Point

North Rim

Havasupai
Point

Bright
Angel Creek

Kaibab Trail

Cape
Royal

Pima
Point

Hopi
Point

SEE INSET

Yaki
Point

Granite Gorge

Lipan
Point

Desert
View

Hermits Rest

West Rim
Drive

South Rim

Grand
Canyon
Village

East Rim
Drive

Tusayan Ruins
and Museum

64

South
Entrance

Grandview
Point

Moran
Point

East
Entrance

Grand Canyon
Airport

Tusayan
Tusayan
Camper Village

TO CAMERON
AND FLAGSTAFF

180

0 ——— 10 miles
0 ——— 15 km

64

TO WILLIAMS
AND FLAGSTAFF

KEY
—— Minor Roads
-- - Unpaved Road
····· Trail
Ranger Station
Campground
Picnic Area
Restaurant
Lodge

KAIBAB NATIONAL FOREST

Colorado River

Marble Canyon

PAINTED
DESERT

Colorado River

Granite Gorge

Colorado River

derness River Adventures (tel. 520/645–3279 or 800/528–6154). Prices for river-raft trips vary greatly: Half-day trips on smooth water run as low as $45 per person, while trips that negotiate the entire length of the canyon and take as long as 12 days can cost more than $2,000. For a complete list of river-raft companies, call 520/638–7888 from a Touch-Tone telephone and press 11, or write Grand Canyon National Park to request a *Trip Planner.*

SCENIC DRIVES AND VIEWS Perhaps the highlight of any trip to the Grand Canyon is a visitor's first look into the awesome gorge. Mather Point, an ideal spot for this moving experience, is about 24 mi from the east entrance and 4 mi from the south entrance. At the junction of Route 64 and U.S. 180, drive about .75 mi toward Grand Canyon Village on **Village Loop Drive,** and park in the lot. From this lookout, you'll have an extraordinary view of the Inner Gorge and numerous buttes that rise out of the chasm.

The **East Rim Drive** is 25 mi one way and takes visitors to several of the Grand Canyon's most spectacular turnouts. (To get to the drive, turn right on Route 64 East, 3 mi north of the South Entrance Station.) There are four well-marked picnic areas along the route, and rest rooms are available at Grandview Point, Tusayan Museum, and Desert View. From the South Rim Visitor Center, drive a couple of miles east on East Rim Drive, turning left on a short, well-marked road leading to Yaki Point. Here, you'll be treated to an impressive view of Wotan's Throne, a massive flat-top butte about 6 mi to the northeast. This is also the point where the popular but challenging South Kaibab Trail starts its canyon descent (*see* Longer Hikes, *below*). Next, travel about 7 mi east to Grandview Point, one of the higher spots along this drive, which reveals a group of dominant buttes, including Krishna Shrine and Vishnu Temple, as well as a short stretch of the Colorado River below. Here you'll find large stands of piñon and ponderosa pine, juniper, and Gambel oak. Other stops along the route include Moran Point; Tusayan

Ruin and Museum, where you can see evidence of pre-Columbian inhabitants and learn about the ancestral Puebloan people who inhabited the region roughly 800 years ago; and Lipan Point. Desert View and Watchtower, the final stops on the tour, are at the highest point of the South Rim (7,500 ft). The view is enhanced by a climb to the top of the stone-and-mortar Watchtower (cost: 25¢), which replicates early Native American architecture. From here you can see the muted pastels of the Painted Desert to the east, the 1,000-ft Vermilion Cliffs to the north, and an impressive stretch of the Colorado River in the canyon gorge below. If you're without a car, the Fred Harvey Transportation Company (*see* Guided Tours, *above*) gives a twice-daily, four-hour bus tour of the area (price: $13.50).

You cannot use your own car for the 8-mi **West Rim Drive** during the summer—the roads are closed to private automobiles. However, it's still worth making this rewarding trip via the park's free shuttle service. If you are traveling between late October and Memorial Day and have a car, start a little more than a mile west of the South Rim Visitor Center. Then head west on West Rim Drive, where you'll encounter 10 scenic turnouts. First you'll come to Trailview Overlook, from which you can see the San Francisco Peaks, Red Butte, and Bill Williams Mountain all to the southeast. There's also a good canyon view of where Bright Angel Trail (*see* Longer Hikes, *below*) loops its way down to the Inner Gorge. Subsequent stops along this road are the Powell Memorial, a large granite monument dedicated to the early canyon explorer John Wesley Powell; Hopi Point, where you can see down to the Colorado River at one of its widest points (350 ft); Mojave Point, which reveals three sets of white-water rapids in the river below; the Abyss, where there is a sheer canyon drop of 3,000 ft to the Tonto Platform; and Pima Point, which offers a clear view of the Tonto Trail as it winds its way for more than 90 mi through the canyon. The last stop on this tour is Hermits Rest, named for a reclusive 19th-century prospector, Louis Boucher, who lived in the canyon. The stone building at this vista point sells refreshments and is the site of the only rest rooms on the West Rim.

The **drive from the South Rim to the North Rim** is one very long journey: 235 mi to be exact. From Grand Canyon Village, take Route 64 east out of the park for 55 mi, turn left onto U.S. 89, and head north another mile to the Cameron Trading Post (tel. 520/679–2231 or 800/338–7385). Founded in 1916, this historic establishment has an extensive stock of authentic Native American jewelry, rugs, baskets, and pottery. There's also a restaurant, cafeteria, art gallery, and motel. As you continue north on U.S. 89, the road on the right is bordered by the Painted Desert, which consists of thousands of square miles of mesas and windswept plains "painted" by nature. Forty miles north of the trading post, drive beside the **Echo Cliffs,** which rise to more than 1,000 ft in many places. At Bitter Springs, bear left onto U.S. 89A. Driving west 14 mi, cross over the canyon on the new (completed 1995) bridge built to replace the 1929 **Navajo Bridge;** both hang 500 ft over the Colorado River. The old bridge, listed in the National Register of Historic Places, is still used as a pedestrian overpass, and an interpretive area and rest rooms are being designed for its former parking lot. About a mile east of Navajo Bridge, at Marble Canyon Lodge, you'll see a turnoff for historic **Lees Ferry,** 3 mi away. Situated on a sharp bend in the Colorado River at a break in the surrounding Echo Cliffs, Lees Ferry is considered mile zero of the river; it's the spot where most of the Grand Canyon river rafts start out. As you proceed west from Marble Canyon Lodge a few miles through the sparsely populated land of the Arizona Strip, you'll come to two other small way stations—Vermilion Cliffs and Cliff Dwellers—that offer gas, food, and motel rooms. Here you'll also be treated to views of the Vermilion Cliffs. These rock formations, among the most spectacular in the world, rise more than

1,000 ft from the plateau floor. As you continue west, 18 mi from Marble Canyon, you will pass the **San Bartolome Historic Site.** Pull into the parking area and read the plaques that tell the tale of the Escalante and Dominguez expedition—one of the earliest undertaken by white men in this harsh and forbidding wilderness—which traversed the river near this point in 1776. (This is also a good spot to look out for California condors, which are among America's most endangered birds; you can recognize them by their immense wingspan—up to 9½ ft.) At Jacob Lake, 55 mi past Marble Canyon, turn left and drive south on Route 67; the remaining 45 mi to the North Rim of the Grand Canyon lie ahead. Along this road, you'll drive over the summit of the 9,000-ft Kaibab Plateau.

On the North Rim, one final scenic drive to a pair of the area's best-loved canyon vistas awaits you. Starting at Grand Canyon Lodge, drive north on the **Cape Royal Road** for a couple of miles, and bear left at the fork. Continue north 11 mi to Point Imperial—at 8,803 ft, it's the highest vista on either rim. Point Imperial affords visitors an excellent view of the canyon, not to mention thousands of square miles of the surrounding countryside in all directions. After stopping here, backtrack the 11 mi to the fork and head southeast on the road to Cape Royal: It's about a 15-mi drive on paved road. This is the site of Angel's Window, a giant, erosion-formed hole through which you can see South Rim across the canyon; it's just beyond the trailhead for Cliff Springs Trail (*see* Nature Trails and Short Walks, *below*). The drive back to Grand Canyon Lodge is 23 mi.

HISTORIC BUILDINGS AND SITES Nearly everyone who comes to the South Rim visits the lobby and public areas of the magnificent **El Tovar Hotel** (*see* Lodging, *below*). Built in 1904 by the Fred Harvey Company, this historic hotel is named in honor of the Spanish explorer Pedro de Tovar. Constructed to resemble a European hunting lodge, it was designed by architect Charles Whittlesey and incorporates native stone and Oregon pine. The hotel is on Village Loop Drive, a short walk from the visitor center, in the heart of the South Rim's historic district. A number of buildings in this area, most of them open to the public, date back to the early part of the century. Within short walking distance of each other are the **Kolb Studio,** built in 1904, where the Kolb brothers showed films and held dances throughout the early half of the century; the 1914 **Lookout Studio** (a competitor of the Kolb brothers' establishment), which was built with rough-cut limestone and now houses a gift shop, and lookout loft; the **Buckey O'Neill Cabin,** the oldest surviving structure on the rim; **Hopi House,** built in 1905 as an outlet for Native American crafts and now one of the best-stocked gift shops in the area; the **Santa Fe Railway Station,** which received train passengers to the park for nearly 70 years until ending service in 1968 (it resumed service in 1989); and the **First National Park Service Administration Building,** erected in 1921 and indicative of the park service's attempt to design buildings that fit in with their natural environments. Finally, a restful place to finish your tour of the district is the **Bright Angel Lodge** (*see* Arizona Steak House *in* Dining, *below*), another of the canyon's historic hotels. The hotel has a dining room and a soda fountain.

Rugged and spacious, created of massive stone walls and timber ceilings, the **Grand Canyon Lodge** sits at the very edge of the North Rim. Built by a subsidiary of the Union Pacific Railroad and opened in 1936, the complex originally consisted of a main building and 125 cabins scattered in the deep forest. Its architect, Gilbert Stanley Underwood, also designed the national-park hotels in Yosemite Valley and Bryce Canyon. The lodge is listed in the National Register of Historic Places.

NATURE TRAILS AND SHORT WALKS In Grand Canyon National Park the opportunities to walk and explore on foot are many. The most popular walking path at the South Rim is the 10-mi one-way **Rim Trail,** which runs along the edge of the canyon from Yavapai

Museum in Grand Canyon Village west to Hermits Rest. This walk, which is paved to Maricopa Point, allows visits to several of the South Rim's historic landmarks (*see* Historic Buildings and Sites, *above*). Start at the **Yavapai Observation Station** (on the east side of Grand Canyon Village, tel. 520/638–2631), where polarized picture windows provide excellent views into the depths of the gorge. Purchase natural-history and geology booklets at the station (25¢ apiece) for your self-guided tour along the rim. From here, take the paved, level Rim Trail west for easy access to many views of the canyon. You'll pass Bright Angel Trailhead (*see* Longer Hikes, *below*), a well-maintained avenue to the bottom of the canyon for mules and foot traffic. Beyond this you'll walk roughly a mile paralleling West Rim Drive (*see* Scenic Drives and Views, *above*) to reach Maricopa Point. You can continue beyond this point to Hermits Rest, but be warned that this stretch of the Rim Trail is unpaved and runs close to the edge in places. Those uncomfortable with heights should stop at Maricopa Point.

Popular walks at the North Rim are the 1.5-mi **Transept Trail,** which starts near the Grand Canyon Lodge, and **Cliff Springs Trail** near Cape Royal. This easy 1-mi round-trip walk leads you through a ravine to another excellent view of the canyon.

LONGER HIKES Treks into the canyon are rewarding for their views, but be prepared for their considerable difficulty. Bright Angel, Hermit, and South Kaibab trails are the most popular from the South Rim; North Kaibab Trail is the best from the North Rim. When hiking down the South Kaibab Trail, be sure to stand quietly by the side of the trail when the mule trains pass by.

Caution: A hike down into the Grand Canyon may be relatively easy, but, beware: Coming back up can be painfully exhausting. For every hour you hike downhill, allow two hours for the uphill return. Wear hiking or running shoes, and dress appropriately for the season (*see* What to Pack, *above*). Always carry food and water, and consult

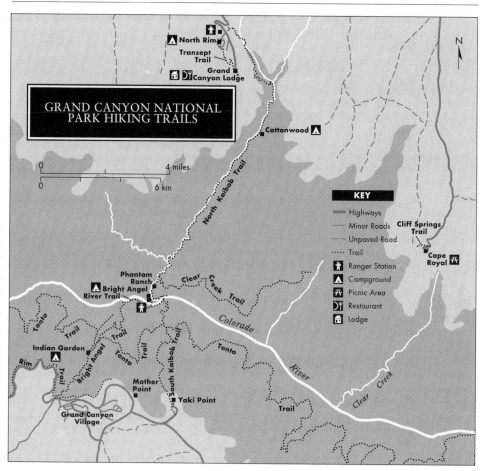

GRAND CANYON NATIONAL
PARK HIKING TRAILS

KEY

Highways
Minor Roads
Unpaved Road
Trail
Ranger Station
Campground
Picnic Area
Restaurant
Lodge

park rangers before you set off (remember, all overnight hikes require a backcountry permit). Summer temperatures in the canyon frequently exceed 100°F, and hikers run the risk of heat exhaustion. Journeys to the bottom of the canyon are recommended only for people in good physical condition and those with backcountry hiking experience. The park service specifically advises against attempting to hike from the rim to the river and back in one day, as heat exhaustion and dehydration are common occurences.

From a trailhead on the South Rim near Grand Canyon Village, **Bright Angel Trail,** almost 8 mi long, descends 4,460 ft to the Colorado River. Phantom Ranch (*see* Lodg-

ing, *below*) awaits hikers at the bottom of the canyon. This historic route was used by Native Americans for centuries before the arrival of Europeans. Drinking water is available May through September at the resthouses 1.5 and 3 mi into the canyon, and at the 4.5-mi point down year-round.

The 9-mi (one-way) **Hermit Trail,** which begins on the South Rim beyond Hermits Rest, drops more than 5,000 ft to Hermit Creek, which flows year-round. This trail is partially responsible for the lush growth and abundant bird- and animal life in the campsite area. You might see desert bighorn sheep on this strenuous hike, which should be attempted by serious hikers only.

The **South Kaibab Trail** starts at Yaki Point, 4 mi east of Grand Canyon Village. This is a steep trail, so many hikers return via the less-demanding Bright Angel Trail. During this 7-mi trek to the Colorado River, you're likely to encounter mule trains and riders. At the river, the trail crosses a suspension bridge and runs on to Phantom Ranch.

On the North Rim, the trailhead to the **North Kaibab Trail** is about 2 mi north of the Grand Canyon Lodge and is open only from May through October. This is a long, steep hike that drops 5,840 ft over a distance of 14.5 mi and is recommended for experienced hikers only. After about 7 mi, you might stop at the Cottonwood Campground, which has drinking water, rest rooms, shade trees, and a ranger. Like the Bright Angel and South Kaibab trails, this one also leads to Phantom Ranch.

OTHER ACTIVITIES **Biking.** Cyclists will find miles of scenic roads to ride on, including paved roads for all types of bicycles and dirt roads for mountain bikes. However, most dirt roads open to mountain bikers are in the national forest lands that border the park to the north and south. Roads are generally level at the South Rim and gently rolling with some steeper hills on the North Rim. Be aware that bicycles are not permitted on any of the walking trails in the national park. Bring your own bike; there are no rentals in or near the Grand Canyon.

Fishing. The high plateau country of northwestern Arizona is a land of limited rain and quick runoffs. Fishing opportunities are few. However, Lake Powell, on U.S. 89, 140 mi north of the South Rim, is known for its largemouth, smallmouth, and striped bass; northern and walleye pike; catfish; and crappie. The Colorado River, below Lake Powell's Glen Canyon Dam and as far south as Lees Ferry, yields trophy-size trout. Before wetting your line, be sure to obtain an Arizona fishing permit, available at marinas and sporting-goods stores in the vicinity of Page and at Marble Canyon Lodge (*see* Lodging, *below*).

Horseback and Mule Riding. On the South Rim, horses can be rented from April through November from **Apache Stables** (tel. 520/638–2891 or 520/638–2424) at Moqui Lodge in Tusayan. Rentals cost $25 per hour, $40 for two hours. At the North Rim, guided mule rides are offered from mid-May to October by **Canyon Trail Rides** (tel. 801/679–8665) at the Grand Canyon Lodge; these trips are extremely popular so reserve far in advance. A trusty mule rents for about $15 per hour, $35 for a half day, and $85 for a full day. In addition, full-day and overnight mule rides are available at the South Rim (*see* Guided Tours, *above*).

Rafting. Very experienced rafters can bring their own rafts to the canyon, but the waiting list for private permits is six to eight years long. White- and smooth-water guided trips through the canyon are offered (*see* Guided Tours, *above*).

Ski Touring. Though you can't schuss down into the Grand Canyon, you can cross-country ski in the woods near both rims when there's enough snow. **Babbits General Store** in the South Rim's Grand Canyon Village (tel. 520/638–2262) rents equipment and can guide you to the best trails. When there's enough snow, the **Kaibab National Forest** (tel. 520/638–2443) sets 22 mi of track, beginning at the junction of the Arizona Trail and the East Rim Drive (east of Grandview Point). In ski season, when the road to the North Rim of the national park is closed, the **North Rim Nordic Center** (c/o Canyoneers, Inc., Box 2997, Flagstaff 86003, tel. 520/526–0924; 800/525–0924 outside AZ) transports visitors via SnowVan from Jacob Lake to the Kaibab Lodge, where they can traverse 52 mi of regularly groomed trails in a spectacular wooded setting.

CHILDREN'S PROGRAMS Family-oriented activities and programs abound here, and children can take part in nearly everything available to their parents. On the South Rim, kids can try horseback riding, and, on the North Rim, mules are available (*see* Other Activities, *above*). On both rims, the

National Park Service has free daily programs that change seasonally and are listed in *The Guide* (*see* Publications, *above*). Typical programs and activities are nature walks, geology talks, and natural-history discussions. Also, children will enjoy the film *Grand Canyon, Hidden Secrets,* shown outside the park at the IMAX Theater in Tusayan (*see* Orientation Programs, *above*).

EVENING ACTIVITIES Entertainment and nightlife in this part of the world often consists of watching a full moon hover above the soaring buttes of the Grand Canyon, roasting marshmallows over a crackling fire, and crawling into your sleeping bag beside a lonely canyon trail. However, there are a few cocktail lounges in Grand Canyon hotels and motels. The **El Tovar Hotel** has a bar that hosts bands on holiday weekends. On Wednesday through Saturday nights, the **Bright Angel Restaurant** has live music, mostly folk along with some blues and classic rock. **Maswik Lodge** is home of the region's sports bar, with darts, a pool table, and a jukebox; call 520/638–2632 for information. The **Grand Canyon Lodge** (tel. 520/638–2611) on the North Rim also has a lounge.

In addition, the National Park Service at both rims presents informative evening programs on subjects related to the Grand Canyon. For a complete daily schedule of these activities, consult a copy of the free newspaper, *The Guide.*

DINING

Throughout Grand Canyon country, restaurants cater to tourists on the move, with simple, reasonably priced American fare. If you want a more elaborate dining experience try the El Tovar Hotel dining room, but be prepared to pay as much as $35 for a complete dinner.

NORTH RIM **Grand Canyon Lodge Dining Room.** The historic lodge, built of native stone and logs, houses a huge, high-ceiling dining room with spectacular views and very good food; you might find pork medallions, red snapper, or spinach linguine with red clam sauce on the sophisticated dinner menu. *Grand Canyon Lodge, Bright Angel Point, tel. 520/638–2611. AE, D, DC, MC, V. Closed winter. $$–$$$*

Grand Canyon Lodge Snack Bar. Dining choices are very limited on the North Rim, so this is your best bet for a meal tailored to a budget. The selections—hot dogs, burgers, sandwiches, yogurt—are standard but sufficient. *Grand Canyon Lodge, Bright Angel Point, tel. 520/638–2611. Reservations not accepted. AE, D, DC, MC, V. Closed winter. $*

NEAR NORTH RIM **Vermilion Cliffs Bar and Grill.** If you make the long drive up U.S. 89 to the North Rim, you'll need at least one food stop, and this may be the best along the route. Popular with river rafters, it's a rustic, rock-walled room with surprisingly good American fare such as steaks and freshly caught fish. *Lees Ferry Lodge, U.S. 89A, 4 mi west of Navajo Bridge, tel. 520/355–2231. Reservations not accepted. MC, V. $–$$*

SOUTH RIM **El Tovar Dining Room.** For decades El Tovar Hotel's restaurant has enjoyed a reputation for fine food served in a classic 19th-century room of hand-hewn logs and beamed ceilings. The Southwest-inspired menu changes seasonally but Atlantic salmon with lemon-lime salsa might appear among the innovatively prepared dishes. *El Tovar Hotel, Grand Canyon Village, tel. 520/638–2631. AE, D, DC, MC, V. $$$*

Arizona Steak House. This casual, Southwestern-style steak house has wrought-iron wall sconces, Native American–inspired prints, and superb canyon views. For dinner, there's good prime rib, rack of lamb, and blackened swordfish. *Bright Angel Lodge, Grand Canyon Village, tel. 520/638–2631. Reservations not accepted. AE, D, DC, MC, V. $$–$$$*

Fred Harvey Cafeterias. There are three cafeterias at the South Rim, all run by the Fred Harvey Company. Two are in Grand

Canyon Village at **Maswik Lodge** and **Yavapai Lodge** (tel. 520/638–2631 for both); the third is at **Desert View Trading Post** (tel. 520/638–2360), 23 mi east of Grand Canyon Village on Rte. 64. The coffee shop in the Bright Angel Lodge, another Fred Harvey concession, is another good option. *AE, D, DC, MC, V. Yavapai Lodge cafeteria closed winter.* $

NEAR THE PARK **Moqui Lodge Restaurant.** A good option for an informal meal just ¼-mi south of the South Rim entrance to the park, the Moqui Lodge's dining room serves decent Mexican food, including combination plates as well as burgers and sandwiches. The dining room, with its exposed wood beams, has an appropriately rustic feel. *Moqui Lodge, .25 mi before entrance to national park on U.S. 180, 1 mi north of Tusayan, Kaibab National Forest, tel. 520/638–2631. Reservations not accepted. AE, D, DC, MC, V. Closed Dec.–Feb. 15.* $$

PICNIC SPOTS There are a number of designated picnic areas within the national park at both rims. The free newspaper *The Guide* points out their locations. On the South Rim, try the picnic area east of **Grandview Point** on the East Rim Drive. At the North Rim, a truly scenic spot is near the parking area at **Cape Royal** (there are pit toilets here).

LODGING

For summer lodging reservations, call as far in advance as possible. Often, hotels and motels on the South Rim are booked for the summer season six months to a year in advance. If you can't get rooms at or near the South Rim, you're likely to find vacancies in Valle, Flagstaff, Williams, or at the Cameron Trading Post (tel. 520/679–2231 or 800/338–7385) on U.S. 89. Motels outside the park frequently lower prices during the colder months. The more remote North Rim is less crowded; Page in Arizona, and Kanab and Fredonia in Utah are additional options if you can't find rooms in or closer to the national park.

NORTH RIM **Grand Canyon Lodge.** Just a few yards from the canyon rim, the historic main building has massive limestone walls and timber ceilings. There are also cabins (both rustic and more luxurious) and traditional motel units scattered among the pines. *Bright Angel Point, Grand Canyon Lodge North Rim, 86502, tel. 303/297–2575 reservations, 520/638–2611 information, fax 303/297–3175. 201 rooms. Facilities: restaurant, lounge, snack bar. AE, D, DC, MC, V.* $$–$$$

Kaibab Lodge. In the woods just 5 mi from the entrance to the North Rim, this 1920s property has rustic cabins with plain, motel-style furnishings. *AZ 67, 26 mi south of Jacob Lake, HC 64 Box 30, Fredonia 86022, tel. 520/638–2389 in season, 520/526-0924 or 800/525–0924 in winter. 24 cabins. Facilities: restaurant. D, MC, V. Closed Nov.–early Dec. and late Mar.–mid-May.* $$–$$$

NEAR NORTH RIM If you are unable to obtain rooms at the North Rim, there are some no-frills, roadside motels—ranging from Native American–style rock-and-mortar units to frame cabins—on the North Rim approach on U.S. 89A: **Marble Canyon Lodge** (.5 mi west of Navajo Bridge on U.S. 89A, Box 6001, Marble Canyon 86036, tel. 520/355–2225 or 800/726–1789, fax 520/355-2227), D, MC, V; **Lees Ferry Lodge** (4 mi west of Navajo Bridge on U.S 89A, HC 67, Box 1, Marble Canyon 86036, tel. 520/355–2231), MC, V; and **Cliff Dwellers Lodge** (9 mi west of Navajo Bridge on U.S. 89A, Box HC 67-30, Marble Canyon 86036, tel. 520/355–2228 or 800/433–2543, fax 520/355–2229), D, MC, V, closed January and February. These are all 70 to 80 mi from the North Rim. **Jacob Lake Inn** (Jacob Lake, U.S. 89A and Rte. 67, 86022, tel. 520/643–7232, fax 520/643–7898), AE, D, DC, MC, V; 45 mi from the North Rim. All four motels are in the $$–$$$ range.

SOUTH RIM **El Tovar Hotel.** Built in 1905 of native stone and heavy pine logs, El Tovar reflects the style of old European hunting lodges and is regarded as one of the finest national park hotels. *Grand Canyon Village, tel. 303/297–2575 reservations, 520/638–2631 information, fax 303/297–3175. 80 rooms and suites. Facilities: restaurant, lounge. AE, D, DC, MC, V. $$$*

Grand Canyon National Park Lodges. In addition to the Bright Angel Lodge and El Tovar Hotel, Grand Canyon National Park Lodges operates five other clean, comfortable, and nicely appointed properties at the South Rim: the 278-room **Maswik Lodge; Yavapai Lodge,** with 358 rooms; **Moqui Lodge,** with 136 rooms (closed Dec.–Feb. 15); the 49-room **Kachina Lodge;** and **Thunderbird Lodge,** which has 55 rooms. *In or near Grand Canyon Village, tel. 303/297–2575 reservations, 520/638–2631 switchboard, fax 303/297–3175. AE, D, DC, MC, V. $$$*

Bright Angel Lodge. This rustic hostelry, built by the Fred Harvey Company in 1935, sits within a few yards of the canyon rim. It has rooms in the main lodge and in quaint cabins. *Grand Canyon Village, tel. 303/297–2575 reservations, 520/638–2631 switchboard, fax 303/297–3175. 144 rooms, 19 with shared or ½ bath. Facilities: restaurant, lounge, beauty salon. AE, D, DC, MC, V. $$–$$$*

Phantom Ranch. Mule riders and hikers with backcountry permits frequent this no-frills lodging at the bottom of the Grand Canyon. There's a dormitory ($21 per person) accessible only to hikers; cabins are exclusively for mule riders (*see* Guided Tours, *above*). *Tel. 520/638–2631. AE, D, DC, MC, V. $*

NEAR SOUTH RIM **Best Western Grand Canyon Squire.** Lacking some of the charm of the older lodges in Grand Canyon Village, this upscale motel compensates with cheerful southwestern-style rooms and a huge list of amenities. *1.5 mi south of South Rim entrance on U.S. 180 (Hwy. 64), Tusayan 86023, tel. 520/638–2681 or 800/528–1234, fax 520/638–0161. 250 rooms. Facilities: restaurant, coffee shop, lounge, pool, beauty salon, hot tub, bowling, billiards, travel services. AE, D, DC, MC, V. $$$*

Grand Canyon Suites. Opened in 1996, this all-suites property has western-theme rooms: You might wake up surrounded by mug shots of John Wayne or by chairs upholstered with Route 66 fabric. Coffeemakers, microwaves, refrigerators, and two TVs in each room make this a good choice for families. *1.5 mi south of South Rim entrance on U.S. 180, Tusayan 86023, tel. 520/638–3100 or 888/538–5353, fax 520/638–2747. 32 suites. AE, MC, V. $$$*

Quality Inn. The attractive atrium here is a good place for drinks. Rooms are well designed, clean, and comfortable. In addition to standard guest rooms, there are 56 one-bedroom suites, each with two TVs, a refrigerator, and microwave. *6 mi south of rim on U.S. 180, Tusayan 86023, tel. 520/638–2673 or 800/221–2222, fax 520/638–9537. 232 rooms. Facilities: restaurant, lounge, pool, hot tub, airport shuttle. AE, D, DC, MC, V. $$$*

CAMPING

All campgrounds in and around the park are in gorgeous country, most of it pine forest. If you can't get a site in the park, you can camp in the surrounding Kaibab National Forest, provided you have a backcountry permit. Reservations are advised wherever you can make them.

Three backcountry campgrounds in the park—**Indian Garden** (15 sites), **Bright Angel** (33 sites), and **Cottonwood** (12 sites)—charge $4 per site and are open year-round, but only Bright Angel has flush toilets. All have drinking water. Fires are forbidden. The requisite backcountry permit serves as a reservation (*see* Visitor Information, *above*).

NORTH RIM In a grove of pines near a general store 3 mi north of the rim, the aptly named **North Rim Campground** is open mid-May through mid-October. Its 83 RV and tent sites (no hookups) cost $12 per night and are available on a first-come, first-served basis. Facilities include flush

GRAND CANYON CAMPGROUNDS

Region	Campground	Total number of sites	Sites suitable for RVs	Number of hookups	Drive to sites	Hike to sites	Flush toilets	Pit/chemical toilets	Drinking water	Showers	Fire grates	Swimming	Boat access	Playground	Disposal station	Ranger station	Public telephone	Reservation possible	Daily fee per site	Dates open
NORTH RIM	North Rim	83	83	0	●		●		●	●	●				●	●	●	●	$12	mid-May–mid-Oct.
NEAR NORTH RIM	Demotte (National Forest)	22	22	0	●			●	●		●						●			mid-May–mid-Oct.
NEAR NORTH RIM	Jacob Lake (National Forest)	53	53	0	●			●	●		●						●		$10	mid-May–mid-Oct.
NEAR NORTH RIM	Kaibab Lodge Camper Village	130	80	70	●			●	●		●				●		●	●	$12–$22	mid-May–Nov.
SOUTH RIM	Desert View	50	50	0	●		●		●		●				●	●	●	●	$10	Apr.–Nov.
SOUTH RIM	Mather	319	319	0	●		●		●	●	●				●	●	●	●	$12	year-round
NEAR SOUTH RIM	Trailer Village	78	78	78	●				●										$17	year-round
NEAR SOUTH RIM	Grand Canyon Camper Village	260	200	200	●				●	●	●				●		●	●	$13–$20	year-round
NEAR SOUTH RIM	Ten X Campground	70	0	0				●	●										$10	May–Sept.
INNER CANYON	Indian Garden	15	0	0		●		●	●									●	$4	year-round
INNER CANYON	Bright Angel	33	0	0		●	●		●									●	$4	year-round
INNER CANYON	Cottonwood	12	0	0		●		●	●									●	$4	year-round

toilets, fire grates, showers, drinking water, a disposal station, and a ranger station.

NEAR NORTH RIM DeMotte Campground (tel. 520/643–7395), open mid-May to mid-October, is operated by the U.S. Forest Service. It's in a beautiful area surrounded by tall pines, 20 mi north of the rim on Route 67. Its 22 RV and tent sites (no hookups) cost $10, including use of pit toilets, picnic tables, fire grates, and drinking water.

In the secluded pine country of the Kaibab Plateau at the junction of U.S. 89A and Route 67, about 45 mi north of the north rim, **Jacob Lake Campground** (tel. 520/643–7395) is also run by the forest service; it's closed from mid-October through May. Its 53 tent and RV sites (no hookups) cost $10 and are near pit toilets, fire grates, drinking water, and a visitor-information station. Demotte and Jacob Lake both have evening programs.

Also at the junction of U.S. 89A and Route 67, **Kaibab Lodge Camper Village** (tel. 520/643–7804 in season, 520/526–0924 in winter) is the closest campground to the North Rim with full hookups. It's in a wooded area near a store, gas station, and restaurant and has 80 RV sites ($22 per night for full hookups, $12 for no hookups) and 50 tent sites ($12 per night). Facilities include pit toilets, fire grates, drinking water, and a disposal station. The campground is closed from November through mid-May, depending on weather.

SOUTH RIM A grocery store, service station, and trading post make **Desert View Campground** (tel. 520/638–7888) a favorite—and there's a spectacular view of the canyon from nearby Watchtower Lookout. The campground is on Route 64, 23 mi east of Grand Canyon Village. The 50 tent and RV sites (no hookups) cost $10 per night, including flush toilets, drinking water, fire grates, and a ranger station. The

campground is open from April through November.

In the heart of Grand Canyon Village near the South Rim Visitor Center, **Mather Campground** has 319 tent and RV sites (no hookups) that are heavily booked in summer (they're open year-round). Make reservations through Destinet (tel. 520/638–7888) as early as the campground will accept them. Mather is equipped with flush toilets, showers, drinking water, fire grates, a disposal station, and a ranger station. Sites cost $12 per night.

There are 78 50-ft RV sites with full hookups at **Trailer Village** (tel. 303/297–2575 for reservations, 520/638–2631 for switchboard) near the South Rim Visitor Center and Mather Campground, just a five-minute walk from the general store. Every site has fire grates, and the facility has potable water, a dump station, flush toilets, and phones. There are hot showers at Mather. Sites cost $17 per night and are open year-round.

NEAR SOUTH RIM The commercially operated **Grand Canyon Camper Village** (tel. 520/638–2887) is generally rated among the best in the South Rim area; it's also one of the easiest to find—just 2 mi south of the park entrance on U.S. 180. There are 200 RV sites ($20 for full hookups, $18 for water and electricity) and 60 tent sites ($13); all are open year-round. Facilities include flush toilets, showers, drinking water, fire grates, and a disposal station.

In Kaibab National Forest, about 9 mi south of the park, **Ten X Campground** (tel. 520/638–2443) is run by the Forest Service and has 70 family sites ($10 per night) plus a group site (available for groups of up to 100 people), with drinking water and pit toilets. No reservations are accepted (except for the group site). The campground is closed from October through April.

Grand Teton National Park

Wyoming

Updated by Candy Moulton

Many travelers treat Grand Teton National Park simply as a strip of Rocky Mountain scenery crossed on the way to Yellowstone National Park's roadside wonders. Its intimidating profile makes Grand Teton seem less accessible than its neighbor to the north: The jagged vertical peaks of the Teton Range rise precipitously, as high as 7,000 ft above the Snake River plain (13,000 ft above sea level), north of Jackson, Wyoming. You can't drive into those steep peaks the way you can cruise over Yellowstone's mountain passes.

But those who venture even a few hundred yards off the Jackson Hole Highway, which crosses the east side of the park's 310,000 rugged acres, are quickly rewarded. Mountain glaciers creep imperceptibly down 12,605-ft Mt. Moran; multicolored wildflowers cover the Jackson Hole valley floor; and Wyoming's great abundance of wildlife scampers about the meadows and mountains.

A drive along Teton Park Road affords close-ups of magnificent peaks; as you pull off Jenny Lake Road at Cathedral Group Turnout, the Grand Teton, Owen, and Teewinot mountains dominate the massif that rises abruptly from the valley floor. Short trails lead through sagebrush near the Snake River and through willow flats near Jackson Lake; concession-operated boats skim the waters of Jackson and Jenny lakes, depositing visitors on the wild western shore of the latter; and guided float trips meander down a calm stretch of the tortu-ous Snake River. A trip to the backcountry—which has more than 200 mi of trails, from the novice's Cascade Canyon to the expert's Teton Crest—reveals the majesty of what the Gros Ventre and Shoshoni tribes called Teewinot (Many Pinnacles).

French trappers, who entered the region about 1820, named the range Les Trois Tetons (the Three Breasts). Today, as you drive through the park, the three most prominent peaks—Grand, Owen, and Teewinot—come into view around Moose Junction, on the west side of the road. Beneath these 12,000- to 13,770-ft peaks stretches a 40-mi-long valley, which the American trappers who arrived after the French dubbed Jackson's Hole (after David E. Jackson, a trapper who reportedly spent the winter of 1829 along Jackson Lake). Through this valley the Snake River winds in braided channels for more than 40 mi. Between the Snake and the Tetons lies a string of sparkling lakes: Phelps, Taggart, Jenny, Leigh, and Jackson, to name only a few.

Jackson Hole was first settled during the 1880s, and it quickly became a splendid hunting ground, with locals leading wealthy outsiders into the Tetons. But early conservationists soon recognized the environmental significance of the area and proposed that it be added to Yellowstone National Park. As early as 1897, environmentalists successfully lobbied Congress and President Grover Cleveland to establish the Teton Forest Reserve, which covered much of the valley floor. The reserve became Teton National Forest in 1908. In

1929 Congress set aside 96,000 acres—covering the main part of the Teton Range itself and most glacial lakes at the base of the mountains—as Grand Teton National Park.

Meanwhile, John D. Rockefeller, Jr., started buying land in Jackson Hole, intending to preserve the wild and scenic character of the mountains, as well as their valley foreground. In 1943 President Franklin D. Roosevelt established Jackson Hole National Monument, whose 221,000 acres included some of the national forest and federal land in Jackson Hole. The Rockefellers donated nearly 33,000 acres to the monument in 1949, and in 1950 Congress merged the park and the monument into today's Grand Teton National Park.

Opportunities for rigorous hiking, climbing, and rafting at Grand Teton are many, but you can also opt for a gentle meander around Jenny Lake or for an evening drink looking out over the Tetons from the veranda of the Jackson Lake Lodge. And if you still have energy to spare, you can always spend the night whooping it up at a cowboy bar in Jackson Hole.

ESSENTIAL INFORMATION

VISITOR INFORMATION For detailed information about the park, write to the Superintendent, **Grand Teton National Park,** Drawer 170, Moose, WY 83012, or call 307/739–3399. **Colter Bay Visitor Center** (tel. 307/739–3594) has information on activities at Jackson Lake. The park's largest lodging, dining, and tour concessionaire is **Grand Teton Lodge Company** (Box 240, Moran, WY 83013, tel. 307/543–2811, 307/543–3100, or 800/628–9988).

For information on Jackson and its environs contact **Jackson Hole Chamber of Commerce** (Box E, Jackson, WY 83001, tel. 307/733–3316); **Jackson Hole Visitors Council** (Box 982, Dept. 8, Jackson Hole, WY 83001, tel. 307/733–7606 or 800/782–0011, fax 307/733–5585); or **Wyoming Division of Tourism** (I–25 at College Dr.,

Cheyenne, WY 82002, tel. 307/777–7777 or 800/225–5996, fax 307/777–6904).

Backcountry permits, which must be obtained in person at the Moose or Colter Bay visitor centers or the Jenny Lake Ranger Station, are free and required for all overnight stays outside designated campgrounds. Unlike Yellowstone, Grand Teton allows off-trail hiking. Pets, which must be leashed at all times, are not permitted on trails. Campfires are prohibited in the backcountry except at designated lakeshore campsites.

FEES Park entrance fees are $20 per vehicle, $10 per individual on foot, or bicycle, and $15 for motorcycle or snowmobile and are payable at the Moose and Moran entrances. Passes are good for seven days in both Grand Teton and Yellowstone parks. Annual passes are $40. Boat permits, available at the Moose visitor center year-round and at Colter Bay, Signal Mountain, and Buffalo ranger stations during summer, cost $10 for motorized craft and $5 for nonmotorized craft.

PUBLICATIONS The *Grand Teton Official Map and Guide* and the seasonal park newspaper, *Teewinot,* are distributed free at park entrances. **Trails Illustrated** (Box 3610, Evergreen, CO 80439, tel. 800/962–1643) sells an excellent waterproof, tearproof topographic map of the park. That map and all 13 park USGS quadrangle topographical maps are available from the **Grand Teton Natural History Association** (Box 170, Moose, WY 83012, tel. 307/739–3403). This nonprofit organization, which operates bookstores at both park visitor centers, also has a wide range of adult and children's books and videos on the park and its environs. Among the best books are: *Guide to Exploring Grand Teton National Park,* by park naturalists Linda Olson and Tim Bywater, which contains natural history, scenic drives, and tips for exploring; *Creation of the Teton Landscape,* by J. D. Love and J. C. Reed, a classic short geologic history with color illustrations and maps; *Birds of Grand Teton and the Surrounding*

Area, by Bert Raynes; *Plants of Yellowstone and Grand Teton,* by Dr. J. Richard Shaw, with black-and-white illustrations; *Wildlife of Yellowstone and Grand Teton,* by F. Douglas and Suvi Scott; *Legacy of the Tetons: Homesteading in Jackson Hole,* by Candy Vyvey Moulton; and *Origins: Place Names of Grand Teton,* by Cynthia Nielsen and Elizabeth Weid Hayden.

GEOLOGY AND TERRAIN As recently as 9 million years ago, the dramatic sawtooth Teton skyline lay under a flat layer of sandstone that today lies more than 4.5 mi beneath the earth's surface. You can still see sections of this sandstone on top of Mt. Moran.

To get an idea of why the valley of Jackson Hole sits beside the immense Teton Range without even the slightest foothill between them, picture the preformed mountains as a flat, rectangular block of granite and gneiss. Tension in the earth's crust caused several vertical breaks in the overlying layer of sandstone. The Teton Fault, the most intense of these breaks, appeared as a vertical fissure broken top to bottom through the block's midsection. The land east of the fault sank, while the block to the west of the fault rose sharply above the landscape.

Several conditions account for the jagged, unpredictable appearance of today's Teton Range. Essentially, the park is set on two blocks of stone: The range, thrust upward and west of the fault, is the higher block, while Jackson Hole dropped downward to the east. During three ice ages that followed the great rift, and the warming spells that followed the ice ages, glaciers—some as thick as 3,000 ft—cut uneven gorges out of the uplifted fault block, creating vast canyons such as Cascade and Leigh. These same glaciers carried layer upon layer of sedimentary rock east of the fault. As the glaciers melted, the numerous lakes that now occupy Jackson Hole formed, as a result of natural damming, in the shadow of the mountains.

Glaciers are responsible for the Teton Range's sheer walls, rugged ridges, and sharp peaks, and a dozen remnant glaciers now slowly flow from the sharp, angular amphitheaters (also called cirques) cut out of the mountainsides by their ice-age ancestors. Schoolroom Glacier, visible up close from the South Fork of Cascade Canyon Trail, has an easily recognizable cirque and outflow. Another good spot for seeing glaciers is Mt. Moran Turnout, also on Teton Park Road, where you have a good view of Mt. Moran, home to Skillet Glacier on its east face and Falling Ice Glacier on its southeast face.

Originating near Yellowstone's South Entrance, the Snake River flows into Jackson Lake and exits through Jackson Lake Dam, rushing eastward through an ice-age glacial trough. The Snake turns suddenly southwest at Moran Junction, following the widened bed of the ancestral river, carved 20,000 years ago by the last ice-age advance down from Yellowstone Plateau. Visible from Jackson Hole Highway, the sagebrush flats along the Snake River's twisting southern path were created when torrential glacial meltwaters washed away moisture-holding clay.

FLORA AND FAUNA Close to 900 wildflower varieties bloom in the park's three-phase explosion of summer color. Following the receding snow on the valley floor are sagebrush buttercups, then spring beauties and yellowbells. In late June the valley is covered with blue lupine, yellow balsamroot, scarlet gilia, and purple larkspur. In July and August, wildflowers flourish in meadows along canyon trails at 7,000 to 10,000 ft. In August, at alpine elevations of over 9,000 ft, a low, brilliant cushion of color includes the official park flower, the alpine forget-me-not. Visitor centers distribute a free wildflower checklist, and the Grand Teton Natural History Association (*see* Publications, *above*) sells more-extensive wildflower guides.

The Snake's ongoing pattern of floods and channel-changing (a fine example of the latter is visible at Oxbow Bend Turnout) keep spruce trees from dominating the land close to the river. Thanks to nature's upheavals, tall cottonwoods and low willows compete with spruce in the valley, creating a perfect moose-and-beaver habitat. As you move up into the mountains you'll find the mix of trees turning to spruce, fir, aspen, and lodgepole pine.

Elk are the region's most common large mammals. The best place to view the herd during the winter is south of the park on the National Elk Refuge, where some 7,500 of them spend the colder months. In summer, elk and mule deer haunt forest edges along Teton Park Road at sunrise and sunset. Oxbow Bend and Willow Flats are good places to look for moose, beaver, and otter. Pronghorn antelope and, occasionally, bison appear in summer along Jackson Hole Highway and Antelope Flats Road (especially at dawn and dusk), and black bear inhabit the backcountry, although sightings are not common. Birds include bald eagles and ospreys, which can be spotted along the Snake, as well as a colony of great blue herons that lives near Oxbow Bend. In addition, there are killdeer in marshy areas and trumpeter swans, mallards, and Canada geese around ponds.

WHEN TO GO July and August are the park's most crowded months. In winter, when park lodgings close, the crowds are genuinely sparse, and, although most of Teton Park Road is also closed, Jackson Hole Highway remains open, providing access to cross-country ski trails and frozen Jackson Lake. (Moose Visitor Center stays open all winter, except on Christmas Day.) Winter dining and lodging rates at Teton Village are often higher than in summer because of the popularity of nearby downhill skiing. In Jackson, rates are generally higher during the summer; the lowest rates, and smallest crowds, can be found during spring and fall. In April most of Teton Park Road is open to bicyclists and hikers only, an off-season treat for observers of wildlife.

The average high temperature in Grand Teton in July is 81°F, the average low, 41°F. Locals say there are three seasons here:

July, August, and winter. Although that is an exaggeration, snow is possible year-round. A spring of mild days and cold nights extends into June, when the average high is 71°F and the average low 37°F. Snow begins falling in October, with temperatures averaging a high of 57°F and a low of 24°F. In January the thermometer can drop as low as −46°F and rise as high as 50°F but usually falls between 2°F and 25°F. The park averages 49 inches of snow in January and 160 inches each year. July and August are generally the driest months, and May is the rainiest, with an average of 3 inches of rain.

SEASONAL EVENTS Unless otherwise noted, more information on the following events can be obtained from the Jackson Hole Chamber of Commerce and the park visitor centers (see Visitor Information, above).

Early April: The **Pole-Pedal-Paddle** is a ski-cycle-canoe relay race starting at Jackson Hole Ski Resort and finishing down the Snake River. **Mid-May:** At the **Elk Antler Auction** in Jackson you'll find roughly 3 tons of antlers shed by the herd that winters at the National Elk Refuge. **Late May: Old West Days** in Jackson includes a rodeo, Native American dancers, a Western swing contest, and cowboy poetry. **May to August: Teton County Historical Society** (tel. 307/733–9605) sponsors monthly field trips to regional sites. **Early June to late September: Teton Science School** (tel. 307/733–4765) conducts one- to six-day natural-science seminars at its park campus. Topics include flora and fauna field study, wilderness skills and ethics, and geology. Enrollment costs $50 to $300 (see Children's Programs, below). **June to September: Jackson Hole Summer Rodeo** (tel. 307/733–2805) runs Wednesday and Saturday near downtown Jackson. **Early July to late August:** The **Grand Teton Music Festival** schedules nightly classical and modern orchestral concerts performed at Teton Village by more than 115 musicians from orchestras worldwide. **Mid-September to early October: Jackson Hole Fall Arts Festival** (tel. 307/733–3316) includes gallery shows, artists' workshops, concerts, dance, and theater. **Early October: Quilting in the Tetons** features workshops and exhibits in Jackson. **Early December to early April: Ski races** for qualifying amateurs and the general public are sponsored by Jackson Hole Ski Club (tel. 307/733–6433), Grand Targhee Resort (tel. 307/353–2300), and Snow King Resort (tel. 307/733–5200). **December to March: Winter Speaker Series** sponsored by Teton Science School (tel. 307/733–4765) features twice-monthly natural-science speakers. **Year-round:** Teton County Historical Center (tel. 307/733–9605) sponsors a **speaker series,** including monthly lectures that focus on regional history.

WHAT TO PACK There's a wind-chill factor even in July, so pack extra warm clothing and rain gear. Wearing several layers is the best safeguard against Grand Teton's fickle weather. In summer, shorts and a light cotton shirt should suffice, but have a wool sweater or thick sweatshirt handy, as well as a hooded nylon windbreaker and long pants. Walking shoes—and hiking boots if you plan on hitting the trail—are essential. Wool socks and extra warm clothing are recommended if you're taking a Snake River float trip (*see* Guided Tours, *below*). Insect repellent, sunscreen, sunglasses, and a hat are also worth carrying.

GENERAL STORES **Colter Bay Grocery and General Store,** along with **Colter Bay Tackle and Gift Shop** (both tel. 307/733–3100), is open daily from 7:30 AM to 10 PM between mid-May and late September. **Flagg Ranch Grocery Store** (tel. 307/543–2861 or 800/443–2311), 4 mi north of the park, is open daily from 8 AM to 10 PM in summer; hours vary the rest of the year. **Dornans' Grocery** (tel. 307/733–2415), west of Moose Junction, which is open daily from 8 to 8 between May and October and from 9 to 6 at other times, has an ATM. **Jenny Lake Store** (tel. 307/733–3708), on Jenny Lake Road, is open daily from 8 to 7 between June and October. **Signal Mountain Lodge Convenience Store** (tel. 307/543–2831), on Teton Park Road, is open

daily from 7 AM to 9 PM between mid-May and mid-October. These stores sell canned, frozen, and some fresh food, as well as most outdoors essentials (from ponchos to camping knives), but don't plan to stock your entire camping trip at any of them. Instead, rely on supermarkets in Jackson for provisions.

Nearby **Jackson** is a shopper's mecca of Western wear, gear, crafts, and souvenirs, with several minimalls off its old-fashioned downtown boardwalks. Some of the more popular stores include the **Hole Works** (tel. 307/733–7000); **Warbonnet Indian Arts** (tel. 307/733–6158), with its fine selection of Navajo rugs; and **Valley Bookstore** (tel. 307/733–4533), with numerous books on regional history, mountaineering, and travel.

ARRIVING AND DEPARTING The park is just over 7 mi from Yellowstone's south entrance on the John D. Rockefeller, Jr., Memorial Parkway, which is often crowded in July and August. Less crowded is the eastern entrance on U.S. 26–287 from Dubois, Wyoming, through Moran Junction. The busiest route is through bustling Jackson, 12 mi south of the park on the Jackson Hole Highway. This is also the most scenic route, with panoramic views of Jackson Hole, the Gros Ventre Range to the east, and the Teton Range to the west.

The cities nearest Grand Teton are: Rock Springs, Wyoming, 177 mi southeast of Jackson on U.S. 191; Pocatello, Idaho, 150 mi from Jackson on U.S. 89 and Route 30; and Salt Lake City, Utah, 269 mi from Jackson on U.S. 89 and I–15.

By Bus. Jackson Hole has no interstate bus service. **Grand Teton Lodge Company** (*see* Visitor Information, *above*) runs daily buses from Jackson Hole Airport to Jackson Lake Lodge for $12.50 one way or $25 round-trip; it also shuttles passengers between Jackson Lake Lodge and Colter Bay Visitor Center hourly from 7 to 5, between early June and mid-September. Jackson's **START Bus** runs regularly from Town Square to Teton Village, from late

May to mid-September and from early December to early April from 6 AM to 11 PM. Fares are $2, with multiride discounts. **National Park Tours** (1680 Martin La., tel. 307/733–4325) makes regular day trips during the summer from Jackson to Grand Teton National Park for $38 per person, round-trip.

By Car and RV. Jackson Hole Highway (U.S. 26–89–191) runs the entire length of the park, from Jackson to Yellowstone's South Entrance. This road is open all year from Jackson to Moran Junction and north to Flagg Ranch, 2 mi south of Yellowstone. (The road into Yellowstone, however, is closed in winter.) The section of the highway that runs east from Moran Junction over Togwotee Pass (U.S. 26–287) is also open year-round.

Depending on traffic, the southern Moose Entrance to Grand Teton is about 20 minutes from downtown Jackson. West Yellowstone, Montana, the western gateway to Yellowstone park, is 58 mi, or two hours, from Teton park via Yellowstone's often crowded Lower Loop Road.

Two back-road entrances require proper equipment. The Moose–Wilson Road passes Teton Village resort 12 mi from Jackson before continuing another 3 unpaved mi to the Moose Entrance; it is closed to trucks, trailers, and RVs. Even rougher is the 60-mi Grassy Lake Road, which heads east from Ashton, Idaho, through Targhee National Forest to the John D. Rockefeller Jr. Memorial Parkway (a park, not a road). The dirt-and-gravel Grassy Lake Road is off Route 32 just a mile south of Ashton. Because much of it is one lane, it's closed to trailers and large RVs. Both roads are closed by snow and are heavily rutted through June.

By Plane. Jackson Hole Airport (tel. 307/733–7682), 8 mi north of town, off Jackson Hole Highway, receives daily flights connecting from Denver and Salt Lake City, home of the closest international airport. **Grand Teton Lodge Company** (*see* Visitor Information, *above*) runs a shuttle between

the airport and Jackson Lake Lodge several times daily for $12.50 per person one way, plus park entrance fees, and some Jackson lodgings provide free airport shuttle service for guests. One-way taxi fare from the airport to Jackson is about $12–$15; taxi companies include **All Star Transportation** (tel. 307/733–2888), **Buckboard Cab** (tel. 307/733–1112), and **All Trans Company** (tel. 307/733–3135). Car-rental agencies at the Jackson Airport include **Avis** (tel. 307/733–3422 or 800/331–1212), **Hertz** (tel. 307/733–2272 or 800/654–3131), **Budget** (tel. 307/733–6868), and **Rent-a-Wreck** (tel. 307/733–5014).

EXPLORING

Unlike Yellowstone's Grand Loop, Grand Teton's road system doesn't allow for easy tour-bus access to all major sights. Only a car will get you close to Jenny Lake, into the remote eastern hills, and to the top of Signal Mountain. Easy interpretive trails make some sights accessible to most visitors. If your time and ability allow it, bicycling is easier here than in Yellowstone: Teton Park Road and Jackson Hole Highway are either flat or have long, gradual inclines, with well-marked shoulders and less traffic than the roads at Yellowstone. While you can breeze through the park by car in two to three hours, you'd do well to spend a couple of days in Grand Teton. Dedicated hikers and outdoor enthusiasts could easily find two weeks worth of adventurous camping.

THE BEST IN ONE DAY Get to Moose Visitor Center in time for a 9 AM, two-hour, guided Snake River float trip (make reservations in advance with one of the dozen or so outfitters that offer the trip). Although mild white water is the roughest stuff you'll experience, this is an exhilarating ride, and you might see moose and bison along the way. When you're back on dry ground, drive north on Teton Park Road, stopping at scenic turnouts—don't miss Teton Glacier—until you reach Jenny Lake Road. Because traffic on this road runs in only one direction, you

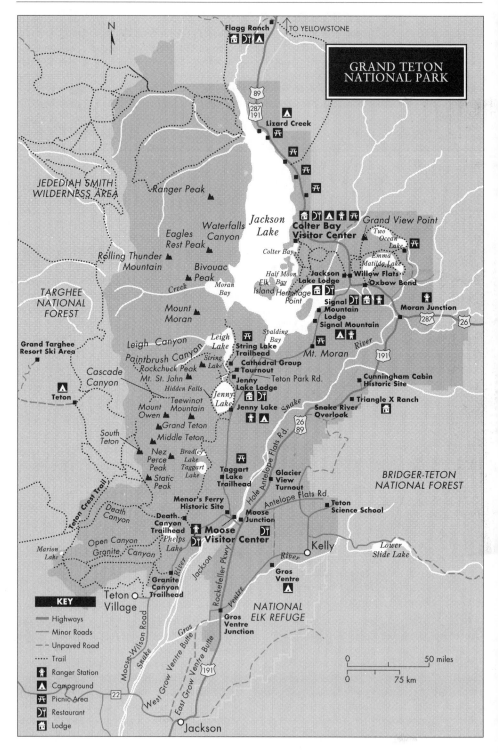

will have to drive to the far end of the road, turning left onto it at North Jenny Lake Junction. After a brief stop at Cathedral Group Turnout, from which you'll see Grand, Owen, and Teewinot peaks up close, park at the South Jenny Lake Ranger Station and take the 20-minute boat ride to Cascade Canyon Trailhead. An easy .5-mi walk up Cascade Canyon Trail takes you to Hidden Falls, a shaded, pine-scented picnic site. Return to your car by early afternoon, drive back to Teton Park Road, and head north to Signal Mountain Road, a spur road that leads to a top-of-the-park view of the Tetons. In late afternoon descend the mountain and continue north on Teton Park Road. At Jackson Lake Junction, you can go east to Oxbow Bend or north to Willow Flats, both excellent spots for wildlife viewing. An early dinner in Jackson Lake Lodge looking out at the Tetons will rejuvenate you just enough for the trip north to Colter Bay Marina, from which you can take a 1½-hour sunset cruise across Jackson Lake to Waterfalls Canyon (*see* Guided Tours, *below*). The nearest Yellowstone lodgings are slightly more than an hour away from Colter Bay, but consider staying in cabins at Colter Bay or back at Jackson Lake Lodge. Do not go on to Yellowstone expecting a room without a reservation.

You can reverse this route if you're heading south from Yellowstone: Start the day with a 7:30 breakfast cruise from Colter Bay, and end it with a sunset float down the Snake.

ORIENTATION PROGRAMS Colter Bay Visitor Center auditorium hosts several free daily programs. A 30-minute ranger lecture, "Teton Highlights," provides tips on park activities daily at 11 and 3. Several times daily, Colter Bay shows "The Nature of Grand Teton," a 15-minute slide show on park geological history, and "Bald Eagles," a 10-minute slide show. Two 25-minute movies—*Song Dog,* about coyotes, and *Elk of the Northern Herd*—are each shown once daily. Every other day, Colter Bay shows the 25-minute film about Native Americans, *In Quest of a Vision.*

Moose Visitor Center plays video versions of *The Nature of Grand Teton* and *Teton Highlights. Song Dog* and *Elk of the Northern Herd* are among the videos shown on rainy days.

GUIDED TOURS **Grand Teton Lodge Company** (Box 240, Moran, WY 83013, tel. 307/543–2811, 307/543–3100, or 800/628–9988; fax 307/543–3143) runs 1½-hour Jackson Lake cruises ($11) from Colter Bay Marina throughout the day, between mid-May and mid-September; narrators on these cruises discuss geology and wildlife. Sunset cruises to the base of Waterfalls Canyon also cost $11 and run from mid-June to mid-August. Daily breakfast cruises ($20) depart from the marina from late May to late September. On Wednesday and Saturday evenings from early June to mid-September, you may also sign up for steak-fry cruises, which cost $35.

Access Tours (Box 2985, Jackson, WY 83001, tel. 307/733–6664 or 800/929–4811) caters to people with physical disabilities, with educational, multiday park tours that include overnight stays in motels. **National Park Tours** (Box 411, Jackson, WY 83001, tel. 307/733–4325, fax 307/733–2689) picks up passengers at local hotels for a daily (9 to 3:30) $38 guided park tour.

There are many guided float trips through calm-water sections of the Snake River; these pick up clients at the Float Trip parking area near Moose Visitor Center for a 10- to 20-minute drive to upriver launch sites. Ten-mile floats last two to three hours and 5-mi floats last one to two hours. All concessionaires provide ponchos and life preservers. Early-morning and evening floats are your best bets for wildlife viewing; be sure to carry a jacket or sweater, and wear soft-soled shoes. Oarspeople provide a narrative. Float season runs mid-May to mid-September. **Barker-Ewing Scenic Float Trips** (Box 100-J, Moose, WY 83012, tel. 307/733–1000 or 800/365–1800) specializes in 10-mi floats. They cost $30. Dinner trips cost $10 more per person. **Grand Teton Lodge Company** (*see above*) gathers floaters from Colter Bay and Jackson Lake

Lodge for 10-mi trips ($33), lunch floats ($38), and supper floats ($44). National Park, Osprey, and Triangle X float trips are all part of **Triangle X Ranch** (Moose, WY 83012, tel. 307/733–6445 for park trip, 307/733–5500 for the others), which is between Moose and Moran junctions off Jackson Hole Highway; pickups are in downtown Jackson, Moose parking lot, and Triangle X Ranch, depending on the float. Ten-mile sunrise wildlife float trips and evening wildlife trips are $30; 5-mi trips cost $20; supper floats are $40. **Signal Mountain Lodge** (*see* Lodging, *below*) takes floaters from the lodge for 10-mi trips ($32).

Rangers lead free walks, from a one-hour lakeside stroll at Colter Bay to an all-day, 10-mi mountain hike from Moose from early June to early September. Some of these require reservations; call the park (*see* Visitor Information, *above*) in advance. **National Elk Refuge Horse-Drawn Sleigh Rides** (Box C, Jackson, WY 83001, tel. 307/733–9212) depart continuously from 10 to 4, late December to late March, from the National Wildlife Art Museum; fares are $10. **Teton Village Aerial Tram** (Teton Village, WY 83025, tel. 307/733–2292) departs every half hour from late May to late September for a 20-minute ride with an informal conductor's narrative up 10,450-ft Rendezvous Mountain, which has a viewing platform, snack bar, and trailhead. Tickets cost $15 and must be purchased in person. **Wild West Jeep Tours** (Box 7506, Jackson, WY 83001, tel. 307/733–9036) depart from Jackson two times daily early June to early September, for rides through the Teton backcountry; the fare is $30. **Jackson Hole Museum** (Box 1005, Deloney and Glenwood Sts., Jackson, WY 83001, tel. 307/733–2414) leads walking tours of historic Jackson. These depart from the museum Monday through Saturday at 11, from early June to late September ($2).

SCENIC DRIVES AND VIEWS Starting at Moose, you can combine several park roads for a 60-mi, three- to five-hour loop past major sights. Displays at Teton Park Road and Jackson Hole Highway turnouts identify mountains and explain geology. Watch carefully for oncoming traffic at turnouts north of Jackson Lake Lodge; the road is narrow and the curves are sharp.

Your first stop on **Teton Park Road** is just a few hundred yards past Moose Entrance, where a short road leads to the Chapel of the Transfiguration. The chapel was built in 1925, and its altar window frames the Grand Teton. Past Teton Park Road's Windy Point and Teton Glacier turnouts, one-way **Jenny Lake Scenic Drive** provides the park's best roadside Teton close-ups. The road winds south past groves of lodgepole pine and open meadows from North Jenny Lake Junction, 12 mi north of Moose. Roughly 2 mi down Jenny Lake Road, the Cathedral Group Turnout faces 13,770-ft Grand Teton (the range's highest peak), which is flanked by 12,928-ft Mt. Owen and 12,325-ft Mt. Teewinot. Just before you rejoin Teton Park Road at South Jenny Lake Junction, you'll see Jenny Lake, named after a Native American who was married to a mountain man; today it's a favorite hiking area. Beware: Steep, unguarded drop-offs border the right side of the road.

Back on Teton Park Road, Mt. Moran Turnout provides a first glimpse of the northern Tetons that surround 12,605-ft Mt. Moran. A detour on **Signal Mountain Road** leads to an 800-ft climb on a 5-mi stretch of switchbacks, with Mt. Moran dominating the view. The trip ends with a sweeping view of Jackson Hole and the entire 40-mi Teton Range. Sunset is the most scenic time to make the climb up Signal Mountain, so you may want to return later. Back on Teton Park Road, continue north to the log Chapel of the Sacred Heart, which has a picnic area overlooking southern Jackson Lake. A mile north of Jackson Lake Junction, Willow Flats Turnout surveys Mt. Moran, 10,825-ft Bivouac Peak, 10,908-ft Rolling Thunder Mountain, 11,258-ft Eagles Rest Peak, and 11,355-ft Ranger Peak. The willow thickets here are an excellent wildlife habitat and are especially lively in the morning. Scan the flats with binoculars to find moose feeding.

Colter Bay Visitor Center, at the north end of this driving tour, has an airy, three-level Native American Arts Museum with displays of hide paintings, beadwork, headdresses, weapons, and tools. When you're through browsing in the museum, backtrack on Teton Park Road to Jackson Lake Junction and turn left onto **Jackson Hole Highway** toward Moran Junction. One mile down this road, Oxbow Bend Turnout overlooks a quiet backwater left by the Snake River when it cut a new southern channel. White pelicans stop here on their spring migration (many stay on through summer); trumpeter swans visit frequently; and a colony of great blue herons nests amid the cottonwoods along the river. Use binoculars to search for these waterfowl as well as for bald eagles, ospreys, moose, beaver, and otter. The Oxbow is also known for the reflection of Mt. Moran that marks its calm waters in early morning.

At Moran Junction bear right, continuing south on the Jackson Hole Highway. Nine miles south, at Snake River Overlook, you may recognize the view of this river bend— it is immortalized in an Ansel Adams photograph. Five miles farther south, stop at Glacier View Turnout for a look at Teton Glacier. About 2 mi before you reach Moose Junction, turn left onto **Antelope Flats Road,** which wanders eastward through ranches and over rolling plains and river flats that are home to antelope, as well as bison and moose during the spring and fall. Turning right off this road at the four-way intersection, you can loop around past Kelly and the Gros Ventre campground and back to the highway at Gros Ventre Junction.

HISTORIC BUILDINGS AND SITES To reach the **Menor's Ferry Historic Site,** take the .5-mi Menor's Ferry Interpretive Trail at the Chapel of the Transfiguration parking lot, just past Moose Entrance. The easy ½-hour riverside walk passes a small, free history museum; 19th-century homesteader Bill Menor's log cabin, which now houses a small general store; the old site of the Snake River Ferry; and an indoor historic-photo exhibit. These exhibits are open

year-round, and a pamphlet on the area is available for 25¢ at the trailhead.

Six miles south of Moran, a gravel spur road leads to the **Cunningham Cabin Historic Site.** An easy .75-mi trail runs through sagebrush around Pierce Cunningham's 1890 log-cabin homestead. Cunningham, an early Jackson Hole homesteader and civic leader, built his cabin in Appalachian dogtrot style, joining two halves with a roofed veranda. Watch for badgers, coyotes, and Uinta ground squirrels in the area. The site is open year-round, and a 25¢ pamphlet is available at the trailhead.

NATURE TRAILS AND SHORT WALKS Beginning at the Death Canyon Trailhead, the **Phelps Lake Overlook Trail** is an easy 1-mi round-trip walk up conifer- and aspen-lined glacial moraine to views of this valley lake, accessible only by trail. Expect abundant bird life: Western tanagers, northern flickers, and ruby-crowned kinglets thrive in the bordering woods, and hummingbirds feed on scarlet gilia beneath the overlook. To reach the trailhead from Teton Park Road, turn left onto Moose–Wilson Road just before the Moose Entrance, go 4.5 mi, and turn right. The trailhead and parking area is near the White Grass Ranger Station, just 1.5 mi ahead.

Off Jenny Lake Road, before it reaches Jenny Lake, you'll come to the String Lake parking area and trailhead, from which two easy hikes begin. The flat 2-mi, one-hour round-trip **Leigh Lake Trail** follows String Lake's northeastern shore to Leigh Lake's south shore. You can extend this hike into a still-easy 7.5-mi, four-hour round-trip by following the forested east shore of Leigh Lake to Bearpaw Lake. Along the way you'll have views of Mt. Moran across the lake, and you may be lucky enough to spot a moose. Also starting from this parking area is the 3.5-mi, three-hour **String Lake Trail** loop, which sits in the shadows of 11,144-ft Rockchuck Peak and 11,430-ft Mt. Saint John.

Lunchtree Hill Trail, one of the park's easiest, begins at Jackson Lake Lodge and leads

.5 mi to the top of a hill above Willow Flats; the round-trip walk takes no more than one half-hour. This area's willow thickets, beaver ponds, and wet, grassy meadows make it a birder's paradise. Look for sandhill cranes, hummingbirds, and the many types of songbirds described in the free bird guide available at visitor centers. Another very easy two-hour walk is the **Colter Bay Nature Trail Loop,** a 1.75-mi round-trip excursion with views of Jackson Lake and the Tetons. Start at the Colter Bay Visitor Center and walk about .3 mi to the trailhead, where you can pick up a trail leaflet. As you follow the level trail along the forest's edge, you may see lakeside moose and bald eagles. Also starting from this trailhead, the 3-mi, two-hour, mostly level **Heron Pond–Swan Lake Trail** passes through areas with willows and aspens and traverses a marshy, stream-crossed terrain favored by beaver and waterfowl.

You can take the 20-minute boat ride from the Jenny Lake dock to the **Cascade Canyon Trailhead,** which is the start of a gentle, .5-mi climb one way to 200-ft Hidden Falls, the park's most popular and crowded trail destination. Listen here for the distinctive bleating of the rabbitlike pikas among the glacial boulders and pines. Or skip the boat ride and walk to Hidden Falls from the Jenny Lake Ranger Station by following the mostly level **Jenny Lake Trail** around the south shore of the lake and joining the Cascade Canyon Trail to the falls. The Jenny Lake Trail continues around the lake for 6.5 mi, an easy hike that takes about four hours and offers views of the Tetons from the eastern shore.

LONGER HIKES From the Death Canyon Trailhead, you can hike out to the Phelps Lake Overlook (*see* Nature Trails and Short Walks, *above*), then continue down to the lake via the **Death Canyon Trail.** This 4-mi, three-hour hike entails a steep return hike.

You can also take the **Death Canyon Trail** from Phelps Lake Overlook up into Death Canyon. The trail passes wildflower meadows and follows the north side of Death Canyon Creek for a 7.5-mi, six-hour round-trip from the Death Canyon Trailhead to the Static Peak Trail Junction and back. As you ascend the canyon, listen for the whistle of marmots and the bleating of pikas, two small mammals that are common in the park, and keep an eye out for moose, mule deer, and the occasional black bear. From the junction, the **Static Peak Divide Trail** switchbacks through a whitebark-pine forest, then climbs a steep slope to the foot of Static Peak. This is one of the roughest trails in the park, and to traverse it early in the season you must use an ice axe (check conditions at the Jenny Lake Ranger Station). Static Peak Divide, at 10,800 ft in altitude, is the highest point on a maintained trail in the park. Your reward on this 15.5-mi, 10-hour round-trip hike from Death Canyon Trailhead will be sweeping views of the Tetons and Jackson Hole.

A somewhat less strenuous southern-Tetons day hike is the 17.5-mi round-trip **Marion Lake Trail,** which climbs nearly 3,000 ft from Granite Canyon Trailhead, off the Moose–Wilson Road (the trailhead is about 2 mi south of the turnoff for the Death Canyon Trailhead). About 1.5 mi in from the trailhead you'll climb through a talus field and then follow Granite Creek for about 4 mi, sometimes winding through willows close to the creek, where chances of moose sightings are excellent. The trail traces Granite Canyon up to subalpine meadows near Marion Lake that in August are brilliantly painted with wildflowers. Just above the tree line, turn right for a brief stretch on the Teton Crest Trail until you reach tiny Marion Lake. It will take about 12 hours to hike to Marion Lake and back. You can shorten this hike—and make it even more spectacular—by returning south from Marion Lake along the **Teton Crest Trail,** past the turnoff for the Granite Canyon Trail, and looping eastward to the top of the tram that runs from Teton Village. The tram will take you down to the village, where you should have parked a car. To get from Granite Canyon Trailhead to Teton Village via the Marion Lake Trail and the tram, you must cover 12.5 mi, a seven-hour journey.

Two more-moderate hikes in the southern Tetons are the **Bradley Lake** and **Taggart Lake–Beaver Creek** trails, which begin as one trail at the Taggart Lake Trailhead, about 3 mi north of the Moose Visitor Center on Teton Park Road. Each of these trails is 4 mi round-trip and takes about three hours to hike, and both pass through a major portion of land burned during a 1985 fire. The Bradley Lake Trail branches north (right) 1 mi from the trailhead, and the Taggart Lake Trail continues west (left) .5 mi to Taggart Lake's south end, climbing glacial moraines surrounding the lake. When you reach Taggart Lake you may continue along its east shore to the north end, climbing the moraine between Taggart and Bradley lakes to join the Bradley Lake Trail. This adds about a mile to the hike and makes it a little more difficult, but it also increases your chances of spotting wildlife.

At Jenny Lake the **Cascade Canyon Trail** past Hidden Falls (*see* Nature Trails and Short Walks, *above*) becomes strenuous as it climbs another .5 mi to Inspiration Point, from which there are sweeping views of Jenny Lake and Jackson Hole below, and Cascade Canyon's wall of mountains above. The Cascade Canyon Trail up to Inspiration Point is the park's most crowded, but beyond that point the crowds thin. The trail continues up the canyon, where there are great views of Mt. Teewinot, Mt. Owen, and Grand Teton (in that order, on your left). At times the trail crosses talus slopes where, in August, wild raspberries and thimbleberries grow. A couple of stream crossings along the way make good lunch spots. To get from the trailhead to the point where the trail forks (it follows the two forks of Cascade Creek) and back, you'll hike 13 mi in about seven hours.

The **Grand View Point Trail** is a good introduction to the backcountry in the northeastern section of the park. The trailhead is at the end of a 1-mi dirt road that turns right off U.S. 89–191–287 about 2.5 mi north of Jackson Lake Junction. Watch for moose in the marshy area at the base of the trail, which switchbacks up moderately through old-growth Douglas firs that support woodpeckers, many kinds of songbirds, and grouse. From the 7,327-ft summit, you'll see long, sparkling Two Ocean Lake below to the northeast and Emma Matilda Lake to the southeast. Red-tailed hawks, pelicans, and eagles may be sighted above the waters. The hike to the summit and back is just over 2 mi and will take about two hours. If you want to go farther, continue down through stands of pine and aspen to the northwest shore of Two Ocean Lake, circle around the lake's north shore, and then trace the north shore of Emma Matilda Lake, returning to the Grand View Point Trailhead. On this route you'll hear many more songbirds, and you will likely see trumpeter swans near the lakes. The loop around the lakes covers approximately 10 mi from the trailhead and takes about five hours.

From the Colter Bay Trailhead (*see* Nature Trails and Short Walks, *above*), the **Hermitage Point Trail** traverses gentle terrain with pine forests and willow thickets that are prime moose and beaver territory. Watch for ducks at Swan Lake and Heron Pond along the way. The trail covers a 9-mi loop to Heritage Point on Jackson Lake and takes about four hours to hike.

OTHER ACTIVITIES **Back-Road Driving.** Except for short dirt roads to trailheads and the two back-road entrances (*see* Arriving and Departing, *above*), no back-road driving is allowed inside the park. Four-wheeling is, however, possible in national forests outside Grand Teton.

Biking. Jackson Hole's long, flat profile and mountain scenery attracts even novice 10-speed and mountain bikers. The River Road, 4 mi north of Moose, is an easy four-hour mountain-bike ride along the Snake River. A bike lane allows for northbound bike traffic along the one-way Jenny Lake Loop Road, a one-hour ride. A four-hour, moderate ride on paved road goes from Gros Ventre Junction to Lower Slide Lake. The three-hour Shadow Mountain Road loop off Antelope Flats Road gives experienced mountain bikers an aerobic workout and spectacular Snake River views. For a true bike odyssey, try all or part of the 60-mi Grassy Lake Road (*see* Arriving and Departing, *above*). Bicycles are not allowed on trails or in the backcountry.

The closest bike-rental and repair shop is **Mountain Bike Outfitters** (Box 303, Moose, WY 83012, tel. 307/733–3314), which gives excellent advice on cycling. The shop is at Dornan's, just before Moose Visitor Center. Mountain bike rentals cost $6 per hour, $16 per half day, and $24 for a full day; sport bikes are $7 per hour, $20 per half day, and $28 for a full day, including water bottle, cage, helmet, and lock. **Teton Cyclery** (175 N. Glenwood St., Jackson, WY 83001, tel. 307/733–4386) has in-town rentals and repairs.

Bird-Watching. Among Teton-country birds are great blue herons and osprey, which nest at Oxbow Bend from spring through fall. White pelicans also stop at the Oxbow on their southward journey in spring, and bald eagles remain all year to fish in the shallow water. Nearby Willow Flats is host to similar bird life. Trumpeter swans, rare in Yellowstone, are more common in Grand Teton; look for them at Oxbow Bend and Two Ocean Lake. Look for songbirds, such as pine grosbeaks and Cassin's finches, in surrounding open pine and aspen forests. Similar songbirds inhabit Grandview Point, as do blue and ruffed grouse. Keep binoculars handy while traveling along Antelope Flats Road: You may spot red-tailed hawks and prairie falcons. At Taggart Lake you'll see woodpeckers, bluebirds, and hummingbirds.

Boating. Motorboats are allowed on Jenny (7½-horsepower maximum), Jackson, and Phelps lakes. **Grand Teton Lodge Company** (tel. 307/543–3100, 307/543–2811, or 800/628–9988; fax 307/543–3143) rents 9.9 HP motorboats at Colter Bay Marina for $16 per hour and $105 per eight-hour day, with a $50 deposit. A two-hour minimum is required. Rowboats and canoes are $8 per hour. Reservations are not accepted. **Signal Mountain Lodge Marina** (tel. 307/543–2831) rents pontoon boats ($130 half day, $180 full day), deck cruisers ($180 half day, $225 full day), motorboats ($65 half day, $105 full day), and rowboats and canoes ($30 half day, $60 full day). The **Teton Boating Company** (tel. 307/733–2703) operates a shuttle across Jenny Lake to Hidden Falls. It costs $4 round-trip.

Fishing. Native cutthroat, rainbow, brook, and lake trout inhabit Grand Teton National Park waters. The Snake's 120 mi of river and tributary are world-renowned. Unlike Yellowstone, the park requires a Wyoming fishing license, which costs $15 for residents and $65 for nonresidents for the entire fishing season. Short-term and full-season nonresident licenses are also available. Fishing licenses are available at the Wyoming Game and Fish Department (Box 67, 360 N. Cache St., Jackson, WY 83001, tel. 307/733–2321), Colter Bay Marina, and most of the area's sporting-goods stores. Jenny and Leigh lakes are open for fishing year-round, Jackson Lake is closed to anglers during October, and the Snake River is closed from November 1 to March 31. Only in the park's northern half, including Jackson Lake, are you allowed to use live bait. **Grand Teton Lodge Company** (*see* Guided Tours, *above*) has guided Jackson Lake fishing trips with boat, guide, and tackle costing $52 per hour for up to three people and $10 per hour for each additional person, with a minimum of two hours, or $325 per day for three people. **Signal Mountain Lodge** (*see above*) leads similar trips costing $50 per hour for up to two people and $10 per hour for each additional person, with a minimum of two hours—or $160 half day, with a $30 fee for each extra person.

Horseback Riding. Grand Teton Lodge Company (*see* Guided Tours, *above*) runs one-hour to half-day trail rides from the Jackson Lake Lodge and Colter Bay Village corrals, ranging in price from $19 to $46 per person. One-hour rides give an overview of the Jackson Lake Lodge area; two-hour rides depart from the lodge corral to Emma Matilda Lake, Oxbow Bend, and

Christian Pond, or from Colter Bay to a variety of destinations. Half-day trips, for advanced riders only, depart from Jackson Lake Lodge Corral to Two Ocean Lake and from Colter Bay Village Corral to Hermitage Point. There are horseback and wagon rides at breakfast and dinner: Breakfast rides cost $32 on horseback, and $18 by wagon. Dinner rides cost $36 on horseback; $24 in a wagon.

Rafting. If you're floating the Snake River on your own, check at visitor centers or the Buffalo Ranger Station near Moran Junction for current conditions. Permits, which are required, cost $5 per raft and are valid for the entire season. There are a variety of guided trips as well (*see* Guided Tours, *above*).

Rock Climbing. The Teton Range offers the nation's most diverse general mountaineering. Excellent rock, snow, and ice routes abound for climbers of all experience levels. Among the peaks that can be ascended in a day are Cube Point, a moderate climb approached via Hanging Canyon west of Jenny Lake, and nearby Symmetry Spire, which has long, moderately difficult pitches. Grand Teton itself is one of the world's classic two-day climbs: Moderately difficult Exum Ridge is the most popular ascent, but the original Owen-Spalding Route is easier. Mt. Moran has the range's most commanding views, with two-day ascents via the standard route or Skillet Glacier, the range's most popular snow climb. Mt. Owen's two-day Koven Route and the more difficult East Ridge both combine rock with steep snow up to the Tetons' most difficult summit. Between June and mid-September all climbers can sign in and out at Jenny Lake Ranger Station and from mid-September to May at Moose Visitor Center. **Exum Mountain Guides** (Box 56, Moose, WY 83012, tel. 307/733–2297) runs one-day basic ($50), intermediate ($70), and advanced ($90) schools from June through September, as well as a winter Snow School. **Jackson Hole Mountain Guides** (Box 7477, Jackson, WY 83001, tel. 307/733–4979) has similar courses.

Ski Touring. Grand Teton has some of North America's finest and most varied cross-country skiing. Ski the gentle 3-mi Swan Lake–Heron Pond Loop near Colter Bay Visitor Center, the mostly level 9-mi Jenny Lake Trail, or the moderate 4-mi Taggart Lake–Beaver Creek Loop and 5-mi Phelps Lake Overlook trail, which have some steep descents. Advanced skiers should head for the Teton Crest Trail. During the winter all overnight backcountry travelers must register at park headquarters in Moose to obtain a free permit.

Rossignol Nordic Ski Center (Box 290, Teton Village, WY 83025, tel. 307/739–2629), at Teton Village, rents skis and maintains about 10 mi of groomed trails. **Jack Dennis Outdoor Shop** (50 E. Broadway, Jackson, tel. 307/733–3270; Teton Village, tel. 307/733–6838), **Wildernest Sports** (Teton Village, tel. 307/733–4297), and **Teton Village Sports** (Teton Village, tel. 307/733–2181) also rent equipment.

Snowmobiling. Designated unplowed sections of Teton Park Road are open to snowmobiles, and you can also snowmobile on Jackson Lake. Annual $5 permits must be purchased at Moose Visitor Center or Colter Bay Ranger Station (*see* Visitor Information, *above*). The speed limit is 45 mi per hour. **Flagg Ranch Village** (Box 187, John D. Rockefeller Jr. Memorial Pkwy., Moran, WY, tel. 307/543–2861) and **Cowboy Village Resort at Togwotee** (Box 91, U.S. 26–287, Moran, WY, tel. 307/543–2847 or 800/543–2847) rent snowmobiles.

CHILDREN'S PROGRAMS The **Teton Science School** (tel. 307/733–4765) conducts weekday Young Naturalists programs for children in grades 3 and 4 from late July through early August. Children may be enrolled in the program for up to 10 days, at a cost of $11 to $14 per day, depending on length of enrollment. The Junior Science School program, for children in grades 5 through 7, runs from June through August and costs $95 to $115 per week, depending on the number of weeks the child is enrolled (there's a nine-week limit). These outdoor programs are led by experienced environmental educators. In previous years, program topics have included "Making Your Own Nature Journal," "Weird Science," and "Wild Animals Need Wild Lands."

EVENING ACTIVITIES Ranger-led activities include campfire programs with nightly slide shows from June through September, at the Colter Bay, Gros Ventre, and Signal Mountain amphitheaters. The **Flagg Ranch Campfire Program** is held several times a week. On Tuesday, Thursday, Friday, and Saturday evenings from July through mid-August, the **Jackson Lake Lodge Wapiti Room** hosts a slide-illustrated ranger talk, where you'll learn about park wildlife, geology, flora, and more. On Monday and Wednesday nights square dancing and Western swing dancing take place in the Wapiti Room. Church services are held on Sunday evening.

DINING

Though the park itself has some excellent restaurants, don't miss dining in Jackson, the hub of Rocky Mountain cuisine. Several innovative restaurants combine native game, fowl, and fish with Old World preparations and New-Age health consciousness. Steaks are usually cut from grass-fed Wyoming beef. Poultry and pasta dishes are still heavily influenced by Alpine tradition, but new styles of preparation are catching on. Whole-grain breakfasts and homemade soups are crowding out eggs and burgers, too.

INSIDE THE PARK **Jackson Lake Lodge Mural Room.** The ultimate park dining experience is found right off the lodge's Blue Heron Lounge. Raised, rose-color banquette tables face tall windows that look out at Mt. Moran and the neighboring northern Tetons. The room gets its name from a mural painted by western artist Carl Roters on 11 8-ft-tall rosewood-and-walnut panels covering 700 square ft. The mural details an 1837 Wyoming mountain-man rendezvous and covers two walls of the dining room. The larger East Mural Room toward the back of the restaurant looks out on Gravelly Peak, best seen at sunset or sunrise. Try sautéed Snake River trout topped with hazelnuts and grapes, or smoked and roasted Wyoming buffalo sirloin in a three-peppercorn sauce. Recommended appetizers include the cured salmon in sweet mustard and sage, and the onion au gratin and mushroom soups. *Jackson Lake Lodge, Moran, tel. 307/543–2811. AE, DC, MC, V. Closed mid-Oct.–late May. $$–$$$*

The Aspens. Part of Signal Mountain Lodge, this casual, modern, lavender room has exposed ceiling beams and big square windows overlooking southern Jackson Lake and the Tetons. The emphasis here is on fish: Rocky Mountain trout is marinated, lightly floured, and grilled, or simply grilled and topped with lemon-parsley butter. *Signal Mountain Lodge, Teton Park Rd., Moran, tel. 307/543–2831, fax 307/543-2569. AE, D, MC, V. Closed mid-Oct.–mid-May. $$*

Jackson Lake Lodge Pioneer Grill. With an old-fashioned soda fountain, friendly service, and seats along a winding counter, this eatery recalls the pre-yuppified Middle American luncheonette. It's favored by families and senior citizens: Tour groups crowd the counter at lunch, often ordering the daily specials, such as hot-dog-and-potato casserole or chicken and dumplings. The buffalo-and-barley soup is excellent. Dinner specials include grilled pork chops with home fries and applesauce, and local trout in egg batter with home fries. The walls are decorated with antique ranch tools. *Jackson Lake Lodge, Moran, tel. 307/543–2811, ext. 1911. Reservations not accepted. AE, DC, MC, V. Closed early Oct.–late May. $–$$*

John Colter Grill and **Chuckwagon Restaurant.** This grill and restaurant are connected in a sprawling, pine-shaded building across from Colter Bay Marina. Both draw families staying at Colter Bay's lodgings as well as sightseers from Jackson

Lake's boat tours. Fare and decor are bland compared to the equally budget-friendly Pioneer Grill (*see above*). On the meat side, the all-you-can-eat cowboy beef stew is plain but hearty. As for fish, Jackson Lake fisherfolk often come here to eat trout they've caught themselves, which must be cleaned and presented to the chef by 4 and can be served any time between 5:30 and 9, when the restaurant is open for dinner. *Jackson Lake Lodge, Colter Bay Village, Moran, tel. 307/543–2811. Reservations not accepted. AE, DC, MC, V. Closed late Sept.–late May. $–$$*

NEAR THE PARK **The Granary.** Located on a butte just north of town, this restaurant, part of Spring Creek Resort, is known for its consistently fine nouvelle Western cuisine and stunning views of the Teton Range. (Sit outside in the summer, when the deck is open.) The downstairs open-beam lodgepole-pine interior is decorated with Northern Plains Native American art and Teton photos. Outstanding entrées include sautéed elk medallions in morel-port sauce with spaetzle; poached salmon in cucumber-dill sauce; and a mixed grill of quail, lamb, and elk with roasted garlic. For starters, try pheasant-and-duck pâté with cranberry-bourbon relish. *1800 Spirit Dance Rd., Jackson, tel. 307/733–8833 or 800/443–6139, fax 307/733–1524. AE, D, DC, MC, V. $$$*

Louie's Steak and Seafood. Louie's is one block north of Town Square, in a 1930s log house with red window frames and a giant wood butterfly on the siding near the door. Three intimate, lavender-wallpapered rooms are furnished with simple pine tables and decorated with the region's omnipresent Teton wildlife photos. Try the swordfish steak over lime *beurre blanc,* or Wyoming Wellington, a beef fillet with mushroom pâté baked in a pastry shell with bordelaise sauce. Sautéed breaded shrimp dipped in a sauce of artichoke hearts and mustard is a popular appetizer. *175 N. Center St., Jackson, tel. 307/733–6803. Reservations essential. AE, MC, V. No lunch. $$$*

Sweetwater Restaurant. A three-room, historic downtown log cabin enhanced by stained-glass windows, a chandelier, and a deck, Sweetwater is crowded with locals drawn by its Greek and American fare. Especially good are the mesquite-grilled Atlantic salmon with raspberry-cream sauce and the moussaka. *Kolokythopita* (feta and Parmesan cheeses with zucchini, baked in phyllo) is an outstanding appetizer. *King and Pearl Sts., Jackson, tel. 307/733–3553. MC, V. $$$*

Cadillac Grille and **Billy's Burger Bar.** These two adjoining restaurants in downtown Jackson are popular with locals. The Cadillac is as slick as Jackson's eateries get: art-deco decor, glass tabletops, classic-car photos, low ceiling fans, and a marble floor. Unfortunately, the nouvelle Western menu doesn't always live up to the restaurant's pretensions. Among entrées that do are buffalo in zinfandel-blackberry sauce with polenta, venison medallions with chanterelle mushrooms and ancho chili sauce, and blackened orange roughy in pineapple butter. Exotic renditions of antelope, wild boar, caribou, and pheasant are sometimes available. Across the front lobby of the Cadillac Grille is Billy's, with a tiled diner floor and reliable food. The biggest burgers in Jackson are cooked at the counter right before your eyes. *Cache St. on Town Square, Jackson, tel. 307/733–3279. Reservations essential for Cadillac; not accepted at Billy's. AE, DC, MC, V. Cadillac $$–$$$; Billy's $*

Anthony's. Inconspicuously set on a downtown Jackson side street, this local favorite, run by a New York émigré, has the homey but funky mood of a Greenwich Village eatery. Past a lounge with an antique barber chair and '60s kitsch tables rescued from a local bar (the owner is also an antiques dealer), you'll find southern Italian abundance. Anthony's minestrone comes with a thick, spicy broth; his chicken Marsala is smothered in mushrooms and prosciutto. Lasagna and a spicy Cajun fettuccine with chicken, shrimp, and sausage are also good choices. *62 S.*

Glenwood St., Jackson, tel. 307/733–3717. MC, V. No lunch. $$

The Bunnery. This lively, pine-paneled whole-grain restaurant and bakery is hidden in a bustling nook called Hole-in-the-Wall Mall. A favorite hearty breakfast, Mother Earth, includes mushrooms, tomatoes, and broccoli piled on a bed of home fries and smothered with melted cheddar. For lunch and dinner, there are hot sandwiches (served on the Bunnery's multigrain bread), burgers, and Mexican fare. Daily baked specials are available, and beer and espresso are served. 130 N. Cache St., Jackson, tel. 307/733–5474. Reservations not accepted. MC, V. No dinner early Sept.–early June. $$

Bar J Chuckwagon Suppers. Jackson Hole's Western lifestyle is the theme at this "best buy" in the valley. Besides an all-you-can-eat meal of barbecued beef, potatoes, beans, biscuits, cake, and coffee or lemonade, you get a first-class Western show featuring the Bar J Wranglers. Recalling the days of cattle drives and the Old West, the show provides a full hour of entertainment in the form of cowboy yodeling, cowboy poetry, and Western music and stories. Teton Village Rd., Wilson, tel. 307/733–3370. AE, MC, V. $

Bubba's Bar-B-Que. Not your average beef 'n' beans joint, this traditional favorite has wood booths, antique signs, and paintings of Western gunmen, as well as groaning beef, pork, turkey, and chicken barbecue platters. Chili, chocolate-buttermilk pie, and the tremendous salad bar are also popular with locals and families. 515 W. Broadway, Jackson, tel. 307/733–2288. Reservations not accepted. D, MC, V. $

Jedediah's House of Sourdough. Mountain-man memorabilia decorates this laid-back, somewhat noisy, log-cabin breakfast-and-lunch spot, which serves sourdough and whole-grain pancakes, waffles, and biscuits—not to mention buffalo burgers. 135 E. Broadway, Jackson, tel. 307/733–5671. Reservations not accepted. AE, MC, V. No dinner. $

PICNIC SPOTS The park has 11 designated picnic areas, each with tables, grills, pit toilets, and water pumps or faucets. Those at **Signal Mountain Lodge** and **Colter Bay Visitor Center** are also close to flush toilets and stores. Colter Bay's big picnic area, spectacularly located right on the beach at Jackson Lake (continue north past the visitor center to reach it), gets crowded in July and August. The Signal Mountain Lodge picnic area is a slightly less crowded alternative; it, too, can accommodate a big group and is also lakeside. A more intimate lakeside picnic area is near the **Chapel of the Sacred Heart**, on Jackson Lake, about a mile north of Signal Mountain Lodge. From here you can see across southern Jackson Lake to Mt. Moran.

Another scenic but crowded picnic area is at the **String Lake Trailhead.** To reach it, turn right onto the spur road off Jenny Lake Road, just north of Jenny Lake. Jenny Lake itself has no designated areas, but you can improvise along the Jenny Lake Trail or at popular Hidden Falls (buy supplies at the Jenny Lake Store). Farther south, just north of the **Taggart Lake Trailhead,** on the east side of Teton Park Road, a picnic area looks out on the Snake River Valley to the east and the southern Tetons to the west.

One of the park's most isolated and uncrowded picnic sites is in the **Two Ocean Lake** area. Drive about 1 mi north of Moran Junction on the Jackson Hole Highway, then turn right onto the Pacific Creek Road, following signs to the lake for about 4 mi. North of Colter Bay, four scenic roadside picnic areas dot the east shore of Jackson Lake. The northernmost, near **Lizard Creek Campground,** is closer to the Flagg Ranch Village stores than it is to Colter Bay's facilities.

LODGING

The park itself doesn't have Yellowstone's quantity or variety of accommodations. A much better range is available in Jackson and Teton Village, which have everything from bare-bones hostels to expensive time-share condominiums. Here you can expect to rub elbows with the likes of Harrison Ford and Bill Clinton—but expect to pay premium rates for rooms. Jackson also has several excellent bed-and-breakfasts at more standard rates. Make reservations for July and August park lodgings two months ahead. Outside the park, ski season raises winter rates $10 to $40 per night. Many lodgings offer April and May shoulder-season bargains. You can reserve some rooms outside the park through **Jackson Hole Central Reservations** (Box 510, Teton Village, WY 83025, tel. 307/733–4005 or 800/443–6931), which handles hotels as well as B&Bs.

INSIDE THE PARK **Jackson Lake Lodge.** Built in 1955, John D. Rockefeller, Jr.'s contribution to park architecture is a massive stone edifice perched on a bluff overlooking the Willow Flats. Even if you're not staying here, the lobby is worth a visit: The walls are bordered with Native American designs and buttressed by giant concrete beams stained to resemble wood and Idaho stone columns. To complete the rustic mood, there are two walk-in fireplaces, a 60-ft-high window overlooking Willow Flats, and comfortable old leather chairs and sofas. A 1989 addition to the main lounge, the Blue Heron cocktail lounge also has big windows. In comparison to the lounges' sumptuous furnishings, the 37 rooms within the lodge are a letdown: They lack adequate ventilation, and they're the smallest and least desirable rooms in the complex. On the other hand, the 343 motor-lodge rooms on either side of the main building are a pleasant surprise. Each room has log partitions, oak furniture, Native American quilts, ceiling fans, and 19th-century prints of the Tetons. Half of them were renovated in 1990, and renovations on the rest were completed by 1993. An outdoor heated pool has a tepee-shape cabana. *Grand Teton Lodge Company, Box 240, Moran, WY 83013, tel. 307/543–2811, 307/543–3100, or 800/628–9988; fax 307/543–3143. 385 rooms. Facilities: 2 restau-*rants, bar, pool, business services. AE, DC, MC, V. Closed early Oct.–late May. $$$*

Jenny Lake Lodge. This is the most expensive—some say overpriced—lodging in the entire national park system. Nestled well off Jenny Lake Road (only the main building is visible from the road), the lodge borders a wildflower meadow, and its guest cabins are adequately spaced in lodgepole-pine groves. The main guest lounge is of open-beam construction with a tidy raised stone fireplace and pine furniture. Cabin interiors, with their sturdy pine beds and handmade quilts and electric blankets, live up to the elegant rustic theme, and cabin suites have fireplaces. Lodging is on the Modified American Plan, with breakfast and dinner in the excellent lodge restaurant included. *Grand Teton Lodge Company, Box 240, Moran, WY 83013, tel. 307/543–2855, fax 307/543–3143. 37 cabins. Facilities: restaurant, bar. AE, DC, MC, V. Closed mid-Oct.–late May. $$$*

Signal Mountain Lodge. The only park lodging not run by Grand Teton Lodge Company, Signal Mountain Lodge is a refreshing change of pace from Colter Bay's commotion and Jackson and Jenny Lake lodges' toniness. The main building's volcanic travertine and pine-shingle exterior gives way to a cramped lobby and cozy lounge with Adirondack stick furniture, a fireplace, a piano, and a television (a rarity within the park). Out back is a grand, pine deck. The rooms here are not in the lodge; instead, there are clusters of four cabinlike units with modern upholstered furniture, sleek kitchens, and pine tables. The larger units sleep up to six people. Numbers 151 to 178 overlook Jackson Lake. Smaller shaded log cabins have carpeting and rustic pine furniture; eight have fireplaces. *Teton Park Rd., Box 50, Moran, WY 83013, tel. 307/543–2831, fax 307/543–2569. 79 units. Facilities: restaurant, bar, dock, meeting rooms. AE, D, MC, V. Closed mid-Oct.–early May. $$–$$$*

Colter Bay Cabins. These log structures, some of which are remodeled settlers' cabins, line a terraced drive overlooking Jackson Lake. Furniture is sturdy, simple pine. Odd-numbered cabins 1001 to 1011 and even numbers 468 to 492 have the best views. *Colter Bay Village, Grand Teton Lodge Company, Box 240, Moran, WY 83013, tel. 307/543–2811, 307/543–3100, or 800/628–9988; fax 307/543–3143. 206 cabins, 176 with bath. Facilities: 3 restaurants, bar, coin laundry. AE, DC, MC, V. Closed late Sept.–mid-May. $$*

Colter Bay Tent Cabins. The walls of these cabins are canvas on log frames, and there are minimal furnishings and shared baths, but the price and central location are unbeatable. Each cabin has an outdoor grill, a wood-burning stove, and two double-decker bunks. The cabins are all set around a circular drive, with rest rooms and showers in the middle. *Colter Bay Village, Grand Teton Lodge Company, Box 240, Moran, WY 83013, tel. 307/543–2811, 307/543–3100, or 800/628–9988; fax 307/543–3143. 66 cabins. Facilities: 3 restaurants, bar, coin laundry. AE, DC, MC, V. Closed early Sept.–early June. $*

NEAR THE PARK **Best Western Inn at Jackson Hole.** Far superior in quality to most of the area's chain motels, the Best Western, set slightly back from the rest of Teton Village's commotion, is actually a distinctive, first-rate hotel. Stone floors, a fireplace, and tree-trunk tables in the lobby are matched by the airy, natural decor of a broad range of rooms. Deluxe rooms with lofts have four-poster lodgepole or bamboo beds, fireplaces, oak or cherry-wood furniture, and a beige color scheme. Even standard and economy rooms have this fine furniture, but the latter are without mountain views. A popular cocktail lounge named Beaver Dick's and two restaurants are in a modern atrium. The inn also has the best outdoor poolside view of the Tetons. *Box 328, Teton Village, WY 83025, tel. 307/733–2311 or 800/842–7666, fax 307/733–0844. 83 rooms. Facilities: 2 restaurants, bar, pool, 3 hot tubs, sauna, coin laundry. AE, D, DC, MC, V. $$$*

Jackson Hole Lodge. Like the Wort Hotel, Jackson Hole Lodge dates from the early '40s, but this in-town lodge has not aged quite as gracefully. Hand-hewn lodgepole pine and a stone fireplace accent the lobby, and stuffed '40s furniture adds character to a comfortable upstairs sitting room. Antique Oregon white pine, originally in the lobby, has been reused in the lodge rooms, which get too much street noise. The condominiums and some motel rooms are quieter. A game room and a big indoor pool keep children happy. *420 W. Broadway, Box 1805–B, Jackson, WY 83001, tel. 307/733–2992, fax 307/739–2144. 26 rooms, 33 condominiums. Facilities: indoor pool, 2 hot tubs, sauna, health club. AE, D, DC, MC, V. $$$*

Spring Creek Ranch. Fifteen minutes from downtown Jackson, yet isolated atop 7,000-ft East Gros Ventre Butte, this elegant group of log buildings occupies 1,000 acres of sagebrush and wildflower meadows adjacent to a mule-deer refuge. Most buildings are of open-beam lodgepole construction, and the main building's intimate lobby is decorated with homey plaid-upholstered chairs. There are four single-bedroom units and blocks of four to six two-bedroom condominiums. All condos have floor-to-ceiling stone fireplaces, pine beds and furniture, Native American hangings and prints, and porches with views of the Tetons. Guided horseback rides are available at Spring Creek, and there are stables where you can board your own horse. The resort also has a Nordic ski center and offers dogsled trips. Shoulder-season specials for couples make this romantic setting especially affordable from April to May and mid-October to November. *1800 Spirit Dance Rd., Box 3154, Jackson, WY 83001, tel. 307/733–8833 or 800/443–6139, fax 307/733–1524. 117 rooms. Facilities: restaurant, bar, kitchenettes, pool, hot tub, 2 tennis courts, horseback riding, Nordic skiing, sleigh rides, concierge, business services. AE, D, DC, MC, V. $$$*

Wort Hotel. Built in 1941, when Jackson was first becoming a winter hideaway for wealthy Hollywood and East Coast residents, this dandy old downtown-Jackson hotel was rebuilt after a 1980 fire and redecorated in 1993. Beyond its stone facade and big front staircase, a pine-panel lounge features southwest-style furniture and a stone fireplace topped by a massive moose head. Halls are lined with photos of the many Hollywood cowboys who worked and played here, among them Alan Ladd, who's renowned for his fight scene in the movie *Shane*, which was filmed in Jackson Hole. A vintage slot machine in the hall is the lone remnant of the Wort's past as an illegal but tolerated gambling house. Look for the old photo of the row of slots that was once hidden under a stairway. Down one hall is JJ's Silver Dollar Bar, inlaid with 2,032 uncirculated 1921 silver dollars. Rooms have western, pine furniture, and some even have Murphy beds. Second-floor rooms are quieter. *50 N. Glenwood, Box 69, Jackson, WY 83001, tel. 307/733–2190 or 800/322–2727, fax 307/733–2067. 60 rooms. Facilities: restaurant, bar, 2 hot tubs, exercise room. AE, D, DC, MC, V. $$$*

Cowboy Village Resort. Log cabins with porches, barbecue grills, and picnic tables make this quasi-rural establishment, on a quiet side street south of downtown Jackson, a desirable home base for families. *Flat Creek Rd., Box 1747, Jackson, WY 83001, tel. 307/733–3121 or 800/962–4988, fax 307/739–1955. 82 cabins. Facilities: kitchenettes, hot tub. AE, D, MC, V. $$*

Cowboy Village Resort at Togwotee. Seventeen miles from the Moran entrance, this big, family-oriented log lodge has a central fireside room and a game room as well as horseback riding and snowmobile rentals. *U.S. 26–287, Box 91, Moran, WY 83013, tel. 307/543–2847 or 800/543–2847. 35 rooms in lodge and log cabins. Facilities: restaurant, bar, hot tub, sauna, coin laundry. AE, D, MC, V. $$*

Flagg Ranch Village. A sprawling year-round resort 4 mi north of the park, Flagg Ranch has attractive cabins with pine furnishings. With its snack bar, float trips that leave from the premises, games, and patio movies, Flagg Ranch is particularly popular with families. *Box 187, John D. Rockefeller Jr. Memorial Pkwy., Moran, WY 83013, tel. 307/543–2861 or 800/443–2311, fax 307/543–2356. 92 cabins. Facilities: restaurant, bar, coin laundry. MC, V. Closed mid-Oct.–mid-Dec. and mid-Mar.–mid-May. $$*

Grand Targhee Ski and Summer Resort. On the west side of the Tetons, this popular ski center is also a summer resort with hiking trails, horseback riding, and other outdoor activities. The motel-style rooms are undistinguished. *12 mi east of Driggs, ID, off U.S. 33 on Grand Targhee Rd., Box SKI, Alta, WY 83422, tel. 307/353–2300 or 800/827–4433, fax 307/353–8148. 97 rooms. Facilities: restaurant, bar, pool, indoor and outdoor hot tubs, cross-country skiing, coin laundry. AE, D, MC, V. $$*

Split Creek Ranch. Modest, carpeted rooms with electric heat in a log lodge are set 1.5 mi west of Gros Ventre Junction south of the park. These are quiet country accommodations without phones or TVs. *Zenith Dr., Box 3463, Jackson, WY 83001, tel. 307/733–7522. 8 rooms. Facilities: hot tub, coin laundry. MC, V. $$*

The Hostel. Favored in summer and winter by young, budget-conscious outdoorspeople, this modest Teton Village lodging has four beds (a bunk bed and two twins) per room. The downstairs lounge has a huge stone fireplace; skiing and mountaineering movies are shown here. The rooms have no phones or TVs. *Box 546, Teton Village, WY 83025, tel. 307/733–3415, fax 307/739–1142. 60 rooms. Facilities: recreation room, coin laundry. MC, V. $*

On the Teton Village Road (Highway 390), about 8 mi from Jackson and 3 mi from Teton Village, you'll find one of the area's best B&Bs, the Painted Porch Bed and Breakfast, as well as the largest condominium-rental complex. The **Painted Porch Bed and Breakfast** (Teton Village Rd., Box 3965, Jackson, WY 83001, tel. 307/733–1981) is a modern house with four guest rooms, each with its own private bath. It also has two Japanese soaking tubs. Right next door is the vast **Jackson Hole Racquet Club Resort** (Teton Village Rd., Box 3647, Jackson, WY 83001, tel. 307/733–3990), which has 120 condos ranging from studios to three-bedroom units. The complex has a restaurant, a bar, a sauna and Jacuzzi, laundry facilities, in-room fireplaces, convention facilities, and a fitness center. Both accommodations are in the $$$ price category, although there is a large gap in price between a single room and a three-bedroom condo.

Jackson has a number of nondescript but adequate lodgings, most of them franchises of large, national hotel chains. These include the **Best Western Executive Inn** (325 W. Pearl St., Box 1101, Jackson, WY 83001, tel. 307/733–4340 or 800/528–1234, $$$), the **Days Inn** (350 South Hwy. 89, Jackson, WY 83001, tel. 307/739–9010, fax 307/733-0044, $$$), the **Forty-Niner Motel** (330 W. Pearl Ave., Box 1948, Jackson, WY 83001, tel. 307/733–7550 or 800/451–2980, $$–$$$), the **Virginian Lodge** (Box 1052, 750 W. Broadway, Jackson, WY 83001, tel. 307/733–2792 or 800/262–4999, fax 307/733–9513, $$–$$$), the **Antler Motel** (43 W. Pearl Ave., Box 575, Jackson, WY 83001, tel. 307/733–2535 or 800/522–2406, $$), the **Super 8 Motel** (Box 1382, 1520 S. U.S. 89, Jackson, WY 83001, tel. 307/733–6833 or 800/800–8000, $$), the **Trapper Motel** (Box 1712, 235 N. Cache St., Jackson, WY 83001, tel. 307/733–2648 or 800/341–8000, fax 307/739–9351, $$), the **Wagon Wheel Motel** (Box 525, 435 N. Cache St., Jackson, WY 83001, tel. 307/733–2357 or 800/323–9279, $$), the **Hoback River Resort** (Star Rte., Box 23, U.S. 89, Jackson, WY 83001, tel. 307/733–5129, $–$$), and the **Motel 6** (1370 W. Broadway, Jackson, WY 83001, tel. 307/733–1620, fax 307/733–9175, $).

CAMPING

Camping possibilities are abundant and varied both inside and outside the park. Inside the park, facilities range from a concessionaire-operated RV site with full hookups to isolated primitive sites in the backcountry. Outside the park there are commercial RV-and-tent campgrounds, as well as roadside campgrounds and backcountry sites on national-forest lands surrounding the park. Always remember that Grand Teton is high, wild country; even if you camp in Colter Bay Village, down the road from a snack bar and laundry, take precautions against bears, and be prepared for temperatures that can dip below freezing even on a night in July.

INSIDE THE PARK Within Grand Teton National Park, the National Park Service operates five campgrounds: Colter Bay, Gros Ventre, Lizard Creek, Signal Mountain, and Jenny Lake. The campground at Jenny Lake allows tenters and small camping vehicles, but no trailers. The others accommodate tents, trailers, and RVs. There are no hookups available in these campgrounds, but all of them have fire grates, drinking water, and modern rest rooms with cold water. Only Colter Bay has hot showers. Fees are $10 per vehicle per night at every National Park Service campground.

A maximum stay of seven days is allowed at Jenny Lake and 14 days at the others. Check in as early as possible—sites are assigned on a first-come, first-served basis, and no reservations are accepted. In July and August most campgrounds are filled by day's end; however, you can usually find a campsite in one of several commercial Jackson Hole campgrounds or in nearby Bridger-Teton and Targhee national forests.

Camping in the park's backcountry is permitted (with the requisite permit) year-round, provided you're able to gain access to it. Remember that snow remains in the high country through much of the summer. Between June 1 and September 15, backcountry campers in the park are limited to stays of fewer than 11 days.

For visitors with RVs, two concessionaire-operated campgrounds, Colter Bay Trailer

GRAND TETON CAMPGROUNDS

	Total number of sites	Sites suitable for RVs	Number of hookups	Drive to sites	Hike to sites	Flush toilets	Pit/chemical toilets	Drinking water	Showers	Fire grates	Swimming	Boat access	Playground	Disposal station	Ranger station	Public telephone	Reservation possible	Daily fee per site	Dates open
INSIDE THE PARK																			
Colter Bay	310	310	0	●		●		●	●	●		●		●	●	●		$10	mid-May–late Sept.
Gros Ventre	360	360	0	●		●		●		●				●	●	●		$10	late Apr.–early Oct.
Jenny Lake	49	0	0	●		●		●		●		●			●	●		$10	late May–late Sept.
Lizard Creek	60	NA	0	●		●		●		●					●			$10	early June–early Sept.
Signal Mountain	86	80	0	●		●		●	●			●		●	●	●		$10	early May–mid-Oct.
Colter Bay Trailer Village	113	113	113	●		●		●	●			●		●	●	●	●	$23	mid-May–late Sept.
NEAR THE PARK																			
Flagg Ranch Village	150	75	75	●		●		●	●	●					●	●	●	$17–$23	mid-May–late Sept.
Bridger-Teton National Forest	39*		0	●			●	●		●							●**	$4–$7	mid-May–mid-Oct.
Targhee National Forest	30*		0	●			●	●		●							●**	$6–$9	Memorial Day–Labor Day

*Number of campgrounds. **Reservation fee charged.

Village and Flagg Ranch Village (on the Rockefeller Parkway), provide hookups.

Busy, noisy, and filled by noon, the **Colter Bay** campground has one great advantage: It's centrally located. There are 310 tent and RV sites, hot showers, a ranger station, a disposal station, and public phones, as well as boat access; Try to get a site as far from the nearby cabin road as possible. Don't confuse this campground with the roadside Colter Bay Trailer Village, operated by Grand Teton Lodge Company, which charges $23 per site with full hookups. Colter Bay is open from mid-May to late September, depending on weather conditions.

Gros Ventre is the park's biggest campground, but it is as isolated as Colter Bay is centrally located. It has 360 tent and RV sites set in an open, grassy area on the bank of the Gros Ventre River, away from the mountains, 2 mi southwest of Kelly (where there's a general store). Here you might see moose and antelope. Try to get a site close to the river. The campground usually doesn't fill until nightfall, if at all; it's open from late April to early October.

The campground at **Jenny Lake** has 49 wooded sites and lovely views across the water that make it the most desirable campground in the park. It is small and quiet and allows tents and small camping vehicles, but no trailers. Close to the Jenny Lake trailhead, this campground is extremely popular and usually fills by 8 AM in July and August. Jenny Lake has phones, boat access, and a ranger station; it is open from the end of May to late September.

With 60 sites, **Lizard Creek** probably has the park's best combination of views and relative isolation, although like Gros Ventre it is far from stores or other facilities. For those you'll have to drive 8 mi north to Flagg Ranch or 8 mi south to Colter Bay. The campground is set on a wooded point of land close to northern Jackson Lake and across the water from Webb Canyon, the park's most primitive hiking area. There is no shuttle-boat service across the lake from

here, but many backcountry hikers use their own boats. Lizard Creek usually fills by 2 PM in summer and is open from early June to early September. RVs longer than 25 ft are not allowed.

Providing much better Teton views than Colter Bay campground, **Signal Mountain** campground has boat access on southern Jackson Lake. Its 86 sites set on the lakeshore are close to nearby stores and services and, in July and August, are filled by 9 AM. Signal Mountain has public phones, a disposal station, and a ranger station. It's open from early May to mid-October.

Colter Bay Trailer Village, near Colter Bay Marina, is ideal for RVers toting boats. The large, often crowded 113-site RV park is also close to horseback riding, stores, and the Colter Bay Visitor Center. An open, flat area, it's not very attractive. Sites are paved or gravel, all with full hookups, and cost $23. Colter Bay Trailer Village has rest rooms with hot showers, boat access, a disposal station, a ranger station, and public phones. LP gas is available at village stores. The trailer park is run by the Grand Teton Lodge Company (Box 240, Moran, WY 83013, tel. 307/733–2811). Reservations are strongly advised in July and August; the campground is open from mid-May to late September.

NEAR THE PARK The **Flagg Ranch Village Campground** (Box 187, Moran, WY 83013, tel. 307/543–2861 or 800/443–2311, fax 307/543–2356), 4 mi north of the park on U.S. 89–287, is reached from a turnoff just north of the main Flagg Ranch Village (*see* Lodging, *above*). It is on the John D. Rockefeller Jr. Memorial Parkway, which is also administered by the National Park Service. Set in a wooded area near the north bank of the Snake River, the campground has 75 RV sites that vary in width and length. Tenters can be accommodated in 75 additional sites. The campground has a ranger station, hot showers, fire grates, and a pay phone. Reservations are advised. RV sites (all with hookups) cost $25; tent sites cost $17. The campground is open mid-May to mid-October.

There are 39 campgrounds scattered across **Bridger-Teton National Forest** (tel. 307/739–5500), a huge expanse of land that stretches south and east of Grand Teton and Yellowstone national parks. These campgrounds are best suited to tent camping (only a few can accommodate RVs) and typically have drinking water, pit toilets, and fire grates, although facilities vary from place to place. Most Bridger-Teton National Forest campgrounds charge $4 to $7 per night, but in some places you can camp for free. The majority of these campgrounds are open from mid-May to mid-September. Reservations ($8) are accepted at 15 of the campgrounds in the Jackson Hole area—through U.S. Forest Reservations (tel. 800/280–2267)—and sites are assigned on a first-come, first-served basis at the rest. You can also camp free in the backcountry here, but be sure to find out about restricted areas and fire dangers before heading out;

stop at the National Forest Service Visitor Center (340 N. Cache, tel. 307/739–5500) in Jackson before you go.

Of the 30 or so campgrounds in **Targhee National Forest** (tel. 208/624–3151) on the west side of the park, 22 are close to Grand Teton. These also typically have drinking water, pit toilets, and fire grates. RVs can be accommodated, but there are no hookups. Most Targhee National Forest campgrounds accept reservations, which must be made through U.S. Forest Reservations (*see above*); sites at others are available only on a first-come, first-served basis. These campgrounds are officially open from Memorial Day to Labor Day, but you may camp in many of them (unless there is a barricade) until access is blocked by snow. Most sites cost $6 to $9. Backcountry camping is allowed in most areas, but be sure to call the forest service to find out about restrictions.

Jasper National Park
Alberta

Updated by Don Thacker

ast and high are the best words to describe Jasper National Park, the most northerly and largest of the national parks of the Canadian Rockies. Of its 10,878 square km (4,200 square mi) of majestic alpine scenery, 40% lies above timberline. This is rugged country, where mountains made of twisted and folded rock jut into the sky, blue-white glaciers contrast with thick evergreen forests and turquoise lakes, and majestic wildlife roams.

Though there is little difference between Jasper and Banff National Parks in terms of scenery, Jasper tends to draw a higher percentage of backpackers and outdoors people than does Banff, thanks to its vast backcountry and smaller selection of shops and services. Its slower pace stems from its relative isolation: The closest major city is Edmonton, four hours to the east, while Calgary is little more than an hour from Banff. Until the early 1990s, when Highway 16 from Edmonton was upgraded to a four-lane highway, the two-lane road to Jasper was slow and sometimes dangerous. Even though the highway has now made Jasper an easy destination, it remains quieter and less visited than Banff.

Jasper National Park is really two parks in one, a southern and a northern half, with the town of Jasper at the center. The area to the south, with most of the park's featured attractions, is by far the more heavily visited. The landscape is quintessential Canadian Rockies: rugged peaks and glaciers. When visitors combine Banff and Jasper national parks in their travels—the two are connected by the spectacular Icefields Parkway—most stay in the town of Jasper and stick to the park's southern half.

The northern half, by contrast, has numerous long trails, but no roads. Although mountains are many, the high, glaciated peaks common in the south are rare. This is getaway land, choice country for wilderness backpackers, packhorse adventurers, and anglers.

It took the Canadian government somewhat longer to create Jasper National Park than it did to create Banff, essentially because of slower railroad development. The priority of the Canadian Pacific Railroad in the late 1800s was to complete an east–west route through the Canadian Rockies. This development led to fears of heavy land speculation, which was one of the major reasons that government officials established Jasper National Park in 1907. The Grand Trunk Pacific Railway Route through Jasper's Yellowhead Pass (through which Highway 16 now passes) was finally completed in 1911.

The park's boundaries did not, however, incorporate what is perhaps the most remarkable mountain in all of the Canadian Rockies: Mt. Robson, at 3,954 meters (12,931 ft), is a stark, often cloud-shrouded colossus of tumbling glaciers and rock walls that loom more than 2 km (1.25 mi) over the valley and are prone to violent weather and avalanches. The area is now protected in British Columbia's Mount Robson Provincial Park, a park contiguous with Jasper National Park, and connected to it via Highway 16 and various hiking trails.

Other Jasper sites of note are the Columbia Icefield, near the park's southern border with Banff; Maligne Lake and Maligne Canyon; Pyramid Lake; and the Whistlers, the mountain near the town of Jasper serviced by an aerial tram. And everywhere, there's the endless expanse of wild terrain that is Jasper's best asset.

ESSENTIAL INFORMATION

VISITOR INFORMATION The major sources of information are **Travel Alberta** (Commerce Pl., 10155 102 St., 3rd floor, Edmonton, AB T5J 4G8, tel. 800/661–8888), **Parks Canada** (Canadian Heritage–Parks Canada, Room 552, 220 4th Ave. SE, Calgary AB T2G 4X3, tel. 403/292–4401 or 800/748–7275, fax 403/292–6004), and **Jasper Tourism and Commerce** (Box 98, 632 Connaught Dr., Jasper, AB T0E 1E0, tel. 403/852–3858). There is also a **Jasper Visitor Centre** run by Parks Canada (Box 10, 500 Connaught Dr., Jasper AB T0E 1E0, tel. 403/852–6176, fax 403/852–6152). All of Jasper National Park is within Alberta; travelers planning to venture into neighboring British Columbia should contact **Tourism British Columbia** (Parliament Bldgs., Victoria, BC V8V 1X4, tel. 800/663–6000).

FEES Canada has recently changed the per-vehicle entrance fee to a per-person entrance fee for visitors to the national parks. A National Parks Day Pass costs $5 per person ($10 per group) and is valid for entry into Banff, Jasper, Yoho, and Kootenay parks. An annual pass, covering 11 national parks in western Canada, is $35 ($70 per group). Travelers in nonstop transit through the parks on Highways 16 and 1 are not charged.

PUBLICATIONS Travel Alberta and Parks Canada (*see* Visitor Information, *above*) have extensive lists of maps, booklets, and brochures. The most comprehensive listing is the free *Alberta Accommodation and Visitors' Guide.* Indispensable for hikers in the park is *The Canadian Rockies Trail Guide,* by Brian Patton and Bart Robinson.

GEOLOGY AND TERRAIN *See* the Banff National Park chapter.

FLORA AND FAUNA *See* the Banff National Park chapter.

WHEN TO GO The park is open year-round, with the high season from about early June to the end of September. Room rates during this period are typically 50% or more above what they are at other times of the year. The period of high-season rates has been gradually lengthening as the park's popularity increases. Until recently, late September was a "best-kept secret"—inexpensive rooms combined with snowcapped mountains, changing foliage, and generally warm days and cool nights. Alas, motels have figured out this secret, so most of the cheap rates are gone until the start of October when the foliage show is over and temperatures have fallen. Though hotels generally stay open for the winter, most cabins and lodges shut down by mid-October. A few restaurants and shops also close for the winter; those that remain open generally shorten their hours of operation.

Jasper is still quite popular in winter, when visitors enjoy downhill and cross-country skiing. The Christmas–New Year's and February break periods are make-or-break periods for downhill ski operators, but the slopes are relatively uncrowded at other times. The ski hills remain open through April or even May, long after the snow has disappeared from the valleys and towns.

Daytime temperatures in summer typically range from the high teens to high 20s°C (60s°F–80s°F), and winter daily maximums typically range from −10°C−−5°C (mid-teens to low 20s°F). But mountain weather is notoriously hard to predict. Occasional summer snowstorms occur above the tree line, and winter temperatures in the valley bottoms can range from bone-chilling −30s°C (−20s°F) to a springlike 10°C (50°F).

SEASONAL EVENTS Winter sees two festivals in Jasper, although the term "festival" is used rather loosely. The main push of the winter-festival concept is to attract visitors to the park—that is, to fill hotel rooms—during normally slow months. Room rates are widely discounted, and special events, many of them ski-related, are promoted. The annual **Winter Festival** runs for 16 days beginning on the third Saturday of January, with numerous ski events and activities for kids. The **Snowdown Festival** is a country and western festival, beginning the last Wednesday in February and running for 12 days. It features a snow rodeo, ribs cook-off, and country-and-western dancing. Begun in 1997, this is planned to be an annual event.

August: In even-numbered years, the **Jasper Folk Festival** attracts musicians, both the famous and the obscure, from the United States and Canada for a series of concerts and informal performances on the first weekend in August. The other notable summer event is the annual **Jasper Indoor Rodeo,** which runs from Tuesday to Saturday during the third week of August. This is a professional rodeo with a full complement of rodeo events, plus dances on the last two nights.

WHAT TO PACK The first rule in packing for the Canadian Rockies is to be ready for almost any weather. In summer, pack a warm wool sweater or synthetic-fleece jacket, warm socks, and a windbreaker, along with your shorts. If you plan on hiking into the high-country, bring extra layers, including polypropylene long underwear, and a headband or warm hat. You might get away with shorts, but it's pretty unpleasant to be caught unprepared. If you plan to spend time at the Jasper Park Lodge, bring something a little more dressy (neat sportswear will do).

GENERAL STORES The only place to buy supplies is in the town of Jasper itself. There is a small convenience store near Pocahontas, at the Miette Hotsprings turnoff, but it's hardly a place for stocking up. The town of Hinton, east of the park gate on Highway 16, is a good place for last-minute shopping before entering the park.

ARRIVING AND DEPARTING **By Bus. Greyhound Lines** (tel. 800/661–8747 in Canada,

800/231–2222 in the U.S.) provides regular service between Edmonton and Vancouver, with a stop at Jasper. **Brewster Transportation and Tours** (Box 1140, Banff, AB T0L 0C0, tel. 800/661–1152; 403/852–3332 in Jasper; fax 403/762–2090) leads half- to multiday sightseeing tours of the parks.

By Car and RV. The main east–west route through the park is Highway 16, the Yellowhead Highway. The town of Jasper is 360 km (224 mi) west of Edmonton on Highway 16, an easy four-hour drive. Many park visitors, however, come into the park from the south—from Banff and Calgary—via Highway 93. The town of Jasper, at the junction of Highways 16 and 93, is 290 km (180 mi) from the town of Banff; the Jasper park border, near the Icefield Centre, is 180 km (110 mi) from the town of Banff. Note: The speed limit within the park is reduced to 90 kph (55 mph).

By Plane. The nearest international airport is **Edmonton International Airport,** served by several major U.S. and Canadian airlines. Travelers making a combined trip to Banff and Jasper national parks might prefer flying into **Calgary International Airport,** which is much closer to Banff.

By Train. VIA Rail Canada (tel. 800/561–8630) provides connecting service between Jasper and Toronto, Edmonton, and Vancouver. **Rocky Mountaineer Railtours** (1150 Station St., Suite 130, Vancouver, BC V6A 2X7, tel. 604/606–7200 or 800/665–7245, fax 604/606–7201) takes passengers on two-day train trips from Vancouver to Jasper, via Kamloops, as well as longer tours through the region. Trips run from mid-May to early October and start at around $500.

EXPLORING

Travelers coming from Banff National Park will hit the **Icefield Centre** at the south end of Jasper, approximately halfway along the Icefields Parkway between Lake Louise (125 km/75 mi) and the town of Jasper (105 km/62 mi). It has interpretive displays, information services, ticket sales, a gift shop, lodging, a cafeteria, and a restaurant, and it's the perfect starting point for people viewing or venturing onto the Athabasca Glacier.

The **Columbia Icefield,** covering approximately 325 square km (125 square mi), is the largest single mass of ice in subarctic North America. It's just one of a number of ice fields in the area that are the collective source of numerous rivers in western Canada. From the Icefield Centre, the Athabasca Glacier, just across the highway, is the most immediate indication of the great store of ice that lies beyond.

Informative exhibits and audiovisual presentations at the center explain the dynamics of this frigid geology. But with an active glacier at your fingertips, it's imperative to get a firsthand look. There are two ways of going about it: by snow coaches (special buses for driving on ice) or by foot, on guided hikes conducted from June through August (*see* Guided Tours, *below*). Venturing onto the ice without a guide is strongly discouraged, as several fatalities have occurred. Note that the midday (11–3) rush—the prime tour-bus time slot—is so intense that even ice-field promotional materials suggest you choose another time of day to come.

Two attractions very close to town are the **Jasper Tramway** and **the Pyramid and Patricia lakes.** The side-by-side lakes, at the foot of Pyramid Mountain, are scenic spots for activities such as hiking, horseback riding, and boating (canoes, pedal boats, and rowboats can be rented at both lakes). The tramway, 7 km (4.3 mi) south of town on Whistlers Road (off Highway 93), rises 976 meters (3,193 ft) up the steep flank of **Whistlers.** The view from the top takes in the Athabasca River valley to the east, and the Miette River valley and mighty Mt. Robson, highest of the Canadian Rockies, to the west (the Miette river valley is unrelated to Miette Hot Springs). The tramway is open from April through October; perhaps the best time to ride is on

a summer evening (the last tram is at 10 PM in summer), to take in the sunset. A restaurant at the upper tramway station serves adequate food. For tramway information, call 403/852–3093.

Perhaps the best way to appreciate Jasper National Park is by venturing into its considerable backcountry. Many long, well-maintained hiking trails—some open to horse-pack trips—establish Jasper's preeminence in making accessible large expanses of wilderness within parks in the North American west (*see* Longer Hikes *and* Other Activities, *below*).

THE BEST IN ONE DAY Because Jasper is such a large park and its best-known sites (the Columbia Icefield, Maligne Lake, Miette Hotsprings) are so widely scattered, it pays to be selective when visiting for a short period.

Assuming that the town of Jasper is your starting point, the drive to the Icefield Centre and back (about a 210-km, or 130-mi, round-trip) is a worthwhile, if time-consuming, venture. Unless you get an early start, don't expect to be back in Jasper before mid-afternoon after the drive and the ice-field tour.

Perhaps a better one-day tour program is to spend the morning driving to Mt. Edith Cavell (named for a British nurse who sacrificed her life in saving Allied lives during the first world war), where you can walk through a landscape that was under ice less than a century ago. This walk leads to a towering cliff where the Angel Glacier flows out of a large bowl carved into the mountain. You can easily make this trip into a full-day excursion by taking the rigorous three- or four-hour return hike up to Cavell Meadows, one of the best alpine wildflower meadows in the Canadian Rockies. The meadows are at their peak from mid-July to mid-August, though the crowds can be thick around midday.

If you return from Mt. Edith Cavell by lunchtime, consider an afternoon drive to Maligne Lake. Rent a boat, take a boat tour

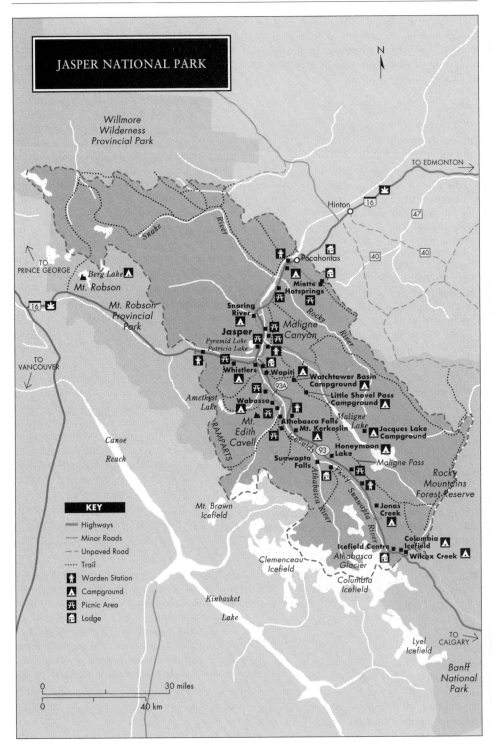

JASPER NATIONAL PARK

Willmore
Wilderness
Provincial Park

N

TO EDMONTON →

Hinton

16

47

40

40

TO
PRINCE GEORGE →

Berg Lake
Mt. Robson

Snake

River

Pocahontas

Miette
Hotsprings

16

Mt. Robson
Provincial
Park

Snaring
River

Jasper

Pyramid Lake
Patricia Lake

Maligne
Canyon

Rocky

River

TO
VANCOUVER

Whistlers

Wapiti

93A

Watchtower Basin
Campground

Little Shovel Pass
Campground

Amethyst
Lake

Wabasso

Maligne
Lake

Athabasca Falls
Mt. Kerkeslin

Jacques Lake
Campground

Mt.
Edith
Cavell

RAMPARTS

Icefields

93

Honeymoon
Lake

Maligne Pass

Sunwapta
Falls

Canoe

Reach

Rocky
Mountains
Forest Reserve

Mt. Brown
Icefield

Jonas
Creek

Athabasca River

Sunwapta River

Pkwy.

Clemenceau
Icefield

Icefield Centre

Athabasca
Glacier

Columbia
Icefield

Wilcox Creek

Columbia
Icefield

Kinbasket

Lake

Lyel
Icefield

TO
CALGARY →

KEY

Highways
Minor Roads
Unpaved Road
Trail
Warden Station
Campground
Picnic Area
Lodge

Banff
National
Park

0   30 miles

0   40 km

or a hike, or have a meal at the restaurant near the boat docks, where the cafeteria-style food is surprisingly good. If time permits, stop along the way for a stroll along Maligne Canyon.

On foul-weather days, Miette Hotsprings—about an hour east of Jasper—is a great place for a soak in hot, sulphurous spring water. Back in Jasper, a drive up to nearby Patricia and Pyramid Lakes or, if the weather has cleared, a sunset dinner at the top of the Whistlers tram, is a nice way to round out the day.

If you prefer a less ambitious itinerary, a good alternative is simply to enjoy Jasper Park Lodge all day. All the activities at your doorstep—including tennis, golf, horseback riding, swimming, and boating—make the lodge seem like an extravagant summer camp. On a hot day, a swim in the crystal-clear Lake Annette or Lake Edith, both near the lodge, is an unsurpassable experience.

ORIENTATION PROGRAMS The **Jasper Visitor Centre** (500 Connaught Dr., Jasper, AB T0E 1E0, tel. 403/852–6176) is administered by Parks Canada. Call or visit for a schedule of programs on the history, geology, and wildlife of the park. For a perspective on what life was like when prospectors, surveyors, and settlers arrived more than a century ago, visit the **Jasper–Yellowhead Museum** (400 Pyramid Lake Rd., tel. 403/852–3013), open mid-May–early September, daily 10–9; early September–mid-May, days and hours vary. Exhibits on the geology, history, and wildlife of the park are also sometimes shown in the **Jasper Activity Centre** (303 Pyramid Ave., tel. 403/852–3381).

GUIDED TOURS Brewster **Transportation and Tours** (main office in Banff: Box 1140, Banff, AB T0L 0C0, tel. 800/661–1152; in Jasper: 607 Connaught Dr., tel. 403/852–3332) runs full- and half-day bus tours of the park, some in conjunction with Maligne Lake boat tours, rafting trips, or tram rides. **Currie's Guiding & Tackle** (Box 202, 416 Connaught Dr., Jasper, AB T0E 1E0, tel. 403/852–5650) conducts four- to six-hour guided van tours, specializing in

wildlife viewing. **Jasper Adventure Centre** (Box 1064, 604 Connaught Dr. [in winter: 306 Connaught Dr.], Jasper, AB T0E 1E0, tel. 403/852–5595; 800/565–7547 in Western Canada) runs three-hour tours to sights near Jasper, including hot spring swims, winter canyon ice walks, birding tours, historical tours, and sightseeing.

Rocky Mountaineer Railtours (1150 Station St., Suite 130, Vancouver, BC V6A 2X7, tel. 800/665–7245, fax 604/606–7201) makes two-day trips from Vancouver to Jasper, with connections available to Edmonton. They run from mid-May to early October and start at around $500. Rocky Mountaineer Railtours also runs longer tours, as well as a deluxe coach service catering specifically to people accustomed to five-star hotels and luxury resorts. The Railtour coaches travel through the Rockies during daylight only.

Maligne Lake is Jasper's boat-tour center. **Maligne Tours** (Box 280, 626 Connaught Dr., Jasper, AB T0E 1E0, tel. 403/852–3370) conducts 1½-hour tours of the lake from mid-May to mid-October (ice conditions permitting); it also conducts winter tours of Maligne Canyon from December through late March. Lake-tour arrangements can also be made through **Brewster Transportation and Tours** (see above).

Audiocassette tapes for self-guided auto tours of Jasper and the neighboring parks are produced by **Audio Tape Tours** and **Rocky Mountain Tape Tours**. Tapes can be rented or purchased at newsstands or gift shops in Jasper.

Snow coaches, buses adapted for travel on glacial ice, carry sightseers onto the Athabasca Glacier. The 1½-hour tours are conducted from May to mid-October. Tickets can be bought at the Columbia Icefield Centre or from **Brewster Transportation and Tours** (see above). Athabasca Glacier Ice Walks (Box 2067, Banff, AB T0C 0C0, tel. 403/347–1828 in-season, 403/852–3803 off-season) runs guided half-day glacier walks from June through August; tickets are also available at the Columbia Icefield

Centre and from Jasper Adventure Centre (tel. 403/852–5595; 800/565–7747 Western Canada).

Jasper Climbing School and Mountaineering Service (Box 452, Jasper, AB T0E 1E0, tel. 403/852–3964) leads hiking and mountaineering tours in summer and ski tours in winter, with private guides available. **Skyline Trail Rides** (tel. 403/852–4215) at Jasper Park Lodge puts on summer evening hayrides, winter sleigh rides, and horseback rides.

SCENIC DRIVES AND VIEWS The scenic roadways of Jasper can be divided into four basic drives: the drive on the Icefields Parkway, and the trips to Maligne Lake, Miette Hotsprings, and Mt. Robson. Each is distinctly different, a testament to Jasper's diverse landscape. On a poor-weather day, the best option is probably the drive to Miette. Not only does the possibility of better weather improve by heading east, but also the broad Athabasca River can be appreciated in sun or gloom, and a soak in the springs seems most enjoyable when the weather is bleak.

The **Icefields Parkway** begins just south of Jasper town and continues southeast through Jasper and Banff national parks for 230 km (143 mi), ending just before Lake Louise. A good day-trip destination is the Columbia Icefield, 105 km (65 mi) south of Jasper. On this drive you travel between major mountain ranges rising steeply on both sides of the road, with numerous scenic pull-offs, wildlife-spotting opportunities, picnic spots, and access to dozens of hiking trails. From the town of Jasper to the ice fields, the road gradually climbs some 800 meters (2,500 ft), which means cooler temperatures and less predictable weather; pack warm clothing even if it is a fine-weather day in Jasper.

Near the Columbia Icefield, you can take a snow-coach ride or guided hike onto the Athabasca Glacier (*see* Guided Tours, *above*), or simply walk to the end of the glacier from the visitor's parking lot. (Be aware that crevasses and hazardous ice con-

ditions make walking onto the glacier without a trained guide extremely dangerous.)

Other options to make this a full day's outing include Sunwapta Falls and Athabasca Falls. The more impressive of the two is **Athabasca Falls,** just off the highway; the violence of the water pounding through a narrow channel makes for a dramatic sight.

Since viewing the falls in either case requires very little hiking, visitors are usually plentiful. An alternative for solitude seekers is the one- to two-hour hike along the Valley of the Five Lakes trail, which skirts five small, clear, turquoise lakes along mostly level terrain 10 km (6 mi) south of Jasper town. This hike is particularly pleasing when the leaves turn color in autumn. The Geraldine Lakes trail, 5.5 km (3.5 mi) along a fire road off Highway 93A near Athabasca Falls, is a more ambitious day hike to two lakes and a waterfall.

Highway 93A, the old highway, departs from Highway 93 8 km (5 mi) south of Jasper townsite, and continues for 23 km (14.5 mi) before rejoining Highway 93. Along this byway are the roads to the Marmot Basin ski area, Mt. Edith Cavell (*see* The Best in One Day, *above*), and the Tonquin Valley, one of the most popular backpacking and horse-packing areas in Jasper National Park. Though Highway 93A is well-maintained, its narrow, winding path makes it seem far more remote than Highway 93.

The drive to **Maligne Lake,** 50 km (30 mi) southeast of Jasper (take Maligne Lake Road from Highway 16 east), is almost obligatory for visitors. The road follows the scenic Maligne River, climbing some 600 meters (2,000 ft) from Jasper to the lake. Although crowds are the norm on summer days, boat rentals and several hiking trails make escaping the masses relatively easy. A big pastime at Maligne Lake is the 1½-hour scenic cruise (*see* Guided Tours, *above*) on the lake.

On the way to or from Maligne Lake, Maligne Canyon is a popular stop-off, where the Maligne River has cut a narrow limestone gorge. At Medicine Lake, about 15 km (10 mi) north of Maligne Lake, an unusual underground drainage system causes huge fluctuations of the lake level over the course of the year.

Another excursion is the drive east along Highway 16 from Jasper to **Miette Hot Springs,** 56 km (35 mi) along the meandering Athabasca River floodplain from Jasper. The 17-km (11-mi) road to the hot springs is a twisting climb into the mountains, with fantastic views of the sheer cliffs of Ashlar Ridge. The sulphurous water of the springs is the hottest in the Rockies, with temperatures reaching 129°F. (The water is diluted with cold water to a bathing temperature of 104°F. A nearby cool pool, used mainly by children, is kept at about 80°F.) At the old hot springs facility, a pleasant 15-minute walk away, several springs seep scalding water into a creek near the abandoned pool buildings.

The fourth drive from Jasper leads westward on Highway 16 for 80 km (50 mi) to **Mt. Robson,** a mountain within the British Columbia provincial park that bears its name. Mt. Robson is the highest peak in the Canadian Rockies, and it's notorious for attracting bad weather. Still, even if Mt. Robson is covered by clouds, excellent mountain scenery can be seen along this entire route, with good wildlife-spotting opportunities at Moose Lake. Mt. Robson is ranked among the world's classic climbs by alpinists, but you needn't climb it to appreciate it. The 5-km (3-mi) hike to Kinney Lake is great for day-trippers, while the 18-km (11-mi) hike to Berg Lake takes backpackers to the snowy north side of the mountain, where icebergs calve off glaciers into the chilly waters of Berg Lake.

HISTORIC BUILDINGS AND SITES Jasper National Park's relatively recent development is responsible for its preservation today as a wild, scenic area. Prospectors, fur traders, and surveyors did not arrive until the latter half of the 19th century, while the town of Jasper itself was not established until the

early 20th century. Most traces of the pathfinding days have vanished, although exhibits and archives at the **Jasper–Yellowhead Museum** (400 Pyramid Lake Rd., tel. 403/852–3013) give some sense of life in the previous century.

Although not especially old, **Jasper Park Lodge** is of some historic significance in being the first resort lodge built in the park—Jasper's equivalent to the much older Banff Springs Hotel in Banff.

NATURE TRAILS AND SHORT WALKS One of the busiest trails in Jasper park is along Maligne Canyon, just a few kilometers from the town of Jasper on the Maligne Lake Road. Here the Maligne River cuts a deep, narrow gorge in the limestone—up to 55 meters (180 ft) deep and, in a few spots, only a few meters (about 10 ft) across. Most visitors follow the walkway from the parking lot at the top of the canyon, where there is a 1-km (.5-mi) loop—the most interesting, and busiest, section of the trail. The trail continues to a parking lot at the "sixth bridge" (the six bridges that cross the river are named rather unimaginatively) a distance of 3.7 km (2.3 mi). Look for winter's frozen ice seeps, which can persist into summer in the cool, dim canyon.

A network of mostly gentle, wooded trails just west of town winds through a cluster of small lakes (Pyramid and Patricia lakes being the best known). The 9-km (5.5-mi) loop to tiny **Mina and Riley lakes** is an easy, half-day jaunt.

A short trail—less than 1.5 km (1 mi)—leads to **Sunwapta Falls,** 50 km, or 30 mi, north of the Icefield Centre. The view of the falls and of distant, glaciated peaks makes the walk well worthwhile, despite the considerable company, and the leg stretch is a good way to break up the drive along the parkway.

LONGER HIKES The best way to experience the vastness and wilderness of Jasper National Park is to hike it. In this national park, it is possible to hike for weeks without crossing a paved road.

The two longest hikes in Jasper, the **North Boundary** and **South Boundary trails,** both exceed 160 km (100 mi). Although neither is known for consistently spectacular scenery, they do present considerable opportunies for wildlife encounters—caribou, elk, goats, bear—while leading hikers into the most remote sections of the park.

The most popular overnight hikes in the park are **Tonquin Valley** and the **Skyline Trail.** Tonquin valley's scenery is highlighted by the twin Amethyst Lakes, lying before the backdrop of a 3,300-ft palisades called the Ramparts. The 21 km (13 mi) to get there on the Maccarib Pass trail makes this is an overnight destination. Rather than returning by the same route, hikers can link up with the Astoria River trail (the other major trail into Tonquin Valley), without changing the overall distance (though transportation would have to be arranged to return to the original trailhead).

The Skyline Trail leads 44 km (27 mi) in a northerly direction from Maligne Lake and is marked by long stretches of alpine meadows strewn with wildflowers in summer. In fact, more than half the length of this trail is above the timberline, providing some of the most expansive views in the park. Heading south from Maligne Lake toward Maligne Pass can be equally rewarding though more rugged, with the trail leading over a series of high passes. Depending on how far you want to go, this southerly route continues for more than 90 km (56 mi) to connect with the trail system of Banff National Park.

Backpackers must obtain permits, and the park does try to keep a limit on backcountry trail-and-campground use. Each trail has a quota, and these can be reached quickly in midsummer—particularly in busy areas such as Tonquin Valley. One-third of each trail's quota is set aside for reservations; permits for the remainder are available one day in advance. Reservations can be made three weeks in advance by writing or calling the Superintendent, Jasper National Park, Box 10, Jasper, AB T0E 1E0, tel. 403/852–6177 in winter, 403/852–6176 in summer.

Longer backpacking trips are Jasper's strong suit; good day hikes are somewhat fewer. Two trails at Maligne Lake climb up onto high hills just above the timberline, where there are expansive views of the lake and surrounding mountains. The **Bald Hills** trail (5 km, or 3 mi) gives the better view, but you must backtrack down the trail, which is merely an old fire road. The **Opal Hills** trail (8 km, or 5 mi) is more rugged, with a nice loop through the alpine tundra. From Miette Hotsprings, the **Sulphur Summit** trail (4 km, or 2.5 mi) is a stiff uphill climb that rewards you with stunning views of sawtooth mountain ridges spreading out from the summit. Near the south end of the park, the hike to **Wilcox Pass** (4 km, or 2.5 mi) leads to a rocky alpine tundra with a wide glacial panorama of the Athabasca and surrounding glaciers. Note that although the distances seem rather short, steep terrain makes the hiking times, round-trip, for all these trails typically about four hours.

OTHER ACTIVITIES **Back-Road Driving.** Off-road driving is prohibited in the park, and roads (much less back roads) are few. Indeed, the way to experience Jasper in its glory is to get off the road, on foot or on horseback. Other than the two main highways (Highways 16 and 93) the park has only a few smaller roads of note: **Miette Hot Springs Road, Maligne Lake Road,** and **Highway 93A,** which connects with Marmot Basin Road and Edith Cavell Road.

Biking. Given the shortage of back roads in Jasper, road cycling is somewhat limited. A good short but steep ride (about 12 km, or 7 mi) is from Jasper to Pyramid Lake and back. Other possibilities from Jasper are the hilly, 50-km (30-mi) ride to Maligne Lake along Highway 16, which gives good views of the Athabasca River, or a trip south along the relatively flat Icefields Parkway, which has better mountain scenery. The Maligne Road route has minimal traffic but virtually no shoulders. The route along the Icefields Parkway, on the other hand, has heavy traffic and wide, paved shoulders.

Mountain bikers are allowed only on a limited number of trails. Before setting out, check with the information centers for a list of those open to cyclists.

Bikes can be rented from **Freewheel Cycle** (611 Patricia St., tel. 403/852–3898), and **Beauvert Boat and Cycle** (tel. 403/852–3301, ext. 6190) at the marina at Jasper Park Lodge (they also rent Rollerblades). **Rocky Mountain Cycle Tours** (333 Baker St., Nelson, BC V1L 4H6, tel. 800/661–2453 or 250/354–1241) conducts tours through Jasper and Banff National Parks.

Bird-Watching. Although such scavenger birds as ravens, jays, and magpies are the most ubiquitous of the more than 200 species in the park, this is the kind of country made for birds of prey. Eagles, hawks, owls, and others can regularly be seen circling on the intense thermal updrafts that build around the mountain flanks rising along the Athabasca River east of Jasper. Sightings also increase near scree (erosion-debris) slopes at higher elevations, where hawks and eagles prey upon rodents, such as pikas, that scurry among the rocks. **Jasper Adventure Centre** (tel. 403/852–5595; 800/565–7547 in western Canada) conducts three-hour "Breakfast and Birding" tours near the town for early risers (starting at 7:30 AM).

Boating. For the most part, boating in the national parks means canoes, kayaks, rowboats, or pedal boats. Rentals are available at Maligne Lake, Pyramid Lake, Patricia Lake, and Lac Beauvert. Maligne Lake, by far the largest, invites serious exploration; the other lakes can be entirely circled in an hour or two, and Lac Beauvert in even less time. Electric motors are allowed in the park, but rentals aren't available. Gas-powered boats, including Jet Skis, are permitted only on Pyramid Lake, and the policy regarding Jet Skis is under review by Parks Canada. You won't make many friends in a powerboat on Pyramid Lake—most visitors tend to regard motorboats and Jet Skis as noisy and incompatible with the park.

Boat rentals are available at Pyramid Lake through **Pyramid Lake Resort** (tel. 403/852–4900); at Patricia Lake through **Patricia Lake Bungalows** (tel. 403/852–3560); at the Maligne Lake boathouse through **Maligne Tours** (tel. 403/852–3370); and at Lac Beauvert through **Beauvert Boat and Cycle** (tel. 403/852–3301, ext. 6190) at the marina at Jasper Park Lodge.

Fishing. Perhaps the best fishing in all of the Jasper-Banff area is in the northern half of Jasper. Because the large tract of land (more than 3,000 square km, or 1,150 square mi) is accessible only on foot or on horseback, the many rivers, lakes, and streams here see relatively few anglers. Fair fishing can also be had at Maligne Lake (where the Alberta-record rainbow trout, weighing over 20 pounds, was caught) and Amethyst Lakes in the Tonquin Valley.

The principal game fish are trout, grayling, and their various cousins. Information on fishing regulations is available at the Jasper Visitors Centre (*see* Visitor Information, *above*). A basic, seven-day fishing license is $6; an annual license is $13. Note that these licenses are valid only in the national parks. Provincial licenses, available at sporting goods stores, are required for fishing outside the parks. Fish stocking is no longer done in the national parks, so better fishing can often be found outside the parks, where stocking programs are common.

Several fishing guides operate within the park; for a recommended guide service (depending on the part of the park and the type of fishing you are interested in), contact **Jasper Tourism and Commerce** (*see* Visitor Information, *above*) or the activities desk at Jasper Park Lodge. **Currie's Guiding & Tackle** (416 Connaught Dr., Box 202, Jasper, AB T0E 1E0, tel. 403/852–5650) sells half- to multiday fishing packages in the park.

Horseback Riding. Depending on trail conditions, the riding season in Jasper runs approximately from May through October. Horse-pack trips are a highlight of any visit to Jasper and the surrounding area; with the large expanses of roadless wilderness, it's easy to understand why. Shorter trips (two- to four-day rides) tend toward Tonquin Valley, but the popularity of the valley make it less than a wilderness getaway. For that, campers on horseback head to the park's northern half for one- and two-week trips.

Several outfitters offer guided horseback-riding trips in and around the park, with rates generally ranging between $100 and $140 per person per day. For a listing of outfitters, see Travel Alberta's *Alberta Accommodation and Visitors' Guide.* For shorter rides (and instruction), there are two stables in Jasper: **Skyline Trail Rides** at Jasper Park Lodge (Box 207, Jasper, AB T0E 1E0, tel. and fax 403/852–4215) and **Pyramid Riding Stables** (Pyramid Lake Rd., Box 787, Jasper, AB T0E 1E0, tel. 403/852–3562).

Rafting. If you're looking for white water, the Maligne River is the place you want to be; if a scenic float is your preference, opt instead for a ride along the Athabasca River. Regardless of your choice, your trip will be relatively short, usually about three hours.

The rafting season generally runs from late May into September, with early-season waters, swollen by snowmelt, usually swifter and more rollicking. **Jasper Raft Tours** (Box 398, Jasper, AB T0E 1E0, tel. 403/852–3613, fax 403/852–3923) runs half-day float trips on the Athabasca River and also has canoe rentals; **Maligne River Adventures** (Box 280, 616 Connaught Dr., Jasper, AB T0E 1E0, tel. 403/852–3370) runs half-day trips on the Maligne River. **Rocky Mountain River Guides** (Box 1447, 600 Patricia St., Jasper, AB T0E 1E0, tel. 403/852–3777) runs trips on both rivers; and **Whitewater Rafting** (Box 362, Block 4142, Stan Wright Industrial Park, Jasper, AB T0E 1E0, tel. 403/852–7238; 800/557–7238 in western Canada) runs trips on the Athabasca, Maligne, and Sunwapta rivers.

Rock Climbing. In general, Jasper is better for ice climbing and glacier travel than it is for rock climbing; the sedimentary underpinnings of many of the mountains here are loose, crumbly rock. Although a park of this size is bound to have something for every type of climber and scrambler, its best offerings are around the ice fields at the southern extreme of the park.

Climbers differ in their opinions of which mountain in this area has the best climbing, but all will agree that any one of the peaks here presents tremendous variety of terrain and breathtaking summit views of the vast ice fields below. The highest peak is Mt. Columbia, at 3,747 meters (12,294 ft), but more accessible climbs are Mt. Athabasca (3,502 meters, or 11,452 ft) and Snow Dome (3,468 meters, or 11,340 ft). All these climbs are almost entirely on ice.

For those seeking a combination of rock and ice, Mt. Edith Cavell, the 3,954-meter (11,033-ft) peak south of the town of Jasper, is a good choice. And for those seeking the ultimate challenge, there is Mt. Robson, just west of the park boundary.

All climbers are urged to register with Parks Canada and/or to sign on with a local guide service before attempting any climb. **Jasper Climbing School and Mountaineering Service** (Box 452, Jasper, AB T0E 1E0, tel. 403/852–3964) leads climbs and offers instruction for climbers of all abilities. Prospective climbers might also want to consider membership in the **Alpine Club of Canada** (Box 8040, Indian Flats Rd., Canmore, AB T1W 2T8, tel. 403/678–3200), which leads climbs and maintains several backcountry huts in and around the park.

Skiing. The one lift-serviced ski area in the park is **Marmot Basin** (Box 1300, Jasper, AB T0E 1E0, tel. 403/852–3816), 19 km (12 mi) south of Jasper. Overshadowed by Banff's ski areas, Marmot Basin tends to be the forgotten ski area of the Canadian Rockies. With 700 meters (2,300 ft) of vertical rise, it has a good variety of open-bowl and trail skiing and a high-speed quad; it's also less crowded than its competitors to the south.

Ski Touring. Track skiers who prefer flat terrain should head for the Jasper Park

Lodge's 25-km (15-mi) groomed-trail network, which loops around Lac Beauvert and the lodge golf course. Those looking for rolling hills should head up to the trail network around Patricia and Pyramid lakes. And for those who can't get enough, the 5-km (3-mi) groomed trail at Whistlers Campground is lit at night.

For touring and backcountry skiing, a logical place to start in Jasper is around Maligne Lake. There's a good mix of terrain here; there's relatively flat skiing along the lake, but those who like moderate climbing and gentle slopes for telemark turning should head for the Bald Hills, overlooking the lake.

Maligne Lake skiing is merely a small taste of the skiing possible in a park with a hiking-trail network of nearly 1,000 km (612 mi). An excellent and popular backcountry tour is the 22-km (14-mi) ski into Tonquin Valley. Small, rustic cabins can be reserved through **Tonquin Valley Pack and Ski Trips** (Box 550, 712 Connaught Dr., Jasper, AB T0E 1E0, tel. 403/852–3909). The sensible plan is to reserve a cabin for at least two nights, to allow time for skiing and exploring around Amethyst Lakes.

All but the most experienced ski tourers and mountaineers are strongly advised to enlist a guide service for longer trips; **Spirit of Skiing** (Jasper Park Lodge, tel. 403/852–3433 or 800/483–8849) can set people up with local guides to suit their needs, and also rents just about anything related to snow sports, including toboggans, snowshoes, skis, and snowboards. Backcountry enthusiasts might also want to contact the **Alpine Club of Canada** (*see above*). The club maintains a hut system within the national parks and organizes outings and expeditions. Full membership isn't necessary to reserve huts or participate in outings, but nonmembers are charged considerably higher rates.

Be aware that avalanches can pose a serious danger in winter and springtime. Enquire about avalanche conditions at visitor centers and warden offices, or by calling 403/852–6177.

Snowmobiling. Snowmobiling, other than for service or emergencies, is prohibited in the park.

Swimming. This is cold-water country, and the antidote is the pool of **Miette Hotsprings** (tel. 403/866–3939), a three-spring combo said to produce the hottest water in the Canadian Rockies. (Actually, the Canoe River hot spring is hotter, but the flow rate is minimal.) The pool is open between late May and early October, from 10:30 AM to 9 PM (from late June to early September, extended daily hours are from 8:30 AM to 10:30 PM); admission is $4–$5, depending on the season. **Jasper Aquatic Centre** (tel. 403/852–3663) has daily public swims (hours vary) for $4 per person. Suits, towels, and lockers can be rented at both places.

Swimming is free at **Lake Annette, Lake Edith,** and **Pyramid Lake.** These lakes have unsupervised beaches, and all are near the town of Jasper. Pyramid Lake is the coldest of the three, Annette the warmest, but even in Annette it has to be a pretty hot day before most bathers will brave the water.

CHILDREN'S PROGRAMS Though there are no programs designated specifically for children, all the activities that appeal to adults—hiking, rafting, horseback riding, boating, swimming—are likely to delight children, too. **Pyramid Lake,** on the outskirts of the town of Jasper, and **Jasper Park Lodge** are the two best places to find a variety of activities in one location; the rates for boat and horse rentals are more modest at Pyramid Lake. There isn't much in Jasper for children on a bad-weather day; the **Jasper-Yellowhead Museum** is worth a visit, but it's hardly a daylong affair.

EVENING ACTIVITIES From July through August, on every night but Sunday, Parks Canada gives interpretive talks on Jasper's flora, fauna, history, and hiking trails, as well as musical theater programs, at several campgrounds in the parks. Programs begin at 8 or 9 PM. Check at the visitor center counters or campground kiosks for a schedule.

DINING

As in Banff, the majority of Jasper's dining options are in town. Though Jasper has fewer restaurants than Banff, there's still a great variety of cuisine. Most restaurants are casual (pizza and burgers are best-sellers), but classy restaurants are easy to find—especially at Jasper Park Lodge.

Beauvert Dining Room, Edith Cavell Dining Room, and **Moose's Nook.** These Jasper Park Lodge restaurants are the epitome of big-hotel–style dining. The Beauvert is the main dining room of the lodge, with a harpist and a view of Lac Beauvert to complement an innovative Continental menu: Try the artichoke pâté and slow-roasted, honey-glazed loin Alberta pork with apricot chutney. The Edith Cavell Dining Room is smaller and more private, with wall tapestries for decoration, a good view of Mt. Edith Cavell, and live classical piano music playing in the background. The French-inspired menu includes an excellent chowder of wild mushrooms and mixed grains. Moose's Nook, the most intimate of the three, serves more basic dishes such as pasta and Alberta prime rib of beef and also has a salad and dessert bar. Moose's Nook is open for breakfast; the Edith Cavell Dining Room and the Beauvert Room are open for dinner only. *Jasper Park Lodge, Hwy. 16, tel. 403/852–3301 or 800/441–1414. Reservations essential for dinner. Jacket required in Edith Cavell Dining Room. AE, D, DC, MC, V. $$$*

Le Beauvallon. When locals go out for a special meal, this is often the place they choose. Inside Chateau Jasper, the elegant restaurant has upholstered chairs, blue tablecloths, and crimson walls with wood trim. House specialties are meat and game; try the double lamb chop, venison Normandy, or fallow deer. The giant Sunday-brunch buffet has epic-feast potential for active outdoorspeople. *96 Giekie St., in Chateau Jasper hotel, tel. 403/852–5644. Reservations essential in summer. AE, DC, MC, V. $$$*

L & W Family Restaurant. Extremely popular with the family crowd, this is perhaps Jasper's busiest restaurant. Expect a lineup during peak dining hours, especially for supper. The simple fare—pasta, burgers, steaks, chicken, sandwiches, and some Greek dishes—is tasty and reasonably priced. If you get here early or late enough, choose a table under one of the domed glass bubbles around the periphery: It's the next best thing to dining outdoors. *Hazel and Patricia Sts., tel. 403/852–4114. Reservations not accepted. AE, MC, V. $–$$*

Palisades Restaurant. A surprisingly rich Greek streak runs through Jasper, and this restaurant is just the place to get a taste of it. The decor evokes a Mediterranean mood, with bright white walls, a partial greenhouse ceiling, and numerous plants. The walls are decorated with works by local artists (for sale). Moussaka and souvlakia, along with baklava for desert, are among the characteristic Greek dishes. Pizzas are also on the menu. *Cedar Ave. near Connaught Dr., tel. 403/852–5222. AE, DC, MC, V. $–$$*

PICNIC SPOTS There are nice picnic spots in the park for anyone willing to walk a kilometer or two. For nonwalkers, picnic areas with tables are scattered around the park. Among the prettiest are those at **Lake Annette, Maligne Lake, Pyramid Lake, Athabasca Falls,** and **Sixth Bridge.** The **Medicine Lake** picnic area, just off the Maligne Lake road, is somewhat more private, but it's also quite small and not especially scenic.

LODGING

Park lodging, for the most part, begins and ends in and around the town of Jasper. The most popular options boil down to cabins or motel-style accommodations, unless there is room in your budget for the high-end Jasper Park Lodge. Cabins tend to be less expensive, but they're also more rustic, with fewer services than motels and hotels. Most cabins are outside the town of Jasper, while motels and hotels are in town (except for Jasper Park Lodge, which comprises its own village near Jasper). Reservation agencies are not regulated in Alberta.

Reservations Jasper (Box 1840, 310 Aspen Ave., Jasper, AB T0E 1E0, tel. 403/852–5488, fax 403/852–5489) books rooms in hotels and private homes for a $15–$30 fee. **Jasper Travel Agency** (Box 320, Jasper, AB T0E 1E0, tel. 403/852–4400) reserves rooms in hotels as well as private homes for a $12 fee. Jasper Travel operates only in the summer.

As for bed-and-breakfast accommodations, don't expect anything fancy; in Jasper, as in Banff, B&Bs tend to be ordinary rooms in private homes. In addition to the above reservation agencies, two agencies specifically handle bed-and-breakfast bookings in the area: **Alberta's Gem B&B Reservation Agency** (11216 48th Ave., Edmonton, AB T6H 0C7, tel. 403/434–6098, fax 403/434–6098) reserves all licensed bed-and-breakfasts, but does not inspect establishments and charges a booking fee. **Bed and Breakfast Agency of Alberta** (410 19th Ave NE, Calgary, AB T2E 1P3, tel. 403/277–8486 or 800/425–8160, fax 403/237–5433) handles only about 50 bed-and-breakfasts, personally inspects each property, and charges a booking fee to the bed-and-breakfast operator, not to the traveler. Individual bed-and-breakfast establishments are listed in Travel Alberta's *Alberta Accommodation and Visitors' Guide.*

Near the eastern (Alberta) periphery of the park are several **guest ranches** and **wilderness lodges** (lodges that are off the-beaten-track but accessible by car). Information about these is included in Travel Alberta's *Alberta Accommodation and Visitors' Guide.* There are also five hostels in Jasper; information and reservations are available through **Jasper International Hostel** (Box 387, Whistler's Mountain Rd., Jasper, AB T0E 1E0, tel. 403/852–3215, fax 403/852–5660).

Alpine Village. A cluster of pine-log cabins 1 km (.6 mi) south of town, this family-run operation is one of Jasper's bargains. The log interior gives a rustic feeling to many of the tidy cabins. All have beamed ceilings and fieldstone fireplaces; two-bedroom cabins have full kitchens. The 12 newer cabins are preferable to the older, smaller ones. The view of Mt. Edith Cavell and the sound of the Athabasca River, just across a small road, create a classic alpine atmosphere. Outside, there's a 5-meter (16-ft) hot tub. *1 km (.6 mi) south of Jasper on Hwy. 93A, Box 610, Jasper, AB T0E 1E0, tel. 403/852–3285. 42 units. Facilities: outdoor hot tub. MC, V. Closed mid-Oct.–Apr. $$$*

Chateau Jasper. Big wood beams cantilevered over the front door suggest a Scandinavian interior. Not so. Rooms are in American motel style, the beds adorned with colonial-style headboards. Low ceilings add a sense of coziness to the large rooms. The hotel's restaurant, Le Beauvallon (*see* Dining, *above*) is excellent. *96 Giekie St., Box 1418, Jasper, AB T0E 1E0, tel. 403/852–5644 or 800/661–9323, fax 403/852–4860. 119 rooms. Facilities: restaurant, indoor pool, hot tub. AE, DC, MC, V. $$$*

Jasper Inn. There are motel-style rooms here as well as two-bedroom condos featuring modern, functional design and architecture. The rates are surprisingly reasonable, given the inn's convenient location and amenities. Most units have kitchenettes and fireplaces. Condo accommodations are especially suitable for families. The full-service restaurant serves pasta and seafood as well as meat entrées. *Giekie St. and Bonhomme Ave., Box 879, Jasper, AB T0E 1E0, tel. 403/852–4461 or 800/661–1933, fax 403/852–5916. 129 rooms, 14 suites. Facilities: restaurant, indoor pool, hot tub, sauna, steam room. AE, DC, MC, V. $$$*

Jasper Park Lodge. This is Jasper's original resort, a lakeside compound northeast of town that hums with on-site activities such as golf, tennis, boating, bicycling, horseback riding, and fishing. The main lodge, overlooking Lac Beauvert and the mountains, has polished-stone floors, totem-pole pillars, and high ceilings; many rooms have fireplaces. Outlying bungalows and rows of cabins comprise most of the accommodation; each has log-cabin walls; bright down comforters; and a balcony, patio, or porch (request one overlooking the lake). Breakfast and dinner are included in most room rates (the priciest in Jasper). There's outdoor swimming in a heated pool year-round—a major draw for winter guests. Overbooking can be a problem in peak season. *4 km (2.5 mi) northeast of Jasper on Hwy. 16, Box 40, Jasper, AB T0E 1E0, tel. 403/852–3301 or 800/441–1414, fax 403/852–5107. 442 rooms. Facilities: 7 restaurants, 3 bars, 18-hole golf course, 4 tennis courts, horseback riding, boating, bicycles, ice-skating, rollerblading, sleigh rides. AE, D, DC, MC, V. $$$*

Patricia Lake Bungalows. Set beside Patricia Lake, this spot is a great place for peace and quiet, just a short drive from Jasper. Cabins are clean and spacious, with basic furnishings—queen-size beds, dressers and tables, a television and a small kitchen. Bathrooms are smallish, with showers, not tubs. This is one of the few remaining bargain accommodations in Jasper. A half dozen motel units have been remodeled into large family units, but the cabin units—especially those nearest the lake—are the most coveted. *Pyramid Lake Rd., 5 km (3 mi) from Jasper, Box 657, Jasper, AB T0E 1E0, tel. 403/852–3560, fax 403/852–4060. 7 rooms, 29 cabins. Facilities: boating, bicycles, coin laundry. AE, MC, V. Closed mid-Oct.–Apr. $$$*

CAMPING

Camping information can be obtained at the **Jasper Information Centre** (500 Connaught Dr., Jasper, AB T0E 1E0, tel. 403/852–6176), from **Parks Canada** (*see* Visitor Information, *above*), or from *Alberta Campground Guide,* published by **Travel Alberta** (*see* Visitor Information, *above*). Drive-in campgrounds are generally open from mid-May to early fall and are first-come, first-served. Camping in the park costs between $10 and $22 per site, depending on whether you require a hookup.

INSIDE THE PARK Because of the park's size, campground selection depends largely on which parts of the park you're most interested in exploring. The drive-in campgrounds listed below are all on or near Highway 16. All have drinking water and public phones.

Pocahontas, in the Athabasca River valley, 44 km (27 mi) north of the town of Jasper, is nearest Miette Hotsprings. It has 130 RV sites and 10 tent sites; the nightly fee is $13. The campground tends to be very crowded on weekends.

Snaring River (48 RV sites, 8 tent sites; $10 per night), **Whistlers** (781 tent and RV sites; $15–$22), **Wapiti** (362 tent and RV sites; $15–$18), and **Wabasso** (232 RV sites, 6 tent sites; $13) are all within 17 km (10 mi) of the center of Jasper. Whistlers is probably the best serviced and most conveniently located in the park, but you must be willing to put up with the high volume of campers.

Thirty-six kilometers (22 miles) south of town is **Mt. Kerkeslin.** With only 44 tent and RV sites ($10 per night), this is a little quieter but more primitive than many of the others. Other smaller grounds between Mt. Kerkeslin and the Columbia Icefield are **Honeymoon Lake** (35 tent and RV sites; $10) and **Jonas Creek** (25 RV sites, 12 tent sites; $10).

In the Columbia Icefield region there are two good campgrounds. Climbers tend to prefer the 33 sites at the somewhat exposed-to-the-elements **Columbia Icefield** campground, since it is a closer starting point for exploring the Athabasca Glacier. The 46-site **Wilcox Creek** is considered more comfortable and is still near all there is to do in the ice-field area of the park. Both of these campgrounds charge $10 per night.

Backcountry campgrounds are scattered throughout the park. These require overnight permits that can be obtained at any of the information centers; the fee is $6 per person per night (to a maximum of $30 per person per trip or $42 annually). They

JASPER CAMPGROUNDS

	Wilcox Creek	Columbia Icefield	Jonas Creek	Honeymoon Lake	Mt. Kerkeslin	Wabasso	Wapiti	Whistlers	Snaring River	Pocahontas
Total number of sites	46	33	37	35	42	238	362	781	66	140
Sites suitable for RVs	46	0	25	35	42	232	362	781	48	130
Number of hookups	0	0	0	0	0	0	40	177	0	0
Drive to sites	●	●	●	●	●	●	●	●	●	●
Hike to sites			●	●		●			●	
Flush toilets						●	●	●		●
Pit/chemical toilets	●	●	●	●	●				●	
Drinking water	●	●	●	●	●	●	●	●	●	●
Showers								●	●	
Fire grates	●	●	●	●	●	●	●	●	●	●
Swimming										
Boat access				●						
Playground						●		●		
Disposal station	●						●	●	●	
Ranger station										
Public telephone	●	●	●	●	●	●	●	●		●
Reservation possible										
Daily fee per site	$10	$10	$10	$10	$10	$13	$15–$18	$15–$22	$10	$13
Dates open	early June–late Sept.	mid-May–mid-Oct.	mid-May–mid-Oct.	mid-May–mid-Oct.	early June–early Sept.	late June–early Sept.	early June–early Sept.	early-May–mid Oct.	mid-May–early Sept.	mid-May–mid-Oct.

are open year-round, but winter camping in this part of the world can be rugged. For backcountry campers, *The Canadian Rockies Trail Guide,* by Brian Patton and Bart Robinson, is a valuable resource. Below is a sampling of Jasper's backcountry sites.

The beauty of **Tonquin Valley** is a draw for many Jasper backpackers, although backcountry campers who aren't fond of sharing their world with horse packers should go elsewhere. There are four campgrounds in the valley as well as small cabins that can be reserved through **Tonquin Valley Pack and Ski Trips** (Box 550, 712 Connaught Dr., Jasper, AB T0E 1E0, tel. 403/852–3909). Because of the popularity of the valley, there is a quota system for campground and trail use.

For a relatively long but flat hike to a pretty backcountry lake, the trip to the **Jacques Lake** campground is tough to beat. For those who prefer camping on high-country meadows, the **Watchtower Basin** campground, a 10-km (6-mi) hike from the Maligne Lake Road, is the place to go, although the hike in is anything but flat.

Perhaps *the* classic backpacking trip in Jasper is the Skyline Trail, which begins at Maligne Lake. A stopover at the **Little Shovel Pass campground,** about 8 km (5 mi) from Maligne Lake, provides a brief introduction to the sprawling meadows and mountain views that lie ahead on a trail that continues for another 37 km (23 mi). Because of the fragile, alpine-meadow vegetation along the trail, campground use is limited by a quota system.

Another classic hike that isn't in the national park (it's in adjoining Mt. Robson Provincial Park) is the trip to the **Berg Lake** campground. It's a fairly long haul for one day—19 km (12 mi)—although there are other campgrounds along the way. The incredible rock-and-glacier mass of Mt. Robson rising above the lake inspires awe—if it's visible. Campers heading for Berg Lake should be prepared for Mt. Robson's often foul weather.

Joshua Tree National Park
California

Updated by Bob Howells

ormon pioneers in the 19th century likened the Joshua trees to a Biblical prophet who, in different versions, was either beseeching the heavens with upraised arms or pointing travelers toward a promised land. There are thousands of Joshua trees in the national park bearing their name. With their multiple and varied arms ending in fists of elongated, needle-like leaves, no two are alike. But not all of the 1.9 million annual visitors to the southern California park come for the Joshua trees; more often, they come for the rocks.

The abundant outcroppings of weathered igneous boulders draw rock climbers from around the world, and on any day of the week, climbers of various abilities can be seen clambering up and around them. Sightseers, too, are drawn to the rocks. Boulder gardens filled with fascinating natural sculptures are the result of the way in which the rocks were formed and have since been eroding.

The park itself has few facilities, but there are towns within a few minutes' drive of any of the three entrances. In addition, Palm Springs is 25 to 50 mi away (depending on which entrance you choose), and Los Angeles, 147 mi. The park gets crowded, especially on weekends from fall through spring, but there are plenty of trails on which visitors can find solitude only a short walk from their car. Since the number of tours available is limited and there is no public transportation within the park, it is difficult to see Joshua Tree without a car. But whether you remain here for one day or one week, you should make it a point to hike away from the roads and the crowds, to let the desert's beauty and solitude seep into your soul.

The park owes its existence to the efforts of Minerva Hamilton Hoyt, a Pasadena resident who, during the 1920s, became concerned with the removal and destruction of Joshua trees and cacti from the area. Vandals were uprooting cacti and palms to transport them to suburban gardens, and Joshua trees were being burned by gold miners to fuel the steam engines in their stamp mills.

Hoyt launched a grassroots campaign to protect the region, lobbying for the creation of an enormous federal desert park. It took several years of battling the bureaucracy and swaying public opinion, but, finally, on August 10, 1936, Franklin D. Roosevelt established the 825,000-acre Joshua Tree National Monument. For more than 15 years, however, prospectors fought for the right to continue searching for new mineral and iron-ore deposits in the park. Fearing the eventual repeal of Roosevelt's original proclamation, conservation groups decided to compromise with the miners and agreed to return over a quarter of a million acres to the public domain. With the passage of the California Desert Protection Act in October 1994, the monument became a national park and 234,000 acres were added to its boundaries. Today, after much give and take, the total area of the park stands at 793,000 acres. Most of the newer acreage is roadless wilderness area.

ESSENTIAL INFORMATION

VISITOR INFORMATION Contact the Superintendent, **Joshua Tree National Park**, 74485 National Park Drive, Twentynine Palms, CA 92277, tel. 760/367–7511.

If you plan to enter the park's backcountry you must self-register at one of 13 designated backcountry boards located throughout the park. Vehicles left overnight anywhere other than at a backcountry board are subject to citation and/or towing. Camping is prohibited within 1 mi of any road, 500 ft of any trail, in washes, and in areas designated for day use only. The latter restriction allows the park's animals to make use of watering holes at night. Pets are prohibited in the backcountry. For maps locating backcountry registration boards and day-use areas, stop by the Oasis Visitor Center at Twentynine Palms or the Cottonwood Visitor Center, at the park's southern entrance; or write to the superintendent (*see above*).

FEES The entry fee is $10 per vehicle and is good for seven days. Bus passengers, cyclists, and travelers on foot pay $5 each. An annual pass for Joshua Tree National Park is $25.

PUBLICATIONS Several publications, in addition to the park's free newspaper, *Joshua Tree Guide,* provide background information and suggestions on what to do and where to go within the park. You can order them through the **Joshua Tree National Park Association** (74485 National Park Dr., Twentynine Palms, CA 92277, tel. 760/367–1488), or look for them at any of the park's three visitor centers.

Joshua Tree National Park, a Visitor's Guide, by Bob Cates, provides most of the basic information necessary for exploring the park. It consists of about 100 pages, including maps, discussions of natural and cultural history, and overviews of various areas within the park. Steve Trimble's *Joshua Tree: Desert Reflections* is filled with four-color photos of the park, with

running text that describes park features and history. Hikers will want to have a copy of *Hikes and Walks, 25 Trails in Joshua Tree,* by Patty Knapp, a pocket-size book that covers the most popular of Joshua Tree's trails. This book will tell you how long and how difficult each trail is. Also useful is a topographic map published by Trails Illustrated and the *Desert Survival Handbook,* which teaches survival techniques for the desert.

GEOLOGY AND TERRAIN Joshua Tree National Park sits at the eastern end of the Transverse Ranges in southern California. Its 793,000 acres straddle the area where two deserts, the Colorado and the Mojave, meet. The eastern side of the park is part of the lower-lying Colorado Desert, where the elevation is generally below 3,000 ft. This area is characterized by creosote bushes, ocotillo, and jumping cholla cactus, the latter named for its propensity to seemingly leap onto the pant legs of those passing through. The western half of the park, most of which sits at elevations exceeding 3,000 ft, is primarily part of the Mojave Desert. Temperatures are cooler here, and the relatively higher precipitation results in more abundant vegetation. It is in these upper elevations that the namesake Joshua tree thrives.

The area's geological instability is responsible for the park's striking landscape, which is characterized by a handful of mountain ranges that rise sharply from the desert floor. A number of major and hundreds of minor faults cut through the park, and over the millennia they have caused huge masses of rock to rise above the desert areas. In fact, the land comprising Joshua Tree has sunk below sea level at least 10 times in the past 800 million years, only to resurface through the radical uplifting of surface rock. Particularly dramatic examples of this uprising are the Pinto Mountains, which form the northern border of the park, and the Little San Bernardino Mountains on the southwestern edge. Other ranges in Joshua Tree are the Hexie Mountains in the park's center, the Cottonwood Mountains to the south, and the Eagle and Coxcomb mountains to the east.

Fault zones have also played an important role in the creation of Joshua Tree's five fan-palm oases. The famous San Andreas Fault skims the park's southwestern border. The movement of earth around this and other faults causes the underground rock to splinter, and the resulting bits of rock form dams that stop the flow of groundwater. The groundwater is then forced to rise through the cracks to the surface, where it gives life to a few plants and animals.

Also look for monzogranite intrusions—boulder gardens filled with multi-ton building blocks stacked in intriguing formations. Their form is the result of spheroidal and cavernous weathering, complicated processes that involve the expansion of fissures (called joints) in the rocks; the chemical and mechanical weathering of the rocks; and the accumulation of minerals, water, and lichen on the rocks, resulting in their decomposition. The Wonderland of Rocks, Ryan Campground, and Split Rock areas are good examples of spheroidal weathering; cavernous weathering was responsible for the formation of Skull Rock, in the Jumbo Rocks area.

FLORA AND FAUNA The desert is a land of precarious existence; plants and animals have adapted to the harsh temperatures and dry climate. To an untrained eye, the desert appears to be relatively devoid of life, but on closer inspection, it becomes apparent that this land is very much alive.

Fifteen species of cactus are found within Joshua Tree National Park. The self-guiding nature trail at the Cholla Cactus Garden takes you through an area concentrated with bigelow cactus, a cholla cactus that is also known as the teddy bear cholla and usually grows taller than waist high. Nearby is the Ocotillo Patch, where the long skinny spines of the ocotillo stretch up to 12 ft into the air. During periods of relatively heavy moisture the ocotillo even produces small green leaves and scarlet blossoms that attract hummingbirds.

Joshua trees can be seen throughout the western portion of the park—generally in elevations above 3,000 ft—and are especially abundant in Queen Valley and Lost Horse Valley. It is difficult to determine the age of a Joshua tree, because, unlike most trees, it has no annual growth ring; its trunk is composed of countless tiny fibers. The Joshua tree, or *Yucca brevifolia,* is a member of the lily family and is also known for its seldom-seen white blossoms, which can appear anytime from February through April but only when the temperature and precipitation in a given year have been just right. You may have to return to the park for many years before you catch a major bloom.

Rising spring temperatures trigger bursts of wildflowers that paint the desert carpet. Among the fields of flowers, you may see the desert five-spot, which draws its name from the dark spot toward the center of each of its five pinkish petals. The pinkish-white desert primrose grows in wide circles of ground cover. Also look for purple lupine, sandmat, and locoweed. These spring blooms vary greatly from one year to the next, depending on rainfall during fall and winter and temperatures in spring. Many of the desert annuals need a good soaking to germinate, usually from September through mid-December; the timing of the fall rains determines what happens in the spring. The lower elevations begin blooming around February, and the upper elevations start in March and April. Some areas above 5,000 ft see blooms as late as June. Spectacular desert blooms typically occur only once every 20 years; one such spectacle was in 1995.

When the sun has set and the air has cooled, the desert's creatures emerge from their hiding places to hunt and forage. The wildlife in Joshua Tree National Park includes coyotes, burrowing owls, kangaroo rats, yucca night lizards, bobcats, sidewinders, roadrunners, golden eagles, bighorn sheep, and tarantulas. The desert tortoise, a protected species, makes its home throughout the park, although it is not commonly seen.

WHEN TO GO It is best to visit Joshua Tree National Park from October through May, when the weather is most comfortable and the number of activities held in the park and nearby communities is greatest. Of course, that is when most of the 1.9 million visitors choose to visit, so the park's roads and campgrounds can become crowded, especially on weekends.

You are most likely to see cacti and wildflowers blooming in March, April, and May. Rainfall is not really a factor at any time of the year, although the wettest month is August, when an average of less then ¾ inch of rain falls each year. The park has an average of 81 days per year above 100°F, with 100-degree temperatures recorded as early as April 18 and as late as October 19. July is the hottest month, with daytime highs averaging 104.7°F. Average high temperatures are 85°F in October, 62°F in January, and 90°F in May. During the summer months, nights usually cool down to around 65°F or 70°F. From November through March, overnight lows get down into the low and mid 30s. Temperatures are 5°F to 10°F cooler in the higher elevations, where the campgrounds are located. With the exception of two campgrounds that may be closed during the summer, the park's facilities are open year-round.

SEASONAL EVENTS **May:** In Yucca Valley, the Grubstake Days (tel. 760/365–6323) are held annually on Memorial Day weekend, with dancing, a parade, and a rodeo. **October:** On the third weekend of the month, Twentynine Palms hosts Pioneer Days, with a rodeo and assorted festivities such as outhouse races, in which five-member teams of enthusiastic potty-pushers compete.

Throughout the year, the **Andromeda Astronomical Society** (tel. 760/228–1977) conducts occasional stargazing programs.

WHAT TO PACK No matter what time of year you visit Joshua Tree, bring a wide-brimmed hat, sunglasses, and sunscreen to combat the heat and glare, but also pack a jacket for the relatively cool nights. A long-sleeved shirt and long pants will help minimize water loss due to perspiration. Carry at least one gallon of water per person for each day you plan to be in the park—whether you are hiking or driving—and bring additional water for your vehicle. Campers must bring their own firewood: Wood gathering is illegal.

GENERAL STORES There are no stores in the park, but there are many in the Morongo Basin, which is traversed by Highway 62. In Yucca Valley, **Von's** (57590 Twentynine Palms Hwy., tel. 760/365–8998), open from 7 AM to 11 PM, sells groceries. Camping supplies can be purchased at **Kmart** (57725 Twentynine Palms Hwy., tel. 760/365–0628), which is open from 8 AM to 10 PM. In Twentynine Palms, groceries can be purchased at **Stater Bros.** (71727 Twentynine Palms Hwy., tel. 760/367–6535), open daily from 7 AM to 10 PM.

ARRIVING AND DEPARTING Joshua Tree National Park is 147 mi northeast of Los Angeles, 50 mi northeast of Palm Springs. There is no public transportation through the park, so the best way to visit is by car. Because the entire park can be seen in one day of driving, it doesn't matter which of the park's three entrances you choose. The west (Joshua Tree) and north (Twentynine Palms) entrances, off Highway 62, are closer to the main loop of the road along which most of the scenic attractions are located. But most visitors wind up heading for the Ocotillo Patch and Cholla Cactus Garden at some point during their stay, and these are closer to the south (Cottonwood Springs) entrance, which is reached off I–10, east of Indio. There are visitor centers at the Twentynine Palms and Cottonwood Springs entrances and an entrance station at the Joshua Tree entrance.

By Bus. Greyhound Lines bus service is available from most major cities to the Greyhound Terminal in Palm Springs (311 N. Indian Ave., tel. 760/325–2053). From there, **Morongo Basin Transit Authority** (tel. 800/794–6282) serves the towns of Yucca Valley, Joshua Tree, and Twentynine Palms. A one-way bus ticket from Palm

Springs to Twentynine Palms costs about $9; it's about a 90-minute ride.

By Car and RV. To reach the park from Los Angeles, take I–10 east to the Cottonwood entrance (a left-hand turn just before Chiriaco Summit), or take I–10 east and turn onto Highway 62 (Twentynine Palms Highway) going northeast. Both the west entrance and the north entrance can be reached from Highway 62; four short spur roads also stem off Highway 62 and dead-end just inside the park boundary. From Palm Springs, take Indian Avenue north 3 mi to I–10 and turn left (west) to reach Highway 62 in 3 mi (it's 29 mi northeast to the west entrance) or turn right (east) on I–10 to reach the Cottonwood entrance in 48 mi.

Those headed to Death Valley have the option of traveling from the park through the Mojave National Preserve, not the shortest route, but certainly the most scenic. From the town of Twentynine Palms, turn north on Utah Trail, then east on Amboy Road. At the east end of town, the road swings north and leads to Amboy. From there, take the Kelbaker Road to Baker, where you can pick up Highway 127 north to Shoshone. From Shoshone, there are numerous options for entering Death Valley (*see* the Death Valley National Park chapter). The scenery along this route— sand dunes and rugged mountains painted by various ores and minerals—makes this a trip to remember. But the way is long and isolated; it covers approximately 260 mi, with a 65-mi stretch between services.

A more populated route from Twentynine Palms starts out on Highway 62 west, then moves north on Highway 247 to Barstow, where you must take I–15 east to Baker. At Baker, Highway 127 runs north to Shoshone.

By Plane. Many major airlines serve Palm Springs Regional Airport (tel. 760/323–8161), 2 mi east of the downtown area. Most hotels provide transportation to and from the terminal, but visitors staying in towns closer to the park should rent a car. Try **Avis** (tel. 800/331–1212), **Budget** (tel. 800/527–0700), **Dollar** (tel. 800/800–4000),

Hertz (tel. 800/654–3131), or **National** (tel. 800/328–4567).

By Train. Amtrak (tel. 800/872–7245) passenger trains service Indio, 25 mi west of the park's south entrance and 20 mi east of Palm Springs. For $3.75 one-way, Greyhound Lines takes passengers from Indio to Palm Springs, where there are buses to Twentynine Palms (*see above*). The bus station is just five blocks from the train station, and taxis meet incoming trains.

EXPLORING

It's easy to motor your way through Joshua Tree in one day. A number of companies offer organized tours of the park for those who would rather leave the driving to someone else, but Joshua Tree is the kind of place where you'll want to pull off the road to explore something that catches your eye. A few of the park's dirt roads are inaccessible to passenger vehicles, so a mountain bike may come in handy. Bikes are permitted on all of the park's dirt and paved roads (they are not permitted off-road), but with motorists constantly craning their necks to look at rock formations and other sites, most of these narrow two-lane roadways aren't ideal for extended bike rides.

Water is not available in the park, so hikers must carry it—a lot of it—making backpacking trips suitable only for the hardiest of visitors. There are, however, many short hikes, and it is easy to take a few of these and still see the park in one day.

THE BEST IN ONE DAY Start out from the Twentynine Palms entrance and drive the 11 mi to the Jumbo Rocks area, a plateau rimmed by huge and splendid boulder formations, formed by the work of 800 million years of tectonic and erosive forces. Head out early enough to catch the sunrise; it paints these giant boulders pink and yellow. By 8 AM the Oasis Visitor Center will open, and it's worth your while to backtrack in order to stop there. You'll learn about the park's natural and cultural his-

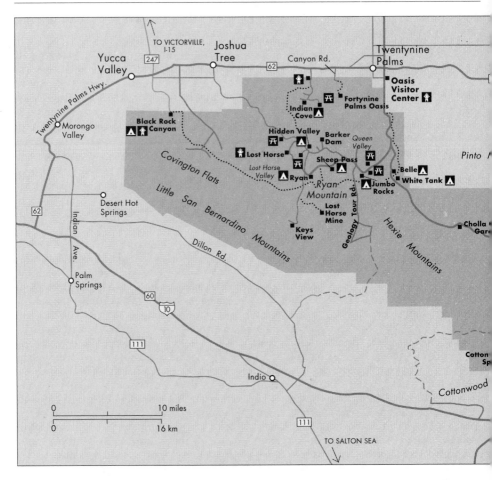

tory and become acquainted with the differences between the two deserts present within the park boundaries. Displays also tell how the plants and animals eke out an existence here. Take the .5-mi nature walk through the nearby Oasis of Mara, which was used by miners, early settlers, and Native Americans. The area is full of cottonwood trees, palm trees, arrowweed, and mesquite shrubs.

From the Oasis Visitor Center, drive up the hill leading back into the park. At about the 5-mi mark, take the fork to the left and continue another 9 mi to the Cholla Cactus Garden, where the sun fills the cactus needles with light. As the road descends, note the transition from high desert to low desert. Get out to take the short self-guiding nature trail, and pick up pamphlets at the site. Then drive back up the hill to the fork in the road; this time turn left toward the Jumbo Rocks (clearly marked with a road sign). After 2 mi, there's a short, well-marked paved road on the left that leads to the Live Oak picnic area.

Continue west on the main road for 1 mi, stopping to view Skull Rock alongside the road (*see* Nature Trails and Short Walks, *below*). As you drive west, you will approach the higher desert and the Jumbo Rocks area, where you may have watched the sun rise. Keep an eye out for rock

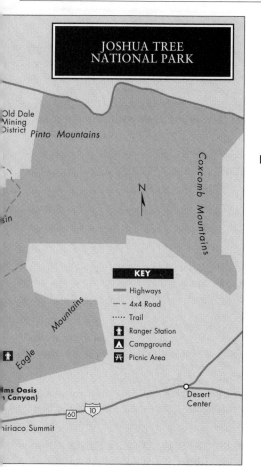

JOSHUA TREE
NATIONAL PARK

Old Dale
Mining
District Pinto Mountains

N

Coxcomb Mountains

sin

KEY

━━ Highways
── 4x4 Road
····· Trail
🛈 Ranger Station
🛆 Campground
🛉 Picnic Area

Mountains

Eagle

ms Oasis
Canyon)

Desert
Center

60 10

iriaco Summit

the Keys View spur road to the main park road and return to Hidden Valley.

At the Hidden Valley campground, look for the signs leading to the Barker Dam Trail (*see* Nature Trails and Short Hikes, *below*). At this point, you have two options: Continue through the park to Highway 62 and the town of Joshua Tree, or return to Keys View to watch the sun set.

ORIENTATION PROGRAMS On Friday, Saturday, and Sunday from mid-October through mid-December and from early February through May, rangers lead a variety of programs, many of which repeat over the course of the day or weekend. Meeting times and places are listed in the *Joshua Tree Guide,* available at any of the visitor or information centers.

Campfire Coffee programs at Hidden Valley, Black Rock Canyon, and Cottonwood campgrounds run from 45 minutes to one hour; coffee, tea, and hot chocolate (bring your own mug) are served while a park ranger or camp host answers your questions. On the **Keys Ranch Tour** you will explore the homestead (also known as Desert Queen Ranch) of one of the few ranchers to successfully endure in this harsh land. The 90-minute tour covers 1 mi and is free. Admission is limited to 20 people on a first-come, first-served basis (*see* Historic Buildings and Sights, *below*).

climbers (binoculars will help you to see their spiderlike feats). By now it should be lunchtime, and the huge boulders in Hidden Valley provide several private places to spread a picnic blanket. Before or after lunch, take an hour to walk the easy 1-mi Hidden Valley Trail, which winds its way through boulders into an area where cattle rustlers once allegedly kept their liberated livestock. From the Hidden Valley area, backtrack to the 6-mi drive out to Keys View (*see* Scenic Drives and Views, *below*). On a clear day (morning is best) you'll be able to see the Coachella Valley, the Salton Sea, and into Mexico. From late fall through early spring it can be chilly at the lookout, so bring a sweater. Backtrack on

There are also several ranger-guided hikes, although they vary from year to year. The **Fortynine Palms Oasis Hike** covers 3 mi in three hours; the 3-mi **Mastodon Peak Hike** explores the Cottonwood area and the Mastodon Gold Mine in 2½ hours; and the 3-mi, three-hour **Ryan Mountain Hike** heads to a summit with some of the best views in the park. On the 1-mi, one-hour **Barker Dam Walk** you will learn about some of the historical uses of Barker Dam, as well as the area's natural history. Covering 2.5 mi in two hours, the **Wall Street Mill Hike** tells the tales of many of the rugged people who mined for gold in the desert. Pick up a pamphlet at the start of the short (.25-mi), self-guided 45-minute

Cholla Walk through the Cholla Cactus Garden and learn how the cholla and the pack rat interact. On the .5-mi **Arch Rock Hike** you'll stroll for 1½ hours among some of the rock formations that make Joshua Tree famous and learn about their origins.

GUIDED TOURS Technical rock-climbing classes, ranging from one to four days for all levels of climbers, are taught by the **Joshua Tree Rock Climbing School** (HCR Box 3034, Joshua Tree, CA 92252, tel. 800/ 890–4745), a school that has been in operation since 1989 and is accredited by the American Mountain Guides Association. The school provides all equipment for the classes, which run from September through June. A two-day basic course is $145 per person; private guides cost $175 per day for one person, with diminishing rates for additional climbers.

The oldest climbing school in the area is **Vertical Adventures** (Box 7548, Newport Beach, CA 92658, tel. 714/854–6250), which has more than 10 years of experience and instructs about 1,000 climbers each year. The school's most popular class is a two-day, $145 beginner's seminar. A two-day intermediate course is $145. Classes run from November through May; sign up at least two weeks in advance.

SCENIC DRIVES AND VIEWS A 6-mi spur road heads south from the park's main road just west of the Ryan campground and leads to 5,185-ft **Keys View,** from which you can see the Salton Sea, the Coachella Valley, the mountains of the San Bernardino National Forest, and—on a rare clear day—Signal Mountain in Mexico. About halfway to the point there is a 4-mi round-trip trail that leads to the Lost Horse Mine, a reminder of the park's gold prospecting and mining history. As you head back north on the road, you'll have an excellent view of the Lost Horse Valley. Keys View is a good place to watch the sunset.

Some of the park's most fascinating landscapes can be observed from the 18-mi **Geology Tour Road,** a dirt road that should be negotiated only with a four-wheel-drive

vehicle. Not only is this road rough and ill-maintained, it also has several sandy stretches that can snag two-wheel-drive vehicles (consider the towing bill). It will take about two hours to make the round-trip journey. Along the way, you'll see a volcanic hill, a 100-year-old stone dam called Squaw Tank, old mines, archaeological sites, and a large plain with an abundance of Joshua trees.

HISTORIC BUILDINGS AND SITES The 150-acre **Keys Ranch** (also known as Desert Queen Ranch) was one of the most successful attempts at homesteading in the area, lasting for more than 50 years. Occupying an open area surrounded by huge boulders, the ranch now consists of the main dwelling and several outbuildings (closed for historic protection), gardens, and some wells. It was started by Bill Keys, who dug the wells by hand, built a concrete dam and an earthen levee, and installed an irrigation system to water his vegetable gardens, fruit orchards, and wheat and alfalfa fields. Free, ranger-led guided tours provide the only access to Keys Ranch; they are held on Saturday and Sunday at 10 AM and 1 PM from October through May and are limited to the first 20 people to arrive at the ranch gate.

NATURE TRAILS AND SHORT WALKS Starting at the White Tank campground, a .3-mi loop leads to **Arch Rock.** Signs along the trail give information on the geology of the area and the formation of this natural arch. A 1-mi loop beginning 2 mi northeast of the Hidden Valley campground passes **Barker Dam,** built by early cattle ranchers to provide water for their stock. After the dam, this trail proceeds past a group of Native American petroglyphs, which, unfortunately, were once painted over by a film crew attempting to make them more visible. One of the park's top geology trails begins at the **Cap Rock** parking area and makes a .5-mi loop through fascinating rock formations. Along the way, signs explain the geology and plant life of the Mojave Desert.

Twenty miles north of the Cottonwood Visitor Center is the **Cholla Cactus Garden,** where you can walk the .25-mi loop through a dense concentration of bigelow cholla. A brochure available at the start of the trail helps identify the well-camouflaged homes of pack rats in the garden. Head to the **Cottonwood Springs Oasis** via the 1-mi round-trip trail that begins at sites 13A and 13B of the Cottonwood campground. Signs tell about the plants and animals of the Colorado Desert.

The **High View Nature Trail** is a 1.3-mi loop that climbs nearly to the top of Summit Peak (elevation 4,500 ft). The view makes the moderately steep, 300-ft elevation gain worth the effort. Start .5 mi west of the Black Rock Canyon campground. Look for wildlife along the .5-mi loop of **Indian Cove Trail,** but observe from a distance—animals are protected by federal law. This trail begins at the west end of Indian Cove campground and follows a desert wash. The 1.75-mi loop of the **Skull Rock Trail** begins near the Loop E entrance at Jumbo Rocks campground and guides hikers through boulder piles, desert washes, and a rocky alley. Don't miss the .5-mi paved **Oasis of Mara** trail or the 1-mi **Hidden Valley** loop (*see* The Best in One Day, *above*).

LONGER HIKES The **Fortynine Palms Oasis Trail** is a 3-mi round-trip that begins at the end of Canyon Road, which is off Highway 62, 4 mi west of the town of Twentynine Palms. Hikers should allow three hours for this moderately strenuous walk. The trail makes a steep climb into the hills, from which there is a good view of the lush oasis, then drops down into the canyon where the oasis is found. Sights within the oasis include fan palms, pools of water, and evidence of fires built by Native Americans for cooking and, occasionally, warmth. Petroglyphs can be found in some of the canyons above the oasis.

The 4-mi round-trip **Lost Horse Mine Trail** makes for a fairly strenuous hike along a former mining road to the site of a well-preserved stamp mill. The mill was used during the late 1890s to crush rock mined from the

nearby mountain in a search for gold. The operation was one of the most successful in the area, and the mine's cyanide settling tanks and stone buildings are the area's best preserved. You'll notice the relative absence of Joshua trees, which were used for fuel and have yet to regenerate. The hike begins at the parking area 1.25 mi east of Keys View Road. From the mine area, a short but steep 10-minute side trip takes you to the top of a 5,278-ft summit. Allow three to four hours for the entire walk.

Set aside four to six hours for the moderately strenuous, 7.5-mi round-trip **Lost Palms Oasis Trail,** which leads from Cottonwood Springs campground to the largest palm oasis in the park, with more than 100 palm trees set at the base of rugged canyon walls. The spring here bubbles from boulders, but disappears into the sandy, boulder-strewn canyon. This area, in the park's southeast corner, is one of the places where you might be lucky enough to spot bighorn sheep. From this trail, there are more technical side trips into Munsen Canyon that involve boulder scrambling.

The **Mastodon Peak Trail** is a 3-mi loop that starts at the Cottonwood Spring Oasis and climbs 420 ft in elevation. Gold was mined along this trail from 1919 to 1932. Be careful not to walk too close to the mouths of open mines. Southeast of the mining area, the trail heads for the peak. Some easy-to-moderate boulder scrambling is required to reach the top, but from the 3,371-ft summit, there are views of the Hexie Mountains, the Pinto Basin, and the Salton Sea. The peak draws its name from a large rock formation that miners during the late 1890s believed looked like the head of a prehistoric behemoth. It takes about two hours to hike to the top and back.

One of the best panoramic views in the park is your reward for hiking to the top of 5,461-ft **Ryan Mountain.** It's a 3-mi round-trip journey that will take two to three hours to complete, with an elevation gain of 981 ft. From the top, you can see Mt. San Jacinto, Mt. San Gorgonio, Lost Horse Valley, the Pinto Basin, and Queen and Pleasant valleys.

The 16-mi round-trip **Boy Scout Trail** runs through the westernmost edge of the Wonderland of Rocks. The northern trailhead is up the road from Indian Cove ranger station; the southern trailhead is about 4 mi west of Hidden Valley Campground along the main park road. On this moderately difficult trail you will see some of the park's most fascinating rock outcroppings.

The **California Riding and Hiking Trail** stretches for 35 mi between Black Rock Canyon Campground, in the west, and the north entrance, in the east. It is accessible to hikers and horseback riders. You can reach sections of the trail at its junction with Covington Flats, Keys View, and Geology Tour (near Squaw Tank) roads and at Ryan Campground—which means you don't have to cover the entire 35 mi, a trek that takes two to three days. The trail will give you a feeling for the higher elevations of Joshua Tree.

OTHER ACTIVITIES **Back-Road Driving.** Vehicles are not allowed off-road in Joshua Tree National Park, but there are a limited number of roads where four-wheel-drive is recommended. Before venturing out on any of these roads check with park officials. (For road description, *see* Biking, *below*.)

Biking. Cyclists should restrict the amount of time they spend on the park's fairly narrow main roads, where two-way traffic can be heavy. Mountain bikes are welcome in Joshua Tree, although they must remain on established roads. This is critical in this fragile environment, where off-road tracks can last for many years. Some suggested routes for mountain biking follow.

Beginning at the Cottonwood Visitor Center, the challenging 20-mi **Pinkham Canyon Road** travels along Smoke Tree Wash, then cuts down Pinkham Canyon. The road crosses soft sand and rocky flood plains and ends at a service road near I–10. The **Black Eagle Mountain Road** is a dead end that begins 6.5 mi north of the Cotton-

wood Visitor Center. This road runs along the edge of Pinto Basin (a flat, sandy, dry lake bed), then crosses a number of dry washes before navigating several of Eagle Mountain's canyons. The first 6 mi are within the park. Beyond is Bureau of Land Management land and a number of side roads. Stay away from the old mines you may see along the way. Beginning at the same place as the Black Eagle Road is the 23-mi **Old Dale Road.** The first 11 mi of this route run across Pinto Basin. The road then ascends a steep hill, crossing the national park boundary. At this point several side roads head off toward old mines and private residences. If you stay on the main road, you will come out on Highway 62, 15 mi east of Twentynine Palms.

A network of roads, totaling 13.5 mi, winds through **Queen Valley** and a huge grove of Joshua trees. You can begin at the Hidden Valley campground or at the dirt road across from the Geology Tour Road. Bike racks at the Barker Dam and Hidden Valley trailheads allow riders to lock up their bikes and go hiking. The **Geology Tour Road** turns south from the main paved road 2 mi west of Jumbo Rocks. The first sandy and bumpy 5.5 mi downhill leads to Squaw Tank, where a 6-mi circular route can be taken through Pleasant Valley. A guide to Geology Tour Road is available at the beginning of the road and at visitor centers.

Several roads in the **Covington Flats** area provide access to some of the park's largest Joshua trees, in addition to piñon pines, junipers, and areas of lush desert vegetation. One suggested ride runs from the Covington Flats picnic area to Eureka Peak, 3.75 mi one way. The dirt road is steep toward the end, but at the top riders are rewarded with views of Palm Springs, the surrounding mountains, and the Morongo Basin.

Rock Climbing. Joshua Tree National Park is one of the most popular climbing areas in the world, with more than 4,000 climbing routes. Climbers are asked to use existing trails to reduce vegetation trampling; contact any of the visitor centers for information on specific climbing routes. At least two companies have schools for climbers of varying abilities (*see* Guided Tours, *above*). The Joshua Tree climbers' brochure, written by climbers and park staff members, gives suggestions for reducing the impact of climbing on natural resources. Read it before you start out for the day.

CHILDREN'S PROGRAMS Programs designed to help children and their parents explore the desert environment are available from time to time, depending largely on the park's budget and staff during the given year. Call the superintendent's office (*see* Visitor Information, *above*) for current details. The park also has programs for school groups on a limited basis; prior arrangements are necessary.

EVENING ACTIVITIES Park rangers or volunteers present one-hour traditional campfire or slide programs every Saturday night from October through April. Topics include history, wildlife, and park management. The programs begin at 7 PM from October through the beginning of daylight savings time (early April), then move to 8 PM through the end of May. They may be held at the Black Rock Canyon information center or the Jumbo Rocks, Cottonwood, or Indian Cove campground amphitheaters. Check visitor centers for a current schedule.

DINING

There are no restaurants within Joshua Tree National Park, but there is a wide selection in the Morongo Basin, which borders the park's northern boundary. The area's eateries range from moderately priced to inexpensive and include plenty of fast-food franchises.

Stefano's. The best Italian restaurant in the basin, this small brasserie has only 16 tables set in two bright, airy, plant-filled dining rooms. The Venetian-style cuisine includes such specialties as chicken in marsala sauce with mushrooms and veal *à la limon*. Also popular are the daily fish combinations such as red snapper and salmon. Stefano's is on Highway 62, 2 mi west of the turnoff to the park's Black Rock entrance. *55509 Twentynine Palms Hwy., Yucca Valley, tel. 760/228–3118. AE, D, MC, V. No lunch Sun. $$*

Twentynine Palms Inn Restaurant. In its own building on the grounds of the historic Twentynine Palms Inn, this informal restaurant feels like a resort. A dozen interior tables share a room with a cocktail bar, and outside, diners at the half dozen tables encircling the pool are warmed with portable heaters. The service is friendly and efficient. Local residents mix with first-time and returning guests. The fare is primarily steak and seafood, but chicken and vegetarian dishes are available as well. The breads are homemade, and the herbs, in season, come from the inn's garden. The restaurant serves Sunday brunch. *73950 Inn Ave., Twentynine Palms, tel. 760/367–3505. AE, D, DC, MC, V. $$*

Edchada's. Rock climbers have long flocked to this Mexican restaurant, which recently opened a Twentynine Palms location in addition to the original in Yucca Valley. Both branches are large, crowded, and noisy—but everyone has a good time. Servings are huge. *56805 Twentynine Palms Hwy., Yucca Valley, tel. 760/365–7655. 2nd location: 73502 Twentynine Palms Hwy., Twentynine Palms, tel. 760/367–2131. AE, MC, V. $*

Finicky Coyote. A deli, specialty shop, and coffee house all in one, this place has Greek sandwiches, gyros, salads, soups, homemade fudge, yogurt, and espresso. It's a good place to stock up on picnic supplies or enjoy a meal on the patio to the sound of a trickling waterfall. *73511 Twentynine Palms Hwy., Twentynine Palms, tel. 760/367–2429. D, MC, V. $*

Ramona's. On the main drag at the west end of Twentynine Palms, Ramona's has a no-frills interior with Formica tables and amiable service. But it's what comes out of the kitchen that counts here. Try the burrito *ranchero,* an all-beef burrito with gua-camole, sour cream, green chilies, onions, and a special ranchero sauce; or the large combo, which includes two tacos, a chicken enchilada, a chili relleño, rice, and beans. *72115 Twentynine Palms Hwy., Twentynine Palms, tel. 760/367–1929. MC, V. Closed Sun. $*

Rocky's Pizzeria. Residents of Twentynine Palms come here when the urge for pizza strikes. You order your food at the counter, but it is served to you at your table or booth. The often-crowded restaurant can hold 185 people, and a party room seats 45. Rocky's is simple but neat; there are no tablecloths on the Formica tables, and the plates are plastic. The large selection of pizzas is sup-plemented by lasagna, spaghetti, and sand-wiches—including meatball, pastrami, and a supersub served hot or cold. *73737 Twen-tynine Palms Hwy., Twentynine Palms, tel. 760/367–9525. MC, V. $*

PICNIC SPOTS Since there are no stores or restaurants inside the park, you will have to pack a picnic lunch. Several stores in the Morongo Basin sell groceries and sand-wiches to go, and the restaurant at the Twentynine Palms Inn, off the park's north entrance, sells tasty box lunches for $7.50.

One standout spot for shelter and solitude amid the giant boulders is the designated picnic spot at **Hidden Valley,** where a lim-ited number of tables are shaded by trees. A 1-mi self-guided tour of the area provides an easy after-lunch walk. Nearby is **Live Oak,** which has tables, rock formations, and Joshua trees. Across the main road from the entrance to the Hidden Valley pic-nic area is a dirt road leading to **Barker Dam,** a refreshing spot for a picnic.

LODGING

Although there are no accommodations within the park's boundaries, lodgings in the Morongo Basin are open year-round. Among the pickings are bed-and-breakfasts with only two guest rooms, standard motor

lodges, and resorts that are more than 60 years old. If you are looking for a luxury hotel, however, you'll have to travel the 40 mi to Palm Springs. Lodgings in Twenty-nine Palms and Yucca Valley are within a few minutes' drive of the park's two north-ern entrances. The more desirable locations usually require reservations 30 days in advance for in-season weekends and the month of April.

Best Western Gardens. This two-story motel is on the Twentynine Palms High-way, close to the Twentynine Palms entrance to the park. It is in a business dis-trict and has no view and no trees, but it does provide Best Western–standard rooms. Suites with kitchenettes are next to the pool. *71487 Twentynine Palms Hwy., Twentynine Palms, CA 92277, tel. 760/367–9141, fax 760/367–2584. 84 rooms, 12 suites with kitchenettes. Facilities: pool, hot tub. AE, D, DC, MC, V. $$–$$$*

Twentynine Palms Inn. This inn in the Oasis of Mara has been in the family of owner Jane Grunt-Smith since it was built in the 1920s, before Joshua Tree became a national monument. The grounds comprise 30 acres with fan palms, a garden, and a 1-acre pond with ducks and a houseboat. The 17 separate cabins each accommodate two to five guests; 10 of them are constructed from adobe and 10 have a fireplace. All have porches. The inn gets a lot of repeat customers who cherish its intimacy and don't mind its offbeat nature. *73950 Inn Ave., Twentynine Palms, CA 92277, tel. 760/367–3505, fax 760/367–4425. 17 units. Facilities: restaurant, bar, pool, hot tub. AE, D, DC, MC, V. $$–$$$*

Circle C. Don't let the cinder-block con-struction of this Twentynine Palms motel fool you. Owners Frank and Cathie Kreutzberg have worked to make guests feel at home. The 12 units have kitchens stocked with a stove, refrigerator, microwave, toaster, coffeepot, dishes, and utensils. Rooms here average 450 square ft and have a TV and VCR. The two wings enclose a large, private garden area with a pool,

Jacuzzi, barbecue pits (necessities provided), and picnic tables. Each morning the staff sets out a Continental breakfast in the motel reception room. *6340 El Ray Ave., Twentynine Palms, CA 92277, tel. 760/367–7615, fax 760/361–0247. 12 units. Facilities: pool, hot tub. AE, D, DC, MC, V. $$*

Roughley Manor. This three-story, 1926 stone home sits on 25 palm-shaded acres. There's a hot breakfast every morning, and owner Jan Peters will pack a picnic lunch for $5 per person. *74744 Joe Davis Dr., Twentynine Palms, CA 92777, tel. 760/367–3238, fax 760/367–1690. 6 rooms. AE, MC, V. $$*

Tower Homestead. At the corner of Amboy and Mojave roads in Twentynine Palms, this circa-1932 bed-and-breakfast sits on 160 acres at the edge of town. The two high-ceiling guest suites are filled with functional antiques; each has its own living room and fireplace. *Box C-141, Twentynine Palms, CA 92277, tel. 760/367–7936. 2 rooms. No credit cards. $$*

Yucca Inn Motor Hotel. A convenient location—a few miles from the park's Black Rock entrance and very near a golf course—makes up for the nondescript decor. *7500 Camino Del Cielo, Yucca Valley, CA 92284, tel. 760/365–3311. 74 rooms. Facilities: restaurant, pool, hot tub, sauna, exercise room. AE, D, DC, MC, V. $*

CAMPING

INSIDE THE PARK Joshua Tree National Park has nine campgrounds with a total of 494 individual campsites and 22 group sites. On many weekends in fall and spring, all these campgrounds will fill up, so plan on arriving by Friday morning at the latest if you expect to find a site (especially from mid-March through mid-May). If you arrive later, try Cottonwood, Indian Cove, or Black Rock Canyon campgrounds first; these are usually the last to fill up. At press time, all campgrounds filled up on a first-come, first-served basis, though a new reservations system for particular camp-

grounds was expected to be in place by spring 1998.

Although RVs are permitted at all campgrounds, no hookups are available. Note that Belle and White Tank campgrounds have small sites with very little space for large vehicles to maneuver. Dump stations are at the Black Rock Canyon and Cottonwood campgrounds.

Camping within the park leans toward the primitive. Only Cottonwood and Black Rock Canyon have flush toilets and drinking water. All other campgrounds have chemical toilets and no water; be sure to bring a gallon of water per person per day. None of the campgrounds has showers. Each individual site can accommodate two cars, two tents, and six people, and each has a fire grate and picnic table. Campfires are allowed only in fire grates, and all wood must be brought in. It is illegal to collect and burn any vegetation in the park. Night temperatures at Joshua Tree can be cool any time of the year—bring a sweater or light jacket. The area is noted for its clean air, which makes for great stargazing.

At the south end of the park, at an elevation of 3,000 ft, the **Cottonwood Campground** is usually the last to fill up with 62 individual sites and three group sites that hold 10 to 25 people. The individual sites cost $8 per night per campsite, and the group sites are $25 per night for the entire site. Stays are limited to 30 days; no more than 14 of these days may be between September and May. The campground has flush toilets, drinking water, a disposal station, and a ranger station. It is open year-round.

Moving toward the interior of the park, **Belle** and **White Tank** campgrounds are next to each other at an elevation of 3,800 ft. These small, quiet campgrounds are very similar to each other: Belle has 17 campsites, White Tank has 15, and they both tend to draw a lot of families. Both have pit toilets, but no water; the nearest water is found at the Oasis Visitor Center, 9 mi away. There are a few big boulders to scramble on in this area, and a trail from White Tank leads to a natural arch. Belle is usually open from September through May, and White Tank is usually open year-round. (Both will close if the number of visitors to the park drops greatly, so it's best to call ahead.) There is no fee to camp at either place.

There are four campgrounds in the center of the park, around the perimeter of Queen Valley: Jumbo Rocks, Ryan, Hidden Valley, and Sheep Pass. They are at elevations of 4,200 to 4,500 ft, with cool nights from fall through spring. All four of these areas are very popular with climbers and tend to fill first.

Jumbo Rocks, with 125 sites, is in the heart of the park, near Geology Tour Road. There are pit toilets and no water. The campground is open year-round, with no fee for camping. **Ryan Campground** sits at the base of Ryan Mountain and has 29 free sites. This is one of two areas in the park where horses are permitted overnight, although the only corral is at Black Rock Canyon Campground (*see below*). It is also one of the more vegetated areas. Of these four campgrounds, **Hidden Valley** is the most popular among rock climbers, especially when Yosemite Valley becomes too cold for climbing. The free 39-site campground tends to be crowded until about June, when the rocks get too hot for climbers. It is situated among large boulders and relatively abundant vegetation, just off a dirt road that leads to Barker Dam. The **Sheep Pass Campground** is much like the Hidden Valley site, but it is reserved for groups only. There are six sites that accommodate 10 to 50 people each. The fee is $10 per night for the entire site, with a 14-day maximum stay. At 4,500 ft, Sheep Pass is the highest campground in the park. It is an isolated area, set among large boulders and relatively dense vegetation. The nearest water is at the Oasis Visitor Center, 16 mi away.

The 107-site **Indian Cove Campground** is also very popular with the climbing community, primarily because it sits at the base of the Wonderland of Rocks. The Wonderland, which separates this campground from the balance of the park, is so named for the more than 50 square mi of rugged mountains and boulder formations. At an elevation of 3,200 ft, Indian Cove can only be reached via a spur road off Highway 62, between Joshua Tree and Twentynine Palms. The campground has pit toilets, and water is available at the Indian Cove ranger station 2 mi away. Indian Cove is open year-round and charges $10 per night. (Its 13 group sites cost $20–$35 per night.)

Finally, there is the **Black Rock Canyon Campground,** reached via a 5-mi drive off Highway 62, just east of Yucca Valley. The 100 campsites sit among piñon pines, junipers, and Joshua trees. There are flush toilets and drinking water, and a ranger station is nearby. Horses are permitted. The fee is $10 per vehicle per night.

NEAR THE PARK In Twentynine Palms, the **Twentynine Palms RV Resort** (4949 Desert Knoll Ave., Twentynine Palms, CA 92277, tel. and fax 760/367–3320) has 198 full hookups, tennis courts, hot tub, sauna, exercise room, and a pool. The setting is a barren desert, but the resort is adjacent to a golf course. Rates are $22 per night, $105 per week.

Also in Twentynine Palms is the city-operated **Knott's Sky RV Park** (6897 El Sol Ave., Twentynine Palms, CA 92277, tel. 760/367–9669), which has 39 sites, all with water and electric hookups (25 of them have full hookups, including sewer and cable TV), a dump station, and rest rooms with showers. This RV park is also in a desert setting, but it has a grass playground, a few trees, and picnic tables. Tent camping is allowed. The area tends to draw senior citizens and international visitors. The park is gated and has a security patrol. Rates are $10.70 per night for a site with water and electricity, $16.16 for a full-hookup site.

Kenai Fjords National Park
Alaska

By Bill Sherwonit

nown for its abundant marine wildlife, tidewater glaciers, and the coastal fjords for which it is named, Kenai Fjords National Park is one of only three national parklands connected to Alaska's road system. This combination of diverse natural wonders and easy access—at least by Alaskan standards—has, in recent years, drawn steadily increasing numbers of visitors to the park. Still, most people see and touch only the park's outermost fringes; those who go beyond the coastal boat tours and limited trail system are almost guaranteed wilderness solitude in one of the nation's premier marine parklands.

Located along the southern edge of the Kenai Peninsula in Alaska's Southcentral region, 670,000-acre Kenai Fjords National Park was established in 1980, making it one of the state's newer parklands. As its name suggests, the park's landscape is dominated by a series of mountain fjords: long and steep-sided valleys carved by glaciers and now filled with seawater. No roads lead to these fjords; they are accessible only by floatplane or boat. During the summer, tour boats visit the fjords almost daily, though coastal storms and rough seas sometimes make boat travel impossible. Based in the nearby gateway community of Seward, the boats take visitors on daylong cruises into Holgate Arm and Aialik Bay, the best known of the park's fjords. Here, stopped in front of tidewater glaciers, you can sit among icebergs and listen to the sharp cracks and thunderous booms of calving ice, which may be heard from miles away.

Besides introducing visitors to glaciers, fjords, and steep-sided mountains, the coastal tours of the Kenai Fjords provide excellent opportunities to watch Alaska's marine life: In one tour alone, you may very well see orcas, humpback whales, sea otters, harbor seals, sea lions, tufted and horned puffins, kittiwakes, cormorants, and bald eagles. Sometimes, black bears are seen along the shore, and mountain goats are spotted in alpine meadows. For anglers, there are also opportunities to catch salmon and halibut in the park's coastal waters.

Beyond Aialik and Holgate are several more fjords, rarely visited except by boaters, fishermen, backpackers, and other adventurous explorers familiar with wilderness travel. These remote coastal areas are especially popular with sea kayakers, who camp on sand or gravel beaches or perhaps stay in one of the four public-use cabins built along the Kenai Fjords coast.

Looming high above the rugged coast is the Harding Icefield, one of only four in the United States. Fed by more than 400 inches of snow each year, the icefield and its dozens of glaciers cover more than 700 square mi. Isolated mountain peaks that rise above the ice are known as *nunataks,* an Eskimo name that means "lonely peaks." Few people visit here, except for occasional mountaineers and trekkers familiar with the dangers of glacier travel. It is possible, however, for day hikers to follow a safe trail that looks out over the icefield.

For all of Kenai Fjords' coastal splendors, its chief attraction is an inland glacier fed by the Harding Icefield. Two-thirds of all park visitors take the 9-mi gravel road that connects the Seward Highway to Exit Glacier. A gentle trail leads to the glacier's snout, where large mounds of rock debris have been deposited, while a steeper path enables visitors to peer into caverns beneath the ice and sometimes hear its groaning movements. There's a ranger cabin near Exit Glacier and naturalist programs are scheduled daily in summer. The road to Exit Glacier is the only one into Kenai Fjords National Park; it is open seasonally, usually from May through early October or until closed by snow.

ESSENTIAL INFORMATION

VISITOR INFORMATION Visitors can obtain information from park headquarters, near the small boat harbor at 1212 4th Avenue in Seward, or by writing to Superintendent, **Kenai Fjords National Park** (Box 1727, Seward, AK 99664, tel. 907/224–3175, fax 907/224–2144). The park also has recorded information at 907/224–2132. The **Alaska Public Lands Information Center (APLIC)** (605 W. 4th Ave., Anchorage, AK 99501, tel. 907/271–2737) provides information about state and federal park lands throughout Alaska. **Seward Chamber of Commerce** (2001 Seward Hwy., tel. 907/224–8051).

No backcountry permits are required at Kenai Fjords, but anyone heading into the backcountry is advised to get up-to-date information from park staff and to leave a travel itinerary with someone responsible. Though backcountry camping is still allowed throughout Kenai Fjords, up to 70,000 acres of parkland—mainly along the coast—have recently been transferred to nearby Native communities, because of land claims filed through the Alaska Native Claims Settlement Act. Coastal explorers should therefore contact **park headquarters** in Seward (see above) to check on the current land status of areas they plan to visit. Eventually, park maps will show how the boundaries have changed.

FEES Vehicles entering Kenai Fjords National Park at Exit Glacier must pay a $5 entry fee. Those who use any of the park's five public cabins are required to pay $30 per night (see Lodging, below).

PUBLICATIONS The park publishes an annual newspaper, *The Nunatak,* which includes information on glaciers, cabins, trails, no-trace camping, park programs, recreational activities, and other nearby parks, refuges, and national forest land. The newspaper, Kenai Fjords brochures, and other publications are available at park headquarters.

Books and maps about Kenai Fjords National Park can also be obtained through the **Alaska Natural History Association (ANHA),** in Anchorage's APLIC building (see above). *The Complete Guide to Kenai Fjords National Park, Alaska,* by Jim Pfeiffenberger, describes the area's geology, plants, animals, and human history and offers tips on what to see and do. **Trails Illustrated** (tel. 800/962–1643) has a detailed, water- and tear-proof map of Kenai Fjords, also available through ANHA. Another good reference is *A Guide to Alaska's Kenai Fjords,* by David William Miller.

GEOLOGY AND TERRAIN From its ocean shorelines to mountain peaks that reach elevations nearly 6,000 ft high (though most are less than 5,000), Kenai Fjords National Park encompasses a steeply rugged and starkly beautiful coastal region whose landscape is still being actively—sometimes violently—shaped by the forces of plate tectonics and glaciers. At the southern edge of the Kenai Peninsula, two of the Earth's crustal plates—the North American and Pacific—slowly grind against one another. This process has melted rocks, caused earthquakes, and built mountain ranges of mixed volcanic, sedimentary, and granite rocks. Yet even as uplift occurs in other areas, landmasses along the intersection of these plates are pulled downward. Over the millennia, high coastal peaks belonging to the Kenai Mountains have been dragged into the sea; former alpine valleys once filled with glaciers have become deepwater fjords, flanked by steep, forested rock walls; and high mountain peaks have been transformed into sea stacks or islands. As they push and grind against each other, the crustal plates sometimes produce large fault movements. In March 1964, the largest earthquake ever recorded in Alaska dropped the shoreline here 6 ft in a single day.

Even as these coastal lands slowly subside into the ocean, other forces are at work. Sitting a mile or more above the saltwater is Kenai Fjords' most dominant single feature, the Harding Icefield. The icefield had been known for centuries by native peoples living in the region, but it wasn't discovered by scientists until early in this century, when geologists mapping the peninsula realized that several coastal glaciers were being fed by the same massive ice system. Thirty-five miles long and 20 mi wide, the 300-square-mi ice field receives an estimated 35 to 65 ft of snow annually. Over time, the snow is transformed to ice, which in turn is acted upon by gravity and the pressure of its own weight to move slowly downslope.

The Harding Icefield feeds more than 30 named glaciers, plus many more that remain unnamed. As they move, these rivers of ice carve and gouge the landscape to form U-shape valleys and knife-edged ridges called arêtes. Eight of the park's glaciers flow right into the ocean; these so-called tidewater glaciers frequently calve huge blocks of ice into the ocean, some larger than houses. Such tidewater glaciers (in combination with the plate tectonics described above) helped form today's coastal fjords. During the Pleistocene Ice Ages, some glaciers cut trenches far below the present sea level; as the climate warmed, glaciers gradually retreated and the sea level rose, thus inundating what had been coastal valleys with ocean water.

Another glacier, Exit, is the park's primary visitor attraction, mainly because it's so easy to reach. A half mile wide, Exit Glacier descends about 2,500 ft over its 3-mi

length. Fed by the Harding Icefield, it is currently moving forward about 2 ft per day; but at the same time, it is melting 2½ ft per day—the net effect, therefore, is glacial retreat. Since 1750, Exit Glacier has retreated nearly 2 mi; in doing so, it has left several large piles of rock debris, called terminal moraines, where its leading edge once stood. Although there are few large streams within Kenai Fjords, Exit Glacier feeds one that runs along the park's northeastern edge, the Resurrection River. There are few lowland areas within the park boundaries; 90% or more of Kenai Fjords is at elevations above 2,000 ft.

FLORA AND FAUNA Most of the Kenai Fjords landscape consists of snow, ice, and rock. Along the park's shores, plant life is largely restricted to thin bands of coastal flatlands and the steep sides of mountains below the zone of perpetual snow and ice. Intertidal areas have a variety of algaes, including various seaweeds and kelp. Here you can also find snails, hermit crabs, mussels, clams, sea urchins, starfish, and sponges.

Beyond the intertidal zone, with its mud, sand, gravel, and rock beaches, is coastal forest, concentrated in a narrow zone from sea level to about a 1,000-ft elevation. The forest's trees are mostly Sitka spruce and two types of hemlock—mountain and western. But there are also pockets of birch and cottonwood trees. The most ancient of Kenai Fjords' evergreens may be 700 to 800 years old. Within these old-growth stands, the forest understory supports lush patches of blueberries and bright red or pale yellow salmonberries, prickly devil's club, ferns, and mosses. The berries and greens provide food for songbirds, voles, and even black bears. Scattered among the forest are other plant communities: bogs, marshes, and wildflower-rich lowland meadows with fireweed, lupine, chocolate lily, and beach pea. There are also patches of nearly impenetrable alder and willow.

Higher on the mountainsides are alpine tundra communities, with their complex mix of lichens, mosses, grasses, heathers, sedges, berries, dwarf willows, and wild-flowers. In midsummer, the tundra is a riot of color, with purplish-blue lupine, sky-blue Alaska forget-me-nots (the state flower), lavender wild geraniums, yellow paintbrush, red western columbine, deep purple monkshood and larkspur, fuchsia shooting stars, and white mountain avens. In autumn, as wildflowers go to seed, the willows and berry plants set the tundra ablaze with their mix of reds and golds.

Kenai Fjords' beaches, meadows, forests, and tundra are home to more than 30 species of land mammals, while its coastal waters are seasonally inhabited by a dozen or more marine mammals, five species of Pacific salmon, and numerous bottomfish, including halibut. More than a hundred species of birds have been identified here.

Especially popular with visitors are the marine animals, most easily seen on coastal boat tours. Sea otters, the smallest of the marine mammals, are often found floating on their backs among kelp beds, eating their favorite foods: mussels, clams, and sea urchins. A more high-profile coastal water dweller is the orca, also known as killer whale. Look for groups of them traveling in family pods; they are easily recognized by their white and black bodies and large dorsal fins. While many of the orcas are residents of the region, their cousins, the humpback whales, travel thousands of miles to come here each year, to feed in the biologically rich waters. Humpbacks are known to breach, or leap out of the water. Other marine mammals seen along the Kenai Fjords coast are sea lions; harbor seals; harbor and Dall's porpoise; and fin, gray, minke, and sei whales.

The coast is also summer home to dozens of shorebird species, including the black-legged kittiwake, common murres, rhinoceros and parakeet auklets, and—a visitor favorite—tufted and horned puffins. The horned puffin is recognized by its white breast, red-and-yellow bill, and hornlike bit of fleshy tissue above each eye. Tufted puffins have orange bills, all-black bodies, and yellow tufts of hair that trail from their heads. Bald eagles can often be spotted perched in spruce trees above the water, or soaring overhead. Also inhabiting the park are numerous types of waterfowl, including four species of loons, several species of owls and hawks, the rufous hummingbird, and dozens of songbirds, including black-capped chickadees, yellow-rumped warblers, American robins, and ruby-crowned kinglets.

Among the land mammals, perhaps the easiest to spot are mountain goats, often seen as distant white dots on mountainsides. In summer they inhabit the park's high alpine areas, grazing on grasses, herbs, and low-growing shrubs; in winter, most descend to the tree line or below, though some remain on windswept ridges. Look for their small, black spiked horns during coastal tours and on the mountainsides near Exit Glacier. Another high-profile alpine resident in the Exit Glacier area is the hoary marmot, a tundra rodent that grows up to 10 pounds or more. Marmots are known for their alarm call, a loud, high-pitched whistle. Less commonly seen but also present in the high alpine are grizzly bears, which feed on a mix of plants, carrion, and other mammals.

Forest residents include black bears, moose, red squirrels, wolverines, porcupines, coyotes, and wolves. One of the few places in Kenai Fjords that moose are likely to be seen is the Exit Glacier area, where they feed on willow and other browse. Black bears are common throughout the park's forested areas and may be spotted as they feed on plants near the tree line or fish for salmon in coastal streams.

WHEN TO GO Summer is by far the most popular time to visit Kenai Fjords: The weather is mild, and wildlife-viewing is at its peak. Most people visit from mid-May through mid-September; tours are most frequently booked in July and August. Even in summer, overcast and cool days are the norm, with daytime temperatures ranging from the mid-40s into the low 70s. Nighttime temperatures occasionally dip below freezing, especially at higher altitudes. May is the driest of the warm-weather months, with succeeding months increasingly wet and stormy; however, fierce coastal storms may occur at any time. The road to Exit Glacier opens in spring when the snow has melted and remains open in fall until snow makes it impassable, usually in early to mid-October.

SEASONAL EVENTS **Fourth of July.** Seward, the gateway to Kenai Fjords, has gained a reputation as one of the best places in Alaska to celebrate **Independence Day.** The town's primary attraction is the Mount Marathon Race. For more than 80 years, mountain runners have competed in this annual race to the top of Mount Marathon, a 3,022-ft peak that overlooks Seward and Resurrection Bay. The race annually attracts hundreds of runners and thousands of spectators, as Seward, population 2,500, swells with 10,000 to 15,000 people. Though the race is the day's big event, Seward also hosts a July Fourth parade, softball games, fireworks, arts and crafts displays, and dozens of food stands. For more information, contact the Seward Chamber of Commerce (*see* Visitor Information, *above*).

WHAT TO PACK Cool and often wet weather demands clothing that will keep you warm and dry; a wool cap and gloves or mittens are especially important. Knee-high rubber boots are recommended for coastal visits.

There are no places to purchase food within the park, but supplies are available in Seward. Food on tour boats is expensive, so many people bring their own bag lunches. Given the abundance of wildlife, binoculars and camera or video gear are highly recommended.

Mosquitoes, biting flies, and flealike critters known locally as no-see-ums can be a problem throughout the spring, summer, and fall, so insect repellent is a must.

GENERAL STORES Seward has two stores stocked with food, fuel, and other camping supplies. The **Eagle Quality Store** (tel. 907/224–3698) is open seven days a week, 24 hours a day year-round, while **Pace Co.** (tel. 907/224–2081) is open daily from 6 AM to 10 PM in summer and from 8 to 8 in winter.

ARRIVING AND DEPARTING Most of Kenai Fjords is easily accessible only by plane or boat, though the Exit Glacier area is connected to the state's highway system by a 9-mi gravel road. Most coastal tours begin in Seward, while plane rides into the park may be arranged in either Seward or Homer. Seward, the principal gateway into Kenai Fjords, can be reached via the Seward Highway or the Alaska Railroad; Homer can be reached by Seward and Sterling highways. Both towns also have regularly scheduled commuter flights to and from Anchorage in summer.

By Boat. Ferries within the **Alaska Marine Highway System** (Box 25535, Juneau, AK 99802-5535, tel. 800/642–0066) won't take you into the park, but they regularly visit Seward during the summer. Costs depend on your point of origin. Several **cruise ship** lines also regularly visit Seward in summer; check with the Seward Chamber of Commerce (*see* Visitor Information, *above*) for specifics. Once in Seward, you can arrange transportation to and from the park with the many charter-boat businesses that operate in Kenai Fjords. A list of boat charters based in Seward can be obtained from *The Nunatak* or the Seward Chamber of Commerce (tel. 907/224–8051); *see also* Guided Tours, *below.*

By Bus. The **Seward Bus Line** (Box 1338, Seward, AK 99664, tel. 907/224–3608 or 907/563–0800) provides daily service between Anchorage and Seward year-round; the one-way fare is $30. **Grayline of Alaska** (745 W. 4th, Suite 200, Anchorage, AK 99501, tel. 907/277–5581) has daily motor-coach service from May through September; its one-way fare is $40. Grayline also has tour packages that combine motor-coach travel with coastal tours into Kenai Fjords as well as motor-coach–railroad combination trips (*see* Guided Tours, *below*).

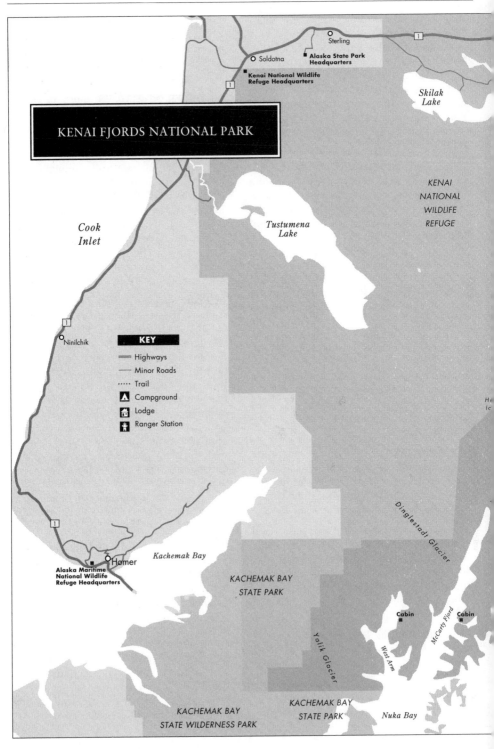

KENAI FJORDS NATIONAL PARK

Sterling

O Soldotna

■ Alaska State Park
Headquarters

■ Kenai National Wildlife
Refuge Headquarters

1

*Skilak
Lake*

*KENAI
NATIONAL
WILDLIFE
REFUGE*

*Cook
Inlet*

*Tustumena
Lake*

1

O Ninilchik

KEY

▬▬ Highways

— Minor Roads

···· Trail

▲ Campground

⌂ Lodge

🛉 Ranger Station

Dinglestadi Glacier

1

O Homer

■ Alaska Maritime
National Wildlife
Refuge Headquarters

Kachemak Bay

*KACHEMAK BAY
STATE PARK*

Cabin ■

McCarty Fjord

■ Cabin

Yalik Glacier

West Arm

*KACHEMAK BAY
STATE WILDERNESS PARK*

*KACHEMAK BAY
STATE PARK*

Nuka Bay

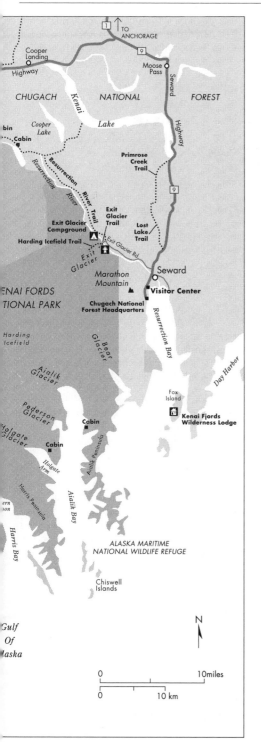

By Car or RV. Kenai Fjords is approximately 120 mi south of Anchorage via the Seward Highway, one of Alaska's most scenic roadways. As you leave Anchorage bound for Seward, the highway winds along Turnagain Arm, a scenic stretch of Cook Inlet; it then passes through the beautiful Chugach and Kenai mountains and along turquoise-colored Kenai Lake. Total travel time between the communities is about 2½ hours in summer. The only road entering Kenai Fjords is at milepost 3.7, where a 9-mi road leads to the Exit Glacier, the park's top visitor attraction.

RV rentals are available in Anchorage; the daily cost averages $125 to $150 for a four-person motor home. Call **Murphy's RV** (Box 202063, Anchorage, AK 99520-2063, tel. 907/ 276–0688), **ABC Motorhome Rentals** (2360 Commercial Dr., Anchorage, AK 99501, tel. 907/279–2000), or **Clippership Motorhome Rentals** (5401 Old Seward Hwy., Anchorage, AK 99518, tel. 907/562–7051).

By Plane. Most backcountry travelers wishing to explore the Kenai Fjords coast charter floatplanes in Seward, though some of the park's westernmost bays and fjords are more conveniently reached from Homer, another small coastal town. The park's newspaper, *The Nunatak,* lists air-taxi and flight-seeing operations based in Seward, Homer, and other Kenai Peninsula towns.

By Train. The **Alaska Railroad** (Box 107500, Anchorage, AK 99510-7500, tel. 907/265–2494 or 800/544–0552) doesn't pass through Kenai Fjords, but it does take passengers from Anchorage to Seward from mid-May to mid-September. From there, passengers can arrange boat or plane rides into the park. From mid-May through September 1, the train leaves Anchorage daily at 6:45 AM and arrives in Seward at 11:15 AM. It then departs Seward at 6 PM and gets back to Anchorage at 10:30 PM. In September, the train operates on weekends only. The peak-season (June 4 to September 1) fare is $50 one way or $80 round-trip. The off-season fare is $45 one way or $68 round-trip.

EXPLORING

The best and easiest way to see Kenai Fjords' rugged coastline and wildlife is to go with one of the many coastal tour boats that visit the park's more accessible fjords daily in summer. Flightseeing trips allow you to see the park's ruggedly beautiful land- and seascape from above. A third option is to drive to Exit Glacier, where trails bring you close to the ice that continues to shape this landscape. Although maintained trails are few, there's one that brings hikers to a ridge that overlooks the Harding Icefield.

Wilderness adventurers may wish to explore the park's remote coastal areas by sea kayak, and either camp on one of its many beaches or stay at one of the remote public-use cabins. For experienced mountaineers and trekkers, there's also the challenge of crossing the Harding Icefield.

THE BEST IN ONE DAY If you only have a day, you can spend it visiting Exit Glacier or taking a coastal tour. Given the long daylight hours of Alaska's summers, it's possible to do both. And you might be able to sneak in a flight-seeing tour, or take in a naturalist program as well.

Coastal boat tours into the park last from eight to nine hours. These allow you to visit the steep-sided coastal fjords for which the park is famous. Moreover, these tours afford the greatest opportunities to see the park's marine life: You're almost certain to encounter sea otters, puffins, bald eagles, sea lions, and seals—and there's a good chance that you'll also see a humpback or killer whale, not to mention mountain goats and black bears. Weather permitting, the boats will take you near a tidewater glacier, where, if you're lucky, you'll see and hear huge chunks of ice crashing into the ocean.

At Exit Glacier, you'll have a chance to approach one of Alaska's most accessible "rivers of ice"—but you don't want to get too close; visitors are required to stay off the glaciers, which can be extremely dangerous with their crevasses and occasional ice falls. In summer, park rangers lead daily guided activities, including nature walks and campfire programs. For more adventurous hikers, a steep alpine trail leads into the mountains above Exit Glacier (*see* Longer Hikes, *below*).

Take time to explore the valley below Exit Glacier: Here the relationship of plant communities to recently glaciated areas is wonderfully displayed. As glaciers recede, they leave bare rock or sterile, rocky debris. Over time, this "barren" ground is recolonized by a series of well-defined plant communities. This so-called plant succession begins with lichens and mosses and is followed by early colonizer wildflowers such as fireweed and dryas. These, in turn, are followed by dense alder-willow thickets, cottonwood trees, and eventually, a "climax forest" of Sitka spruce and hemlocks. From start to finish, it takes about 300 years to move from bare ground to spruce-hemlock forest. All stages of this succession can be identified in this single valley.

ORIENTATION PROGRAMS Interpretive programs take place at **park headquarters** (tel. 907/224–3175) in Seward and at the **Exit Ranger glacier station** (*see* Visitor Information, *above*). Free naturalist and ranger-led activities occur daily in summer, including guided nature walks through the forest and to the snout of Exit Glacier. There are also self-guided walks with natural-history displays that explain glacial processes and describe the types of wildlife found in the park. A 12-minute slide show on the park is given several times daily at headquarters; natural history or adventure films are occasionally shown as well. Recorded information on park programs can be obtained by calling 907/224–2132.

GUIDED TOURS The most popular guided activities are the coastal boat tours that leave Seward several times each day during the summer. It's possible to take half-day tours of Resurrection Bay, but to enter one of the park's fjords you must take a daylong cruise. Weather and ocean conditions permitting, the boats may visit Aialik Bay or, less commonly, Northwestern Fjord. There you'll get close-up looks at one of Kenai Fjords' tidewater glaciers (from a safe distance, of course); and you'll see abundant wildlife (see The Best In One Day, above). Most tours also include stops at sea lion and seabird rookeries in the Chiswell Islands, which are part of the Alaska Maritime National Wildlife Refuge. There are few other places in Alaska where such a variety of marine life can be viewed within a short distance of town.

Mariah Tours (3812 Katmai Circle, Anchorage, AK 99517, tel. 907/243–1238 or 907/224–8623) offers a "small ship alternative" to coastal sightseeing, with boats that carry no more than 22 passengers (the larger tours may carry 100 or more). Mariah schedules four-hour tours of Resurrection Bay and 8- to 9½-hour tours to Aialik Bay and Northwestern Fjord, respectively, from mid-April through the end of September. Costs range from $63 to $121. Prices don't include meals. Mariah also provides drop-off and pick-up service for sea kayakers who want to explore the park's backcountry coastline on their own. **Kenai Fjords Tours** (Box 1889, Seward, AK 99664, tel. 907/224–8068 or 800/478–8068) leads a three-hour natural-history tour of Resurrection Bay, a five-hour whale-watching tour (April 1 to mid-May only), and full-day cruises to Aialik Bay or Northwestern Fjord. Costs, including meals, range from $57 to $146. The company also has tour packages that include rail and/or motor-coach transportation to and from Anchorage, plus two overnight tours that include a one-night stay at Kenai Fjords Wilderness Lodge (see Lodging, below). **Major Marine Tours** (Box 338, Seward, AK 99664, tel. 907/274–7300 or 800/764–7300) has afternoon and evening half-day tours that cost $72 with an all-you-can-eat buffet, or $63 without; its all-day tour to Holgate Glacier in Aialik Bay includes natural-history presentations by a park ranger. It also has junior ranger programs for children. The

eight-hour tour costs $103 with buffet, $93 without.

Tour packages that combine coastal boat tours into Kenai Fjords with motor-coach and/or railroad transportation between Anchorage and Seward can be arranged through either **Kenai Fjords Tours** (see above) or **Grayline of Alaska** (see Arriving and Departing, above). Costs range from $129 to $209. Another option is **Alaska Snail Trails** (Box 210894, Anchorage, AK 99521, tel. 907/337–7517), which conducts 10-day minibus tours between Seward and Denali national parks, including a six-hour coastal tour of the Kenai Fjords. The company specializes in people with disabilities and senior citizens; group size is limited to 12 people. The cost is $2,550.

Sunny Cove Sea Kayaking Company (Box 111283, Anchorage, AK 99511, tel. 907/345–5339) leads weeklong trips in and around Kenai Fjords National Park, including five nights of camping at Northwestern Fjord. There, kayakers can paddle among icebergs, seals, and seabirds, as tidewater glaciers calve in the distance. The cost, $1,295, includes one night at Kenai Fjords Wilderness Lodge (see Lodging, below). The company also teams up with Kenai Fjords Tours for a combination one-day wildlife cruise and three-hour wilderness paddle, and can arrange custom trips into the park. Guided sea-kayak trips in Kenai Fjords are also available from **Dennis Eagen** (Box 110047, Anchorage, AK 99511, tel. 907/653–7575), who specializes in five- to 10-day customized expeditions for one to six people. Both novice and experienced kayakers are welcome. Costs average $1,200 for a five-day trip. **Coastal Kayaking and Custom Adventures Worldwide** (414 K St., Anchorage, AK 99501, tel. 907/258–3866 or 800/288–3134) leads guided day trips in Resurrection Bay for $95 and also organizes longer customized expeditions into Kenai Fjords for groups of up to 10 people. Prices vary, depending on the number of people and length of trip. The company also rents kayaks for those who wish to go exploring on their own. **Alaska Kayak Paddlesport Outfitters** (Box 233725, Anchorage, AK 99523, tel. 907/243–2998) leads custom trips into Aialik Bay for five to seven days, with groups of up to eight people; costs vary but average about $1,000 to $1,400. **Fox Island Charters** (Box 695, Seward, AK 99664) provides boat transportation from Seward into the park for sea kayakers and other coastal explorers. Costs depend on destination and number of people.

Scenic Mountain Air (Box 4, Moose Pass, AK 99631, tel. 907/288–3646 or 907/224–7277) provides flight-seeing tours over the Harding Icefield and along Kenai Fjords' remote outer coast; flight time ranges from 40 minutes ($99) to 1½ hours ($199). Scenic Mountain also conducts wildlife-viewing flights and fly-in-and-hike tours. Other air-taxi operators that fly backcountry travelers in and out of Kenai Fjords are **Kachemak Air Service** (Box 1769, Homer, AK 99603, tel. 907/235–8924), **Bald Mountain Air Service** (Box 3134, Homer, AK 99603), and **Bear Lake Air** (HCR 64, Box 386, Seward, AK 99664). Prices depend on the length of the flight and number of passengers.

SCENIC DRIVES AND VIEWS The only drive into Kenai Fjords is the 9-mi road to Exit Glacier. The last couple miles afford excellent views of the glacier, the Kenai Mountains, and the Resurrection River valley.

NATURE TRAILS AND SHORT WALKS The park's only developed trail system is in the Exit Glacier area. A network of short trails begins at the ranger station; the most popular is the flat, half-mile-long **Exit Glacier Trail** that leads to the glacier's face (the first .25 mi is paved; the remainder is gravel). As you approach Exit Glacier, you can wander along the flat outwash plain or ascend a steeper side trail that passes along the glacier's edge. Whichever route you take, flat or steep, it's less than a mile's walk from the parking lot to the glacier. There's also a 1- to 1.5-mi nature-trail loop that begins at the ranger station and winds through forest and along Exit Glacier Creek. Interpretive displays at the ranger station and a small shelter along the main trail provide information on Kenai Fjords' glaciers, the Harding Icefield, and resident wildlife.

LONGER HIKES The **Harding Icefield Trail** is Kenai Fjords' only maintained backcountry trail—and one of the few anywhere in the world that leads to an ice field overlook. The 4-mi ice field trail branches off the Exit Glacier Trail about a half mile past the ranger station. Rising 3,000 ft, this often steep path passes through thick forest; then, after a series of switchbacks, it rises above the tree line and into alpine tundra. In midsummer, the tundra is beautifully colored by dozens of wildflower species. Several points along the way provide sweeping panoramic views of the Kenai Mountains, Resurrection River valley, and pale-blue glaciers. Walking through the tundra, you're also likely to see marmots, mountain goats, and perhaps even a brown or black bear. Eventually the trail moves beyond the tundra onto bare rock and remnant snowfields. If you follow it to the end, you'll pass a small mountain shelter and come out on a rocky ledge where you can look out over the vast expanse of the Harding Icefield. Allow four to eight hours to complete the entire round-trip journey. The trail rises steeply in places, making the hike somewhat strenuous for anyone who is not in good physical shape. Because it traverses fragile tundra, park managers ask visitors to stay on the designated path, to prevent trampling of the vegetation and subsequent erosion.

Beyond its limited trail system, Kenai Fjords presents unlimited hiking, mountaineering, and trekking opportunities for experienced backcountry travelers. Those who leave the trail system should be educated in wilderness travel and no-trace camping techniques. Whenever heading into the backcountry, leave an itinerary with someone you trust and notify park rangers of your plans, including your expected return date. The **University of Alaska Anchorage's Alaska Wilderness Studies Program** (AWS/UAA, College of Community and Continuing Education,

3211 Providence Dr., K134, Anchorage, AK 99508, tel. 907/786–4066) and **Mountaineering Club of Alaska** (Box 102037, Anchorage, AK 99510) sometimes organize wilderness treks across the Harding Icefield.

OTHER ACTIVITIES Fishing. Many of the park's remote streams have salmon runs, though the number of salmon may be small. One major fly-in fishing destination is the Delight Spit area within McCarty Fjord, where a large run of silver salmon returns each summer. Halibut-fishing charters in Resurrection Bay and nearby coastal waters are also available. **Miller's Landing Fishing Camp** (Box 81, Seward, AK 99664, tel. 907/224–5739) has guided fishing charters for salmon, halibut and other bottomfish, as well as boat rentals, water-taxi services, tent camping, oceanfront fishing cabins, bait, tackle, and "fishing advice." A complete list of fishing-charter businesses can be obtained from the **Seward Chamber of Commerce** (tel. 907/224–8051). Licenses are required for both fresh and saltwater fishing. The cost for a three-day, non-resident license is $15; they can be purchased at most general stores in Anchorage or Seward.

Flight-Seeing. Small-plane tours of Kenai Fjords give you a different perspective on the park's rugged landscape and its vast wilderness (*see* Guided Tours, *above*).

Sea Kayaking. Aialik and Harris Bays, Northwestern Lagoon, McCarty Fjord, and North Arm are major destinations among sea kayakers. Experienced long-distance paddlers sometimes begin their journeys in Seward, but most kayakers arrange either boat or plane transportation into the park and then spend their time exploring one or more of its fjords. For those who enjoy backcountry solitude, kayaking is a wonderful way to see marine wildlife in the park's most remote corners, far from tourboat traffic. Kayakers may either camp in tents or stay in one of the park's public-use cabins, which must be reserved in advance (*see* Lodging, *below*).

Kayakers may rent equipment from **Kenai Fjords Kayaks** (tel. 800/992–3960), **Coastal Kayaking and Custom Adventures Worldwide** (tel. 907/258–3866 or 800/288–3134), or **Sunny Cove Sea Kayaking Company** (tel. 907/345–5339). Because the park's coastal areas are frequently subject to stormy weather, only experienced paddlers should attempt their own sea kayaking trips into the park. Another option is to arrange a guided kayaking expedition (*see* Guided Tours, *above*). An information packet on kayaking opportunities and destinations can be obtained from park headquarters (*see* Visitor Information, *above*).

Ski Touring and Snowmobiling. In winter, Exit Glacier Road closes to cars and opens to skiers, snowshoers, mushers (dogsledders), and snowmobiles. Winter visitors who wish to remain in the park overnight may either camp or stay at the Exit Glacier public-use cabin, which must be reserved in advance (*see* Lodging, *below*).

Wildlife Viewing. Kenai Fjords' abundant marine wildlife is one of its primary visitor attractions. The best way to see marine mammals, eagles, and seabirds is to take one of the coastal boat tours (*see* Guided Tours, *above*). Viewing opportunities are best from May through September. Visitors are also likely to see many birds and mammals—everything from sparrows and squirrels to marmots, eagles, moose, and mountain goats—while hiking the Exit Glacier and Harding Icefield trails.

EVENING ACTIVITIES Campfire programs are sometimes presented by park rangers or naturalists. Pick up a schedule at **park headquarters** or the **Exit Glacier ranger station** (along the path to Exit Glacier).

DINING

Standard diner-type restaurants with a small-town atmosphere serve mostly seafood.

NEAR THE PARK Christo's Palace. One of the oldest restaurants in Seward, Christo's has an eclectic menu of Mexican, Italian, and traditional American fare. Meals are served in a simply decorated, casual setting. After 5 PM there's a free pizza-delivery service. *133 4th Ave., Seward, tel. 907/224–5255. AE, D, DC, MC, V. $–$$*

Harbor Dinner Club. Run by the same family since 1958, this newly expanded eatery serves local seafood and other standard fare in a simple, comfortable dining room with a view of Resurrection Bay and the surrounding mountains. *220 5th Ave., Seward, tel. 907/224–3012. AE, D, DC, MC, V. $–$$*

Peking Restaurant. The Chinese menu is supplemented by the standard halibut and salmon selections. *338 4th Ave., Seward, tel. 907/224–5444. D, MC, V. $–$$*

Ray's Waterfront. As the name suggests, this restaurant is near the Seward harbor and has views of Resurrection Bay. Clam chowder is a specialty. *Seward small-boat harbor, tel. 907/224–5606. AE, D, DC, MC, V. Closed in winter. $–$$*

PICNIC SPOTS The park has one picnic area, with tables and a nearby water pump, along the Exit Glacier Trail. The area is enclosed, to offer some protection from the region's often wet and cool weather.

LODGING

No privately owned accommodations are operated within the park, but Seward has plenty of hotels, inns, and cabins. The Seward Chamber of Commerce (tel. 904/224–8051) lists more than three dozen bed-and-breakfasts in and around Seward. There are also a couple of lodges near the park. Backcountry hikers and sea kayakers also make use of several public-use cabins.

IN THE PARK **Public-use Cabins.** Of Kenai's five public-use cabins, four are located along the coast, at Aialik Bay, North and Holgate Arms, and Delight Creek. Accessible by boat or floatplane, these coastal cabins are for summer use only and must be reserved in advance, by mail or by phone,

through the park headquarters in Seward (*see* Visitor Information, *above*). The rental cost is $30 per night, with a three-night limit at all but North Rim, where the limit is nine nights. Cabins can accommodate up to eight people; amenities include oil-burning stoves to heat the cabins (users must provide their own fuel), pit toilet, bunkbeds, table and chairs, countertops and shelves for food storage, and porches. Cabin users must provide their own cooking stove and cooking fuel, bedding, and eating utensils. Water is available in nearby streams and should be treated; food must be properly stored.

The park's only winter cabin, at Exit Glacier, is used by skiers, mushers, and snowmobiles. This cabin is a little more luxurious than the others; it comes equipped with two bedrooms, table, chairs, sofa, and bunkbeds with mattresses. It is propane-heated, so there's no need for fuel; and there's a stove with a range for cooking, plus kitchen utensils. Users must supply their own water, however. As with the others, the Exit Glacier cabin has a three-night limit.

NEAR THE PARK **Kenai Fjords Wilderness Lodge.** An hour's boat ride from Seward, this wilderness lodge sits within a quiet, forest-lined cove on Fox Island in Resurrection Bay. Cabins are tucked inside the spruce forest beside a small lake; each has expansive views of the bay and surrounding mountains, as well as private baths with shower, two beds, and woodstoves. Meals are served family-style in the main lodge building. Guided kayak trips and coastal wildlife and glacier tours can be arranged upon request, and hiking trails abound. *Box 1889, Seward, AK 99664, tel. 907/224–8068 in summer, 907/276–6249 in winter, 800/478–8068 for reservations, fax 907/224-8934. 4 rooms in main lodge, 6 cabins. Facilities: dining room, hiking. AE, D, MC, V. Closed in winter. $$$*

Seward Windsong Lodge. Built in 1997, this lodge sits in a forested setting near the banks of the Resurrection River. It's near mile 0.6 of Exit Glacier Road, a short drive from both the glacier and downtown Seward. The lodge has modern rooms with double beds, full private baths, and coffeemakers; you also get a view of the mountains or the river. Continental breakfast is served, and sandwiches or snack food can be prepared upon request. Guided tours can be arranged through Kenai Fjords Tours; shuttle-bus service to the Alaska Railroad depot can also be arranged. *Box 221011, Anchorage, AK 99515, tel. 907/ 245–0200 or 800/265–0201. 24 rooms. AE, D, MC, V. Closed in winter. $$$*

Best Western Hotel Seward. Decorated in gold-rush style, this downtown hotel has rather fancy rooms with phones, VCRs, and king- or queen-size beds. Several of the rooms have views of Resurrection Bay. The hotel runs shuttles to the harbor and is close to the ferry terminal. *221 5th Ave., Box 670, Seward, AK 99664, tel. 907/224– 2378 or 800/528–1234, fax 907/224–3112. 38 rooms. AE, D, DC, MC, V. $$–$$$*

Van Gilder Hotel. This aging but dignified three-story stucco building is listed on the National Register of Historic Places. Some rooms have brass beds, pedestal sinks, and claw-foot tubs. *308 Adams St., Box 2, Seward, AK 99664, tel. 907/224-3079; 800/ 204–6835 outside AK; fax 907/224–3689. 25 rooms. AE, D, DC, MC, V. $$*

CAMPING

INSIDE THE PARK With only one small campground inside Kenai Fjords park, most of the camping around here is backcountry-style, usually along the coast. Wilderness campers are asked to use no-trace camping techniques to minimize impact on the landscape. Recommended practices are discussed in the park's newspaper, *The Nunatak,* available from either park headquarters or APLIC (*see* Visitor Information, *above*).

INSIDE THE PARK **Exit Glacier Campground.** A quarter-mile hike from the parking area, this small campground has eight walk-in sites, available on a first-come, first-served basis. There are no facilities, and camping is free. Call park headquarters (*see* Visitor Information, *above*) for information.

NEAR THE PARK **Seward Municipal Campground** (tel. 907/224–3331) lies along Resurrection Bay and has a 25 designated sites with electrical hookups, in addition to limited space for tent and RV camping. It's available on a first-come, first-served basis. Hookup sites cost $15 per night; undesignated sites cost $6 for tents and $8 for RVs.

A Creekside RV Park (tel. 907/224–3647), at mile 6.5 of the Seward Highway, has 20 tent sites ($15 per night) and 20 RV sites ($26 per night). Amenities include showers, firewood, and picnic tables. The campground is closed in winter.

A half mile up Bear Creek Road, at milepost 6.5 of the Seward Highway, **Bear Creek RV Park** (tel. 907/224–5725) is open year-round and caters to RV owners. Fifty sites with full hookups cost $22 per night.

The family-operated **Miller's Landing Fishing Camp** (tel. 907/224–5739) sits along the Resurrection Bay shoreline on a former homestead; it can be reached by driving out Lowell Point Road, south of town. The 50 campsites, some in the forest and some facing the beach, cost $15 per night, $20 with electrical hookups; the fee includes bathroom and shower facilities. In addition, the Millers rent out four cabins for $40 to $60 per night; although outfitted with wood-burning stoves, they have no electricity or plumbing (there is a water source nearby). Millers Landing also has boat rentals, a boat-launching service, fishing charters, water-taxi services, general store, and kayak drop-offs and pickups. The campground is closed in winter.

Mesa Verde National Park
Colorado

Updated by Diana Lambdin Meyer

he Four Corners area, where Arizona, Utah, New Mexico, and Colorado square off, has long drawn visitors with a sense of wonder about those who inhabited this land more than a millennium ago. Signs of complex societies, some of them extremely well preserved, are widespread throughout the region—in Arizona's Canyon de Chelly, for example, and New Mexico's Chaco Canyon. Perhaps no more illuminating experience of our nation's cultural past can be found than in southwest Colorado, at Mesa Verde National Park, where the dwellings of the ancestral Puebloan people remain.

Rising dramatically from the San Juan Basin, Mesa Verde is much more than an archaeologist's dreamland. The Spanish translation, "Green Table," accurately describes the lushness of the area: It was the piñon pine-juniper forest blanketing the slopes of this flat-topped mountain that first attracted the nomadic ancestral Puebloan people to settle here. A series of complex canyons cut the park into a number of smaller mesas, allowing for spectacular views across to the cliff dwellings and sheer mountain faces. As you wind your way up along the park's twisting roads, sudden sweeping vistas of the Mancos and Montezuma valleys unfold. The sand-color dwellings dwarfed by towering cliffs appear almost as a natural occurrence in the midst of the desert's harsh beauty.

The inhabitants of Mesa Verde, called Anasazis by the Navajo people, lived peacefully in the area for 700 years, from about AD 500 to 1300. Their reasons for leaving the region have been the subject of widespread speculation, but it's clear that a prolonged drought was in large part responsible. The history of these people unfolds as you walk through sites ranging from the simple pit houses built before AD 750 to huge multistory complexes constructed less than 100 years before their builders migrated south.

Spanish and Mexican explorers used the mesa as a landmark in the 18th and early 19th centuries, but didn't penetrate its interior. In the 1870s, a few of the cliff dwellings were discovered by U.S. adventurers, but it wasn't until the Wetherill family began to explore—some would say exploit—the mesa in 1888 that the full extent of its treasures became widely known. Due in large part to the efforts of Virginia McClurg and Lucy Peabody, who campaigned tirelessly to protect the dwellings, Mesa Verde National Park was created in 1906. In order to divert crowds from the increasingly popular Chapin Mesa sites, Wetherill Mesa was opened to the public in 1972. In 1978 Mesa Verde became one of the first eight places to be designated a World Cultural Heritage Site by the United Nation's UNESCO.

ESSENTIAL INFORMATION

VISITOR INFORMATION To get information about the park by mail, contact the Superintendent, **Mesa Verde National Park** (Mesa Verde, CO 81330, tel. 970/529–4461). Backcountry permits are not available: Because of the extreme fragility of the cliff dwellings, it is forbidden to wander beyond the sanctioned trails. To find out about Mesa Verde road conditions, call 970/529–4461 or, as you approach the park, tune your radio to the Traveler's Information Station, at 1610 AM.

Visitor resources within the park include the **Far View Visitor Center,** 15 mi from park entrance, and the **park headquarters,** 20 mi from the park entrance (tel. 970/529–4475). The former is the only place to purchase tickets for the guided cliff dwelling tours, but both have bookshops and rangers on hand to answer questions.

The best walk-in resource for data on the area surrounding Mesa Verde—including dining, lodging, and attractions in the nearby towns of Cortez, Dolores, and Mancos—is the **Colorado Welcome Center** in Cortez, about 10 mi west of the national park (928 E. Main St., tel. 970/565–3414). For a visitor's guide to the area and additional pamphlets on cross-country skiing, biking, and fishing, you can also write to the **Mesa Verde Country Visitor Information Bureau** (Box HH, Cortez, CO 81321, tel. 800/253–1616). The best source of material on Durango, about 36 mi east of Mesa Verde, is the *Official Visitors Guide* published by the **Durango Area Chamber Resort Association** (Box 2587VG, Durango, CO 81302, tel. 800/525–8855 or 970/247–0312).

FEES The fee to enter Mesa Verde National Park is $10 per car. This allows visitors to come and go from the park for five days. An annual pass to the park is $20.

PUBLICATIONS The tabloid-style *Visitor Guide* and the glossy park service *Mesa Verde* pamphlet—available free at park entrances—have excellent maps of the park. In addition, at all the major trailheads and overlook points, you'll find self-guided tour pamphlets that detail the history as well as the flora and fauna of the site.

The park's two bookstores are in the visitor center and the museum; the latter has the more comprehensive selection of literature. Good introductions to the cultural history of the park include *The Story of Mesa Verde National Park,* by Gilbert H. Wenger, and *The People of Mesa Verde,* by Anne Markward. *Mesa Verde National Park,* by Duane A. Smith, focuses on the story of how Mesa Verde became part of the national parks system. *Mesa Verde: A Complete Guide,* by Gian Mercurio and Maxymilian L. Peschel, gives a concise overview of the park's current attractions and facilities. For basic background on the former inhabitants of the area, pick up the inexpensive *Indians of the Mesa Verde,* by Don Watson.

GEOLOGY AND TERRAIN Mesa Verde's archaeological sites are spread out over 52,000 acres of land. In addition to viewing the traces of human occupation, visitors can also envision a portion of the park's geological history.

The gray rock visible along the road at the entrance to the park, for example, is Mancos shale. It was formed by mud and limestone deposited 65 million years ago, when a shallow sea covered the Four Corners area. The fluctuations in this body of water eventually resulted in a series of sandstone layers, the uppermost of which is called Cliff House sandstone. It was this portion of rock that eroded into the niches and alcoves in which the park's cliff dwellings perch.

The mesa was part of a final uplift of the San Juan Mountains that occurred millions of years later. It slopes gently southward from a high point of 8,572 ft to a low elevation of roughly 6,000 ft. Mountain streams slowly created a network of dramatic canyons in the mesa. The streams had disappeared by the time humans arrived, but the land was made habitable by snowmelt and summer rainfall, along with the fertile wind-blown soil called loess, which layers the mesa top.

FLORA AND FAUNA Tall trees such as Douglas fir grow at park elevations above 8,000 ft, where moisture is derived from both rain and snow. Lower down, but still above 7,000 ft, the landscape is dominated by "mountain scrub," which includes the diminutive Gambel oak and the rosebushlike Utah service berry. By far the largest portion of Mesa Verde, however, is covered with piñon pine and Utah juniper. The pine provided building materials for the mesa's inhabitants, and the juniper's shaggy bark was used, among other things, to make diapers for babies. In addition, both pine nuts and juniper berries were important supplemental food sources. Yucca plants, scattered throughout the park, are not only edible, but also have fibers from which capes, sandals, and cord were made.

Brightly colored blossoms fill the canyons and roadsides in the early summer months. The Perky sue, an abundant yellow flower, blooms in May and June. Sand-loving lupines, a soft blue flower, are seen along the roadways in the higher elevations. Bright red Indian paintbrush are scattered throughout the rocky, arid cliffs. There is also abundant sage and mountain mahogany.

The wildlife that once fed the people of the pueblos still inhabit Mesa Verde. Mule deer, thus named because of their large ears, are the most frequently sighted of the park's larger animals. Coyotes are also abundant; they often run alongside or across the road. In August and September you may spot American elk at the canyon bottoms, and in late spring there are bighorn sheep in Cliff Canyon. Another native is the black bear. About 200 species of birds inhabit Mesa Verde, including red-tailed hawks, great-horned owls, and golden eagles (*see* Bird-Watching *in* Other Activities, *below*).

WHEN TO GO Mesa Verde National Park may be entered year-round, but the major cliff dwellings on Chapin Mesa are open to the public only from late April through mid-October, which is also when the park's campground and lodge operate. Wetherill Mesa is open for an even shorter stretch, from Memorial Day through Labor Day.

Mid-June through August are Mesa Verde's most crowded months. Better times to visit are late May, early June, and most of September, when the weather is fine but the crowds have thinned. Winter is also an interesting time for day trips from surrounding areas; the sight of the sandstone dwellings sheltered from the snow in their cliff coves is spectacular.

Temperatures range from about 85°F to 100°F during daylight in summer; nights are cooler, averaging 55°F to 65°F. Winter highs hover around 40°F to 50°F, but the mercury can plummet below zero at night. The mesa gets as many as 100 inches of snow during the winter. Snow may fall as late as May and as early as October, but there's rarely enough to hamper travel. Afternoon thunder showers are common in July and August.

SEASONAL EVENTS **Late May to early June:** The **Ute Bear Dance** (tel. 970/565–3751), held on a Ute reservation in the nearby town of Towoac, celebrates springtime and the legacy of the bear who taught the Ute people its secrets. **July:** The only annual event in the park itself is the three-day **Indian Arts and Crafts Festival** (tel. 970/529–4475) at the Morefield Campground in the latter part of the month. **August:** Balloonists from all over the country congregate for the three-day **Hot Air Balloon Rally** (tel. 970/565–8155), at the Conquistador Golf Course in Cortez. **October:** On Columbus Day weekend, the **Indian Summer Run** (tel. 970/565–3414) is a half marathon from Mesa Verde National Park to Centennial Park in Cortez. **December:** Cortez's Main Street hosts a parade of floats and fanfare during the **Parade of Lights** (tel. 970/565–8939), held on the last weekend of the month. Write to Mesa Verde–Cortez Visitor Information Bureau (Box HH, Cortez, CO 81321) for a current calendar of events.

WHAT TO PACK Bring layers, since temperatures drop dramatically at night and even during the day when the sun ducks behind the clouds. Be prepared for sudden thunderstorms.

GENERAL STORES The **general store** (tel. 970/529–4474) in Morefield Village, at the entrance to the park's campground, is well stocked with groceries and basic camping supplies; it's open from 7 AM to 9:30 PM daily from early May through mid-October.

In Mancos, about .5 mi east of the turnoff road to the park, the **Wild Wild Rest** (37101 U.S. Hwy. 160) complex has a convenience store (tel. 970/533–9747) that's open daily, year-round, and a sporting goods outlet called **Sequel** (tel. 970/533–9717), open daily from mid-April through December.

ARRIVING AND DEPARTING Although the nearby towns of Durango and Cortez both have airports and Durango also has a Greyhound bus station, there's no public transportation from either Durango or Cortez to the national park. **Durango Transportation** (547½ W. 2nd Ave., Durango, CO 81301, tel. 970/259–4818 or 800/626–2066) is the only tour operator in the area that runs bus trips to Mesa Verde.

Cortez is 10 mi west of Mesa Verde via Highway 160; Durango is 36 mi east of Mesa Verde, also via Highway 160. Mesa Verde is close to a number of other Native American historical sites. **Hovenweep National Monument,** on the Utah-Colorado border, is 1½ to two hours from the park; from Cortez (9 mi west of the park entrance on U.S. 160), take the unnumbered but well-marked road that starts just south of town. **Aztec Ruins National Monument,** just east of Farmington in New Mexico, is also about two hours away: Take U.S. 160 east to Durango, then U.S. 550 south to Aztec. If you continue south another 45 minutes from Aztec on New Mexico Interstate 44, you'll see a turnoff for **Chaco Culture National Historical Park;** from there, it's another 20 mi via dirt road to the park. You can get to **Canyon de Chelly National Monument** in Arizona in about three hours: Take U.S. 160 west from Cortez to U.S. 191 South.

By Bus. There's a **Greyhound** (tel. 970/259–2755 or 800/231–2222) and **TNM&O** (tel. 806/763–5329) depot in Durango (275 E. 8th Ave.), about a 45-mi drive from the park. **Budget** (tel. 970/259–1842), **Rent-A-Wreck** (tel. 970/259–5858), and **Thrifty** (tel. 970/259–3504) provide rental cars at the bus station.

By Car and RV. North of Mesa Verde, I–70 is the major east–west interstate. Along this route, about four hours north of the park, lies Grand Junction, Colorado, the nearest city. I–40 runs in an east–west direction, to the south of Mesa Verde; this is the route that leads to Farmington, New Mexico, about two hours from the park.

By Plane. Cortez's Montezuma County Airport (tel. 970/565–7458) is serviced by **United Express** (tel. 970/565–9510 or 800/241–6522), a subsidiary of Mesa Airlines. **U-Save Auto Rental** (tel. 970/565–9168) has car rentals at the airport, which is on the south side of town, about 12 mi from the entrance to Mesa Verde. From the airport, take County Road G to Highway 160, which runs through town to the national park.

The Durango–La Plata Airport (tel. 970/247–8143) receives flights from **America West Express** (tel. 800/235–9292), **United Express** (tel. 800/241–6522), and **Mesa Airlines** (tel. 800/637–2247). You can rent a car at the airport from **Avis** (tel. 970/247–9761 or 800/831–2847), **Budget** (970/259–1841 or 800/527–0700), **Dollar** (970/259–3012 or 800/800–4000), **Hertz** (970/247–5288 or 800/654–3131), or **National Interrent** (tel. 970/259–0068 or 800/227–7368). The airport is about 12 mi east of Durango. To drive from there to Mesa Verde, take Highway 172 west toward Durango; in 6 mi, you'll come to the turnoff for Highway 160. Make a left and continue west on 160 for 36 mi, when you'll see the turnoff for the park entrance.

By Train. The nearest **Amtrak** station is in Denver, 370 mi northeast of the park.

EXPLORING

For a full perspective of Mesa Verde, try to take at least one ranger-led hike to a major cliff dwelling site, as well as a few self-guided tours. Plan ahead: It takes about 45 minutes to reach the visitor center from the park entrance, and another 45 minutes to get to the sites at Wetherill Mesa. If possible, stay over for at least one night: Sunrise, sunset, and the starry-night sky from the top of this world are rarely matched on any other point on earth.

THE BEST IN ONE DAY Start your day at the Far View Visitor Center (open 8 AM to 5 PM, summer only), where you can pick up park information and purchase tickets for the Cliff Palace or Balcony House tours on Chapin Mesa and Long House on Wetherill Mesa. All three of these tours require some degree of physical stamina, but Balcony House is the most physically challenging and should be avoided by those with a fear of heights. If it's going to be a hot day, you might want to take an early-morning or late-afternoon tour. If picture taking is a prime consideration, it's best to sign on for a mid- to late-afternoon tour.

After you've gotten your tickets, drive to the Chapin Mesa Museum to learn about the area and its history. Just behind the museum, the .5-mi-long Spruce Tree House trail leads to the best preserved cliff dwelling in the park. Getting in and out of your car to explore the various overlook points on the Mesa Top Loop Road (comprising two 6-mi loops) should keep you busy for the rest of the day.

If Wetherill Mesa is open during your visit, an alternative would be to buy tickets for a late-afternoon Cliff Palace or Balcony House tour and then drive out to Wetherill as soon as the road opens (9 AM). You'll be there in time for the first ranger-led Long House tour, which takes off at 10 AM. After that you can take the free minitram to various overlooks before heading back to Chapin Mesa for the afternoon. Or spend the entire day at Wetherill Mesa; there are plenty of sights and trails, and it's far less crowded than Chapin Mesa.

ORIENTATION PROGRAMS At the Chapin Mesa Archaeological Museum (tel. 970/529–4475), the history of Native American life in the area is traced through dioramas, craft displays, photographs, and even stuffed animals. An orientation program is a good supplement to the museum's exhibits, and rangers are on hand to answer questions. The museum is open daily; call for the current schedule.

GUIDED TOURS The most popular cliff dwellings—Balcony House and Cliff Palace on Chapin Mesa, and Long House on Wetherill Mesa—can only be explored by **ranger-led tours,** which last about an hour. You must buy tickets for these at the Far View Visitor Center on the day of the tour. In high season, tours of Cliff Palace take place every half hour from 9 AM to 6 PM; Balcony House every half hour from 9 to 5; Long House, every half hour from 10 to 5. Some stair climbing and road ascents are involved in all three tours, but at Balcony House visitors are also required to climb a 32-ft wooden ladder and crawl through a short but narrow tunnel.

Aramark (tel. 970/529–4421), the National Park Service's authorized concessionaire, runs bus excursions around the mesa rim. The morning tour visits pit houses and early village sites. Afternoon guides discuss the architecture and culture of the last 100 years (AD 1200 to 1300) from various overlook points. On the full-day tour, visitors get the complete survey and also spend an hour in Cliff Palace. Each of the half-day tours lasts three hours and costs about $17. Full-day tours, which run about seven hours (including time on your own for shopping and lunch) are about $21. Morning tours leave from Morefield Campground at 8:30 AM and from Far View Lodge at 9 AM; afternoon tours depart only from Far View Lodge at 1 PM. Full-day tours have campground pickups at 9 AM and lodge pickups at 9:30 AM.

SCENIC DRIVES AND VIEWS Among the most spectacular Mesa Verde drives is from the **park entrance to the Far View Visitor Center,** where 15 mi of switchbacks reveal far-ranging vistas of the surrounding areas. There are a couple of minor overlooks along the way, but hold out for **Park Point,** which, at the mesa's highest elevation (8,572 ft), affords unobstructed 360-degree views. On the clearest days, you can see Utah's Manti-LaSal Mountains, 110 mi to the northwest; you'll also recognize such landmarks as Shiprock, New Mexico (32 mi south), and

Colorado's Ute Mountain (13 mi west). Wetherill Mesa is closed during winter, and from 4:30 PM until 9 AM in summer.

Running along the rim of Chapin Mesa, the **Mesa Top Loop Road** is not only scenic but also key to understanding the park. Here, a series of interpretive signs explains the cultural development of Mesa Verde. The first of two 6-mi loops introduces the nomadic Basket Maker people—so called because they used woven vessels for cooking and storage—who preceded Mesa Verde's inhabitants. As you walk around the loop's 12 stops, you'll view increasingly complex structures: The simple mud-and-wood pit houses built starting around AD 550 evolve into kivas (ceremonial rooms) about 200 years later, and eventually into such edifices as the multistory Sun Temple, left unfinished around 1276 (*see* Historic Buildings and Sites, *below*). In addition to Sun Temple, highlights of this loop include the **Sun Point Overlook,** from which you can see Cliff Palace, Sun Temple, Sunset House, and other sites. The second loop, which leads to the trailheads for Cliff Palace and Balcony House (*see* Historic Buildings and Sites, *below*), affords some good overlook points, such as the **House of Many Windows** and the **Cliff Canyon Overlook.** You can also pick up the **Soda Canyon Overlook Trail** (*see* Nature Trails and Short Walks, *below*) on this loop.

HISTORIC BUILDINGS AND SITES Mesa Verde is the only national park set up to protect the works of human beings rather than those of nature, so its main interest lies in its archaeological sites: There are more than 4,000, including some 600 cliff dwellings; 35 are open to the public. Most of the sites on the short list that follows are cliff dwellings, which represent the last and most advanced stage in the development of the Mesa Verde peoples; they didn't start building in the park's sandstone alcoves until around AD 1200. Balcony House, Cliff House, and Long House can be entered only by ranger-led tour. Interpre-

tive placards and/or self-guided pamphlets are available to help visitors explore the other sites. Unless otherwise indicated, all are on Chapin Mesa.

Balcony House. You'll be impressed by the stonework of this medium-size cliff dwelling, which housed 40 or 50 people in about 40 rooms, but you're likely to be even more awed by the skill it took to reach this place. Perched in a sandstone cove 600 ft above the floor of Soda Canyon, Balcony House seems almost suspended in space. Even with the aid of modern steps and a partially paved trail, today's visitors must climb two wooden ladders (the first one 32 ft high) to enter. Surrounding the house are a courtyard with a parapet wall, a 12-ft-long exit tunnel, two separate water sources, and the intact balcony for which the house is named.

Cliff Palace. Cliff Palace was originally thought to have contained 23 kivas (ceremonial chambers) and 217 rooms on four terraced levels; however, recent findings indicate the dwelling contained about 150 rooms. The 14 rooms on the uppermost level are believed to be storage units. You can still see some bits of the plaster that originally covered these structures, which were made out of sandstone blocks held together with adobe mortar. The wooden beams that protrude from the base of the alcove wall are among Mesa Verde's few intact timbers dating back to prehistoric days. Excavated pottery shards, bone, and discarded clothing and tools indicate that the talus slope in front of Cliff Palace was originally used as a refuse heap and burial ground. The exit trail from Cliff Palace is thought to be the same trail used by the Anasazi. Hand and toe holes are within reach as you climb the 700 ft out of Cliff Palace.

Far View Village Complex. This is believed to have been one of the most densely populated areas in Mesa Verde, comprising as many as 50 villages in a .5-square-mi area. (The reason may be that this area receives

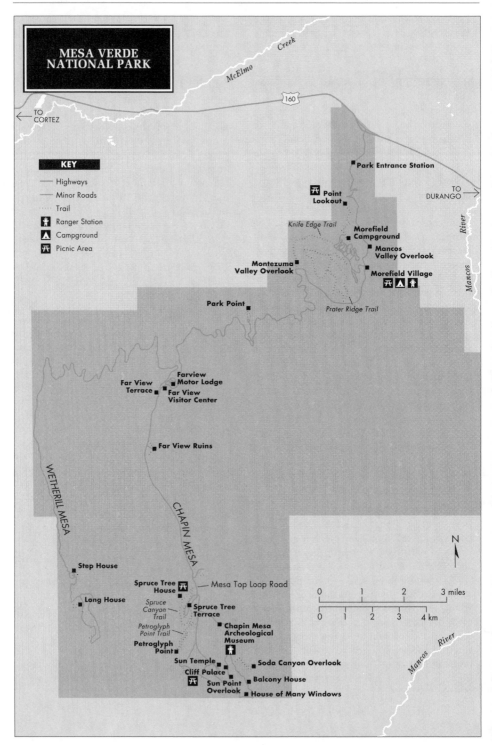

more moisture than other places in the park.) Most of the sites date from between AD 900 and AD 1300, though occupation is hypothesized to have gone back even earlier. Highlights include Far View House, a rectangular pueblo with a particularly large kiva as well as 40 unusually symmetrical rooms; Pipe Shrine House, where a number of decorated clay pipes were discovered; and the mysterious Mummy Lake, which may have been a man-made reservoir. You'll see signs for this complex on the main road between the Far View Visitor Center and Chapin Mesa Archeological Museum.

Long House. Excavated in 1959–1961 as part of a larger attempt to divert crowds from Chapin Mesa, this Wetherill Mesa cliff dwelling is the second largest in Mesa Verde. It is believed that 150 or 160 people lived in the Long House, so named because of the size of its cliff alcove. The 21 kivas uncovered at the site suggest that it was probably a center of activity for the entire mesa. The complex includes one of only two large central plazas found at Mesa Verde (the other is at Chapin Mesa's Fire House). The seep spring at the back of the cave, which provided its inhabitants with water, is still active today.

Spruce Tree House. This is the only dwelling in the park where visitors may enter a kiva via a short ladder just as the builders did. (The kiva was a religious structure and park rangers will remind you to enter it with respect.) Spruce Tree House is thought to have been home to about 100 people, with 114 rooms and eight kivas. Like the other cliff dwellings, it has been protected from the elements by an overhang and has required little protective maintenance from the National Park Service. It looks much the same now as it did when it was found by the Wetherill brothers in 1888. Although the tour through this site is self-guided, there's always a park ranger around to answer questions.

Sun Temple. Perhaps not as important to archaeologists as some of the other sites at Mesa Verde, Sun Temple is nevertheless intriguing for the many questions it leaves unanswered. Although they assume it was probably a ceremonial structure, researchers are unsure of the purpose of this capital D–shape complex that has no doors or windows in most of its chambers. Because the temple was not quite half finished when it was left in 1276, there are those who surmise it might have been constructed to stave off whatever disaster caused its builders to leave. It is the only structure that appears to have been planned and built as a multi-community effort. A stop here in the early-evening hours provides great photo opportunities.

Step House. Step House on Wetherill Mesa is so named because of the prehistoric and now crumbling stairway leading up from this now-ruined dwelling. On the site lay the ruins of two separate occupations—a modified Basket Maker site and the classic Pueblo masonry dwelling. The short but steep trail to the dwelling is paved, making it a good alternative to the longer, more strenuous tours of the other cliff dwellings.

NATURE TRAILS AND SHORT WALKS Three of the park's major trails branch off from a single trailhead just behind the park's museum and ranger headquarters. For safety reasons, hikers are required to register at the Chief Ranger's Office for the Petroglyph Point and Spruce Canyon trails, but not for the short one (about .5 mi round-trip) that leads to **Spruce Tree House** (*see* Historic Buildings and Sites, *above*). On the last, you'll be quickly descending 170 ft, so you might find yourself puffing a bit on the way back up. Signs along the trail point out plants that abound in this area—juniper, piñon pine, yucca—and, less appealing, poison ivy.

Petroglyph Point Trail, the longest of the three, is 2.8 mi round-trip, with a total elevation change of 330 ft; allow two to three hours. After heading south for a bit into Spruce Tree Canyon, the trail ascends to the plateau's rim and follows it back to the museum area. The flora, fauna, geological features, and marks of human activity along the route are detailed in a trail guide pamphlet. The highlight of this trek is the misnamed Pictograph Point, where you'll see the largest and best known group of petroglyphs in Mesa Verde (pictographs are painted onto rock, whereas petroglyphs are carved into it).

If you're interested in exploring a canyon bottom, take the mildly difficult 2.1-mi-long **Spruce Canyon Trail.** Its highest elevation is 7,000 ft, its lowest 6,440 ft. There's a picnic area at the top, with shaded tables, grills, and rest rooms.

The park's other sanctioned trails are in the Morefield Campground area. You don't need permits for any of them, but stop at the entry station to pick up a map that will direct you to the trailheads. **Knife Edge Trail** is an easy 2-mi round-trip walk around the north rim of the park. If you stop at all the flora identification points that the trail guide pamphlet suggests, the hike should take about 1½ to two hours. The patches of asphalt you're likely to spot along the way are leftovers from Knife Edge Road, built in 1914 as the main entryway into the park. The Montezuma Valley Overlook is a superb spot for viewing the sunset.

The 2.3-mi-long **Point Lookout Trail** has a total elevation change of only 400 ft—its lowest point is at about 7,600 ft, its highest at 8,000—but the switchbacks up the rear of Point Lookout make the hike more difficult. Still, it's well worth the effort for those in good shape. Point Lookout, which affords spectacular vistas of both the Mancos and Montezuma valleys, may have been used by the U.S. cavalry in the 19th century as a signal relay point.

One of the easiest and most rewarding strolls in the park is the **Soda Canyon Overlook Trail,** which stretches 1.5-mi round-trip through the forest on almost completely level ground. The trailhead is about .25 mi past the Balcony House parking area, and the overlook is an excellent place to photograph the famous cliff dwelling.

LONGER HIKES No backcountry hiking is permitted in Mesa Verde. The only long

(7.8 mi round-trip) hike you can take inside the park is on **Prater Ridge Trail,** which begins and ends on the west side of the Morefield Campground. The south section of this double-loop trail affords fine views of Morefield Canyon, while the northern portion looks off toward the San Juan Mountains. Although you'll be ascending from 7,600 to 8,300 ft, this is not an especially difficult hike; there are only about 15 minutes of hard climbing at Prater Ridge.

OTHER ACTIVITIES **Bird-Watching.** The park is in a transition zone between the low desert and the southern Rockies, so many birds either live here year-round or migrate through the area annually. Turkey vultures can be seen between April and October, large flocks of ravens hang around all summer, and ducks and waterfowl fly through from mid-September through mid-October. Among the park's other large birds, mostly found on the northern escarpment, are redtailed hawks, great-horned owls, and a few golden eagles. The dark blue Steller's jay frequently pierces the piñon-juniper forest with its cries, and hummingbirds dart from flower to flower. Ask for a checklist of the park's birds, including about 200 species, at the museum desk.

Boating and Fishing. The marina at McPhee Lake, the second largest lake in Colorado, is about 10 mi northeast of Cortez. Fishing boats, pontoons, and waver runners can be rented here by the full or half day; tackle, poles, reels, and fishing licenses are also available. For more information, call the **McPhee Marina** (tel. 800/882–2038). You can find out about other good fishing spots in the area by contacting the Mesa Verde Country Visitor Information Bureau (*see* Visitor Information, *above*). A fishing license is required in Colorado for all lakes, streams, and reservoirs; licenses are sold at many retail outlets.

Horseback Riding. You can easily find a mount in the immediate area around the park. Among the outfitters in nearby Mancos is **Echo Basin Ranch** (Box 602, Mancos CO, 81328, tel. 970/533–7000 or 970/533–7588), which offers trail rides, pack trips, hay rides, and more. In addition, the Durango Area Chamber Resort Association (*see* Visitor Information, *above*) can give you the names of the many ranches in that area.

Rafting. Everything from white-water rafting in class-five rapids to gentle float trips is available around Mesa Verde, where the Dolores, San Juan, Gunnison, and Animas rivers run through beautiful mountain country. The Animas is the most popular river. Most outfitters operate out of Durango; contact the Durango Area Chamber Resort Association (*see* Visitor Information, *above*) for information.

Ski Touring. Mesa Verde's Cliff Palace/Balcony House road is closed to automobile traffic in winter, but it's open for ski-touring when there's enough snow. Along this easy 6-mi loop through piñon pine and juniper forest are several overlooks of the cliff dwellings. There are also 3 mi of beginner's trails in the Morefield campground. Contact the Park Ranger's Office (tel. 970/529–4461) for permission before setting out in the park. In addition, U.S. Forest Service trails abound in the area around the park; for detailed maps and for information about weather and snow conditions, contact the **San Juan National Forest** (Mancos District: 41595 E. Hwy. 160, Mancos, CO 81328, tel. 970/533–7716; Dolores District: 100 N. 6th St., Dolores, CO 81323, tel. 970/882–7296). In Cortez, you can rent skis at **Slavens** (237 W. Main St., tel. 970/565–8571).

CHILDREN'S PROGRAMS In summer, different children's programs take place every day at the Chapin Mesa Archaeological Museum. Naturalists might talk about the uses Native Americans would have made of local plants, and children might make papier-mâché replicas of the park's sites. An ongoing Junior Ranger program also helps educate kids about the park: Children who successfully complete a two-page questionnaire about the park—available from the Far View Visitor Center or the museum—may receive official Junior Ranger certification.

EVENING ACTIVITIES Mesa Verde was the first national park to institute a campfire program, and it continues to this day at the Morefield Campground Amphitheater. Every summer night at 9 PM, park rangers supplement your park explorations with free talks or slide shows. Inquire about the program at the visitor center or at park headquarters. At the Far View Lodge (*see* Lodging, *below*), experts on such subjects as the history of the pre-Puebloan peoples of the San Juan Basin give lectures at 7:30 PM; admission is $3.

DINING

You won't go hungry in the Mesa Verde area, nor will you have to rely on fast food, though there's no shortage of that if you want it. In the park itself there are two cafeterias, an upscale dining room, and, on Wetherill Mesa, a snack bar; breakfast and dinner are also available at Morefield Campground (*see* Camping, *below*). Mancos, the closest town to Mesa Verde (7 mi away), has some good restaurants, and there's an even larger selection in Cortez, about 15 minutes from the park entrance.

INSIDE THE PARK **Metate Room.** Tables in this Southwestern-style dining room may be candlelit and cloth-covered, but the atmosphere is casual. A wall of windows affords wonderful Mesa Verde vistas. The menu includes American staples like steak and seafood, but more unusual dishes such as quail, venison, and rabbit may appear as well. For appetizers, try Anasazi beans and Mesa bread. *Far View Lodge, across from Far View Visitor Center, tel. 970/529–4421. AE, D, DC, MC, V. Closed late Oct.–early Apr. No lunch. $$$*

Far View Terrace. This full-service cafeteria may not be as atmospheric as the Metate Room, but views aren't lacking, choices are plentiful, and the price is right. Fluffy blueberry pancakes are often on the breakfast menu. Dinner options might include a heaping Navajo taco made with shredded chicken, pizza, or fried chicken. A salad bar and fresh fruit are available for lighter appetites. Pies, frozen yogurt, and homemade fudge round out the selection. The big adjoining gift shop is excellent if pricey. *15 mi from park entrance (.5 mi from Far View Lodge), tel. 970/529-4444. D, MC, V. Closed late Oct.–early Apr. $*

Knife's Edge Cafe. Though it's in the Morefield Campground, the café is open to all visitors. An all-you-can-eat pancake breakfast is served every morning from 7:30 to 10 for $3.50; at night, there's an all-you-can-eat barbecue dinner from 5 until 8 for $6.50. *4 mi from park entrance, tel. 970/565-2133. AE, D, MC, V. Closed Labor Day–Memorial Day. No lunch. $*

Spruce Tree Terrace. There's not much of a selection at this cafeteria: If you don't want beef, you might be out of luck for hot food (except French fries or beans), and the cold sandwich selection is limited, too. But the patio is pleasant, and this is the most convenient refueling stop for all the Chapin Mesa rim and cliff-dwelling tours. It's also the only food concession open year-round. *21 mi from park entrance, across from Chapin Mesa Archaeological Museum, tel. 970/529-4521. AE, D, DC, MC, V. No dinner in winter. $*

NEAR THE PARK **Millwood Junction.** This rustic, rambling restaurant, made out of wood from seven local barns, has everything you'd want for a fun night out: good drinks, good food, and, on summer weekends, top-notch entertainment. An excellent Friday-night seafood buffet (all you can eat for $13.95) draws folks from four states. *Junction of Hwy. 160 and Main, Mancos, tel. 970/533-7338. MC, V. No lunch. $$*

Nero's. The menu is mainly southern Italian—lasagna, linguine marinara, eggplant parmigiana—but the atmosphere is Southwest, with the owner's collection of prints, sandpaintings, and ceramics adorning the cozy dining room. Regional influences turn up in such nightly specials as grilled shrimp in mango-tequila-lime sauce. *303 W. Main St., Cortez, tel. 970/565-7366. AE, MC, V. No lunch. $$*

M&M Family Restaurant and Truckstop. Sure it's a truck stop, but who ever said truckers don't like good food? Come here for good, inexpensive versions of all the American classics—meat loaf, burgers, chicken-fried steak—and huge breakfasts 24 hours a day. In a concession to the '90s, there are even some low-fat selections. *7006 Hwy. 160 S, Cortez, tel. 970/565-6511. Reservations not accepted. AE, MC, V. $*

PICNIC SPOTS In addition to the picnic area at the top of Spruce Canyon Trail (*see* Nature Trails and Short Walks, *above*), outdoor diners can take advantage of the tables, grills, and rest rooms near the Chapin Mesa Archaeological Museum. Drive just past the museum on the loop road and you'll see a sign.

LODGING

There's only one place to sleep inside the park itself, but inexpensive and comfortable rooms are easy to find in the Mesa Verde vicinity. In Cortez, motels line the main drag, Highway 160. In recent years, bed-and-breakfasts have proliferated around Cortez, Mancos, and Dolores. Contact the **Southwest Colorado B&B Association** (tel. 800/745-4885). You can find brochures for many other B&Bs at the Colorado Welcome Center in Cortez (*see* Visitor Information, *above*). If you're willing to splurge and don't mind the extra driving time from the park, you might also consider two outstanding historic properties in Durango. Along with the General Palmer Hotel, listed below, the slightly less expensive **Strater Hotel** (699 Main Ave., 81302, tel. 970/247-4431 or 800/247-4431) is a step back to the 1860s, when the hotel was built. Price categories are based on summer rates, which may be considerably higher than winter ones.

INSIDE THE PARK **Far View Lodge.** The walls are thin and the furniture generic at this motel-style complex, but all the rooms are spotless and have terrific views from private balconies. The only hotel in the park, Far View is not only convenient, but more than adequate for the price. *15 mi from park entrance. Reservations: ARA Mesa Verde, Box 277, Mancos, CO, 81328, tel. 970/529-4421 or 800/449-2288, fax 970/529-4411. 150 rooms. Facilities: restaurant, bar. AE, D, DC, MC, V. Closed mid-Oct.–mid-Apr. $$$*

NEAR THE PARK General Palmer Hotel. Anchoring Durango's historic downtown district, this 1898 Victorian beauty is in prime condition. The romantic rooms with antique reproductions have all the modern amenities. *567 Main Ave., Durango 81301, tel. 970/247-4747 or 800/523-3358. 39 rooms. Facilities: restaurant, bar, concierge. AE, D, DC, MC, V. $$$*

Holiday Inn Express. On the western end of Cortez (the one closest to Mesa Verde), this motel has all the standard comforts and more, including complimentary Continental breakfast, indoor pool, sauna, exercise room, and VCR and movie rentals. Many rooms have mountain views. *2121 E. Main St., Cortez, CO 81321, tel. 970/565-6000 or 800/626-5652, fax 970/565-3438. 100 rooms. Facilities: bar, indoor pool, sauna, exercise room. AE, D, DC, MC, V. $$–$$$*

Enchanted Mesa Motel. This is the place to come for a quiet, inexpensive room in Mancos, a delightful Western town as close to Mesa Verde as you can get. Accommodations are basic, but comfortable and clean; units overlook a grassy courtyard. *862 Grand Ave., Box 476, Mancos, CO 81328, tel. 970/533-7729. 10 rooms. AE, D, MC, V. $*

CAMPING

It's easy to find a spot to pitch a tent or park an RV in Mesa Verde's environs, but there's little reason to stay outside the park: The huge Morefield Campground—almost never full, but closed in winter—has everything you'd ever want. Two pleasant places in the immediate vicinity are listed below as back-

ups, but be sure to check Morefield first. For information on camping in the San Juan National Forest, call 800/283-2267.

INSIDE THE PARK Four miles past the park entrance, **Morefield Campground** (tel. 970/565-1675 in summer) is an appealing minicity for campers, with a gift shop, laundromat, coin-op showers, flush toilets, disposal stations for RVs, grocery store, tour desk, full service gas station, and the Knife's Edge Cafe (*see* Dining, *above*). Morefield's capacity is huge: There are more than 450 tent sites ($10 per night) and 84 RV sites ($17), 15 with hookups. On summer evenings, rangers give campfire talks at the amphitheater. The campground's lush green grass and Gambel oaks attract deer (remember, don't feed them) and three of the park's main hiking trails depart from the area. The campground is closed from mid-October through mid-April.

NEAR THE PARK Just across the highway from the park entrance, the **A&A Mesa Verde R.V. Park–Resort** (tel. 970/565-3517 for information, 800/972-6620 for reservations, fax 970/565-7141) has a heated pool and spa, a playground, sports field, store, laundry, showers, and kennel. There are 20 sites without hookups ($17), 11 sites with water and electricity ($21), and 18 with full RV hookups ($21). If more than two people occupy one site, there's a $2.50 fee for each additional person. Some of the sites are shaded by trees, and all except the pull-throughs have grills. There are also five rustic log cabins that sleep five and cost $30.

The 43 sites at **Mesa Verde Point Kampark** (tel. 970/533-7421 or 800/776-7421), on Highway 160 near the park, can be used either for tents or RVs. Sites cost $21.50 to $24.50, plus a $3 additional fee for more than two people per site. Facilities include showers, laundry, pool, and spa. In the evenings, campers congregate in the poolroom near the front office. The campground is closed during January and February.

Mt. Rainier National Park
Washington

Updated by Alex Aron

he awestruck local Native Americans called it Tahoma, "the mountain that was God," and dared not ascend its eternally icebound summit. In 1792 the first European to visit the region, the British explorer George Vancouver, gazed in amazement at its majestic dome and named it after his friend Rear Admiral Peter Rainier.

Two centuries later, Mt. Rainier, visible from a distance of 200 mi, still fills visitors and natives with wonder. Like a mysterious white-clad virgin, often veiled in cloud even when the surrounding forests and fields are bathed in sunlight, the 14,411-ft mountain is the centerpiece of Mt. Rainier National Park in northwest Washington. Surrounded by some of the finest old-growth forests left on earth, gnawed at by the most extensive system of glaciers in the contiguous United States, supporting diverse plant and animal life, Mt. Rainier rewards day-trippers as well as experienced mountaineers.

At one time an unbroken wilderness stretched for hundreds of miles in every direction around this summit, but today Mt. Rainier National Park is an oasis of wilderness in a sea of clear-cuts. Its 235,612 acres were preserved by President McKinley in 1899, who proclaimed Mt. Rainier the nation's fifth national park. Today, its cathedral-like groves—some more than 1,000 years old—are the grandeur of America's now nearly vanished old-growth forests. Water and lush greenery are everywhere in the park, and dozens of waterfalls, accessible from the road or by a short hike, fill the air with thundering mist.

Higher, above the timberline, are flower-filled meadows thronged with life during Rainier's brief 11-week summer. Higher still, the mountain's glaciated ridges are studies in the elemental forces of geology. Nearly 3 mi high, Rainier's summit is one of the Cascade Range's most challenging mountaineering adventures; serious climbers use Rainier's walls and crevassed ice fields to prepare for such Himalayan peaks as Everest. Every year 10,000 climbers take on the Rainier challenge, though only about half reach the summit.

Most visitors to Mt. Rainier, however, aren't prepared for or inclined to participate in dangerous climbs. A well-designed road system at the park allows casual summer visitors to get a sense of the mountain's greatness without leaving their cars. Most head first to gorgeous Paradise Valley, high on the mountain's south flank, half an hour's drive from the Nisqually entrance. From there they might choose to hike a few of the 240 mi of maintained trails, or even to circle the mountain on the spectacular 93-mi loop of the Wonderland Trail.

Close to the densely populated area of Puget Sound, the park is accessible to anyone who cares to explore it: More than 2 million visitors arrive every year. But mountain wilderness lovers will still find Rainier just the way it has always been: majestic, beautiful, and remarkably unspoiled.

ESSENTIAL INFORMATION

VISITOR INFORMATION Contact the Superintendent, **Mt. Rainier National Park,**

Tahoma Woods, Star Route, Ashford, WA 98304, tel. 360/569–2211.

Wilderness use permits are available from the visitor centers at Longmire, Paradise, Ohanapecosh, and Sunrise; at the hiker information centers at Longmire and White River; and at any of the park's ranger stations. These permits are required for all overnight stays in the park's wilderness areas and are distributed on a first-come, first-served basis.

FEES Single-visit passes at Mt. Rainier, valid for seven days, cost $10 per vehicle. Bicyclists, bus passengers, and travelers on foot pay $5 each. Annual passes are available for $20.

PUBLICATIONS The park service has free fliers, brochures, and maps covering various aspects of Mt. Rainier ecology, geology, history, trails, camping, and climbing opportunities. To get copies of these write or call the superintendent (*see* Visitor Information, *above*). The office also distributes a useful, free four-page guide for those planning overnight trips in the backcountry, "Wilderness Trip Planner: A Hiker's Guide to the Wilderness of Mt. Rainier National Park." The free, quarterly *Tahoma* newsletter lists current information on roads, campgrounds, and the like; it's available at visitor centers.

The best general guide to the park, *A Traveler's Companion to Mt. Rainier National Park,* is available through the **Northwest Interpretative Association**, Longmire, WA 98397, for $5, as is a list of books and park publications, the "Catalogue of Books and Maps—Mt. Rainier National Park." You can also purchase books at the Longmire Wilderness Information Center, the Longmire Museum, the Jackson Visitor Center at Paradise, and the Ohanapecosh and Sunrise visitor centers.

One publication worth considering is *Forests of Mount Rainier,* by William H. Moir, a fine overview for those interested in the flora, fauna, and geology of the park. Other recommended trailside companions are *Cascade and Olympic Natural History,*

by Daniel Mattews; *Mt. Rainier: The Story Behind the Scenery,* a colorful backgrounder by Ray Snow; and *Wilderness Above the Sound,* an illustrated history by Arthur Martinson.

For a concise and useful map and guide to Rainier's trail system, buy *50 Hikes in Mt. Rainier National Park,* by Ira Spring and Harvey Manning. If you are curious about glaciers, Carolyn Driedger's pamphlet "Visitor's Guide to Mt. Rainier's Glaciers" will give you an easy-to-understand explanation of the forces that continue to shape the mountain. *Timberline: Mountain and Arctic Forest Frontier,* by Stephen Arno and Ramona Hammerly, is consistently recommended by experts.

GEOLOGY AND TERRAIN Mt. Rainier rises abruptly from its surrounding terrain in northwest Washington, towering above a series of jagged, heavily forested ridges in the Cascade Range. From an airplane the land surrounding the mountain's base looks like a crumpled sheet of green paper; roads and trails within the park's 378 square mi are steep and winding.

Rainier is a young mountain, less than a million years old. And the area that now comprises Mt. Rainier National Park was not always part of a mountain range. Fifty million years ago, the Cascades did not exist. This area was lowland, with rivers, lakes, and even saltwater bays. Volcanic eruptions in these lowlands spread layer upon layer of debris in the form of ash and lava flows that hardened into rock, which later broke and folded and was eventually uplifted into mountains. The mountains wore away, the Cascade Range began to form across the low hills that remained, and rivers cut rugged paths through the range. Before the birth of Rainier the highest point in the Cascades was only 6,000 ft.

Rainier was formed between half a million and a million years ago, when a weak spot in the earth's crust allowed deeply buried molten rock to ooze to the surface. Lava flowed from Rainier's central vent as far as 15 mi through the Cascades' deep valleys.

The high cone of the mountain was formed later, by lava flows that were smaller and thinner and thus did not travel as far from the vent. When the Mt. Rainier volcano calmed, it immediately began to undergo erosion from wind, rain, and ice; the results of this process are visible in the mountains' rounded contours and deep glacial valleys. There are now three "summits" to Mt. Rainier: Liberty Cap and Point Success, the sides of the old cinder cone, and Columbia Crest, the top of a more recently formed cone and the highest point, at 14,411 ft.

Deep valleys; serrated, sheer-sided ridges; and lesser mountains 6,000 to 10,000 ft high radiate outward from Rainier's domed summit. Those smaller peaks on the westward, or windward, side of Rainier are covered with the dripping green of rain forests at their lower elevations, and, at higher elevations, an average of 620 inches of snow falls during the long winters. To the east, Rainier's vast bulk casts a considerable "rain shadow," and the vegetation in this shadow, though still impressive, is sparser. The twisting 14-mi road from the park's eastern entrance, at White River, to the 6,400-ft Sunrise Visitor Center passes through stately lowland, silver fir, and subalpine forests, emerging from the timberline at about 5,500 ft in a zone of verdant alpine meadows. The visitor center provides what many consider to be the park's most breathtaking views of the mountain and its Cascade neighbors.

This is a peak shaped by fire and ice. An active volcano, it is capable of the same suicidal violence that decapitated nearby Mt. St. Helens in May 1980. In fact, Rainier used to be 2,000 ft taller. About 5,000 years ago the mountain's volcanic grumblings triggered a vast mud slide. When it was over, the unstable summit had vanished, and debris covered nearly 200 square mi around the mountain's base. The volcano's last major eruption occurred about 2,500 years ago, but scientists expect another outburst some time in the next 500 years.

Further change is wrought by Rainier's 25 named glaciers and 50 smaller ice patches, which, combined, contain more than a cubic mile of ice and are fueled by as much as 90 ft of fresh snow every year. The glaciers continually eat away at the mountain's sturdy flanks; some creep downhill more than a foot a day. Carbon Glacier, on the mountain's north face, is the longest (5.7 mi) in the continental United States; Emmons Glacier, on the northeast side, has the largest surface area (4.3 square mi) of any glacier in the contiguous United States.

At Kautz Creek, just east of the park's Nisqually entrance, rank upon rank of dead weather-silvered snags march toward the mountain's slopes, silent witnesses to the destructive power of Rainier's glacier-spawned jökulhlaups (pronounced yo-kul-loips), outburst floods that can cause debris flow. In 1947 torrential rains weakened the front edge of the Kautz Glacier, and a roaring wall of mud and debris swept down, carrying along boulders up to 13 ft in diameter, snapping ancient firs like pencils, and burying the landscape in an estimated 50 million cubic yards of cementlike mud. Scientists believe that jökulhlaups like this one occur when glacial cavities that are filled with water from snow, ice melt, and rain are "opened" by increased water pressure, and the stored water is released in violent flows.

Because it is the highest peak in the Cascades, Mt. Rainier has a profound effect on local weather, which in turn affects the geology of this young mountain. Moisture-laden storms off the Pacific rise to pass over Rainier's summit; as the moisture rises, it cools and condenses into snow, which begets glaciers. Over the course of millions of years these glaciers will reduce Mt. Rainier and the Cascades to the stature of the East Coast's Blue Ridge and Catskill mountains.

FLORA AND FAUNA The undisturbed forest and alpine biosphere of Mt. Rainier supports dozens of mammal species, 150 bird species, more than 100 different flowering plants, and hundreds of trees, shrubs, and other plants. These interact with a temperate lowland climate and plentiful rainfall to weave a complex and interdependent tapestry of life. Scientists are only now beginning to unravel its secrets. Trees and plants provide food and shelter for the animals, which in turn fertilize the plant life and, by scattering seeds, help them to reproduce. The visitor centers and naturalist activities at Longmire, Sunrise, Ohanapecosh, and Paradise each address different facets of park ecology.

The park's flora runs the gamut from the tiny to the tremendous. Immense old-growth Douglas firs shade minuscule ferns and epiphytes, or "air plants." Roosevelt elk inhabit the park in summer; their mating bugles resound through the high ridges on the east side of the park in September. The best place to see them is the Shriner Peak area, reached by trail from Ohanapecosh. Their smaller cousins, the shy black-tailed deer, are often seen from the park roads in early morning and at twilight; spotted, wobbly legged fawns appear in May and June.

White-wooled mountain goats bound from crag to crag near the snow line on their strong legs and soft black hooves. They are most common at Van Trump Park, west of Paradise; at Emerald Ridge, in the southwest corner of the park; in the Colonnades, just east of Sunset Park; and at Cowlitz Chimneys, on the east side of the park.

Black bears are present but rarely seen. More common are Rainier's chubby raccoons and porcupines, which prowl the lowland forests nibbling the tender inner bark of young trees. Pikas, timid ground-dwelling rodents with soft gray fur, rounded ears, and no discernible tail, inhabit the talus slopes and rock piles of the highlands, gathering forage for winter. Watch for their tiny piles of "hay" drying in the sun on rocks, and listen for their shrill "eek!"s of alarm. There are also plenty of pine martens and marmots.

Rainier is particularly rich in avian life. In the winter, pigeon-size ptarmigan turn snow white and travel on feathery "snowshoes." Flycatchers, hawks, owls, pileated woodpeckers, and the occasional golden eagle roost in snags in the lowland forest. The cheerful, bubbling calls and sprightly antics of the gray-and-black water ouzel charm hikers along forest streams.

These and dozens of other species depend on the dense woodland to survive. The Douglas fir, monarch of the Northwest forest, towers hundreds of feet in the air. Crinkle-barked spruce and hemlock and thick-boled cedar can grow almost as large. The trees in the Grove of the Patriarchs, in the park's southeast corner, protected from fire by nearby rivers, are thought to be more than 1,000 years old. In their shadows grow slimy 6-inch banana slugs, mushrooms, mosses, ferns, and a particularly nasty lowland species called devil's club, whose extravagant spines and serrated barbs make it the punk rocker of local plant life. Fortunately—or, perhaps, unfortunately—devil's club grows only in the Pacific Northwest.

Rainier's extensive alpine meadows, accessible by car at the Paradise and Sunrise visitor centers, are one of the park's special attractions. From late June to early September flowers follow the retreating snows and bloom in profusion, sometimes thrusting their blossoms through several inches of snow in their haste to reproduce. Avalanche lilies, penstemon, monkey-flower, partridge-foot, cinquefoil, and dozens of other species bring color to the meadows, then wither away before the arctic blasts of winter.

WHEN TO GO The ideal time to visit Mt. Rainier is September through the first week of October. Although the wildflowers have vanished by then, the weather is still fine, the huckleberries and vine maples turn brilliant fall colors, all the park's roads and facilities (except the ones at Sunrise) are still open, and most important of all, the summer crowds have melted away. Half of Rainier's 2 million annual visitors arrive in July and August, a human flood that continues into early September.

From December to April deep winter grips the park, burying the lodge at Paradise up to its high-gabled roof in snow and closing access to most of the park. Only the road from Nisqually to Paradise is kept plowed; the north and east sides of the park are completely inaccessible by vehicle. The cross-country skiing and snowshoeing, however, are exquisite, and the crowds thin (only about 100,000 people visit the park in winter). At this time, the mountain, covered with a deep blanket of fresh snow, is at its most beautiful—when it can be seen, that is. In winter, the mountain is frequently socked in for weeks on end, and many visitors depart without ever seeing it. Of course, even in summer, fog and clouds rising from Rainier's extensive glaciers can hide it from view.

SEASONAL EVENTS **May to early June:** The birth of fawns to the park's black-tailed deer herds occurs. **December to April:** Ski season (*see* Other Activities, *below*). **Last week of June to first week of September:** Enjoy the colors of the wildflower season in subalpine meadows. **September to early October:** During elk-mating season the bulls bugle and fight for harems of females.

WHAT TO PACK Over the years, visitors to this inclement mountain have bestowed on it the sardonic nickname Rainiest. Campers and hikers in particular should be sure to bring adequate rain gear. Those planning extended stays in the backcountry will need to bring some means of purifying drinking water: vessels for boiling or lightweight, hand-pumped filters.

GENERAL STORES The **General Store at Longmire's National Park Inn** (tel. 360/569–2411) stocks food, gifts, camping supplies, and other basic necessities. It's open from 8 to 8 between mid-June and mid-October, and from 10 to 5 throughout the rest of the year. A limited supply of groceries is also available at **Sunrise Lodge** (tel. 360/569–2211, ext. 2357), which is open from early June to early September, 10 to 6.

Outside the park, the nearest gas and groceries are found at **Ashford,** near the park's Nisqually entrance; at **Packwood,** near the Ohanapecosh Visitor Center; and at **Fairfax,** near the Carbon River entrance. The nearest grocery stores are the **Eatonville Market** (tel. 360/832–4551) and the **Plaza Market** (tel. 360/832–6151), both in Eatonville.

ARRIVING AND DEPARTING The vast majority of visitors to Mt. Rainier National Park arrive via Highway 706 and the Nisqually entrance, at the park's southwest corner. Highways 410 and 123 enter the park from the east and southeast, respectively; both routes are closed in winter. Highway 165 leads to Ipsut Creek Campground through the Carbon River entrance and to Mowich Lake, in the park's northwest corner. (The Carbon River Road was closed at press time; call the visitor center for an update.) The Nisqually entrance is preferred because of its proximity to I–5, and because the road from it links the popular Paradise area with Ohanapecosh and Sunrise. In winter, this route dead-ends at Paradise, but the other roads within the park are not plowed at all.

By Bus. Gray Line (tel. 360/544–0739 or 800/426–7532) runs buses between Seattle and Mt. Rainier National Park from May through mid-October.

By Car and RV. Seattle is 80 mi from the park, and Tacoma is 55 mi. It takes about two hours by car to get to the Nisqually entrance from Seattle and 1½ hours from Tacoma. From both cities, take I–5 south to Highway 7 east, which will bring you to Route 706 and Mt. Rainier.

A scenic alternate route (impassable in winter) starts in Renton, 10 mi southeast of downtown Seattle. Follow Highway 169 east from Renton and pick up Highway 410 at Enumclaw. This road follows the eastern edge of the park to Chinook Pass, where you pick up Highway 123 south to its junction with Stevens Canyon Road. Take Stevens Canyon Road west to its junction with the Paradise–Nisqually entrance road, which runs west through Longmire and exits the park at Nisqually. This route covers about 100 mi and will take you three to four hours to drive with minimal stops.

If you are coming from the east through Yakima, take Highway 12 northwest. Just past Naches the road will split: You can either continue on Highway 12 and pick up Highway 123 north to Ohanapecosh, or take Highway 410 west to Chinook and Cayuse passes and enter the park via the White River entrance.

From Portland, take I–5 north toward Olympia, then take Highway 12 east to Route 7 at Morton and finally Highway 706 to Mt. Rainier.

By Plane. The nearest airport is Seattle–Tacoma International, 70 mi and two hours northeast of the park. **Rainier Express** (tel. 360/569–2331) and **Rainier Overland** (tel. 360/569–0851) provide van shuttle service to Mt. Rainier from May through October. All major car-rental agencies service Seattle and Tacoma. Try **Budget** (tel. 800/345–6655; 800/435–1880 in WA) or **Avis** (tel. 360/433–5231).

By Train. There is no commercial rail service to the park; the nearest **Amtrak** (tel. 800/872–7245) station is in Tacoma, about 60 mi away. **Budget** (tel. 800/345–6655; 800/435–1880 in WA) and **Hertz** (tel. 360/922–6688) provide free shuttle service from the station to their offices. From May to October, the **Mount Rainier Scenic Railroad** (tel. 360/569–2588) runs 90-minute round-trip excursions from Elbe to Mineral Lake.

EXPLORING

A single, narrow, winding paved road links the main attractions at Rainier, and during the peak months of July and August, traffic can be torturously slow and heavy. Despite this, a combination of driving and hiking is your best bet for exploring the park. The ideal trip would include 10 to 14 days to hike the Wonderland Trail (*see* Longer Hikes, *below*), the magnificent 93-mi circuit of Mt. Rainier; but time and rugged terrain may make this option impractical.

The main park road from Nisqually climbs through towering forests toward Paradise, then loops around the east side of the mountain and exits at the park's northeast corner, a total of about 50 mi. The unpaved Westside Road runs northward 3 mi into the mountains from the Nisqually entrance. Two short gravel roads in the northwest corner of the park dead-end at Mowich Lake Campground and Ipsut Creek Campground. (At press time, the latter road was closed due to storm damage; call the visitor center for an update.) The rest of the park interior is roadless, and feet, horses, cross-country skis, and snowshoes are the only means of exploration.

It is possible to sample Rainier's main attractions—Longmire, Paradise, the Grove of Patriarchs, and Sunrise—in a single day by car, but you should plan on spending at least two days or, better, three, hiking the park's many forest, meadow, and high mountain trails.

Every year, nearly 10,000 people take the most adventurous exploring option of all—a climb up the steep face of Mt. Rainier. (Only about half that number reaches the mountain's 14,411-ft summit.) Novice climbers complete a one-day snow- and ice-climbing school taught by park concessionaire Rainier Mountaineering Inc. (*see* Other Activities, *below*), then make the two-day climb to the top. This transcendent mountain adventure, open to all regardless of previous climbing experience, is one of Mt. Rainier's most distinctive experiences.

THE BEST IN ONE DAY The best way to get a complete overview of Mt. Rainier in a day or less is to enter via Nisqually and begin your tour by browsing in the Longmire Museum. The .5-mi Trail of the Shadows nature loop will acquaint you with the environment in and around Longmire Meadow, as well as with the overgrown ruins of the Longmire Springs Hotel.

From Longmire, the road climbs northeast into the mountains toward Paradise. Take a moment to explore gorgeous Christine Falls, just north of the road 1.5 mi past Cougar Rock Campground, and Narada Falls, 3 mi farther on; both are spanned by graceful

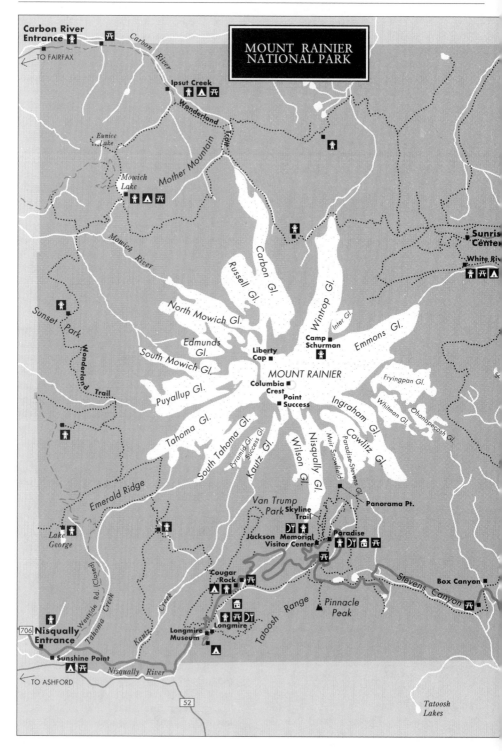

MOUNT RAINIER
NATIONAL PARK

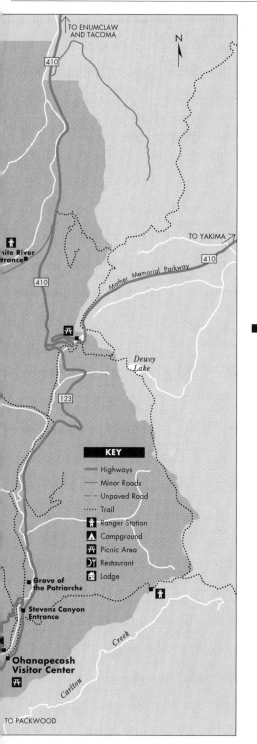

TO ENUMCLAW
AND TACOMA

N

410

TO YAKIMA

410

ite River
rance

410

Mather Memorial Parkway

Dewey
Lake

123

KEY

Highways
Minor Roads
Unpaved Road
Trail
Ranger Station
Campground
Picnic Area
Restaurant
Lodge

Grove of
the Patriarchs

Stevens Canyon
Entrance

Creek

Ohanapecosh
Visitor Center

Carlton

TO PACKWOOD

stone footbridges. Fantastic mountain views, alpine meadows crosshatched with nature trails, a welcoming lodge and restaurant, and the excellent Henry M. Jackson Memorial Visitor Center combine to make lofty Paradise the primary goal of most park visitors. One outstanding (but grueling) way to explore the high country is to hike the 5-mi Skyline Trail to Panorama Point, which rewards you with stunning 360-degree views (*see* Longer Hikes, *below*).

Continue eastward 21 mi and leave your car for an hour to explore the incomparable, thousand-year-old Grove of the Patriarchs, a small, protected island where a 1.3-mi nature trail leads through towering Douglas fir, cedar, and hemlock. Afterward, turn your car north toward White River and the Sunrise Visitor Center, from which you can watch the alpenglow fade from Mt. Rainier's domed summit.

ORIENTATION PROGRAMS From the Fourth of July weekend through Labor Day, park rangers and naturalists lead frequent nature walks and illustrated campfire talks at Paradise, Longmire, Sunrise, and Ohanapecosh. See bulletin boards at campgrounds, ranger stations, and visitor centers for dates, times, and subjects; or call the main park phone number (tel. 360/569–2211).

The park's four visitor centers each focus on a different aspect of park ecology, and each is worth a visit. The **Longmire Museum**'s glass cases contain preserved plants and animals from the park, including a large, friendly-looking stuffed cougar. Historical photographs and geographical displays provide a worthwhile overview of the park's history. Longmire is open daily all year, from 9 to 4:15.

At disk-shape **Jackson Memorial Visitor Center** in Paradise, high on the mountain's southern flank, exhibits focus on geology, mountaineering, glaciology, winter storms, and alpine ecology. Multimedia programs repeat at half-hour intervals. The center is generally open daily from May to mid-October, and on weekends and holidays only throughout the rest of the year. Call for exact hours.

At **Ohanapecosh Visitor Center,** near the Grove of the Patriarchs, you can learn about the region's dense old-growth forests from late May to October, daily from 9 to 6.

The **Sunrise Visitor Center,** open daily from 9 to 6 between early July and Labor Day, has exhibits on that region's sparser alpine and subalpine ecology.

GUIDED TOURS Gray Line of Seattle (tel. 206/624–5813) runs daily bus tours to Mt. Rainier, with stops at Paradise and Longmire, from May 1 through mid-October. The tours leave at 8 AM from the Convention Center, downtown at 8th Avenue and Pike Street, and cost $45 per person. Lunch is not included in the price of this 10-hour trip. Reservations are required. **Cascade** (tel. 800/824–8897) bus service also runs tours to Mt. Rainier.

SCENIC DRIVES AND VIEWS Four paved roads form one continuous route through the park, with a spur road from the White River entrance to the Sunrise Visitor Center. The main road starts at the Nisqually entrance and traces the southern boundary of the park, turning north in the southeast corner, and traveling along the east side of the mountain until it exits the park in the northeast corner (*see* The Best in One Day, *above*). Every foot of this 50-mi route is scenic. Along the 7 mi of road between the Nisqually entrance and Longmire, deer stalk the shadows, and the narrow thoroughfare, wrapping around gigantic old trees, gives the right-of-way to nature. This is one of the most beautiful stretches of forest road in the world.

The kinks and twistings of the 15-mi spur road from the White River entrance to Sunrise give the best views of the mountain.

Two unnamed roads that start near the Carbon River entrance lead to some of the park's steepest, wildest, and most densely wooded sections. These roads are not plowed in winter and are often closed by mud slides (one of them was, indeed, closed at press time), but in dry summer months you can cover them even without a four-wheel-drive vehicle. Be careful—the roads are narrow and winding. One of the two northern roads ends at Ipsut Creek campground, the other at Mowich Lake. The latter road is usually open only from July through mid-October.

HISTORIC BUILDINGS AND SITES The **Paradise Inn,** in continuous operation since 1917, has sheltered the likes of Shirley Temple, Cecil B. DeMille, John D. Rockefeller, and Tyrone Power. Its high, gable roof, massive beams, and parquet floors were constructed from Alaska cedars salvaged during the building of the road to this high mountain meadow. Through the inn's tall, many-paned windows you will be treated to unequaled views of the mountain. The property is on the National Register of Historic Places.

A smaller sister establishment, the **National Park Inn at Longmire,** is also a national historic landmark, and like many of the park service buildings at Longmire, it is worth a look for its massive stone-and-timber construction and hand-forged wrought iron. Its rooms lost much of their historic character in a 1990 renovation.

NATURE TRAILS AND SHORT WALKS The .5-mi **Trail of the Shadows** begins just across the road from the National Park Inn at Longmire. It's notable for the insights it provides into meadowland ecology, its colorful soda springs, James Longmire's old homestead cabin, and the foundation of the old Longmire Springs Hotel, which was destroyed around the turn of the century.

A 1.3-mi loop takes hikers through one of the park's most stunning features, the **Grove of the Patriarchs,** a lush old-growth forest in Rainier's southeastern corner. The trail begins just west of the Stevens Canyon entrance and leads over a bridge to an island covered with thousand-year-old trees, among the oldest in the Northwest; they have been protected from forest fires and other disasters by the rushing waters.

The mile-long loop of the **Sourdough Ridge Self-Guiding Trail** takes you through the delicate subalpine meadows near the Sunrise Visitor Center. The trail begins at the north side of the parking area; a gradual climb to the ridge top yields magnificent views of Mt. Rainier and neighboring peaks Baker, Adams, Glacier, and Hood.

Equally popular in summer and winter, the 1.25-mi round-trip **Nisqually Vista Trail** heads out from the Jackson Visitor Center at Paradise, through subalpine meadows, to an overlook point for Nisqually Glacier. In winter, the snow-covered, gradually sloping trail is a favorite venue for cross-country skiers. In summer, listen for the shrill alarm calls of the area's marmots.

LONGER HIKES All other Mt. Rainier hikes pale in comparison to the stunning 93-mi **Wonderland Trail,** which completely encircles the mountain. The Wonderland passes through all the major life zones of the park, from the old-growth forests of the lowlands to the wildflowers and goat-haunted glaciers of the highlands. It's a rugged trail; elevation gains and losses totaling 3,500 ft are common in a day's hike, which averages 8 mi. Most hikers start out from either Longmire or Sunrise and take 10 to 14 days to cover the 93-mi route. Snow lingers on the high passes well into June, and you can count on rain any time of year. Campsites are primitive trailside areas with pit toilets and water that must be purified before drinking. Only the hardy and well-equipped should attempt this trip, but those who do will be amply rewarded.

Those who lack the time or the conditioning to complete the entire Wonderland loop can sample an 18-mi section of the trail that leaves Stevens Canyon Road at Box Canyon, runs northward along the mountain's east flank, and connects with the road to Sunrise near the White River entrance to the park. In three or four days of hiking, you can cover a microcosm of Rainier's scenic glories.

The 5-mi loop of the **Skyline Trail,** one of the highest in the park, beckons day-trippers with an exhilarating *Sound of Music* vista of alpine ridges and, in summer, meadows filled with brilliant flowers and birds. At 6,800-ft Panorama Point, the spine of the Cascade Range spreads away to the east, and Nisqually Glacier grumbles its way downslope. The trail begins and ends in the Paradise parking lot, just west of the inn.

OTHER ACTIVITIES **Back-Road Driving.** All vehicles are required to stay on constructed roads; off-road vehicles are not allowed in the park.

Biking. This is not a prime activity in the park. Bikes are allowed, but only on constructed roads; your best bets are usually Westside Road, which is closed to vehicles, and Carbon River Road, which was closed at press time. Off-road mountain biking is prohibited. Park roads are narrow, winding, and, in summer, extremely crowded with cars. Bike rentals are not available within the park.

Bird-Watching. Watch for kestrels, red-tailed hawks, and, occasionally, golden eagles on snags in the lowland forests. Rarely seen, but also present at Rainier, are great horned owls, spotted owls, and screech owls. Iridescent hummingbirds flit from blossom to blossom in the drowsy summer lowlands, and there are sprightly water ouzels in the many forest creeks. Raucous Steller's jays and gray jays scold passersby from trees, often darting boldly down to steal morsels from unguarded picnic tables. At higher elevations, look for the pure white plumage of the white-tailed ptarmigan as it hunts for seeds and insects in winter. Waxwings, vireos, nuthatches, sapsuckers, warblers, flycatchers, larks, thrushes, siskins, tanagers, and finches are common throughout the park in every season but winter.

Boating. There are no boat rentals inside the park. Nonmotorized boating is permitted on all lakes inside the park except Frozen Lake, Ghost Lake, Reflection Lakes, and Tipsoo Lake.

Fishing. Fishing in Rainier's unstocked lakes and rivers is apt to be an unproductive experience; the park isn't known for its fishing, but you're welcome to try. Small trout are the main quarry, and park rangers encourage "fishing for fun," with barbless hooks. No license is required, but seasonal regulations are enforced. The Ohanapecosh River and its tributaries are open to fly-fishing only.

Horseback Riding. Horseback riding is permitted on nearly 75 of the park's 240 mi of maintained trails, most of which are accessible from mid-July to September. Parties with horses may use four backcountry camps—Deer Creek, Mowich River, North Puyallup River, and Three Lakes. Neither saddle nor pack animals are permitted in auto campgrounds or picnic grounds, or within 100 yards of trail shelters or campsites. A horse trail map is available at ranger stations. There are no horse rentals within the park.

Mountain Climbing. The highly regarded concessionaire **Rainier Mountaineering Inc.**, cofounded by Himalayan adventurer Lou Whittaker, makes climbing the Queen of the Cascades an adventure open to anyone in good health and physical condition. The company teaches the fundamentals of mountaineering at one-day classes held during the climbing season, from late May through early September. Participants in these classes are evaluated for their fitness for the climb; they must be able to withstand a 16-mi round-trip with a 9,000-ft gain in elevation. Those who meet the fitness requirement choose between guided two- and four-day summit climbs, the latter via more-demanding Emmons Glacier. Experienced climbers can fill out a climbing card at the Paradise, White River, or Carbon River ranger stations and lead their own groups of two or more. Climbers must register with a ranger before leaving and check out upon return. There is a $15 per person fee for a single trip, or a $25 annual climbing fee. Otherwise, contact Rainier Mountaineering Inc. (Paradise, WA 98398, tel. 206/627–6242 in winter, 360/569–2227 in summer).

Ski Touring. Mt. Rainier is a major Nordic ski center. Equipment rentals are available at the **Longmire Ski Touring Center** (tel. 360/569–2411), adjacent to the National Park Inn at Longmire, for $10.50 per day. (No rentals are available on the eastern side of the park.) Though trails are not groomed, those around Paradise are extremely popular; if you want to ski with fewer people, try the trails in and around the Ohanapecosh/Stevens Canyon area, which are just as beautiful. Visitors should never ski on the plowed main roads, especially in the Paradise area—the snow-plow operator can't see you.

Snowmobiling. Snowmobiling is allowed on the east side of the park, between Highway 410 and White River Campground; and between the Ohanapecosh Visitor Center and Highway 123, which becomes Steven Canyon Road at Box Canyon. A $10 State of Washington Sno-Park permit, available at stores and gas stations throughout the area, is required to park in the area near the north park entrance arch.

Snowshoeing. Deep snows make Mt. Rainier a snowshoeing capital. Rentals are available at the **Mt. Rainier Guest Services Ski Shop** (tel. 360/569–2411), adjacent to the National Park Inn, for $12 per day. On weekends and holidays from late December through April, park rangers lead snowshoe walks that start at Jackson Memorial Visitor Center at Paradise and cover 1.2 mi in about two hours; there is no official fee for these, but a donation is requested. Check park publications for dates. The network of trails in the Paradise area makes it the best choice for snowshoers, but the park's east side roads, Highways 123 and 410, are unplowed and provide another good snowshoeing venue.

Swimming. There are 62 lakes and countless streams and rivers within the park, but all are fed by glacial snowmelt. Unless your tolerance for bone-chilling cold exceeds that of a walrus, it is best to avoid Rainier's waters. Reflection Lake, Frozen Lake, and Tipsoo Lake are closed to swimming.

CHILDREN'S PROGRAMS A Junior Ranger program for children ages 6 to 12 runs from July 4 through August; check park publications for the schedule. Also in summer, naturalists escort visitors on a two-hour, .5-mi walk through old-growth forest around Ohanapecosh Campground; you can also meet a park naturalist at the Cougar Rock Campground Amphitheater for a two-hour, .5-mi walk that includes nature activities (for scheduling information consult park publications or call the park headquarters at 360/569–2211). Both outings are geared toward children as well as adults.

EVENING ACTIVITIES Rangers and naturalists lead campfire talks and slide shows at park campgrounds from late June to mid-September. Consult bulletin boards at the campgrounds, visitor centers, and ranger stations for dates, times, locations, and subjects.

DINING

Dining options inside Mt. Rainier National Park are somewhat better than average because of the capable chefs at the National Park Inn at Longmire and (in summer) the lofty Paradise Inn. Outside park boundaries, dining options are relatively austere. Meal prices include a Washington sales tax of about 8%.

INSIDE THE PARK **Paradise Inn.** Where else can you get a decent Sunday brunch in a historic heavy-timbered lodge halfway up a mountain? Tall, many-paned windows provide terrific views of Rainier, and the warm glow of native wood permeates the large dining room. The lunch menu is simple and healthy—grilled salmon, salads, and the like. For dinner, you might find London broil with apple demi-glaze, Mediterranean chicken, and poached salmon with blackberry sauce. *Paradise, tel. 360/569–2413. Reservations not accepted. MC, V. Closed Oct.–late May. $$–$$$*

National Park Inn. This historic inn at Longmire was completely remodeled in 1990, a process that robbed it of some of its old-fashioned rustic charm but left it looking more cheerful. Photos of Mt. Rainier taken by some of the Northwest's top photographers adorn the walls of the inn's large

dining room—a bonus on the many days the mountain refuses to show itself. Meals are simple but tasty: maple hazelnut chicken, tenderloin tip stir-fry, and grilled red snapper with black bean sauce and corn relish. For breakfast, don't miss the home-baked cinnamon rolls with cream-cheese frosting. The inn is the only year-round lodging in the park, and it makes a great base camp for day explorers. *Tel. 360/569–2411. Reservations not accepted. MC, V. $$*

The **Paradise** and **Sunset visitor complexes** also have modestly priced snack bars serving burgers, sandwiches, and salads.

NEAR THE PARK **Alexander's Country Inn.** Without a doubt, this Victorian inn has the best food in the area. Fresh seafood figures heavily in the permanent menu: Try Alexander's rainbow trout, fresh from their own pond and panfried; salmon francaise, baked with a scampi-style sauce; and shrimp scampi. Other great choices are raspberry chicken, bourbon T-bone steak, and roasted duck with brandied cherry sauce. Don't forget homemade blackberry pie for dessert. Ceiling fans and wooden booths lining the walls make it look like a country kitchen. *37515 Hwy. 706 E, 4 mi east of Ashford, tel. 360/569–2300 or 800/654–7615. MC, V. Closed weekdays (except holidays) Nov.–mid-May. $$–$$$*

Wild Berry Restaurant. This ramshackle eatery just down the road from Alexander's is where the mountain's laid-back ski-and-hot-tub crowd stokes up for a long day in the woods. Salads, pizzas, crepes, sandwiches, and home-baked desserts are served in relaxed, friendly surroundings. *37720 Hwy. 706 E, 4 mi east of Ashford, tel. 360/569–2628. MC, V. $*

PICNIC SPOTS The picnic areas at **Sunrise** and **Paradise** are justly famous, especially in summer, when wildflowers fill the meadows and friendly yellow pine chipmunks dart hopefully about in search of handouts. After picnicking at Paradise, you can take an easy hike to one of the numerous waterfalls in the area—Sluiskin, Myrtle, or Narada, to name a few. Both areas are open from July through September only.

LODGING

The Mt. Rainier area is singularly bereft of quality lodging, a fact that may be a result of its proximity to Seattle. The two national park lodges, at Longmire and Paradise, are attractive and well maintained, and ooze history and charm, but unless you've made your summer reservations a year in advance, your chances of getting a room are slim. There are dozens of motels and cabin complexes near the park entrances, but the vast majority are disappointingly plain, overpriced, or downright dilapidated. With just a few exceptions, you're better off camping. The room tax in Washington is 9.8%.

INSIDE THE PARK **National Park Inn.** This smaller, more modern, and more intimate version of the Paradise Inn (*see below*) lost a little of its old rustic flair but gained a lot of comfort in an extensive 1990 renovation. The old stone fireplaces are still here, but the public areas suffer from generic prefab country touches. The small rooms mix budget-motel functionality (though without TVs and telephones) with such wistful backwoods touches as antique bentwood headboards and graceful wrought-iron lamps. A good restaurant serves Northwestern specialties including seafood and hearty spaghetti. Located down the hill at heavily wooded Longmire, the inn is the only year-round lodging in the park, and it makes a great base camp for day explorers. Reservations up to a year in advance are highly recommended. *Box 108, Ashford, WA 98304, tel. 360/569–2275. 25 rooms, 18 with bath. Facilities: restaurant. MC, V. $$*

Paradise Inn. With its hand-carved cedar logs, burnished parquet floors, stone fireplaces, Native American rugs, and glorious mountain views, this 80-year-old inn is loaded with high-mountain atmosphere. Its smallish, sparsely furnished rooms, however, are not equipped with TVs or telephones and have thin walls and showers that tend to run cold during periods of peak use. The attraction here is the 5,400-ft alpine setting, so lovely you expect Julie Andrews to stroll by singing at any moment. There's a small, crowded bar and a competent dining room as well. Reserve well in advance. *Box 108, Ashford, WA 98304, tel. 360/569–2275. 127 rooms, 96 with bath. Facilities: restaurant, bar, snack bar. MC, V. Closed early Oct.–late May. $$*

NEAR THE PARK **Wellspring.** This collection of cabins is the creation of Sunny Thompson-Ward, a massage therapist, and is the area's only retreatlike alternative. A choice of nine log cabins—each tastefully designed to optimize views of the surrounding woodland—share the compound with a couple of spas (huts sheltering outdoor hot tubs, saunas, and massage rooms). Cabins are individually decorated: The extremely romantic "Nest" has a suspended bed over a pillow-strewn floor; the "Tatoosh" has a huge stone fireplace and can accommodate 10 people. The fee structure is an à-la-carte menu of options involving therapeutic massage and use of the spas. A breakfast basket is delivered to the cabins in the morning. *Hwy. 706 E (4 mi east of Ashford), Ashford, WA 98304, tel. 360/569–2514. AE, DC, MC, V. $$–$$$*

Alexander's Country Inn. Right down to the fairy-tale turret, Alexander's is Victorian in every detail; it was built in 1912. There's no lack of modern comforts, however. A large hot tub overlooks the trout pond out back, and a second-floor sitting room has a fireplace, stained-glass doors, and complementary evening wine. There are also two separate three-bedroom ranch houses next door, the Forest House and the Chalet. The Chalet has more of the country-quaint qualities found in the Inn; the Forest House has scant decor, but it does have a private moss-covered backyard. A hearty farm breakfast is included in the price of an overnight stay. *37515 Hwy. 706 E (4 mi east of Ashford), Ashford, WA 98304, tel. 360/ 569–2300 or 800/654–7615. 12 rooms, 2 guest houses. Facilities: restaurant, hot tub, fishing. MC, V. $$*

Nisqually Lodge. Built in 1989, this motor lodge has a faux Swiss-chalet feel, with a big stone fireplace, exposed beams, and lots of knotty pine in the lobby. Although it is decorated with budget furniture and institutionlike amenities, the lodge retains an airy, comfortable atmosphere. A Continental breakfast is included in the room price. *31609 Hwy. 706 E (2 mi east of Ashford), Ashford, WA 98304, tel. 360/569–8804. 24 rooms. Facilities: hot tub. AE, DC, MC, V. $$*

Whittaker's Bunkhouse. In 1991 Lou Whittaker of Rainier Mountaineering bought this vintage-1908 motel. In those days it housed loggers and was nicknamed "The place to stop on the way to the Top." Now, as then, it's a comfortable hostelry, with extremely inexpensive single bunks as well as larger private rooms. Guests are invited to bask in the hot tub; there's also an espresso café. *30205 SR 706 E, Ashford, WA 98304, tel. 360/569–2439. 19 rooms. Facilities: café, hot tub. MC, V. $–$$*

Between the park's Nisqually entrance and the town of Ashford, 11 mi east, Highway 706 is crowded with privately owned bed-and-breakfasts, motels, and cabin complexes. Though most are small and primitive, they fill up quickly in summer. These include the **Gateway Inn** (tel. 360/569–2506), the **Growly Bear Bed & Breakfast** (tel. 360/569–2339), **Mountain Meadows Inn** (tel. 360/569–2788), **Mounthaven** (tel. 360/569–2594), and **Rainier Country Cabins** (tel. 360/569–2355).

CAMPING

INSIDE THE PARK There are five drive-in campgrounds in the park—Cougar Rock, Ipsut Creek, Ohanapecosh, Sunshine Point, and White River—with almost 700 campsites for tents and RVs. All these campgrounds have parking spaces, drinking water, garbage cans, fire grates, and picnic tables with benches. There are ranger stations, flush toilets, and concrete parking pads at Cougar Rock, Ohanapecosh, and White River. None of the park

campgrounds has hot water, and RV hookups are not available. (Showers are available only at Jackson Memorial Visitor Center.)

Just 5 mi past the Nisqually entrance is **Sunshine Point,** which has 18 Class B sites that are the only drive-in sites open all year. It's a pleasant, wooded riverside campground. Sites cost $10 per night.

Farther up the road, 2.5 mi north of Longmire, is **Cougar Rock,** a very popular, secluded, heavily wooded campground. It has 200 sites, including 60 pull-throughs— as well as five group sites. Open from late May to mid-October, Cougar Rock has an amphitheater and a trailer dump station. The fee is $10 per site; group sites can be reserved for $3 per person, per night, with a minimum of 12 people per group.

In the southeast corner of the park is lush, green **Ohanapecosh,** with 205 sites, including 10 walk-ins. Open from May to late October, Ohanapecosh has a visitor center, amphitheater, dumping station, and self-guided trail. The fee is $12 per site.

The **White River** campground, in the northeastern section of the park, has 117 sites that are available from late June to late September for $10 per site. At an elevation of 4,400 ft, White River is the highest and least-wooded campground in the park; it has partial views of Mt. Rainier's summit. Here you can also enjoy campfire programs and self-guided trails.

Isput Creek, which has only 31 sites and two group sites with no potable water, is the quietest park campground, but also the most difficult to reach. In the remote northwest corner of the park, it is open from May through October, though at press time it was closed to car campers, due to storm damage. Set in the middle of a wet, green, and rugged wilderness, this campground is near many self-guided trails.

Except for group sites, reservations are not accepted at any of the campgrounds; it's strictly first-come, first-served. Sunshine Point, Cougar Rock, and Ohanapecosh tend to fill up first; White River, the highest and last to open, is also busy but harder to get to. Cougar Rock, Ohanapecosh, and Sunshine Point have the best RV access. The road to White River is paved. Ipsut Creek is accessible only by a 5-mi, convoluted gravel road, which was closed at press time.

Camping is also allowed throughout the wilderness, but you must have a wilderness permit—ask at the visitor centers (*see* Visitor Information, *above*). Primitive sites are spaced at 7- or 8-mi intervals along the Wonderland Trail. A copy of "Wilderness Trip Planner: A Hiker's Guide to the Wilderness of Mt. Rainier National Park," available from any of the park's four visitor centers or through the superintendent's office (*see* Visitor Information, *above*), is an invaluable guide for those planning overnight backcountry stays.

Olympic National Park
Washington
Updated by Alex Aron

Just off the Washington coast, where the farthest northwestern horn of the continental United States gores the Pacific, the mournful lighthouse atop Destruction Island warns ships away from the rock-fanged coast of the Olympic Peninsula. To the north, the coast of the Olympic Peninsula curves gracefully outward toward Japan, a wild, lush coastline without roads, souvenir shops, golf courses, or crowded resorts. Marked only by the tracks of black bear, Roosevelt elk, bobcat, and other wildlife, these are the last wilderness beaches left in the contiguous United States, and just one area of Olympic National Park.

Traveling east from the coastline, you will reach the gateway to the park's most remarkable zone: a rare temperate rain forest. This type of rain forest exists only here on the northwest coast and in a few other isolated areas of the world.

The jagged Olympic Mountains gash the passing Pacific storm fronts, causing the forests and highlands to soak up as much as 200 inches of rain and snow each year—up to 11 inches in one day. Olympic National Park contains the largest, wildest ancient forest in the lower 48, with vast old Douglas fir, western hemlock, Sitka spruce, and western red cedar whose shallow roots spread over the mountains that feed them. The heavily forested park is divided into five biological zones: lush, mossy temperate rain forest in the coastal valleys; richly diverse lowland forests at elevations up to 3,000 ft; the snowier but still biologically

dense montane forest, from 3,000 to 4,500 ft; the austere subalpine forest from about 4,500 to 6,500 ft; and alpine meadows on the highest slopes.

A range of sharp, snow-frosted peaks rules the interior of the peninsula. In the regal shadow of 7,965-ft Mt. Olympus lie alpine meadows bursting with frantic life during the all-too-brief summer, glacial lakes of sapphire blue, lonely hiking trails to fill the soul with wonder, and living glaciers that advance or retreat a few feet each year.

Olympic is one of the least sullied national parks, partly because it is one of the least accessible. Although more than 12 roads enter the park from different directions, none traverse it, and none penetrate more than a few miles. In most of the park's interior, horses and hiking boots are the only means of transportation.

The secrets of the Olympic Peninsula have always been guarded well. Two of the first seaborne expeditions to alight here— Bodega y Quadra's in 1775 and Captain Charles Barclay's in 1787—suffered massacres at the hands of northwest coast Native Americans. It wasn't until 1889 that the first organized exploration of what is now Olympic National Park took place. The expedition, sponsored by the *Seattle Press*, took almost six months to hack its way from Port Angeles to Lake Quinault, about 50 mi south.

These virgin forests were preserved for posterity by federal mandate in 1897 and further protected by Theodore Roosevelt, who proclaimed the area a national monument in 1909. Official national park status was conferred in 1938.

ESSENTIAL INFORMATION

VISITOR INFORMATION For more information about the park, write to Superintendent, **Olympic National Park,** 3002 Mt. Angeles Road, Port Angeles, WA 98362; or call 360/452–0330.

Olympic's wilderness is a fragile web of life, and park regulations are designed to keep it as healthy and unspoiled as possible. A copy of "Olympic National Park: Backcountry Use Guidelines," available from any of the park's visitor centers or through the address above, is an invaluable guide for those planning overnight stays in the park.

Backcountry permits, which cost $5 per group, plus $2 per person per night, are required for all overnight stays in the park's wilderness areas. They are available at some ranger stations or the Wilderness Information Center (tel. 360/452–0300).

FEES Visitors to Hurricane Ridge, Hoh, Staircase, Elwha, and Sol Duc are charged $10 per vehicle, or $5 per noncommercial bus passenger. If you enter at the more isolated, Lake Ozette you'll only have to pay a $1 parking fee.

PUBLICATIONS The park service publishes a variety of free fliers on specific aspects of the park, including "Suggested Day Hikes," "Facilities and Services," and "Climate and Seasons." You can pick these up at the visitor centers, or write to the park superintendent (*see* Visitor Information, *above*).

A handy mail-order catalog of books and maps of the park is available from the **Northwest Interpretive Association** (3002 Mt. Angeles Rd., Port Angeles, WA 98362, tel. 360/452–4501, ext. 239), as are the following books:

Robert L. Wood's *Olympic Mountains Trail Guide* is a bible for both day hikers and those planning longer excursions. Stephen Whitney's *Field Guide to the Cascades and Olympics* is an excellent trailside reference covering more than 500 plant and animal species found in the park. Rowland W. Tabor's *Geology of Olympic National Park* provides a detailed history of the forces that shape the Olympic Peninsula and guides geophiles to geologic points of interest within the park. Robert Steelquist's *Olympic National Park and the Olympic Peninsula* is a lavishly illustrated overview of the park, complete with detailed maps.

GEOLOGY AND TERRAIN The rocky 57-mi coastal strip of Olympic National Park has claimed hundreds of ships over the years, and their weedy bones protruding from the surf at low tide lend poignancy to the gorgeous vistas of wave-tortured stone. Hikers who explore the long, driftwood-choked gray-sand beaches linked by slick, steep forest trails find teeming tide pools, vast galleries of rock sculptures, and brooding, forested headlands. The incoming tides are strong and fast, and the surf often carries logs that can weigh several tons and have killed some unwary waders and swimmers over the years.

The coastal portion of the park is separated from its mountainous interior by a broad band of land, most of which was logged off early this century. Passing through this belt of savage clear-cuts—a zone of stumps and erosion-gashed hillsides—you will enter the dense, protected virgin forests along the Olympic Mountains' western slopes in the lush valleys of the Hoh, Queets, Quinault, and Bogachiel rivers. These valleys were scoured out of the basalt mountains by glaciers and water, a process that continues to this day.

Towering above, the Olympic Mountains are an austere rampart of glacier-carved stone 1.5 mi high, pocked with waterfalls, meadows, and clear glacial lakes. Less than 30 million years ago the Olympic peninsula was under water. When the tremendous tectonic forces of the Pacific's "Ring of Fire" crumpled the floor of the sea and thrust it skyward, the mountains rose and intercepted moisture from the Pacific. Streams and glaciers formed, and the intricate carving of the Olympics began. Today the park contains some 60 named glaciers, vast sheets of ice in constant slow motion. The Blue, White, and Hoh glaciers of Mt. Olympus are the most impressive.

FLORA AND FAUNA A mild climate, torrential rainfall, warm sunlight, and a wealth of plant and animal species have combined to produce the complex ecological system of Olympic's temperate rain forest. Gigantic, elephant-bark Douglas fir, shaggy cedar, and lordly Sitka spruce thrust hundreds of feet heavenward. One Douglas fir, on the South Fork of the Hoh River, stands 298 ft high; another, near the Queets River, is 44 ft in circumference. A thick carpet of moss cushions the forest floor, and dense fern glades provide cover for small animals. Epiphytes, or "air plants," pluck moisture from the musky air.

As the elevation increases, the lowland and montane forests give way to a sparser subalpine zone of stunted, widely spaced clumps of subalpine fir, Western hemlock, and yellow cedar. Above the timberline, where the snow can last into August, magnificent alpine meadows bloom with wildflowers during the brief summers (mid-July to mid-September). At this time, there is a profusion of lupines, wallflowers, paintbrushes, phlox, and monkeyflowers, as well as some species that are found only in the Olympics, such as the delicate, six-petaled Pipers bellflower.

Herds of Roosevelt elk, some weighing 1,000 pounds, wander the park, their bellows of challenge echoing through the forest during the September mating season. Black bears, coyotes, and cougars haunt the highlands (Olympic is believed to contain the largest cougar population of any national park). Black-tailed deer are also plentiful—and unafraid of human visitors.

Among the park's most unique and charming inhabitants is the chubby and gregarious Olympic marmot. These cat-size rodents, related to the eastern woodchuck, inhabit the high meadows and talus slopes of the park. This species of marmot is found nowhere else in the world. Their shrill whistles of alarm greet hikers throughout the high country, and their friendly antics are an inexhaustible source of entertainment. Squirrels, chipmunks, weasels, river otters, and hundreds of other mammals also inhabit the park.

A colony of sea otters, re-introduced after the original population was hunted to extinction, cavorts in the offshore kelp beds, in full view of coastal hikers. Seals are plentiful, and in late March and early April pods of Pacific gray whales pass on their way north to Alaska. In early fall most return, heading south to Baja, California.

Avian life thrives from the coastal estuaries to the high mountain crags. Bald eagles and red-tailed hawks ride the winds in search of prey. Great blue herons, with their 6-ft wingspans, stalk the estuaries. Glossy, long-billed black oyster catchers patrol the shoreline, while brilliant hummingbirds dip nectar from the flowers. The water ouzel, found in forest streams from the high slopes to the sea, dives and walks along the river bottom to find its meals. The crow-size pileated woodpecker, with its red head and haunting call, is another star performer.

There are those who believe Olympic National Park's vast wilderness houses another rare and timid species: Bigfoot, or Sasquatch, whose tracks local residents occasionally claim to find. When asked about the legendary creature, park rangers usually wink and smile.

WHEN TO GO Because of the park's vastly varied terrain, it's difficult to generalize about weather at Olympic. Even at the height of summer (late July to early September) the temperature rarely exceeds 85°F anywhere on the peninsula; in general, it ranges between 45°F and 75°F. Autumn is usually cool and wet, with temperatures in the 35°F to 60°F range. In winter, the park's windward mountains receive as much as 100 ft of snow, though the lowlands seldom receive more than a few inches at a time; temperatures are generally in the 40s during the day, dropping down to the high 20s and low 30s at night. Springs are wet, mild, and windy throughout the park. Three-quarters of Olympic's considerable precipitation falls between October 1 and March 31.

The coastal lowlands and forested areas of the park, accessible year-round, always teem with plant and animal life. The highlands tend to be snowed in well into summer; the best time to observe the flora and wildlife is during July, August, and September. Like most national parks, Olympic is most crowded in July, August, and September, when the weather is drier and plant and animal life are at their peak.

Starting in June, park rangers give free nature walks, lectures, and in the evenings, campfire programs on various aspects of park ecology. Overall, the weeks from mid-September to early October provide the best balance between plant and animal activity, good weather, and diminished crowds.

The dense snowpack in the mountains begins to accumulate in October, and from December to late March the area around Hurricane Ridge is a good place for Nordic skiing.

SEASONAL EVENTS July to early September: Park rangers lead nature walks, lectures, and fireside programs. See the park newspaper (available at the visitor centers and campgrounds) for dates, times, and subjects. **Late March to early November:** The **Olympic Park Institute** (111 Barnes Point Rd., Port Angeles, WA 98363, tel. 360/928–3720 or 800/775–3720) runs seminars on various aspects of park ecology, history, native culture, and such arts as writing, painting, and photography. The institute also organizes one- to five-day hiking and guided backpacking trips in the summer and fall, as well as whale- and bird-watching in the spring. Classes are led by wildlife experts, local artists, and park rangers and cost $12 to $290 per person. **Late March to mid-April:** Coastal hikers can watch the

stately passage of Pacific gray whales on their 12,000-mi annual migration from the Sea of Cortez to the Bering Sea. In October they pass in the opposite direction.

WHAT TO PACK Visitors to the peninsula, particularly campers and hikers, should be sure to bring adequate rain gear. Those planning extended stays in the backcountry will need to bring some means of purifying drinking water: vessels for boiling or lightweight, hand-pumped filters.

GENERAL STORES The main shopping area for the park is **Port Angeles,** the Olympic Peninsula's largest community, at the northern (Hurricane Ridge) entrance to the park.

Elsewhere, stores are fewer and farther between. Continuing counterclockwise around the park, there is a small general store at **Fairholm** (tel. 360/928–3020), at the west end of Lake Crescent. Food, gas, camping supplies, fishing tackle, and boat rentals are available there. The store is open daily from April 1 to October 1, from 9 to 6; between Memorial Day and Labor Day it stays open from 8 to 9.

Gas, food, and other supplies are available from several stores in the town of **Sappho** and its larger neighbor, **Forks.**

A small store at **Sol Duc Hot Springs Resort** (tel. 360/327–3583), in the northwestern corner of the park, stocks food, fishing tackle, and camping supplies; it's open from 8 AM to 9 PM, mid-May through late September.

Another general store is at **Kalaloch Lodge** (pronounced Clay-lock) (tel. 360/962–2271), on Highway 101, at the southern end of the park's coastal strip. It sells gas, food, fishing tackle, and camping supplies, and is open daily from 8 AM to 9 PM year-round.

ARRIVING AND DEPARTING The best way to reach Olympic National Park is by car. Though no roads traverse the park, and much of the coastline is roadless, Highway 101 circles the park, and spur roads provide access to it at various points. Visitor information is available at the Olympic

Park Visitor Center, in Port Angeles, and the Hoh Rain Forest Visitor Center, in the western section of the park, as well as at the Storm King Information Station, on Lake Crescent, and the Kalaloch Information Station, on the southern coast. The long stretch of highway from Kalaloch to Port Angeles, along the western and northwestern edges of the park, has the best views of ocean, forest, and mountains.

By Bus. Port Angeles, the park's northern gateway, is served by **Olympic Bus Lines and Tours** (tel. 360/452–3858). Buses depart daily from Seattle and Sea-Tac Airport. Fares are $20 one-way, $30 round-trip. **Clallam Transit** (tel. 360/452–4511 or 800/858–3747) provides commuter bus service to Sequim, Lake Crescent, Forks, and La Push (75¢–$1 one-way).

By Car and RV. The eastern boundary of the park is less than 50 mi from downtown Seattle as the crow flies; unfortunately, the Puget Sound lies in between, and the drive from Seattle to Kalaloch takes four to five hours. From Seattle or parts north, drivers can either cross the spectacular Tacoma Narrows Bridge or take a quick ferry ride, a relaxing way to see the island-dotted expanse of Puget Sound and catch rewarding glimpses of the Olympics. Seattle–Winslow, Seattle–Bremerton, and Edmonds–Kingston are the most popular ferry routes to the peninsula. Call 206/464–6400 for scheduling information. The one-way cost for a car and driver is $7.10 in summer, or $5.90 in winter, plus $3.50 for each passenger. Foot passengers pay $3.50 westbound only. The Bainbridge and Bremerton ferries depart downtown Seattle from Pier 52. The Edmonds–Kingston ferry departs from Edmonds, 15 mi north of Seattle: From I–5, take the Edmonds exit and follow the signs to the ferry terminal. Once you are in Bremerton, drive north on Route 3, turn left onto Route 104, and then turn right onto Highway 101, which leads directly to Olympic's main entrance, in Port Angeles. From Bainbridge, take 305 north to Route 3 and follow the directions above, and from Kingston drive west on 104, also following the directions above. The drive from each of these three towns is between 70 and 75 mi and takes roughly 1½ hours. Those arriving from the south via I–5 should turn westward on Highway 101 at Olympia.

By Plane. Visitors can fly into either **Seattle-Tacoma International Airport,** 10 mi south of downtown Seattle and a three-hour drive from the park, or **Fairchild International Airport,** at Port Angeles, the park's northern gateway. Both airports are served by **Horizon Air** (tel. 800/547–9308). Dozens of car-rental firms service Seattle's airport, the region's busiest; call **Sea-Tac information** (tel. 360/433–5217) for specific agencies. In Fairchild, try **Budget Rent-A-Car** (tel. 360/457–4246).

By Train. There is no passenger train service on the Olympic Peninsula. Seattle, Tacoma, and Olympia are served by **Amtrak** (tel. 800/872–7245). Rental cars are available in all three cities.

EXPLORING

You can acquire an overview of the park by driving up the coast from Kalaloch, visiting the Hoh Rain Forest, then continuing on to Hurricane Ridge, but only if you're willing to hike a few miles off the main roads will you discover the park's hidden grandeur. Plan to spend at least a day in each of the park's three wilderness environments: coastal, forest, and mountain. Try camping in several of the 17 campgrounds, or break up your visit with a stay at Kalaloch Lodge or one of the bed-and-breakfasts near the park.

THE BEST IN ONE DAY Those who have just one day to see Olympic National Park and want to see a variety of ecosystems must have a car. It's best to start in the mountains and work your way toward the sea. Begin your tour at Hurricane Ridge, 17 mi south of Port Angeles. There are soul-stirring mountain views from this point, 5,200 ft up in the Olympics, and in summer, the green alpine meadows are grazed by shy black-tailed deer. A warm, modern lodgelike visitor center with food service and observation plat-

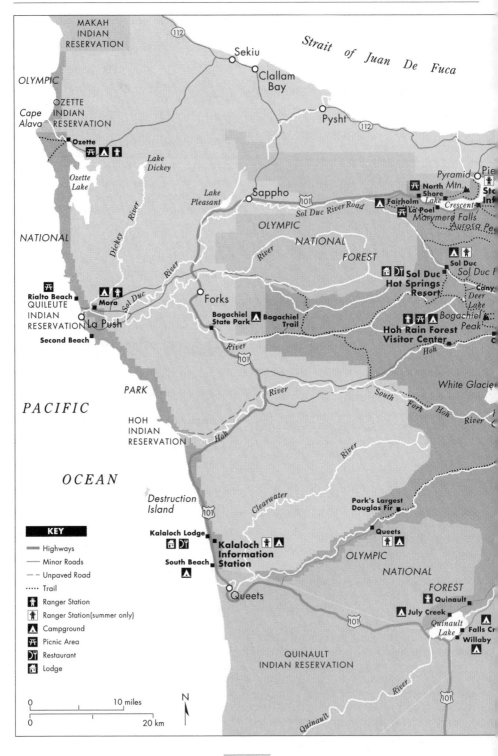

MAKAH
INDIAN
RESERVATION

112

Sekiu

Clallam
Bay

Strait of Juan De Fuca

OLYMPIC

OZETTE
INDIAN
RESERVATION

Cape
Alava

Pysht

112

Ozette

Ozette
Lake

*Lake
Dickey*

Pyramid   Pie

North Mtn.
Shore

Sto
Inf

NATIONAL

*Lake
Pleasant*

Sappho

101

Sol Duc River Road

Fairholm

La Poel
Marymere Falls

Crescent

Aurora Pe

Dickey River

OLYMPIC

NATIONAL

FOREST

Sol Duc

Sol Duc

River

Sol Duc R

Rialto Beach
QUILEUTE
INDIAN
RESERVATION

Mora

Sol Duc

Forks

Sol Duc
Hot Springs
Resort

Cany

Deer
Lake

La Push

Bogachiel
State Park

Bogachiel
Trail

Hoh Rain Forest
Visitor Center

Bogachiel
Peak

C

Second Beach

River

101

Hoh

PACIFIC

PARK

HOH
INDIAN
RESERVATION

River

Hoh

South

Fork

Hoh

White Glacier

River

OCEAN

Destruction
Island

101

Clearwater

Park's Largest
Douglas Fir

Queets

OLYMPIC

Kalaloch Lodge

Kalaloch
Information
Station

River

NATIONAL

South Beach

FOREST

Quinault

Queets

101

July Creek

*Quinault
Lake*

Falls Cr

Willaby

QUINAULT
INDIAN
RESERVATION

River

101

KEY

━━━ Highways
---- Minor Roads
- - - Unpaved Road
····· Trail
🛉 Ranger Station
🛉 Ranger Station (summer only)
▲ Campground
🛉 Picnic Area
🍴 Restaurant
🏠 Lodge

0   10 miles
0   20 km

N

Quinault

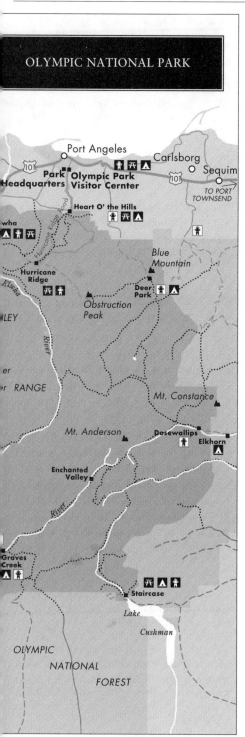

OLYMPIC NATIONAL PARK

Port Angeles
Carlsborg
Sequim
Park Olympic Park
Headquarters Visitor Cernter
TO PORT
TOWNSEND
Heart O' the Hills
wha
Blue
Mountain
Hurricane
Ridge
Deer
Park
Obstruction
Peak
ILEY
RANGE
Mt. Constance
Mt. Anderson
Dosewallips
Elkhorn
Enchanted
Valley
Graves
Creek
Staircase
Lake
Cushman
OLYMPIC
NATIONAL
FOREST

forms serves as a base for visitors. Hikes, short and long, radiate from the ridge in all directions. To get a good introduction to the mountains take the 1.5-mi-long paved Hurricane Hill Lookout Trail, which leaves the parking lot and climbs through meadows and stands of fir to the site of a former fire lookout.

Returning to Highway 101, drive west to limpid, mountain-girded Lake Crescent, and take the trail to Marymere Falls. This short, 1-mi trail ascends through dense forest to the base of the falls, a 90-ft cascade falling into a moss-hung grotto.

Continue along Highway 101 until you reach the sign for Mora, Rialto Beach. Follow the 14-mi spur road, stopping for lunch in the tiny community of Three Rivers, then drive on to Rialto Beach. Here, the restless Pacific has slashed away at the rocky coast, creating a series of much-photographed natural pillars, monoliths, sea stacks, and offshore islands. The beach is adjacent to the parking lot. Look for shells and green-glass fishermen's floats from Japan along the shore. Watching a melancholy sunset through the rocks and driftwood is a fitting end to any tour.

An alternate plan is to spend the day exploring the Hoh Rain Forest. Enter the park on the western side and take Highway 101, stopping for lunch in the town of Forks. Staying on the same road—the only road—travel south and follow the signs toward the Hoh Rain Forest, 18.5 mi from the Highway 101 turnoff up the Hoh River. A somewhat rudimentary visitor center will acquaint you with the basic ecology of the ancient forests that blanket this portion of the park. Behind the building is the beginning of the Hall of Mosses nature trail, an easy .75-mi loop over chuckling creeks and through stately, somber forests that have never known an ax. Signs explain many facets of the rich and complex forest biosphere.

ORIENTATION PROGRAMS The best place to get a quick overview of the park is the **Olympic Park Visitor Center** (3002 Mt. Angeles Rd., Port Angeles, tel. 360/452–

0330), which is open year-round, daily from 9 to 4, with extended hours from July through Labor Day. Here you'll find written materials as well as displays on park geology, history, and wildlife. A 13-minute slide show provides an excellent survey of the history and main features of the park.

The park's other information centers are at Hoh Rain Forest, Hurricane Ridge, Kalaloch, and the ranger stations at Dosewallips, Elwha, Mora, Ozette, Queets, Lake Quinault, Sol Duc, and Staircase. These tend to be more limited in scope, providing information more specific to the area in which they are located. Several visitor centers close seasonally; call the main visitor center to find out which are open.

From July 1 through Labor Day, park naturalists lead nature walks that last from one to several hours through Olympic's forests, meadows, and tidal areas. These highly informative walks give visitors a hands-on experience and are an excellent way to get to know different aspects of park ecology. Weekly schedules are posted on the bulletin boards at visitor centers and campgrounds. Also in summer, a newsletter lists naturalist activities.

GUIDED TOURS An area native with a genuine love for the park leads trips in air-conditioned 10-passenger vans to Hurricane Ridge, through a service called **Olympic Van Tours** (Box 273, Port Angeles, WA 98362, tel. 360/452–3858). The three-hour tour departs from downtown Port Angeles two times a day from mid-June to Labor Day and costs $13 per person, and an all-day trip is also available. Tours to the Hoh Rain Forest, Lake Crescent, Marymere Falls, and other destinations can be arranged upon request. Full-day trips take visitors through the full range of the Peninsula's ecosystems, including the shore (Rialto Beach), the forest (Hoh Rain Forest), and the mountains (Lake Crescent and Hurricane Ridge). The cost is $48 per person (price includes picnic lunch).

Four backcountry operators lead guided backpacking trips through Olympic National Park: **America's Adventure Inc.** (2245 Stonecrop Way, Golden, CO 80401, tel. 303/526–0806); **Mountain Madness Inc.** (4218 S.W. Alaska, Suite 206, Seattle, WA 98116, tel. 360/937–8389, fax 360/937–1772); **Trailmark Outdoor Adventures Inc.** (16 Schuyler Rd., Nyack, NY 10960, tel. 914/358–0262); and **Wilderness Ventures Inc.** (Box 2768, Jackson, WY 83001, tel. 307/733–2122).

Olympic's rugged wilderness also lends itself well to travel with llamas, who carry the equipment while you walk. Three local firms lead llama pack trips: **Kit's Llamas** (Box 116, Olalla, WA 98359, tel. 360/857–5274); the **Woolley Packer Llama Co.** (5763 Upper Hoh Rd., Forks, WA 98331, tel. 360/374–9288); and **Olympak Llamas** (3175 Old Olympic Hwy., Port Angeles, WA 98362, tel. 360/452–4475).

SCENIC DRIVES AND VIEWS **Highway 101** circles the park, and those who take the time to explore its length will find much to enthrall them. The 95-mi drive from Kalaloch to Port Angeles offers an ever-changing series of shoreline, forest, lake, and mountain views. Clear-cuts mar the road from the Hoh River to Sappho; take a good long moment to contemplate the destruction. Stop and stretch your legs at La Poel Picnic Area, on the south shore of the deep blue-green Lake Crescent. The snowcapped ramparts of the Olympics lie beyond.

To get a look at a forest in restoration—that is, a heavy second-growth forest—as well as an old-growth forest, backtrack 2 mi and turn left down **Sol Duc River Road.** This paved spur road runs for about 12 mi and ends at the trailhead to lovely Sol Duc Falls, about a mile's hike one-way.

The 17 serpentine mi of **Hurricane Ridge Road** run from Port Angeles into the mountains, providing unequaled glimpses of the peninsula's glacier-sculpted interior. At the 9-mi point, the wayside at Lookout Rock overlooks the Strait of Juan de Fuca, Dungeness Spit, and Vancouver Island. Following a paved path at Lookout Rock, you'll be rewarded with views of the crags of the Olympics.

NATURE TRAILS AND SHORT WALKS Olympic National Park abounds in short exploratory walks showcasing various aspects of park ecology. Probably the best known of these is the **Hall of Mosses Trail,** which begins at the Hoh Rain Forest Visitor Center. This gentle .75-mi loop takes hikers through the forest and into a fanciful grove of maple and alder dripping with green-gold moss.

At **Second Beach,** 14 mi west of Highway 101 on the La Push Road, a .5-mi trail leads to a broad, tide pool–filled beach with excellent views of the offshore sea stacks.

The **Quinault Rain Forest Nature Trail,** also known as the Maple Grove Nature Trail, leads through one of the finest groves of old-growth Douglas fir left in the world. These magnificent, near-primeval evergreens are remarkable for their uniform age and size—500 years old and 250 to 275 ft tall. The .5-mi (one-way) trail meanders through the somber forest, and benches are placed along the way for quiet contemplation. The trailhead is at the parking area west of Willaby Creek, 1.5 mi northeast of Highway 101 on Lake Quinault's South Shore Road.

LONGER HIKES Olympic's 600 mi of trails require 23,000 man-hours of maintenance work annually, and many of the park's most precious treasures are accessible only on foot.

Wilderness beaches provide the park's most unusual hiking experience: an opportunity to explore a green Pacific coastline essentially unaltered by humans. Raccoons waddle from the forest to pluck dinner from the tide pools; bald eagles stoop over fantastic tangles of bleached drift-logs, the bones of ancient forests. The three-day hike from Rialto Beach to Cape Alava is especially rewarding. Hikers—equipped with backcountry permit, current tide table and a watch (many headlands can only be crossed at low tide), a durable tent, and rain gear—generally camp on the beach. To reach Rialto Beach take Highway 101 to the point just north of Forks where signs point the way west to the shore. Park at the picnic area.

One note of caution: Beach hikers should beware of the peninsula's strong incoming tides and beach logs, some of which weigh several tons. Logs roll unpredictably in the surf and have killed unwary waders and swimmers over the years. You should also use extreme caution when hiking around the park's many protruding headlands— incoming tides may trap you, rendering it impossible to advance or retreat. When hiking the coastal strip, always carry a watch and a current tide table, available at all visitor centers and many stores.

For a long hike combining the best of Olympic's forest and mountain areas, take Sol Duc River Road to the end and park at the trailhead. The 8.5-mi **Sol Duc Trail** first passes Sol Duc Falls, then follows the river through colonnades of huge Douglas fir, hemlock, and cedar. The trail climbs steeply after the falls, toiling toward its junction with the spectacular **High Divide Trail** at Sol Duc Park, a perfect base camp for an exploration of the alpine meadows and peaks nearby. Turning west along the High Divide Trail, you'll enjoy incredible mountain vistas in every direction, particularly of Mt. Olympus and the Bailey Range. The trail tightropes along the spine of the mountains for a little over 2 mi; at Bogachiel Peak, turn north on the **Bogachiel Trail** toward Deer Lake, reentering the forest. After about 4 mi you'll reach the lake and the junction of the **Canyon Creek Trail,** which leads you back to Sol Duc Falls. The loop totals about 17.5 mi and runs through steep and mountainous terrain; plan on taking your time and spending two or, better, three nights along the trail.

For all their splendor, the trails in the Sol Duc region are probably the most-trampled trails in the park. Rangers, fearing the long-term environmental effects of heavy wear on the trails, have instituted a quota system during the summer months: Between July 1 and September 30, check in at the Sol Duc Ranger Station before setting off on these trails. If the area is too crowded, the rangers will suggest alternative trails in quieter, but no less spectacular, regions of the park. To avoid being turned away, skip Sol Duc and head to the Dosewallips or Staircase ranger stations for information on crossing the park along the Dosewallips River in the southeastern corner of Olympic.

OTHER ACTIVITIES **Back-Road Driving.** No roads penetrate more than a few miles into the park, and vehicles are prohibited.

Biking. Mountain bikes are allowed on only two trails at Olympic: Spruce Railroad Trail (north shore of Lake Crescent) and Olympic Hotsprings Trail (in Elwha Valley). Bikes are not allowed off the trails. Roads in and around the park are generally narrow, winding, steep, and, particularly in the summer, crowded with automobile traffic. There are no bike rental facilities inside the park. **P.T. Cyclery** (100 Tyler St., tel. 360/385–6470), on the beach in Port Townsend, rents bikes by the day and the hour.

Bird-Watching. With its proximity to both shoreline and mountains, Olympic is one of the truly outstanding national parks for bird-watchers. Bald eagles are found throughout the coastal reaches of the park; look for them soaring on the offshore breeze or nesting in the branches of Sitka spruce. Graceful great blue herons stalk the coastal estuaries on stiltlike legs, watching keenly for fishy morsels. In the forests, look for the large rectangular holes carved by redheaded pileated woodpeckers in standing dead trees called snags. Wild ducks, particularly mergansers and harlequins, bob along on calm stretches of forest streams; the charming water ouzel floats and dives, then walks along the streambed searching for its meals. Higher up, in the alpine meadows, the gray-crowned rosy finch flits about in search of insects. Hurricane Ridge is the best place to observe blue grouse, whose booming calls attract females during the mating season. In early April, thousands of hawks congregate at the tip of Cape Flattery (at the northwestern end of the peninsula) on their way to their breeding grounds to the north.

Boating. Lake Crescent, one of the largest of Olympic's lakes, is the prime spot for boaters. Paddleboats, rowboats, and canoes

are available for rent at the **Log Cabin Resort** (tel. 360/928–3325), at the lake's northeast end. The resort is open from mid-February through December. The **Fairholm General Store** (tel. 360/928–3020), at the western end of the lake, rents boats from May 1 to September 30; it's generally open from 8 to 7 in summer and from 9 to 6 the rest of the year. A U.S. Coast Guard courtesy inspection is required for any boat on the lake.

Fishing. Licenses are not required in the park, except at the Pacific coast. The many streams and lakes at Olympic contain rainbow, brook, and sea-run cutthroat trout. A unique and beautiful species of trout, the crescenti, is found only in Lake Crescent. Most prized of all are the huge and belligerent steelhead that spawn in the coastal streams each fall. To fish for these, or for the coho and chinook salmon that throng the ocean and the sound, anglers need a State of Washington punch card, available from any general store or sporting goods outlet in the vicinity.

Rock Climbing. Although the tallest of the park's peaks, Mt. Olympus, is only 7,965 ft high, many of the Olympic Mountains present more climbing challenges than their diminutive stature would suggest. Each year avid climbers converge here to try their skills on these jagged walls of rock. Mt. Olympus, with its crevassed glaciers and vertical rock walls, is known for excellent snow and ice climbing. Mt. Storm King (4,534 ft), Mt. Ellinor (5,944 ft), and the Brothers (6,866 ft) are popular, but less demanding. Mt. Constance (7,743 ft) and Mt. Anderson (7,365 ft) present more exciting challenges for top-notch climbers. Climbing parties must register at the ranger station nearest their route. One tour operator—**Mountain Madness** (*see* Guided Tours, *above*)—provides climbing instruction, equipment rentals, and guided climbing excursions.

Snowshoeing and Ski Touring. Ski and snowshoe rentals and instruction are available at the Hurricane Ridge Visitor Center as long as the snow lasts, but the best conditions are from mid-December through late March. The most popular route for day-mushers is the 1.5-mi Hurricane Hill Road, just west of the parking area. A marked snow-play area with trails and gentle hills has been set aside near the center for cross-country skiers, snowshoers, inner tubers, and children.

Swimming. The Pacific is a dangerous playground this far north: Even in summer, ocean temperatures seldom exceed 50°F, and ocean currents are vicious. The park's best swimming areas are at Lake Crescent, whose cool and inviting green water is distilled from the glaciated peaks that surround it. At Fairholm Campground, on the lake's west end, there is a small sandy beach with a roped-off swimming area. At the opposite end of the lake, East Beach Picnic Area has a larger beach and, often, warmer air and water temperatures.

CHILDREN'S PROGRAMS Olympic has few programs for children. However, children may be interested in the park's summertime naturalist programs, which are geared to all ages. Consult the bulletin boards at the visitor centers and campgrounds for information on location, subject matter, and scheduling.

EVENING ACTIVITIES On summer nights after the sun goes down, park naturalists give fireside lectures, illustrated with slides and movies, at the park's main campgrounds: Fairholm (Thursday through Saturday), Heart O' the Hills, Hoh, Mora, Sol Duc, and Kalaloch. Consult park bulletin boards for scheduling and subject information.

DINING

Surrounded by the fruitful waters of the Pacific and protected, island-flecked Puget Sound, the Olympic peninsula is seafood territory; tiny, delicate Quilcene oysters, rich chinook salmon, and, best of all, sweet, heavy-clawed Dungeness crab dominate menus. A bowl of creamy clam chowder is the perfect antidote to the chill of a hike through the cool, damp woods. One local specialty, the geoduck (pronounced goo-ey duck) clam, looks like something from a science-fiction movie when first plucked from the brine, its lank, leathery neck dangling a foot or more from the shell. But don't be scared off: The geoduck's flesh, pounded tender and quick-fried, is a famous local delicacy that every visitor should try.

Within the park, dining options are extremely limited. You'll have better luck in the peninsula's more sophisticated communities, particularly Port Angeles, Port Townsend, and Sequim (pronounced squim). A 7.7% Washington sales tax is added to the bill.

INSIDE THE PARK **Kalaloch Lodge.** You can count on finding fresh seafood and well-aged beef at this popular seaside resort, just within the southern boundary of the park's coastal strip. The menu changes seasonally, but it's hard to go wrong with the local oysters, crab, and salmon, often served baked or broiled with a simple lemon-butter sauce. The Salmon Oscar topped with Dungeness crabs is especially good. Dinner is also served in the upstairs cocktail lounge—which, like the restaurant, has unobstructed ocean views. *Hwy. 101, Kalaloch, tel. 360/962–2271. AE, MC, V. $$*

NEAR THE PARK **C'est Si Bon.** French expatriates Norbert and Michele Juhasz run this locally famous French restaurant, the most elegant eatery on the decidedly informal Peninsula. The food is outstanding—escargots in Pernod and a hearty onion soup are typical appetizers; outstanding entrées include *pavée du roi* (filet mignon with Dungeness crab), and sturgeon baked in phyllo pastry. There is an excellent wine list, and desserts are also good—especially the chocolate mousse. With its large European oil paintings hanging against bold red walls, and ornate lighting fixtures, C'est Si Bon has a distinctly playful ambience. A romantic balcony overlooks the room with four small tables, and views of the rose garden and the Olympic Mountains add to the allure. *2300 Hwy. 101 E (4 mi east of Port Angeles), tel. 360/452–8888. AE, DC, MC, V. Closed Mon. No lunch. $$$*

Fountain Café. This small, funky café filled with artwork and creative knicknacks is a quintessential Port Townsend restaurant run by a longtime town resident. Old standards like oysters Dorado remain by popular demand, but there are also plenty of creative new dishes. Look for seafood and pasta specialties with imaginative twists such as smoked salmon in light cream sauce with hint of scotch. *920 Washington St., Port Townsend, tel. 360/385–1364. Reservations not accepted. MC, V. Closed Tues. in winter. $$–$$$*

The Greenery. Fresh, healthy salads, thick deli sandwiches, and a flair for homemade pasta have long made this a favorite with locals. Preparations are simple and unpretentious; try a cheesy open-face Dungeness crab sandwich, or fettuccine with smoked salmon, fresh tomato, mushrooms, garlic, and cream. The staff is friendly and attentive. *117-B E. 1st St., Port Angeles, tel. 360/457–4112. AE, MC, V. Closed Sun. Dec.– Mar. $$*

Three Crabs. An institution since 1958, this large crab shack on the beach specializes in Dungeness's famed specialty. The clawed creatures are served many ways, but because these crabs are so fresh, it's best to have them the simple way: chilled, with lemon and butter. The large menu also accommodates non-seafood eaters and children. The ambience is vaguely nautical, with knotty-pine walls and views of New Dungeness Bay. *11 Three Crabs Rd. (5 mi north of Sequim, on the bay), tel. 360/683–4264. MC, V. $$*

Timber House. Quilcene is famous for its oysters, and this friendly, rustic restaurant is the place to get them—plump, sweet, and delicate. Try them raw on the half shell, with a squeeze of lemon and a dollop of horseradish–tinged cocktail sauce, or baked in the shell with drawn butter. Local Dungeness crabmeat, sautéed with butter, garlic, and wine, is outstanding. *.5 mi south of Quilcene, on Hwy. 101. tel. 360/765–3339. MC, V. Closed Tues. $$*

Swan Cafe. At this unpretentious, plant-filled storefront café near the Port Angeles ferry terminal, the chef/owner shows a light and deft touch with fresh local oysters, prawns, calamari, and other seafood. Try the oysters Dorado, in which the tiny, succulent bivalves are tossed with pepper linguine, mushrooms, and eggplant. *222 N. Lincoln St., Port Angeles, tel. 360/452–2965. D, MC, V. Closed Tues. $–$$*

Salal Café. Ample breakfasts are served around the clock on Sunday at this informal, brightly lit restaurant known for its hearty, healthy cuisine. For lunch there's standard American fare, with plenty of vegetarian options. Dinners are more exotic, with entrées like tofu stroganoff, mushroom risotto with oysters, and curried sea scallops. Try to get a table in the glassed-in back room, which faces a plant-filled courtyard. *634 Water St., Port Townsend, tel. 360/385– 6532. Reservations not accepted. No credit cards. No dinner Tues. or Thurs. $–$$*

Coffee House Restaurant and Gallery. This urban anomaly jump starts its daily horde of loyal customers with espresso drinks, homemade pastries, and sprouty vegetarian fare. Cheery, eclectic, and cheap, it's a good bet for a meal any time of day. *118 E. 1st St., Port Angeles, tel. 360/452–1459. No credit cards. $*

La Casita. This family-run Mexican restaurant overlooking Port Angeles harbor leans heavily on old standbys and combination plates, but what sets it apart is its artful use of local fish. The seafood chimichanga is a crisp-fried burrito filled with Dungeness crab, bay shrimp, fresh cod, Monterey jack cheese, tomato, and chilies. Other standouts: Dungeness crab enchilada; and crab-stuffed cod Veracruz, poached in salsa and topped with gooey jack cheese. Don't overlook the *pollo asado* (boneless chicken breasts marinated in tequila and orange juice and charbroiled). *203 E. Front St., Port Angeles, tel. 360/452–2289. AE, D, MC, V. $*

Shanghai Restaurant. The peninsula's best Chinese food is here. The huge menu features specialties from Szechuan and Hunan, most ranging from spicy to volcanic. The kimchilike Shanghai cabbage is enough to bring tears to your eyes, and the seafood items are masterfully done—tender, fragrant, and delicately sauced. The gingery kung pao shrimp is especially good. *265 Point Hudson, at eastern tip of Port Townsend, tel. 360/385–4810. D, DC, MC, V. $*

PICNIC SPOTS Olympic abounds with congenial spots for al fresco dining. So long as you pack out everything you brought in, any of the park's beaches, forested areas, and mountain meadows are suitable. Among Olympic's many official picnic areas, **Rialto Beach** is the best on the coast, **North Shore** is the most beautiful and least crowded on Lake Crescent, and **Hurricane Ridge** has the most tables and best views in the mountains.

LODGING

Although there are a few national and regional chain properties on the Olympic Peninsula, most of the lodgings are independently owned. For a rustic, woodsy atmosphere try the historic lodges at Kalaloch, Lake Quinault, and Lake Crescent. If it's pampering you want, an ever-growing population of Northwest-flavor bed-and-breakfasts cater to romantics. Families seeking practicality will find numerous small, clean, budget hotels and cabin resorts.

As in most national parks, the busy season at Olympic runs from mid-June to early September, and the best lodgings are booked months in advance. In the off-season, particularly during the stormy "monsoon" months (December through March), there are some lodging bargains to be had: Expect to pay 20% to 25% less per night during the winter and early spring months. Bear in mind, however, that several of the charming old lodges inside the park—Lake Crescent Lodge, the

Log Cabin Resort, and Sol Duc Hot Springs Resort—are closed from October or November through early May.

INSIDE THE PARK **Kalaloch Lodge.** This cedar-sided two-story lodge, built in 1953, sits on a low bluff overlooking the Pacific, just inside the southern boundary of Olympic's coastal strip. The informal lodge has eight rooms; in addition, 40 small cabins and a modern 10-room minimotel, Sea Crest House, straggle southward along the crest. The cabins are unadorned and rustic, but comfortable; most have terrific ocean views and fireplaces. A few of the larger cabins have private outdoor picnic areas in the greenery around the beach. Decor tends toward knotty pine and earth tones, with deep comfortable couches looking seaward out of picture windows. At night, fat raccoons waddle from the shore pines to press their noses against the windows. There are no phones or TVs in the rooms, but there is a common room off the lounge. Cabins 1 through 16 and the Macy and Overly cabins have the best ocean views. *Hwy. 101, HC 80, Box 1100, Forks, WA 98331, tel. 360/ 962–2271. 18 rooms, 40 cabins. Facilities: restaurant, coffee shop, kitchenettes, library. AE, MC, V. $$$*

Lake Quinault Lodge. Set on a perfect glacial lake in the midst of the Olympic National Forest, the lodge is within walking distance of spectacular old-growth forests and Lake Quinault, where there's abundant salmon and trout fishing. The complex consists of a medium-size central lodge with 33 rooms, 16 fireplace units attached to the lodge, and 43 units in the lakeside addition, a half block away on the lake. The main lodge was built in 1926 of cedar shingles. Though rooms are sparsely furnished and lack the sophistication of the grand lobby, all have antique furniture and a large stone fireplace. Most of the accommodations have views of the gently landscaped lawns and the lake beyond. The restaurant cuisine is excellent, and there's an old-fashioned, lively bar. Hiking and jogging trails begin right across the street. *South Shore Rd. (follow signs from Hwy. 101), Box 7, Quinault,*

WA 98575, tel. 360/288–2900 or 800/562–6672. 92 rooms. Facilities: restaurant, bar, pool, hot tub, sauna, boating, recreation room. AE, MC, V. $$$

Log Cabin Resort. This rustic hostelry is in an idyllic setting at the northeast end of Lake Crescent. Settle in to one of the A-frame chalet units, standard cabins, "camping cabins" (wooden tents with shared bathroom), motel units, or RV sites. Twelve of the units are on the lake. You can rent paddleboats or kayaks to use by the day. 3183 E. Beach Rd., Port Angeles, WA 98363, tel. 360/928–3325. 28 units, 3 with kitchen; 4 cabins; 40 RV sites with hookups. Facilities: restaurant, dock, fishing, coin laundry. D, MC, V. $$–$$$

Sol Duc Hot Springs Resort. This 32-unit cabin resort lies deep in the brooding forest along the Sol Duc River, surrounded by 5,000-ft mountains. Bubbling, steaming sulfur springs fill the three large outdoor pools, which range from 98°F to 106°F. Nearby is a swimming pool, filled with slightly warmed glacial runoff. The resort was built in 1910; a 1988 renovation added fresh paint and bathrooms to each unit. Rooms are functional, even spartan, but after a day's hiking in the rugged Seven Lakes Basin nearby, a dip in the pool, and dinner at the surprisingly sophisticated restaurant in the lodge, you'll hardly notice. Sol Duc River Rd. (follow signs from Hwy. 101 between Forks and Port Angeles), Box 2169, Port Angeles, WA 98362, tel. 360/327–3583. 32 rooms, 6 cabins with kitchens. Facilities: restaurant, bar, snack bar, pool. AE, D, MC, V. Closed Oct.–mid-May. $$–$$$

Lake Crescent Lodge. Nestled deep in the forest at the foot of Mt. Storm King, its broad veranda and picture windows framing a view of its brilliant aquamarine namesake, historic Lake Crescent Lodge has been beguiling visitors to the peninsula since 1916. There are 30 motel rooms, 17 modern cabins, and five lodge rooms, all but the latter with private bath. The grand old, two-story cedar-shingle lodge has an acceptable restaurant and a lively lounge; rooms are clean, functional, and heavy on the hand-rubbed wood. There are no phones or TVs in the rooms. Four of the cabins have fireplaces; all have small, private porches. Barnes Point, south side of Lake Crescent (follow signs from Hwy. 101), HC 62, Box 11, Port Angeles, WA 98362, tel. 360/928–3211. 35 rooms and 17 cabins (5 rooms share 2 baths). Facilities: restaurant, lounge, boating. AE, DC, MC, V. Closed Oct. 31–Apr. 25. $$

NEAR THE PARK **Best Western Olympic Lodge.** Rooms at this fresh, cheerful 106-room motel are up to Best Western standards, though a little on the smallish side. The pleasant lobby has tall windows and a fireplace of rustic stone. The motel is just off Highway 101 in Port Angeles; across the street, an unaffiliated 18-hole golf course has a spectacular view of the jagged Olympic peaks. 140 Del Guzzi Dr., Port Angeles, WA 98362, tel. 360/452–2993 or 800/600–2993, fax 360/452–1497. 106 rooms. Facilities: restaurant, pool. AE, D, DC, MC, V. $$$

Ft. Worden. The 330-acre Ft. Worden was built as a turn-of-the-century gun emplacement to guard the mouth of the Puget Sound. Its mighty cannons are long gone, and enterprising souls have now turned the 32 spacious Victorian homes on officer's row into one of the more memorable lodgings on the Olympic Peninsula. There are no phones, no TVs, no restaurant, and no lounge, but each house has a kitchen, and all are furnished with antique reproductions. The houses have a spare charm, and the old fort is a magical place for children. The abandoned gun emplacements echo eerily; there's an artillery museum, a bronze foundry, a marine science center, a dirigible hangar, and a graceful old lighthouse. You can rent a single-bedroom house or even the entire complex, through the Ft. Worden State Park Conference Center; reserve at least a year in advance. The film An Officer and a Gentleman was shot here. Ft. Worden State Park Conference Center (1 mi north of Port Townsend), 200 Battery Way, Port Townsend, WA 98368, tel.

360/385–4730. *2 single-bedroom houses, 10 2-bedroom houses, 19 larger houses, 80 campsites with full hookups. Facilities: restaurant. D, MC, V. $$$*

Red Lion Bayshore Inn. This Washington-based chain is a regional favorite, charging a little more than most motels in the area but providing additional amenities. With 187 renovated units, it's the largest motor inn on the peninsula. Most of the spacious, modern rooms overlook the Strait of Juan de Fuca or the bay, and are decorated in earth tones. There's a lively bar and a surprisingly good restaurant next door. *221 N. Lincoln, Port Angeles, WA 98362, tel. 360/ 452–9215 or 800/547–8010. 187 rooms. Facilities: restaurant, lounge, pool. AE, D, DC, MC, V. $$$*

Manitou Lodge. A golden retriever named Bosco greets guests at this remote and unusual forest lodge. The towering A-frame common room, complete with a 30-ft stone fireplace, is larger than all five lodge guest rooms put together. There is also an additional guest cottage with two units. Room furnishings are a little austere, but the central areas are warm and inviting. There's a broad porch with comfortable chairs for sunset-watching. The coast is nearby, as are the trout-stocked Sol Duc and Bogachiel rivers. This small, popular inn fills up quickly, so book well ahead for summer and weekends. *Kilmer Rd. (follow La Push Rd. west from Hwy. 101, then follow signs toward Mora), Box 600, Forks, WA 98331, tel. 360/374–6295. 7 rooms. MC, V. $$*

Aggie's Inn. The 114 rooms here look like something from the 1972 Sears catalog; there's hardly a square inch of wall covering or upholstery that's not petroleum-derived. Still, this place is clean, friendly, and near the waterfront in downtown Port Angeles. *602 E. Front St., Port Angeles, WA 98362, tel. 360/457–0471. 114 rooms. Facilities: restaurant, bar, indoor pool, sauna. AE, D, DC, MC, V. $*

Bed-and-Breakfasts. With its laid-back charm, proximity to Seattle, Victoria, and the national park, and its wealth of well-pre-served Victorian structures, **Port Townsend** is the peninsula's B&B capital, a haven of ornate guest houses and charming small hotels. Rates run from $65 to $165 per night, but most rooms are in the $75 to $95 range. Among the most esteemed are the 13-suite **Bishop Victorian** (714 Washington St., 98368, tel. 360/385–6122 or 800/824–4738); the fanciful, towered eight-room **F. W. Hastings House Old Consulate Inn** (313 Walker St., 98368, tel. 360/385–6753); the immaculate, six-room **Heritage House** (305 Pierce St., 98368, tel. 360/385–6800); the five-room **Holly Hill House** (611 Polk, 98368, tel. 360/ 385–5619), with its private, guests-only restaurant; the ornate, friendly **Lizzie's** (731 Pierce St., 98368, tel. 360/385–4168), with eight rooms; the 15-room **Palace Hotel** (1004 Water St., 98368, tel. 360/385–0773), formerly a bordello; the refreshingly modern, eight-unit **Ravenscroft Inn** (533 Quincy St., 98368, tel. 360/385–2784); and the beautiful 11-room **Ann Starrett House Inn** (744 Clay St., 98368, tel. 360/385–3205 or 800/321– 0644), almost baroque in its extravagance.

Most famous of all is the 12-room **James House** (1238 Washington St., 98368, tel. 360/385–1238 or 800/385–1285), considered by many to be the state's—and maybe the region's—premier B&B. The beauty of the century-old house, its unrivaled views of the sound, sumptuous furnishings, and the impeccable hospitality of its owners all justify its reputation.

Hard-working Port Angeles, at the park's northern gateway, has nearly as many B&Bs as Port Townsend but lacks that town's Victorian charm. Port Angeles's inns are a disparate group, smaller and less ornate than their Port Townsend counterparts. One exception is **Domaine Madelaine** (146 Wildflower La., 98362, tel. 360/457–4174, fax 360/457–3037), an oasis of garden-girt European charm perched high above the Strait of Juan de Fuca. On fine days, you can see Victoria across the water. Chef and owner Madelaine Chambers rules the premises with a near-obsessive attention to detail, which shows up in everything from the faultless housekeeping to the crab omelet on your breakfast plate. Inside, the sprawling, modern house has a vaguely Oriental feel; outside are acres of gardens, some patterned after Monet's gardens at Giverny. Some guests have been known to journey all the way across the country just to stay here.

Another Port Angeles standout is the **Tudor Inn** (1108 S. Oak St., 98362, tel. 360/452–3138), a sprawling half-timbered mansion built by Dr. Harold Butler, an English dentist who moved to the peninsula in 1902. Beautifully furnished with antiques collected during the owners' eight years in Europe, the inn has six smallish rooms and a venerable Elizabethan feel. Dark wood, vibrant colors, leaded-glass windows, mirrored armoires, and distinctive touches, such as the 1848 vintage Broadwood & Sons grand piano, lend character to every room. There's a well-stocked library off the dining room, and a good selection of videocassettes. Owners Jerry and Jane Glass, born in Houston but Anglophiles to the core, spent years understudying at top-quality European inns. From the furnishings to the sumptuous afternoon tea, the influence shows.

For a free listing of accommodations in Port Angeles, contact the **Port Angeles Chamber of Commerce** (tel. 360/452–2363).

CAMPING

The best and most popular accommodations at Olympic are the 17 campgrounds, which range from primitive backcountry sites reached only after grueling hikes to paved handicapped-accessible trailer parks with toilets and nightly naturalist programs. There are no showers at park campgrounds, and some are open in summer only. More intrepid hikers camp on the park's wilderness beaches or virtually anywhere in the mountain and forest areas of the park. The only requirements: You must have a backcountry use permit (*see* Visitor Information, *above*), and you must choose a site that is at least .5 mi inside the park. Some backcountry campgrounds require

reservations as well; contact the park for details.

Altogether there are about 925 formal sites in Olympic's campgrounds. Not surprisingly, the park's drive-in facilities are the most heavily used, particularly those at **Altaire** (30 sites, flush toilets, drinking water, fire grates), **Elwha** (41 sites, flush toilets, drinking water, fire grates, boat access, ranger station, public phone), **Fairholm** (87 sites, flush toilets, drinking water, fire grates, swimming, boat access, disposal station, public phone), **Heart O' the Hills** (105 sites, flush toilets, drinking water, fire grates, ranger station, public phone), **Hoh** (89 sites, flush toilets, drinking water, fire grates, disposal station, ranger station, public phone), **Kalaloch** (177 sites, flush toilets, drinking water, fire grates, disposal station, ranger station, public phone), **Mora** (94 sites, flush toilets, drinking water, fire grates, boat access, disposal station, ranger station, public phone), **Sol Duc** (80 sites, flush toilets, drinking water, fire grates, swimming, disposal station, ranger station, public phone), and **Staircase** (59 sites, flush toilets, drinking water, fire grates, ranger station, public phone). These campgrounds are the only ones that charge for sites ($10 per night). No reservations are accepted at any of the campgrounds; all space is allocated strictly on a first-come, first-served basis. On summer weekends, plan to arrive by Thursday night if possible.

Olympic's wilderness beaches provide a camping experience unmatched at other national parks. There is nothing quite like watching a Pacific sunset through a beach-log fire out of sight of another person. Hikers can camp anywhere they like, provided it's well above the high-tide mark. Remote **Queets Campground** (20 sites, pit toilets, fire grates, ranger station, no water) is in lush old-growth forests in the southwestern corner of the park, near the park's largest Douglas fir tree. **July Creek Campground** (29 sites, pit toilets, drinking water, fire grates, swimming) has gorgeous views of Quinault Lake and the rugged mountains beyond; nearby **North Fork** (7 sites, pit toilets, fire grates, ranger station, no water) and **Graves Creek** (30 sites, flush toilets, drinking water, fire grates, ranger station) campgrounds lie deep in the forested foothills of the mountains.

There are also thousands of isolated sites in the park's interior. Perhaps the most beautiful of these are in **Enchanted Valley,** accessible via a 13-mi hike along the Enchanted Valley Trail, in the southeastern section of the park. This valley is known as Olympic's mountain-girded miniature Yosemite and is often called the Valley of a Thousand Waterfalls, because as the snow melts in late spring and early summer, hundreds of seasonal cascades appear on the valley walls.

Point Reyes National Seashore
California

By Pam Earing

Updated by Kristina Malsberger

oint Reyes, the only National Seashore on the West Coast, feels like the end of the earth. A 10-mi peninsula buffeted by crashing waves and heavy winds, it's a land apart, where time is measured by the ebb and flow of the tides, the migrations of birds and whales, and the seasonal growth of wildflowers.

In this rugged coastal wilderness, the winds on the Great Beach are so strong you sometimes can't open the door to your car. But Point Reyes has two faces: windswept and wild, it is also quiet and serene. Twisting, two-lane roads ride the undulating hills past grazing sheep and cattle, ranches with hitching posts, and springtime meadows splashed with color. There are shaded trails surrounded by sweet-smelling Douglas fir and Bishop pine, and open paths through tall grasses on the edge of salty esteros, or estuaries.

It was at Drakes Estero that Sir Francis Drake is said to have landed in 1579. There he encountered the Coast Miwok Indians, a group of hunters and gatherers who lived well on the area's bounty of acorns, berries, game, and fish. After Drake's short visit, other explorers came and went. In 1603 the Spanish explorer Don Sebastian Vizcaino named the area La Punta de Los Reyes for the Point of the Three Kings, but it wasn't until almost 200 years after Drake's visit that settlers began to arrive.

Ruled successively by Spanish, Mexicans, and Californians, Point Reyes finally became home to a number of dairy farms, which still operate on almost 18,000 acres of the park's land, through long-term lease arrangements. In 1962 President John F. Kennedy signed legislation authorizing the establishment of Point Reyes National Seashore.

ESSENTIAL INFORMATION

VISITOR INFORMATION Information about the park can be obtained by writing to the Superintendent, **Point Reyes National Seashore** (Point Reyes Station, CA 94956).

Bear Valley Visitor Center (tel. 415/663–1092), at the main entrance, is the largest visitor center in the park and is open weekdays from 9 to 5 and weekends from 8 to 5. The **Kenneth C. Patrick Visitor Center** (tel. 415/669–1250) on Drakes Bay is open weekends and holidays from 10 to 5, as well as Monday through Wednesday 10 to 5 from Memorial Day through Labor Day; the **Point Reyes Lighthouse Visitor Center** (tel. 415/669–1534) is open Thursday through Monday from 10 to 5. The park's beach areas are open from sunrise to sunset. Recorded information and weather can be obtained by calling 415/663–1092, ext. 402.

Permits are required for the four hike-in camps; call 415/663–8054 weekdays between 9 AM and 2 PM. The park administration accepts both individual and group reservations but recommends that they be made over the telephone rather than in writing. Camping is limited to a total of four nights per visit, with a maximum of 30 nights per year. There are no drive-in sites in the park.

FEES There are no entrance fees at the park.

PUBLICATIONS An assortment of one-page fact sheets outlining park information is available at the visitor centers. Point Reyes National Seashore publishes a newsletter three times a year listing interpretative programs and special events. You can also pick up the brochure, "Point Reyes Official Map and Guide" and detailed maps of the roads and trails in the park's North and South districts. The fact sheets, newsletter, maps, and brochure are free; pick them up at the visitor centers or write to the Superintendent (*see* Visitor Information, *above*).

The Bear Valley Visitor Center has a bookstore that sells publications about the park. The following are helpful guides.

Point Reyes National Seashore: A Hiking and Nature Guide (Martin Press) by Don and Kay Martin, which contains detailed trail descriptions and maps; *Family Guide to Point Reyes* (Chardon Press) by Karen Gray, a wonderfully illustrated guide that outlines activities for the whole family; and *Natural History of Point Reyes* (Point Reyes National Seashore Association), by Jules Evens, which takes a comprehensive look at the park's diverse ecosystems.

The most accurate topographical map of the park is the *Trail Map of Point Reyes National Seashore and Vicinity* by Tom Harrison. It's published by **Tom Harrison Cartography** (2 Falmouth Cove, San Rafael, CA 94901-4465, tel. 415/456–7940) and is available at the Bear Valley center for $6.95. Older but equally detailed is the park map published by the **United States Geological Survey** (USGS Map Sales, Box 25286, M.S. 306, Denver, CO 80225, tel. 303/202–4700), which costs $5.60.

GEOLOGY AND TERRAIN Point Reyes National Seashore comprises 71,046 acres, or approximately 100 square mi, and has more than 140 mi of trails. It is distinguished by a hammerhead-shape peninsula that extends 10 mi from the coastline.

The San Andreas Fault is responsible for the park's diverse topography. Two tectonic plates, the North American and the Pacific, come together in a dramatic meeting, forming a rift zone that runs straight through the park. The entire Point Reyes peninsula rides on the eastern edge of the Pacific Plate, which moves steadily northwestward at a rate of about 2 inches a year. The San Francisco earthquake of 1906, whose epicenter was here, thrust the peninsula almost 20 ft northwestward.

The bedrock of 65- to 100-million-year-old granite lying west of the fault is completely different from the 150-million-year-old Franciscan Formation rock lying to the east. Consequently, the soil is different, and this affects the types of plants found on either side of the Inverness Ridge.

The ridge forms a spine that runs parallel to the fault, and its eastern slopes are covered with dense forests of Douglas fir and Bishop pine that descend sharply into the pastures of the Olema Valley. On the seaward side of the ridge, the hills are covered with more than 20 species of shrub and chaparral-type growth, and they slope gently down to rolling pastures, finally ending at Limantour and Drakes beaches. Large, fingerlike estuaries indent the coastline here, creating muddy marshes that teem with bird life. (The esteros are places where fresh and salt water mix.) Sweeping pastureland lies to the northwest, between the Pacific Ocean and Tomales Bay. At the tip of the peninsula, the promontory of Point Reyes rises above the sea. Miles of sandy beaches with rough, hazardous surf line the western coast north of the point, and the more sheltered Drakes Bay forms a curving coastline below the point.

FLORA AND FAUNA Each season the park offers a range of activities that correspond to the presence of the varied plant and animal life found within its borders. Recent budget cuts have resulted in abbreviated schedules, but visitors can still choose from several free talks and guided tours given by naturalists or rangers. Call any of the visitor centers for information.

Its diversity of habitats has made Point Reyes a haven for birds. More than 440 species have been observed here—that represents about 45% of the recorded species in North America. Because the peninsula extends 10 mi out into the ocean it attracts many fall migrants. Seabirds include gulls, cormorants, herons, brown pelicans, and ducks. Land birds include pigeons, kites, wrens, woodpeckers, and turkey vultures, as well as songbirds such as chestnut-backed chickadees and song sparrows. Hawks are common in the pasturelands. During the fall and winter, Limantour and Drakes esteros are feeding grounds for many species of waterfowl and shorebirds. Other great viewing spots are Five Brooks Pond, Olema Marsh, Tomales Bay, Bolinas Lagoon, and Abbotts Lagoon. A bird check-list is available for $1 at the visitor centers.

The observation platform at Point Reyes Lighthouse (about 21 mi from the Bear Valley Visitor Center) is the best place to see gray whales on their 10,000-mi round-trip migration along the coast. In late fall the whales travel south from the cold Alaskan waters to the west coast of Baja, where they calve and breed; the majority of these southbound pods pass Point Reyes in late December and January. Then in mid-February they begin the return trip north to their nutrient-rich feeding grounds in Alaska. During the peak months of January and March it is possible to see up to 100 whales a day, and they often swim surprisingly close to shore. Another good viewing spot is Chimney Rock. On busy weekends and holidays when the parking lot at the lighthouse is full, the park service runs a shuttle bus from another parking lot—usually at South Beach or the Kenneth C. Patrick Visitor Center—up to the observation platform.

The Sea Lion Overlook, near the lighthouse, is usually an excellent spot any time of year for viewing harbor seals and sea lions. These creatures cannot maintain their body temperature if they remain in cold water all the time, so they "haul out" on land. Their preference is for sandy beaches, mudflats, and reefs. Pupping season occurs from March through June. Do not disturb lone pups on the beach—the mother is usually a short way off feeding in the water. If seals and sea lions even sense your presence, there is a chance they will abandon their hauling areas. Federal law prohibits approaching marine mammals, and visitors are advised to stay at least 100 yards away from them at all times.

The tule elk was once abundant in the grassy habitats of this coast, but by 1860, hunting had killed off nearly the entire herd. In 1875 a single pair was discovered near Bakersfield, California. From these two animals, the herd has slowly been expanded and transplanted to reintroduction sites like Tomales Point, which received seven members of the herd in 1978. There are now about 465 tule elk contained on 2,600 acres of grassland and scrub.

Deer are a common sight within the park—so common that park officials have had to initiate a deer-management program for non-native species. There are three wild and reproducing species living here. Native black-tailed deer, numbering about 2,500, are spotted mostly in open pastures feeding in early evening. Native to India and Ceylon, the axis deer, or chital, are usually reddish-brown with white spots. They were introduced into the park in 1947 and 1948, and it is now estimated that the population has grown from the original eight to more than 400. Axis deer can be seen in large herds, usually in areas of coastal scrub or open grassland. Fallow deer, native to the Mediterranean region, were introduced into the park between 1942 and 1954, and there are now about 500 of them. Their coat colors range from white or buff to charcoal or brown with white spots. The white deer are especially beautiful. Fallow deer can be seen in most areas of the park.

Skunks, foxes, bobcats, gophers, weasels, rabbits, and raccoons are among the more common small mammals in the park.

During the spring and early summer you may find small, jellyfish-like Velella, or "by-the-wind-sailors," washed up on the sand. These blue or clear offshore animals live on the water's surface and differ from true jellyfish in that they have no tentacles and therefore cannot change the direction in which they travel.

Tidepooling is a favorite activity at Point Reyes. The best tidepools occur during a minus low tide (when the water recedes farther than usual) and can be found at Palomarin Beach, Sculptured Beach, and Chimney Rock. Depending on the intertidal zone, you may encounter such diverse organisms as purple sea urchins, ocher stars, ribbed limpets, and lined shore crabs.

There are 860 species of plants within the park, which account for 17% of all plant species in California. Most of the low hills facing the sea are covered with grasses. Exotics, such as blue gum eucalyptus and Monterey cypress, can be found in the pastoral areas, and lupines and European dune grass are prevalent in the bluffs above the beaches. The freshwater and saltwater marshes are full of pickleweed. In addition to the Douglas fir and Bishop pine forests, mixed evergreen trees that are native to central California, such as bay laurel, buckeye, and coast live oak, are common.

Wildflowers bloom from February through June, with April and May being the peak months. Look for them in coastal areas where salty winds have prevented the growth of large conifers that would block the sun. The most common wildflowers are California poppy (the state flower); checkerbloom (a wild cousin of hollyhock); the lavender and purple Douglas iris, especially along the coast, or in the Bishop pine or Douglas fir forests; yellow composites, such as gumplant and tidytips; lupines, along the bluffs and dunes and in the coastal hills; and wild radish, as well as wild mustard, in the fields and along the roadsides. The best place in the park to view wildflowers is Chimney Rock, followed by the Abbotts Lagoon and Tomales Point trails.

Note: Poison oak, identified by leaves in groups of three that are glossy green in summer and bright red in late summer and fall, is common on the peninsula. It is especially prevalent on the old, unmaintained trails in the southern portion of the park. When traveling cross-country or on narrow or unmaintained trails, wear long pants and long sleeves.

WHEN TO GO The park's climate is similar to that of the Mediterranean, characterized by warm, dry summers and cool, rainy winters. However, the weather may vary dramatically—not only from one side of the fault to the other, but also from hour to hour. Summer days on the eastern side of the Inverness Ridge may be warm and sunny, differing in temperature by as much as 20 degrees from the ocean side, which is often blanketed in thick, chilly fog.

Expect constant, moderate to strong winds on the exposed headlands and beaches. Winds are generally northwesterly, with an average maximum velocity of 43 mph, although winds up to 130 mph have been clocked. They are strongest in November and December and tend to be lighter on the eastern side of the ridge.

The peninsula is the second-foggiest place on the continent, after Nantucket Island; up to 2,700 hours of fog have been recorded annually. July, August, and September are the foggiest months, so a windbreaker or light jacket is advised.

Annual rainfall averages 11½ inches at the Point Reyes Lighthouse. A few miles inland, at the Bear Valley headquarters, the rainfall is much greater, averaging 36 inches a year. The heaviest rains are from December through March, and although there is scarcely any rain from mid-April through October, fog keeps the land damp.

The moderating effect of the Pacific Ocean creates an even climate with no great extremes in temperature from month to month. In midsummer the average temperature at the coast is 55°F, while the average midwinter temperature is 50°F. Still, there can be notable temperature differences on the same day in different areas of the park.

From April through October, mild weather creates good conditions for hiking, but wildflowers bloom only from March through

May. Summer is an excellent time to explore the cool forests of the Inverness Ridge. Bird-watching is best in fall, and whale-watching peaks during January and March.

SEASONAL EVENTS The exact dates of the following festivals and events vary from year to year. Call the visitor centers for details (*see* Visitor Information, *above*).

July: Native American Celebration at Kule Loklo gives you a modern-day look at Native American life with dancing, demonstrations of traditional skills, and items available for sale. **October: Dairy Day at Historic Pierce Point Ranch** celebrates early farming on the peninsula with demonstrations of milking, butter making, hauling, and other activities. **Point Reyes Field Seminars** conducts seasonal programs and events, including seminars with well-known wildlife photographers. Write or call for a brochure and listings: Point Reyes Field Seminars, Point Reyes National Seashore, CA 94956, tel. 415/663–1200.

WHAT TO PACK There is only one food concession in the park, so you'll probably want to pack a lunch. If you hike for one day at a time, as most people do, you'll need only a knapsack and a water bottle or canteen (in some areas the water is not potable, so bring your own to be safe). Heavy boots are unnecessary for trail hiking in Point Reyes—a lightweight trail boot or hiking shoe is sufficient. Unpredictable fog and winds make jackets and windbreakers a good idea any time of the year. If it's warm enough, bring along a swimsuit and towel for the beach. You may also want to bring long pants and long sleeves to avoid poison oak and ticks.

GENERAL STORES Just 4 mi from park headquarters is the **Inverness Store** (tel. 415/669–1041), which sells sandwiches, deli items, beer, wine, and liquor. It is open Monday through Saturday from 9 to 7 and Sunday from 8:30 to 6:30, with slightly shorter hours in the off-season.

Perry's Delicatessen (tel. 415/663–1491) in Inverness Park sells sandwiches, cold meats, and beach and picnic supplies. It is open daily from 7 to 10.

Three miles from the park in Point Reyes Station is **Palace Market** (tel. 415/663–1016), a full-size grocery store open Monday through Saturday from 8 to 8, Sunday from 8 to 7 (in summer Monday–Thursday and Sunday 8–8, Friday and Saturday 8–9). In addition to sandwiches, deli items, beer, and wine, you can also buy liquor, toiletries, and fishing bait.

Sandwiches, deli items, beer, and wine are also sold at the **Olema Country Store** (tel. 415/663–1479), just 1 mi from the park. Daily summer hours are 9:30 to 8:30; winter hours, 10:30 to 8. Also in Olema is **Olema Liquor & Deli** (tel. 415/663–8615), which sells sandwiches, drinks, and—best of all—ice cream, daily from 7 AM to 10 PM.

ARRIVING AND DEPARTING A good place to begin is the Bear Valley Visitor Center, which serves as an excellent introduction to the park and the starting point of several short nature walks. There are no visitor centers at the other road entrances.

By Bus. To reach Point Reyes from San Francisco, you must first take the No. 80 bus from 7th and Market streets to San Rafael; before getting off the bus, ask for a transfer to the No. 65 bus. From San Rafael, the No. 65 bus runs on weekends and holidays only, stopping at Samuel P. Taylor Park, Olema, park headquarters, Point Reyes Station, and Inverness. Only two buses a day (one in the morning and one in the afternoon) make the round-trip between San Rafael and the park, so plan accordingly. The entire trip costs $4. Call **Golden Gate Transit** (tel. 415/453–2100) for information, as schedules and fares vary.

By Car and RV. Point Reyes National Seashore is an hour's drive north of San Francisco. The quickest route is north on Highway 101, then west on Sir Francis Drake Boulevard, which turns into Sir Francis Drake Highway. Take this road to Olema, where signs point the way to park headquarters, 1 mi farther west.

If you're feeling adventurous, exit Highway 101 onto Highway 1, a sometimes-harrowing drive along the coastal cliffs north out of San Francisco to Olema. This route is longer and may be difficult at night or in bad weather, but the stunning views will make getting there a memorable part of your trip. On sunny weekends from spring through fall, southbound traffic to the Golden Gate Bridge can be backed up between 3:30 and 7.

By Plane. San Francisco International Airport and Oakland International Airport are both roughly 70 mi (1½ hours by car) from the park. Car rentals are available at both airports.

By Train. Amtrak (tel. 800/872–7245) service from Chicago, Denver, Seattle, and Los Angeles stops in Emeryville before terminating at the Jack London Square station in Oakland. Amtrak stations provide no car rentals, but you can rent a car at the Oakland International Airport, only 15 to 20 minutes away from the Oakland station by cab.

EXPLORING

Though park managers and Point Reyes residents regularly push for more public transportation, there is no transportation system within the park; without a car, bike, horse, or strong legs, you will be limited to the small area of trails around the Bear Valley Visitor Center.

Some park sites, such as Alamere Falls and Arch Rock, can be reached only on foot or by horseback. These are part of a large section of the park, 32,730 acres, that has been designated wilderness and is off-limits to bicycles and motorized vehicles. The best way to explore the Point Reyes backcountry is to park at one of the four major trailheads and proceed on foot. For campers, this is a necessity: None of the four camping areas within the park is accessible by car. Cyclists and horseback riders can make use of many backcountry trails in the park, but not all of them. Check at the visitor centers to see which trails you can use (some are restricted on weekends; others are always restricted).

The park is small, and visitors traveling by car can easily get a good sense of the varied terrain within a day. The three major roads—Limantour, Pierce Point, and Sir Francis Drake—run by beaches, wooded area, and pastureland, but trying to cover all three roads in a day would not make for a very relaxing visit. Plan on a leisurely two-day stay, with an overnight at one of the campgrounds, the hostel, or a nearby inn.

THE BEST IN ONE DAY Day-trippers to Point Reyes should begin by getting an overview of the park at the Bear Valley Visitor Center. Take the half-hour hike along the flat, paved Earthquake Trail (*see* Nature Trails and Short Walks, *below*) and visit the Kule Loklo village (*see* Historic Buildings and Sites, *below*). You might also follow the scenic 4.1-mi Bear Valley Trail (*see* Longer Hikes, *below*) out to the ocean at Arch Rock, stopping en route for a picnic at Divide Meadow.

If you return to the trailhead by mid-afternoon, take the 21-mi drive to the lighthouse, especially if it's whale-watching season. At other times, a good option is to drive to Chimney Rock for wildflowers and ocean views. If you have less time, head for Drakes Beach, where high white cliffs meet the shore; in the nearby estero, shorebirds are plentiful. Wading and bird-watching are also favorite pastimes at Limantour beach and estero. Cap off your visit with a drive to Mt. Vision Overlook (*see* Scenic Drives and Views, *below*) for a dramatic sunset view of the entire peninsula. This area is particularly beautiful during wildflower season.

ORIENTATION PROGRAMS The three visitor centers provide information on local weather, safety, and tide conditions. They also have exhibits and post information about park programs.

The main center at Bear Valley has an auditorium, an exhibit area, and a bookstore with an excellent selection of books and trail maps. Also worth looking at (or keep-

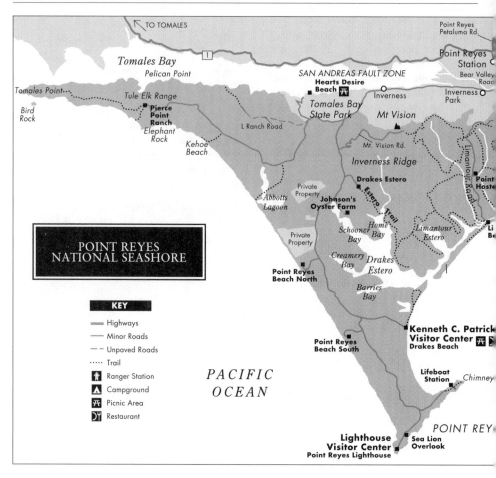

ing an eye on) is the center's seismograph, which records the movement of the earth's plates from an underground signal sent from the San Andreas Fault, just east of the visitor center.

A 20-minute slide show, "Enchanted Shores," is shown on request at the Bear Valley center. The slides give an overview of the park and its varied ecosystems. Rangers are available to answer questions.

The Ken Patrick Visitor Center at Drakes Beach has educational exhibits on the Drakes Beach area, including the unique whale fossil beds of the estero.

The Lighthouse Visitor Center, at the very tip of the peninsula, has exhibits about the maritime history of the area, whales and sea lions, and headland wildflowers. The historic lighthouse is 302 steps down from the visitor center.

GUIDED TOURS The park service leads a series of walks, talks, and educational programs on weekends and holidays. Rangers and naturalists give tours that focus on specific aspects of the park's wildlife, plant life, and history. These are open to the public free of charge.

Several independent groups conduct field trips to the park, including the **Golden Gate Audubon Society** (2530 San Pablo Ave., Suite G, Berkeley, CA 94702, tel. 510/843–2222), which leads three to four birdwatching trips each year. The Marin chap-

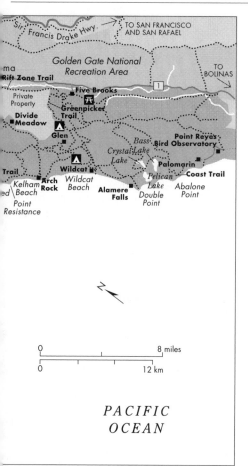

Golden Gate National Recreation Area

TO SAN FRANCISCO AND SAN RAFAEL

TO BOLINAS

Sir Francis Drake Hwy.

ma
Rift Zone Trail

Private Property

Five Brooks

Greenpicket Trail

Divide Meadow

Glen

Bass Lake
Crystal Lake
Lake

Point Reyes Bird Observatory

Palomarin

Trail

Wildcat

Pelican Coast Trail
Lake

Kelham Arch
Rock
ed Beach

Wildcat Beach

Alamere
Falls

Lake
Double
Point

Abalone
Point

Point Resistance

PACIFIC OCEAN

0 ——————— 8 miles
0 ——————— 12 km

ter of the **California Native Plant Society** (Box 589, Inverness, CA 94937, tel. 415/ 669–1686) schedules monthly field trips in Marin County, with several trips each year to the national seashore. Call for a current schedule of excursions.

There are also a few specialized tours:

Sierra Club, San Francisco Bay Chapter (2530 San Pablo Ave., Suite 1, Berkeley, CA 94702, tel. 510/848–0800) conducts field trips to the park that are open to the public for a nominal fee. Topics and routes vary, but often include bird-watching and natural history.

Oceanic Society Expeditions (Fort Mason Center, Bldg. E, San Francisco, CA 94123,

tel. 415/474–3385) runs a whale-watching boat tour between San Francisco Marina and Point Reyes every weekend, weather permitting, from the end of December through the end of April. Naturalists specializing in marine life are on board. The trip takes 6½ hours and costs $48 on weekdays, $50 on weekends. Children under 10 are not permitted.

SCENIC DRIVES AND VIEWS The few roads in Point Reyes may all be twisting and windy, but otherwise they vary considerably in length and terrain. Travelers on Pierce Point Road will be treated to the pastoral scenes of California cattle grazing, while Limantour Road and Mt. Vision Road provide sweeping vistas. In fact, some of the park's best views of Drakes Estero, Tomales Bay, and the Pacific Ocean are seen while buzzing down the tarmac.

The paved, two-lane **Limantour Road** is the most direct route from Bear Valley to the ocean. Start on Bear Valley Road, proceed north for 1.3 mi, then turn left onto Limantour Road. As you make the steep climb over Inverness Ridge, you'll pass through sections of blackened chaparral and Bishop pine— stark reminders of the Mt. Vision fire that swept through this area in 1995. From the ridge top, the road follows sharp curves for 8 mi down to a parking lot; from here it's a flat .25-mi walk through the marshy Limantour Estero to Limantour Beach, a wide expanse of white-sand coastline. This is a windy spot, but many consider the beach's relatively calm but very cold waters excellent for an invigorating ocean dip. Just before the beach, a sandy trail to the right runs along the Limantour Spit, a finger of sand separating the ocean from the estuary. Usually foggy during the summer, the spit is still a fine place to view the egrets, blue heron, snowy plovers, and other shore and low-wading birds inhabiting the waters that surround it. Visitors should proceed with caution beyond the 1-mi trail's end: Harbor seals and sea lions make their home near the tip of the spit, and park goers must not invade their privacy.

To get a feel for the park's varied geography, take the trip out to the **Tule Elk Range** and

Tomales Point. Start on Bear Valley Road and travel north along the eastern edge of the peninsula through the town of Inverness, keeping your eyes open for the unusual wooden houses that exemplify the town's Czech heritage. This relatively straight drive also provides fine views of slender Tomales Bay to your right, and later, of the ocean to your left. A few miles from Inverness, where the road forks, you can either bear right to Tomales Bay State Park's popular, sheltered beach, **Hearts Desire** (where there's a $5 entry fee), or continue along Pierce Point Road, through 6.5 mi of serene dairy and beef cattle country, to the tule elk preserve. Along this route are parking lots from which trails lead to Abbotts Lagoon, popular for birdwatching, and Kehoe Beach. From Pierce Ranch, continue on foot for 5 mi to Tomales Point, the northernmost part of the peninsula (*see* Longer Hikes, *below*).

The 12-mi drive to **Mt. Vision Overlook** is a roller coaster of bumpy, twisting road. From Bear Valley take Sir Francis Drake Highway toward the lighthouse; the turnoff to Mt. Vision (1,282 ft high) will be on your left, 8.75 mi from the visitor center. At one point on this sharply inclined road you'll be treated to one of the park's most expansive views of North Beach and Drakes Estero. From the top of the mountain you can see the curving coastline of Drakes and Limantour beaches, the rocky hammer-shape promontory of Point Reyes, and the long stretch of coast from the lighthouse to Tomales Point.

The longest and most popular drive at the national seashore is the 21-mi stretch out to the **Point Reyes Lighthouse,** which gets especially busy during the winter whale-watching season (January through March). Take Sir Francis Drake Highway south from Bear Valley Road and follow it to the end, stopping at various sites along the way. About 11 mi from the Bear Valley Visitor Center, past the Mt. Vision turnoff and less than a mile past the Estero trailhead turnoff, a .5-mi road on your left leads to Johnson's Oyster Farm. At this family-run business, oysters are farmed using an unusual Japanese method. In the retail sales room you can purchase oysters and pick up recipes and brochures that explain the growing method. Farther along Drake Highway on the right is Point Reyes Beach, a windy, exposed section of coast that is divided into two areas. At the 13.25-mi marker is North Beach and at 15.75 mi is South Beach. These wide stretches of sand are good places to picnic and beachcomb, but the surf is too strong for swimming or wading. Between the South and North beach turnoffs, a road on the left leads to Drakes Beach, a protected part of the coast where you can swim, wade, and picnic. The only food concession in the park is here. As you continue southwest down Drake Highway the road sweeps back away from the ocean, passing several historic ranches and a few miles of coastal grass and shrub. For a view of the lighthouse or to stop by the lighthouse visitor center, bear right where the road forks near the end of the peninsula. From the parking lot at the end of the road you can either walk .5 mi to the visitor center and descend the 302 steps to the lighthouse, or survey the sea lions and harbor seals from the Sea Lion Overlook. If you bear left at the fork instead, the road will take you 1 mi to a short trail leading to Chimney Rock, the best place for viewing wildflowers and elephant seals in spring.

HISTORIC BUILDINGS AND SITES About a half mile from the Bear Valley Visitor Center is **Kule Loklo,** a replica of a typical Coast Miwok village. It is estimated that the Miwoks, who were hunters and gatherers, lived in more than 100 small village communities in Marin and southern Sonoma counties at the time of Sir Francis Drake's visit in 1579. Among the buildings in the replica village are redwood-bark kotcas in which Miwok families lived, an underground sweat lodge, and a ceremonial round house. Great care was taken to construct the buildings to resemble as closely as possible those built by the Miwoks. Follow the .4-mi trail and read the signs to learn about the life and culture of Coast

Miwok villagers. It is not uncommon on Saturday to find volunteers giving demonstrations on arrowhead making or Miwok crafts. Entry to the village is free. It is always open to the public during daylight hours but is not regularly staffed. Schedules of free cultural programs vary; call the Bear Valley Visitor Center (tel. 415/663–1092) before your visit.

Established in 1858, the **Pierce Point Ranch,** at the end of Pierce Point Road, is one of the park's historic ranches. Visitors can take a self-guided tour among the nine outbuildings, where exhibits describe butter churning and hay collecting while providing glimpses of the ranch's history. Once a year in October, the ranch sponsors Dairy Day, with demonstrations of farm activities and an exhibition of farm animals. The site is open seven days a week, from dawn to dusk; there's no admission charge.

The **Morgan Horse Ranch** (tel. 415/663–1763), behind the Bear Valley Visitor Center, is home to its namesake, America's first breed of horse. Dating back to 1789, the Morgan horse was originally bred in Vermont and is renowned for its strength, speed, and endurance. Signs and exhibits on the property detail the history of the Morgan breed, as well as aspects of ranch life such as horseshoeing and grooming. Although the ranch's horse-breeding days are over, several horses are still kept here, and you may be able to observe them on the outdoor obstacle course. The farm is staffed on most days from 8 to 4:30, but visitors are generally left to peruse the grounds on their own.

The historic **Point Reyes Lighthouse** (tel. 415/669–1534), built in 1870, is at the end of Sir Francis Drake Highway, 21 mi from the Bear Valley Visitor Center. The point is a notorious navigational hazard, and the surrounding water is a graveyard of ships—46 shipwrecks were recorded in the first 60 years after the lighthouse was built. It is the windiest point on the West Coast and the second-foggiest place on the continent. The beacon was retired from service in 1975, when the U.S. Coast Guard installed an automated light, but it is still maintained in excellent working condition. This is a prime whale-watching site, especially during the peak months of January and March. When the lighthouse parking lot is full, a bus shuttles passengers from another nearby parking lot, such as Drakes Beach or South Beach. The Point Reyes Lighthouse Visitor Center (tel. 415/669–1534) is a .5-mi walk from the parking lot at the end of Sir Francis Drake Highway. When staff is available, free 10- to 15-minute programs explain how the lighthouse works; ask a ranger for details. At least one is on duty from Thursday through Monday between 10 and 5. From the visitor center it's 302 steps down to the lighthouse building (and 302 calf-breaking steps back up), but the ocean views and the sense of accomplishment are worth it. The lighthouse is open Thursday through Monday from 10 to 4:30, but if wind velocity is more than 40 mph, the lighthouse is closed. You must make a reservation to witness the lighthouse lighting (free), which occurs on certain Saturdays, shortly after the sun sets.

Because of the dangers at the point, a lifesaving station equipped with surfboats was established on the Great Beach just north of the lighthouse in 1889. Men kept vigil in four-hour shifts, looking for people who needed rescuing. Many lives and millions of dollars in cargo were saved. The historic **Lifeboat Station** (tel. 415/669–1534) was later moved to Drakes Bay, near Chimney Rock, before it finally closed its doors in 1969. The defunct station is now open to the public sporadically; call the Bear Valley Visitor Center for scheduled openings.

NATURE TRAILS AND SHORT WALKS Beginning at the Bear Valley Visitor Center, the **Earthquake Trail** is an easy, paved, .5-mi self-guided trail that meanders across Bear Valley Creek, through groves of willow and oak, and along the San Andreas Fault Zone. The trail passes several signposted geological features, including the epicenter of the 1906 San Francisco quake. You can often spot black-tailed deer and the beautiful white fallow deer in the meadow here, particularly at dusk.

The easy .75-mi self-guided **Woodpecker Trail** starts at the Bear Valley Trailhead and runs uphill toward the forest. Woodpeckers are attracted to the coast live oaks and Douglas firs; you'll find evidence of them along this trail, which crosses a meadow and ends at the Morgan Horse Ranch barn (*see* Historic Buildings and Sites, *above*).

Completely flat, the **Kule Loklo Trail** runs alongside eucalyptus groves for .4 mi before it reaches the Coast Miwok replica village, where there is a small native plant garden. Note that many of the tree trunks are pocked with holes made by woodpeckers, which store acorns in them.

LONGER HIKES Free trail maps are available at the visitor centers and topographical maps may be purchased at the Bear Valley center. The principal trailheads are Bear Valley, Palomarin, Five Brooks, and Estero, all of which have parking. Many of the trails in the park were formerly old ranch roads that the park service has mapped and marked. There are many more old roads and trails that are not marked or maintained and are not found on the trail maps. Bring a compass and topographic map if you plan to hike these, and be sure to close all gates behind you, lest the cattle escape.

The most popular trail at the park—for both hikers and cyclists—is the **Bear Valley Trail,** a fairly easy, level walk of just over 4 mi (one way). Starting at the Bear Valley trailhead, the path runs along streams, under tall trees, and through a meadow before reaching Arch Rock, a natural rock formation that curves over the beach. Because most of the way is shaded by forest, this hike is an excellent choice for summer visitors; unfortunately, the trail can also be crowded with as many as 300 people on a good-weather weekend. No drinking water is available on the trail, but a picnic spot and toilets are mid-route.

The 4.5-mi **Estero Trail** passes over undulating grassland and shrubbery, along the shore of Home Bay to Drakes Estero. This is a treeless route, but one on which you can find plenty of wildlife. The mudflats of the estero are a haven for birds. Since much of the area is still devoted to farming, you'll come upon cattle, but deer and harbor seals can be spotted as well.

Rift Zone Trail runs for 4.7 level mi between the Bear Valley and Five Brooks Stable parking lots, along the top edge of the park, parallel to the San Andreas Fault. The trail begins at the Bear Valley trailhead, traverses Bear Valley Creek, then continues to a wooded area of bay laurels and coast live oaks. Groves of eucalyptus and Monterey cypress also line the route. The last 3 mi travel through land that belongs to the Vedanta Society, a religious organization, and hikers must observe the society's rules: You can pass through only from 8 AM until two hours before sunset, and wheeled vehicles, camping, and picnicking are prohibited. Along the way, you'll see the old Shafter mansion, built in 1869 and now headquarters for the Vedanta Society Retreat. Next, the trail moves through forests alternating with meadows and marshes. It then descends to a horse camp and ultimately comes out to the main road headed for the Five Brooks parking lot.

Many consider the **Tomales Point Trail,** which runs high above the crashing Pacific, one of the best trails in the Bay Area. It begins at Pierce Ranch and covers 5 easy mi along level ground, with scenic views of Tomales Bay. Come prepared for foggy or windy conditions—this is exposed terrain. The trail starts out on a gentle incline and gradually descends past Bird Rock, a favorite resting spot for cormorants. The trail is only maintained for the first 3 mi; the last mile is over sand, leading to a bluff that overlooks the entrance to Tomales Bay. Most of the trail runs through the Tule Elk Range, so you're likely to spot the herd grazing in the grasslands. You'll have to walk the 5 mi back to the trailhead.

True to its name, **Coast Trail** skirts the entire coast, from Limantour Beach to the Palomarin Trailhead, with intermittent views of the entire peninsula and the cliffs above Drakes Beach. For an easy 5-mi loop, take Laguna Trail from just past the youth hostel, then descend to Coast Camp on Fire Lane Trail and follow Coast Trail along a flat, open stretch of coastal bluffs back to the youth hostel. Another good hiking stretch begins at the Palomarin Trailhead and runs 2.6 mi past eucalyptus groves and seaside cliffs to tranquil Bass Lake; a mile farther on is Alamere Falls.

Mt. Wittenberg Trail requires a higher level of fitness than the other trails mentioned here. It is a steep 2.5-mi hike that brings you to the highest point in the park—1,407-ft Mt. Wittenberg. Start on the Bear Valley Trail; about .25 mi along, Mt. Wittenberg Trail branches off to the right. It is heavily forested with Douglas fir and California bay, and carpeted with ferns. An occasional meadow provides a rest stop. From the summit of Mt. Wittenberg, the peninsula, the ocean, and the valleys and mountains lying beyond the park's boundaries will take your breath away. You can reach Sky Camp via this route, although the Sky Trail approach is shorter and less strenuous.

OTHER ACTIVITIES **Biking.** The park's paved roads are not recommended for cycling, especially on weekends, when traffic can be heavy—but there are 38 mi of dirt trails open to cyclists. Mountain bikes are best for negotiating the rough terrain. Check at the visitor centers for information on trail use and restrictions. You must stay on the trails, pedaling at a maximum speed of 15 mph, and bicycles are prohibited on the 32,730 acres designated as wilderness areas.

Some of the more popular trails follow (distances are one way): Bear Valley Trail is a moderate-to-easy 3.3 mi along a wide dirt trail. The final .8 mi of the trail is off-limits to bikes because it's in a designated wilderness area; lock your bike at the bike rack and continue on foot to the beach. Coast Trail is a moderate-to-easy 2.8-mi fire road with some beach access; park at the Point Reyes Hostel off Limantour Road. Stewart Trail starts at the Five Brooks Trailhead and climbs steeply through old-growth forest before branching off to Glen Camp (total 5 mi) or Wildcat Beach Camp (total 6.7 mi).

Estero Trail is a moderate-to-difficult route that starts at the Estero Trailhead and runs along exposed grasslands to the beach; the first 3 mi are fire road, and in the 1.5 mi after that the trail becomes less distinguishable and the terrain rougher.

If you need to rent a bike, try **Trail Head Rentals** (Hwy. 1 and Bear Valley Rd., Olema, tel. 415/663–1958), which has 18-speed mountain bikes for $24 a day on weekends and holidays, $20 on weekdays. In the afternoon, you can rent bikes for $7 an hour on weekends and $6 an hour on weekdays, with a two-hour minimum. Trail Head is open Thursday to Tuesday from 10 to 6.

Bird-Watching. The park attracts serious bird-watchers from throughout the United States, and many educational walks and seminars are available. More than 400 species, many of them migratory, can be found at the seashore. During fall and winter, the wetlands of Limantour Estero and the mudflats at Drakes Estero are home to several types of migrating shorebirds and waterfowl, including ring-necked ducks and green-winged teals. In winter, hooded mergansers and green-backed herons can be spotted in the secluded Five Brooks Pond. Abbotts Lagoon is a prime nesting area for many birds, including the endangered snowy plover. Land birds and birds of prey thrive in the pasturelands of Pierce Point road. You can rent binoculars from **Trail Head Rentals** (Hwy. 1 and Bear Valley Rd., Olema, tel. 415/663–1958) for $5 to $6 a day.

The **Point Reyes Bird Observatory** (tel. 415/868–0655 or 415/868–1221) is an independent, nonprofit research and conservation organization that has a field station on Mesa Road, .5 mi south of Palomarin Trailhead. Visitors can observe bird banding (the tagging of birds in order to monitor the area's species and population patterns) starting at sunrise and continuing for six hours, on Wednesdays and weekends from Thanksgiving through April, and then from Tuesday through Saturday between May and November; there is no fee. The visitor center and exhibits at the station are open to the public year-round from dawn to dusk.

Fishing. Persons 16 and older must have a valid California fishing license to take any fish, mollusks, or crustaceans in the park. Licenses are available at many of the local stores, including Builders Supply (tel. 415/663–1737) on Highway 1 in Point Reyes Station. Licenses cost $27 for the season ($15 for saltwater fishing only) and $5 for a one-day license. Regulations for fishing hours, limits, and methods are found in the pamphlet "California Sport Fishing Regulations," available at stores selling licenses, bait, and equipment. These regulations are very specific to certain areas in the park and are strictly enforced. From May 1 through October 31, the State Department of Health places an annual quarantine on mussels because of algae-associated toxins. Point Reyes Headlands Reserve and Estero de Limantour Reserve are off-limits—all marine life is protected within their boundaries—and fishing is not permitted in inland streams. Extreme caution should be observed at ocean beaches, where the heavy surf is dangerous. Many fishing areas can be reached only by foot trails, and some beaches only by boat.

Surf casters can catch flounder, surfperch, and sea trout. Along the shore, you'll find clams, cockles, mussels, and crabs.

Horseback Riding. More than 100 mi of trails are open to horseback riders, as are all beaches except Drakes. A trail map and information on restrictions is available at the visitor centers; it's a good idea to consult a topographic map before setting out, as some trails are quite steep. The shortest trails to the coast generally require two hours of riding time, and horses must be kept on trails. Plenty of drinking water for the horses can be found in streams, and hitching racks are provided at the four camps and at Kelham Beach. Camping with horses is permitted by reservation through the Bear Valley Visitor Center at all park campgrounds except for Glen Camp. If you camp overnight, bring your own weed-free feed.

Among the more popular trails are Bear Valley Trail (open to horses only on week-days) and Greenpicker Trail, which begins at the Five Brooks Trailhead.

You can rent a horse at **Five Brooks Ranch** (Hwy. 1, 3 mi south of Olema, tel. 415/663–1570). Guided one- and two-hour rides cost $20 and $35 a person, and guided half- and full-day trips cost $60 and $85 per person. The ranch also leads overnight pack trips, picnic trips, and hayrides. Reservations are recommended.

Kayaking. Kayaking provides an up-close perspective on the park's marine life and allows access to the most remote stretches of seashore. **Blue Water Kayaking** in Inverness (12938 Sir Francis Drake Blvd., tel. 415/669–2600) conducts guided day trips, bird-watching excursions, and moonlight tours in the calm waters of Tomales Bay. No experience is required to rent open-deck kayaks, which cost $35 to $45 per half day and $45 to $65 per day, including orientation and a wet suit. If you paddle on your own, note that Drakes Estero is off-limits to all boats, including kayaks and canoes, during harbor seal pupping season (March 15 to June 30).

Swimming. Some of the best swimming in the area is at the adjacent **Tomales Bay State Park** (tel. 415/669–1140), approximately 20 minutes from park headquarters on Pierce Point Road. Its five small beaches are much less windy than the exposed beaches on the rest of the peninsula, and the water is warmer, calmer, and shallower than that of Drakes Bay. There is no lifeguard here, but there is a dressing room. Day visitors must pay a $5 entrance fee to the park.

Another good choice is **Bass Lake,** a 2.6-mi hike from the Palomarin Trailhead along Coast Trail. Although the park does not officially encourage swimming here due to problems with overuse, it's hard to beat the warmish water and two rope swings.

If you don't mind cold water—average temperatures run from 48°F to 61°F—you can swim at **Drakes** and **Limantour** beaches. There are no lifeguards on duty, and only Drakes Beach has a bathhouse.

Don't consider swimming, or even wading, at the ocean beaches that run from the lighthouse up to Tomales Point. Powerful surf and undertow make these beaches extremely dangerous; lives have been lost here.

CHILDREN'S PROGRAMS Visitors with children will probably want to spend most of their time around the Bear Valley area—at the educational exhibits at the visitor center, the Morgan Horse farm, and the Kule Loklo settlement; children also enjoy hiking the short, self-guided Earthquake and Woodpecker trails. There are shady picnic grounds around here, but you must bring your own food since there is no concession.

All of the park's naturalist programs are open to children, who may especially enjoy talks that focus on the local wildlife, such as "Sharks in Our Waters" and "Encounters with a Screech Owl." Programs change seasonally, so contact the Bear Valley Visitor Center for information.

Point Reyes Field Seminars (Point Reyes National Seashore Association, Bear Valley Rd., Point Reyes Station, CA 94956, tel. 415/663–1200) conducts one- and two-day nature and crafts programs approximately three times per season. Geared toward families, these are often set up like college-extension courses, covering such activities as basket weaving, photography, bird-watching, and local crafts. Prices vary slightly but generally run about $15 per person.

The **Point Reyes National Seashore Association** (*see* Field Seminars, *above*) also runs a summer camp for boys and girls ages seven through 16. The camp has such activities as canoeing and hiking, but the emphasis is on environmental studies. Four- to six-day sessions are scheduled six times each summer and cost $330. At the six-day Adventure Camp, 13- to 16-year-olds backpack and camp out while learning new ways to protect the environment. This camp costs $375.

EVENING ACTIVITIES Included in the park's regular nature series are several events that take place in the evening because of the nocturnal habits of certain animal species. In programs such as **Transition into Night,** visitors explore the behavior and habitats of night-loving creatures such as owls and bats. On the popular **Evening Lighthouse Tour,** the giant lens is lighted at dusk just as it was by the lighthouse keepers until 1975. The free tour takes place on Saturday evenings in summer; reservations are required, so call the Lighthouse Visitor Center (tel. 415/669–1534) early on the day of the tour. Occasionally, visitors are given the chance to explore the coastal forest at dusk and in the early evening on a mildly strenuous three-hour guided hike to **Mt. Wittenberg.** Like other naturalist programs in the park, these evening events are free. Contact the Bear Valley Visitor Center for details.

Point Reyes Field Seminars sponsors a few evening events each season, including the **Full Moon at Abbotts Lagoon,** a moonlight hike on the Estero Trail; **Stories by the Sea,** an evening of storytelling and singing on Limantour Beach; and **Calling All Mammals,** a scientific search for nocturnal mammals. Events cost $14 to $20 and pre-registration is required; call 415/663–1200.

DINING

Considering the wealth of marine life at the ocean and in Tomales Bay, it comes as no surprise that fresh seafood and shellfish are a dominant feature of the local cuisine. Since there is only one concession in the park (which closes at 6 PM), those who plan on having dinner in the area will have to eat at nearby restaurants, most of which are within 5 mi of the park's main entrance. The towns in the Point Reyes area are fiercely opposed to overdevelopment, so don't expect to find fast-food eateries nearby. There are a number of coffee shops and local bakeries for those who prefer a light snack.

INSIDE THE PARK **Drakes Beach Café.** Nestled next to the Kenneth C. Patrick Visitor Center, this is the park's only concession. The café seats 30 indoors, but if it is not too windy, you can enjoy your meal on the outdoor deck looking out at the ocean at Drakes Beach. The simple all-wood structure has a very basic interior, with a woodstove providing warmth on chilly days. Most of the fare is of the hot dog and hamburger variety, but there is also an excellent selection of seafood dishes, including oyster stew, clam chowder, and fish-and-chips. The barbecued oysters are rated as the best oysters in the Bay Area by local food critics. Bring your own alcoholic beverages. *Drakes Beach, Point Reyes National Seashore, tel. 415/669–1297. No credit cards. Closed Tues.–Wed. $*

NEAR THE PARK **Manka's.** Many locals consider this former hunting lodge the finest restaurant in the area. Chef Matt Banks strives to reflect Manka's hunting-lodge past, with hearty American dishes featuring local game, fowl, and fresh whole fish. Set in the hills near Tomales Bay, the romantic dining room is elegantly rustic, with large windows, white linen tablecloths, and a huge centerpiece of garden flowers. The ever-changing specials include venison with wild black currants and swordfish grilled in the fireplace. There are fresh fruit pies for dessert. *Argyle and Callendar Way, Inverness, tel. 415/669–1034. MC, V. Closed Tues.–Wed. $$$*

Barnaby's. This popular seafood restaurant 1 mi north of the Inverness town center is known for its excellent weekend brunches. The spectacular view of Tomales Bay makes up for the rather bland furnishings, which are as casual as the dress code. Sit outside if the weather permits. Cooking is home-style Californian with an Asian accent. Try the fresh local seafood and shellfish, or the applewood-smoked ribs and chicken. *12938 Sir Francis Drake Blvd., Inverness, tel. 415/669–1114. MC, V. $$*

Vladimir's. This authentic Czech restaurant serves up hearty meals to those who need replenishment after a hard day's hiking. About 4 mi from the park, in the center of Inverness, Vladimir's is designed to look like an Old World hunting lodge, with a dark wood interior and a burning hearth. The eccentric owner frequently dons a Czech folkloric costume, and accordion players often entertain patrons with traditional music. Best bets are roast duck in plum sauce, chicken paprikash (cooked on the bone in a paprika sauce), and cabbage rolls. *12785 Sir Francis Drake Blvd., Inverness, tel. 415/669–1021. Reservations not accepted. No credit cards. Closed Mon. No breakfast. $$*

Station House Cafe. The home-style California cuisine here has long been popular with locals and visitors. In the center of Point Reyes Station, the bright, spacious café is simply decorated with wood chairs and tables, and a ceramic boar's head grins benevolently above the open kitchen. There are also 12 coveted tables in the outdoor garden. Among the favorite dishes are those made with oysters, which come from farms in the park. Other specialties are mussels fettuccine and New York steak with blue cheese butter. Expect a wait on sunny weekends. *Hwy. 1, Point Reyes Station, tel. 415/663–1515. D, MC, V. $–$$*

Cafe Reyes. A converted garage with an open ceiling and a cool Southwestern motif, this casual eatery serves salads, burgers, and an esoteric assortment of burritos. Espresso drinks and local beers on tap make this a popular hangout for locals and visitors, and live mariachi music keeps the place hopping on weekends. *Hwy. 1, Point Reyes Station, tel. 415/663–9493. No credit cards. $*

Taqueria La Quinta. Families and hikers on a budget have made this colorful taqueria a popular choice for quick and healthy dining. The room is decorated with colorful Mexican folk art. A free salsa bar features three types of salsa for dipping chips or topping entrées. The menu includes such authentic Mexican fare as chilies rellenos as well as vegetarian dishes and fruit smoothies. *Hwy. 1, Point Reyes Station, tel. 415/663–8868. No credit cards. Closed Tues. No breakfast. $*

PICNIC SPOTS Point Reyes has three designated picnic areas, two of which have picnic tables and/or braziers. The only food
concession in the park is at Drakes Beach,
so you must bring your own picnic basket.
The most accessible and largest area is set
in a picturesque grove of trees near the
Bear Valley Visitor Center. An equally popular spot at **Drakes Beach** has fewer tables
and sits unassumingly on the grass beside
the parking lot. To avoid the crowds, tote
your basket for 1.5 mi along Bear Valley
Trail to the **Divide Meadow** picnic area—a
placid heath without tables. All four hike-
in camps also have picnic tables and braziers. In addition, at the adjacent Tomales
Bay State Park's **Hearts Desire Beach** you
can picnic in a tree-shaded area with
sweeping views of the bay, then stroll down
to the beach for a swim.

LODGING

There are few hotels and motels in the
Point Reyes area, and the youth hostel in
the park fills up quickly, especially on
weekends. If you don't want to stay at the
park's hike-in camps, you can choose a
nearby car campground or one of the many
bed-and-breakfasts or inns. These tend to
be small, and many establishments use the
terms "inn" and "bed-and-breakfast" inter-
changeably. The inns, however, are more
likely to offer complimentary hot tubs, and
the more popular B&Bs require a two-night
minimum stay on weekends. Budget accommodations are sparse here; expect to
pay upwards of $80 for a double room. If
the accommodations near the park are full
or too expensive, consider making the 20-
to 30-minute drive along Point Reyes-
Petaluma Road to Petaluma, where there
are several large budget motels.

INSIDE THE PARK **Point Reyes Hostel (HI).**
Providing a fraction of the luxury of a bed-
and-breakfast at a fraction of the price, the
youth hostel offers dormitory-style lodging
in a secluded valley 2 mi from Limantour
Beach. Groups of up to 20 can pay $240 for
exclusive use of a private redwood bunkhouse, with a large common room and fireplace; the bunkhouse houses individual
guests. There are hot showers in both
buildings and a fully equipped kitchen is
accessible to the entire hostel. Bring your
own soap, towels, sleeping bag, and food;
linens and towels can be rented. Reservations are recommended. Office hours are
daily from 7:30 AM to 9:30 AM and 4:30 PM
to 9:30 PM, with lockout hours between
9:30 and 4:30. There is a maximum stay of
five nights. *Box 247, Point Reyes Station,
CA 94956, tel. 415/663–8811. 44 beds. MC,
V. $12 per night.*

NEAR THE PARK **Blackthorne Inn.** The
imaginative design of this inn, with its
free-form layout, embodies the California
Craftsmen style. Constructed from native
woods—cedar, redwood, and Douglas fir—
and set in a secluded canyon 3 mi from
park headquarters, the inn resembles a
giant four-level tree house. The main level
is surrounded by a 3,500-ft deck, and the
large A-frame sitting room has a stone fireplace. The eclectic rooms blend wicker,
antiques, and country-style furnishings
and do not have TVs. The Overlook is the
most spacious and comfortable room, but
for sheer fantasy try the Eagle's Nest, an
octagonal, glass-enclosed room reached by
a spiral staircase. A buffet breakfast and
use of the inn's hot tub is included in the
price of a night's stay, but there is a two-
night minimum stay on weekends. *266
Vallejo Ave., Inverness Park, Box 712,
Inverness, CA 94937, tel. 415/663–8621. 5
rooms, 3 with bath. Facilities: hot tub. MC,
V. $$$*

Manka's Inverness Lodge. This former
hunting lodge, set in the hills near Tomales
Bay, has the ambience of a rustic Adiron-
dack retreat. Eight rooms (four in the main
house, four in an annex) and two fishing
cabins are simply decorated with Pendle-
ton plaids, Beacon and Yukon blankets,
and beds made of unpeeled Oregon fir.
Rooms are small, but some have a large red-
wood deck that overlooks the bay. In the

sitting room, original furniture from the Arts and Crafts period fronts a stone fireplace that doubles as a cooking grill for the lodge's top-rated restaurant (*see* Dining, *above*). Also on the property are two historic buildings some distance from the main complex: a private, two-bedroom 1850s cabin at the beach and a 1911 boathouse with a kitchen and room for six. *Argyle and Callendar Way, Inverness, CA 94937, tel. 415/669–1034. 8 rooms, 4 cabins. Facilities: restaurant. MC, V. $$$*

Point Reyes Seashore Lodge. Just a half mile from park headquarters, this cedarwood lodge is one of the largest accommodations in the area, with 18 rooms, three suites, and a cottage that sleeps eight. Although the lodge is not as secluded or private as many of the small inns, all rooms overlook a wide lawn that slopes down to a creek; the park itself is just a quick walk over the wooden bridge. The amenities are another perk: Most rooms have balconies or patios, as well as a fireplace or Jacuzzi, and there is a common library and a game room with an antique pool table. Only the cottage has a TV. A complimentary Continental breakfast is served. *10021 Hwy. 1, Box 39, Olema, CA 94950, tel. 415/663–9000. 18 rooms, 3 suites, 1 cottage. AE, D, MC, V. $$$*

Ten Inverness Way. Built in 1904, this romantic B&B is in the village of Inverness, one block from Tomales Bay and an easy walk to shops and restaurants. The large sitting room, paneled in Douglas fir, has a player piano, several comfortable couches, and an immense stone fireplace. Antiques, fresh flowers, handmade quilts, and Oriental rugs give guest rooms a casual elegance. The back rooms overlook a garden, but Room 2, with its view of Tomales Bay, is a favorite. Breakfast time brings homemade banana-buttermilk-buckwheat pancakes and chicken-apple sausages. Guests have use of a hot tub in an adjacent cottage, but don't expect to watch TV. There is a two-night minimum stay on weekends. *10 Inverness Way, Box 63, Inverness, CA 94937, tel. 415/669–1648. 4 rooms, 1 suite. Facilities: hot tub. MC, V. $$$*

Bear Valley Inn. This classic Victorian two-story ranch-house built in 1899 is the closest inn to the park's main entrance. Although it is not as polished as Ten Inverness Way or the Blackthorne Inn—and not as expensive—the small, simple establishment emphasizes comfort and old-fashioned charm, from its lovely garden of herbs and flowers to its wholesome home-cooked breakfasts. The tiny downstairs parlor has a fireplace and is decorated with period pieces, including overstuffed velveteen sofas and handmade rugs. Each room has a different look: Choose either country comfort with handmade quilts and rustic antiques or Victorian elegance with velvet, lace, and a brass bed. There are no TVs. *88 Bear Valley Rd., Olema, CA 94950, tel. 415/663–1777. 3 rooms share bath. AE, MC, V. $$–$$$*

Golden Hinde Inn and Marina. One of the largest accommodations in the area, this inn is set up like a motel, with a small registration office, no lobby or sitting room, and outside entry to each room. The spacious rooms are done up in pale blues and beiges; lava lamps add a quirky touch. Those interested in privacy should request one of the eight units in the adjacent Bayview building, appropriately named for its views of Tomales Bay. Eighteen rooms have fireplaces, 10 have kitchenettes, and all have TVs. There's an outdoor swimming pool, and nearby are a restaurant and a kayaking outfitter. *12938 Sir Francis Drake Blvd., Box 295, Inverness, CA 94937, tel. 415/669–1389. 33 rooms, 2 suites. Facilities: pool. MC, V. $$–$$$*

Contact the following organizations for more information on accommodations in the Point Reyes area: **Inns of Point Reyes** (tel. 415/663–1420), **Bed & Breakfast Cottages of Point Reyes** (tel. 415/663–9445), **West Marin Chamber of Commerce** (tel. 415/663–9232), and **Coastal Lodging of Point Reyes National Seashore** (tel. 415/ 663–1351).

CAMPING

INSIDE THE PARK The fog makes it necessary for campers to have cover for the night—a lightweight tent or a tarp. Since the humidity can run high, fiberfill sleeping bags are better than down. Coast and Wildcat camps are especially damp.

You must have a permit to camp at Point Reyes National Seashore, which has only four hike-in camping areas accommodating a limited number of people. All four charge $10 per site per night. Camping is permitted for only four consecutive nights, with a maximum of 30 days per year. Sites fill up well in advance on weekends and holidays, especially those set aside for groups. You can reserve sites up to two months in advance by calling 415/663–8054 Monday through Friday, from 9 AM to 2 PM.

Most campgrounds have pit toilets, drinking water, and a hitching rail for horses, but there are no troughs provided. Individual sites can accommodate up to eight people and are equipped with space for a tent, a table, and a charcoal grill. Most group sites accommodate up to 25 people; at Wildcat the maximum group size is 40.

Wood fires are prohibited in campgrounds—only charcoal, gas stoves, or canned heat may be used—but you are allowed to make driftwood fires on sandy beaches below the high-tide mark as long as you have a beach fire permit, available at the Bear Valley Visitor Center for free. Sleeping on beaches, however, is prohibited and dangerous because of the rough surf and tides. Raccoons and skunks are numerous and aggressive, so food should be stored in the food lockers at the sites. Littering has been a problem at the sites: You are responsible for hiking out with every piece of trash you produce. Quiet hours are from sunset to sunrise.

There are 12 walk-in sites, including one group site, at **Sky Camp,** on the western side of Mt. Wittenberg. The camp's 1,025-ft elevation means terrific views of Drakes Bay and the surrounding hills of Point Reyes. It's not as crowded here as it is in the two coastal camps, but getting to the campground requires a somewhat hilly 1.75-mi hike from the Sky Trailhead, on Limantour Road.

There are no trees to provide protection from the wind at **Coast Camp,** which sits on an open, grassy bluff about 200 yards above the beach. This heavily trafficked area has 14 sites, including two group sites, and is a flat 2-mi hike along the beach from the Limantour Beach parking lot. You can also park near the youth hostel and make the 1.8-mi hike on Coast Trail. From the Bear Valley Trailhead you will have to hike 5.8 mi.

Those in need of a sound night's sleep will cherish the tranquility of **Glen Camp's** 12 secluded sites in a wooded valley protected from ocean breezes (groups are not allowed here, nor are horses). From Bear Valley Trailhead, it's 4.6 mi of relatively flat walking.

Wildcat Camp is in a green meadow a short walk from the beach. Nearby a small stream flows down to the sea. There are three hard-to-get individual sites, but the camp is much better known for its four group sites, which are often noisy. From Bear Valley Trailhead it's an ambitious 6.3-mi hike traversing meadows and hills; from Five Brooks Trailhead, via Stewart Trail, expect a steeper 6.7-mi hike.

NEAR THE PARK **Tomales Bay State Park** (tel. 415/669–1140), 7 mi north of Inverness on Pierce Point Road, has six hike-in/bike-in campsites available year-round on a first-come, first-served basis. The sites cost $3 per person per night and are set under oak trees near the beach, a .5-mi walk from the parking lot; facilities include toilets, running water, picnic tables, and a communal fire ring.

If getting away from it all isn't an imperative, try the **Olema Ranch Campground** (Hwy. 1, Box 175, Olema, CA 94950, tel. 415/663–8001), just .75 mi from the Bear Valley Visitor Center. The campground has 150 drive-up tent sites, 75 RV sites, and a large group site on 32 acres of grassy meadow, with trees, flowerbeds, and a creek. Children will enjoy the playground, and during summer weekends, campfire storytelling, free movies, and materials for arts and crafts are provided. The privately owned campground has flush toilets, hot showers, fire rings, a disposal station, a post office, laundry facilities, an arcade, and a general store. Rates are $18 per night for a tent for up to two persons ($2.50 per each additional person, $2 per extra vehicle). RV sites with water and electricity cost $23; full hookups cost $25. The charge for dogs is $1 per night. Visitors are welcome year-round.

You must reserve as far as seven months in advance to stay at **Samuel P. Taylor State Park** (Box 251, Lagunitas, CA 94938, tel. 415/488–9897 for information only; 800/444–7275 for reservations), a scenic, wooded campground with 60 tent sites, roughly half of which can accommodate RVs (although there are no hookups). The grounds, located on Sir Francis Drake Highway, 7 mi east of the Bear Valley Visitor Center, are heavily shaded by towering redwoods along with a number of Douglas firs and oak trees. Flush toilets, drinking water, fire grates, and hot showers (for a nominal fee) are available. There's also a disposal station, a public telephone, and a ranger station. Rates are $14 per night between April and October, $12 per night the rest of the year for up to eight people. There's a two-car maximum at each site; the charge for the second car is $5 (the first is free). Dogs can stay (on leash only) for $1 per night. Two of the sites are equipped for visitors with disabilities. AC Transit Bus No. 65 from San Rafael stops here twice a day en route to park headquarters.

Redwood National and State Parks
California

Updated by Kristina Malsberger

nyone who has forgotten what it feels like to be a child should visit the redwoods of northern California. Standing beside their massive trunks, following their graceful lines as they soar toward the heavens, adults will be reminded of the time when they were very small in a very big world.

Redwood National Park was created in 1968 along a thin strip of California coastline surrounding three state parks and stretching for 50 mi along the coast. Ten years later it was further expanded to provide a "buffer" forest to protect the redwoods. Today the park surrounds Prairie Creek Redwoods State Park, Jedediah Smith Redwoods State Park, Del Norte Coast Redwoods State Park, and former timberlands that were privately owned. The name Redwood encompasses both the national and the state parks.

The area has been the focus of environmental concerns since 1918, when the Save-the-Redwoods league was formed. Spurred by deforestation (old-growth redwoods once covered an estimated 2 million acres, but by 1965 only 300,000 acres remained), the group began the push toward national-park status for the area, and it remains active in the redwoods' preservation. At present, work continues to protect the area against erosion by replacing trees taken through logging and eliminating unneeded roads.

Jedediah Smith was the first explorer to travel overland to this then-virgin forest. He came in 1828, but the area remained relatively unpopulated until gold-hungry fortune hunters began to fill the woods in the early 1850s. Plentiful and just as valuable, the real fortune in this area soon proved to be "red gold"—redwood lumber. Though logging is still an important activity in the area, the days when wealth was measured by the board foot are over, and the forest is largely depleted. (Though the park consists of 105,516 acres, only about 39,000 of those acres are old-growth forest.) To make matters worse, tourism has not made up for lost logging income, and the largest town within the park, Crescent City (population 8,000), remains economically strapped.

ESSENTIAL INFORMATION

VISITOR INFORMATION The **Redwood National and State Park Headquarters** (1111 2nd St., Crescent City, CA 95531, tel. 707/464–6101, ext. 5064) is the best place to find books, maps, posters, and general information about the parks. If you're approaching the park from the south, the **Redwood Information Center** (Box 7, Orick, CA 95555, tel. 707/464–6101, ext. 5265), just off U.S. 101 in Orick, is a more convenient stop. Visitors coming from the north can try the **Hiouchi Information Center** (Hiouchi, CA 95531, tel. 707/464–6101, ext. 5067), a smaller center only open May through October. You can get information on the three state parks at park headquarters, or contact **Prairie Creek Redwoods State Park** (Orick, CA 95555, tel. 707/464–6101, ext. 5300) directly for detailed information on that park.

Visitors can request information about lodging, transportation, and local facilities by contacting either the **Crescent City/Del Norte County Chamber of Commerce** (1001 Front St., Crescent City, CA 95531, tel. 707/464–3174 or 800/343–8300) or the **Eureka/Humboldt County Convention and Visitors Bureau** (1034 2nd St., Eureka, CA 95501-0541, tel. 707/443–5097). Those interested in finding out more about redwood preservation can contact the **Save-the-Redwoods League** (114 Sansome St., Room 605, San Francisco, CA 94104, tel. 415/362–2352).

FEES Admission to Redwood National and State Parks is free. The state parks charge a fee of $5 per carload per day if you use any of the park facilities, such as the beach or the picnic areas. This fee covers use of all the state parks during the day of purchase.

PUBLICATIONS The **Redwood Natural History Association** (1111 2nd St., Crescent City, CA 95531, tel. 707/464–9150) sells more than 160 books, posters, maps, coloring books, laminated field-identification cards, videos, and audiotapes on the park and on natural history in general. These materials are available at the park-information stations in Crescent City, Hiouchi, and Orick. You can also order a catalog and place your order by mail.

Books and pamphlets that provide a good introduction to the area include Joseph Brown's *Monarchs of the Mist,* a brief and readable history of the coast redwood and Redwood National and State Parks, and Richard Rasp's *Redwood: The Story Behind the Scenery,* a photo essay on the forest and man's relationship with it. Bill Schneider uses simple text and enchanting watercolors to describe big trees to small readers in *The Tree Giants.* Caranco and Labbe's *Logging the Redwoods,* slanted more toward the loggers-as-hardy-pioneers than the save-the-trees set, provides valuable historic information and photos detailing early logging practices in the area.

If you plan to hike even a single trail, purchase the Redwood Natural History Association's *Redwood National Park Trail Map* from any park information center, or order one in advance from the Redwood Natural History Association. It lists all the area's trails, with mileage, and elaborates on each trail's best and worst features. Nature buffs might appreciate Macs Field Guides' *Northwest Waterbirds, Northwest Invertebrates,* or *Northwest Wildflowers*—double-sided laminated cards with illustrations of local flora and fauna.

GEOLOGY AND TERRAIN Ocean, rain forest, and rugged mountains crowd each other here. The redwoods that thrive within 30 mi of the coast disappear in the higher and drier areas, replaced by Douglas fir, oak, and red alder. It is these dramatic differences that make the park so interesting.

This variety is the result of centuries of shifting in the earth's crust. Geologists theorize that the north coast was created from rocks that were pushed up from below the Pacific Ocean about 170 million years ago. These were eventually shifted toward the coast, shoving tons of ocean sediment ahead of them. When the sediment collided with the North American continent, the folding and faulting of earth created the coastal mountains and left an inland strip of sedimentary earth between the Coast Range mountains and the volcanoes of the Sierra Nevada range.

All this geological gyration has led to an amazing array of stone for rock hounds. The northern California coast holds everything from the sea-foam green serpentine that covers so many area beaches and the Smith River to the flecks of gold that brought the California Gold Rush of the mid-1800s. But it is the rich earth from the former ocean sediment that is probably most geologically crucial to the region, since it is part of the precise equation that helps nurture the prehistoric redwoods.

Since sediment is the product of settling rather than heat, such ground is prone to erosion. Given the rain-forest-like climate on the coastal side of the mountains— where between 63 and 122 inches of rain falls annually—and the cobweb of rivers and streams that pass through here on their way to the Pacific, erosion is a nagging problem in the park. As a result, many more acres of trees have been protected along the park's boundaries to form a stabilizing watershed area.

FLORA AND FAUNA A common adage on the northern California coast says that everything here will either rust, root, or rot—bad news for everyone except the coast redwoods. The moisture-loving giants thrive in this area precisely because of the moderate temperature, excessive rainfall, and omnipresent fog.

Although the sand verbena and evening primrose that grow along local beaches are charming, the area really gained its national-park status because of the unique and magnificent local trees. The coast redwood, more properly known as Sequoia sempervirens, is a botanical kissing cousin to the giant sequoia of drier central California's Sierra Nevada mountains. Most coast redwoods are between 500 and 700 years of age, though they may live as long as 2,000 years—still a good 1,200 years younger than the oldest giant sequoias. But although they may be younger, the redwoods are definitely taller: It is a coast redwood that holds the title of world's tallest tree—nearly 366 ft. This particular beauty, which is more than 600 years old, can be found in the Tall Trees Grove at the south end of the park.

The coast redwood is not only taller than the giant sequoia, it is also more popular—at least in everyday use. The giant sequoia is cursed (or blessed) with brittle wood that is unsuitable for lumber, but the durable coastal redwood is favored by consumers for backyard picnic tables and garden trellises. The redwood is a tough tree. It suffers from no known mortal diseases, is virtually impervious to insects, and routinely survives lightning strikes. It exhibits amazingly tenacious growth habits, too: Cutting down a single redwood can cause a small grove to sprout. Stumps commonly send up several new shoots, and minor damage to a limb may result in an entirely new tree shooting up from a horizontal branch. A wind-toppled trunk will routinely put out new skyward shoots like a row of soldiers standing at attention along the massive log.

The north coast redwoods have developed over many centuries into what botanists call a climax forest, a mature mix of plants and animals, all of which thrive in the dense shade the tall trees provide and the moist air of the region. As a result, plants here grow to a size that is much larger than would be common in other parts of the country. Humidity-loving fuchsias, the wild ancestor of the familiar garden plant, grow in lengthy, tangled vines. Native sword ferns form groves beneath the trees, thrusting their sawtooth fronds 6 to 8 ft high. Redwood sorrel, a cousin of the tiny clover that grows in northern lawns, forms 10-inch-high clumps with shamrock leaves that are 2 to 4 inches across.

A few plants grow to more traditional dimensions but are no less distinctive. Native rhododendron enjoys an extended blooming season under the forest canopy and can still be found in full flower in late July. The petite woodland iris, no taller than the oxalis, or redwood sorrel, decorates the woods in shades ranging from off-white through purple, nearly all with a splash of yellow in the center. The curious-looking tan oak is another resident of the woods. Although its mature foliage is leathery and dark green, new growth is tan. Also look for thimbleberries, blackberries, and huckleberries.

As the elevations become higher and drier—coast redwoods do not typically grow above 3,000 ft in elevation—the forest turns to Douglas fir, alder, and oak. Another common sight is the madrone tree, which ranges in height from shrub size to nearly 100 ft and is distinctive for its peeling reddish or reddish-orange bark. Keep an eye out for rash-inducing poison oak, distinguished by shiny green leaves in clusters of three, which turn red in the fall. It's common in both the redwood lowlands and higher altitudes.

Wildlife is nearly as plentiful as plant life in the park, but may not be as visible. Backcountry hikers will usually have much more luck than drive-through park visitors in spotting local animals, though Roosevelt elk are readily visible along Newton B. Drury Scenic Parkway, and especially just off U.S. 101 at Davison Road.

Backcountry campers may also observe mountain lions, black bears, and blacktail deer. Near the water, look for smaller animals such as the river otter, beaver, and mink. Local rivers and streams are a fisherman's paradise, filled with silver and king salmon, as well as rainbow, coast cutthroat, and steelhead trout.

Along the coastline you'll be able to see plenty of the ocean's mammals, including gray whales, seals, and sea lions.

Bird-watchers can enjoy a front-row seat for the Pacific Flyway, one of North America's four major bird-migration routes. Owing to this small area's diversity of environments, an amazing 370 species of bird have been sighted in the park, including both rare and unusual species such as blue herons, brown pelicans, pileated woodpeckers, spotted owls, and marbled murrelets; as well as more-common birds such as kingfishers, three species of warbler, wood ducks, ravens, and hawks.

WHEN TO GO Campers and hikers flock to the park from mid-June to early September, the driest and busiest months. In winter, frequent rains, sinister potholes, and abbreviated facility hours are the prices you'll pay to enjoy a mist-enshrouded seascape uncluttered by tourists. Bird-watchers prefer to visit during the spring and fall migrating seasons; the best whale-watching occurs also during fall and spring migrations, with peak sightings in December and March.

Temperatures vary widely throughout the park, with marked differences between the foggy coastal lowland and the interior's higher altitude. In summer, temperatures along the coast usually remain in the mid-60s, though they can rise into the 70s. It's much hotter in the interior, with highs ranging from 80°F to 100°F. Winter temperatures throughout the park hover between 30°F and 50°F. Crescent City averages more than 65 inches of rain a year, and throughout the park the rainy season lasts roughly from late October through April. The weather here is fickle, so be prepared for unexpected showers.

SEASONAL EVENTS **February:** For more than 30 years competitors from California and Oregon have gathered for the **World Championship Crab Races** (tel. 800/343–8300), held on President's Day Weekend in Crescent City. The two-day event features races of locally caught crabs and an all-out chow down at the accompanying crab feed. **June:** Testosterone levels rise during the two-day **U.S. National Jet Boat Races** (tel. 800/200–2335), a display of speed and splashing on the Klamath River. **July 4:** The large **Fourth of July Celebration** (tel. 800/343–8300) held in Crescent City features fireworks, food stalls, and a parade. **August:** Of interest to foodies are the **Klamath Salmon Festival** (Klamath, tel. 707/482–7165), a two-day Native American celebration held by the local Yurok tribe, and the **Del Norte County Fair** (Crescent City, tel. 707/464–9556), a four-day festival that includes a carnival. The most unusual event in August, however, is certainly the **Banana Slug Derby** (tel. 707/464–6101, ext. 5300) held in Prairie Creek Redwoods State Park, where competitors race large, yellow slugs—that's right, slugs. They also elect a banana-slug queen or king to lead the banana slug parade. **October:** The **Noll Longboard Classic** (tel. 707/465–4400), held on Crescent City's wide South Beach, is a two-day competition that brings more than 200 participants to California's northernmost surfing outpost.

WHAT TO PACK Temperatures in the park can be unpredictable, so bring layered clothing. Sturdy shoes with nonslip soles are necessary during the rainy season, when the eroding hillsides are especially slippery. There's abundant poison oak here, so wear long pants whenever possible.

GENERAL STORES Although there are no general stores inside the park, more than two dozen grocery stores dot the map in the small towns surrounding it. Most of the better prospects are in Crescent City. On Highway 101 in Crescent City you can find grocery supplies at **Safeway** (475 M St., tel. 707/465–3353), open daily 24 hours. For general merchandise, including cosmetics, hardware, auto parts, sports equipment, and camera supplies, try **Payless Drugstore** (575 M St., tel. 707/465–3412), also on Highway 101 and open Monday through Saturday from 9 to 9, Sunday from 9 to 7. If you are in the southern half of the park, visit the smaller **Orick Market** (U.S. 101, tel. 707/488–3225) in Orick. This general store is open daily from 8 to 7:30 in summer; and Monday through Saturday from 8 to 7, Sunday from 9 to 6 in the off-season.

ARRIVING AND DEPARTING Since access to Redwood National and State Parks by public transportation is extremely limited, visitors will find that driving their own car or RV into the park is easiest. Redwood National and State Parks are about 375 mi from San Francisco and 350 mi from Portland, Oregon. Crater Lake National Park is 175 mi northeast of Redwood, and Point Reyes National Seashore is about 350 mi to the south.

By Bus. Crescent City is served by **Greyhound** (tel. 707/464–2807), which operates two buses per day to San Francisco and two per day to Portland. The bus also makes stops at Orick and at the Redwood youth hostel on U.S. 101 in Klamath. The local bus company, called **Dial-A-Ride** (tel. 707/464–9314 or 707/464–4314), provides on-call, door-to-door service within Crescent City and sends two vans a day to Klamath.

By Car and RV. Most drivers approach the park from San Francisco in the south via U.S. 101. This eight-hour drive is a pleasant one, past numerous stands of redwoods and through many lovely small towns.

If you are arriving from Seattle or Portland, follow either I–5 or U.S. 101 south. Those using I–5 should exit at Grants Pass, Oregon, and take U.S. 199 to its termination at U.S. 101 just north of Crescent City. This route allows for a side trip off U.S. 199 at Cave Junction to the Oregon Caves National Monument—but factor in at least an extra half day to visit the caves. Drivers, particularly those in RVs, should be aware that U.S. 199 is very narrow, especially on the southbound side. Although it's a considerably slower drive than I–5, coastal U.S. 101 has the advantage of leading straight into the park. To get onto U.S. 101, those coming from the direction of Seattle should head south on I–5 to Olympia, then take Highway 8 west to the coast. Those driving from the Portland area should take Highway 99W southwest to Highway 18, which climbs the Coast Range mountains and joins U.S. 101 just north of Lincoln City.

Although traveling by car or RV is the easiest way to reach and explore the park, drivers should be aware that many of the park's most scenic roads are not paved, and winter rains can turn these routes into pothole-riddled obstacle courses that are sometimes closed to vehicles completely. In the dry summer season, these routes are passable by almost all vehicles, but RVs and trailers are not advised or not permitted beyond various points. Check your route with a ranger in advance to avoid disappointment later.

By Plane. Commercial air service to Crescent City and to Eureka/Arcata airport, 32 mi south of Orick, is provided daily by **United Express** (tel. 800/241–6522) from San Francisco.

Car-rental services in Eureka include **Avis** (tel. 707/839–1576), **Hertz** (tel. 707/839–2172), and **National** (tel. 707/839–3229). In Crescent City, try **Enterprise** (tel. 707/464–4228) and **U-Save Auto Rental** (tel. 707/464–7813).

By Taxi. Del Norte Taxi Service (tel. 707/464–6030) is the area's one taxi service. It is based in Crescent City but provides out-of-town service and tours through the red-woods.

EXPLORING

Driving along U.S. 101, you will pass through Redwood National and State Parks for an hour or so and will see many of the famed redwood trees. But these monarchs, towering taller than 35-story skyscrapers, are not the only wonders in the park. There are also sandy beaches, pillared-rock sea stacks, cliffs and coves, oak-lined prairie, and crystal-clear streams and rivers. Seeing the plant-rich estuaries, the driftwood-strewn beaches, and the most impressive redwood groves requires a short detour from the main route.

THE BEST IN ONE DAY If time is short, don't give in to the temptation to simply rubber-neck while passing through. Tree-hugging is essential to the traveler's sense of wonder here. For a good, hands-on overview of the park, with minimal hiking, explore Howland Hill Road in the morning and Gold Bluffs Beach in the afternoon.

Start the day by taking U.S. 101 south from Crescent City, making a left on Elk Valley Road, and turning right at the Stout Grove sign onto Howland Hill Road, in the Jedediah Smith Redwoods State Park. This one-lane gravel road can be negotiated by most vehicles, but the park service does not rec-ommend the trip for RVs and trailers. Although Howland Hill Road is only 12 mi long, you'll want to allow at least 40 min-utes for the trip so you'll have time to wan-der into the forest. About 10 mi into the drive, you'll reach Stout Grove, where a flat, 1-mi loop leads along the Smith River and past the Stout Tree, one of the largest redwoods in the park. Two miles farther, Howland Hill Road runs into U.S. 199.

Return to U.S. 101 and head south for about 35 mi through the Del Norte Coast Red-woods State Park, taking a worthwhile detour from the highway along the Newton B. Drury Scenic Parkway. After re-entering Prairie Creek Redwoods State Park, turn right onto Davison Road. Follow this wind-ing, gravel road (trailers or RVs over 24 ft in length or 8 ft in width are prohibited) for 4 mi or so until you reach Gold Bluffs Beach and Campground for a leisurely picnic lunch and a short hike. There is a state-park day-use fee of $5 per vehicle.

Roosevelt elk frequent the lovely beach here. Follow the trail at the north end of the beach, and, after wading across a shal-low creek several times, you will arrive at Fern Canyon (*see* Nature Trails and Short Walks, *below*). Try to time your visit for late afternoon, when the lighting is partic-ularly dramatic.

ORIENTATION PROGRAMS From Memorial Day through Labor Day the National Park Service and the three state parks sponsor free, ranger-led programs on topics such as the redwoods, tide pooling, geology, and local Native American culture. The topics vary according to available staff, so consult the information desk at the visitor centers throughout the parks for a schedule of events.

GUIDED TOURS Owing to recent budget cuts, the park service has phased out many of its guided nature walks and tours. Call any of the visitor centers for information about existing tours, which usually take place during summer.

SCENIC DRIVES AND VIEWS Five paved roads provide scenic routes through the park. To reach 2.3-mi **Enderts Beach Road,** follow U.S. 101 south from Crescent City for 2 mi, then make a right. This route takes you to several beaches and to the 50-mi Coastal Trail. **Requa Road,** off U.S. 101 some 16 mi south of Crescent City, is a good choice for hikers, picnickers, and whale-watchers. After winding uphill for 2.5 mi, the road reaches Klamath Overlook, a windy point perched 600 ft above the mouth of the Kla-math River; here you might stop and enjoy the view or set off down the Coastal Trail, which can be picked up here. **Bald Hills Road,** which begins just 1 mi north of Orick, leads to Lady Bird Johnson Grove,

Tall Trees Grove, and plenty of elk, but, because of its steep grade, the 35-mi road is not recommended for trailers. Visitors to Tall Trees Grove must have a permit, available from the Redwood Information Center on a first-come, first-served basis.

You can pick up **Coastal Drive** from two points on U.S. 101, north of Prairie Creek Redwoods State Park. The scenery along this 8-mi drive, parts of which are unpaved and not recommended for trailers, alternates between dense forest and ocean, with plenty of hiking, picnicking, whale-watching, and sightseeing opportunities. Note the World War II radar station that's disguised as a farmhouse and barn. Formerly part of U.S. 101, the flat, well-graded **Newton B. Drury Scenic Parkway** is an excellent option for bicyclists and RVers. This redwood-lined, 10-mi route, great for camping and hiking, is between Klamath and Orick; take the Prairie Creek State Park exit from U.S. 101.

The park also has four unpaved but well-graveled scenic routes. The 12-mi **Howland Hill Road,** northeast of Crescent City, accesses Stout Grove and is great for photo opportunities. **Cal-Barrel Road** is a 3-mi tour through Prairie Creek Redwoods State Park, 6 mi north of Orick. (Note that there is no turnaround for RVs.) Both routes are well endowed with the dense, old-growth redwood groves that make the park so popular. The 1-mi **Lost Man Creek Road,** 5 mi north of Orick, leads to the Lost Man Creek picnic area and serves as the terminus for the Holter Ridge Mountain Bike Trail. **Davison Road** is a 9-mi route through a mixed redwood and spruce forest that leads to Gold Bluffs Beach. From this beach, you can walk to Fern Canyon (*see below*).

NATURE TRAILS AND SHORT WALKS Allow one hour to explore the 1.5-mi round-trip **Fern Canyon Trail,** accessible from Davison Road. Carved away by erosion from Home Creek, the .75-mi canyon has 60-ft walls covered with sword, maidenhair, and five-finger ferns. The trail ends at an abandoned mining town left over from the gold-

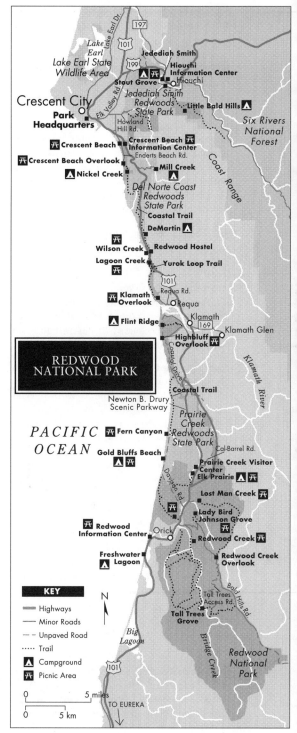

rush days. From the north end of Gold Bluffs Beach it's an easy walk, although you do have to wade across a small stream several times. **Lady Bird Johnson Grove Nature Loop** is a 1-mi round-trip trail that begins on Bald Hills Road about 2.75 mi east of U.S. 101. The wheelchair-accessible trail follows an old logging road through a mature redwood forest. Allow 45 minutes to complete the loop. Beginning at the Lagoon Creek picnic area, **Yurok Loop Trail** is also a 1-mi round-trip nature trail, with good bird-watching opportunities. Visit in the spring to enjoy a riot of wildflowers. You'll need about 45 minutes here.

LONGER HIKES The almost 120 mi of trails in Redwood National and State Parks are rated according to six classifications of difficulty. A trail's difficulty is determined according to the steepness of the grade, the number of switchbacks, and the length of the trail. For a complete review of the park's trails, buy a copy of the trail guide at any visitor center.

Although the **Coastal Trail** runs the entire 50-mi length of the park, smaller sections are accessible by frequent, well-marked trailheads. The difficulty of each section varies, depending on which part of the trail you decide to tackle. The 4-mi-long **Hidden Beach** section connects the Lagoon Creek picnic area with Klamath Overlook and provides a view of the coast as well as whale-watching opportunities. The somewhat more difficult **DeMartin** section, which you can pick up at milepost 15.6 on U.S. 101, leads past 5 mi of mature redwoods and through prairie. Those who feel up to a real workout will be well rewarded for hiking the brutal but stunning **Flint Ridge** section. This 4.5-mi stretch of steep grades and numerous switchbacks starts at the Douglas Bridge parking area at the north end of Coastal Drive and leads past redwoods and Marshall Pond.

Day hikers looking for a satisfying, moderately strenuous trek should try the **West Ridge–Friendship Ridge–James Irvine Loop,** accessible from the Prairie Creek

Redwoods State Park headquarters off the Newton B. Drury Scenic Parkway. The 12.5-mi loop's greatest asset is the variety of its terrain. The West Ridge Trail passes redwoods looming above a carpet of ferns; the Friendship Ridge Trail slopes down toward the coast, playing host to the Sitka spruce and Western hemlock that thrive near the ocean; and the James Irvine Trail winds along a small creek and through old-growth redwood groves.

OTHER ACTIVITIES **Bird-Watching.** Welcome to some of the best and most varied bird-watching in the West. Some of nature's rarest and most striking winged specimens inhabit the area, including brown pelicans, great blue herons, pileated woodpeckers, spotted owls, and marbled murrelets. The Lagoon Creek picnic area, just south of the Redwood hostel on U.S. 101, is an easily accessible place to marvel at the park's feathered inhabitants.

Fishing. Both deep-sea and freshwater fishing are popular sports here; anglers often stake out sections of the Klamath and Smith Rivers in their search for salmon, steelhead, and trout. Lunker Fish Trips (2095 U.S. 199, Hiouchi, tel. 707/458–4704) provides guide service along the Smith River for $250 per day for two people, including boat, equipment, and bait. For information on the local deep-sea fishing companies that offer charter and/or guide service, contact the Crescent City/Del Norte County Chamber of Commerce (tel. 800/343–8300). Fishing licenses, available at Payless Drugstore (575 M St., Crescent City, tel. 707/465–3412) for $26.50, are required for both river and ocean fishing.

Less serious anglers can get in on the action by crabbing or clamming on the coast. You can rent crab pots at Popeye's Landing at the pier at the southern end of B Street in Crescent City. No license is necessary to spend a lazy day on the pier trying your luck.

Kayaking. With the many miles of often shallow rivers and streams in the area, kayaking is a popular pastime in the park.

Lunker Fish Trips (2095 U.S. 199, Hiouchi, tel. 707/458–4704) rents kayaks in the summer for $20 a day; for an extra $10 they will drive you and your trusty craft to a put-in point on the Smith River and pick you up when you're done. Children must be accompanied by an adult 18 years or older, and reservations should be made a day or two in advance. Ranger-led kayaking trips through the Klamath River Estuary take place in summer; the cost is $20 per person (including kayak), and the minimum age is 10. For reservations, call 707/464–6101, ext. 5265.

Swimming. Though the Pacific Ocean may seem inviting, the pounding surf and rip currents are so deadly that rangers suggest visitors never swim in the ocean, even if it appears calm. The Smith River is a better bet for swimmers; many people brave the cold waters for a dip or an inner-tube ride down the river.

Whale-Watching. There are several good vantage points for whale-watching, including Crescent Beach Overlook, Klamath Overlook, the Redwood Information Center in Orick, and points along the Coastal Drive. The best months for watching the whales varies from year to year, but late October through January are usually good months to see their southward migrations.

CHILDREN'S PROGRAMS All of the state parks run a Junior Ranger program, in which rangers instruct children ages 7 to 12 on bird identification, outdoor survival skills, and more. The program typically runs every morning in summer: Check with Park Headquarters (tel. 707/464–6101, ext. 5064) for specific locations.

EVENING ACTIVITIES Inquire at a visitor center or check campground bulletin boards during the summer to find out the schedule of evening programs. All three state parks have campfire programs in addition to talks and demonstrations covering such topics as local plants and wildlife, geology, forestry practices, and local Native American culture. Or just take a stroll down the Crescent City pier after sunset, when the lights of the harbor shine over the ocean.

DINING

A handful of surprisingly good dining choices can be found in the small towns surrounding the park, but the biggest selection of eateries is in Crescent City. Most menus feature simply prepared dishes that highlight the region's plentiful seafood. Good food comes at reasonable prices here, and servings are sized for big appetites.

Requa Inn. A hidden treasure overlooking the mouth of the Klamath River, this former stagecoach inn is well worth seeking out. Specialties include grilled ocean salmon and charbroiled filet mignon smothered in mushroom sauce. *451 Requa Rd., Klamath, tel. 707/482–8205. AE, D, MC, V. $$–$$$*

Beachcomber Restaurant. Fresh seafood and ribs or chicken grilled over an open-pit barbecue are the house specialties at this local favorite with a view of the waterfront. The decor is unmistakably nautical—diver's helmets, portholes, and brass ship's bells. *1400 U.S. 101 S, Crescent City, tel. 707/464–2205. MC, V. Closed Wed. and Nov.–Feb. 15. No lunch. $$*

Da Lucianna Ristorante Italiano. Classier than Crescent City's boisterous seafood restaurants, Da Lucianna serves excellent Italian cuisine in casual, dimly lit surroundings. Authentic dishes such as gnocchi with bolognese sauce or veal scallopini are the house specialties; steak, barbecued chicken, and pork are always on the menu, but on weekends they are cooked out back on the open-pit barbecue. The friendly staff is happy to field special requests. *575 U.S. 101, Crescent City, tel. 707/465–6566. MC, V. No lunch weekends. $$*

Harbor View Grotto. If you have ever had difficulty conceptualizing the food chain, then eat at the Grotto: The fish comes straight from the boat, into the restaurant, and onto your plate. Besides serving the north coast's best fresh seafood, this casual eatery is known for immense portions—scallops come in heaps of a dozen or more to a plate—making the so-called Lite Eater's Menu a wise choice. The white two-story building is marked only by a neon sign saying "Restaurant"—keep your eyes open. *150 Starfish Way, off U.S. 101, Crescent City, tel. 707/464–3815. MC, V. $$*

Rolf's Park Cafe. After driving past the few greasy spoon diners in Orick, you might be surprised to find such fine dining at Rolf's Park Cafe. German chef Rolf Rheinschmidt's specialties are German Farmer's Omelette, served family style for two or more, and all sorts of game dishes. Enjoy elk steaks with wild mushroom sauce and cranberries in the casual interior, or out on the patio, where you may spot a few live elk in the distance. *U.S. 101 at Davison Rd., 2 mi north of Orick, tel. 707/488–3841. MC, V. Closed late Nov.–early Mar. $$*

Good Harvest Cafe. Not only is the Good Harvest's casually funky atmosphere a welcome reprieve from Crescent City's strip-mall aesthetic, but this place serves the best breakfasts in town: Locals and visitors flock here for vegetarian dishes like tofu rancheros and old favorites like eggs Benedict and French toast. A lunch menu of salads and sandwiches is served after 11 AM, and you can get your caffeine fix all day long from the espresso bar. *700 Northcrest Dr., Crescent City, tel. 707/465–6028. D, MC, V. No dinner. $*

Los Compadres. This family-run restaurant is little more than a roadside shack, but you can practically taste its pride in the authentic Mexican food. It's known for the super burritos—giant bundles of meat and vegetables that live up to their name. Eat in the lackluster sitting area or get your food to go. *457 Hwy. 101 S, Crescent City, tel. 707/464–7871. No credit cards. $*

Palm Cafe. Dishes at this funky diner in Orick have memorable names like the Vagabond (a bacon burger with cheese), the Long Hand (steak and two eggs), and Old Hen on the Nest (chicken strips, fries, and toast). It's no bastion of haute cuisine, but it is a good place to join the local loggers for a quick cholesterol fix on your way through

the park. *121030 U.S. 101, Orick, tel. 707/488–3381. AE, D, DC, MC, V. $*

PICNIC SPOTS A brief glance at a park-service map will tell you Redwood has more than a dozen picnic grounds, some of them quite small. Among the best are: **Jedediah Smith,** 10 mi east of Crescent City on U.S. 199; **Crescent Beach,** just 2 mi south of Crescent City on Enderts Beach Road; **Lagoon Creek,** where you can also beachcomb, fish the freshwater lagoon, or choose from several area hiking trails; **Highbluff,** on the Coastal Drive, where the sunsets and whale-watching are unequaled; Gold Bluffs Beach, where Roosevelt elk stroll the beach (Fern Canyon is nearby); and Elk Prairie, where you'll also find a campground, nature trail, ranger station, and many, many elk. All grounds have tables and toilets.

LODGING

If you think plush accommodations are a necessary part of travel, make your visit to Redwood National and State Parks a day trip. A youth hostel is the only accommodation inside the park, and you won't find anything too fancy in the towns around it. There are, however, three historic properties: a bed-and-breakfast inn, a former-stagecoach-stop-turned-rustic-lodge, and a youth hostel. Though most of these hotels are no-frills, good service and genuine friendliness are the general rule.

Holiday Inn Express. Built in 1993, this motel exudes an aura of modern efficiency that makes you understand why the word "express" is in its name. The rooms are decorated in muted pastels with light wood accents and have TVs and phones. Rates include Continental breakfast, which is served in the lobby. *100 Walton St., off Hwy. 101, Crescent City, CA 95531, tel. 707/464–3885, fax 707/464–5311. 46 rooms. Facilities: coin laundry, meeting room. AE, D, DC, MC, V. $$–$$$*

Requa Inn. In a restored 1915 stagecoach inn overlooking the Klamath River, this bed-and-breakfast has 10 individually decorated rooms with redwood wainscoting and Craftsman furniture that mirrors the building's architectural style. Seven rooms are still equipped with claw-foot bathtubs; the other three have modern showers. In keeping with the old-fashioned ambience, rooms have neither TV nor telephones, and no smoking is permitted. *451 Requa Rd., Klamath, CA 95548, tel. 707/482–8205. 10 rooms. Facilities: restaurant. AE, D, MC, V. $$–$$$*

Bayview Inn. The Bayview is perhaps the best lodging value in Crescent City: Plush carpets, delicate prints, and amenities like cable TV, coffeemakers, and full baths in every room means plenty of luxury for the same price as the other motels. The staff is friendly and professional, and will gladly book you a room with a view at no extra charge. *310 U.S. 101 S, Crescent City, CA 95531, tel. 707/465–2050 or 800/446–0583, fax 707/465–3690. 65 rooms. Facilities: coin laundry. AE, D, DC, MC, V. $$*

Best Western Northwoods Inn. Modern and tastefully furnished in neutral colors, this motel is in the center of town, across from the harbor. The spotless rooms testify to the manager's obsession with cleanliness, but the best reason to stay here is the complimentary breakfast, which you order from the adjacent restaurant. *655 U.S. 101 S, Crescent City, CA 95531, tel. 707/464–9771 or 800/528–1234, fax 707/464–9461. 89 rooms. Facilities: restaurant, spa. AE, D, DC, MC, V. $$*

Curly Redwood Lodge. This motel's official claim to fame is that all the redwood you see—from the outside paneling to the mailbox and garbage cans in the lobby—was cut from a single tree. Not just any tree, either: a redwood tree whose rippling or "curly" grain is extremely rare. But the real reason that it's so popular is the unobtrusive, yet ever-present service staff. Don't expect deluxe surroundings—the rooms look as if they haven't been remodelled since the '70s—but Curly Redwood Lodge is a great value. *701 U.S. 101 S, Crescent City, CA*

95531, tel. 707/464–2137, fax 707/464–1655. 36 rooms. AE, MC, V. $$

Hiouchi Motel. This spartan but reliable sportsman's motel near the Smith River in the Hiouchi Hamlet complex makes plain its purpose by proudly advertising plenty of freezer space for your catch. Still, it's not a bad little place for a nonfishing family to use as a modestly priced home base while exploring the surrounding redwoods. *2097 U.S. 199, Hiouchi, CA 95531, tel. 707/458–3041. 17 rooms. Facilities: restaurant. D, MC, V. $$*

Pacific Motor Hotel. In that only-in-California tradition, half of the lobby in this sprawling wooden structure is a retail liquor store. Dark green carpet in the rooms combines with mauve bedspreads to create a decorative eyesore, but the rooms are clean and many come with microwaves and minirefrigerators. Guests have free use of the health club next door. *440 U.S. 101 N, Box 595, Crescent City, CA 95531, tel. 707/464–4141 or 800/323–7917, fax 707/465–3274. 62 rooms. Facilities: refrigerators, spa. AE, D, DC, MC, V. $$*

Patrick's Creek Resort. Getting away from it all is easy at this rustic (some might say primitive) inn built in 1926, 25 mi east of Crescent City. The original was an 1880s stagecoach inn. This is a true backcountry fishermen's lodge with fishing 100 ft from the resort. *13950 U.S. 199, Gasquet, CA 95543, tel. 707/457–3323. 16 rooms, 1 cabin. Facilities: bar, restaurant, pool. AE, DC, MC, V. $$*

Royal Inn Motel. This centrally located facility has easy access to shopping and restaurants, and it's just around the corner from the Crescent City Chamber of Commerce and Redwood National and State Parks Headquarters. The rooms are a bit musty, but the motel is a good choice for families on a budget: Seven of the units have kitchenettes, and another 10 have microwave ovens and minirefrigerators. *102 L St., Crescent City, CA 95531, tel. 707/464–4113 or 800/752–9610. 36 rooms. AE, D, MC, V. $$*

Palm Cafe & Motel. This tacky but endearing little roadside motel is most notable for its namesake palm tree sprouting from the roof and a funky mural on the outside of the building that integrates the real windows with the trompe l'oeil. The furniture and decor are somewhat schizophrenic, but the outdoor swimming pool provides an easy escape from the circus-theme paintings in the rooms. *121130 U.S. 101 S, Orick, CA 95555, tel. 707/488–3381. 18 rooms. Facilities: restaurant, pool. AE, D, MC, V. $*

Redwood AYH Hostel. Travelers of all ages are welcome to stay in this vintage 1908 two-story Edwardian building. The enthusiastic staff and oceanside location can't be beat, but you'll have to contend with a 9:30 to 4:30 lockout and an 11 PM curfew. There are three dormitory-style rooms, plus three private rooms; bring a sleeping bag or rent a sleep sheet here for a nominal fee. Kitchen and laundry facilities are available, and a wood-burning stove often warms the common room. *14480 U.S. 101, Klamath, CA 95548, tel. 707/482–8265, fax 707/482–4665. 34 beds, 3 shared bathrooms. MC, V. $*

CAMPING

The north coast has campgrounds both primitive and well-equipped, and the region's temperate winter climate makes camping possible year-round. Within a 30-minute drive of Redwood National and State Parks there are nearly 60 public and private camping facilities with tent, RV, and trailer sites. In addition, there are backcountry sites for those wishing to immerse themselves in the magnificent wilderness.

Disposal stations are available at campgrounds in Jedediah Smith, Del Norte Coast, and Prairie Creek state parks, as well as at private campgrounds. None of the national-park, state-park, or national-forest campgrounds has RV hookups.

INSIDE THE PARK Redwood National and State Parks operate five primitive camping areas on national-park land. Four of these—Little Bald Hills, Nickel Creek, DeMartin, and Flint Ridge—are backcountry sites that can only be reached by hiking in .25 to 4.5 mi. There is no camping fee for these sites and no permit is needed, but stop at a ranger station to inquire about availability. The fifth site, Freshwater Lagoon, is a drive-in area that is actually a state right-of-way. Because it is not officially run by the park service, a $6 donation is requested. With a backcountry permit, available at any of the park's visitor centers, campers can also pitch a tent on gravel bars in certain areas along Redwood Creek.

The **Little Bald Hills** area, a 4.5-mi hike from the trailhead at the east end of Howland Hill Road, has 5 sites with amazing ridge-top vistas. There are chemical toilets, picnic tables, potable water, and fire rings here. **Nickel Creek** has five sites just .5 mi from the end of Enderts Beach Road on the Coastal Trail. The campground is near tide pools and has great ocean views. Facilities include a composting toilet, picnic tables, and fire rings; there is no potable water. Two and a half miles from the Coastal Trail trailhead, near the Redwood AYH Hostel, is the **DeMartin** camping area, which has 10 sites in a grassy prairie with a panoramic view of the ocean. DeMartin has a composting toilet, picnic tables, and fire rings, but no potable water. **Flint Ridge,** with 10 campsites on a scenic coastal bluff, is approximately .25 mi from the Flint Ridge-trailhead parking area on the Coastal Drive. There's a composting toilet here, as well as potable water and fire rings.

At **Freshwater Lagoon,** 1.5 mi south of Orick, you'll find unlimited primitive camping sites along a strip of sand on the west shoulder of U.S. 101, with the ocean on one side of the road and the lagoon on the other side. Car and tent camping are permitted at this unofficial campground, but most sites are taken by RVs and trailers. There is a 15-day maximum stay. Facilities are limited to chemical toilets, fire rings, and tables. There are no hookups and no water. The Redwood Information Center is just .25 mi north of here.

REDWOOD CAMPGROUNDS

	INSIDE THE PARK					INSIDE STATE PARKS				IN NEARBY NATIONAL FOREST			
	Little Bald Hills	Nickel Creek	DeMartin	Flint Ridge	Freshwater Lagoon	Mill Creek	Elk Prairie	Gold Bluffs Beach	Jedediah Smith	Panther Flat	Grassy Flat	Patrick Creek	Big Flat
Total number of sites	5	5	10	10	8	145	75	24	106	39	19	13	30
Sites suitable for RVs	0	0	0	0	8	145	75	0	106	39	19	13	30
Number of hookups	0	0	0	0	0	0	0	0	0	0	0	0	0
Drive to sites					•	•	•	•	•	•	•	•	•
Hike to sites	•	•	•	•									
Flush toilets						•	•	•	•	•		•	
Pit/chemical toilets	•	•	•	•	•					•	•		•
Drinking water	•		•	•		•	•	•	•	•	•	•	
Showers							•	•	•	•			
Fire grates	•	•	•	•	•	•	•	•	•	•	•	•	•
Swimming									•	•	•	•	•
Boat access									•				
Playground													
Disposal station						•	•		•				
Ranger station							•		•				
Public telephone							•		•			•	
Reservation possible						•¹	•¹		•¹	•	•	•	
Daily fee per site	free	free	free	free	$6	$16*	$16*	$16*	$16*	$12	$8	$10	$5
Dates open	year-round	year-round	year-round	year-round		year-round	year-round	year-round	year-round	year-round	late May–mid-Sept.	late May–mid-Sept.	year-round

¹Reservation fee charged.   *$14 off-season.

The four campgrounds on state-park land are the most expensive, charging $16 in season ($14 off-season) for overnight use and $5 for day use only. They are also the most likely to fill up first during the high season. All are developed campgrounds, open year-round, with flush toilets, drinking water, and fire grates. All but Gold Bluffs Beach have disposal stations and hot showers (Gold Bluffs has solar showers), and at all but Gold Bluffs Beach you can make reservations, from Memorial Day to Labor Day only, through Mistix (tel. 800/444–7275). There is a $6.75 reservation fee.

Mill Creek, in Del Norte Coast Redwoods State Park, has 145 sites, and is 7 mi south of Crescent City on U.S. 101. In Prairie Creek Redwoods State Park, **Elk Prairie,** 6 mi north of Orick on the Newton B. Drury Scenic Parkway, has 75 sites, a ranger station, and a public phone; and **Gold Bluffs Beach,** with 24 sites, is reached by traveling 8 mi on unpaved Davison Road south of Prairie Creek. Note: Trailers are prohibited on Davison Road, as are any vehicles more than 24 ft long and 8 ft wide. The beautiful **Jedediah Smith** campground in Jedediah Smith Redwoods State Park has 106 sites in groves of mature redwoods 8 mi northeast of Crescent City on U.S. 199. There's a ranger station and public phone here as well as a boat ramp, available only November to March (nonmotorized boats only). Jedediah Smith is on the Smith River,

which makes it popular with summer campers who like to swim.

NEAR THE PARK The **U.S. Forest Service** (tel. 707/457–3131 or 800/280–2267) runs four campgrounds on national-forest lands surrounding the park, all in prime fishing areas. These campgrounds have either flush or pit toilets and fire grates, as well as swimming. None has a disposal station, and only Panther Flat has a shower. All but Big Flat have potable water. Three campgrounds are strung along U.S. 199, northeast of Redwood National and State Parks, on the popular Smith River. These generally charge between $8 and $12 per site per night in season. Closest to the park is **Panther Flat,** with 39 sites, 2 mi east of Gasquet on U.S. 199. Two miles farther along U.S. 199 you will come to **Grassy Flat,** which has 19 sites and is closed from mid-September through mid-May. **Patrick Creek,** with 13 sites, is 3 mi farther east on U.S. 199, and is also closed from mid-September through mid-May. On the South Fork of the Smith River, 13 mi southeast of U.S. 199 on South Fork Road, **Big Flat** has 30 sites where you can camp for $5.

For an up-to-date listing of the many tent, RV, and trailer parks in the area, contact the **Crescent City/Del Norte County Chamber of Commerce,** the **Eureka/Humboldt Convention and Visitors Bureau,** or **Redwood National and State Parks** (*see* Visitor Information, *above*).

Rocky Mountain National Park
Colorado

Updated by Jane McConnell

nyone who delights in dizzying heights should consider Rocky Mountain National Park, where a single hour's drive leads from a 7,800-ft elevation at park headquarters to the 12,183-ft apex of Trail Ridge Road, the highest continuous paved road in the United States. From this vantage, sweeping vistas take in high-country lakes, meadows flushed with wildflowers, rushing mountain streams, and cool dense forests of lodgepole pine and Engelmann spruce. Above, snow-dusted peaks dotted with small glaciers and patches of blue Colorado columbine seem to float in the sky. The fragile, treeless ecosystem of alpine tundra is seldom found outside the Arctic, but it makes up one-third of the park's terrain. Rocky Mountain National Park isn't a pretty passage; it is a moment of grandeur.

More than 3 million people experience that grandeur annually, 80% of them in summer. That's roughly the same number of people that visit Yellowstone, which is nine times Rocky Mountain's size. They come for the 355 mi of hiking trails, as well as saddle rides, bus tours, rock climbing, fishing, seminars, and more. In summer, traffic jams clog the small town of Estes Park, at the park's eastern entrance.

But even though Rocky Mountain is far more crowded than it once was, there are places in the backcountry that look and feel as wild as they did when Native Americans roamed these woods. If you choose to come in early fall, after the crush of people and cars has gone and before the cold weather sets in, you'll enjoy brilliant autumn foliage and a better chance of spotting wildlife, which begin moving down from the higher elevations at this time. In winter, the backcountry snow can be 4 ft deep and the wind brutal at high elevations, but ski touring, snowshoeing, and ice fishing still draw the cold-weather adventurer.

Of course there is one very good reason to put up with the summer crowds: Only from Memorial Day to mid-October can you make the unforgettable drive over Trail Ridge Road, a ride that carries you high into the Rockies and makes you shake your head in wonder. Just steps from your car you'll discover the park's oldest rocks and traces of volcanic ash. From this vantage point, the mountains are not just a backdrop, but rather wild products of nature, with a dynamic past and an infinite future.

Rocky Mountain National Park comprises lands that were part of the Louisiana Purchase, acquired by the U.S. government in 1803. Fifty-six years later, the first white settler, Joel Estes, moved his family into a cabin in what would become Estes Park, and by 1909 a naturalist named Enos Mills had moved here and begun the campaign to save the area. In 1915 President Woodrow Wilson set aside 358.5 square mi of this land, near the heart of Colorado, to be preserved and protected as a national park (an additional 46.5 square mi were added 75 years later); since then, Rocky, as the locals call it, has been welcoming people from around the globe.

ESSENTIAL INFORMATION

VISITOR INFORMATION For general information on the park contact the Superintendent, Park Headquarters, **Rocky Mountain National Park**, Estes Park, CO 80517, tel. 970/586–1206. For information on the area surrounding the park contact **Estes Park Chamber of Commerce** (tel. 970/586–4431 or 800/443–7837) or the **Grand Lake Chamber of Commerce** (tel. 970/627–3402 or 800/531–1019).

If you are planning an overnight trek into the backcountry, you must have a permit. From May through October the cost is $15 (it's free throughout the rest of the year); it can be picked up at two locations: just east of headquarters at the park's Backcountry Office (Estes Park, CO 80517, tel. 970/586–1242) and at the Kawuneeche Visitor Center (tel. 970/627–3471). Phone reservations for summer must be made between March 1 and May 15; after that reservations must be made by mail or in person. Include the nights and sites you are interested in, with a second and third choice; the number in your party; and your return address, and a reply will be mailed within 24 hours. You pay for your permit when you pick it up.

FEES Entrance fees are $10 per week per vehicle. Visitors entering the park on bicycles, mopeds, motorcycles, or on foot pay $5 for a weekly pass. Passengers on bus tours also pay $5. The park's Annual Area Pass, which allows you to come and go for a year from the date of purchase, costs $20.

PUBLICATIONS The **Rocky Mountain Nature Association** (Rocky Mountain National Park, Estes Park, CO 80517, tel. 970/586–1265), a nonprofit organization that works with the National Park Service, has an outstanding selection of books, guides, postcards, and videos on the park. Books include such historical accounts as *Magnificent Mountain Women,* by Janet Robertson; *Rocky Mountain Wildflowers,* by Kent and Donna Dannen; and the *Mountain Wildlife Coloring Book,* by Marj Dunmire.

The association also sells geologic maps of Rocky Mountain National Park and the more detailed United States Geological Survey (USGS) maps. You can buy detailed maps of the area from **Trails Illustrated** (tel. 303/670–3457).

The park itself sells numerous guides, maps, and books in its five visitor centers. The most useful of these are *Hiking Rocky Mountain National Park,* by Kent and Donna Dannen; and *A Roadside Guide to Rocky Mountain National Park,* by Beatrice Elizabeth Willard and Susan Quimby Foster. The *High Country Headlines,* a free park publication available at the visitor centers, entrances, and ranger stations, has a schedule of ranger programs.

A good reference book for the park's flora is *From Grassland to Glacier,* by Mutel Cornelia Fleischer and John C. Emerick. Other good sources are *Rocky Mountain Flora,* by William A. Weber, and *Rocky Mountain National Park Natural History Handbook,* by John C. Emerick. Look for *Rocky Mountain Mammals,* by David M. Armstrong, for background on local wildlife.

GEOLOGY AND TERRAIN Rocky Mountain National Park comprises 415 square mi and has 114 named peaks over 10,000 ft. For 40 mi it strides the Continental Divide, the range of high peaks that determines whether a stream will flow east toward the Atlantic Ocean or west to the Pacific. The park's east side is dominated by deep valleys, cirque lakes (small bodies of water cut out by glaciers), and harsh mountain faces. The weather here is unpredictable; thunderstorms occur nearly every summer afternoon. The western side of the park is wetter and denser, with pine forests and a gentler slope to the land. In wintertime, more snow falls here, but winds are diminished, which is an important fact: At these heights a breeze can knock you down.

Today, you can see evidence of the park's long (1¾ billion years) and varied past. Scientists estimate that 530 million years ago the park was covered by water, but a highland was created when the earth's internal forces pushed the land under the sea upward. Consequently, the water receded over time and left tropical plains inhabited by dinosaurs. Continued uplift and faulting raised the Rockies above the surrounding terrain. Finally, glaciers from the Ice Age left the park as it looks now, full of scooped-out valleys and peaks carved by ice.

The park is divided into three ecosystems, which correspond to elevation. The Montane ecosystem, from 7,000 to 9,000 ft above sea level, is full of slopes, valleys, and stands of ponderosa pines. The subalpine ecosystem, which is found from 9,000 to 11,500 ft, straddles the tree line and supports forests of Engelmann spruce and subalpine fir along with a plethora of wildflowers. Finally, the alpine tundra—over 11,500 ft—has arctic temperatures, strong winds, and barren stretches. Trees vanish and a meadowland of flowering grasses, mosses, and lichens appears briefly in the summer, only to change color with the onset of autumn.

FLORA AND FAUNA Rocky has one of the most diverse tundra ecosystems in North America: There are 65 species of mammal, 260 species of bird, and more than 300 species of plant. Montane vegetation includes ponderosa pine in the drier regions and Douglas fir on the damp north slopes; willow and birch thrive in meadows fed by underground streams. Local wildflowers include the wood-lily and the yellow lady's slipper orchid.

The subalpine ecosystem supports lodgepole pine, Engelmann spruce, aspen, huckleberry, and subalpine fir. Some of these trees have been sculpted into bizarre shapes by the wind. Stunted trunks and branches, known as *krummholz* (German for "crooked wood"), live in this zone, often surviving for several centuries. A member of the orchid family called fairy slipper grows in the lower range of this area.

Plants that can survive at the elevation of the alpine tundra are few. They generally resemble mossy clumps with long roots, although many startlingly beautiful wildflowers such as alpine avens, dwarf clover, and the alpine forget-me-not bloom briefly in late June or early July.

Birds and animals add color to Rocky's land, trees, and sky. The broad-tailed and the rufous hummingbirds are summer favorites at the park, along with woodpeckers, peregrine falcons, Steller's jays, mountain bluebirds, and Clark's nutcracker. The white-tailed ptarmigan—utterly white in its winter plumage—can be spotted throughout the year on the alpine tundra. Park authorities ask that visitors not feed any animals; abundant forage grows in the park throughout the year. Rangers will tell you about the best sites for bird-watching.

In the early part of the century black bears were scarce in the park, and today they hide in the backcountry, rarely spotted by hikers. Mountain lions and bobcats are, likewise, seldom seen. Bighorn sheep, however, are a more common sight, especially along Big Thompson Canyon and in Horseshoe Park. If you're lucky, you might spot moose in the willows of the Kawuneeche Valley, but you're more likely to see mule deer wandering along the main roads of the park, and you can often hear the soulful sound of coyotes baying at the moon at night. In autumn, herds of American elk (or wapiti, as the Shawnee people called them) roam down to lower elevations and are frequently visible near the park's eastern entrances during early morning or evening hours. Beavers live near ponds and streams, although they usually work after dark. Squirrels, chipmunks, and marmots are common, but beware: They sometimes carry such serious diseases as bubonic plague and rabies and should not be approached or fed.

WHEN TO GO Only in summer can you drive the 45-mi Trail Ridge Road, for many the highlight of a trip here. The road closes with the first heavy snowfall—typically around mid-October—and usually reopens by Memorial Day. The other great advantage of traveling to Rocky in the summer is that the climate is tame, making it possible to hike through much more of the 265,727 acres. Moreover, summer activities far outnumber winter ones. In summer you'll find biking, fishing, backpacking, horseback riding, and a number of local celebrations and festivals in the Estes Park area. The pleasures of summer touring are no secret, though; some drives through Rocky remain crowded well into September and even later into the leaf-gazing season.

Although the higher elevations are somewhat inaccessible in winter, there are still many trails where snowfall is minimal, and many hikers choose to take advantage of the solitude of cold-weather hiking. You can also snowmobile on some roads (on the west side only), snowshoe, and cross-country ski in the park, but be prepared for fierce winds and icy conditions.

Always keep in mind that, due to the altitude and the shape of the landscape, weather in the park, even in summer, can vary tremendously. On summer days, temperatures reach into the 70s or 80s but drop into the 40s or 50s at night. Fortunately, all of the drive-in campgrounds are below 9,400 ft, and the weather there is usually better than at higher elevations. On Trail Ridge Road it can snow in July.

January and February are the coldest months, with an average temperature of 15°F to 45°F in the day and 20°F to −10°F at night, and a snowfall that may leave up to 25 inches. March and April bring moisture, high winds, and higher temperatures. Throughout the summer, late-day showers are common. July checks in as the warmest month; the temperature may reach 85°F in the daytime and fall to as low as 35°F at night. The wettest time of year is August, whose last days are marked by cold fronts. Mixed rain and snowfall occur in September, with temperatures rising to 75°F in the daytime and slipping to 30°F at night. October is colder and snowier, particularly on the west side, but snowfall in November and December is usually light. December registers high winds and even colder temperatures, anywhere between 20°F to 50°F in the daytime and 30°F to −5°F at night. In winter, be mindful that the wind-chill factor is severe at higher elevations. Beware: At any time the climate can suddenly turn harsh, and roads may become slick, snow-packed, icy, and potentially dangerous.

SEASONAL EVENTS **May:** The town of Grand Lake, just outside the southwestern boundary of Rocky Mountain National Park, hosts several **fishing derbies** in which tagged trout are caught from Grand Lake and the tags redeemed for prize money. Contact the Chamber of Commerce (tel. 970/627–3402) for details. **July 4:** The **Fourth of July Celebration** (tel. 970/586–4431) in Estes Park features fireworks, an outdoor barbecue, and a John Philip Sousa concert at the Stanley Hotel. **Mid-July: Rooftop Rodeo and Western Week** (tel. 970/586–6104) in Estes Park includes an arts-and-crafts fair, a parade, and a rodeo full of cowboys. Grand Lake has **Buffalo Barbecue Weekend** (tel. 970/627–3402) with fireworks, a parade, and barbecued buffalo. **Early August:** The **Lipton Cup Regatta** (tel. 970/627–3402) takes place on Grand Lake. The story goes that when the Grand Lake Yacht Club was founded in 1905, several of its members persuaded Sir Thomas Lipton, the English tea baron, to donate a trophy for their annual regatta. Thus, a mountain tradition was born. The solid sterling silver cup is now worth $500,000. **Mid-September:** Estes Park holds a Long's Peak **Scottish Festival** (tel. 800/903–7837), a weekend affair alive with highland dancing, sheepdog contests, and bagpipe and drum-major competitions. Estes Park also holds an **arts-and-crafts festival** (tel. 970/586–8585) in Bond Park, one of the largest such juried shows in the state of Colorado.

More than 70 seminars, conducted by the **Rocky Mountain Nature Association** (*see* Publications, *above*), are held each summer, with topics ranging from "Rocky Mountain Bird-watching" to "Opaque Watercolor Technique" to "Introduction to Mushrooming." Hidden Valley Lodge, 10 mi west of Estes Park along Trail Ridge

Road, is the center of this activity on the park's east side. Seminars west of the Continental Divide are held at Camp Kawuneeche, 8 mi north of Grand Lake. College credit is given for most of the sessions, which can last anywhere from one to six days; tuition varies from $45 to $175. Call the Rocky Mountain Nature Association (tel. 970/586–1258) for details.

WHAT TO PACK Even in summertime, be prepared for wet, chilly interludes. Rain gear and extra clothing are always a wise idea. Because the sun is intense in the Rockies, bring sunglasses and sunblock.

GENERAL STORES Within the park, there is only one snack bar and souvenir shop, the **Trail Ridge Store,** which has been around for 50-odd years. Near the Alpine Visitor Center, Trail Ridge stocks sweatshirts and jackets, postcards, and assorted crafts items, and serves light meals, including chili, burgers, soup, and sandwiches. Picnic supplies are available at **Safeway** (tel. 970/586–4447) in Estes Park. For camping and outdoors supplies, try **Colorado Wilderness Sports** (tel. 970/586–6548), the **Hiking Hut** (tel. 970/586–0708), or **Outdoor World** (tel. 970/586–2114), all in Estes Park.

ARRIVING AND DEPARTING **By Bus. Charles Tour and Travel** (Box 4373, Estes Park, CO 80517, tel. 970/586–5151) provides year-round van service between Denver and Estes Park. The 10- to 14-seat vans make six daily trips June through September, and four trips daily October through May. It's a two-hour ride, and tickets cost $50 round-trip, $28 one-way. The company also runs tours of the park (*see* Guided Tours, *below*).

By Car and RV. The best way to reach the east side of the park by car or RV is on Highway 34 or 36. The 65-mi ride from Denver to Estes Park should take about 1½ hours. Inside the park, Highway 34 becomes the touted Trail Ridge Road, which carries you across the Continental Divide and into Grand Lake.

If you want to enter the park's western boundary at Grand Lake, count on a two-hour drive from Denver: Take I–70 west to Highway 40 and turn north. Just past Granby go north on Highway 34 toward the park. Although Grand Lake is about 85 mi northwest of Denver, this western route, through Winter Park, Granby, and Grand Lake, is the more scenic.

By Plane. The nearest major airport is **Denver International Airport,** 75 mi southeast of the park.

By Train. Amtrak (tel. 800/872–7245) trains from around the country arrive at and depart from Union Station in Denver, 70 mi away southeast of the park.

EXPLORING

Though you can get a good enough feel for the park by exploring it by car, bus, or bicycle, you'll see far more by walking. Trails take off in every direction, and a one- to two-hour hike upcountry will lead you to quiet isolation, even during the summer season. Although backpacking is still popular in America, in the 1990s only half as many backpackers have been coming to Rocky annually as they did at the height of the craze, in the mid-1970s.

To help visitors get out on the trail faster—without the hassles of driving in traffic and finding a parking space—the park runs a free shuttle bus daily in summer from the Glacier Basin parking lot to Bear Lake. Buses leave every half hour from 8:30 AM to 9:30 AM and approximately every 15 minutes between 9:45 and 5:30. After Labor Day to the end of September, the shuttle runs only on Fridays, Saturdays, and Sundays, from 10 AM to 5:30 PM, every 30 minutes.

THE BEST IN ONE DAY If you are just passing through the Colorado Rockies and haven't much time, don't resist the temptation to drop in at Rocky Mountain National Park. A single day here is sure to be memorable enough to make you want to come back.

Start your day at Estes Park, driving west on Highway 36 into Rocky and stopping for an hour at the visitor center. Watch the 22-

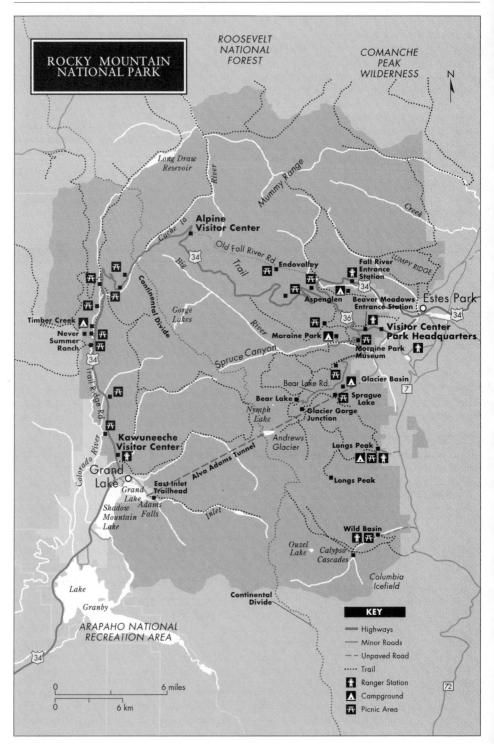

ROOSEVELT
NATIONAL
FOREST

COMANCHE
PEAK
WILDERNESS

N

**ROCKY MOUNTAIN
NATIONAL PARK**

*Long Draw
Resevoir*

River

Mummy Range

Creek

**Alpine
Visitor Center**

Cache la

Old Fall River Rd.

Trail

34

Endovalley

**Fall River
Entrance
Station**

BUMPY RIDGE

34

Aspenglen

**Beaver Meadows
Entrance Station**

Estes Park

Big

*Gorge
Lakes*

River

Moraine Park

36

**Visitor Center
Park Headquarters**

Timber Creek

Continental Divide

**Moraine Park
Museum**

**Never
Summer
Ranch**

Spruce Canyon

34

Bear Lake Rd.

Glacier Basin

7

Bear Lake

*Nymph
Lake*

**Sprague
Lake**

**Glacier Gorge
Junction**

Trail Ridge Rd.

**Kawuneeche
Visitor Center**

Colorado River

*Andrews
Glacier*

Alva Adams Tunnel

Longs Peak

**Grand
Lake**

**East Inlet
Trailhead**

*Grand
Lake*

*Adams
Falls*

Longs Peak

*Shadow
Mountain
Lake*

Inlet

Wild Basin

*Ouzel
Lake*

*Calypso
Cascades*

*Columbia
Icefield*

Lake

Granby

**Continental
Divide**

KEY

**ARAPAHO NATIONAL
RECREATION AREA**

34

Highways

Minor Roads

Unpaved Road

Trail

Ranger Station

Campground

Picnic Area

72

0		6 miles
0	6 km	

minute film and peruse the exhibits to get acquainted with the park. You can also pick up a map and various informative booklets.

Passing through the Beaver Meadows Entrance Station, continue driving northwest on Highway 36, past the juncture with Trail Ridge Road (bear right at the fork), until you reach Fall River Road. Turn left, and drive straight through, toward Endovalley, to Old Fall River Road, which begins where the paved road ends. This 9-mi gravel route, with a 15-mi-per-hour speed limit, runs one way uphill to the Alpine Visitor Center, where you'll find the Trail Ridge Store, the park's only gift store and snack bar. While you're here, you can attend one of the free ranger-led walks or lectures at the center. Vehicles longer than 25 ft are prohibited on Old Fall River Road, which opens July 4 and closes at the same time as Trail Ridge Road.

Next, take Trail Ridge Road back toward Estes Park, stopping at overlooks along the way, until you get to Highway 36 (about 17 mi from the Alpine Visitor Center); take this south to the 9-mi Bear Lake Road. Follow Bear Lake Road south, stopping at Sprague Lake to walk the .5-mi trail around it (see Nature Trails and Short Walks, below). Another 3 mi up the road will bring you to Bear Lake, where you can relax quietly by the water or stretch your legs on a stroll to Nymph Lake (see Nature Trails and Short Walks, below). At this point you'll be ready to head back to your camp or hotel.

ORIENTATION PROGRAMS If you enter the park from the east, through Estes Park on Highway 36, a stop at the visitor center/park headquarters will help you get acquainted with Rocky. The center has a relief model of the park and shows a 22-minute film. You can also pick up informational booklets and maps here. Entering from the west, through Grand Lake, you will find exhibits on hiking, wildlife, and history at the Kawuneeche Visitor Center. At the Alpine Visitor Center, on Trail Ridge Road, you will learn about the ecology of the alpine tundra through exhibits on geology, harsh weather, and the adaptations of plants and animals.

GUIDED TOURS All-day outings in Rocky, originating in Denver and Boulder, are offered year-round by **Scenic Mountain Tours** (100½ E. Cleveland, Lafayette, CO 80026, tel. 303/665–7625). **Best Mountain Tours** (3003 S. Macon, Aurora, CO 80014, tel. 303/750–5200) runs a sightseeing-van service when at least six passengers sign up for its 14-seat loads. A 10-hour comprehensive trip through Rocky, starting in Denver, is available through **Gray Line Tours** (Box 17646, Denver, CO 80217, tel. 303/289–2841 or 800/348–6877), in summer only. **Charles Tour and Travel** (Box 4373, Estes Park, CO 80517, tel. 970/586–5151) also runs van tours in the park from Memorial Day through Labor Day.

Don't miss the park's ranger-led walks and talks. More than 150 programs are scheduled each summer, on both the east and west sides of the park, with topics covering every aspect of local wildlife, geology, vegetation, and the history of the park. Special activities are available for people with disabilities. Look for the program schedule and designations of accessibility in *High Country Headlines* (see Publications, *above*).

The visitor centers also provide brochures for many of the park's most popular trails, ranging from easy .5-mi strolls to more invigorating nature walks above the tree line. The tundra walks involve two to three hours of hiking at high altitude, coupled with discussions of alpine plants, climate, and the process of adaptation to high elevations by living organisms.

SCENIC DRIVES AND VIEWS There are only three paved roads in the park, but all of them have spectacular views. In normal summer traffic, 45-mi **Trail Ridge Road** is about a two-hour drive from the east side of the park to the west, but it's best to give yourself three to four hours to allow for leisurely stops at the numerous overlooks. From the road's topmost points you will get a glimpse of all 415 square mi of Rocky and discover arcticlike conditions in a world more than 11,000 ft above sea level. The road climbs gradually, so its grade never exceeds 7%. Of the many turnoffs, don't miss Never Summer Ranch (tel. 970/627–3652), near the park's west boundary. This was a working ranch at the turn of the century. From the road it's a short walk to the ranch. Free daily self-guided tours take place throughout the summer.

Nine-mile **Bear Lake Road** travels from Highway 36 to a high mountain basin very popular with tourists. The road dead-ends at Bear Lake and the Bear Lake Trailhead. Count on full parking lots on summer days between 10 and 3. If you can't avoid traveling at those times, park your car at the shuttle bus parking area and take the park's free summer shuttle bus to Bear Lake (*see above*). Along Bear Lake Road, adjacent to the Moraine Park Museum, is the William Allen White Cabin, named after the famous Kansas journalist who wrote at Rocky in the summer. Visiting artists use the cabin in the warm months, so it's not open to the public. Schedule an hour for the full round-trip ride on Bear Lake Road.

The park's other driving option, the 9-mi, one-way **Old Fall River Road**, has a gravel surface and many switchbacks. The first road leading to the high country, it begins at the Endovalley picnic area and stays open from July to September, weather permitting. Along this road you'll see avalanche areas, waterfalls, flower-strewn meadows, alpine tundra, and wapiti.

HISTORIC BUILDINGS AND SITES On Trail Ridge Road near the west boundary of the park, **Never Summer Ranch** is the site of the Holzwarth homestead, which was built at the turn of the century as a cattle ranch and later used as a dude ranch until the 1920s. The ranch has been restored and is now used as an interpretive center. You can take a free guided or self-guided tour to view the original lodge, workshops, icehouse, and taxidermy building. The ranch is open from mid-June through Labor Day, daily from 10 until 5. It is a .5-mi hike off Trail Ridge Road, .5 mi from Timber Creek Campground.

Just west of Moraine Park Museum is the **William Allen White Cabin,** site of the park's artist-in-residence program. The cabin was built in the late 1800s by Pulitzer prize–winning newspaper editor William Allen White and has hosted such dignitaries as Dwight D. Eisenhower. The cabin is not open to the public, but you can drive up to its stone front porch for a glimpse.

The **Beaver Meadows Visitor Center,** designed in 1966 by the Frank Lloyd Wright School of Architecture at Taliesen West, is now on the National Register of Historic Places. The surrounding utility buildings, also on the National Register, are noteworthy examples of the "Rocky Mountain rustic"–style buildings that the Civilian Conservation Corps constructed during the Depression.

NATURE TRAILS AND SHORT WALKS Starting at Bear Lake (9,475 ft), try the .5-mi one-way walk to **Nymph Lake,** an elevation gain of 225 ft. Another walk begins at the East Inlet Trailhead (8,391 ft) on the western boundary of the park; the .3-mi one-way trail climbs 79 ft in elevation to **Adams Falls,** an excellent spot for a picnic. The self-guided **Sprague Lake Nature Trail** begins at the Sprague Lake Picnic Area and loops around the lake for about .5 mi. The trail is easily accessible to people with disabilities, and there are picnic tables, livery stables, and rest rooms at the trailhead. If you have an hour, the paved .5-mi one-way **Tundra Nature Trail** is a good bet. Signs along the way will teach you about the fragile ecosystem above the tree line. The trailhead is on Trail Ridge Road, about 4 mi southeast of the Alpine Visitor Center.

LONGER HIKES Follow Bear Lake Road for 1 mi, and, just past the Moraine Park Museum, turn right onto the spur road that leads to the **Cub Lake Trailhead.** The moderate 2.3-mi one-way trek to Cub Lake climbs only 540 ft in elevation; it will take you about three hours to hike in and out. A moderately difficult hike with steep terrain and brilliant views of the Rockies is from the **Wild Basin Ranger Station** (8,500 ft), in the southeast corner of the park, to **Calypso Cascades**. It is 1.8 mi one-way, with an elevation gain of 700 ft. A more strenuous trek, starting from the same point, is up to **Ouzel Lake**, a trip of 5 mi one way and a gain of 1,510 ft in elevation. Another rigorous outing, where you can see firsthand how the park was carved by ice, is from **Glacier Gorge Junction** (9,240 ft), at the south end of Bear Lake Road, **to Andrews Glacier**, a 5-mi one-way journey with a gain of 2,460 ft in elevation.

The **Keyhole Route**, from Longs Peak Ranger Station, 10 mi south of Estes Park off Highway 7, to Longs Peak (14,255 ft) requires ice axes, ropes, and crampons for all but a few weeks (usually in August) of the year. The peak lies 7.5 mi from the trailhead, but due to the difficulty of the last 2-mi leg of the trek, be advised that this is a 12- to 15-hour endeavor. The hale and hardy are advised to set off by 3 AM to approach the summit by noon and thereby escape afternoon lightning storms. Anyone who tackles this route should be in good condition and be able to maneuver ledges and steep ascents. Printed advice on what to expect on the climb is available at the ranger station or visitor centers and should be scrutinized before your trip.

OTHER ACTIVITIES **Back-Road Driving.** Vehicles are not allowed off-road anywhere in the park, but rugged routes abound in the surrounding national-forest lands. For information, call 970/887–4100.

Biking. There are no bike paths in the park, and bikes are not allowed on trails. Trail Ridge Road has spectacular views but is too strenuous for most people. Remember, although the grade of this road doesn't exceed 7%, it *begins* at an altitude most people will have trouble with, and going from east to west there's a 15-mi uphill stretch. At the top, you'll have to contend with winds that can reach 70 mi per hour. If you want to cycle, it's probably best to stay around the campgrounds. Rentals are available at **Colorado Bicycling Adventures** (tel. 970/586–4241).

Bird-Watching. Spring and summer are the best times for bird-watching at Rocky. Go early in the morning, before the crowds arrive. Lumpy Ridge is the nesting ground of the rare raptor; prime viewing is after mid-July (the area is closed until then so the birds won't be disturbed). You can see migratory songbirds from South America in their summer breeding grounds along Endovally Road. Alluvial Fan, along the Roaring River, is an excellent place for viewing birds, including broad-tailed hummingbirds, hairy woodpeckers, robins, the occasional raptor, and ouzels, which frequent rapid streams and rivers. McGregor Ranch, along Black Canyon, and Adams Falls, due east of Grand Lake, are also prime spots for seeing wildfowl and flowers.

Boating and Rafting. No motorized boating is allowed inside the park. Nearly all of the lakes within Rocky are accessible only by hiking in, so you must carry your inflatable boat with you. For those willing to do this, **Sprague Lake** is an easy walk and a rewarding destination—it is directly accessed off Bear Lake Road.

The main location for water sports is not inside the park itself but at the privately owned **Grand Lake.** Rent boats at Beacon Landing on Grand Lake (tel. 970/627–3671) or Trail Ridge Marina on Shadow Mountain Lake (tel. 970/627–3568). You can also boat in the nearby **Arapaho National Recreation Area** (Sulphur Ranger District, Box 10, Granby, CO 80446, tel. 970/887–4100), just outside the southwest corner of the park in the Arapaho Forest.

Within Estes Park, **Lake Estes** has a marina for those who want to rent boats (tel. 970/586–2011), but the action here is limited. This is primarily a "wakeless" body of water—waterskiing is permitted only Tuesday through Thursday from 5 PM until dark.

If you're interested in rafting outside the park, **Rapid Transit Rafting** (Box 4095, Estes Park, CO 80517, tel. 970/586–8852 or 800/367–8523) has trips of moderate difficulty, good for beginners. **Colorado Wilderness Sports** (358 E. Elkhorn Ave., Estes

Park, CO 80517, tel. 970/586–6548) runs raft trips on the Cache la Poudre River, north of Estes Park, and other half- and full-day trips on the Cache and Colorado rivers. Prices start at $29 for half-day trips, $52 for full-day. Reservations are advised.

Fishing. Rocky is a wonderful setting for fishing—home to brown, brook, rainbow, Colorado River cutthroat, and greenback cutthroat trout—but not the best place for a catch. Special regulations for fishing within Rocky Mountain National Park apply: Each person is allowed to have only one rod, and only artificial flies and lures are permitted, with exceptions for children under 12. In some areas you are required to release the fish you have caught, and some waters are closed because native greenback cutthroat trout are being reintroduced in them. Rangers recommend the more remote back-country lakes, since they are less crowded. You'll need a Colorado fishing license, which costs from $5.25, for a one-day license, to $40.25, for a yearly nonresident license. These can be obtained at local sporting-goods stores.

Outside the park your chances are better. Lake Estes, on the east side of town, is frequently stocked with foot-long rainbow trout. The **Lake Estes Marina** (1770 Big Thompson Ave., tel. 970/586–2011) sells fishing licenses and tackle and rents boats. Head a few miles downstream from Lake Estes, and you'll discover fine fishing on the Big Thompson River.

The town of Grand Lake is known for its big brown trout, 20-pound Mackinaw, and kokanee salmon. In fact, between Grand Lake, Lake Granby, Shadow Mountain Lake, and the nearby Colorado River, an angler can stay pretty busy. Rainbow and brown trout are more active in the spring and early summer, while kokanee bite all year long. When the water freezes, try your hand at ice fishing on Grand Lake or Shadow Mountain Lake.

Horseback Riding. Within the park, **High Country Stables** owns two operations. One is Glacier Creek Stables (tel. 970/586–

3244), near Sprague Lake, and the other, Moraine Park Stables (tel. 970/586–2327), just beyond Moraine Park. Two-hour rides from these stables run about $32, but visitors are hardly confined to a single program; those who are so inclined can even ride for as long as eight hours. Outside the park try one of two **Sombrero Stables** locations (Box 1735AC, Estes Park, CO 80517, tel. 970/586–4577; or 304 W. Portal Rd., Grand Lake, CO 80447, tel. 970/627–3514). Reservations are necessary for rides that last more than two hours, and also for the steak fry and breakfast rides at Sombrero.

If you're interested in llama trekking (outside the park only), contact the **Keno Ranch** (Box 2385, Estes Park, CO 80517, tel. 970/586–2807). Llamas carry all the food and supplies, while as many as 10 or 12 participants walk through mountainous areas about 4 mi outside of Estes Park for a daylong adventure that includes a lunch cookout. Reservations are required.

Rock Climbing. There are hundreds of classic climbs here for novices as well as technical rock climbers. **Longs Peak** and the 2-mi-long **Lumpy Ridge** provide every level of challenge, from basic to highly advanced. Many first-timers learn the art of technical climbing at Lumpy Ridge, 1.5 mi north of Estes Park, although some routes there are closed from March to July, due to nesting birds. Its rock outcroppings rise behind the Stanley Hotel and can be seen from the town itself. If you're interested in a spectacular setting, try **Petite Grepon,** an internationally famous spire that attracts groups from all over the world who are keen on a highly technical climb.

The **Colorado Mountain School** (Box 2062, 351 Moraine Ave., Estes Park, CO 80517, tel. 970/586–5758) holds classes for those who want to learn more about climbing before taking on the Rockies. The exclusive climbing concessionaire in the park is an invaluable resource. Sixteen full-time guides work throughout the summer, leading everything from half-day introductory courses to daylong climbs to international expeditions. Equipment rentals and guided climbs are available. During the summer peak season, make reservations as far as six weeks in advance for climbs.

Ski Touring. On Rocky's east side the **Bear Lake Trailhead** is the point of departure for many winter activities. It is a fairly easy .5-mi one-way climb of several hundred feet to Nymph Lake. Dream Lake is only .5 mi beyond the west shore of Nymph Lake, and .7 mi beyond that is Emerald Lake. To reach these lakes you must be an experienced skier. These routes run through densely forested areas and provide breathtaking views of the high peaks. The one- to three-hour intermediate trek from Glacier Gorge Junction to Sprague Lake follows the summer trail on the south side of Glacier Creek. All ski trails can be icy and windswept.

On the west side of the park is the **Tonahutu Creek Trail**—a gently sloping route that traverses broad expanses of meadowland. Leave your car at the Kawuneeche Visitor Center and ski east, away from the parking lot, then cruise the easy 2-mi trip down to Grand Lake. Warning: Skiers should beware of high winds and avalanches.

There are no ski rentals within the park; however, **Never Summer Mountain Sports** (tel. 970/627–3642), in Grand Lake, rents backcountry skis for $12 per day. **Grand Lake Ski Shop** (tel. 970/627–8008) maintains groomed trails that you can use for a $7 trail fee. The shop rents skis for use on its trails only; the cost is $8 for a half day.

Snowmobiling. Only on the west side of the park are you permitted to think snowmobile. Snowmobilers can leave from the Kawuneeche Visitor Center and use the first 15 mi of Trail Ridge Road. Snowmobiling is also common on the streets of Grand Lake, and drivers have the same rights (and responsibilities) as vehicular traffic. For rental information, call the **Grand Lake Chamber of Commerce** (tel. 970/627–3402).

Snowshoeing. There are good snowshoeing opportunities on all of the park's hiking trails, especially those around Bear Lake, off

Old Fall River Road, and at Longs Peak. **Colorado Wilderness Sports** (358 E. Elkhorn Ave., Estes Park, tel. 970/586–6548) rents equipment for $10 per day, and the **Colorado Mountain School** (351 Moraine Ave., Estes Park, tel. 970/586–5758) charges $12 for one day or $9 per day for multiple days. Another option is the **YMCA** (just outside Estes Park, tel. 970/586–3341), which charges nonmembers $3 per day for a pass that lets you rent snowshoes for $10. (Members pay the rental fee only.)

Swimming. Since streams and lakes in the park are fed by melting snow and ice, they stay cold. You can swim in Lake Estes, but be advised that it's a chilly dunk. You might spare yourself some agony by calling the **Lake Estes Marina** (tel. 970/586–2011) to rent a wet suit.

The **YMCA** (tel. 970/586–3341) just outside of Estes Park has an indoor pool, as does the **Estes Park Aquatic Center** (660 Community Dr., tel. 970/586–2340), just south of Lake Estes.

Wildlife Viewing. Rocky has such an abundance of wildlife that you can usually engage in prime viewing from the seat of your car. Mid-March to mid-July is the best time to see the bighorn sheep that congregate in the **Horseshoe Park/Sheep Lakes** area, just past the Fall River entrance on Highway 34. This is one of the few places where wildlife has the right-of-way—rangers will stop traffic for sheep to cross. Wapiti elk can be seen year-round throughout the park, but the bulls and their harems are especially plentiful in **Horseshoe Park, Moraine Park,** and **Upper Beaver Meadows** during mating season, from September to early October.

CHILDREN'S PROGRAMS Children ages six to 12 will find many educational programs at Rocky, including puppet shows, bird walks, photo talks, and numerous safety seminars. Parents must accompany their children to these free gatherings.

One popular guided tour for children, called "Rocky's Engineers," explores the beaver ponds. "Junior Ranger Adventure" is a program of hands-on projects that teach children about the park ecosystem and how people affect it. Consult *High Country Headlines* for current programs (*see* Publications, *above*).

EVENING ACTIVITIES Every evening from mid-June to Labor Day, nature programs are held at park headquarters, Aspenglen Campground, Glacier Basin Campground, Moraine Park Campground, and Timber Creek Campground. In summer, evening slide shows and lectures take place at campgrounds throughout the park and at the visitor centers. Consult the free *High Country Headlines* (*see* Publications, *above*) for times and details. From September through May, programs are held at the park's two main visitor centers on Saturday night only.

In Estes Park during summer, all ages will enjoy the **Stanley Hotel Theatre/Fine Arts Series** (tel. 970/586–3371). A number of bars on Elkhorn Avenue have live music, including **Lonigan's** (110 W. Elkhorn Ave., tel. 970/586–4346). The **Lazy B Ranch** (1915 Dry Gulch Rd., tel. 970/586–5371 or 800/228–2116) hosts a chuck-wagon supper and Western show appropriate for the whole family, also in summer.

Grand Lake has the rustic **Stagecoach Inn** (tel. 970/627–8079), with a dance floor and live country and western music on the weekends, and the **Lariat Saloon** (1141 Grand Ave., tel. 970/627–9965), a watering hole for local cowboys.

DINING

Inside the park there is only a lonely snack bar to feed the hungry hordes. But don't despair: Right outside the park, nearly 100 dining options in and around Estes Park and Grand Lake lie at your feet, with everything from Mexican to Cajun to French to Chinese fare. Many restaurants offer not only fine cuisine but also great views of Rocky. The majority of local cafés are modest, but the pricier ones are worth the splurge.

Dunraven Grille at the Stanley Hotel. When you enter the lobby of the Stanley Hotel, you'll feel as if you are attending a coronation ball. Everything is fresh, white, and elegant. The space has retained its original turn-of-the-century fixtures, including glass-etched, globe chandeliers. In the dimly lit, wood-paneled room, indulge in smoked breast of duck, charbroiled buffalo steak, and crab ravioli. Consider the Sunday champagne brunch at the McGregor Room—a local favorite—served between 10 and 2. *333 Wonderview, Estes Park, tel. 970/586–3371. Reservations essential in summer. AE, D, DC, MC, V. $$–$$$*

Dunraven Inn. This is a favorite of both locals and out-of-towners. Home-style Italian cooking, a long wine list, a dark interior, and walls decorated with signed dollar bills from playful clientele entertain scads of repeat customers. The most popular dishes are lasagna, scampi, and veal parmigiana. In summertime the Dunraven is jammed, so be prepared for a wait. *Hwy. 66, 4 mi southwest of Estes Park, tel. 970/586–6409. AE, D, MC, V. $$*

Grand Lake Lodge Restaurant. Built in 1921, this restaurant has very large, high, timber-vaulted ceilings and a spectacular view of Grand Lake. Other delights include the Sunday champagne brunch and numerous mesquite-grilled dishes. The restaurant serves breakfast, lunch, and dinner and has a children's menu. *Off Hwy. 34, .25 mi north of Grand Lake, tel. 970/627–3967. AE, D, MC, V. Closed late Sept.–early June. $$*

La Chaumière. This small French restaurant is not in Estes Park but southeast of the town, a pretty drive down Highway 36 on a summer's evening. The exterior is rustic, with a setting that may seem unlikely for a fine dining experience, but the food is country French and a delight. The menu changes frequently, but certain entrées are standard: house-smoked salmon and trout, sweetbreads with pine nuts, and the signature homemade ice cream. *12 mi southeast of Estes Park on Hwy. 36, Pinewood Springs, tel. 303/823–6521. AE, MC, V. Closed Mon. $$*

Donuthaus. No trip to Rocky is complete without a stop at this small take-out donut shop. The coffee is hot, the price is right, and the sheer goodness and variety of donuts will cause you to loosen your everything-in-moderation standards, not to mention your belt. Try to leave room for the long johns (long, custard-filled donuts) and cake donuts. What's more, the neighborly atmosphere makes you feel as if you've lived in town for years. *Hwy. 36 between Estes Park and Park Headquarters, tel. 970/586–2988. Reservations not accepted. No credit cards. Closed Wed. $*

Estes Park Brewery. Cap off a day in the park by sipping a Longs Peak Raspberry Wheat ale on the outdoor deck. The beers brewed here—including the popular Stinger Wild Honey-Wheat—are gaining national renown. Fresh-brewed root beer and cream soda are available as well; burgers, brats, and pizza make a meal. Upstairs are billiard tables; downstairs is a tasting room with brewery souvenirs and retail sales of the beers. *470 Prospect Village Dr., tel. 970/586–5421. AE, D, MC, V. $*

La Casa. This Mexican restaurant on the main street of Estes Park has indoor dining in a south-of-the-border setting as well as a riverside glass-enclosed patio in the adjoining Casa Grande room. Choose between Mexican dishes such as Estorito—a glorified burrito with everything you can imagine on it—and an interesting mix of Cajun dishes, including blackened shrimp or fish and gumbo. There's also an extensive salad bar. Sip a margarita (on tap) and listen to live music (offered nightly). *222 E. Elkhorn Ave., Estes Park, tel. 970/586–2807. AE, D, DC, MC, V. $*

Mountain Home Café. Estes Park is full of good breakfast spots, but the Mountain Home is unique. Located in a shopping-center complex a block from downtown, the restaurant has a simple, homey atmosphere. Service is amiable, and the food outstanding. Made-from-scratch best-sellers include Swedish pancakes, waffles, and Swedish potato pancakes. Lunch and din-

ner are of equally high caliber, especially some of the demonic desserts that ought to come with danger warnings: chocolate mousselike French Silk Pie, English Toffee Pie, and various tortes. The kids' menu is handy for scaled-down portions. *Upper Stanley Village Shopping Center, Estes Park, tel. 970/586–6624. D, MC, V. $*

Mountain Inn. When it's time to feed the family after a long day in the park, this rustic restaurant in Grand Lake is the place to go. The atmosphere is casual and the service friendly. Specialties include fried chicken, prime rib, and a giant chicken pot pie. Vegetables are served family-style in big bowls. *612 Grand Ave., Box 300, Grand Lake, tel. 970/627–3385. Reservations required in summer. D, MC, V. $*

PICNIC SPOTS Most picnic areas within the park consist of widely spaced single tables and are not for large parties. One such spot, **Endovalley,** on the east side of Rocky, is found at the start of Old Fall River Road. The views here include beautiful Fan Lake, Fall River pass, and aspen groves. Picnic tables, fire grates, and rest rooms allow comfortable outdoor eating. On the west side of the park, near the Continental Divide, is **Lake Irene,** which also has fire grates, tables, and rest rooms.

LODGING

There are no hotels within Rocky Mountain National Park itself, but in the surrounding area you can check in at an expensive hotel, a bed-and-breakfast, a cabin, or a guest ranch. Contact the **Estes Park Chamber of Commerce Lodging Referral Service** (tel. 970/586–4431 or 800/443–7837) for information.

Aspen Lodge. Eight miles south of Estes Park, the "ultimate family resort" has your pick of family-reunion packages—and every kind of activity, from snowmobiling and sleigh rides to fishing and horseback riding. The log-and-stone lobby, complete with a vast fireplace, sets the tone for this Western-style guest ranch. You can choose between a room in the main lodge (all have balconies) or a rustic cabin. During summer, meals are included in the cost of a room, and there's a three-night minimum stay. *6120 Hwy. 7, Estes Park, CO 80517, tel. and fax 970/586–8133 or tel. 800/332–6867. 36 rooms, 23 cabins. Facilities: pool, hot tub, sauna, tennis, exercise room, racquetball, volleyball, ice-skating, cross-country skiing, sleigh rides, tobogganing. AE, D, DC, MC, V. $$$*

Riversong Bed and Breakfast Inn. The living room of this romantic retreat holds an impressive library, where guests are known to settle down with a book by the fireplace and not emerge for hours—it's that relaxing. Bedrooms are luxurious, with antique furniture and fireplaces; some even have a big sunken bathtub. The showpiece is Forget-Me-Not: a large room with a huge picture window, a whirlpool in front of the fireplace, and marble floors in the bathroom and shower. A fishing stream and private hiking trails run through the spacious grounds. *Box 1910, Estes Park, CO 80517, tel. 970/586–4666. 9 rooms. Facilities: hiking, fishing. MC, V. $$$*

Stanley Hotel. F. O. Stanley, who invented the Stanley Steamer automobile, built the Stanley Hotel in 1909; since that time it has competed with other hotels of its size throughout the world, and it is now on the National Register of Historic Places. The white-painted wood exterior may be familiar from the ABC miniseries "The Shining." Each room is different, but all are furnished with period antiques, and have modern, renovated bathrooms. Deluxe rooms have views of the Continental Divide. In addition to fine cuisine in the Dunraven Grille (*see* Dining, *above*), the hotel hosts theater performances and concerts. Summer reservations must be made at least two months in advance. *333 Wonderview, Box 1767, Estes Park, CO 80517, tel. 970/586–3371 or 800/976–1377, fax 970/586–3673. 133 rooms. Facilities: 2 restaurants, pool, 2 golf courses (18-hole and 9-hole), hiking, horseback riding, meeting rooms. AE, D, DC, MC, V. $$$*

Taharaa Moutain Lodge. On a plateau overlooking the Continental Divide, this luxury bed-and-breakfast commands sweeping views from wraparound decks (accessible from every room). The log-and-stone, board-and-batten retreat is built in the style of the grand lodges of the Adirondacks. Each room has a fireplace and a unique theme, from the Ute room with a Native American carved bed, to the Southwestern Taharaa suite, featuring a Taos drum coffee table, private deck, and double Jacuzzi tub. After a day of exploring the park, enjoy afternoon treats by the huge fireplace in the great room. *Box 2586, Estes Park, CO 80517, tel. 970/577–0098 or 800/597–0098, fax 970/577–0819. 12 rooms. Facilities: hot tub, sauna, exercise room. AE, MC, V. $$$*

Grand Lake Lodge. Built of lodgepole pine in 1921, this accommodation is known as "Colorado's favorite front porch." With both Grand and Shadow Mountain lakes below, the lodge is a gathering place for guests who wish to observe the calming vista at their leisure or who amble over to the in-house restaurant (*see* Dining, *above*) for breakfast. For those who crave peace and quiet, two-unit cabins (with bath) grant secluded sanctuary in the hills, away from summer crowds. The entrance to the lodge is .25 mi north of the Grand Lake turnoff on Highway 34. *Box 569, Grand Lake, CO 80447, tel. 970/627–3967, fax 970/627–9495 summer; or 4155 E. Jewel, Suite 104, Denver, CO 80222, tel. 303/759–5848, fax 303/759–3179 off-season. 56 units. Facilities: restaurant, pool, hot tub, horseback riding, playground, recreation room. AE, D, MC, V. Closed mid-Sept.–early June. $$–$$$*

Hi Country Haus. This condominium complex is in the town of Winter Park, just south of Grand Lake. In addition to luxury studio rooms, it has one-, two-, and three-bedroom condos with linens, fireplace, and a complete kitchen. You'll find whirlpools, an indoor swimming pool, a sauna, and a stocked trout pond on the property complex. During the cold months, Winter Park is one of Colorado's favorite ski resorts; summer activities include rafting, alpine sliding, rodeos, golf, tennis, and a jazz festival. *Box 3095, Winter Park, CO 80482, tel. 970/726–9421 or 800/228–1025, fax 970/726–8004. 145 condominiums. Facilities: indoor pool, hot tub, sauna, fishing. AE, D, MC, V. $$–$$$*

Lemmon Lodge. On the banks of Grand Lake, this hideaway has 24 cabins, each accommodating anywhere from two to 12 people, that are usually booked at least a year in advance. Each one is distinctive, and all but one have kitchens. There's a sandy beach with a private dock for those who bring a boat. During the summer, a minimum stay of four days is required. *Box 514, Grand Lake, CO 80447, tel. 970/627–3314 summer, 970/725–3511 winter. 24 cabins. Facilities: beach, dock. MC, V. Closed Oct.–mid-May. $$–$$$*

Telemark Resort. At night as you lie in bed in your cabin, you can hear the Big Thompson River rushing down from the mountains. In summer, guests can let their children loose to enjoy the grounds—picnic tables, horseshoe pits, and a play area for youngsters allow young and old to relax. Trout swim the rivers, and deer graze nearby. In winter, the Telemark caters primarily to skiers, hikers, and snowshoers. All cabins have color TV, fireplaces, and screened porches. Just outside Estes Park, Telemark is on Highway 36 as you drive west toward Rocky. *Box 100B, Estes Park, CO 80517, tel. 970/586–4343 or 800/669–0650. 26 cottages. Facilities: picnic areas. AE, MC, V. $$*

Estes Park Center/YMCA of the Rockies. This is not your typical Y. Many people consider it the ideal resort for those traveling with children. Throughout the summer, lots of activities are planned for the kids—horseback riding and hayrides, basketball, tennis, and swimming. In winter, there's cross-country skiing on adjacent park acreage, plus ice-skating and snowshoeing. Equipment can be rented on the premises. The 860-acre resort has 200 cabins, a restaurant, a library, a grocery store, and a museum. Cabins have full bedrooms and kitchens, and some have fireplaces. Large groups and conferences are welcome. The Y is 5 mi southwest of Estes Park. *Estes Park Center/YMCA, 2515 Tunnel Rd., Estes Park, CO 80511-2550, tel. 970/586–3341, fax 970/586–6078. 200 cabins with bath. Facilities: 3 restaurants, library. No credit cards. $–$$*

CAMPING

There are five designated drive-in campgrounds at Rocky Mountain National Park and numerous opportunities for backcountry camping. In addition, visitors can choose from the many sites in the Arapaho National Recreation Area, near Grand Lake; in the surrounding Arapaho National Forest; and in private campgrounds in Estes Park.

INSIDE THE PARK Three of the drive-in campgrounds at Rocky (Timber Creek, Aspenglen, and Longs Peak) assign sites on a first-come, first-served basis; at the other two (Moraine Park and Glacier Basin) reservations are required from late May through the first week in September and can be made through Destinet (tel. 800/365–2267). Camping fees are $12 for nonreserved sites or $14 per night for reserved sites in summer. (Prices are reduced in winter, when the water is shut off.) The 12 group sites at Glacier Basin each cost $30 to $60 per night and can accommodate 10 to 50 people, depending on the site. From June through September, camping within the park is limited to seven days, three days at Longs Peak. During the summer, most campgrounds have nightly campfire programs.

RVs are welcome at all campgrounds except Longs Peak. RV spaces are standard width and 27 to 32 ft long, and some of the RV sites in the park are paved. There are no hookups or showers in the park. Disposal stations are at Moraine Park, Glacier Basin, and Timber Creek.

Just a mile from Estes Park on Bear Lake Road, at the Cub Lake Trailhead turnoff, is **Moraine Park Campground** ($14 per night,

ROCKY MOUNTAIN CAMPGROUNDS

	INSIDE THE PARK					NEAR THE PARK			
	Moraine Park	Glacier Basin	Longs Peak	Timber Creek	Aspenglen	Arapaho National Recreation Area	Estes Park Campground	KOA	Spruce Lake RV Park
Total number of sites	247	150	26	100	54	324	65	99	110
Sites suitable for RVs	63	85	0	70	49	289	12	62	110
Number of hookups	0	0	0	0	0	20	0	62	110
Drive to sites	•	•	•	•	•	•	•	•	•
Hike to sites									
Flush toilets	•*	•*	•*	•*	•*	•	•	•	•
Pit/chemical toilets	•	•	•			•	•		
Drinking water	•*	•*	•*	•*	•*	•	•	•	•
Showers							•	•	•
Fire grates	•	•	•	•	•	•	•	•	•
Swimming									•
Boat access						•			
Playground							•	•	•
Disposal station	•*	•*		•*		•	•	•	•
Ranger station	•	•	•	•	•				
Public telephone	•	•		•	•		•	•	•
Reservation possible	•*	•*				•	•	•	•
Daily fee per site	$14**	$14	$12**	$12**	$12	$8–$17	$17.95	$14–$19	$16–$26.25
Dates open	year-round	mid-June–Labor Day	year-round	year-round	late May–late Sept.	Memorial Day–Labor Day	Memorial Day–mid-Sept.	Apr.–mid-Oct.	Apr.–mid-Oct.

*In summer only. **Reduced fees in winter.

$10 in winter), open year-round. This campground has 247 sites (55 open in winter), with flush and pit toilets, drinking water in summer, fire grates, a ranger station, and a public phone. This is the most open campground setting, in a ponderosa-pine woodland on a bluff overlooking the Big Thompson River and 8,150-ft Moraine Park.

Three miles farther down Bear Lake Road, you will reach the 150-site **Glacier Basin Campground** ($14 per night), which closes from Labor Day to mid-June. Here you'll find flush toilets, drinking water in summer, fire grates, a ranger station, and a public phone. The campground is near Sprague Lake and is 300 ft higher in elevation than Moraine Park Campground. It is in a denser, lodgepole-pine forest and looks out on the Continental Divide and three glaciers.

The 26-site **Longs Peak Campground** ($12 per night, $10 in winter) is about 11 mi from Estes Park, off Highway 7, and a long way from Trail Ridge Road. It is open year-round, but RVs are not allowed here—a rule that contributes to the campground's sense of quiet and isolation. Facilities include flush and pit toilets, drinking water in summer, fire grates, and a ranger station.

Also open year-round is the **Timber Creek Campground** ($12 per night), which is off Trail Ridge Road, 8 mi inside the west entrance of the park, just north of Never Summer Ranch. This 100-site campground has flush and pit toilets, drinking water in summer, fire grates, a ranger station, and a public phone. It is beside the Colorado River, which makes it an angler's paradise.

The small, 54-site **Aspenglen Campground** ($12 per night) is closed from late September to late May. Set in open pine woodland by Fall River, it does not have the views of Moraine Park or Glacier Basin, but it is the first campground to fill up on the east side of the park in summer. Just .5 mi into the park and 5 mi from Estes Park, off Highway 34, Aspenglen has some excellent walk-in sites for those who want to pitch a tent away from the crowds but still close to the car. There are flush toilets, drinking water in summer, fire grates, a ranger station, and a public phone.

To camp in the **Rocky Mountain backcountry,** you must obtain a backcountry permit for $15 (*see* Visitor Information, *above*).

There are a few designated campsites with fire rings in the backcountry. If you want still-more-primitive conditions, ask the rangers about camping in cross-country zones, which are farther back into the wilderness and have no designated sites. Be aware that special regulations apply to cross-country zones; the rangers will tell you what you need to know. At any backcountry campsite, you should follow basic camping rules: bury human waste, do not dump food scraps or soapy water into streams and lakes, and carry out any garbage you may accumulate. Wood fires are restricted to specific areas; you are encouraged to use a portable stove. Remember, pets are not allowed in the backcountry—it is dangerous for them, for you, and for the wildlife.

NEAR THE PARK There are many campgrounds and backcountry sites in the area surrounding Rocky Mountain National Park. Campsites in the **Arapaho National Recreation Area** (tel. 970/887–4100) range from $8 to $17 per night; call to find out about public facilities. Among the numerous privately owned campgrounds are **Estes Park Campground** (tel. 970/586–4188), which has 65 sites that cost $17.95 per night; **KOA** (tel. 970/586–2888), where 99 sites range from $14 to $19; and **Spruce Lake RV Park** (tel. 970/586–2889), where 110 sites range from $16 to $26.25.

Saguaro National Park
Arizona

By Edie Jarolim

Saguaro poised against a starry sky, standing sentinel in the desert. Although this poignant desert image is inevitably associated with the Southwest, today office buildings are cropping up far more quickly in this part of the country than the slow-growing cacti. There's no better encapsulation of this changing contemporary landscape than Saguaro National Park, a Sonoran Desert preserve sliced into two distinct sections by the sprawling city of Tucson.

Contrary to the Hollywood images of saguaros towering taller than John Wayne in Wyoming or Montana, these plants grow only in northwest Mexico and in southern Arizona, where Saguaro National Park hosts the world's largest concentration of them. Soaking up as much as 11 inches of rain a year, the portion of the Sonoran Desert that lies in the Tucson Basin sustains a startling array of plant and animal life. To further contradict the prevailing image of the dry, flat, desert, Tucson is actually surrounded by five mountain ranges, and both national park districts encompass some impressive peaks.

Viewed in a group, the upright saguaro cacti with their limblike appendages have a distinctly human air. The Tohono O'odham people, whose reservation adjacent to Tucson is second only in size to that of the Navajo, incorporated the saguaro into their creation myth, which holds that they were put on earth to inspire humans with their stalwartness and dignity. These desert dwellers consider the cactus literally as well as spiritually nourishing, and every summer they celebrate the harvest of its sweet fruit. They use the plant's woody skeleton, called saguaro ribs, to build fences and building supports.

The Tohono O'odham's ancestors (thought to be descendants of the Hohokam), who occupied the Tucson Basin from around AD 300 to 1450, also enjoyed the fruit and the wood of the saguaro; and the adobe homes of the Spanish, who settled the area in the late 17th century, utilize saguaro ribs as cross beams. Although it's illegal now to destroy these giant plants, you'll still see their remains in many contemporary Southwest furnishings.

Some human interactions were less than benign. Overgrazing by local cattle ranchers threatened the once-thick stands of cactus to the east of Tucson and led Herbert Hoover to create Saguaro National Monument in 1933. Even after what is now known as the Rincon Mountain District was established, however, federal permits still allowed cattle to denude the land; the grazing didn't stop until 1979, when the last permit expired. On the west side, copper, gold, and silver mining posed the greatest danger to the cactus. Throughout the Tucson Mountain District, you can still spot remnants of some of the 100-odd shafts and tunnels dug before 1961, when John F. Kennedy signed off on this portion of the national monument. A bit of additional land was added to the western unit when national park status was conferred in 1994: Today, the eastern side has 67,293 acres, the more-visited western side 24,034.

ESSENTIAL INFORMATION

VISITOR INFORMATION You can enter both sections of Saguaro National Park every day from sunrise to sunset. The visitor centers—the new Red Hills complex in the west district, and the headquarters in the east district—are open daily from 8:30 to 5. For additional information, contact **Saguaro National Park** (3693 S. Old Spanish Trail, Tucson AZ 85730-5699, tel. 502/733–5153 for Saguaro West, 520/733–5158 for Saguaro East). If you'd like to know more about lodging, dining, and additional sightseeing options nearby, contact the **Metropolitan Tucson Convention and Visitors Bureau** (130 S. Scott Ave., Tucson 85701, tel. 520/624–1817 or 800/638–8350). At press time, the CVB was planning to move to a new, undetermined address; call for an update.

Neither side of the park has lodging or drive-in camping facilities, and backcountry camping is permitted only at certain designated sites in the Rincon Mountain District. You can pick up the required free camping permit from the east-side visitor center, or request it by mail as early as two months in advance. If you opt for the latter, write the park and request an application form, which must be sent back at least two weeks in advance of the date you wish to visit.

FEES Admission to the Tucson Mountain District of the park is free. You'll pay $4 per car to drive into the Rincon Mountain District, $2 if you're coming in on bicycle or by foot.

PUBLICATIONS You can pick up printed flyers on various aspects of the park—geology, hiking trails, and the like—at the visitor centers. The bookshops in both units carry USGS maps (important if you're planning on exploring the east-side backcountry) and the *Tucson Hiking Guide* by Betty Leavengood, a useful and entertaining book that includes day hikes on both sides. General introductions to the park and its landscape include *Saguaro National Park*, by Doris Evans, and *Sonoran Desert: The Story Behind the Scenery*, by Christopher L. Helms. For a poetic take by a naturalist, try Gary Nabhan's *Saguaro: A View of Saguaro National Monument and the Tucson Basin*. The little *Hohokam Indians of the Tucson Basin* by Linda M. Gregonis and Karl J. Reinhard provides some background on the area's earliest inhabitants. The last is out of print, but the visitor center may have copies.

GEOLOGY AND TERRAIN You'd be hardpressed to match Saguaro National Park for what might be termed, in the words of William Butler Yeats, "a terrible beauty." Dense, spiny cactus forests, stark granite outcroppings, sheer-cut canyons, and dry arroyos that fill up astonishingly fast are among its most striking characteristics. Although both sides of the park are equally scenic, their origins are not necessarily identical. Geologists can determine with some certainty how the eastern section was formed, but the exact origins of the west side still elude them.

The entire area was once covered by a vast inland sea that deposited a layer of limestone, sandstone, and shale onto the earth's molten crust. The eastern district's broad, rounded Rincon Mountains were created about 20 to 30 million years ago when that crust began to pull apart, distorting the sandstone into unusual shapes and bringing the lower layers of gneiss up to the surface. Of the major fissures that occurred at the time, you can best see the north–south Catalina Fault, which roughly bisects the eastern district's Cactus Forest Drive.

The western side is more mysterious, an amalgam of eroded volcanic rocks so anarchic that it's been dubbed the Tucson Mountain Chaos. Current theory has it that the Tucson Mountains were originally part of the Rincon and Santa Catalina chains, but then slowly shifted some 20 or 30 mi west to the other side of the Tucson Valley.

In geological terms—and even in relation to the three other North American deserts, the Mohave, the Chihuahuan, and the Great

Basin—the Sonoran Desert is a mere babe, about 10,000 years old. At around the time it was formed, the wet Pleistocene climate warmed and dried, causing the mammoths and other large mammals that roamed the area to became extinct. Today the Sonoran is the most complex of all the North American deserts, with the greatest variety of plant and animal life; it receives rain in both winter and summer, thus ensuring year-round vegetation.

On the west side of the park, you can move beyond the low, hot desert scrub region to a higher elevation, but the changes are far more pronounced in the Rincon Mountain District, where the highest peak, Mica Mountain, rises 8,666 ft. From the cactus forest, you'll ascend through six different life zones, going beyond desert grassland and oak woodland to pine and mixed conifer forest on the tallest north-facing slopes. Because there's never been a major road built into the Rincons, the thick growth on top is unusually pristine, and the vistas of southeast Arizona from these "sky islands" are outstanding.

FLORA AND FAUNA Saguaro National Park's namesake cactus is famous for its size (it can tower as high as 40 or 50 ft and may weigh up to 8 tons); its longevity (frequently more than 150 years); and its arms, which reach out in strange configurations. Some of these plants become local legends: In 1993 Tucson newspapers announced the death of Old Granddad, a 54-arm saguaro that had resided in the eastern section of the national park for perhaps 300 years. It takes the saguaro at least 15 years to grow 12 inches and twice as long to start producing flowers and fruit. Not until it's at least 10 ft tall and approximately three-quarters of a century old does it begin sprouting arms.

The saguaro is ribbed vertically with accordion-like pleats that expand to store moisture gathered through its shallow roots during desert rain showers; water can comprise up to 95% of the saguaro's bulk, which is supported by a circular column of woody internal ribs. From around late April through May, the giant cactus sprouts a party hat of white blossoms. These waxy blooms—Arizona's official state flower—are actually quite large, but not in comparison with the cactus. In June and July the red, sweet fruit of the saguaro ripens and its seeds are disseminated.

The saguaro may be the most showy of the Sonoran Desert plants, but the national park sustains about 2,700 additional species of flora, including 50 types of cactus. Among the most common are the prickly pear, barrel cactus, and teddy bear cholla, the last so named because it appears deceptively cuddly. Although not a cactus, the skinny, sticklike ocotillo is duplicitous in a different way: It often looks dead in dry weather, but when it gets wet it quickly perks up, sprouting leaves up to seven or eight times a year. The palo verde tree has bright green trunks and branches. The rather nondescript creosote bush, widespread throughout North American deserts, is easily recognized when it rains because it gives off a wonderfully fresh smell (putting one of its branches in a glass of water does the trick, too).

One of the great surprises of the desert is its wildflowers. Dominating the landscape are the yellow, daisylike flowers of brittlebush. Other yellow-gold flowers are the Mexican gold poppy, marigolds, and evening primrose. Whimsical fairy dusters add splashes of red, and desert verbena, lupines, owl's clover, and penstemon provide a purple haze.

For many of the desert fauna, the saguaro functions as a kind of high-rise hotel. The gila woodpecker and the gilded flicker peck holes and nest in the cactus each spring. When they give up their temporary digs, elf owls, cactus wrens, sparrow hawks, and other avians move in, as do insects such as honeybees. Larger birds—great horned owls and red-tailed hawks, for example—frequently rest in the arm joint of the saguaro. Other creatures such as long-nosed bats and white-winged doves eat the nectar of the saguaro flowers. Large desert critters—coyotes, foxes, skunks, javelinas, squirrels, and wood rats—feast on any saguaro fruit that hits the ground.

Though six different species of rattlesnake inhabit the park, you are not likely to encounter any. Still, use common sense: Don't stick your hands or feet under a rock or crevice where a snake might be lurking. If you should get bitten, don't panic—more than half the time it will be a "dry" (non-venomous) bite. If you're far from your car, some experts recommend using a product called The Extractor (*see* General Stores, *below*). Your best bet is to get to a clinic or emergency room quickly.

WHEN TO GO Spring is the best time to see wildflowers. When there's been a lot of rain, the period around the end of March and early April is best, but wildflowers at higher elevations turn up about four to eight weeks later than those on the desert floor. Some types of cactus flower in April, while others wait until May or June; you'll even see some (including the fishhook barrel cactus and the chainfruit cholla) blooming in August and September.

In both spring and fall, temperatures are usually moderate (not generally higher than the low 90s during the day), though summer heat hangovers and early warming can raise the temperature significantly. Winters are mild, with the average temperature hovering at around 50 to 60. In the Rincon Mountains, there's frequently snow at higher elevations. Most of the park's interpretive programs take place from around Christmas to Easter.

Unless you want to remove yourself to the cool mountain reaches of Saguaro National Park East, you're best off avoiding a trip in summer. In summer, lodging prices are greatly reduced, and mornings are relatively cool. It can cost as much as 70% less to stay in a Tucson resort or hotel at this time of year than it would in winter. And there's nothing like the smell of the desert after heavy rains, which normally occur throughout August.

WHAT TO PACK Since temperatures can cool considerably in the late afternoon, it's best to wear layered clothing—especially if you're planning to hike beyond the desert floor. Various cactus, especially cholla, will attach themselves to you if you brush up against them, which makes lightweight slacks a much better choice than shorts. Pack a pocket comb, a pair of tweezers, and adhesive tape, all helpful for removing prickly spines; the comb will allow you to remove large pieces of cactus while the tape is good for removing bristles that aren't deeply embedded. And be sure to pack sunscreen, a hat, sunglasses, and a large canteen or water bottle.

GENERAL STORES **Bob's Bargain Barn** (2230 N. Country Club Rd., tel. 520/325–3409) and **Summit Hut** (5045 E. Speedway Blvd., tel. 520/325–1554) are two excellent places in Tucson to pick up any hiking or camping supplies you may have forgotten. Both carry The Extractor snakebite kit.

ARRIVING AND DEPARTING Though some tour operators will take you to Saguaro National Park (*see* Guided Tours, *below*), there is no public transportation to either section; a car is a necessity. All the major car-rental companies are represented at Tucson International Airport. **Enterprise** (tel. 800/736–8222) is the only company with an office downtown, near the Amtrak and Greyhound depots. **Alamo** (tel. 800/327–9633), **Budget** (tel. 800/527–0700), and **National** (tel. 800/227–7368) will pick you up and drop you off for free no matter where you arrive.

By Bus. Greyhound Lines (2 S. 4th Ave., at E. Broadway, tel. 520/792–3475) will take you into downtown Tucson from most major cities.

By Car. I–10, the southernmost coast-to-coast highway in the United States, is also the major north–south artery through the city of Tucson; unless you're coming north from Mexico (in which case you'll take I–19), you'll have to hook up with I–10 sooner or later. If you're headed eastbound on I–10, take exit 242, Avra Valley Road, to reach the west side of the park; westbound, get off at exit 275, Houghton Road, for the eastern district.

To go from the center of town to the west unit of Saguaro National Park, take Speedway Boulevard west over Gates Pass to Kinney Road, where the Red Hills Visitor Center is located. To reach the east unit, drive on Broadway Boulevard or 22nd Street to Old Spanish Trail, and turn left when you see the sign for the visitor center. Both sides are about 15 mi from central Tucson. Note: Oversized vehicles are prohibited from going over Gates Pass. If you're driving an RV, take I–19 to Ajo Way (AZ86), then go west to Kinney Road, which will lead you northwest to the park (it only goes in this one direction from Ajo Way).

By Plane. U.S. carriers that fly into **Tucson International Airport** (tel. 520/573–8000) include **Aerocalifornia** (tel. 800/237–6225), **American** (tel. 800/433–7300), **America West** (tel. 800/235–9292), **Continental** (tel. 520/623–3700), **Delta** (tel. 800/221–1212), **Great Lakes Aviation** (tel. 800/274–0662), **Northwest** (tel. 800/225–2525), **Reno Air** (tel. 800/736–6247), **Southwest** (tel. 800/435–9792), and **United** (tel. 800/241–6522).

By Train. Amtrak serves Tucson with westbound and eastbound trains three times a week. The station is downtown at 400 East Toole Street, tel. 520/623–4442.

EXPLORING

THE BEST IN ONE DAY Pack a picnic lunch before setting off for either side of the park. In the western district, start out by watching the 15-minute slide show in the Red Hills Visitor Center, then take the .5-mi-long Desert Discovery Trail, about a mile north on Kinney Road from the visitor center. Continue along Kinney Road until you reach the graded dirt Bajada Loop Drive; you'll soon see a turnoff for the Hugh Norris Trail. After ascending for about 45 minutes, you'll reach the first ridge, a perfect

spot for a picnic. Hike back down and drive along the Bajada Loop Drive until you come to the turnoff for Signal Hill. It's a short, gentle walk to the petroglyphs (*see* Historic Buildings and Sights, *below*), no more than about 15 minutes each way. When you finish the loop drive, you'll be back on Kinney Road.

If you're on the east side, start at the visitor center, where you can pick up a free detailed map of the hiking trails (it's easy to get lost even in the most established part of the park). From there, take the paved Cactus Forest Loop to the Javelina Picnic Area, where you'll see signs for the Freeman Homestead Nature Trail, an easy 1-mi loop. After that, if you're a reasonably fit hiker, you might want to follow the first part of the Tanque Verde Ridge Trail, which also begins near the Javelina Picnic Area. After about 1.5 mi you'll reach a ridge that affords excellent views and is a good halfway point for a picnic. Alternatively, there are plenty of flatter trails across the lowlands: You'll see a sign on the northern part of the Cactus Forest Loop road for the Cactus Forest Trail, which branches off into several level paths. Consult your map and choose the distance you'd like to hike (the scenery doesn't vary much, no matter what direction you take) and spend the rest of the afternoon strolling among the saguaro.

ORIENTATION PROGRAMS From late December through April, both park units have daily programs introducing various facets of the desert. You might find ranger talks or slide shows on topics such as bats, birds, or desert blooms. On the west side, you can always catch the excellent 15-minute slide show. There's an older, more conventional program on the east side.

GUIDED TOURS Most Tucson tour companies don't include Saguaro National Park on their itineraries, but you can arrange a specialized excursion with **Old Pueblo Tours** (tel. 520/795–7448). Guided tours in both sections of the park might range from a 30-minute stroll through the cactus garden near the visitor center to a three-hour

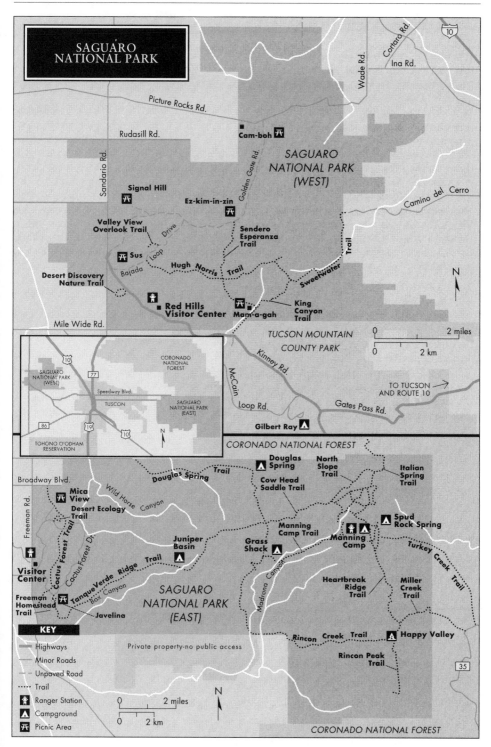

SAGUARO
NATIONAL PARK

Picture Rocks Rd.

Rudasill Rd.

Cam-boh 🏕

SAGUARO
NATIONAL PARK
(WEST)

Wade Rd.

Cortaro Rd.

Ina Rd.

Golden Gate Rd.

Camino del Cerro

Signal Hill

Ez-kim-in-zin

Valley View
Overlook Trail

Sandario Rd.

Drive

Loop

Bajada

Sus

Desert Discovery
Nature Trail

Mile Wide Rd.

Sendero
Esperanza
Trail

Hugh Norris Trail

Sweetwater Trail

Red Hills
Visitor Center   Mam-a-gah

King
Canyon
Trail

TUCSON MOUNTAIN
COUNTY PARK

0   2 miles
0   2 km

Kinney Rd.

McCain

Loop Rd.

Gates Pass Rd.

TO TUCSON
AND ROUTE 10

Gilbert Ray

Inset map:
CORONADO
NATIONAL
FOREST
SAGUARO
NATIONAL PARK
(WEST)
Speedway Blvd.
TUSCON
SAGUARO
NATIONAL PARK
(EAST)
TOHONO O'ODHAM
RESERVATION
N

CORONADO NATIONAL FOREST

Douglas Spring Trail

Douglas
Spring

North
Slope
Trail

Italian
Spring
Trail

Broadway Blvd.

Mica
View

Wild Horse Canyon

Desert Ecology
Trail

Cow Head
Saddle Trail

Freeman Rd.

Cactus Forest Trail

Cactus Forest Dr.

Juniper
Basin

Manning
Camp Trail

Spud
Rock Spring

Visitor
Center

Tanque Verde Ridge Trail

Box Canyon

Grass
Shack

Manning
Camp

Turkey Creek Trail

Freeman
Homestead
Trail

Javelina

SAGUARO
NATIONAL PARK
(EAST)

Madrona Canyon

Heartbreak
Ridge
Trail

Miller
Creek
Trail

Rincon Creek Trail

Happy Valley

KEY

Private property-no public access

Rincon Peak
Trail

35

Highways

Minor Roads

Unpaved Road

Trail

🏕 Ranger Station

▲ Campground

🏕 Picnic Area

0   2 miles
0   2 km

N

CORONADO NATIONAL FOREST

347

morning hike. Most of the organized activities take place from December through April.

SCENIC DRIVES AND VIEWS It's hard to beat the Gates Pass section of the drive from central Tucson to the western unit of the park for sheer drama—the sharp descent down the mountain road is guaranteed to get your adrenalin going. Within the park, the 6-mi **Bajada Loop Drive** winds through thick stands of saguaro and other desert vegetation. Though the drive is unpaved and bumpy, some slight discomfort is a worthwhile trade-off for access to some of the park's densest desert growth. In the eastern unit, the paved 8-mi **Cactus Forest Drive** is a quicker route through the park, providing a great overview.

The eastern district's **Cactus Forest Drive** has several unnamed turnouts for people who want to stop and linger over the scenery. Be sure to bring your camera on this drive.

HISTORIC BUILDINGS AND SITES In the 1930s, the Civilian Conservation Corps built a number of **picnic shelters** in what is now the western unit of the park out of native rock and wood. Over the years, most have been massively revamped, but the check dams (dams built to control flash floods) and bathrooms remain largely intact. In this district, you'll also come across a number of **abandoned mine shafts,** all off limits to visitors.

Although Hohokam petroglyphs (pictures pecked in stone) are scattered throughout both sections of the park, the most impressive ones, and the only ones with interpretive signs, are at **Signal Hill,** on the Bajada Loop Drive. This is one of the largest gathering of petroglyphs in the Southwest; it's also one of the most accessible. Walking on the rocks is prohibited, but you'll still have a close-up view of the designs left by the Hohokam sometime between AD 900 and 1200. No one is entirely sure what they mean—they may have religious significance or they may be a form of ancient graffiti. Most distinctive among them are the

large spirals that some believe are astronomical markers.

It's more difficult to see the main historic site in the Rincon Mountain unit, **Manning Camp**: The former summer home of Levi Manning, a onetime Tucson mayor, sits at an elevation of 8,000 ft (it's accessible by four of the unit's five high-country trails). It's hard to imagine getting the family furnishings, including a piano, hauled up to this remote spot on a rough wagon road, and even harder to imagine that, until the land became public and Manning had to give it up, this was a popular gathering spot for Tucson's elite. Located at the largest of the park's six backcountry campgrounds, Manning's original log cabin is now used as a fire lookout and temporary quarters for park service staff.

NATURE TRAILS AND SHORT WALKS Adjacent to the two visitor centers are **cactus gardens** with signs identifying the plants you're likely to come across on longer treks. One mile northwest of the west-side visitor center, the gentle, .5-mi round-trip **Desert Discovery Trail** interprets the native plants, animals, and ecology of the region. Also in the west unit, the .25-mi-long **Signal Hill Trail** is an easy, rewarding ascent (*see* Historic Buildings and Sights, *above*).

On the east side, the paved **Desert Ecology Trail,** a .25-mi loop near the Mica View Picnic Area, has exhibits explaining how local plants and animals subsist on a limited supply of water. As its name suggests, the 1-mi-loop **Freeman Homestead Nature Trail** gives a bit of the history of homesteading in the desert at the turn of the century; it's accessible from the Javelina Picnic Area. In addition, visitors can devise their own short hikes on the flatlands of the park by consulting the map of the Cactus Forest Trail system available at the visitor center.

On the west side, **Signal Hill** (*see* Historic Buildings and Sites, *above*) is an easy walk to a good vantage point. The aptly named **Valley View Overlook Trail** takes you up to a ridge with splendid vistas of Avra Valley; on clear days, you can also spot the distinctive slope of Picacho Peak to the north. The 1.5-mi, round-trip trail, built by the Civilian Conservation Corps in the 1930s, can be reached on the Bajada Loop Drive, 3.5 mi north of the Red Hills Visitor Center.

LONGER HIKES Covering a total distance of 10 mi, the Tucson Mountain Unit's **Hugh Norris Trail** is one of the most impressive treks in the Southwest. Named after a former chief of the Tohono O'odham Indian police, it starts at the Bajada Loop Drive (2.5 mi north of the visitor center) and leads to the crest of the Tucson Mountains, terminating at Wasson Peak (elevation: 4,687 ft). It's full of switchbacks and some sections are moderately steep, but at the top you'll enjoy vistas of the saguaro forest spread across the *bajada* (Spanish for the gently rolling hills at the base of taller mountains) and of the valleys and mountains around Tucson.

The 7-mi round-trip **King Canyon Trail** starts 2 mi south of the visitor center, directly across the road from the Arizona-Sonora Desert Museum. This is the shortest, but steepest, route to the top of Wasson Peak, meeting up with the Hugh Norris Trail about a third of a mile from the summit. Named after the Copper King Mine, the trail was developed in 1917, and many scars from the search for mineral wealth remain. Look for petroglyphs around this area.

One and a half miles east of the intersection of Bajada Loop Drive and Golden Gate Road, you can pick up the 6.4-mi **Sendero Esperanza Trail.** You'll be following a sandy former mine road for the first mile, then ascending, via a series of switchbacks, to the top of a ridge where you'll come to the intersection with the Hugh Norris Trail. Descending on the other side of the ridge, you'll meet up with the King Canyon Trail. The trail is rocky in parts and some of the switchbacks are steep, but rewards include ruins of the 1907 Gould Mine and many spectacular views.

In the east-district high country, hikes are considerably longer. The 13.8-mi **Tanque**

Verde Ridge Trail, which begins to the right of the Javelina Picnic Area, follows its namesake landmark, the Tanque Verde Ridge, to Juniper Basin, site of one of the park's backcountry campgrounds. The hike brings you through Sonoran desert scrub at the trailhead to oak, alligator juniper, and piñon pine at the top, doubling its elevation from about 3,000 to 6,000 ft. Until you're a couple of miles from the campground and among thicker trees, overlooks of the city and surrounding mountain ranges from both sides of the ridge are spectacular.

Slightly shorter at 11.8 mi round-trip, but equally difficult, the **Douglas Spring Trail** begins at the east end of Speedway Boulevard and heads almost due east into the Rincon Mountains. After a half mile through a dense concentration of saguaros, you'll reach open desert grassland. Farther along, Bridal Wreath Falls is worth a slight detour in early spring, when snowmelt creates a large flow of water. Blackened tree trunks at the Douglas Spring Campground, your final destination, are one of the few vestiges of a huge lightening fire that swept through the last 6 mi of the trail in the summer of 1989; most of the affected area has already been filled in with new growth.

Caution: Be sure to bring at least 2 quarts of water per person on any extended hike; on hot days, a gallon is recommended. Not only are you likely to get dehydrated in the hot, dry air, but you can't depend on finding water should you run out.

OTHER ACTIVITIES **Biking.** On the west side, only roads, not hiking trails, are open to bicyclists. Many mountain bikers like touring the **Bajada Loop,** a 6-mi dirt road whose bumpy "washboards", worn into the ground by seasonal drainage, make biking a challenge. In 1991 Saguaro was the first national park in the country to open a trail to mountain bikers: The 2.5-mi **Cactus Forest Trail** (in the east unit) a sandy single track with varied terrain, is good for beginning cyclists. The trailhead begins about a mile past the visitor center, off **Cactus For-**

est Drive—a paved, but curvy and hilly 8-mi loop also popular with bikers.

Bird-Watching. If you're looking for avian action, focus your binoculars on the saguaros, where many birds make their home (*see* Flora and Fauna, *above*).

Horseback Riding. Horses are permitted on the park's designated trails. Many people stay at a nearby guest ranch (*see* Lodging, *below*) so they can spend a few days cantering among the cactus. If you want to go on a day ride, check the Yellow Pages under "Horse Rentals and Riding." **Pantano Riding Stables** (tel. 520/721–1971) is one reliable, long-standing operator on the east side. Horses have the right of way over hikers and bikers.

CHILDREN'S PROGRAMS A Junior Ranger program allows children to check out a Discovery Pack with tools for completing an educational activity booklet; when completed, the child earns a badge and certificate. Discovery Packs must be checked out before 2:45 PM and returned by 4:45 PM.

In addition, a Junior Ranger camp offered in the east unit four times during the month of June includes daily hikes and activities such as pottery- and petroglyph-making. Sessions run three consecutive mornings from 7:30 AM to 12:30 PM (call the visitor center for exact dates); cost is $10 per participant, including a daily snack. Applications are accepted after May 1 on a first-come, first-served basis. Similar workshops lasting a single day and costing $2.50 are held on the west side every Friday from mid-June through mid-August. Call the visitor center for details.

EVENING ACTIVITIES From December through April, evening programs at both visitor centers might include ranger talks on such topics as wildlife, geology, and archaeology; call ahead for schedules. The most popular event, however, takes place on the west side once a month during this period: A few nights before the full moon, a park volunteer leads a hike up to Wasson Peak via the Sendero Esperanza Trail (*see*

Longer Hikes, *above*). You'll reach the top just in time to enjoy a sunset picnic (bring your own) and then descend by the light of the moon. It's not an easy excursion; don't be fooled by the fact that the volunteer who has led it for the past few years is in his 70s. There's also a shorter sunset hike to the Hugh Norris Ridge line. Sign up for these gatherings in advance at the visitor center.

DINING

Visitors to Saguaro National Park have Tucson's vast selection of restaurants to choose from. There are no dining facilities, or even vending machines, inside either section of the park, although both sides have scenic picnic areas. If you're on the east side and don't mind spending a bit more time in the car, you'll find many good restaurants on Tanque Verde Road: Fuego!, Jonathan's Cork, City Grill, and the Olive Tree are among the best. For west-side visitors willing to go the extra miles, Tucson's small downtown doesn't have quite as many eateries, but Cafe Poca Cosa is tops for regional Mexican food and Janos—a big-splurge option—features innovative Southwestern cuisine in a historic setting. In addition, there are plenty of casual eateries in Old Tucson, a former film studio–turned–theme park about 10 minutes from Saguaro National Park West.

NEAR THE WEST DISTRICT **Scordato's.** Tidy up from your hike before you come here. The white tablecloths and formal service at this upscale Italian restaurant call for clean khakis, at least. Since 1972, this place has attracted diners with its superb mountain and city views. You might start with stuffed mushrooms followed by veal *stresa* (with prosciutto and mozzarella in a Marsala sauce). All the desserts are made on the premises. *4404 W. Speedway Blvd., tel. 520/624–8946. AE, D, DC, MC, V. Closed Mon. No lunch. $$$*

Fred's Arena Bar & Steak House. Area ranchers come around to enjoy the mesquite-grilled steak and chicken, and, occasionally, to ride in the restaurant's rodeo shows. Dinners include chili, salad, and thick hunks of white cowboy bread. You'd be hard-pressed to find more local color. *9650 S. Avra Rd., tel. 520/883–7337. No credit cards. $–$$*

Ocotillo Cafe. You'll have to pay $8.95 to enter the Arizona-Sonora Desert Museum (about five minutes from the park visitor center) in order to have lunch here, but it's well worth the surcharge. A zesty selection of Southwestern-inspired salads and other light lunches are served in a bright, contemporary room or on the adjacent patio. The afternoon high tea is lovely, too. *Arizona-Sonora Desert Museum, 2021 N. Kinney Rd., tel. 520/883–5705. AE, MC, V. No dinner (except Sat. June–Sept.). $–$$*

Los Nopales. This unpretentious Mexican restaurant in a shopping center south of the park serves tasty, fresh food at reasonable prices. *3051 S. Kinney Rd., tel. 520/883–5353. MC, V. Closed Sun.–Mon. $*

NEAR THE EAST DISTRICT **Webb's Steak House.** Enjoy a red-meat fest at this down-home restaurant: A 20-ounce T-bone, baby-back ribs, or a huge burger with baked potato and salad. The barbecue chicken is also a treat. Killer frozen margaritas will remind you that Tucson is close to the Mexican border. *5400 S. Old Spanish Trail, tel. 520/885–7782. AE, D, MC, V. No lunch. $$*

Saguaro Corner. The '50s meet the '90s in this combination restaurant, cocktail lounge, and nature viewing center, just down the road from the park visitor center. The frozen-in-time decor and menu (basic burgers, soups, and sandwiches) stand in odd but interesting juxtaposition to huge picture windows looking out on the local wildlife. Prices are pleasantly retro, too. *3750 S. Old Spanish Trail, tel. 520/886–5424. AE, D, DC, MC, V. Closed Mon. $*

Tony's. If you're heading to the park's east district from the center of town, stop at this New York–style Italian deli to pick up some picnic fixings: a prosciutto and provolone hero, say, accompanied by imported olives

and potato salad. And if you need some comfort food after a hard day of hiking, come by for a lasagna dinner on the way back. *6219 E. 22nd St., tel. 520/747–0070. Reservations not accepted. AE, D, MC, V. Closed Sun. $*

PICNIC SPOTS There are five picnic areas on the west side of the park, four of them accessible by car: **Ez-kim-in-zin** (named after an Apache Indian Chief), **Sus** (short for Jésus), **Signal Hill,** and **Cam-boh** (a Spanish word for camp). You'll need to hike a mile on the King Canyon Trail to get the fifth one, **Mam-a-gah** (referring to the deer dance of the Tohono O'odham Indians). Because of the nearby petroglyphs, Signal Hill is the most popular. Each picnic area has shaded tables and an accessible pit toilet, but there's no drinking water at any of them.

In the eastern district, **Mica View Picnic Area** can't be accused of false advertising: It gives you an eyeful of Mica Mountain, the park's highest peak. You can't be equally certain of seeing any piglike creatures at the **Javelina Picnic Area,** but there's a good chance some desert critters will come by begging for picnic scraps (park rangers ask that you refrain from feeding them). Both picnic areas have accessible bathrooms, but neither has drinking water and only Javelina's tables are shaded.

LODGING

Although there is no lodging inside the park, the many guest ranches and bed-and-breakfasts inns near both districts will give you a feel for the desert landscape and for western architecture. If you book a room at one of the guest ranches, you can fulfill your Western fantasies by trotting off into a saguaro-filled sunset. In addition to riding, a ranch stay also includes three meals and a number of other activities. The B&Bs all serve full breakfasts, with the exception of Hacienda del Desierto, which lays on a Continental spread.

NEAR THE WEST DISTRICT **Car Mar's.** The handwriting on the wall—a unique place for gathering guest comments—reveals that visitors enjoy warm hospitality here. Not quite as isolated as some of the other lodgings near the park, Car Mar's compensates with extras such as plush robes, evening turndown, and an on-site massage therapist. Rooms incorporate desert colors and designs. *6766 W. Oklahoma St., 85746 tel. 520/578–1730. 3 rooms, 1 with bath; 1 suite. Facilities: pool. No credit cards. $$$*

Casa Tierra Adobe Bed & Breakfast. Rooms in this lovely hacienda-style lodging, five minutes from the national park, all have private entrances, terraces, and kitchenettes. They're attractively furnished with Mexican *equipale* chairs, cool tiled floors, and viga-beam ceilings. A central courtyard looks out onto dense desert foliage. There's a two-night minimum stay. *11155 W. Calle Pima, 85743, tel. and fax 520/578–3058. 3 rooms. Facilities: kitchenettes, hot tub. No credit cards. Closed June–mid-Sept. $$$*

Lazy K Bar Guest Ranch. At this family-oriented guest ranch in the Tucson Mountains, riders are entertained with tales of the Old West as they trot through Saguaro National Park West. Guest rooms in the older stucco *casitas* (cottages) have fireplaces and wood-beam ceilings; rooms in the newer, adobe-brick buildings are larger and more modern. There's a three-night minimum stay. *8401 N. Scenic Dr., 85743, tel. 520/744–3050 or 800/321–7018, fax 520/744–7628. 23 rooms. Facilities: pool, library. AE, D, MC, V. $$$*

Rancho Quieto. Here you get both the desert and an oasis: This beautifully landscaped B&B has a 9-ft-deep pool and adjacent waterfall, as well as a hot springs–like pond nestled among palm trees; all use recycled well water. The two-level suites, done in contemporary Southwestern style, all have full kitchens, fireplaces, and patios. *12051 W. Fort Lowell Rd., 85743, tel. 520/883–3300. 3 suites, 1 guest house. Facilities: kitchens, hot tub. No credit cards. Closed June–Sept. 15. $$$*

Sahuaro Vista Guest Ranch. Built in the 1930s, Sahuaro Vista was originally a cattle ranch; its other incarnations have included a stint as a guest ranch, and even as a drug rehab center. Now a bed-and-breakfast, the place brims with local character. Although it doesn't have all the usual dude ranch amenities on site, there are stables nearby, and there's a restaurant with updated Continental cuisine on the premises. Rooms are comfortable but rather plainly furnished, and they have no TVs or phones. The 27-acre property is only about a mile from the north end of the national park and boasts similarly impressive desert growth. *7501 N. Wade Rd., 85743, tel. 520/579–2530. 20 units. Facilities: restaurant, pool. MC, V. $$$*

White Stallion Ranch. A number of scenes from *High Chaparral* were shot on this homey, family-run ranch, which sits on 3,000 acres abutting Saguaro National Park West. Children especially enjoy the petting zoo. Horseback rides, a weekend rodeo, cookouts, and hikes along mountain trails are among the activities available. There are no telephones or TVs in the spare but comfortable rooms. *9251 W. Twin Peaks Rd., 85743, tel. 520/297–0252 or 888/977–2624, fax 520/744–2786. 32 rooms. Facilities: bar, pool, hot tub, 2 tennis courts, basketball, horseback riding, Ping-Pong, shuffleboard, volleyball, billiards. No credit cards. Closed May–Sept. $$$*

NEAR THE EAST DISTRICT **Bienestar.** Enjoy contemporary Southwestern comfort, including delicious, healthful breakfasts made with whole grains and free-range eggs, very close to the park. High tea is served near the large pool or around a blazing fire in the living room in winter. No pets are allowed—except horses (there are paddocks on the property). *10490 E. Escalante Rd., 85730, tel. 520/290–1048, fax 520/290–1367. 1 room, 1 suite, 1 casita. Facilities: pool. MC, V. $$$*

Hacienda del Desierto. Ideal for families and extended stays because of the variety of room layouts and availability of kitchen facilities, this B&B is only a few minutes from the park entrance. An idyllic desert setting and fascinating architectural details add to the appeal. *11770 Rambling Trail, 85747, tel. 520/298–1764 or 800/982–1795, fax 520/722–4558. 1 room, 1 suite, 1 casita. Facilities: kitchenettes, hot tub. No credit cards. $$$*

Rimrock West Hacienda. About 7 mi north of the park, this B&B on 20 acres has a panoramic view of Tucson. The artwork in the adobe ranch house is all by the innkeepers and their son; their studio is on the property. Attractive rooms open onto a sunny brick courtyard; a kidney-shape pool occupies its own walled enclosure. The single cottage has a kitchen. *3450 N. Drake Pl., 85749, tel. 520/749–8774. 2 rooms, 1 cottage. Facilities: pool. No credit cards. $$$*

Tanque Verde Ranch. The most upscale of Tucson's guest ranches and one of the oldest in the country, Tanque Verde rests on more than 600 acres in the Rincon Mountains between Coronado National Forest and Saguaro National Park. Most of the tastefully furnished rooms in the main ranch house or in private casitas have patios, and some have fireplaces. *14301 E. Speedway Blvd., 85748, tel. 520/296–6275 or 800/234–3833, fax 520/721–9426. 70 rooms, 4 houses. Facilities: indoor pool, outdoor pool, 5 tennis courts, basketball, exercise room, horseback riding, horseshoes, volleyball, fishing. AE, D, MC, V. $$$*

CAMPING

There's no drive-up camping in the park, and backcountry camping is permitted only in designated campgrounds on the east side. Just over 4 mi south of the west district, however, Tucson County Park has a 152-site campground that's open year-round. Within the park, five free, primitive campgrounds—**Spud Rock Spring, Happy Valley, Juniper Basin, Grass Shack,** and **Douglas Spring**—have three sites, which will fit up to six people each; **Manning Camp** has six sites. Only Manning Camp has water year-round, and it frequently has to be treated. Inquire about the status of the water at Manning Camp and all the other campgrounds at the visitor center, where you'll also need to pick up your free backcountry permit (*see* Visitor Information, *above*). You can camp in the backcountry for a maximum of 14 days. Hikers are encouraged to set out before noon.

Sequoia and Kings Canyon National Parks

California

Updated by Jonathan Leff

lthough Sequoia and Kings Canyon are often obscured by the shadow of Yosemite to the north, famed naturalist John Muir didn't think any less of the former. He called the Kings Canyon "a rival to Yosemite Valley" and proclaimed the sequoia trees "the most beautiful and majestic on earth." Visit Sequoia and Kings Canyon National Parks and you will undoubtedly concur. You will walk, as Muir did, awestruck among the silent giants, marveling at the deep granite canyons and the snowcapped peaks.

The two parks share a boundary and are administered as one. They encompass more than 1,300 square mi that are rivaled only by Yosemite National Park in terms of rugged Sierra beauty. The topography runs from foothill chaparral, at an elevation of 1,500 ft, in the west, to the giant sequoia belt at 5,000 to 7,000 ft, to the towering peaks of the Great Western Divide and the Sierra Crest. Mt. Whitney, the highest point in the contiguous United States at 14,494 ft, is the crown jewel of the east side.

Many of the major attractions in both parks can be reached by automobile, but the majority of acreage is without roads. If you expect simply to drive through, you may be disappointed: Although the panoramic views and striking geological features found in other national parks exist here, they are less accessible. If you want to explore these parks, you will have to hike. And you'll have more than 800 mi of trails from which to choose.

Today, almost 2 million people visit the parks annually. They come to while away peaceful hours on uncrowded trails through meadows and conifer groves, or to head into the rugged grandeur of the backcountry. There was a time, beginning in the 1860s, when people came to these timberlands to cut trees, and in some places the scars are still evident. By 1890, however, the area's beauty was officially recognized, as was its value as a watershed, and the destruction was checked by the establishment of a 50,000-acre Sequoia National Park, the country's second national park. This was followed by the designation of the tiny 2,560-acre General Grant National Park a week later. At that time, additional acreage was granted to Sequoia; although this nearly tripled its size, Sequoia remained small by national park standards. Years of prodding by environmentally minded people resulted in further growth of Sequoia. It wasn't until 1940 that the General Grant Park was expanded to include the high country around the South Fork Kings River and renamed Kings Canyon National Park; and in 1965, Cedar Grove and Tehipite Valley were protected within the Kings Canyon domain.

ESSENTIAL INFORMATION

VISITOR INFORMATION You can get information about the two parks (plus road and weather information) by contacting the Superintendent, **Sequoia and Kings Canyon National Parks** (Three Rivers, CA 93271, tel. 209/565–3341, fax 209/565–3730). **Sequoia/**

Kings Canyon Park Services, the concessionaire that manages accommodations in the parks, can be reached at 209/335–5500, or by fax at 209/335–5502.

Free wilderness permits are required for all overnight trips into the backcountry (tel. 209/565–3708). Reservations are accepted only by mail, beginning with March 1 postmarks; they must be made at least three weeks in advance. You have the best chance of getting a permit on the dates you request if you choose to travel on weekdays rather than weekends; also avoid holidays. Without a reservation, you may still get a permit: One-third of them are distributed on a first-come, first-served basis starting at 1 PM the day before you plan to hike. If you plan to travel with horses, mules, burros, or llamas, find out in advance about regulations for trails and forage areas.

FEES The $10 per vehicle fee allows you to enter both parks for one week; those on foot, bicycle, bus, or any other noncar vehicle pay $5 for a pass good for seven days. An annual pass to the two parks is $20 for the calendar year.

PUBLICATIONS In addition to the quarterly *Sequoia Bark,* given out for free at the entrances, the **Sequoia Natural History Association** (HCR 89, Box 10, Three Rivers, CA 93271, tel. 209/565–3758) will send you a brochure listing its numerous maps, books, pamphlets, and video- and audiocassettes. Its 212-page *Sequoia and Kings Canyon Official National Park Handbook* ($6.50) includes color photos and covers such topics as the area's climate, plant and animal adaptations, sequoias, and man's impact on the park. One section is devoted to the high country. *Wildflowers of Sequoia and Kings Canyon National Parks* ($5.25) divides the parks' flowers by color to help neophyte botanists identify species. It has 48 pages with 90 color photos, covering wildflowers from the foothills to the high country. With 229 pages and many color plates, *Discovering Sierra Birds* ($6.95), by Edward C. Beedy and Stephen Granholm, can help both novice and expert birders

learn more about the parks' winged creatures. *Sequoia Yesterdays* ($3.95), a paperback featuring black-and-white historical photographs, documents the power of the timber industry, congressional acts, the Sierra Club's work at the parks, and the early park service years. Larry Dilsaver and William Tweed's *Challenge of the Big Trees* ($9.95) is a 379-page history of the parks, covering the natural world, Native Americans, explorers and exploiters, the forests, and the selling of the sequoias. Spelunking enthusiasts might order Joel Despain's *Crystal Cave: A Guidebook to the Underground World of Sequoia National Park* ($8.95), featuring photos of the largest cave system in California and its geological history. A topographic map ($7.95) of Sequoia and Kings Canyon, printed on tear-proof, waterproof fabric, is a fine companion for all hikers.

GEOLOGY AND TERRAIN About 225 million years ago, this area of California was at the ocean's edge and the meeting point of two tectonic plates: The heavier plate formed an ocean basin, and the lighter plate was that of the North American Continent. These two plates collided, and slowly the heavier one slipped beneath the continent, a process called subduction. The collision created heat and pressure that eventually melted the lower rocks and pushed them toward the surface. A string of volcanoes venting magma formed along the coast, and the eruptions left beds of sediment, both marine and terrestrial, that in turn were covered and cracked by subsequent eruptions.

Much of the magma never made it to the surface. Instead, it began to cool and harden, and after tens of millions of years masses of this igneous material accumulated on the edge of the continental plate. The angle of collision between the two plates changed, and the line of igneous rock moved to the east. This igneous, or "fire-caused," rock is the granite rock at the surface of today's Sierra.

Eighty million years ago this granite was mostly covered by sedimentary and metamorphic rock. But when the forces pushing the two plates together shifted, about 25 million years ago, and continental stretching and uplift began, the once-molten rock began to move toward the surface. The overlying layers of rock weathered away and exposed the granite. For 10 million years the granite rock that forms the Sierra Nevada has been rising.

The two parks are comprised of more than 860,000 acres on the western flank of the Sierra and can be divided into three distinct zones cut by stream and river canyons. In the west are the lower elevation foothills—rolling hills covered with shrubby chaparral vegetation or golden grasslands dotted with oaks. At the middle elevation, from about 5,000 ft to 9,000 ft, there are rock formations mixed with meadows and huge stands of conifers. The giant sequoia belt is here. The high alpine section of the parks is extremely rugged, a land of harsh rock formations in a string of peaks reaching above 13,000 ft and towered over by Mt. Whitney.

To the north, the Kings River cuts a swath through the backcountry and over the years has formed a granite canyon that, in places, towers nearly 4,000 vertical ft above the canyon floor. From Junction Overlook, on the drive to Cedar Grove, visitors can observe the drop from 10,051-ft Spanish Mountain to the Kings River, a distance of 8,200 ft. Spanish Mountain sits approximately 2.5 mi north of the river. The confluence of the Middle and South forks of the Kings River can also be seen from the overlook.

FLORA AND FAUNA As the elevation of these parks changes, so do the wildlife and plants that inhabit the various ecological zones. Spring usually arrives in the foothills in early March, its telltale signs moving like a shadow of light up the Sierra's side, so that by mid-July the wildflowers blossom in the higher elevations.

The gently rolling foothills, ranging in elevation from 1,500 ft to 4,500 ft, are primarily oak woodland and chaparral. Chamise

and red-barked manzanita grow here, as does the occasional yucca plant, a veritable vegetative porcupine. The amount of groundwater determines the density of the oak groves, which, in early spring, are carpeted with knee-high grass. In spring, fields of white popcorn flower also cover the hillsides, and the yellow fiddleneck flourishes too. In summer, intense heat and absence of rain cause the hills to turn golden-brown. Small creatures stalk these lands, including the bushy-tailed California ground squirrel, which scours the countryside for berries, acorns, and grasses. Black bears, coyotes, skunks, and gray fox are also present, as is the noisy and sassy scrub jay, a blue and gray bird that seems to delight in scolding anyone who crosses its path.

It is the parks' mid-zone forests, home to the sequoias, that draw the crowds. But in addition to these giant trees, there are such evergreens as red and white fir, western juniper, incense-cedar, and pines—Jeffrey, lodgepole, sugar, and ponderosa. Wildflowers include yellow blazing star and red Indian paintbrush. Animals in this area are golden-mantled ground squirrels, Steller's jays, chipmunks, gray squirrels, mule deer, and, of course, black bears. One of the most obvious inhabitants is the Douglas squirrel, or chickaree, who spends most of his days policing his territory in noisy fashion, all the while clipping cones from the tops of the firs, pines, and sequoias.

The high country, with its fierce weather and scarcity of soil, is sparsely vegetated. Foxtail and whitebark pines have gnarled and twisted trunks, the result of years of high wind, heavy snowfall, and freezing temperatures. Life is smaller here than at lower elevations, and in summer, you will see yellow-bellied marmots, pikas, weasels, mountain chickadees, and Clark's nutcrackers. Leopard lilies and shooting stars grow near streams and meadows.

WHEN TO GO In summer, daytime highs usually run in the 70s in the middle elevations, where the parks' most popular attractions are found. Overnight lows average 50°F. The lower elevations often experience temperatures above 100°F, with overnight lows averaging in the mid 60s. Summer thundershowers are not uncommon, and the weather can change quickly in the mountains.

In winter, mid-elevation temperatures usually range from the low 20s to mid-40s, with overnight lows in the single digits, and low-hanging clouds can move in and obscure the countryside for days. Most of the 40 to 50 inches of precipitation this elevation receives falls during the winter, which means that much of the area is covered deep in snow from December to May. Highway 198 to Giant Forest and Highway 180 to Grant Grove are open year-round but are subject to brief closures or chain restrictions due to snowfall. The Generals Highway, which connects the two areas, is usually open year-round, but it, too, often closes for days at a time in winter.

The best times to visit the parks are late spring and early fall, when the temperatures are still moderate and the crowds thin. The parks draw their heaviest crowds in July and August and over holiday weekends. If you plan to visit in summer, be forewarned that you will be approaching the parks from the west, across the San Joaquin Valley, where temperatures often exceed 100°F from late May through early September.

SEASONAL EVENTS April: The **Jazzaffair,** held in the town of Three Rivers, is a festival of mostly swing jazz held at several locations, with shuttle buses between sites. **Early May:** The **Redbud Festival,** in Three Rivers, is a two-day arts-and-crafts festival; the **Woodlake Rodeo,** in Woodlake, is a weekend event that draws large crowds. **Early December:** Carolers gather at the base of the General Grant Tree, the nation's official Christmas tree. (For more information on these and other events, contact the **Visalia Chamber of Commerce,** tel. 209/734–5876.)

WHAT TO PACK Bring the essentials for high mountain country: layered clothing, waterproof gear, and sunscreen.

GENERAL STORES Small stores carrying most essential items and foods are in the lodging centers at **Lodgepole** (near Giant Forest), **Grant Grove, Cedar Grove,** and **Stony Creek.** In summer the stores are generally open from 8 AM to 9 PM, with shorter winter hours (call ahead). The stores at Lodgepole, Cedar Grove, and Stony Creek are closed in winter. Contact **Sequoia/Kings Canyon Park Services** (Box 909, Kings Canyon National Park, CA 93633, tel. 209/335–5500, fax 209/335–5502) for specific information about the stores.

ARRIVING AND DEPARTING There is no public transportation to the parks, and public tours are limited (*see* Guided Tours, *below*). San Francisco is 280 mi from the parks, a five-hour drive; Los Angeles is 240 mi and four hours away. Fresno, the largest city near the parks, is 54 mi from Grant Grove; Visalia, 36 mi away from the southern entrance of the parks on Highway 198, is also used as a base for exploring the area. Many people stay in Three Rivers, just outside Sequoia, on Highway 198. Other National Park Service areas that are fairly close by western standards are Death Valley, an eight-hour, 345-mi haul, and Yosemite, a four-hour, 185-mi drive.

By Bus. Both Fresno and Visalia have **Greyhound Lines** (tel. 209/268–1829 in Fresno; 209/734–3507 in Visalia; or 800/231–2222) depots, with buses that come from San Francisco and Los Angeles. A round-trip ticket from Los Angeles to Visalia costs about $37; from San Francisco, about $40.

By Car and RV. Only two roads lead into the parks, and both approach from the west. Highway 180 from Fresno passes through the peninsula-like Grant Grove in the southwestern section of Kings Canyon National Park; travels north, then east through the national forest; reenters the park as the Kings Canyon Highway; then dead-ends in Cedar Grove. It takes about two hours to make the round-trip drive from Grant Grove. Highway 198 travels 36 mi from Visalia, entering Sequoia National Park from the southwest at Ash Mountain. It eventually turns into the Generals Highway, a winding 56-mi road that connects with Highway 180, linking the two parks. Progress along this byway will be even slower than normal for at least the next five years, as road improvements to the entire stretch may cause delays of up to an hour. No roads enter the parks from the east, but three spur roads off U.S. 395 come within 3 to 5 mi of the east boundary. These head west from Lone Pine, in the south; Independence, near the middle; and Big Pine, in the north. Highway 168, which stems off U.S. 395 at Bishop, leads to Kings Canyon's northernmost boundary. All of these spur roads have campgrounds.

If you are traveling in an RV or with a trailer, study a map of the parks and the restrictions on these vehicles. RVs longer than 22 ft and autos pulling trailers are advised to use Highway 180 from Fresno to the park, a straighter, easier route than Highway 198. From Highway 198 to Giant Forest, the Generals Highway is extremely narrow and climbs 5,000 ft in 20 mi. Maximum vehicle length is 40 ft, or 35 ft for trailers. Steep grades (5%–8%) and heavy traffic may cause vehicles to overheat; overheated brakes are common.

By Plane. The **Fresno Airport** (tel. 209/498–4700), which services American, Delta, United, United Express, and US Airways, in addition to several smaller airlines, is about 10 mi from downtown Fresno and at least an hour from the parks. At the **Visalia Municipal Airport** (tel. 209/738–3201) commercial passengers may arrive on **United Express** (tel. 800/241–6522), which flies directly to San Francisco. **Hertz** (tel. 800/654–3131) rental cars are available at both airports. Additional rental-car companies at the Fresno Airport include **Avis** (tel. 209/251–5001), **Budget** (tel. 209/251–5515), **Dollar** (tel. 209/252–4000), and **National** (tel. 209/251–5577). In addition, the larger hotels in Fresno provide free shuttles from the airport.

By Train. Amtrak (tel. 800/872–7245) has stations in Fresno and Hanford, which is 15 mi from Visalia.

From Los Angeles, a late-night bus carries train passengers from downtown to the train station at Bakersfield, where they can board the train for **Hanford** (the fare is $20 one-way, $40 round-trip, and includes the bus transfer). Near the Hanford train station is **Budget** car rental (tel. 209/583–6123).

From the Ferry Building in San Francisco, a bus takes train passengers to the Emeryville station, where they can catch the train to **Fresno** ($25 one-way, $50 round-trip, including the bus). In Fresno, car rentals are available from **Enterprise** (tel. 209/442–0902) and **Budget** (tel. 209/224–2066), both of which have free shuttles from the train station to their offices, and **Hertz** (tel. 209/251–5055), which will reimburse customers for their cab fare from the train station.

EXPLORING

There are three main centers of interest in the two parks: In Kings Canyon, there is the eponymous river and its surrounding canyon, with a small development called Cedar Grove, as well as Grant Grove; in Sequoia most people flock to Giant Forest. From early May through October all the roads in the parks are usually open, providing access to some spectacular scenery. But these parks are best appreciated on foot. If you have only one or two days and want to see all three of these areas, your best bet is to stay in Grant Grove, which is a one-hour drive from both Cedar Grove and Giant Forest (along the Generals Highway). If you do not plan on extensive hikes, two to three days is ample time to get a sense of the two parks.

THE BEST IN ONE DAY From late spring through early fall you will probably be able to drive the major roads within the parks in three or four hours. Start out on Highway 198 and enter Giant Forest in the early morning, heading straight for the visitor center at Lodgepole. A half hour here will give you a good overview of the area and an

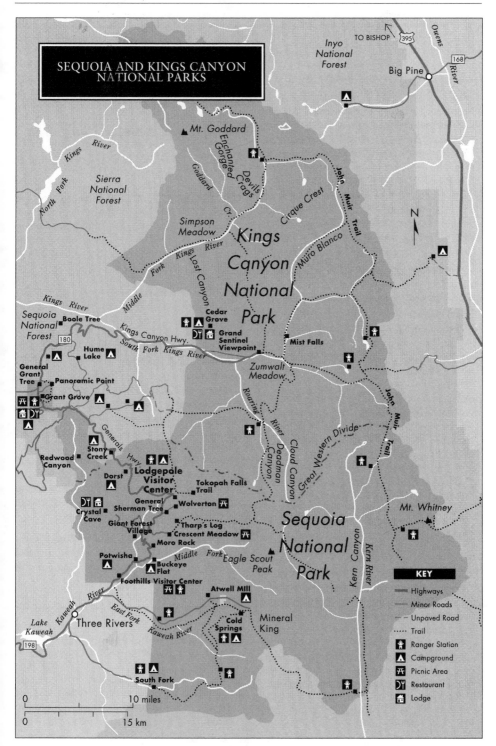

SEQUOIA AND KINGS CANYON
NATIONAL PARKS

TO BISHOP

Inyo
National
Forest

Big Pine

Owens River

Mt. Goddard

Enchanted Gorge

Devils Crags

Goddard Cr.

Cirque Crest

John Muir Trail

Sierra
National
Forest

North Fork

Kings River

Simpson
Meadow

Kings

Middle Fork Kings River

South Fork Kings River

Lost Canyon

Múro Blanco

Canyon

National

Park

Kings River

Sequoia
National
Forest

Boole Tree

Hume Lake

Kings Canyon Hwy.

Cedar Grove

Grand Sentinel Viewpoint

Mist Falls

General Grant Tree

Panoramic Point

Grant Grove

Zumwalt Meadow

Generals Hwy.

Stony Creek

Redwood Canyon

Dorst

Lodgepole Visitor Center

Tokopah Falls Trail

General Sherman Tree

Wolverton

Crystal Cave

Giant Forest Village

Tharp's Log
Crescent Meadow

Moro Rock

Roaring River

Deadman Canyon

Cloud Canyon

Great Western Divide

Sequoia

National

Mt. Whitney

Kern Canyon

Kern River

Potwisha

Buckeye Flat

Foothills Visitor Center

Middle Fork

Eagle Scout Peak

Park

Atwell Mill

Lake
Kaweah

Kaweah River

Three Rivers

East Fork

Kaweah River

Cold Springs

Mineral King

South Fork

KEY

— Highways
— Minor Roads
-- Unpaved Road
····· Trail
Ranger Station
Campground
Picnic Area
Restaurant
Lodge

0   10 miles

0   15 km

idea of what you might want to see in your limited time at the parks. In summer, a half-hourly shuttle van makes the round-trip journey from Lodgepole Campground through Giant Forest Village to Moro Rock and Crescent Meadow.

From the visitor center, backtrack on Generals Highway 2.5 mi to reach the General Sherman Tree, the world's largest living tree. It is just a short walk from the parking area; signs clearly mark the way. This giant is between 2,300 and 2,700 years old, 275 ft high, and has a base diameter of 36.8 ft and a circumference of 102.6 ft; its trunk weighs about 1,385 tons. First-time visitors with time to spare should stroll down the Congress Trail, an easy 2-mi loop through the heart of the sequoia forest that takes one to two hours to complete (*see* Nature Trails and Short Hikes, *below*).

Next, head farther south and turn onto the Moro Rock–Crescent Meadow Road (*see* Scenic Drives and Views, *below*). Make the effort to climb the steep .25-mi staircase leading to the summit of Moro Rock, a large granite dome from which you can gaze out over the western end of Sequoia National Park. Even from a short distance up you'll get a wonderful view. Nearby Crescent Meadow gives an excellent midsummer wildflower show, and a 2-mi round-trip hike from the meadow leads to Tharp's Log, the summer home of Hale Tharp, built inside a fallen sequoia (*see* Historic Buildings and Sites, *below*).

Back on Generals Highway, head north to Grant Grove, where the General Grant Tree has been standing for 1,800 to 2,000 years. You can reach the tree, which President Calvin Coolidge ordained as the Nation's Christmas Tree in 1926, via a half-mile loop trail. Nearby, a 2.3-mi (one-way) spur road (not recommended for trailers and RVs) leads to Panoramic Point, from which you can see the jagged shards of granite peaks looming some 20 mi in the distance (*see* Nature Trails and Short Walks, *below*).

From Grant Grove take Highway 180 east. You will drive along the scenic Kings River

Canyon, and in an hour you'll descend to Cedar Grove, which occupies the upper end of a "yosemite" valley (*yosemite* is the generic term given to glacial U-shape valleys). While this valley lacks the towering waterfalls of the Yosemite Valley in Yosemite National Park, it is full of huge granite cliffs similar to those in the more northern park. Cedar Grove is a good place to sit on a rock next to the Kings River and watch the sinking sun cover the granite faces in a golden wash.

ORIENTATION PROGRAMS Slide shows are presented year-round at the Grant Grove visitor center, and in the summer at Lodgepole. They usually last about 20 minutes and cover such topics as the geological and political creation of the parks.

GUIDED TOURS Private tour companies lead guided tours of the parks; Park Headquarters (tel. 209/565–3341) can provide a complete listing. **Sequoia/Kings Canyon Park Services** (tel. 209/335–5500, fax 209/335–5502) didn't know at press time if they would run tours of the parks; call for more information. The **Sequoia Natural History Association** (tel. 209/565–3758) offers tours of Crystal Cave; these cost $5; tickets must be purchased at the Lodgepole and Foothills visitor centers. They also give nighttime wild-cave tours on weekends from June through September; tickets for these very popular spelunks are available through a lottery held in May; contact the Association for more information.

SCENIC DRIVES AND VIEWS The **Kings Canyon Highway** winds alongside the powerful Kings River, below the towering granite cliffs and past two tumbling waterfalls in Kings Canyon. One mile past the Cedar Grove Village turnoff, the U-shape canyon becomes broader, and you can witness its glacial past. In the granite walls you can see the work of glaciers, wind, rain, and river. Four miles farther along is the Grand Sentinel Viewpoint, where you will see the 3,500-ft tall granite monolith and some of the most interesting rock formations in the canyon. The drive takes about one hour each way. Take Highway 180 east from Grant Grove.

The **Moro Rock–Crescent Meadow Road** is a 3-mi paved spur road that begins at Giant Forest Village and explores the southwest portion of the village's sequoia grove. Among the odd attractions on this road are the Auto Log and the Tunnel Log (*see* Historic Buildings and Sites, *below*). For excellent views of the Great Western Divide and the western half of Sequoia National Park, you will have to climb a steep quarter-mile staircase to the summit of Moro Rock. About 100 yards from the end of the road is Crescent Meadow, John Muir's "gem of the Sierra," where brilliant wildflowers bloom in midsummer. Many trails begin here, including the 1-mi route to Tharp's Log (*see* Historic Buildings and Sites, *below*) and the High Sierra Trail, which runs 71 mi to the summit of Mt. Whitney. This drive is not recommended for RVs or trailers. It is not a steep road, but it has many sharp curves and is closed in winter, when it is used as a ski trail. The road may also soon be closed to private cars in the summer; in this event, it will be serviced by a shuttle.

Generals Highway, which connects Grant Grove with Giant Forest and the foothills to the south, is a narrow, twisting road that runs past Stony Creek, the Lost Grove, Little Baldy, the General Sherman Tree, Amphitheater Point, and the Foothills Visitor Center. Under normal driving conditions it takes approximately two hours to complete the drive, but in summer this is the most heavily traveled road in the park and traffic can slow you down; also, construction on the road may slow (or temporarily halt) progress. Several trailheads lead off the Generals Highway, including the Congress Trail (*see* Nature Trails and Short Walks, *below*), the Trail for All People at Round Meadow, and the Hazelwood Nature Trail. Also on this road, 4.5 mi north of Giant Forest Village, is the Lodgepole Visitor Center, which has excellent exhibits and audiovisual programs describing the Sierra Nevada and the natural history of the area.

HISTORIC BUILDINGS AND SITES During the Roaring '20s, wealthy Santa Barbara businessman George Knapp commissioned extravagant fishing expeditions into Kings Canyon. To store quantities of gear he built a small cabin, which still stands. **Knapp's Cabin** is a short walk from a turnout about 2 mi east of the Cedar Grove Village turnoff.

You can drive your car onto the top of the **Auto Log,** a fallen giant sequoia that is about 1 mi from Giant Forest on the Moro Rock–Crescent Meadow Road, and you can actually drive through **Tunnel Log,** a giant fallen sequoia 2.75 mi from the Giant Forest Village on the same road. A bypass is available for larger vehicles.

A 2-mi trail that begins at Crescent Meadow in Giant Forest clearly marks the way to **Tharp's Log,** which is named for Hale Tharp, the first non–Native American resident in the sequoia forest. When Tharp ran cattle there in the 1860s, he built a cabin onto the end of this giant sequoia log, which was hollowed out by fire; the cabin still stands.

During the 1920s and 1930s Shorty Lovelace trapped in what is now the southern section of Kings Canyon National Park, later moving his operation into Sequoia National Forest. There he erected a series of **cabins** along his trapline, each a day's walk apart. Some of his weather-beaten cabins have been preserved, though none can be reached within a day's hike from the road. They sit far into the backcountry and are seen only by the occasional backpacker.

Even tall people can walk through the entire 100-ft length of the **Fallen Monarch,** a hollowed-out, fallen sequoia near the General Grant Tree. Early explorers, cattle ranchers, and Native Americans used the log for shelter, and soldiers who began patrolling the area during the late 1880s used it to stable their horses.

A walk up the General Grant Trail will lead you to the **Gamlin Cabin,** built by brothers Thomas and Israel Gamlin as a summer cabin in 1867. The brothers used it primarily for storage as they moved their cattle through the area or logged sugar pines; they operated in the area until the 1880s. The cabin, which is listed on the National Register of Historic Places, was returned to an area close to its original site in 1931 and was rehabilitated in 1981. The roof and lower timber are giant sequoia.

Built as a mill pond, **Hume Lake** supplied water for a flume that floated rough-cut sequoia lumber to the planing mill at Sanger, 54 mi below in the San Joaquin Valley. The lake is just outside the parks in Sequoia National Forest and is ideal for swimming, fishing, boating, and camping. Drive 8 mi north of Grant Grove on Highway 180, then 3 mi south on Hume Lake Road.

NATURE TRAILS AND SHORT WALKS Sequoia National Park. Two miles north of the Giant Forest Village is the 1,385-ton General Sherman Tree, the biggest of the big trees; those who take the time to read the text at the nearby sequoia slab will learn how these big trees depend on fire for their existence. The easy 2-mi **Congress Trail** is a largely paved loop that starts out near the General Sherman Tree and winds through the heart of the sequoia forest. In the one to two hours it takes to complete the loop you will pass groups of trees known as the House and Senate, and individual trees called the President and McKinley.

Crystal Cave (tel. 209/565–3758), a marble cavern with stalactites, cave pearls, and flowstone, is at least a 45-minute drive from Giant Forest Village; follow the twisting 7-mi road that leads west from Generals Highway just south of Giant Forest Village. Daily tours depart on the half hour, between mid-June and early September, from 11 to 4, and on the hour Friday through Monday during May and September (*see* Guided Tours, *above*). You must buy tickets ($5, $2.50 children 6–12, free children under 6) at the Lodgepole or Foothills visitor centers.

Kings Canyon National Park. One of the shortest trails in the parks is the one that leads to the **General Grant Tree,** the third-largest living tree in the world. President Calvin Coolidge designated the tree the Nation's Christmas Tree (not to be confused with the national Christmas tree, which appears on the Capitol mall each winter). President Eisenhower pronounced the tree a national shrine, making it the nation's only living memorial to American soldiers who have died while fighting for the United States in its wars. The trail is only .3 mi, but it passes the Gamlin Cabin and the Fallen Monarch (*see* Historic Buildings and Sites, *above*). Paved and fairly level, it begins 1 mi northwest of the Grant Grove Visitor Center.

While in Grant Grove take the time to walk out to **Panoramic Point,** which you can reach via a spur road that heads east through the visitor center parking lot, curves left around a meadow, then splits; bear right at the intersection, marked Panoramic Point, which is 2.3 mi farther along. (Trailers and RVs are not permitted on the steep and narrow road.) A .25-mi walk from the parking lot leads to a viewpoint from which you can see the High Sierra, from Mt. Goddard in northern Kings Canyon National Park to Eagle Scout Peak in Sequoia. Mt. Whitney can't be seen from the west side of the park because of the height of the Great Western Divide. The Park Ridge Trail, a 4-mi round-trip, begins here (*see* Longer Hikes, *below*).

LONGER HIKES Sequoia National Park. The moderate **Tokopah Falls Trail** follows the Marble Fork of the Kaweah River for 1.75 mi one way and dead-ends below the impressive granite cliffs and cascading waterfall of Tokopah Canyon. It will take you 2½ to four hours to make the 3.5-mi round-trip journey. The trail starts .25 mi north of Lodgepole Campground, 4.5 mi north of the Giant Forest Village, and passes through a lodgepole pine forest.

Little Baldy Trail climbs 700 vertical ft in 1.75 switchbacking miles and ends at a mountain summit with a great view of the peaks of the Mineral King area and the

Great Western Divide. The trail begins at Little Baldy Saddle, 11 mi north of the Giant Forest Village on the Generals Highway; the walk to the summit and back takes about four hours.

Kings Canyon National Park. The **Don Cecil Trail** climbs the cool north-facing slope of Kings Canyon, passing Sheep Creek Cascade and providing several good views of the canyon and the 11,000-ft Monarch Divide. The trail leads to Lookout Peak, which affords an incredible panorama of the park's backcountry. It is a strenuous, all-day hike of 13 mi (round-trip) that climbs 4,000 ft.

From the canyon floor at Cedar Grove take the **Hotel Creek Trail** up a series of switchbacks until it splits. Follow the route left through chaparral to the forested ridge and rocky outcrop known as Cedar Grove Overlook, from which you'll see Kings Canyon stretching below. This strenuous 5-mi round-trip hike gains 1,200 ft and takes three to four hours to complete. If you take the right fork of the Hotel Creek Trail, you will descend to the **Lewis Creek Trail,** about 1.25 mi past the overlook junction. Turn left onto this trail, which passes through a huge area that was burned in 1980. From the beginning of the Hotel Creek Trail to the end (really the trailhead) of the Lewis Creek Trail, you will cover 8 mi with a 1,200-ft elevation gain and loss; it will take about five hours to hike this route.

The sandy **Mist Falls Trail** follows the glaciated South Fork Canyon through forest and chaparral, past several rapids and cascades, to one of the largest waterfalls in the two parks. This 9-mi round-trip hike is relatively flat, but climbs 600 ft in the last mile. It takes four to five hours to complete. The trailhead is at Road's End, 5.5 mi east of the Cedar Grove Village turnoff.

Hikers may want to explore the area in Sequoia National Forest called **Converse Basin,** once the largest grove of sequoias in the world. Early in the century practically every mature tree in this area was cut down, and today it is still barren, with only a small amount of brush growing among the granite boulders. The Boole Tree was one of the few giants to be spared; one of the oldest-known giant sequoia, the Muir Snag, is also found here. It was more than 3,000 years old when it died. The basin is 6 mi north of Grant Grove; you can reach it via a graded dirt road off Highway 180. Maps of the area are available at visitor centers.

The **Park Ridge Trail** begins at the end of the road to Panoramic Point, in Grant Grove. It is a fairly flat 4-mi hike to the Park Ridge fire lookout and back. If you are lucky enough to make this hike on one of the few days when western views are not smoggy, you will be able to see the San Joaquin Valley. More likely, however, you'll see only the great peaks of Kings Canyon, to the east.

About 8 mi southeast of Grant Grove on Generals Highway, a turnoff west onto a bumpy dirt road dead-ends after about 2 mi, at Redwood Saddle. Here is the trailhead to **Redwood Canyon,** where a 10-mi trail leads through the world's largest grove of the world's largest trees. Take in the cascades, the quiet pools of Redwood Creek, and the mixed conifer forest on a short walk, day hike, or overnight backpacking trip.

OTHER ACTIVITIES No off-road driving is allowed in the parks. Boating, rafting, and snowmobiling are also prohibited.

Biking. Those who would rather travel by bicycle than by car may be disappointed in Sequoia and Kings Canyon. Bicycles are allowed only on the paved roads, and the steep highways have such narrow shoulders that cyclists should be extremely cautious.

Bird-Watching. Not seen in most parts of the United States, the white-headed woodpecker and the pileated woodpecker are common in most mid-elevation areas here. There are also many hawks and owls in these two parks, including the renowned spotted owl. Ranger-led bird-watching tours are held on a sporadic basis. Visitors should call the parks' information number (tel. 209/565–3341).

Fishing. There is a limited amount of trout fishing in the parks' creeks and rivers—primarily in the Kings and Kaweah rivers—from late April through mid-November. Those venturing into the backcountry on multiday trips will find some good fishing in some of the parks' secluded lakes. A California fishing license ($9.45 for one day, $26.50 for 10 days) is required for persons 16 and older; anglers should check state and park fishing regulations for special closures and restrictions. Licenses and fishing tackle are usually available in Lodgepole, Grant Grove, and Cedar Grove. Only Grant Grove is open year-round.

Horseback Riding. Four private operators run everything from one-hour jaunts to full-service, multiday pack trips into the backcountry. One-day destinations out of Cedar Grove include Mist Falls and Upper Bubb's Creek. In the backcountry, many equestrians head for Volcanic Lakes or Granite Basin, ascending trails that reach elevations of 10,000 ft. Costs per person range from $15 for a one-hour guided ride to $150 per day for fully guided trips on which the packers do all the cooking and camp chores, leaving the riders to spend their nonriding time as they please. Contact **Cedar Grove Pack Station** (Box 295, Three Rivers, CA 93271, tel. 209/565–3464), **Mineral King Pack Station** (Box 63, Sequoia National Park, CA 93262-0063, tel. 209/561–3030), or **Wolverton Pack Station** (same address as Mineral King Pack Station, tel. 209/565–3039).

Ski Touring. There are cross-country touring centers and marked trails at **Wolverton** (tel. 209/565–3435), in Giant Forest, and **Grant Grove** (tel. 209/335–2314). At the former, qualified instructors give two-hour group lessons that cost $18 per person (reservations are suggested); both areas have rentals for $16 per day. The centers operate daily from 9 to 5 between Thanksgiving and March, depending on snowfall. Primitive backcountry lodging costs $15 a night at the **Pear Lake Ski Hut.** The 7-mi trail to the hut is extremely difficult and should be attempted by expert skiers only. Pear Lake is open from mid-December to mid-April. Space is limited; call the Sierra Natural History Association (tel. 209/565–3759) well in advance to check on availability.

Sledding. The Wolverton area near Giant Forest and the Big Stump and Azalea areas in Grant Grove allow sleds, inner tubes, and platters.

Snowshoeing. There may be naturalist-guided snowshoe walks on weekends and holidays at Grant Grove and Giant Forest, as conditions permit (usually from mid-December to mid-March). Reservations are recommended and can be made through the visitor center (tel. 209/335–2856 for Grant Grove, 209/565–3763 for Giant Forest). Snowshoes are provided for a $1 donation. Otherwise, you can rent snowshoes at the Wolverton and Grant Grove ski touring centers for $11 per day. Snowshoers may stay at the Pear Lake Ski Hut (*see* Ski Touring, *above*); reservations are required.

Swimming. Due to swift currents, cold waters, and treacherous footing, the scenic, sometimes raging rivers in the area are not conducive to swimming or wading. **Lake Kaweah** (tel. 209/561–3155 or 209/597–2301), about 10 mi outside the park's southern entrance, is a lower elevation lake where boating, swimming, and fishing are prime. There are bathrooms and primitive campsites at the lake. Another option for swimming is **Hume Lake** (tel. 209/338–2251), which is in Sequoia National Forest, 8 mi north of Grant Grove on Highway 180, then 3 mi south on Hume Lake Road. You can also fish in Hume Lake, where boat and bike rentals are available.

CHILDREN'S PROGRAMS Look for kids' programs in June, July, and August at Grant Grove, Cedar Grove, and Lodgepole. Among the most popular is the Patch Program, where kids earn badges by participating in free ranger-led activities, including nature walks. Buy the $1 Junior Ranger booklet at any visitor center.

EVENING ACTIVITIES In summer, evening campfire lectures and slide shows are held at many of the parks' campgrounds. In winter, programs are held sporadically at the Grant Grove visitor center, with additional programs on some holidays. Program schedules are posted on bulletin boards around the park.

DINING

Each of the major areas within the park has only one restaurant, serving breakfast, lunch, and dinner. Most are simple, no-frills eateries where basic American meals—steak, hamburgers, pancakes, and eggs—are served at moderate prices. Health-conscious eaters will find an expanding, but still limited selection of foods, including salad bars, fruit platters, pastas, and fish (primarily salmon and halibut). All the restaurants within the parks are managed by **Sequoia/Kings Canyon Park Services** (Box 909, Kings Canyon National Park, CA 93633, tel. 209/335–5500, fax 209/335–5502), which also handles reservations. The Grant Grove restaurants are open year-round. Most restaurants are open from 7 AM to 9 PM in summer and from 7 AM to 7 PM in winter. Should the closure of Giant Forest Village go as planned, Beetle Rock and the Village Restaurant will be gone by 1999. All eateries within the parks accept MasterCard and Visa.

INSIDE THE PARKS **Cedar Grove Restaurant.** Patrons order their food at a counter and then carry it themselves to a table. The menu has recently expanded beyond hamburgers and hot dogs to include stir-fry and a terrific trout plate; eggs, bacon, and toast are still the norm for breakfast. *$–$$*

Giant Forest Village Restaurant. This buffet-style restaurant has a changing selection of hot entrées and a well-stocked salad bar. Open for breakfast, lunch, and dinner, it's a vital mid-Sequoia fuel-up point. The nearby **Fireside Pizza Pub,** in a historic knotty-pine building with a cozy stone fireplace, serves beer and wine in addition to pizza and calzones. *$*

Grant Grove Restaurant. To feed the whole family on a budget, fill up your plate and take a wooden seat at this all-you-can-eat buffet-style restaurant. American standards are served all day long: Feast on eggs, burgers, and steak. A full salad bar, fruit platters, and seasonal fish specials round out the selection. *$*

Lodgepole Delicatessen. For a quick bite any time of day, try this tiled deli for hot and cold sandwiches, hamburgers, and other short-order items. One favorite: the Sequoia Sub, made with several meats and cheeses on a choice of breads. Indoor and outdoor tables seat about 60. *$*

NEAR THE PARKS **White Horse Inn.** Easily the finest dining near either of the parks, the White Horse has a dimly lit dining room packed with antiques, a smattering of mirrors, and wedding pictures. The restaurant is known for its salads, which are prepared tableside. These can be ordered à la carte, but you'll get one automatically with the house special, a succulent prime rib served with baked potato. Other good choices are teriyaki chicken and duck à la Montmorency (half a roasted duck in a cherry wine sauce). For dessert, try the mousses and tarts. *42975 Sierra Dr., Three Rivers, tel. 209/561–4185. AE, D, MC, V. Closed Mon.–Tues., also Wed.–Thurs. in winter. No lunch. $$*

Noisy Water. Yet another family-style establishment, the Noisy Water is named for the Kaweah River, which flows within view of the restaurant's many windows. Try the eggs, pancakes, or French toast for breakfast, French-grilled sourdough burger at lunch, and the 16-ounce T-bone or 10-ounce lobster for dinner. Several menu selections are geared toward vegetarians and health-conscious diners. A glass-enclosed patio provides stunning views of the river. *41775 Sierra Dr., Three Rivers, tel. 209/561–4517. AE, MC, V. $–$$*

Cider Mill Cafe. Although the painted riverside landscape at this apple-themed restaurant doesn't quite make up for the obscured view, happy patrons seem so focused on their American and Mexican meals that they don't mind. Their menu ranges from taquitos to T-bone, and they've been making their own cider since 1928. You'll always find a few vegetarian offerings; one meatless favorite is *chilaquiles,* a Mexican mash with corn tortillas, enchilada sauce, various spices, and cheese. If you're still hungry for a vista, cross the street for free wine tastings on the patio at **Bullene Vineyards**; they also have picnic fixings and serve small sandwiches. *40311 Sierra Dr., Three Rivers, tel. 209/561–4157. No credit cards. $*

Clingan's Junction Restaurant. Not far from the entrance to Kings Canyon National Park, this place keeps the hungry happy. For breakfast you'll be treated to omelets or huge flapjacks with gobs of potatoes; at lunch try the grilled chicken-breast sandwich with jack cheese and mushrooms. A chicken-fried steak dinner might start with homemade soup and include fresh-baked breads and pies. Dieter's specials are available, and if you don't see what you want on the menu, just ask. *35591 E. Kings Canyon Hwy. (Hwy. 180), Clingan's Junction, tel. 209/338–2559. AE, MC, V. $*

PICNIC SPOTS The picnicking options in these two parks are unlimited. Numerous creeks and streams and countless stands of pine and sequoia provide thousands of peaceful, scenic places to take a midday meal. Food, beverages, and ready-made sandwiches and bag lunches can be purchased at any of the general stores in the park villages.

There are two designated picnic areas in Kings Canyon and five in Sequoia. All are spacious, with picnic tables, grills, and rest rooms. The **Columbine** area, shaded by pine trees, is in Kings Canyon's Grant Grove, roughly 1 mi north of the visitor center on the road to the Grant Tree. Less than a half mile inside the park entrance on Highway 180 is the **Big Stump** picnic area, which is more open than Columbine. Near Sequoia's Giant Forest, 2 mi north of the General Sherman Tree on the Generals

Highway and another 2 mi along the Wolverton Road, the **Wolverton** picnic area sits among white and red firs and pines. There is also a picnic area at **Halstead Meadow** on the Generals Highway. Near the parks' southern entrance above Highway 198, just before the road to the Buckeye Flat campground, is the **Hospital Rock** picnic area, which is in a foothills setting. You can also picnic on the lawn near the **Foothills Visitor Center.**

LODGING

A new concessionaire has made big strides in improving park accommodations, but there were many unresolved plans at press time. The Giant Forest motel is expected to be demolished by the end of 1998, though a new lodge may eventually replace it in a development just north of Lodgepole. An additional 30-room lodge is scheduled to be built by the end of 1998. All of the parks' lodges and cabins are open in summer months, but in winter only those in Grant Grove remain open. The room tax in California is 10%.

Lodging facilities within the parks are operated by Sequoia/Kings Canyon Park Services, an authorized concessionaire of the National Park Service. They also manage the Snowline and Stony Creek lodges, in Sequoia National Forest. Reservations should be made months in advance. All the park lodges accept MasterCard and Visa, and all have simple, inexpensive restaurants on the premises. *For information and reservations, contact Sequoia/Kings Canyon Park Services, Box 909, Kings Canyon National Park, CA 93633, tel. 209/335–5500, fax 209/335–5502.*

INSIDE THE PARKS Cedar Grove. At the bottom of Kings Canyon, in one of the prettiest areas of the parks, Cedar Grove is a good place for those who plan on staying a few days and doing a lot of day hiking. Although it's near a roaring river, the lodge manages to retain a quiet atmosphere. Those who don't want to camp will have to book a room well in advance. Each room is air-conditioned and carpeted and has a private shower and two queen-size beds. *Hwy. 180, Kings Canyon National Park. 18 rooms. Closed mid-Oct.–mid-May. $$$*

Stony Creek. Sitting at 6,800 ft among the peaceful pines, Stony Creek is on national forest land between Grant Grove and Giant Forest. Rooms are carpeted and have private showers. *Generals Hwy., Sequoia National Forest. 11 rooms. Closed early Sept.–late May. $$$*

Snowline Lodge. Step into the lobby of this bed-and-breakfast-like lodge, with its old-stone walls and log furniture, and you'll know you've stumbled onto something special. The small, country rooms share a patio overlooking the foothills. Book way in advance. *44138 E. Kings Canyon Rd., Hwy. 180. 8 rooms. $$–$$$*

Grant Grove. Scheduled to be built by the end of 1998, this will be the park's most luxurious accommodation, with modern, hotel-style rooms as well as carpeted cabins—some with private bath, others sharing a rest room and shower facility. All will have electricity and heaters, though the bathless cabins will also have wood-burning stoves. Rooms and cabins will be set back from the road amid a stand of wide pines, so that the place will feel secluded without being far from the thick of things. *Hwy. 180, Sequoia National Forest. 30 rooms. $–$$$*

NEAR THE PARKS The only nearby lodging outside the parks is in Three Rivers, where several motels charge from $45 to $70 per night. Reservations there can usually be made with little advance notice; call the Three Rivers Reservation Center (tel. 209/561–0410). Staying inside the parks' boundaries, however, will save driving time and give you a better feel for the area. As a last resort, you can get a room in either Visalia or Fresno, about an hour from the south and north entrances, respectively.

In Three Rivers the best choices are **Best Western** (40105 Sierra Dr., Three Rivers, CA 93271, tel. 209/561–4119); 54 rooms. Facilities: pool, spa, basketball court, playground. AE, D, DC, MC, V. $$–$$$; **Buckeye Tree Lodge** (46000 Sierra Dr., Three Rivers, CA 93271, tel. 209/561–5900); 12 rooms, all with river views. AE, D, DC, MC, V. $$; and **Lazy J Ranch** (39625 Sierra Dr., Three Rivers, CA 93271, tel. 209/561–4449 or 800/341–8000), recommended for families; 12 rooms and 6 cabins, some with kitchenettes. Facilities: pool, river access. AE, D, DC, MC, V. $$.

CAMPING

Campgrounds are by far the most economical accommodations in Sequoia and Kings Canyon National Parks, and they are probably the most fun. Located near each of the major tourist centers, the parks' 1,200-plus campsites are equipped with tables, fire grills, drinking water (except for South Fork), garbage cans, food lockers, and either flush or pit toilets. At press time, all campgrounds assigned sites on a first-come, first-served basis, though a new reservations system for Lodgepole and Dorst (both in Sequoia National Park) was expected to be in place by spring 1998. Beware: Campgrounds often fill up by Friday afternoon on weekends in July and August. Most campgrounds permit a maximum of one vehicle and six persons per site. Note: Campers must store food and other scented items in the provided food lockers, since bears have been a recurrent problem in the parks.

RVs are permitted in all areas except for the Buckeye Flat and South Fork campgrounds in the Foothills area and either of the Mineral King campgrounds. Sanitary disposal stations are available year-round in the Potwisha and Azalea areas (snow permitting); from Memorial Day to mid-October in Lodgepole; from Memorial Day to Labor Day in Dorst; and from May to mid-October in Sheep Creek. There are no hookups in the parks, and only a limited number of campsites can accommodate vehicles longer than 30 ft.

SEQUOIA AND KINGS CANYON CAMPGROUNDS

Campground	Total number of sites	Sites suitable for RVs	Number of hookups	Drive to sites	Hike to sites	Flush toilets	Pit/chemical toilets	Drinking water	Showers	Fire grates	Swimming	Boat access	Playground	Disposal station	Ranger station	Public telephone	Reservation possible	Daily fee per site	Dates open
INSIDE SEQUOIA																			
South Fork	13	0	0	•			•	•		•						•		$6**	year-round
Potwisha	44	44	0	•		•		•		•				•		•		$12	year-round
Buckeye Flat	28	0	0	•		•		•		•								$12	mid-Apr.–mid-Sept.
Lodgepole	250	149	0	•		•		•	•*	•				•***	•	•	•***	$14**	year-round
Dorst	218	200	0	•		•		•		•				•***			•***	$14	Memorial Day–Labor Day
Atwell Mill	21	0	0	•			•	•		•								$6	Memorial Day–mid-Nov.
Cold Springs	40	0	0	•			•	•		•					•	•		$6	Memorial Day–mid-Nov.
INSIDE KINGS CANYON																			
Azalea	114	88	0	•		•		•	•*	•				•***	•	•		$12	year-round
Sunset	119	154	0	•		•		•	•*	•					•	•		$12	Memorial Day–mid-Sept.
Crystal Springs	66	41	0	•		•		•	•*	•					•	•		$12	mid-May–late Sept.
Sentinel	83	83	0	•		•		•	•*	•				•***	•	•		$12	mid-May–mid-Oct.
Moraine	120	120	0	•		•		•	•*	•				•***		•		$12	mid-May–mid-Oct.
Sheep Creek	111	111	0	•		•		•	•*	•				•***		•		$12	mid-May–mid-Oct.
Canyon View	37	0	0		•	•		•	•*	•				•***		•		$12	mid-May–mid-Oct.

*Pay showers nearby. **Free in winter. ***Available summer only.

Lodgepole, Potwisha, Azalea, and South Fork campgrounds stay open all year. Other campgrounds open between mid-April and Memorial Day and close either after Labor Day or later in September or October. Campers should be aware that the nights, and even the days, can be chilly into early June, especially at higher elevations.

In the foothills area of Sequoia, the **South Fork Campground** (13 sites, pit toilets) tends to remain fairly quiet, largely because of its isolated location and its lack of drinking water. Sites cost $6 per night. **Potwisha** (44 sites, flush toilets, disposal station, public phone) and **Buckeye Flat** (28 sites, flush toilets) are at 2,100 ft and 2,800 ft, respectively. There are more families with children here than at South Fork. Both charge $12 per site, per night.

The two largest campgrounds in the parks (and the only ones that require reservations in summer) are north of Giant Forest Village: **Lodgepole** (250 sites, flush toilets, pay showers nearby, launderette, disposal station, ranger station, public phone) and **Dorst** (218 sites, flush toilets, disposal station, public phone). Sites cost $14 per night at both locations. Lodgepole is .25 mi from the visitor center, restaurants, and service station and is a 10-minute drive from Giant Forest. With so many campers, Lodgepole tends to be among the noisiest campgrounds in the parks, but even here the noise dies down at night.

Atwell Mill (21 sites, pit toilets, public phone) and **Cold Springs** (40 sites, pit toilets, ranger station, public phone), in the Mineral King area of Sequoia, are fairly isolated but still get heavy use. Both are for tent campers only and are favored by those making day hikes to the area's lakes, streams, and peaks. To get here you must travel on a steep, winding road not recommended for RVs. Nearby is Silver City, a private community where pay showers are available. Atwell Mill is at 6,650 ft in a second-growth sequoia forest. Cold Springs, at 7,500 ft elevation, is in a subalpine area. Sites at both campgrounds cost $6 per night.

The campgrounds in Grant Grove—**Azalea** (114 sites, flush toilets, disposal station, ranger station, public phone), **Sunset** (119 sites, flush toilets, public phone), and **Crystal Springs** (66 sites, flush toilets, public phone)—are similar to Lodgepole and Dorst, in that they are situated near the giant sequoias and close to restaurants, stores, and other facilities. Sites cost $12 at all of them. There are pay showers at the lodge, nearby. Although these campgrounds are smaller than Lodgepole and Dorst, they get almost as much traffic.

There are four additional campgrounds in the Cedar Grove area of Kings Canyon National Park—**Sentinel** (83 sites), **Moraine** (120 sites), **Sheep Creek** (111 sites), and **Canyon View** (37 sites). These are open summer only and cost $12 a night. Facilities include flush toilets, a public phone, pay showers, a market, coin laundry, a gas station, and a visitor center nearby. Rangers lead regularly scheduled interpretive walks and talks at these campgrounds.

Waterton/Glacier International Peace Park
Alberta/Montana

By Bud Journey

Glacier National Park embodies the essence of the Rocky Mountains. The massive peaks of the Continental Divide constitute its backbone, where ribbons of pure, clear streams, from melting snow and alpine glaciers, form the headwaters of the Columbia River to the west and the Mississippi to the east. Coniferous forests, rocky mountaintops, thickly vegetated stream bottoms, and green-carpeted meadows and basins provide homes and sustenance for all kinds of wildlife. Flora is profuse, and raw nature dominates.

The northern boundary of Glacier National Park coincides with the international border and with the southern boundary of Canada's Waterton Lakes National Park. Together, the two parks are called Waterton/Glacier International Peace Park.

Access by car is limited in both parks, but the few roads can take you through a range of settings—from densely forested lowlands to craggy heights. The Going-to-the-Sun Road, which snakes through the precipitous center of Glacier National Park, is one of the most dizzying rides on the North American continent. Navigating the narrow, curving highway, built from 1922 to 1932, you will understand why access to it is restricted. Vehicles more than 21 ft long and 8 ft wide (including mirrors) are not allowed to drive over Logan Pass—a restriction that is enforced at checkpoints at the east and west entrances.

Driving through Waterton/Glacier International Peace Park allows you to see much of both parks' spectacular scenery; and wildlife, both great and small, often appears along roads, especially in the early morning and late afternoon. The hiking routes through various sections of the parks present a chance to delve deep into the area's natural richness. At times, exploring Waterton/Glacier is like stepping into the past for a glimpse of what the frontier was like.

Most development and services in these two parks are concentrated around St. Mary Lake, on the east side of Glacier; Lake McDonald, on the west side of Glacier; and the town of Waterton at about the center of the Canadian park. There's development also at Many Glacier, in the northeastern part of Glacier; at Logan Pass Visitor Center, at the summit of Going-to-the-Sun Road on the Continental Divide; and at Apgar Village, at the foot of Lake McDonald.

The Peace Park has all kinds of accommodations, from tent camping to castlelike hotels, and food services from the most basic to gourmet. But the focus of a trip here remains the region's natural wonders, and the opportunities to see those wonders up close are many.

Waterton Lakes National Park was established in 1895; its main proponent was Frederick William Godsal. Glacier National Park was established on May 11, 1910, largely through the efforts of George Bird Grinnell, editor of *Forest and Stream* magazine. During the early years Glacier was essentially roadless, and a saddle-horse concession transported about 10,000 yearly visitors around the park on more than 1,000 horses. In 1932 the Going-to-the-Sun Road was completed, and motor vehicles took over as the primary mode of transportation in the park, giving today's 2 million-plus annual visitors a far easier passage. Through the efforts of the U.S. and Canadian Rotarians, the two parks joined to form the first International Peace Park in 1932.

ESSENTIAL INFORMATION

VISITOR INFORMATION Contact Glacier Park Headquarters, **Glacier National Park,** West Glacier, MT 59936, tel. 406/888–7800; or the Superintendent, **Waterton Lakes National Park,** Waterton Park, AB, Canada T0K 2M0, tel. 403/859–2224, fax 403/859–2650. The same information on Waterton is available through the **Waterton Chamber of Commerce and Visitors Association,** Box 55, Waterton Lakes National Park, AB, Canada T0K 2M0, tel. 403/859–2203.

Backcountry hikers who plan to stay overnight or have a campfire must obtain a backcountry use permit, available at park headquarters and all ranger stations and information centers within the parks. Permits are free in Glacier, but cost $5 per site per night per group in Waterton.

FEES A seven-day vehicle pass to Glacier costs $10. Those entering on foot, motorcycle, or bicycle pay $5 per day. A Glacier park pass, valid 12 months from the day of purchase, costs $20. A day pass for Waterton costs $4; a daily group fee (carload) is $8. Four-day permits in each of these categories cost double the one-day fee. Annual fees are $28; annual group fees are $50. A 10% discount is available if you purchase your permit before June 1. Note: All fees for Waterton are quoted in Canadian dollars.

PUBLICATIONS Park headquarters at both Waterton and Glacier have pamphlets and maps about the region, some of them free.

Probably the best device for familiarizing yourself with Waterton/Glacier International Peace Park is the newspaper *Waterton/Glacier Guide.* Produced jointly by the two parks, it contains articles on the many activities available in the parks, including special events, wildlife-interpretive programs, and religious services. It also makes suggestions for excursions, gives camping information, and issues warnings about park hazards. The newspaper is available at park entrances and visitor centers, and by mail from Park Headquarters (*see* Visitor Information, *above*).

Glacier Natural History Association (West Glacier, MT 59936, tel. 406/888–5756) publishes a free catalog of books, maps, and videos about the Glacier area, and **Waterton Natural History Association** (Box 145, Waterton Park, AB, Canada T0K 2M0, tel. 403/859–2624) does the same for Waterton. Both are recommended.

Free printed works distributed by the parks include: "Ski Trails of Glacier National Park," "Nature With a Naturalist," "Backcountry, Glacier National Park," "Glacier National Park," "Waterton/Glacier International Peace Park Map," "Waterton/Glacier Guide," "Fishing Regulations" (for both parks), "The Trees and Forests of Waterton Lakes National Park," "You Are in Bear Country," "Checklist of Birds Found in Waterton Lakes National Park," and "Waterton Lakes National Parks Visitors Guide."

These short publications may provide all the information you'll need prior to visiting the park, but for those who want more in-depth data, here is a list of some larger publications sold by the natural-history associations.

Geology Along Going-to-the-Sun Road: Glacier National Park—A Self-Guided Tour for Motorists, applicable to both parks; *Hiker's Guide to Glacier National Park; Short Hikes and Strolls in Glacier National Park; The Grizzlies of Glacier,* by Walter L. Hanna; *A Climber's Guide to Glacier National Park,* by Gordon J. Edwards; *Glacier—The Story Behind the Scenery,* by Kathleen E. Ahlenslager; *The Story of the Highway Across Glacier National Park: Going-to-the-Sun Road,* by Rose Houk; *Waterton and Northern Glacier Trails,* by

Charles Russell, Beth Russell, Valerie Haig-Brown, and John Russell, an excellent description of hiking routes in Waterton, updated in 1991; *Montana's Continental Divide,* by Bill Cunningham, Montana Geographic Series No. 12, published by *Montana Magazine,* Inc.; and *Waterton Lakes National Park,* by Heather Pringle, a sightseeing-tour guide with trail descriptions, history, and background on flora and fauna.

GEOLOGY AND TERRAIN The Continental Divide cuts through Waterton/Glacier from north to south, forming the western boundary of Waterton. Glacier's western boundary is marked by the meandering, clear waters of the North Fork of the Flathead River, and to the north and east only a brief transition of rolling hills separates the high Rockies from the expansive Great Plains. In Waterton that transition does not exist; the change is sudden and dramatic, giving the park its claim to fame as the place where "the mountains meet the prairie." To the south of Glacier lies the vast 1½-million-acre Bob Marshall Wilderness Area and to the northwest of both parks the Rockies continue to Canada's Banff and Jasper national parks.

Glacier is the fourth-largest national park in the contiguous 48 states, with more than 1,600 square mi. It's about 40 mi wide at the international boundary and about 53 mi long from north to south. The highest point, just south of the international boundary in the northeast part of the park, is 10,448-ft Mt. Cleveland. The lowest point is at the confluence of the North and Middle forks of the Flathead River, at an elevation of 3,150 ft along the western border of the park.

Glacier's partner to the north, Waterton, contains about 202 square mi; it is about 23 mi wide and 14 mi long. The highest point is 9,600-ft Mt. Blakiston, in the northwestern part of the park, and the lowest point, at an elevation of 4,050 ft, is at Waterton River, which runs south to north through the park.

Glacier National Park has 50 glaciers, 200 lakes, and 1,000 mi of streams where native trout thrive. Lake McDonald, near the west entrance to the park, is the largest lake in the park, at 10 mi long and 1 mi wide. St. Mary Lake, near the east entrance, is slightly smaller. Other sizable lakes include Kintla, Bowman, Quartz, and Logging along the west slope of the park and Two Medicine, Sherburne, Glenns, and Cosley along the east slope.

Upper Waterton Lake is the largest lake in Waterton Lakes park, nearly 7 mi long and 1 mi wide. It's also the deepest lake in the Canadian Rockies and once yielded a huge 51-pound, 12-ounce lake trout to an angler from nearby Lethbridge. The other large lakes in the park include Middle and Lower Waterton lakes to the north and east of Upper Waterton and Cameron Lake in the extreme southwestern corner. Rivers and streams also abound in the park.

FLORA AND FAUNA With the park's great differences in elevation comes a wide variety of plant species. Among the trees, conifers are most prevalent, with 15 species at various elevations: western white pine, lodgepole pine, whitebark pine, ponderosa pine, western larch, subalpine larch, Engelmann spruce, subalpine fir, grand fir, Douglas fir, western red cedar, Pacific yew, western hemlock, Rocky Mountain juniper, and common juniper.

Lodgepole pine grows in old burns at all elevations. Cedar, yew, and hemlock form dense thickets in low, dark, wet areas on the western side of the Continental Divide. Western white pine and ponderosa pine are also found only on the west side of the divide; they are low- to mid-elevation trees that can grow to great sizes, often with no branches for the first 20 to 30 ft. Mature ponderosa, found only in the North Fork area of Glacier, often have a yellowish-brown tinge and are sometimes called yellow pine. One of the most interesting trees is the larch, the only deciduous conifer; its needles turn golden in the fall before falling off. The whitebark pine is an often stunted tree that grows at high elevations, usually on the dry, east side of the divide.

At least 10 broadleaf species are also present in the park, most found at lower elevations. They are black cottonwood, quaking aspen (so named for the trembling of its leaves in the breeze), willow, paper birch, chokecherry, pin cherry, black hawthorn, alder, and maple.

From early spring to late summer, Waterton/Glacier is covered with more than 1,000 species of flowers, including glacier lilies, pale-blue forget-me-nots, false dandelions, red paintbrush, and red-purple fireweed. At times, whole basins are virtually ablaze. One of the most unusual wildflowers is beargrass, which is not grass and is not eaten by bears. Beargrass is actually a variety of lily with tough grasslike leaves that were sometimes used by Native Americans for weaving baskets. It is also called squaw grass.

Despite the breadth of plant life in the parks, animals often steal the show. Among the animals, none draws more attention than the bear. Waterton/Glacier has many black bears, and it's one of the few parks with a substantial number of grizzlies. Backcountry hikers should be out only during the day, and they should make lots of noise as they walk through bear country by singing loudly, carrying on a loud conversation, or performing some other noisy activity that will warn away bears. People who camp in the backcountry must wash their utensils after every meal and hang their food in a tree, well away from sleeping areas. Campers who use drive-in campgrounds must store their food in a closed, hard-side vehicle. Never approach a bear, no matter how cute, cuddly, and harmless it may appear.

Park officials warn visitors not to feed any of the park wildlife. Feeding animals is not only a hazard to humans, who may become the victims of aggressive animals that have lost their fear of people, but also a hazard to the animals, bears especially: When it becomes necessary to keep wildlife away from humans, rangers must either move the animal, in which case it may be injured, or

kill it. The animals here are sometimes visible and approachable, but they are best observed from a distance.

Bears are not the only animals in the park. Another high-profile animal that is making a comeback in Waterton/Glacier is the gray wolf. Wolves were almost totally absent from the U.S. side of the border for about 50 years. Then, in the early 1980s, a female wolf linked up with a male along the international boundary. These two animals produced a litter that researchers dubbed the Magic Pack because of their ability to disappear and reappear. From that original pack, several others have formed, denning in Glacier National Park. Wolf numbers have sporadically increased in recent years, and one pack has ranged as far south as Dixon, only 40 mi northwest of Missoula, Montana.

Mountain goats are also found in generous numbers in Glacier National Park and can often be seen along the Going-to-the-Sun Road and Highway 2 at the park's southern boundary. At the Goat Lick (a natural exposure of mineral salts) at the extreme southern tip of Glacier, you can almost always see goats and other wildlife.

Bighorn sheep and mule deer are usually present in and around the town of Waterton. Elk are a common sight on the prairie in fall, winter, and spring, but they are rarely seen in or near town. White-tailed deer, moose, and coyotes are also found in the parks. Other large animals that live in the park are bobcats, lynx, mountain lions, foxes, and wolverines. Smaller animals include ground squirrels, pikas, snowshoe hares, porcupines, martens, beavers, marmots, and chipmunks.

At least 250 species of birds, including songbirds and raptors, live in both parks. Bald eagles and osprey are among the raptors. Franklin, ruffed, and blue grouse have also been spotted here, as have Canadian jays and kingfishers. The parks are well known for the large numbers of migratory waterfowl on lakes and rivers in autumn.

Among the fish inhabiting the park's waters are burbot (ling), northern pike, whitefish, kokanee salmon, grayling, sculpin, and a few varieties of trout, including cutthroat, brook, rainbow, and lake. All except sculpin are considered sport fish and can be caught with angling equipment.

Ticks and mosquitoes are rampant here. Ticks are most common in spring, and although Lyme disease has not been reported in the immediate area, it's always a good idea to check for them after walking through shrubs and high grasses. Mosquitoes, on the other hand, can be quite a nuisance. The mosquito problem is worse in early and midsummer than it is in late summer and early fall. To get away from them, stay away from dark, damp places, where they tend to congregate. If you have a choice of campsites, try to pick one in a dry, open spot, where a breeze may blow the mosquitoes away. A good insect repellent will help.

WHEN TO GO Snow removal on the Going-to-the-Sun Road is usually completed by mid-June. That event opens Glacier National Park to summer activities, and by July 1 all naturalist programs are operating. Canada's Victoria Day, celebrated with a long weekend in late May, marks the beginning of summer activities in Waterton. Most people prefer traveling to this part of the country in summer, when the snow has receded substantially. The wildflower displays begin on the prairie in spring, and by early summer (late June and July) flowers bloom throughout the parks. You'll catch the highest alpine blooms in late summer and autumn.

Summer is the time that wildlife redistributes itself throughout the parks after spending the long winter in dens and lowland winter ranges. It's when a profusion of flora covers the landscape with new grasses, flowers, and budding trees. The moisture that's been trapped in snowfields and glaciers is released into lakes by ribbons of water splashing down rocky mountainsides, accentuating the rugged scenery.

More and more people, however, are taking advantage of the parks in winter. Some facilities remain open throughout the cold season, serving those who come for the skiing and other cold-weather recreational opportunities.

Temperatures can reach into the 90s in the summer and dip as low as -40°F in the winter (primarily east of the Continental Divide). But if there is one constant, it is that the weather is unpredictable: It can vary considerably, even within a single day. In Waterton, another weather constant is the wind, which is often fierce.

The weather is usually most consistent in early September, and since by then the crowds have substantially decreased, this is a favored month to visit Waterton/Glacier.

SEASONAL EVENTS **Late April to early May:** One of the biggest events of the year at Glacier is Show Me Day, when you get a chance to watch the plowing of the Going-to-the-Sun Road. Spectators park downhill from the work site, then are shuttled up the hill to a spot across the canyon from the plowing. From there, you can watch road crews plow tons of packed snow from the mountaintop road, creating man-made avalanches in the process. Park-service employees provide spotting scopes and disperse information to the people watching the show. Unfortunately, this event is governed by so many uncontrollable variables in the weather that it doesn't come off every year. **July 1 (Canadian Independence Day) to July 4:** The Days of Peace and Friendship focus on the International Peace Park theme, and are acknowledged by both parks each year with special programs. **August:** The annual **Beargrass Festival** (tel. 403/859–2042) in Waterton is sponsored by the Waterton Community Association, in the town of Waterton. The event may include Native American dancers, a storytelling contest, a fiddling competition, cowboy poetry, a golf tournament, and a chili cook-off.

Every summer the Waterton Natural History Association (tel. 403/859–2624) (*see*

Publications, *above*) sponsors the **Heritage Education Program,** in which qualified instructors teach courses on archaeology, bears, flora, birds, and other related topics. Photography workshops are another option. Prices range from $25 to $100 per course. The number of participants is limited. Park personnel also conduct natural history programs.

WHAT TO PACK Bring clothes for all kinds of weather. In summer you may find yourself in shorts and a T-shirt one day and heavily insulated foul-weather gear the next. Layered clothing is a good idea, as is sound footwear suitable for walking over wet, uneven terrain. Rain gear is also a must, as thunderstorms can develop at any time. Don't forget to bring insect repellent.

GENERAL STORES In Glacier and Waterton, general stores are small and have limited inventories. Most sell fishing and camping supplies as well as food and drink.

For information on Glacier's camp stores, contact the concessionaire **Glacier Park, Inc.** (VIAD Corporate Center, Phoenix, AZ 85077, tel. 602/207–6000, fax 602/207–5589). Its small stores are in several commercial areas of Glacier, such as Apgar Village, Lake McDonald, Rising Sun, Swiftcurrent, and Two Medicine.

There are also stores just outside the park at West Glacier, East Glacier, and St. Mary.

The best place to pick up food supplies in Waterton is the **Rocky Mountain Food Mart** (tel. 403/859–2526, fax 403/859–2665), which is open daily from 8 AM to 10 PM in July and August, with hours varying in other months. Camping equipment is sold at **Waterton Sports and Leisure** (tel. 403/859–2378).

ARRIVING AND DEPARTING Glacier National Park is in northern Montana, just off the northernmost federal highway, U.S. 2. It has an east entrance and a west entrance, but your entry point probably will depend on the direction in which you're traveling; there is no particular advantage to entering at either place. Provincial Roads 5 and 6

enter Canada's Waterton Lakes National Park, in Alberta.

You can reach Glacier National Park by plane and train, but you'll want to rent a car or take the shuttle service to see the Going-to-the-Sun Road.

Waterton/Glacier is 230 mi south of Banff and 350 mi south of Jasper. Yellowstone lies about 400 mi south.

By Car and RV. U.S. 2 skirts the south end of the park, and the west entrance is directly off this highway at West Glacier. The east entrance is just off U.S. 89 at St. Mary. U.S. 89 connects with U.S. 2 at Browning, about 30 mi south of St. Mary.

U.S. 2, the northernmost federal highway, is a two-lane road that runs across northern Montana. If you're coming from the south on I–90, the best roads to take to U.S. 2 are U.S. 15, beginning near Butte, Montana, and U.S. 93, starting 9 mi west of Missoula. U.S. 2 is an uncrowded road that gives you a glimpse of rural Montana, including plenty of wildlife.

Waterton is approachable from the east by Provincial Road 5 and from the north by Provincial Road 6. These roads come together on the north end of the park, and Provincial 5 leads to the interior. The best approach to Waterton from the United States is U.S. 89 to State/Provincial 17, known as the Chief Mountain International Highway. This road closes when the customs station closes, from mid-September to mid-May. When it is closed, take U.S. 89 north to the border, where the customs station remains open. The road becomes Provincial Road 2 and runs north to Cardston, where you can pick up Provincial Road 5 west to the park.

By Plane. Glacier Park International Airport (tel. 406/257–5994, fax 406/257–5960), about 30 mi southwest of the park, between Kalispell and Whitefish, serves Glacier Park. **Delta** (tel. 800/221–1212), **Northwest** (tel. 800/225–2525), and **Horizon** (tel. 800/547–9308) run daily flights to and from the airport. Rental cars are available at the airport through **Hertz** (tel. 406/758–2220 or 800/654–3131), **National** (tel. 406/257–7144 or 800/328–4567), **Avis** (tel. 406/257–2727 or 800/331–1212), and **Budget** (tel. 406/755–7500 or 800/527–0700).

Flathead/Glacier Transportation Company (tel. 406/892–3390) runs eight-passenger vans from the airport to the park. To get to West Glacier, just outside the west entrance of the park, the rate is $32 for the first passenger and $2 for each additional passenger. To the town of East Glacier Park (commonly called just East Glacier), on the southeast side of the park, it's $100 for the first passenger and $2 for each additional person. To Many Glacier, a developed area on the northeast side of the park, the fare is $160 plus $2 for each additional rider.

Flathead Area Custom Transportation (tel. 406/752–4022 or 800/872–8294) runs small transit buses that hold up to 14 passengers from the airport to points in the park. The rate for one to three people from the airport to West Glacier is $32, to East Glacier is $125, and to Many Glacier is $150. Each additional passenger pays only $2.

The nearest commercial Canadian airport is at **Lethbridge** (tel. 403/382–3165), about 70 mi northeast of Waterton (about a 1½-hour drive). It is served by **Canadian Regional** (tel. 800/426–7000), a subsidiary of Canadian Airlines, and **B.C. Air** (tel. 800/776–3000).

By Shuttle. Glacier Park, Inc. (VIAD Corporate Center, Phoenix, AZ 85077-0928, tel. 406/226–9311, fax 406/226–9221) operates a shuttle service along the Going-to-the-Sun Road from July 1 through September. Buses make stops at major trailheads, campgrounds, and other developed areas between Lake McDonald Lodge and Rising Sun Motor Inn, with two buses making the circuit constantly during the day. Rates vary according to the length of the ride.

By Train. Amtrak (tel. 800/872–7245) stops at West Glacier regularly and at East Glacier during busy seasons. There is no train to Waterton.

EXPLORING

You can explore Waterton/Glacier by touring in a car or RV or by boating, horseback riding, or walking. Those who prefer an urban setting might choose to view the scenery and observe the wildlife while playing the Waterton golf course or walking the streets of Waterton. Just about everyone will want to head out on a car, shuttle, or bus tour of the precipitous Going-to-the-Sun Road, but those with more time and a bent for adventure might try a more vigorous activity such as exploring on horseback or on foot.

THE BEST IN ONE DAY It's hard to beat the Going-to-the-Sun Road for a one-day trip in Glacier National Park (*see* Scenic Drives and Views, *below*). Although the road passes through only a fraction of the park, it does travel from the lowest elevations to the summit of the Continental Divide. Many species of flora and fauna appear along the road, and numerous turnoffs scattered along the way provide stops for viewing, resting, or photographing the scenery. The trip is short enough to allow brief excursions on some of the many trails, along with a visit to the Logan Pass Visitor Center, about halfway through the park at the highest point of the road.

The Going-to-the-Sun Road is a narrow, winding route flanked by precipitous mountainsides. Those who feel uneasy about driving on such a road can take a tour in a charming, old-fashioned tour bus with a removable top. These tours are run by Glacier Park, Inc. (*see* Guided Tours, *below*), the same people who run the lodging and food services in Glacier. Another option is the shuttle operated by Glacier Park, Inc. (*see* Arriving and Departing, *above*).

Waterton is a much smaller park than Glacier, so a one-day excursion allows time for more than one driving route. The Chief Mountain International Highway is the longest road, and from it you will see the Rocky Mountain Front, the area where the mountains meet the prairie. The Akamina

Parkway goes to Cameron Lake, at the base of the Continental Divide, just below the ridge where Alberta, British Columbia, and Montana meet. The Red Rock Parkway takes you from the prairie up a major valley to Red Rock Canyon, where water has cut through the earth, exposing red sedimentary rock. Wildlife viewing is also a highlight on this drive. You can easily cover all three routes in a single day. There are numerous picnic areas, pullouts, and exhibits along these roads and at Cameron Lake and Red Rock Canyon, which both serve as major trailheads for short and long hikes.

ORIENTATION PROGRAMS In Glacier National Park, the visitor centers at Apgar, Logan Pass, and St. Mary all have displays describing the park's geology and history, as well as brochures with suggested hiking routes. The only Waterton National Park visitor center is just across the street from the turnoff to the Prince of Wales Hotel, at the entrance to the townsite. Here you'll find books about the park, as well as brochures and hiking maps.

GUIDED TOURS A bus tour of Going-to-the-Sun Road can be exciting, and a cruise on Waterton Lake, St. Mary Lake, Lake McDonald, Two Medicine Lake, or Many Glacier can give you a close-up look at the great natural attributes of the Peace Park.

Glacier Park, Inc. (VIAD Corporate Center, Phoenix, AZ 85077-0928, tel. 602/207–6000) conducts guided tours in vintage 1936 Red Buses, with roll-back tops. These driver-narrated tours cover just about every part of Glacier National Park accessible by road. The costs range from $8 for short trips to $60 for full-day circle tours. Babies who don't occupy a seat ride free.

An international guided boat tour starts in the town of Waterton and cruises Upper Waterton Lake across the border into Goat Haunt, Montana. It's run by **Waterton Inter-Nation Shoreline Cruises** (Box 126, Waterton, AB, Canada T0K 2M0, tel. 403/859–2362, fax 403/938–5019); the narrated tour costs $18.

Glacier Park Boat Company (Box 5262, Kalispell, MT 59903, tel. 406/257–2426) runs summer cruises on Lake McDonald and Many Glacier, Two Medicine, and St. Mary lakes. Cruises last from 45 minutes to 1½ hours. Naturalist hikes are available with the boat rides. Rates range from $7.50 to $9.50. Small-boat rentals are also available: Nonmotorized boats cost $6 per hour or $30 per 10-hour day; small motorboats cost $12 per hour or $60 per day. Larger motorboats cost a little more. You can rent a canoe for $6.50 an hour.

SCENIC DRIVES AND VIEWS Entering Glacier National Park at the west entrance, you come to a stop sign about a mile inside the park. If you turn left, you will reach Apgar Village, on the southwest end of Lake McDonald. Apgar is a tiny community that's the hub of activity for the west side of the park. It has lodging, food, gift shops, a campground, a picnic area, rest rooms, swimming, boating, and a visitor center. Just about a mile north of the village, make a right onto the 43-mi **North Fork Road**, which follows the west boundary of the park and parallels the North Fork of the Flathead River. This winding dirt road runs through an area that is among the lowest in elevation in the park. It consists of river-bottom terrain and is marked by lodgepole-pine flats. Glimpses of the Whitefish Range appear to the west. The road continues north to Bowman Creek, where a spur road leads to Bowman Lake, then it continues on to Kintla Lake, where it dead-ends. Both Bowman and Kintla lakes have campgrounds and good trout fishing. Allow six hours for the round-trip drive to Kintla Lake.

Back at the stop sign just inside the west entrance, turn right to get on the **Going-to-the-Sun Road**—probably the biggest single attraction in Glacier National Park. This road travels along the southeastern side of Lake McDonald, past the Lake McDonald Lodge, where you need a room reservation about six months in advance. The Lake McDonald Coffee Shop and the lodge dining room, however, are fine places to stop

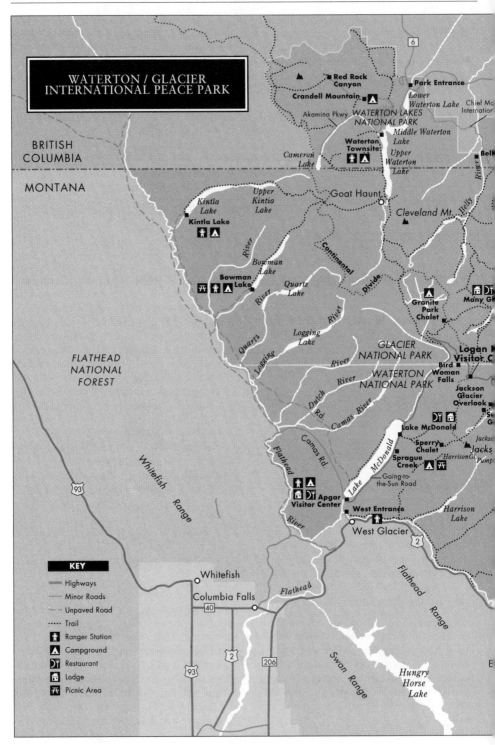

WATERTON / GLACIER
INTERNATIONAL PEACE PARK

Red Rock
Canyon

Crandell Mountain

Park Entrance

Lower
Waterton Lake

Chief Mo
Internatior

Akamina Pkwy.

WATERTON LAKES
NATIONAL PARK

Middle Waterton
Lake

Waterton
Townsite

Upper
Waterton
Lake

Bel

River

BRITISH
COLUMBIA

Cameron
Lake

MONTANA

Goat Haunt

Cleveland Mt.

Belly

Kintla
Lake

Upper
Kintla
Lake

Kintla Lake

Continental

River

Bowman
Lake

Quartz
Lake

Divide

Granite
Park
Chalet

Many Gl

Bowman
Lake

River

River

FLATHEAD
NATIONAL
FOREST

Quartz

Logging
Lake

River

GLACIER
NATIONAL PARK

WATERTON
NATIONAL PARK

Bird
Woman
Falls

Logan
Visitor C

Logging

River

Jackson
Glacier
Overlook

Dutch

Rd.

Camas River

S
G

Camas Rd.

Lake McDonald

Sperry
Chalet

Jacks

Flathead

Sprague
Creek

Harrison Gl

Jacks
Pump

93

Whitefish Range

Camas Rd.

Lake McDonald

Going-to-
the-Sun Road

Apgar
Visitor Center

West Entrance

Harrison
Lake

River

West Glacier

2

KEY

Highways

Minor Roads

Unpaved Road

Trail

Ranger Station

Campground

Restaurant

Lodge

Picnic Area

Whitefish

Columbia Falls

Flathead

Flathead Range

40

2

206

93

Swan Range

Hungry
Horse
Lake

E

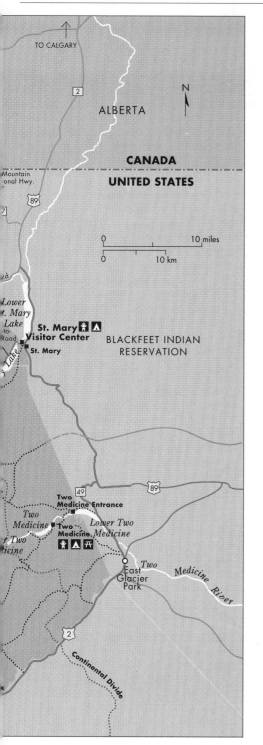

for breakfast or lunch. (If you're not in a hurry, rent a small boat or canoe here or take a guided cruise on the lake.)

As you leave Lake McDonald behind and begin the long, winding climb to Logan Pass, stop to visit McDonald Falls, which can be reached via a short trail on the left side of the road. In this same area you can see the treeless avalanche chutes on the mountainsides, where bears are often visible, especially during late spring.

At the first big switchback on Going-to-the-Sun Road, you can park your car and make the 4-mi climb on foot to the Granite Park Chalet. The chalet has recently reopened after repairs, with bunks and a communal stove. Hikers must bring their own food and bedding.

When you resume your trip to the summit, you'll find ample turnoffs where you can stop to enjoy the colors and shapes of the high country. You'll probably want to photograph Bird Woman Falls across the canyon.

At the Logan Pass summit, stop at the Logan Pass Visitor Center to listen to a talk about the alpine environment, pick up a book on the local flora and fauna, or enjoy the exhibits. Then take a short hike along the Highline Trail for a look at the scenery. Have a friend take your picture as you follow this trail, which has been cut out of a sheer cliff. At Logan Pass, you can also choose an alternate 3-mi round-trip hike to Hidden Lake Overlook.

The trip down the east side of the Continental Divide is shorter than the drive up the west side. The terrain here, where the road was carved out of the mountain, is slightly more friendly than the terrain on the west side of the divide, where the road was blasted out of solid rock.

Among the attractions on this stretch of Going-to-the-Sun Road is the East Side Tunnel, just over the hump from Logan Pass. The tunnel cuts through a rock point, and the road passes by the imposing 9,642-ft Going-to-the-Sun Mountain, before descending to St. Mary Lake. Along the way, flowers color the grassy basins, with beargrass dominating from mid- to late summer.

Just as the Going-to-the-Sun Road descends into the trees, you will pass Jackson Glacier looming in a rocky pass across the canyon. According to a roadside marker, the glacier is shrinking and may disappear in another 200 years.

Traveling another 2 mi down the road, you will see Virginia Falls, which empties into St. Mary Falls, which in turn runs into the upper end of St. Mary Lake. It's a fairly short walk from the road to the falls. Drive another .75 mi, where a 25-yard walk will take you up to Sunrift Gorge.

At Rising Sun, on St. Mary Lake, you may choose to take advantage of the first rest room since the summit, stop for something to eat at the coffee shop, or take a boat tour. The St. Mary Visitor Center is just up the road. If you're tired, you can stay overnight at the Rising Sun campground or, if you've made reservations, at St. Mary Lodge Motel (*see* Lodging, *below*). It will take you about two hours to drive back to the west entrance.

The best time to drive the Going-to-the-Sun Road is the last two or three hours before dark; that's when the lighting is best for photos, the wildlife is most likely to appear, and the crowds have left the road.

The **Many Glacier Road** enters the northeast side of the park, west of Babb, Montana, and travels along Sherburne Lake for almost 5 mi, penetrating a glacially carved valley surrounded by mountains. As the road moves toward the mountains, it passes through a scrubby forest of lodgepole pines, aspen, and cottonwood, with meadows that are covered with grass and flowers during summer. (The road is often closed by snow during winter, usually from October to May.) The farther you travel up the valley, the more clearly you'll be able to see Grinnell and Salamander glaciers. Formed only about 4,000 years ago, these two glaciers were one ice mass until 1926, and they continue to shrink.

After driving 12 mi you will arrive at Swiftcurrent, the end of the road. Here you can camp, fish, ride horseback, hike, take a boat cruise, or stop for a meal at the coffee shop. If you camp or stay at the motel, you can attend the rangers' campfire talks. Swiftcurrent is also the starting point for a number of long and short hikes, including one to Grinnel Glacier. The high basin on the north side of the valley, visible from the Swiftcurrent parking lot, is a good place to spot bears, mountain goats, and sheep.

The **Chief Mountain International Highway** leads northwestward from the U.S. side of the international boundary toward the town of Waterton. It starts in the rolling hills at the edge of the prairie and climbs through open fields and patches of cottonwood and aspen trees. As the road climbs, the surrounding forest thickens, and deciduous trees begin to give way to mixed conifers, mostly lodgepole pine and spruce. The road then passes through the extreme northeastern corner of Glacier before entering Canada's Waterton Lakes National Park, heading down toward Waterton Lakes, and passing through a similar succession of vegetation in reverse. (The road closes in the fall, when the customs station closes, and reopens in late spring.) The Lewis Overthrust becomes visible on the left, and a roadside marker tells you that you're looking at 1.6-billion-year-old rock that has been thrust over 100-million-year-old rock by movement in the earth's crust. (If you have a good pair of binoculars, you might spot grizzly bears, mountain goats, or other wildlife on the grassy, parklike hills of the Lewis Overthrust.) On the final descent into the valley, Waterton unfolds before you in one of the most comprehensive views of the park. This road is 22 mi long and takes about an hour to drive one way.

NATURE TRAILS AND SHORT WALKS In Glacier, one of the most popular hiking areas is **Logan Pass,** at the summit of the Going-to-the-Sun Road on the Continental Divide. The easy 1.5-mi one-way self-guided Hidden Lake Nature Trail runs southwest from Logan Pass Visitor Center to Hidden Lake

Overlook, from which you can see the lake and McDonald Valley.

Trail of the Cedars, a .5-mi boardwalk loop trail through an ancient cedar-and-hemlock forest, starts a few miles northeast of Lake McDonald on the Going-to-the-Sun Road. At the end of the trail, there's a view of Avalanche Gorge. It's a favorite of families with small children, senior citizens, and people with disabilities.

The **Bear's Hump Trail** is a .75-mi trail that starts at the Waterton Information Centre. It is a fairly steep climb, but from it you get a great view of the town, the chain of Waterton Lakes, and surrounding mountains.

LONGER HIKES The **Highline Trail** goes north from the Logan Pass Visitor Center to the Granite Park Chalet and beyond, starting out in spectacular fashion. Cut out of a sheer rock cliff, it winds along for 7.5 mi and overlooks a vast portion of the southwest side of the park.

Many Glacier Hotel is the starting point for several trails running south, west, and north. A day hike can take you within viewing distance of glaciated canyons, steep mountains, and profuse flora, as well as a variety of wildlife. This can also be the starting point for overnight hiking to the interior of the park.

Two Medicine is the access point for hiking the southeastern part of Glacier. From there, you can get to Appistoki Falls, Paradise Point, and Rockwell Falls, as well as backcountry sites in the southern part of the park.

Backcountry lakes that can be accessed by trails from the North Fork Road on the west side of Glacier National Park include Logging (about 8 mi round-trip), Quartz (about 15 mi), Rogers (10 mi), and Trout (12 mi) lakes. On the northeast side of the park, trails provide the only access to Cosley (15 mi), Glenns (18 mi), Helen (25 mi), and Elizabeth (16 mi) lakes.

The **Lakeshore Trail** begins at the Waterton Townsite and parallels the west side of Upper Waterton Lake, passing Boundary Bay and the international boundary before reaching Goat Haunt in Glacier National Park. It's about 3.5 mi one way to Boundary Bay and about 8.5 mi one way to Goat Haunt, where you may see goats grazing. A Canadian park interpreter and a U.S. ranger lead the International Peace Park Hike along this trail on Saturdays during July and August.

The **Snowshoe** and **Blakiston Valley** trails, which skirt the north and south sides of Anderson Mountain in the northwest part of Waterton, play host to an abundance of wildflowers and wildlife. These trails are major access routes for several backcountry destinations. The two trails form a 15-mi loop around the mountain, starting from the Red Rock Canyon Trailhead, at the end of the Red Rock Parkway.

OTHER ACTIVITIES **Biking.** Pedaling is as good a way as any to see both parks. Cyclists in Glacier National Park should stay on the main roads, but even they tend to be narrow and steep. Many Glacier Road and the roads around Lake McDonald have mild slopes and are not difficult to bike. The Two Medicine Road is an intermediate route, with a mild grade at the beginning, becoming steeper as you approach Two Medicine. Restrictions apply during peak traffic periods. Going-to-the-Sun Road is closed to bikes from 11 to 4. Mountain biking is not allowed on park trails.

Waterton National Park allows bikes on some designated trails: Check with park headquarters for updated information. Red Rock Canyon Road has a mild slope, making it a relatively easy ride. The Cameron Lake Road is an intermediate route.

Bird-Watching. The Peace Park is home to more than 260 avian species, from songbirds to raptors. Among the species that get the most attention are birds of prey, including ospreys and bald eagles. Waterfowl are numerous along the parks' waterways, particularly in fall; look for Canada geese and the rare harlequin duck.

Fishing. Both parks have a number of lakes and rivers where the fishing is good. In fact, you can fish in most waters of the parks, but the best fishing is generally in the least accessible spots. The sportfishing species include burbot (ling), northern pike, whitefish, kokanee salmon, grayling, and cutthroat, rainbow, lake (Mackinaw), and brook trout. In Waterton, a license costs $4 per day, $6 per week, and $13 annually. In Glacier, a license is not required. Special restrictions apply in several areas, so visitors should read the regulations before fishing. A catch-and-release policy is encouraged in both parks.

Golf. It costs $28 to play 18 holes and $16 to play nine holes at the **Waterton golf course** (tel. 403/859–2114), just outside town. Don't be surprised if you see moose, elk, deer, bighorn sheep, and other wildlife on the greens while playing. **Glacier Park Lodge** (tel. 406/226–9311, fax 406/222–9221), in East Glacier, has a nine-hole course, which you can play for $15 (nine holes) or $28 (18 holes). **Glacier View Golf Course** (tel. 406/888–5471), in West Glacier, is an 18-hole course. The greens fees are $12 for nine holes and $20 for 18 holes.

Horseback Riding. Mule Shoe Outfitters (tel. 406/257–5009) runs the horseback riding concession in Glacier from early June on, as the weather allows. Rates run $20 for one hour, $35 for two hours, and $42 for three hours. An all-day rate runs from $90 to $100, depending on the service you choose. For Waterton, rates run from $15 per person per hour, to $77 per day. Contact **Alpine Stables** (tel. 403/859–2462).

Rafting. You can either bring your own boat or choose from four outfitters that lead guided white-water rafting in the pristine waters of the Flathead River drainages: **Glacier Raft Company** (Box 218, West Glacier, MT 59936, tel. 406/888–5454 or 800/235–6781, fax 406/888–5541); **Glacier Wilderness Guides and Montana Raft Company** (Box 535, West Glacier, MT 59936, tel. 406/387–5555 or 800/521–7238, fax 406/387–5656), **Great Northern Whitewater** (Box 278, West Glacier, MT 59936, tel. 406/387–5340 or 800/735–7897, fax 406/387–9007), and **Northwest Voyagers** (Box 272B, West Glacier, MT 59936, tel. 406/387–9453 or 800/826–2724, fax 406/387–9454).

Ski Touring. Cross-country skiing is increasingly popular in the Peace Park, especially on the U.S. side. It's a good way to observe wildlife, but be careful not to chase the animals; it causes unnecessary stress that may hamper their ability to survive the winter. Glacier National Park distributes a free pamphlet entitled "Ski Trails of Glacier National Park," which describes 16 ski trails that have been identified by the park.

Skiing in Waterton Lakes National Park is concentrated along the Akamina Parkway, especially near Cameron Lake. Don't expect to ski around Waterton town; the wind usually blows the snow away. The free pamphlet "Winter Activities" has additional information.

Swimming. You can swim in some of the lakes in both parks, but these mountain lakes can be very cold and rough. The best choices are Apgar Village beach on Lake McDonald and the Waterton town beach on Upper Waterton Lake, which is often windy and cold.

Tennis. There are free, public tennis courts at Waterton town, adjacent to the campground. These are available on a first-come, first-served basis, but there is rarely a wait. The courts are open year-round, although the nets are taken down for winter at the end of September.

CHILDREN'S PROGRAMS The many children's programs at Glacier vary from year to year. In one program a ranger leads kids in a role-playing skit about bears that teaches youngsters how difficult it can be for injured bears to survive and build up enough fat reserves to get them through the winter.

EVENING ACTIVITIES Waterton Lakes National Park conducts educational programs every evening in the summer, from 8:30 to 9:30 (admission is charged). At Waterton there are bars and a summer cinema.

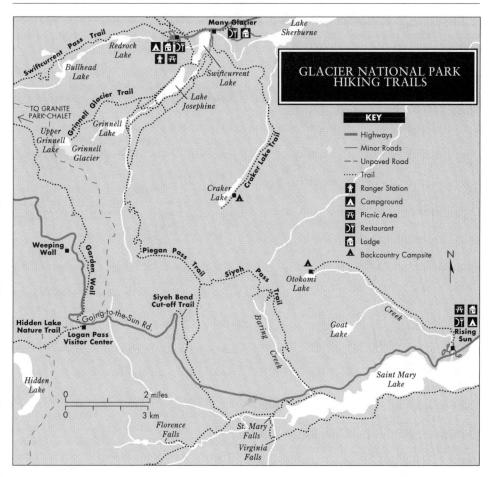

Many campgrounds at Glacier also host evening campfire programs, and adults can settle in for the night at one of the lounges in the park's hotels and lodges.

DINING

Dining generally takes a back seat to other attractions in and around Waterton/Glacier; however, prepared foods ranging from ice cream to complete dinners can be found in small, commercially developed areas. Healthy eating is not a priority in the Peace Park, but at least one dining room (at Waterton's Kilmorey Lodge) has "Heart Smart" entrées, and most eating places will

custom-cook your food to cut down on fat and sodium, if you so request.

INSIDE WATERTON **Bayshore Dining Room.** The view of the lake and mountains makes this an ideal place to enjoy Western specialties. One popular dish is fresh trout stuffed with crab and shrimp. *Waterton Ave., downtown Waterton, tel. 403/859–2211, fax 403/859–2291. AE, D, MC, V. $$*

Kilmorey Lodge (Lamp Post Dining Room). This full-service, sit-down restaurant is that rarest of breeds in Waterton: a health-conscious restaurant. The menu has several vegetarian and "Heart Smart" entrées, and since everything is made from scratch, special diets can generally be accommodated.

At breakfast, make for the Saskatoon berries, a tarter version of the huckleberry. *Next to lake on left as you enter town of Waterton, tel. 403/859–2334, fax 403/859–2342. AE, DC, MC, V. $$*

Prince of Wales Lodge Dining Room. In this century-old chalet high on a peninsula with a dazzling view of Waterton Lake, you can enjoy cuisine that's a step above standard as well as a fine selection of wines. From 2 to 5 every afternoon a British high tea is served in Valerie's Tea Room (with the same great view); true to form, this includes finger sandwiches and scones, plus an array of chocolate-dipped fruits and pastries. *On hill overlooking Upper Waterton Lake, north side of Waterton, tel. 403/859–2231. D, MC, V. $$*

Zum-M-M's. This family-oriented restaurant has a wide range of American standards, including trout and fried chicken and bumbleberry pie—a combination of blueberries, blackberries, raspberries, rhubarb, and apple. *Waterton Ave., downtown Waterton, tel. 403/859–2388, fax 403/859–2010. AE, MC, V. $–$$*

New Frank's Restaurant. Another family-style establishment, this restaurant lays out a Chinese buffet from 5 to 9 each night—the only Chinese food you'll find in the parks. There are also some Western selections on the menu. *Waterton Ave., downtown Waterton, tel. 403/859–2240. AE, MC, V. $*

Pearl's. This squeaky-clean deli-café exhibits sandwich ingredients in a glass display case, but the main attractions are the homemade muffins and pies. *Windflower Ave. (1 street west of Waterton Ave.), in Waterton, tel. 403/859–2284. MC, V. $*

Waterton Park Cafe. Western food is served at this small, tidy café in downtown Waterton. There is also a children's menu. *Waterton Ave., tel. 403/859–2055. V. $*

INSIDE GLACIER **Lake McDonald Lodge Dining Room.** Apple bread pudding with caramel-cinnamon sauce is a favorite at this historic lodge and restaurant. Pasta, steak, and salmon are standards on the menu. *Off Going-to-the-Sun Rd. about halfway along south side of Lake McDonald, tel. 406/888–5431. D, MC, V. $$*

Many Glacier Dining Room. Sophisticated cuisine is served in this early 1900s chalet. Each night there's a chef's special. For a true Montana creation, try the huckleberry daiquiris. *Near end of Many Glacier Rd., on south side just before Swiftcurrent Campground, tel. 406/732–4411. D, MC, V. $$*

Cedar Tree Deli. Here you can order sandwiches, ice cream, and yogurt from the counter. There is no sit-down dining. *Going-to-the-Sun Rd., Apgar Village, tel. 406/888–5232. No credit cards. $*

Eddie's Cafe. This casual café's big sellers are the local trout and whitefish fillets, drenched in lemon butter sauce. For dessert, take a swipe at the Bearpaw Pie, a variation of mud pie with coffee ice cream, caramel, and hot fudge, topped with whipped cream. *Going-to-the-Sun Rd., Apgar Village, tel. 406/888–5361. MC, V. $*

Lake McDonald Coffee Shop. A cheaper alternative to the Lake McDonald Lodge dining room, this sit-down café serves an enormous Indian taco—layers of chili, cheese, onions, tomatoes, sour cream, guacamole, and olives on *bannik*, a flat, fried Native American bread. *Next to Lake McDonald Lodge on south side of Lake McDonald, tel. 406/888–5431. D, MC, V. $*

Rising Sun Coffee Shop. This modern coffee shop overlooking St. Mary Lake serves the same Western foods found at Lake McDonald Coffee Shop. *North side of St. Mary Lake, about 5 mi inside east entrance, tel. 406/732–5523. D, MC, V. $*

NEAR GLACIER **Glacier Park Lodge (The Goatlick).** Here you'll enjoy fine dining in a natural megalog structure with all the amenities of a first-class dining room that was originally a steak place. Though the restaurant now serves pasta and chicken as well, ribs and steaks are still the house specialties. *Hwy. 49, next to railroad station in East Glacier, tel. 406/226–9311, fax 406/222–9221. D, MC, V. $$*

St. Mary Lodge Dining Room (Snow Goose Grill). In a ranch-style setting, diners feast on buffalo steaks, St. Mary Lake whitefish, and sour dough scones, as well as pasta, prime rib, and Pacific salmon. The Snow Goose Grill also specializes in huckleberry desserts. *Just outside east entrance of Glacier Park, tel. 406/732–4431, fax 406/ 732–4105. AE, D, MC, V. $$*

PICNIC SPOTS All campgrounds within the Peace Park have picnic areas with tables, water, and cooking grills that can double as barbecue pits. There are also dozens of turnoffs along the park's roads where you can snack while enjoying the scenery. Look for picnic areas at **Fish Creek, Sprague Creek, Avalanche Creek, Sun Point, Two Medicine,** and **Bowman Lake.** Remember, it's important that you don't feed the animals and that you dispose of garbage in the bear-proof waste bins.

LODGING

Lodgings in the Peace Park tend to be fairly rustic and simple, though there are a few grand lodges and some modern accommodations. The emphasis here is on what's outside the rooms: A number of places have lovely settings and magnificent views. Despite the great demand for the limited number of rooms in and around the Peace Park, the rates are surprisingly reasonable. It's best to reserve your rooms from six months to a year in advance—especially for the busy months of July and August. A few rooms usually become available owing to cancellations, but don't count on it.

Two popular historic lodgings in Glacier National Park, the Granite Park Chalet and Sperry Chalet, have been closed for major repairs. The Granite Park Chalet, however, is now open to hikers on a limited basis. It has bunks with no linen and a common stove, but no other accommodations. Sperry Chalet is scheduled to be open, full-service, for hikers by 1998 or 1999, assuming the U.S. Congress appropriates the necessary money. For information about either chalet, call 888/242–5381.

INSIDE WATERTON **Prince of Wales Hotel.** Designed like a Swiss chalet, this grand hotel above Waterton lacks modern amenities, but the view is great, especially from the rooms facing south toward the lake. *5 km from Waterton park entrance. Glacier Park, Inc., VIAD Corporate Center, Phoenix, AZ 85077-0928, tel. 602/207– 6000. 87 units. Facilities: restaurant, bar. D, MC, V. Closed mid-Sept.–mid-May. $$$*

Bayshore Inn. The most modern motel in the Peace Park, the Bayshore Inn has an "L" shape that matches the shoreline of Upper Waterton Lake and parallels a gravel beach. *Box 38, Waterton Townsite, AB T0K 2M0, tel. 403/859–2211, fax 403/859–2291. 70 units. Facilities: restaurant, bar, coffee shop, ice cream parlor, room service, hot tub, coin laundry. AE, MC, V. $$–$$$*

Aspen Village Inn. This motel-style one- and two-story structure in the middle of Waterton has a good view. It's plain but clean. *Box 100, Waterton Townsite, AB T0K 2M0, tel. 403/859–2255, fax 403/859–2033. 51 units (16 cabins), 12 kitchenettes. Facilities: hot tub, playground. AE, MC, V. Closed late Oct.–early May. $$*

Crandell Mountain Lodge. In a tree-covered niche in Waterton, this old, two-story chalet-style building has a front deck with two barbecues and chairs for guest use, as well as 11 units with fireplaces. *Box 114, Waterton, AB T0K 2M0, tel. 403/859–2288, fax 403/859–2288. 17 units. Facilities: kitchenettes. AE, DC, MC, V. Closed late Oct.–Easter. $$*

Kilmorey Lodge. The only year-round full-service lodge in Waterton, the old-style Kilmorey Lodge faces the lake and is surrounded by trees. In keeping with the rustic decor, many rooms have antique furniture and feather quilt–covered beds. *Box 100, Waterton Townsite, AB T0K 2M0, tel. 403/859–2334, fax 403/859–2342. 21 units. Facilities: restaurant, bar, room service. AE, D, DC, MC, V. $$*

El Cortez Motel. The cheapest motel around looks a little down-at-the-heel, but at prices like these it's hard to complain. In downtown Waterton, the motel has a nice mountain view. *Box 67, Waterton Townsite, AB T0K 2M0, tel. 403/859–2366. 35 units. AE, DC, MC, V. Closed Oct.–Apr. $*

INSIDE GLACIER **Many Glacier Hotel.** The most isolated of the grand hotels—it's near Swiftcurrent Lake on the northeast side of the park—this is also one of the most scenic, especially if you nab one of the balcony rooms. There are several hiking trails nearby, and a large wrought-iron fireplace in the lobby where guests gather on chilly mornings. There are nightly cabaret performances. *12 mi west of Babb. Glacier Park, Inc., VIAD Corporate Center, Phoenix, AZ 85077-0928, tel. 602/207–6000. 212 rooms. Facilities: restaurant, bar, snack bar, horseback riding, boating. D, MC, V. Closed mid-Sept.–May. $$$*

Lake McDonald Lodge. Hiking and boating on Lake McDonald and exploring groves of giant cedars are part of the fun of staying at this historic lodge. The lobby is decorated with stuffed and mounted wild animals. Rooms are small but tastefully done. *10 mi east of West Glacier on Going-to-the-Sun Rd., Glacier Park, Inc., VIAD Corporate Center, Phoenix, AZ 85077-0928, tel. 602/207–6000. 100 rooms. Facilities: restaurant, bar, coffee shop. D, MC, V. Closed Oct.–May. $$–$$$*

Village Inn at Apgar. This two-story motel-style wood structure faces Lake McDonald and has a beach. Some rooms have balconies, and all overlook the lake and mountains. *West end of Lake McDonald, in Apgar. Glacier Park, Inc., VIAD Corporate Center, Phoenix, AZ 85077-0928, tel. 602/ 207–6000. 36 units, 12 kitchenettes. D, MC, V. Closed late Sept.–mid-May. $$–$$$*

Apgar Village Lodge. In a lovely, woodsy setting, this historic hotel, built in the early years of this century, is the only lodging in Glacier Park not run by Glacier Park, Inc. The units are plain but meticulously clean. Cabins have kitchenettes. *Box 398, West Glacier, MT 59936, tel. 406/888–5484. 48 units (28 cabins). D, MC, V. Closed Oct.–Apr. $$*

Rising Sun Motor Inn. Though it resembles a barracks from the outside, this motel overlooks St. Mary Lake, and it's clean and neat. *5 mi west of St. Mary's on Going-to-the-Sun Rd., Glacier Park, VIAD Corporate Center, Phoenix, AZ 85077-0928, tel. 602/ 207–6000. 72 rooms. Facilities: coffee shop. D, MC, V. Closed Oct.–early June. $$*

Swiftcurrent Motor Inn. These plain but practical motel and cabin units sitting at the end of Many Glacier Road have spectacular views of the mountains. *13 mi west of Babb. Glacier Park, Inc., VIAD Corporate Center, Phoenix, AZ 85077-0928, tel. 602/207–6000. 88 units (26 cabins, most without bathrooms). Facilities: restaurant, coin laundry. D, MC, V. Closed Sept.–mid-June. $$*

NEAR GLACIER **Glacier Park Lodge.** Originally built in 1913 by the Great Northern Railway, this full-service lodge is supported by 500- to 800-year-old fir and 3-ft-thick cedar logs. There are nightly cabaret performances. *Corner of Highways 2 and 49, East Glacier. Glacier Park, Inc., VIAD Corporate Center, Phoenix, AZ 85077-0928, tel. 602/207–6000. 161 rooms. Facilities: restaurant, bar, snack bar, pool, 9-hole golf course. D, MC, V. Closed mid-Sept.–mid-May. $$$*

Izaak Walton Inn. Halfway between East and West Glacier, this small inn was originally a dormitory for railroad workers. Today it overlooks the train yard; since Amtrak trains stop here, it's best to request one of the quieter rooms at the back. For train buffs, four renovated cabooses have been made into cabin-style accommodations. *U.S. 2, Essex, MT 59916, tel. 406/ 888–5700, fax 406/888–5200. 33 rooms. Facilities: restaurant, sauna, recreation room, laundry. MC, V. $$$*

East Glacier Motel & Cabins. These small, clean, contemporary motel units and cabins make a satisfactory lodging. *Box 93, East Glacier, MT 59434, tel. 406/226–5593. 16* units (9 motel, 7 cabins), 11 kitchenettes. MC, V. Closed late Sept.–early May. $$

River Bend Motel. A small, no-frills, motel sits in a wooded setting on the edge of West Glacier, across the Middle Fork of the Flathead River from Glacier Park. There is a laundromat within 100 yards. *Box 398, West Glacier, MT 59936, tel. 406/888–5662. 32 units (5 cabins), 5 kitchenettes. Facilities: restaurant. D, MC, V. Closed Oct.–mid-May. $$*

St. Mary Lodge Motel. The most eager-to-please motel in the area, this place offers a greater variety of services than any others. It's just outside the east entrance of Glacier Park. *St. Mary, MT 59417, tel. 406/732–4431; 208/726–6279 in winter. 76 units (19 cabins), 6 cottages. Facilities: restaurant, bar, café, pizzeria, kitchenettes, coin laundry. AE, MC, V. Closed Oct. 2–Mother's Day. $$*

Vista Motel. About a mile outside the west entrance, this small, modern motel has comfortable rooms and a great view of Glacier Park. *Box 98, West Glacier, MT 59936, tel. 406/888–5311 or 800/831–7101. 26 units, 2 kitchenettes. Facilities: pool. AE, D, MC, V. Closed Sept. 24–May 30. $$*

Glacier Highland Resort. About .5 mi outside Glacier Park is this old but clean and spruce motel. Its three sprawling buildings are fairly close to one another, and six units stay open in winter. *Box 397, West Glacier, MT 59936, tel. 406/888–5427, fax 406/888–5764. 33 units. MC, V. $*

Jacobson's Cottages. These individual cottages outside Glacier Park in East Glacier are tucked in among trees. Two have kitchenettes. *Box 216, East Glacier, MT 59434, tel. 406/226–4422. 12 cottages. D, MC, V. Closed Oct. 2–May 14. $*

Mountain Pine Motel. This small, modern, one-story motel is in East Glacier. *Box 260, East Glacier, MT 59434, tel. 406/226–4403. 26 units. AE, D, DC, V. Closed Oct.–Apr. $*

Sears Motel and Campground. This bare-bones motel in East Glacier looks better on the inside than the outside, but it's clean.

There are 19 camping units with 15 RV hookups on the grounds. There's a small car rental service here. *Box 275, East Glacier, MT 59434, tel. 406/226–4432, fax 406/226–4432. 16 rooms. D, MC, V. Closed Oct.–early May. $*

CAMPING

INSIDE GLACIER All Glacier National Park campgrounds operate on a first-come, first-served basis, and during the busy months of July and August they usually fill up in the early afternoon. Fees are from $10 to $12 per night, depending on the services available, and are charged only when the water is turned on. No utility hookups or showers are provided in park campgrounds, but showers are available at Rising Sun and Swiftcurrent motor inns for a nominal fee. Drinking water and cement-and-metal fireplaces, which can double as barbecue pits, are found in all campground and picnic areas. Questions about any Glacier National Park campgrounds should be directed to Park Headquarters, Glacier National Park, West Glacier, MT 59936, tel. 406/888–5441.

Apgar Campground is at Lake McDonald, near the west entrance. It's large (196 sites), busy, close to many activities and services (including swimming and boating in the lake), and within a short walking distance of Apgar Village. Facilities include flush toilets, a disposal station, a ranger station, and a public phone. Sites cost $12.

You give up convenience for less-crowded camping at **Bowman Lake Campground,** on the northwest side of the park near Polebridge (at the end of Bowman Lake Road on the west end of Bowman Lake). Its 48 sites cost $10, including use of pit toilets. There's boat access to the lake, and a ranger station nearby.

The 110-site **Many Glacier Campground** has flush toilets, a disposal station, a ranger station, public phone, and boat access; sites cost $12. The campground is nestled in a

WATERTON/GLACIER CAMPGROUNDS

INSIDE GLACIER: Apgar, Rising Sun, Two Medicine, Bowman Lake, Many Glacier, Avalanche, Fish Creek, Kintla Lake, Sprague Creek, St. Mary

INSIDE WATERTON: Waterton Townsite, Belly River, Crandell Mountain

	Apgar	Rising Sun	Two Medicine	Bowman Lake	Many Glacier	Avalanche	Fish Creek	Kintla Lake	Sprague Creek	St. Mary	Waterton Townsite	Belly River	Crandell Mountain
Total number of sites	196	83	99	48	110	87	180	13	25	156	238	24	129
Sites suitable for RVs	196	83	99	48	110	50	80	13	0	5	95	0	60
Number of hookups	0	0	0	0	0	50	80	13	0	5	95	0	0
Drive to sites	•	•	•	•	•	•	•	•	•	•	•	•	•
Hike to sites						•	•	•	•	•	•		
Flush toilets	•	•	•		•						•		•
Pit/chemical toilets				•		•						•	
Drinking water	•	•	•	•	•	•	•	•	•	•	•	•	•
Showers		•			•						•		
Fire grates	•	•	•	•	•	•	•	•	•	•	•	•	•
Swimming	•	•	•	•	•	•							
Boat access	•	•	•	•	•	•							
Playground											•	•	•
Disposal station	•	•	•		•	•				•	•		•
Ranger station	•		•	•	•	•	•	•			•	•	•
Public telephone	•		•	•	•						•		
Reservation possible													
Daily fee per site	$12*	$12	$10	$12	$12	$12	$10	$10	$12	$12	$14–$21**	$10**	$13
Dates open	early May–late Oct.	late May–early Sept.	mid-May–early Sept.	early June–early Sept.	early June–early Sept.	late June–early Sept.	late May–early Sept.	late May–early Sept.	late May–early Oct.	late May–early Sept.	late Apr.–mid-Oct.	late May–mid-Oct.	late May–early Sept.

*Free in winter; no running water. **Canadian dollars.

scenic valley at the end of Many Glacier Road, adjacent to Swiftcurrent Motor Inn; it's the hopping-off place for hiking into the northern part of the park.

Rising Sun Campground has 83 $12 sites with flush toilets; there's also a disposal station. It's on the north side of St. Mary Lake, 5 mi west of the east entrance; there's easy access to water sports such as boating, cruising, paddling, and fishing.

The 99 $12 sites at **Two Medicine Campground** are at Two Medicine Lake, on the southeast side of the park. Though it is not near a town and facilities, the campground is scenic, and it usually fills up later than the others. On the grounds are flush toilets, a disposal station, a ranger station, a public phone, and boat access. It's at the end of Two Medicine Road, next to Two Medicine Store, 11 mi northwest of East Glacier. Some hardy campers swim in the lake.

There are five other campgrounds scattered along the roadways of the park: **Fish Creek** (180 sites, $12); **Avalanche** (87 sites, $12); **St. Mary** (156 sites, $12); **Kintla Lake** (13 sites, $10); and **Sprague Creek** (25 sites, $12).

INSIDE WATERTON Waterton's campgrounds are also available only on a first-come, first-served basis. The town campground operates a waiting-list service: Campers with valid permits report to the campground, and if no campsite is available, a waiting-list ticket will be issued. Sites that become available are listed daily on a bulletin board from 10 AM to 11 AM and 12 PM to 1 PM. For more information contact Waterton Lakes National Park (Waterton Park, AB, Canada T0K 2M0, tel. 403/859–2224).

Waterton Townsite Campground is large and busy, with all the facilities of the town within walking distance. It's on the south end of Waterton and has 95 full-service sites (power, water, sewer) that cost $21; 113 multi-use sites (kitchen shelters with stoves, drinking water, flush toilets, tables) for $16; and 30 walk-in sites (flush toilets and tables) for $15. The campground has washrooms, showers, sewage disposal, and picnic tables, as well as public telephones, an information kiosk, and a playground.

Belly River is a small, tree-covered campground far away from heavy commercial activity. Its 24 sites are close to kitchen shelters with stoves, drinking water, and tables. Other facilities include dry toilets, a washroom, a playground, and fire pits. It's off Chief Mountain Highway, 18 mi east of Waterton, near Belly River. Regular sites cost $10; group camping (available by reservation) costs $2 per person.

There are 129 sites at **Crandell Mountain**, in a heavily treed area without commercial development. Facilities include kitchen shelters with stoves, drinking water, flush toilets, tables, fire pits, washrooms, a playground, and a disposal station. It's off Red Rock Parkway, 11 mi from Waterton, near the center of the park. There is an information kiosk at the campground.

Yellowstone National Park
Wyoming

Updated by Candy Moulton

here else but Yellowstone can you pull off an empty highway at dawn to see two bison bulls shaking the earth as they collide in battle before the herd, and an hour later be caught in an RV traffic jam? For more than 125 years the grandmother of national parks has been full of such contradictions, which usually stem from its twin goals: to remain America's preeminent wildlife preserve as well as its most accessible one.

Evidence remains from the great fires of the summer of 1988. Above the South entrance, along dizzying Lewis River canyon, a landscape of charred trees to the west seems to suggest a disaster that will alter the park's appearance for generations. Yet below the North entrance, the multicolored mosaic of burned, untouched, and regenerating areas along the Gallatin Range reinforces the idea that fire is essential to Yellowstone's natural cycle. Fires sweep out deadwood on the forest floor and release nutritious ash into the watershed. They open the forest canopy to more light, allowing for more grasses and sprouts, which feed mammals ranging from rodents to bison and elk. In the process, meadows of brilliant wildflowers form. The chain of benefits goes on and on. The newly opened canopy makes the smaller rodents more vulnerable to hawks and eagles, thereby increasing the latter's population. Browsers, such as moose and deer, flourish with the new plant life—and they will surely be followed by more predators, like grizzly bears, and such scavengers as coyotes.

The abundance of wildlife in the park has been known for thousands of years to Blackfoot, Crow, Bannock, Flatheads, Nez Percé, and the Northern Shoshone—hunters who frequented the area. (Only one small Shoshone band, named Sheepeaters, lived in what is now the park.) Mountain man John Colter became the first white man to explore Yellowstone in 1807–1808, and his stories about geysers and boiling rivers prompted some mapmakers to dub the uncharted region Colter's Hell.

It is popularly believed that a Sioux description of the yellow rock varieties in the Grand Canyon of the Yellowstone (also called Canyon) gave the park its name, adopted by early 19th-century French trappers. Unverified reports of outlandish natural phenomena continued filtering out of Yellowstone from the 1820s through the 1860s. In 1870 the government agreed that this remarkable land should become a national park, and in 1872 Congress declared Yellowstone the world's first national park.

ESSENTIAL INFORMATION

VISITOR INFORMATION Write to the Superintendent, National Park Service (**Yellowstone National Park,** Box 168, WY 82190, tel. 307/344–7381). Information and reservations for lodging, dining, and activities are available from **Amfac Parks and Resorts** (Yellowstone National Park, WY 82190–9989, tel. 307/344–7311). To find out more about the surrounding towns contact the **Wyoming Division of Tourism** (I–25 at College Dr., Cheyenne, WY 82002, tel. 307/777–7777 or 800/225–5996) or **Travel Montana** (Dept. of Commerce, Helena, MT 59620, tel. 406/444–2654 or 800/541–1447).

Information on facilities and services in Cody, Wyoming, and outside the East entrance can be obtained from the **Cody Visitors and Conventions Council** (Box 2777, Cody, WY 82414, tel. 307/587–2297). If you plan to travel through Jackson, contact the **Jackson Hole Visitors Council** (Box 982, Dept. 8, Jackson Hole, WY 83001, tel. 307/733–7606 or 800/782–0011, ext. 41).

All overnight backcountry camping requires a backcountry use permit, which must be obtained in person no more than 48 hours before the planned trip. For information, call the Backcountry Office (tel. 307/344–2160). In summer you can usually get these free permits seven days a week, from 8 to 4:30, at Mammoth Ranger Station/Visitor Center, Canyon Ranger Station/Visitor Center, Grant Village Visitor Center, South Entrance Ranger Station, Bechler Ranger Station, and Old Faithful Ranger Station. Hours vary off-season. Backcountry camping is allowed only in the park's designated campsites, with exceptions during the winter season (from October 15 to May 15). All backcountry campsites have restrictions on group size and length of stay. Boating is prohibited throughout the backcountry, and pit fires are prohibited at certain campsites.

FEES Entrance fees entitle visitors to seven days in Yellowstone and Grand Teton national parks. The cost is $20 per automobile; $15 per visitor entering by snowmobile, motorcycle, or bus; and $10 per person on a bicycle or on foot. You can buy a calendar-year pass to the two parks for $40.

PUBLICATIONS The National Park Service (*see* Visitor Information, *above*) distributes its yearly "Official Map and Guide" and its seasonal newspaper, *Yellowstone Today,* at park entrances and by mail. You can also request specific seasonal and activity information and bird and wildlife checklists from the park service.

If you plan to hike in the backcountry, get a topographical map. A good one, printed on waterproof and tear-proof plastic, is available from **Trails Illustrated** (Box 3610, Evergreen, CO 80439, tel. 800/962–1643) or from any of the visitor centers in the park. The **Yellowstone Association** (Box 117, Yellowstone National Park, WY 82190, tel. 307/344–2293) sells a Trip Planner Package (roadside, wildlife, hiking, bird, and geological guides, and detailed maps of the park's northern and southern halves) and many other Yellowstone books, posters, and videos at the park's visitor centers.

One of the best historical references is Lee Whittlesey's *Yellowstone Place Names,* a detailed narrative about the park's many sights and sites. The handiest trail guide is Tom Carter's *Day Hiking Yellowstone,* which, despite its title, also details popular overnight trips. The classic geological, ecological, and human history of the park is *The Yellowstone Story,* two volumes by Aubrey L. Haines. For more information on geology, read William R. Keefer's *The Geologic Story of Yellowstone National Park.* A much more critical history is Alston Chase's controversial *Playing God in Yellowstone,* which chronicles a century of government mismanagement. Three other excellent titles are *Roadside History of Yellowstone Park* by Winfred Blevins; *Yellowstone Ecology: A Road Guide,* by Sharon Eversman and Mary Carr; and *Roadside Geology of the Yellowstone Country,* by William J. Fritz, all published by Mountain Press Publishing (Box 2399, Missoula, MT 59806, tel. 800/234–5308). The most beautiful mile-by-mile roadside guide to the park is *National Parkways: Yellowstone National Park,* part of a series by Worldwide Research and Publishing Company (Box 3073, Casper, WY 82602).

Just as striking as its natural wonders are Yellowstone's man-made structures: the elegant Lake Yellowstone Hotel and the magnificently rustic Old Faithful Inn. The two best books on the history, architecture, and trivia of these buildings are *Plain to Fancy: Story of the Lake Hotel,* by Barbara

Dittle and Joanne Mallmann (Roberts Rine-hart Press, 1987) and Susan C. Scofield's *The Inn at Old Faithful* (Crown's Nest Associates, 1979).

GEOLOGY AND TERRAIN Yellowstone is a high plateau ringed by even higher mountains. Roadside elevations range from 5,314 ft at the north entrance to 8,859 ft at Dunraven Pass. The Gallatin Range to the west and north, the Absaroka and Beartooth ranges to the north and east, and the Tetons to the south all have peaks higher than 10,000 ft. Terrain ranges from near high desert around the north entrance to lodgepole-pine forests around the south entrance, and otherworldly landscapes of stunted pine and shrub around the thermal areas.

With some 10,000 geysers, hot springs, fumaroles, and mud pots, Yellowstone's 3,472 square mi contain the world's largest thermal area. Cataclysmic volcanoes "blew" 2 million years ago, then again 1.3 million years ago and 600,000 years ago. The last eruption deposited 240 cubic mi of hot gas, ash, pumice, and rock debris, collapsing a 28- by 47-mi caldera, or basin, now in the park's center. Heat from the magma (molten rock) under the Yellowstone Caldera continues to fuel the park's five most famous geyser basins—West Thumb, Upper Geyser Basin, Midway, Lower, and Norris—which contain most of Yellowstone's 200 to 250 active geysers. Geysers occur when surface water seeping down through the porous rock is superheated and, as it rises to the surface and the pressure decreases, turns into steam. When that water is not superheated or under pressure, it rises to the surface in the form of hot springs, such as those at Mammoth. Fumaroles, visible at geyser basins and elsewhere along the caldera (try the Washburn Hot Springs Overlook, south of Dunraven Pass), result when the water is present in such small quantities that it does not flow out but is continually released as steam. Fumaroles become mud pots, like the stinking, simmering Mud Volcano, between Canyon and Fishing Bridge, when the acidic gases decompose rocks around

the fumarole, turning them into mud and clay.

Although much of the Yellowstone caldera is hard to see, a few major park sites mark its boundaries. The road from Madison to Norris follows the caldera's northwest rim; along the way, Gibbon Falls cascades over the caldera wall. From Washburn Hot Springs Overlook you can see a 35-mi northeastern stretch of the caldera boundary from Mt. Washburn south to the Red Mountains. From Lake Butte Overlook, you can see the caldera boundary 4 mi to the east.

After the volcanic eruptions at least three glacial periods occurred, the last one ending 8,500 years ago. Yellowstone Lake, North America's largest mountain lake, was formed by glaciers. So was Hayden Valley, whose clay soil and fine silt is inhospitable to trees but has produced a rich shrubland teeming with wildlife. At one time glacial debris blocked the Yellowstone River above the Upper Falls, creating a large lake in Hayden Valley. When this natural dam broke, its waters scoured out the Grand Canyon of the Yellowstone. The rounded boulders strewn along the Northeast entrance road also bear witness to the glaciers.

FLORA AND FAUNA The park's most common tree is the lodgepole pine, soaring tall and straight in dense stands with few branches on its lower trunk. Although lodgepole accounts for 80% of all park forests, six other conifers—most notably Engelmann spruce and subalpine fir—are interspersed with it. Sagebrush and rabbitbrush are common around Mammoth Hot Springs, while willows grow in moist sections of the Hayden and Lamar valleys.

Wildflowers abound in July and August in alpine meadows. Most common are Indian paintbrush, lupine, yellow monkeyflower, mountain bluebell, fireweed, and Rocky Mountain fringed gentian (the official park flower), whose blue petals crown 1- to 3-ft-tall stems.

Yellowstone contains the biggest concentration of mammal species in the lower 48 states: seven ungulates (hooved animals), two types of bear, and 49 other mammal species. There are also 290 bird species, five reptile species, and four species of amphibian. Elk, moose, mule deer, and bison are Yellowstone's most commonly seen large mammals. The best times to see these and other wildlife in summer are early morning and late evening. About 30,000 elk, or wapiti, roam meadows, especially around the Midway and Upper geyser basins, the Lewis River area near the south entrance, and Mammoth Hot Springs. Some 500 to 700 moose feed throughout lowland marshy areas in summer, especially in the Hayden Valley and at Pelican Creek east of Fishing Bridge. Mule deer, also called blacktail deer, frequent Old Faithful, Lake, Canyon, and the area between the north entrance and Tower Fall. Bison, the park's largest animals (around 2,000 lbs.) move to upland meadows in the Lamar and Hayden valleys in summer, although lone bison are often seen by roadsides. Despite their ponderous appearance, bison are unpredictable and can sprint at 30 mi per hour, three times faster than an average person can run. Almost every year, several visitors who approach bison too closely are seriously injured.

Bears are Yellowstone's most famous animals. From the 1930s through the 1960s, they frequented roadsides, begging food from obliging tourists. Increasing injuries and property damage forced the park service to wean bears from their human dependence in the early 1970s. Today there are far fewer roadside bears and fewer people injured by bears. Black bears (actually black, brown, or cinnamon) are the most commonly seen. Although they may seem clownish and disinclined to attack people, black bears are still dangerous. Never approach one, especially a female with cubs.

Yellowstone is home to some 200 of the fewer than 1,000 threatened grizzly bears surviving in Montana, Wyoming, and Idaho. They are bigger than black bears (3½ ft high at the shoulders, as opposed to 3 ft when on all 4s) have flat-face profiles and a pronounced hump between the shoulders. They come in a range of colors, from almost-black to light cream. Several park service brochures available at all entrances detail precautions you should take to avoid grizzly encounters, but the park cannot guarantee absolute safety. Grizzlies may attack without warning and for no apparent reason; the last fatal attack on a tourist was in 1986. Grizzlies are solitary animals, partial to the park's deepest backcountry. Most roadside sightings of black bears and occasional grizzlies occur in early morning or evening near tree cover along open areas.

Bighorn sheep, whose males have massive curved horns, mostly stay above timberline among rocky crags. In summer they often appear around Mt. Washburn, 15 to 30 to a flock. Coyotes, which inhabit caves and burrows, appear often in Hayden Valley and the park's northern ranges. Count yourself lucky if you see a bobcat in the backcountry; count yourself blessed if you see a fleeting mountain lion. Badgers, beavers, foxes, marmots, minks, muskrats, otters, and wolverines also inhabit the park.

The Rocky Mountain wolf, an endangered species, returned to Yellowstone in 1995, when a controversial wolf recovery program brought animals from Canada to the park. First placed in enclosed pens in the Lamar Valley in January 1995, the wolves were released to the wild in April of that year. The possibility of reintroducing wolves into the park had been debated for years: Environmentalists believe the predators are essential to the Yellowstone ecosystem, while ranchers outside the park are fearful of losing livestock to wolves.

Backcountry lakes and rivers are especially rich in bird life: Black and white ospreys hover over surfaces, while Canada geese bob and white pelicans dive for fish.

The park service will send you a "Birds of Yellowstone National Park" checklist of the park's 290 bird species and a "Wildlife" checklist, and the Yellowstone Association sells several Yellowstone mammal and bird guides (*see* Publications, *above*).

WHEN TO GO Most people visit Yellowstone in summer. In any given year, more than 3 million visitors will come to the park during summer and only 140,000 in winter. Those winter visitors, however, are the ones who see the park at its most magical—with steam billowing from geyser basins to wreath trees in ice, while bison and elk forage close to roads turned into ski and snow vehicle trails. With the exception of the road from the north entrance at Gardiner, Montana, to the northeast entrance at Cooke City, Montana—which remains open year-round—all Yellowstone roads are closed to wheeled vehicles from early November to early May; they are open to over-snow vehicles from mid-December to mid-March. Spring road openings usually follow this pattern: Mammoth to Norris, mid-April; west entrance, mid-April; east and south entrances, early May; Old Faithful to West Thumb, early May; Beartooth Highway (northeast entrance) and Tower to Canyon, end of May.

The average maximum temperature at Mammoth Hot Spring in July is 80.3°F and the minimum is 45.5°F, with extremes of 96°F and 25°F. August temperatures are similar. When hiking, be prepared for cold rain and temperatures dropping as much as 20 degrees. January average highs and lows are 28.7°F and 9°F, with extremes of 50°F and –41°F. Old Faithful is often 5 to 15 degrees colder than Mammoth. January snowfall at Mammoth averages 17½ inches, although it has reached 77 inches. Snow is possible year-round at high elevations such as Mt. Washburn. June and September are often wet and cloudy throughout the park's lower elevations, but in September, and to a lesser extent October, there are some delightfully sunny days—albeit 5 to 20 degrees cooler than in midsummer. May and June are the best months for seeing baby bison, moose, and other new arrivals.

SEASONAL EVENTS **Mid-March:** The **Rendezvous Ski Race** (tel. 406/646–7701) in West Yellowstone, Montana, is one of eight segments in the cross-country Great American Ski Chase. **Late May to late October:**

The **Yellowstone Institute** (tel. 307/344–2294) sponsors dozens of short, mostly in-the-field courses on park flora, fauna, geology, and outdoor skills. **Late June to early July:** The **Plains Indian Powwow** (tel. 307/587–4771) and **Cody Stampede** (tel. 307/587–2297), both in Cody, Wyoming, celebrate the Native American and cowboy heritages of the Northern Plains. **Mid-August:** The **Festival of Nations** (tel. 406/446–1718) in Red Lodge, Montana, is a nine-day extravaganza of free food, dancing, music, and exhibits celebrating the customs of the various groups who settled this mining town. It takes place at the foot of the spectacular Beartooth Highway, 69 mi from Yellowstone's northeast entrance.

WHAT TO PACK In summer expect intense dry heat, bone-chilling drizzle, and much in between—sometimes on the same day. Layering is the best solution: Try a short-sleeved shirt, sweatshirt, and a hooded windbreaker. Even if it's warm, carry long pants. Gloves and rain gear are also a good idea; you can carry them in a small knapsack. Walking shoes are essential, but hiking shoes are recommended for trails.

Yellowstone's extreme winters make attention to proper clothing critical, even if you plan to stay inside a car or snow coach. You should have thermal underwear, wool socks and outerwear, waterproof boots, a lined coat, and warm headgear. If you're planning on skiing or snowmobiling, consider polypropylene underwear and socks: It resists moisture from outside and wicks away your body's own moisture. Sunscreen, sunglasses, and binoculars for watching wildlife are worth bringing in any season.

GENERAL STORES The oldest national park concessionaire, **Hamilton Stores, Inc.** (Box 250, West Yellowstone, MT 59758) has been serving Yellowstone since 1915. Today it runs 15 park stores, some of which are interesting destinations themselves. The Old Faithful Lower Store, for example, has a knotty pine porch with benches that beckon tired hikers, as well as an inexpensive lunch counter. All stores sell souvenirs ranging from the tacky (cowboy joke items and rubber tom-toms) to the authentic ($60 buffalo-hide moccasins and $200 cowboy coats). Stores are generally open from May through September; Mammoth's is open year-round. The following stores in the park, are listed with their summer hours; in other seasons hours vary.

Old Faithful Basin Store (tel. 307/545–7282), 7:45 AM–9:45 PM; **Old Faithful BAC Store** (tel. 307/545–7237), 7:45 AM–9:45 PM; **Old Faithful Photo Shop** (tel. 307/545–7258), 7:30 AM–10 PM; **Grant Village General Store** (tel. 307/242–7266), 7:45 AM–9:45 PM; **Grant Village Mini Store** (tel. 307/242–7390), 7:45 AM–9:45 PM; **Bridge Bay Marina Store** (tel. 307/242–7326), 7:45 AM–9:45 PM; **Lake General Store** (tel. 307/242–7563), 7:45 AM–9:45 PM; **Fishing Bridge General Store** (tel. 307/242–7200), 7:45 AM–9:45 PM; **Canyon General Store** (tel. 307/242–7377), 7:45 AM–9:45 PM; **Photo Shop** (tel. 307/344–7757), 7:45 AM–10 PM; **Tower Fall Store** (tel. 307/344–7786), 7:45 AM–9:45 PM; **Roosevelt Store** (tel. 307/344–7779), 7:45 AM–9:45 PM; **Mammoth General Store** (tel. 307/344–7702), 7:45 AM–9:45 PM; **Yellowstone Nature Store** (tel. 307/344–7757), 7:45 AM–9:45 PM.

Outside the park, 2 mi below the South entrance, **Flagg Ranch Village** (Box 187, Moran, WY 83013, tel. 307/733–8761 or 800/443–2311) has a grocery store, gift shop, and tackle shop that are open from mid-May to mid-October and mid-December to mid-March. Summer hours for the gift shop are 8 AM to 10 PM, for the grocery store 7 AM to 10 PM, and for the tackle shop 8 AM to 5 PM. Winter hours vary.

In Gardiner, Montana, 5 mi north of Mammoth Hot Springs, the **Conoco Travel Shoppe** (tel. 406/848–7681) is open daily 5:30 AM to 9:30 PM, the **Exxon Convenience Store** (tel. 406/848–7742) is open from 6 AM to 10 PM, and the **North Entrance Food Farm** (tel. 406/848–7524) is open Monday to Saturday from 7 to 8, Sunday from 8 to 7. All are on U.S. 89 and all sell groceries and outdoor supplies year-round.

ARRIVING AND DEPARTING The park has five entrances, all of which join the Grand Loop Road. The most scenic entry is from the northeast on U.S. 212, the Beartooth Highway. The drive along U.S. 89 from Livingston, Montana, to the north entrance is easier; it is also the only entrance open to wheeled vehicles in winter. Those coming from Grand Teton use the south entrance (U.S. 89–191–287). This route, along with U.S. 20 through West Yellowstone to the west entrance and U.S. 14–16–20 from Cody to the east entrance, are the most heavily trafficked. The route from Cody to the east entrance and over Sylvan Pass in the park itself is presently under construction, so expect rough stretches and delays. You can avoid that construction by using the northeast entrance; from Cody take the Chief Joseph Scenic Byway (Wyoming Route 120 and then Wyoming 296).

By Bus. Greyhound Lines (tel. 800/231–2222) serves West Yellowstone, Montana (depot at Menzel's Travel Agency, 127 Yellowstone Ave.), during certain months of the summer, from Salt Lake City, Utah (depot at 160 W. South Temple St.), and from Bozeman, Montana (depot at 625 N. 7th Ave.). Greyhound does not serve Cody or Jackson, Wyoming. **Cody Bus Lines** (tel. 800/733–2304) provides daily service from Billings.

From mid-May to mid-September, several bus lines outside the park shuttle visitors to Old Faithful, where they can make noon connections to Amfac Parks and Resorts tour buses. **Gray Line of Jackson Hole** (1680 Martin La., tel. 307/733–4325) makes regular day trips during the summer from Jackson to Yellowstone National Park for $41 per day, round-trip.

By Car and RV. The 69 mi from Red Lodge, Montana, to the northeast entrance traverse the 11,000-ft Beartooth Pass, whose dizzying switchbacks were cut in the 1930s. The drive from Red Lodge takes about two hours and is best avoided at night, in bad weather, and when traveling by RV. The easier, all-season approach is from the north on U.S. 89, which exits I–90 in Livingston, Montana. This road traverses about 60 mi of the appropriately named Paradise Valley along the Yellowstone River, which is flanked by the gentle Gallatin Range on the west and the towering Absaroka Range on the east, before reaching the 1903 stone arch of the north entrance in the funky old tourist town of Gardiner, Montana. Also good for RVs is the west entrance, 60 mi from Ashton, Idaho, on U.S. 20; the west entrance is 90 mi from Bozeman, Montana, through winding Gallatin Canyon on U.S. 191. Fifty-three miles from Cody, Wyoming lies the east entrance, on U.S. 14–16–20 past the Shoshone National Forest; just past the entrance the road climbs the 8,530-ft Sylvan Pass. From Cody you can also take the newly paved Chief Joseph Scenic Byway (also known as Wyoming Route 120) and then Wyoming 296 to the northeast entrance at Cooke City, Montana. From Jackson, Wyoming, U.S. 89–191–287 travels 57 mi through Grand Teton National Park to the south entrance; this route is fairly easy on RVs. Grand Teton Park, 6 mi from the south entrance, is often visited in conjunction with Yellowstone. Utah's Arches and Canyonlands national parks and Zion National Park are almost 700 mi from Old Faithful. Grand Canyon Village in Arizona is more than 950 mi away, and Colorado's Rocky Mountain National Park is 548 mi from Old Faithful.

By Plane. The two most convenient airports are **Jackson Hole Airport** (tel. 307/733–7682), outside Jackson, Wyoming, 50 mi from the south entrance; and **Yellowstone Regional Airport** (tel. 307/587–5096), outside Cody, Wyoming, 52 mi from the east entrance. Jackson has daily flights connecting through Denver or Salt Lake City on several national and commuter airlines; Cody is served by **GP Express** (tel. 800/525–0280) year-round.

Bozeman's **Gallatin Field** (tel. 406/388–6632), 90 mi from the west entrance and 85 mi from the north entrance, also has daily flights on national airlines connecting through Minneapolis and Denver. **West Yellowstone Airport,** the closest to the park, is served daily by **SkyWest** (tel. 406/646–7351 or 800/453–9417) from June through October, but closed to everything but ski-planes the rest of the year.

During the summer, none of these airports offers public transportation to the park or even into their respective towns, but some lodgings in each town have free airport shuttles. Taxi service from Yellowstone Regional Airport is through **Cody Connection Taxi** (tel. 307/587–9292), which charges $5 for the first person and $1 for each additional person to get into town. **West Yellowstone Taxi** (tel. 406/646–7359) charges about the same from West Yellowstone Airport into town. One-way taxi fares from Gallatin Field into Bozeman and from Jackson Hole Airport into Jackson average $12 to $15 for a carload of people.

Car rentals are available at Cody's Yellowstone Regional Airport, Bozeman's Gallatin Field, West Yellowstone Airport, and Jackson Hole Airport. Try **Avis** (tel. 800/331–1212), **Budget** (tel. 800/527–0700), **Hertz** (tel. 800/654–3131), **National** (tel. 800/328–4567), **Payless** (tel. 800/548–9551), or **Rent-A-Wreck** (tel. 406/587–4551). **Budget** (tel. 406/646–7634) and **Payless** (tel. 406/646–9332) have offices in town with free airport shuttle service. In the town of Jackson, cars are available at **All Trans Company** (tel. 307/733–31359) and **Rent-A-Wreck** (tel. 307/733–5014). In Bozeman, you can rent RVs from **C&T Trailer Supply** (2000 N. 7th Ave., Bozeman, MT 59715, tel. 406/587–8610).

EXPLORING

Although the plane and bus connections to Yellowstone are adequate, the park, like so many others, remains car country. The Grand Loop Road and five entrance roads pass nearly every major park sight and region, with interpretive displays, overlooks, and/or short trails at each. Actual driving times along the 142-mi Grand Loop

Road are difficult to estimate because the maximum speed is 45 mph or lower where posted, roads are narrow and winding, surfaces may be rutted, and traffic may be heavy. If you're nervous about driving steep roads with sharp and sometimes unprotected drop-offs, consider Amfac Parks and Resorts' tour buses (*see* Guided Tours, *below*).

You can drive the Grand Loop Road in a day—but don't do it unless you must. To see Yellowstone's major roadside attractions, you'll need at least three days.

THE BEST IN ONE DAY If you have just one day in Yellowstone, it is best to explore a single area. A good choice would be the five major geyser basins, which all occupy the southwest part of the Grand Loop. At each you can follow short interpretive trails out to major features. Alternatively, you might choose to concentrate on the Grand Canyon of the Yellowstone, taking time to walk either Uncle Tom's Trail or the Lookout Point Trail for close views of the Upper and Lower Falls.

From the North and Northeast. If you are entering the park from the north or northeast, begin at dawn, with wildlife viewing in Lamar Valley. Drive south over Dunraven Pass and spend the morning sightseeing at the Grand Canyon of Yellowstone. Follow the North Rim Drive (*see* Scenic Drives and Views, *below*) stopping to take the very short paved walks out to Inspiration, Grandview, and Lookout points. You can leave the car at either the Inspiration Point or Brink of Upper Falls parking areas and walk all or part of the North Rim Trail (*see* Nature Trails and Short Walks, *below*), which affords views of the river and both the Lower (308 ft) and Upper (109 ft) falls. Return to your car and take Artist Point Drive to Artist Point for the best view of the Lower Falls and much of the canyon (*see* Scenic Drives and Views, *below*). Unwrap a picnic lunch at Chittenden Bridge, where Artist Point Drive connects with the Grand Loop Road.

Continue clockwise around the Grand Loop's north half to Norris. At this point you will have to decide whether you want to veer south for an afternoon around Old Faithful or north to Mammoth Hot Springs. In both areas, many easy walks pass outstanding thermal features. At Old Faithful, you can place the famous geyser into context by walking the 1.3-mi Geyser Hill Loop (*see* Nature Trails and Short Walks, *below*) or a variety of other Upper Geyser Basin trails. Since you've come all this way, you will probably want to join the throngs of visitors waiting for the next eruption: Do it from the deck of the Old Faithful Inn, a building that certainly deserves a bit of your exploring time (*see* Historic Buildings and Sites, *below*).

If you choose Mammoth, park at the base of the Lower Terrace and hike the Lower Terrace Interpretive Trail (*see* Nature Trails and Short Walks, *below*) past Liberty Cap and other strange, brightly colored limestone formations. If you drive 1.5 mi south of the visitor center you will reach the Upper Terrace Drive, from which there are more close-ups of hot springs and an overview of both terraces. (Note: Large RVs and trailers are prohibited on this narrow road.) Later, you can poke around Mammoth's old red-roof Army buildings and finish the day with dinner at the Mammoth Hotel Dining Room or the Terrace Grill.

From the South and West. If you enter the park from the south or west, it makes sense to focus on the geyser basins around Old Faithful, Norris Geyser Basin, Canyon, and Yellowstone Lake. Start with the geysers: Old Faithful's trails are frequently visited by elk in the early morning. After exploring the Upper Geyser Basin around Old Faithful, head north toward Norris Geyser Basin, detouring onto the 3-mi Firehole Lake Drive (*see* Scenic Drives and Views, *below*). When you reach Norris walk the .25 mi out to Steamboat, the world's tallest active geyser (although it seldom erupts), and look around the Norris Museum's geyseriana. At lunchtime, you can drive the 12 mi east to Canyon and eat in Canyon Village, or stop at the Virginia Cascade picnic area, about 5 mi east of Norris.

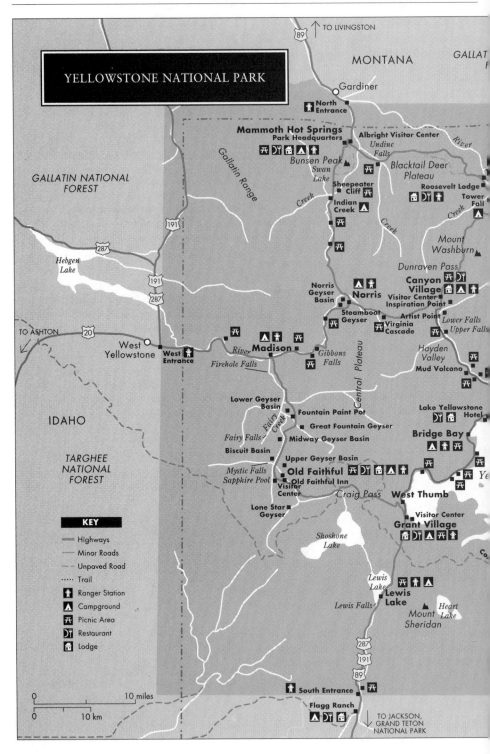

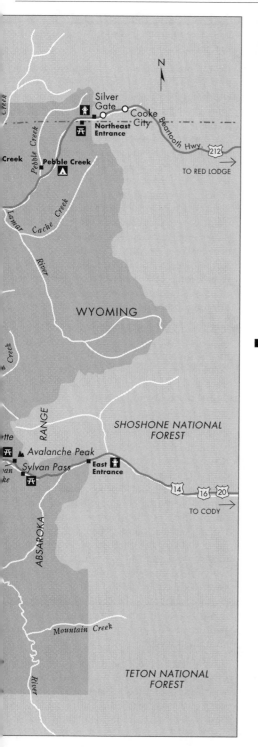

When you're through exploring Canyon (follow the tour described above), head south through Hayden Valley with an eye out for bison and other wildlife. It's 16 mi to Bridge Bay at Yellowstone Lake's northern end. From here take a Scenicruise boat tour (*see* Guided Tours, *below*) of the northern lake, and then have an elegant dinner at Lake Yellowstone Hotel. Drive the 10 mi east to Lake Butte Overlook for spectacular sunset views.

From the East. If you are arriving from the east, start with sunrise at Lake Butte and early morning wildlife viewing in Hayden Valley, moving counterclockwise around the Grand Loop's southern half to morning sightseeing at Canyon, early afternoon at Old Faithful, and back to Yellowstone Lake at West Thumb (*see* tours described *above*). From here follow the lake's western shore back up to Bridge Bay for a late afternoon boat ride and dinner at Lake Yellowstone Hotel.

ORIENTATION PROGRAMS Ranger naturalists give free talks on natural history at all the park's visitor centers in summer, and also lead wildlife field trips (*see* Guided Tours, *below*). At park visitor centers, free films, videos, talks, slide shows, skills workshops, walking tours, campfire programs, and living history demonstrations are geared to various areas in the park. Check *Yellowstone Today,* a seasonal newspaper available at all visitor centers, for details, or call the Office of Interpretation at park headquarters (*see* Visitor Information, *above*). Note that visitor center hours vary depending on the time of year.

Mammoth's Albright Visitor Center (tel. 307/344–2263) alternates the historical film *The Challenge of Yellowstone* with a slide show titled "Winter in Yellowstone" all day during the winter, and has other rotating programs in summer. It is open from 8 to 6 between late May and mid-August, and from 9 to 5 the rest of the year.

Throughout the day the **Old Faithful Visitor Center** (tel. 307/545–2750) shows the nine-minute film *Yellowstone: A Living Sculpture,* which explains the park's geothermal activity. It is open from 8 to 6 between early June and early September, and from 9 to 4:30 between December and mid-March. Spring and fall hours vary but are generally shorter than summer and winter hours.

Canyon Visitor Center (tel. 307/242–2550) focuses on the Grand Canyon of the Yellowstone, with an art exhibit called "Imagine Yellowstone." This center is typically open from 8 to 6 between late May and late September.

GUIDED TOURS Ranger-led programs take place at all visitor centers from mid-June to mid-August. These include one- to three-hour geyser basin hikes at major thermal areas, backcountry orienteering sessions, hawk-watching on the canyon's north rim, bird-watching and "fire of '88" field trips at West Thumb, a six-hour strenuous hike up Specimen Ridge at Mammoth Hot Springs, and photography skills workshops and walks throughout the park. For information call 307/344–7381.

Amfac Parks and Resorts (Yellowstone National Park, WY 82190-9989, tel. 307/344–7311) schedules full-day bus tours from various park locations from mid-May to mid-September ($29, not including lunch). Lower Loop tours leave from Old Faithful and Grant Village; Upper Loop tours leave from Lake, Fishing Bridge, and Canyon. The buses stop frequently, and the guides, mostly college students, are usually knowledgeable and enthusiastic. From early June to late September the company also conducts **Scenicruise Rides,** one-hour boat tours around the northern part of Yellowstone Lake, from which you can view the Absaroka Mountains and the Lake Yellowstone Hotel. The trip is narrated by the captain ($7.50). In winter, Amfac Parks and Resorts has **snow-coach tours** (about $73 round-trip) to Old Faithful and Canyon, full-day **snowmobile tours** ($115 per machine) from Mammoth to Norris Geyser Basin on Thursday, various **cross-country ski tours** ($28–$89), and **winter wildlife bus tours** through Lamar Valley ($14).

National Park Tours (tel. 307/733–4325) leads tours from Jackson, Wyoming, into the park.

If you plan to take a self-guided driving tour of the park, be sure to rent a **Tour-Guide,** a compact-disc player that uses Sony Data Discman CD-ROM technology to teach you about the park. TourGuide has five hours of well-presented audio, covering history, geology, wildlife, ecology, and park services, as well as a few visuals. Blocks of information are numerically coded, and you can easily select what you want to hear by punching the appropriate numbers on the keypad. The unit, which plugs into your car's cigarette lighter and broadcasts over your FM radio, rents for $24.95 per day and is available at nine locations—four just outside the park's entrances and at all hotels within the park. For more information, call 800/247–1213.

SCENIC DRIVES AND VIEWS There are 370 mi of paved roadway within Yellowstone, and the figure-eight pattern of the Grand Loop Road makes all areas of the park accessible. Hardly a segment of road is dull, but the following tour points out various highlights.

In the northwest section of the park, south of Mammoth Hot Springs, the Grand Loop Road passes the inactive hot spring cone called Liberty Cap, which is visible from the Mammoth Hot Springs parking area. Two miles south of Mammoth off the Grand Loop Road is the narrow and tortuous **Upper Terrace Loop Drive,** a 1.5-mi tour past 500-year-old limber pine trees and mosses growing through white travertine, which is composed of lime deposited when Mammoth's hot, acidic springs come in contact with open air. This eerie landscape is further delineated by brilliant orange, yellow, green, and brown algae growing atop the travertine.

If you travel the Grand Loop Road east toward Roosevelt, you will pass the one-way **Blacktail Plateau Drive,** a dirt road that traverses sagebrush hills and pine forests. The 45-minute excursion may reward you with a coyote sighting in early evening.

In the 19 mi from Roosevelt south to Canyon, the **northeastern Grand Loop** passes some of the park's finest scenery, twisting beneath a series of leaning basalt towers 40 to 50 ft high. Take the short path from the Tower Fall store's parking lot to view 132-ft Tower Fall, which is at its best in morning. Ascending through arid sagebrush fields dotted with stands of aspen and heavily burned areas, the road passes 10,243-ft Mt. Washburn. The rough, unpaved **Chittenden Road** leaves the main road for a 2-mi bounce up a north flank of the mountain to a sweeping overlook. You'll have to hike the last 3 mi to reach the Grand Loop's highest point, Dunraven Pass (8,859 ft), which is covered with wildflowers and subalpine fir in spring and summer.

At Canyon Village, the paved 2.5-mi one-way **North Rim Drive** leads first to Inspiration Point, where the Yellowstone River plunges 900 ft below. The often-crowded overlook is a two-minute trek uphill, then down about a dozen steps. The next stop on this detour is Grandview Point, where another short paved trail leads to a view of the 308-ft Lower Falls in the distance. A little farther along is Lookout Point. From here a difficult .5-mi switchback trail descends 600 ft to the Brink of the Lower Falls; this trail is best taken in morning, when sunlight often creates a misty rainbow.

Return to Grand Loop Road. Less than .5 mi along, turn left into Upper Falls Parking Area. From there you can hike the 500-ft trail to a platform hanging over the 109-ft Upper Falls. Drive another .5 mi south on the Grand Loop, turn left onto the Chittenden Bridge, and follow **Artist Point Drive,** which leads to the best Canyon views. The five-minute walk from the parking area ends at a platform perched 700 ft above the canyon's gray, pink, orange, and yellow rhyolite rock—one of the park's most photographed scenes.

Moving south out of Canyon, the 16 mi to Fishing Bridge (turn left onto East Entrance

Road to reach it) crosses Hayden Valley, one of Yellowstone's best roadside wildlife viewing areas. Fishing Bridge, once famous for postcards showing fishermen lining its banks, is now reserved for cutthroat trout spawning and the waterfowl activity that attends it. You can watch from a viewing area on the bridge. Ten miles east, a 1-mi spur road leads to **Lake Butte,** a wooded promontory rising 615 ft above Yellowstone Lake and a prime sunset-watching spot. The **East Entrance Road** continues 16 mi from Lake Butte to the park boundary, winding through the Absarokas. This is the most beautiful alpine setting of any park road.

Traveling west from Fishing Bridge to West Thumb, the Grand Loop Road follows Yellowstone Lake for about 23 mi, with numerous turnoffs and picnic areas. About 12 mi south of West Thumb, the **South Entrance Road** tops the sheer black lava walls of Lewis River Canyon, another place that was heavily burned. Turn into the parking area just before the bridge here for a close-up of Lewis River Falls.

Going northwest 17 mi from West Thumb on the Grand Loop Road, you'll reach **Old Faithful Road,** on your right. Park at the visitor center and walk the few hundred feet to benches surrounding Old Faithful Geyser. Although not the park's biggest geyser, Old Faithful has been the world's most famous geyser since 1870; each of the 18 to 22 daily eruptions is predicted at the visitor center.

About 8 mi north of Old Faithful, on the right, the 3-mi (one-way) **Firehole Lake Drive** passes Great Fountain Geyser, which explodes between 75 and 150 ft into the air, and on occasion reaches as high as 200 ft. If you're touring the park by snow coach in winter, watch for bison here. Just before crossing the Firehole River, you will come to the entrance to the paved 2-mi (one-way) **Firehole Canyon Drive,** on your left. This road twists through a 700- to 800-ft-deep canyon past 40-ft Firehole Falls.

At this point you will have reached Madison. Traveling east, the Grand Loop enters

1,000-ft deep Gibbon Canyon, whose black lava walls contrast sharply with its riverbed reddened by iron deposits. Gibbon Falls drops 84 ft in this canyon; it is actually cascading over a piece of the Yellowstone Caldera's northwest rim. An adjacent picnic area overlooks the canyon. West of Madison, the **West Entrance Road** hugs the Madison River for 14 mi: This is a fine sunset drive, with views of National Park Mountain and the heavily fished Madison River.

Norris Junction, site of Norris Geyser Basin, is 14 mi northeast of Madison on Grand Loop Road. Though oddly not as renowned as Old Faithful's Upper Geyser Basin, Norris is richer in superlatives: North America's hottest geyser basin (highest underground recording: 459°F); Yellowstone's oldest geyser basin (over 115,000 years old); and site of the world's tallest individual geyser (Steamboat Geyser, with rare eruptions over 300 ft—three in 1989, one in 1990, and one in 1991). Norris is divided into the open, concentrated geysers of Porcelain Basin on the east and the forested, scattered geysers of Back Basin on the west, with the quaint 1930 log-and-stone Norris Museum in the middle (*see* Nature Trails and Short Walks, *below*).

Mammoth Hot Springs is 21 mi north of Norris. Eight miles into this stretch on the right you pass Obsidian Cliff, whose volcanic glass was prized by the region's Native American tribes for projectile points. About 5 mi farther north on the right is a .5-mi turnoff to Sheepeater Cliff, where the park's only known year-round Native American inhabitants—a couple of hundred Shoshones nicknamed "Sheepeaters" by other tribes—lived until the 1870s. A small display here describes their meager existence. Immediately north of here the main road opens onto Swan Lake Flats, a prime elk habitat, and then continues to Mammoth.

HISTORIC BUILDINGS AND SITES Among the stern, gray stone buildings at Mammoth is the **Albright Visitor Center,** which was an Army Bachelor Officers' Quarters from 1886 to 1918. Also dating from the time when Mammoth was Fort Yellowstone are the former **Surveyor's Headquarters,** now park offices (next to the hotel), and the former **parade grounds,** now an empty field below the Terrace Restaurant.

Completed in 1891 and restored for its 1991 centennial, the **Lake Yellowstone Hotel** is the oldest surviving lodging in any national park and is listed on the National Register of Historic Places. The hotel was quite plain until a 1903 renovation, when architect Robert Reamer added the columns, gables, and decorative moldings that give it its distinctive neo-Colonial air. In 1923 and 1927 Reamer completed the hotel's transformation from railroad hostelry to elegant resort with lobby and dining room renovations. (*See* Lodging, *below*.)

It is hard to imagine that any work could be done in Yellowstone during the long, cold winter, but the **Old Faithful Inn** was built during the winter of 1903, also under the direction of Robert Reamer. The inn is as massively rustic as the Lake Yellowstone Hotel is elegant, and other than two flat-roof wings added in 1913 and 1927, it looks much as it did in 1904. A foundation of volcanic rhyolite and giant lodgepole pillars support the 79-ft-high structure, one of the world's tallest log buildings. From its steeply pitched roof looms an uneven array of dormer windows with crisscrossed lodgepole decorations. During the summer, an employee dressed as a 1915 chambermaid gives living-history tours of the property. Another 500 tons of rhyolite form the 40-ft-high lobby chimney. The lobby also has a gargantuan popcorn popper and a 14-ft-long clock. (*See* Lodging, *below*.)

NATURE TRAILS AND SHORT WALKS There are 1,210 mi of trails and 85 trailheads in Yellowstone. Because of space limitations, it is impossible to describe all of the trails here, so a sampling is given. Don't be surprised to find some trails closed temporarily due to weather conditions or bear activity. For

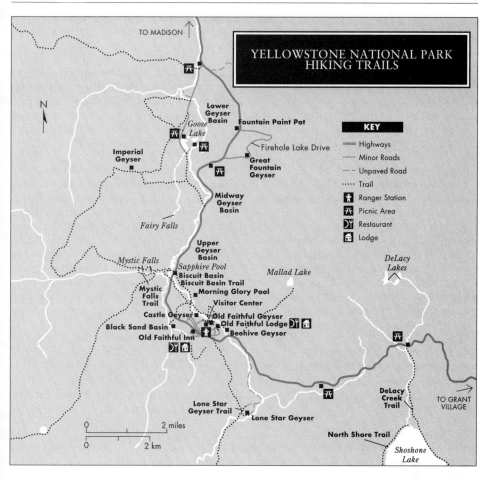

YELLOWSTONE NATIONAL PARK
HIKING TRAILS

TO MADISON

Lower
Geyser
Basin
Goose Fountain Paint Pot
Lake

Imperial
Geyser

Firehole Lake Drive

Great
Fountain
Geyser

Midway
Geyser
Basin

Fairy Falls

Upper
Geyser
Basin
Mystic Falls *Sapphire Pool* *Mallad Lake*
Biscuit Basin
Biscuit Basin Trail
Mystic Morning Glory Pool
Falls Visitor Center
Trail
Castle Geyser Old Faithful Geyser
Black Sand Basin Old Faithful Lodge
Beehive Geyser
Old Faithful Inn

*DeLacy
Lakes*

Lone Star
Geyser Trail
Lone Star Geyser

*DeLacy
Creek
Trail*

TO GRANT
VILLAGE

North Shore Trail

*Shoshone
Lake*

KEY

Highways
Minor Roads
Unpaved Road
Trail
Ranger Station
Picnic Area
Restaurant
Lodge

N

0   2 miles
0   2 km

more information on specific areas of the park, contact the visitor center in that area (*see* Visitor Information, *above*).

From parking areas at the south end of Mammoth village, the **Lower Terrace Interpretive Trail** leads past the most outstanding features of the multicolored, steaming Mammoth Hot Springs. Start at Liberty Cap, at the area's north end, named for its resemblance to Revolutionary War patriots' caps. Head uphill on the boardwalks past bright and ornately terraced Minerva Spring. Alternatively, drive up to the Lower Terrace Overlook on Upper Terrace Drive (*see* Scenic Drives and Views, *above*) and take the boardwalks down past New Blue

Springs (which, inexplicably, is no longer blue) to the Lower Terrace. This route works especially well if you can park a second vehicle at the foot of Lower Terrace. Either route should take about an hour.

From the lookout point at Tower Fall (*see* Scenic Drives and Views, *above*), the .5-mi (round-trip) **Tower Fall Trail** switchbacks down through pine trees matted with luminous green wolf lichen to the base of the waterfall. There, you will find yourself at the northern end of the Grand Canyon of the Yellowstone, whose more famous section lies 18 mi upriver (south).

At Canyon, the 1.75-mi (one-way) **North Rim Trail** from Grandview Point to Chittenden Bridge and the 2-mi (one-way) **South Rim Trail** from Chittenden Bridge to Artist Point connect to all major turnoffs from the North Rim and Artist Point drives. You can take small sections of these trails or combine the two into a three-hour (one-way) Grand Canyon experience far more intimate than you get just scurrying to and from your car along the way (it is, however, helpful to have a car parked at either end). The .5-mi (one-way) section of the North Rim Trail from the Brink of Upper Falls Parking Area to Chittenden Bridge hugs the rushing Yellowstone as it approaches the Canyon. Both trails are partly paved and fairly level, and throughout these walks you'll get spectacular views of the canyon, which is up to 1,200 ft deep and has sheer walls of yellow, red, brown, and white rock; the silvery thread of foam is the river below. To hear and feel the Yellowstone's power, follow the much steeper side trails into the canyon: The **Brink of Lower Falls Trail** switchbacks .5 mi one way from the parking area of that name (it's 1.75 mi south of Inspiration Point on the North Rim Trail) 600 ft down to the brink of Lower Falls.

Even more spectacular—and very strenuous—is the 700-step **Uncle Tom's Trail,** which descends 500 ft from the parking area of that name off Artist Point Drive or from a turnoff at South Rim Trail (both about .5 mi north of Chittenden Bridge) to the roaring base of Lower Falls. Much of this walk is on steel sheeting, which can have a film of ice in early morning or in spring and fall.

At the Mud Volcano parking area, some 10 mi south of Canyon, the .75-mi round-trip **Mud Volcano Interpretive Trail** loops gently around seething, sulfuric mud pots with such names as Sizzling Basin and Black Dragon's Cauldron and around Mud Volcano itself.

Drive another 6 mi south to Lake Junction and 3 mi east on the East Entrance Road to reach the well-marked and mostly flat 1.5-mi loop of **Storm Point Trail,** which leaves the south side of the road for a perfect beginner's hike out to Yellowstone Lake. The trail rounds the western edge of Indian Pond, then passes moose habitat on its way to Yellowstone Lake's Storm Point, named for its frequent afternoon wind storms and crashing waves. Heading west along the shore, you're likely to hear the shrill chirping of yellow-bellied marmots, rodents that grow as long as 2 ft. Also look for ducks, pelicans, and trumpeter swans.

Old Faithful and its environs in the Upper Geyser Basin are rich in short walking options, starting with three connected loops that depart from Old Faithful Visitor Center. The .75-mi **Old Faithful Geyser Loop** simply circles the benches around Old Faithful, filled nearly all day long in summer with tourists. Currently erupting approximately every 79 minutes, Yellowstone's most frequently erupting big geyser—although not its largest or most regular—reaches heights of 100 to 180 ft. Head counterclockwise around the Old Faithful boardwalk .3 mi from the visitor center, crossing the bubbling Firehole River to the turnoff for **Geyser Hill Loop,** a 1.3-mi round-trip from the visitor center. The first attraction is on your left: violent but infrequent Giantess Geyser. Giantess is normally active only a few times each year, but when it does erupt, it spouts 100 to 250 ft high for five to eight minutes once or twice hourly for 12 to 43 hours; the ground shakes from its underground explosions. A bit farther on your left is Doublet Pool, two adjacent springs whose complex ledges and deep blue waters are highly photogenic. Near the loop's end on your right, Anemone Geyser starts as a gentle pool, overflows, bubbles, and finally erupts, 10 ft or more, repeating the cycle every three to eight minutes. **Observation Point Loop,** a 2-mi round-trip from the visitor center, leaves Geyser Hill Loop boardwalk and becomes a trail shortly after the boardwalk crosses the Firehole River; it circles a picturesque overview of Geyser Hill with Old Faithful Inn as a backdrop. A longer but still easy boardwalk trek is the **Morning Glory Pool Trail,** 1.5 mi one way from the visitor center. This route passes stately Castle Geyser, which possesses the biggest cone of any park geyser and currently erupts every 10 to 12 hours, to heights of 90 ft for up to an hour. Morning Glory Pool, named for its resemblance in shape and color to the flower, is a testament to human ignorance: Tons of coins and trash tossed into it over the years clogged its vent, cooling it and allowing brown and green bacteria to spread to the center.

Three miles north of Old Faithful off the Grand Loop Road, the Biscuit Basin Parking Area accesses the 2.5-mi round-trip **Biscuit Basin Trail,** a boardwalk across the Firehole River to colorful Sapphire Pool. From the boardwalk's west end, the **Mystic Falls Trail** (a trail, not a boardwalk) gently climbs 1 mi (3.5 mi round-trip from Biscuit Basin Parking Area) through heavily burned forest to the lava-rock base of 70-ft Mystic Falls, then switchbacks up Madison Plateau to a lookout with the park's least-crowded view of Old Faithful and Upper Geyser Basin.

Directly across Grand Loop Road from the end of Firehole Lake Drive, the **Fountain Paint Pot Nature Trail** is an easy .5-mi loop boardwalk past hot springs, colorful mud pots, and dry fumaroles at its highest point.

At Norris Geyser Basin, **Porcelain Basin Trail** is a .75-mi, partially boardwalked loop from the north end of Norris Museum through whitish geyserite stone and past extremely active Whirligig and other small geysers. **Back Basin Trail** is a 1.5-mi loop from the museum's south end past Emerald Spring, Steamboat Geyser, Cistern Spring (which drains when Steamboat erupts), and Echinus Geyser. The latter erupts 50 to 100 ft every 35 to 75 minutes, making it Norris's most dependable big geyser.

LONGER HIKES Again, space allows for only a sampling of Yellowstone's many longer hikes. Always check at a ranger station for trail and wildlife conditions, sign the trailhead register, and carry a topographical map on backcountry hikes.

At Mammoth, the 2.5-hour, 5-mi round-trip **Beaver Ponds Loop Trail** starts at Liberty Cap, climbing 400 ft through .5 mi of spruce, fir, and open meadows, past beaver ponds (look for their dams) and spectacular views of the Mammoth Terraces on the way down. Moose, antelope, and occasional bears may be sighted.

South of Mammoth on the left side of Bunsen Peak Road, just past the entrance to the road, the moderately difficult 4-mi, three-hour round-trip **Bunsen Peak Trail** climbs 1,300 ft to Bunsen Peak for a panoramic view of Blacktail Plateau, Swan Lake Flats, the Gallatin Mountains, and the Yellowstone River valley (use a topographical map to locate these landmarks). The easier 4-mi, two-hour round-trip **Osprey Falls Trail** starts near the entrance of Bunsen Peak Road. A series of switchbacks drops 800 ft to the bottom of Sheepeater Canyon and the base of the Gardner River's 151-ft Osprey Falls. As at Tower Fall (*see* Scenic Drives and Views, *above*), the canyon walls are basalt columns formed by ancient lava flow.

Starting at Slough Creek Campground some 7 mi east of Tower-Roosevelt Junction off the Northeast Entrance Road, the **Slough Creek Trail** climbs steeply for the first 1.5 mi before reaching expansive meadows and prime fishing spots, where moose are common and grizzlies occasionally wander. From this point the trail, now mostly level, meanders another 9.5 mi to the park's northern boundary.

Nineteen miles east of Lake Junction on the north side of East Entrance Road and across from a parking area, the difficult 4-mi, four-hour round-trip **Avalanche Peak Trail** (closed for construction at press time) climbs 2,150 ft to the peak's 10,566-ft summit, from which you'll see the rugged Absaroka Mountains running north and south. Some of these peaks have patches of snow year-round. Look around the talus and tundra near the top of Avalanche Peak for alpine wildflowers and butterflies. Below you, Yellowstone Lake spreads magnificently; use your topographical map to distinguish its various arms. Don't try this trail before late June or after early September—it may be covered in snow. At any time of year, carry a jacket: The winds at the top are strong.

Starting 1 mi north of Lewis Lake on the east side of South Entrance Road, the very difficult 24-mi, 13-hour round-trip **Heart Lake–Mt. Sheridan Trail** provides one of the park's premier overnight backcountry experiences. After traversing 5.5 mi of partly burned lodgepole pine forest, the trail descends into Heart Lake Geyser Basin, reaching Heart Lake at the 8-mi mark. This is one of Yellowstone's most active backcountry thermal areas (the biggest geyser here is Rustic Geyser, which erupts 25 to 30 ft about every 15 minutes). Circle .5 mi counterclockwise around the northern tip of Heart Lake and camp at one of five designated backcountry sites on the western shore (remember to get your permit beforehand); enjoy the hazy sunrise over the lake next morning. Leave all but essentials here (you'll return by the same route) for the 3-mi, 2,700-ft climb to the top of 10,308-ft Mt. Sheridan. Heart Lake will be directly below you, and Shoshone and Lewis lakes, along with part of Yellowstone Lake, unfold in the distance. To the south, looking very close, you'll see the Tetons.

The **Shoshone Lake–Shoshone Geyser Basin Trail** is a 22-mi, 11-hour moderately difficult overnight trip combining several shorter trails. (It can be abridged into a simple day hike out to Shoshone Lake.) The trail starts as DeLacy Creek Trail 8 mi east of Old Faithful on Grand Loop Road's north side, gently descending for 3 mi to Shoshone Lake's north shore. On the way, look for sandhill cranes and browsing moose. At the lake turn right and follow the North Shore Trail 8 mi, first along the beach and then through lodgepole forest. Make sure you've reserved one of the several good backcountry campsites along this trail. Also take time to explore the Shoshone Geyser Basin, reached by turning left at the fork at the end of the trail and walking about .25 mi. Next

morning turn right at the fork, follow Shoshone Creek for 2 mi, and make the gradual climb over Grant's Pass. At the 17-mi mark the trail crosses the Firehole River and divides; take a right onto Lone Star Geyser Trail and continue past this fine coned geyser through Upper Geyser Basin backcountry to Lone Star Geyser Trailhead, 2 mi east of Old Faithful on the Grand Loop Road.

In the park's far northwest, starting on the east side of U.S. 191, 25 mi north of West Yellowstone, the extremely difficult 16.5-mi, 10-hour **Skyline Trail** is another combination trail that climbs up and over numerous peaks whose ridgelines mark the park's northwest boundary before looping sharply back down to U.S. 191 via Black Butte Creek. Starting at Specimen Creek Trailhead, follow **Specimen Creek Trail** 2.5 mi and turn left at the junction, passing petrified trees to your left past the junction. At the 6.5-mi mark, turn left again at the fork and start climbing 1,400 ft for 2 mi up to Shelf Lake, one of the park's highest bodies of water at 9,200 ft altitude. The lake has two designated backcountry campsites; your night here will be cold even in the heart of summer. Just past the lake begins Skyline Trail proper, which follows the ridge with steep drop-offs on either side and craggy Bighorn Peak looming ahead. Watch for bighorn sheep and marvel at the spectacular vistas as you approach Bighorn Peak's summit. The trail's most treacherous section is just past the summit, where it drops 2,300 ft in the first 2.5 mi of descent; make sure you take a left where the trail forks at the big meadow just past the summit (otherwise you'll keep following Skyline Trail) to reach Black Butte Creek Trail, which hits U.S. 191 just 2 mi north of your starting point. Moose and elk can be seen along this last 2.5-mi stretch.

OTHER ACTIVITIES **Back-Road Driving.** All-terrain vehicles are not allowed on any trails, and all other vehicles are restricted to designated roads.

Biking. More visitors tour parts of the park by bicycle every year, despite the fact that

Yellowstone's roads are typically narrow, rough, and without shoulders. Some 300 mi of roadway are available to bicyclists, but bikes are prohibited on trails and in the backcountry. Blacktail Deer Plateau Road, near Mammoth, allows two-way bike and one-way auto traffic. Bicyclists face stiff climbs at Craig Pass, between Old Faithful and West Thumb; Sylvan Pass, between the East entrance and Fishing Bridge; and Dunraven Pass, north of Canyon.

Some roads restricted to bicycle and foot travel are: the abandoned railroad bed paralleling the Yellowstone River near Mammoth (5 mi); Riverside Trail, which starts at the west entrance (1 mi); the paved trail from Old Faithful's Hamilton Store to Morning Glory Pool (2 mi); and Natural Bridge Road, near Bridge Bay (1 mi).

Bikes can be rented in West Yellowstone, Gardiner, Livingston, and Bozeman, Montana, as well as in Cody and Jackson, Wyoming. A big selection of mountain bikes is available from **Mountain Bike Outfitters** (tel. 307/733–3314) in Moose, Wyoming, north of Jackson, for $6 per hour and $24 per day.

Boating. Boating is allowed on Yellowstone and other lakes, but you must have a permit ($5 nonmotorized), which can be obtained in person at the south entrance, Lewis Lake Campground, Grant Village Visitor Center, Bridge Bay Marina, Lake Ranger Station, or Mammoth Visitor Center. Be aware that Yellowstone Lake is subject to sudden high winds, and its waters are extremely cold. Boating is not allowed on rivers and streams, nor on Sylvan, Eleanor, and Twin lakes.

Amfac Parks and Resorts (tel. 307/344–7311) rents boats at Bridge Bay Marina from mid-June through mid-September (*see* Visitor Information, *above*). Rowboats cost $5.50 per hour or $25 per eight-hour day; 18-ft outboards cost $25 per hour; 22- and 34-ft cabin cruisers with fishing tackle included cost $45 and $59 per hour (minimum two hours); docking slips for private boats cost $8 to $10 per night.

Fishing. The season starts Memorial Day weekend and ends the first Sunday in November. Cutthroat, brook, lake, and rainbow trout, along with grayling and mountain whitefish, inhabit Yellowstone's waters. Everyone 16 and older must have a fishing permit, which is available at any ranger station, visitor center, or Hamilton store. Permits cost $10 for 10 days or $20 for the season. Children age 11 and under need no permit, but they must have supervision. Catch and release is the general policy, but there are exceptions: Get a copy of the fishing regulations at any visitor center. No live bait is allowed; lead-free tackle is required. Prime areas include Yellowstone River north of Canyon; Madison River between Madison and the west entrance; and Yellowstone, Sylvan, and Shoshone lakes. Fishing supplies are available at all Hamilton stores; the biggest selection is at Bridge Bay.

Horseback Riding. Since many of the horses that are used on guided tours have been ridden by too many people, the animals are often unresponsive. Amfac Parks and Resorts (tel. 307/344–7311) runs one- and two-hour guided rides that leave Mammoth from late May through mid-September, Roosevelt and Canyon from late June to mid-September; the trips cost $18.50 for one hour and $28.50 for two hours.

Better than the above guided tours is the nightly trail ride to the Old West Cookout, which leaves from Roosevelt Lodge at 4:30 and 5:15, depending on how long a ride you want to take. This trip is available between early June and early September and costs about $32 for a one-hour ride and $41 for a two-hour ride. Advance reservations are required. Check at lodging activities desks, or contact Amfac Parks and Resorts (tel. 307/344–7311).

About 50 area outfitters also lead horsepacking trips and trail rides into Yellowstone. Expect to pay about $950 for a five-day/four-night backcountry trip, $1,450 for an eight-day/seven-night trip, or $1,550 for nine days/eight nights, including meals, horses, tents, and guides. Try **Schmalz Outfitting** (Box 604, Cody, WY 82424, tel. 307/587–5929 or 800/587–5929), or contact the park (tel. 307/344–7381) for a complete listing. You cannot rent a horse without a guide.

Skiing and Snowshoeing. You can rent touring and telemark skis and snowshoes from Amfac Parks and Resorts at Mammoth Hot Springs Hotel and Old Faithful Snow Lodge. Rentals cost $12.50 per day for touring skis and telemark skis, and $10 for snowshoes. Skier shuttles run from Mammoth Hotel to Mammoth Terraces (free), Mammoth Hotel to Tower ($9 round-trip), and Snow Lodge to Fairy Falls ($7.50, drop-offs only). Canyon, West Thumb, and Madison have intermittently staffed warming huts; huts at Indian Creek, Fishing Bridge, and Old Faithful are unstaffed. All are open 24 hours. At Old Faithful, the easy Lone Star Geyser Trail passes thermal features and links to several other trails ranging from easy to difficult. The Riverside Trail starting at the west entrance follows the Madison River and involves one traverse up a short, steep hill. The Canyon area has trails for beginner to intermediate skiers with some awesome rimside views, as well as dangerous switchbacks for advanced skiers only. Detailed maps are available at the visitor center.

Downhill skiers can head to the slopes in Jackson Hole (*See* Grand Teton National Park chapter for information.)

Snowmobiling. This is one of the most exhilarating ways to see the park and its wildlife. Most of the Grand Loop as well as the west, south, and east entrance roads are open to snowmobiles from mid-December to mid-March; though some roads may be inaccessible due to wildlife concerns (call the visitor center for an update). You must drive on the right and in single file. You must be 16 or older, with a valid driver's license, to ride a snowmobile alone in the park.

Amfac Parks and Resorts (tel. 307/344–7311) rents snowmobiles at Mammoth

Hotel and Old Faithful Snow Lodge for $115 per day. In West Yellowstone try **Ranch Snowmobile Rentals** (tel. 406/646–7388 or 800/234–4083) or **Rendezvous Snowmobile Rentals** (tel. 406/646–9564 or 800/426–7669); at the east entrance, **Pahaska Teepee** (tel. 307/527–7701 or 800/628–7791) rents snowmobiles as well as cabins.

CHILDREN'S PROGRAMS Ranger-led activities at all visitor centers (*see* Orientation Programs *and* Guided Tours, *above*) include seasonal children's programs. Some topics: 19th-century stagecoach robberies, geysers, nature games, bears, and animal tracking. Most are free and aimed at children six to 12, and many are accessible to people using wheelchairs. Some require reservations at visitor centers; baby-sitting is not available.

EVENING ACTIVITIES Mammoth, Canyon, Grant Village, and Bridge Bay amphitheaters hold free ranger-led campfire programs at 9 and 9:30 during summer. Topics may include Yellowstone's food chain, Native American and mountain-man legends, animal bones, bison, and 19th-century photographers.

DINING

The Northern Rockies have come a long way since the days when roadside signs advised "This is cow country—eat beef!" You'll still find excellent steaks and prime rib, cut from grass-fed beef, but new eating habits have also taken hold. Among the offerings are grilled chicken and fish, vegetarian dishes, and light sauces. Expect less formality than you'd find elsewhere, even in the fanciest dining rooms. All restaurants within the park are run by **Amfac Parks and Resorts** (Yellowstone National Park, WY 82190-9989, tel. 307/344–7901 for reservations).

INSIDE THE PARK **Lake Yellowstone Hotel Dining Room.** This double-colonnaded dining room adjoining the hotel lobby has wine-and-green carpeting, peach walls, wicker chairs, and linen napkins—as well as great scenes of wildlife through its big square windows overlooking the lake. The clientele tends to be older and quieter than that at other park restaurants. Specialties include prime rib prepared in a dry marinade of thyme, rosemary, and garlic; fettuccine with smoked salmon, asparagus, and a light dill cream sauce; and Tuscan shrimp, with Tuscan peppers, sautéed mushrooms, and roasted tomatoes, finished with wine and fresh basil. Baked acorn squash filled with cheese, raisins, and apples is a popular entrée. *Lake Yellowstone Hotel, Lake Village Rd. Reservations required for dinner. AE, D, DC, MC, V. Closed early Oct.–late May. $$–$$$*

Grant Village Restaurant. The floor-to-ceiling windows of this lakeshore restaurant provide grand views, but the green director-style chairs are uncomfortable. The most contemporary of the park's restaurants, Grant Village has pine-beam high ceilings and cedar-shake walls. Order the 10-ounce New York strip steak topped with sautéed mushrooms or the fettuccine primavera. *Next to post office on Grant Village Rd. Reservations required for dinner. AE, D, DC, MC, V. Closed late Sept.–late May. $$*

Mammoth Hot Springs Dining Room. A windowed wall in this dining room overlooks what was once the Army's parade and drill field at Mammoth Hot Springs. The airy art deco–style restaurant is decorated in gray, deep green, and burgundy, with upholstered bentwood chairs. The two best entrées here are the nearly boneless panfried Idaho trout topped with slivered almonds, and the fettuccine in pesto sauce with shrimp and scallops. *Across street from Mammoth Hot Springs Hotel. Reservations required for dinner. AE, D, DC, MC, V. Closed mid-Oct.–mid-Dec. and mid-Mar.–mid-May. $$*

Old Faithful Inn Dining Room. Lodgepole walls and ceiling beams, a giant volcanic rock fireplace, and green-tinted windows etched with scenes from the 1920s set the mood here. Soaked in history, the restaurant remains a big, friendly place where servers somehow find time amid the bustle to chat with diners about their home states and the park. Specialties include grilled ahi tuna finished with Arizona chili butter, and grilled chicken breast glazed with honey-lemon butter. Don't pass up the mud pie—coffee ice cream in Oreo cookie crust, smothered in melted fudge, and topped with pecans. The buffet breakfast is daunting. *Old Faithful Inn. Reservations required for dinner. AE, D, DC, MC, V. Closed late Oct.–early May. $$*

Roosevelt Lodge Dining Room. The pine chairs and tables in this rustic eatery are often filled with locals from the towns surrounding the park. Many come to indulge in the restaurant's "family menu," in which each entrée is served with separate bowls of coleslaw, mashed potatoes, corn, baked beans, and cornbread muffins with honey. Good choices are barbecued baby-back pork ribs and fried chicken. *Roosevelt Lodge. AE, D, DC, MC, V. Closed early Sept.–early June. $$*

Old Faithful Snow Lodge Restaurant. Next to the Old Faithful Inn, this unimposing little restaurant has fake wood paneling, oilcloth tablecloths, and low prices that attract families. The menu is the same for lunch and dinner, with hearty soups, hamburgers, and seafood lasagna as top choices. *Old Faithful Snow Lodge, Old Faithful Bypass Rd. AE, D, DC, MC, V. Closed early Oct.–mid-Dec., mid-Mar.–mid-May; no lunch early Sept.–early Oct. $*

A number of park cafeterias serve standard burgers, meat loaf, and sandwiches. These are usually large, bustling places frequented by families, and the volume can be quite loud. They all accept AE, D, DC, MC, and V. Brief reviews follow.

Canyon Lodge Cafeteria. This is the park's busiest lunch spot, serving chili, soups, and such traditional American fare as meat loaf and hot turkey sandwiches. It has a full breakfast menu. *Off North Rim Dr. Closed mid-Sept.–early June. $*

Lake Lodge Cafeteria. Choose from a full breakfast menu as well as hearty lunches and suppers. *Far end of Lake Village Rd. Closed mid-Sept.–early June. $*

Old Faithful Lodge Cafeteria. This cafeteria has the best tableside view of Old Faithful. It serves meat loaf, lasagna, individual pizzas, and more, all day long. *South end of Old Faithful Bypass Rd. Closed mid-Sept.– mid-May. $*

Pony Express Snack Shop. You can get fast-food burgers, sandwiches, and french fries all day. *Off Old Faithful Inn lobby. Closed early Oct.–late May. $*

Terrace Grill. Although the exterior is elegant, only fast food is served. *Side entrance to Mammoth Hot Springs Hotel. Closed late Sept.–mid-May. $*

NEAR THE PARK **Chico Hot Springs Restaurant.** A long, low room in a resort dating from the turn of the century, this is one of Montana's best restaurants. Pine tables, upturned barrels as server stations, and informal young servers give Chico its ranch atmosphere. The clientele is a mix of Yellowstone-bound tourists, local ranchers, and trendy Montanans from as far away as Helena. Especially good are the beef Wellington and the filet mignon cut from grass-fed Montana beef. Outlandish desserts include a Chocolate Oblivion torte. The all-you-can-eat Sunday brunch features custom-made omelets as well as muffins and breads baked on the premises. Behind the restaurant is one of the region's most rollicking saloons, with live country or rock music on weekends. *25 mi south of park on E. River Rd., Pray, MT, tel. 406/ 333–4933. Reservations required for dinner. D, MC, V. $$$*

Livingston Bar and Grill. This spot attracts Paradise Valley locals, who socialize at its mahogany bar. The French Country cuisine includes lamb, duck, rabbit, and a variety of fresh fish and pastas. *130 N. Main St., Livingston, MT, tel. 406/222–7909. MC, V. $$*

Proud Cut. Some of the best prime rib in northwest Wyoming is served in this cow-boy-style restaurant and bar, complete with historic Western photographs. The full menu includes steak, shrimp, crab legs, ½-pound cheeseburgers, homemade soups, and desserts. *1227 Sheridan Ave., Cody, WY, tel. 307/527–6905. AE, D, DC, MC, V. $$*

Bacchus Pub and the Pasta Co. The pub, actually a café with tables and a counter, is in the restored lobby of the former Baxter Hotel. It serves burgers, sandwiches on whole wheat, and hearty soups. The French dip roast beef and meatball subs are especially good. The Pasta Co. is a dinner restaurant set into one of the lobby's darker recesses. It does creditable versions of such regional Italian specialties as baked pasta primavera and fettuccine Alfredo, along with poultry, veal, seafood, and beef entrées. Its Continental menu includes roast prime rib, seared chicken breast, lamb chops, and herb-crusted salmon. *105 W. Main, Bozeman, MT, tel. 406/586–1314. AE, D, MC, V. No lunch at Pasta Co. $–$$*

La Comida. With indoor country Mexican decor and shaded sidewalk tables in downtown Cody, this tourist and lunch-crowd favorite serves better-than-average combination plates of chicken, spinach, pork, and beef enchiladas, burritos, and tacos. *1385 Sheridan Ave., Cody, WY, tel. 307/ 587–9556. AE, D, DC, MC, V. $–$$*

Trapper's Inn. This popular restaurant recalls the days of the mountain men with a menu featuring sourdough pancakes, biscuits, and rolls accompanying massive breakfasts; thick soups; and steak dinners. The decor runs to pine furniture and mountain-man memorabilia. Trout with eggs is one of the best breakfast dishes; lunch standouts include buffalo burgers on sourdough bread, and onion soup. *315 Madison Ave., West Yellowstone, MT, tel. 406/646– 9375. AE, MC, V. $–$$*

Casa Sanchez. The best Mexican food in Yellowstone country is served in two downstairs rooms of a converted house on a Bozeman side street. Casa Sanchez is decorated in turn-of-the-century style, and the hands-on attention from its owner results in superb *chile verde* (green chili with pork), *colorado* (red chili with beef), *carne asada* burritos, and pork or chicken enchiladas. The hot sauce here is extremely hot. Enjoy your meal on the redwood deck in summer. *719 S. 9th St., Bozeman, MT, tel. 406/586–4516. D, DC, MC, V. No lunch Sun. $*

PICNIC SPOTS The park's 49 picnic areas all have tables, but only nine have fire grates: Snake River, Grant Village, Spring Creek, Nez Percé, Old Faithful East parking lot, Bridge Bay, Cascade Lake Trail, Norris Meadows, and Yellowstone River. Only LP gas stoves may be used in the other areas. None of the picnic areas has running water; most have pit toilets.

About 5 mi east of Mammoth on the Grand Loop Road, the **Undine Falls** picnic site is set along Lava Creek, a short walk to the 60-ft falls. On the Northeast Entrance Road, about 4 mi east of Slough Creek Campground Road, a picnic site has superb views of wildlife-rich Lamar Valley. The **Dunraven Pass** picnic area sits at 8,800 ft, with eastward views of Washburn Hot Springs and the Yellowstone caldera border. At **Canyon,** try the picnic area off Artist Point Drive just after it crosses the Yellowstone River. Eight picnic areas line the north and west shores of **Yellowstone Lake,** all with excellent views. Halfway out to the west entrance from Madison, a pretty site sits on the banks of the Madison River. **Gibbon Falls** picnic site east of Madison is the most scenic in this section of the park. The area near **Obsidian Cliff,** about 8 mi north of Norris, occupies prime elk- and moose-viewing terrain.

LODGING

Park lodgings are all run by **Amfac Parks and Resorts** (Yellowstone National Park, WY 82190-9989, tel. 307/344–7311 for reservations). They range from two of the national park system's magnificent old hotels to bland modern motels and simple cabins. Old Faithful and Lake Yellowstone have lodgings in all categories and are the most convenient areas for visiting major sights; they are, however, also the most crowded. Old Faithful Snow Lodge and Mammoth Hot Springs Hotel are the only accommodations open in winter; rates are the same as in summer. Cabins in the park fall under the following categories: Western and Frontier (shower or tub, sink, and toilets); Family (tub, sink, and toilets); Budget (sink and toilets only); Rough Rider and Rustic (no facilities, but showers and toilets nearby). Make reservations at least two months in advance for July and August for all park lodgings. Amfac Parks and Resorts must receive a deposit covering the first night's lodging within 14 days of the date you make your reservation, but reservations made within 14 days of arrival can be guaranteed with a credit card. No park lodgings have room TVs or phones. For all park lodgings, contact the Reservations Department, **Amfac Parks and Resorts** (*see above*).

Outside the park, West Yellowstone remains the most popular gateway lodging area, with about 50 hotels, motels, and cabin clusters. Cooke City and Silver City, at the northeast entrance, look as if they were lifted from the 1950s, with funky old log-cabin motels, neon grizzly bear signs, and a rugged high-country atmosphere. Gardiner, at the north entrance, has about 15 mostly uninspiring motels. Jackson, Wyoming, at the south entrance, and Cody, Wyoming, at the east entrance, both have a full range of hotels and motels, as do Bozeman, Livingston, and Red Lodge, Montana.

INSIDE THE PARK **Lake Yellowstone Hotel and Cabins.** Fresh from its eight-year restoration, the dowager of national park hotels once more exudes 1920s elegance. The distinguished hotel draws mainly older visitors, who come to relax in the lake-facing Sun Room while a string quartet plays in late afternoon, to shop behind the etched green windows of the expensive Crystal Palace Gift Shop, or to warm themselves on chilly days before the tile-mantel fireplace in the colonnaded lobby. Off mauve-carpeted hallways, the rooms have peach carpeting, pine furniture, and brass beds. All have bathrooms. Although the east wing is newer (1923) than the west (1903), both wings have lake-facing rooms; the hotel's cheapest rooms are smaller and don't face the lake. You will have to climb the stairs to get to the first floor of both wings, but elevators access the second and third floors. Set unobtrusively in back of the hotel, the renovated cabins are all Western or Frontier class, with pine beds and paneling. *Near Yellowstone Lake. 296 rooms and cabins. Facilities: bar, restaurant, gift shop. AE, D, DC, MC, V. Closed late Sept.–mid-May. $$–$$$*

Canyon Lodge. With plain pine-frame cabin clusters and a main lodge building, this is one of Yellowstone's more mundane lodgings. Cabins are furnished with modern, inexpensive chairs and sofas. The main lodge is heavily trafficked at lunchtime. This is the park's biggest lodging, and the one you're most likely to end up in if you arrive without reservations. *At first turn into parking lot on North Rim Dr. 572 cabins, 37 annex rooms. Facilities: 3 restaurants, bar, cafeteria, horseback riding, gift shop. AE, D, DC, MC, V. Closed early Sept.–early June. $$*

Grant Village Motel. Yellowstone's newest and least attractive lodging was finished in 1984 amid controversy over whether it detracted from the park's atmosphere. However, it certainly helps relieve the park's room crunch. Cedar shingle siding covers the check-in and restaurant buildings, and six lodge buildings have rough pine exteriors painted gray and rust. Rooms are undistinguished, with standard motel decor. *At end of Grant Village Rd. 300 rooms. Facilities: 2 restaurants, bar, boating, gift shop. AE, D, DC, MC, V. Closed mid-Sept.–late May. $$*

Lake Lodge. The cabin clusters here are similar to those at Canyon Lodge, but there is a much nicer main lodge nestled in the trees overlooking Lake Yellowstone. Parts of the main lodge date from 1920, providing a fine example of earlier park architecture. *At far end of Lake Village Rd. 186 cabins.*

Facilities: bar, cafeteria, gift shop. AE, D, DC, MC, V. Closed mid-Sept.–mid-June. $$

Mammoth Hot Springs Hotel and Cabins. Built in 1937, with one wing surviving from 1911, this hotel has a spacious art deco lobby and small motel-style rooms, as well as cabins in back. The rooms here aren't as nice as those at the other two historic park hotels, but Mammoth is generally less crowded. *North entrance to park. 96 rooms, 67 with bath; 2 suites; 126 cabins, 76 with bath. Facilities: 2 restaurants, bar, horseback riding, gift shop. AE, D, DC, MC, V. Closed mid-Sept.–mid-Dec. and mid-Mar.–late May. $–$$*

Old Faithful Inn. Past its steep rhyolite and lodgepole-log exterior, through the massive veranda and iron-latched red lobby door, you enter a log-pillared lobby that is as national park lodgings were originally meant to be. Thick leather chairs, rockers, and big wool Navajo rugs form three distinct sitting areas in the main lobby, one of which centers around the three-story fireplace. Two balconies above the lobby allow guests to watch the action below from more cozy leather chairs and sofas; pine writing desks are interspersed among the sitting furniture. From the veranda you can watch Old Faithful erupt. Guests range from leather-clad bikers to long-robed Russian Orthodox priests, with families from all over the country predominating. Rooms in the 1904 "old house" section have brass beds, and some have deep, brass-foot tubs. Newer upper-range rooms in the 1913 east and 1927 west wings contain Victorian cherrywood furniture. The east wing was completely renovated in 1993 and rooms now have Stickley furniture; four-poster, queen-size beds; and bathrooms; similar west wing renovations were completed in 1994. An elevator serves the upper floors. First-floor old-house rooms are the hotel's noisiest. Rooms facing Old Faithful geyser cost more, but rear-facing rooms are much quieter. *First left turn off Old Faithful Bypass Rd. 325 rooms, 97 with bath. Facilities: 2 restaurants, bar, gift shop. AE, D, DC, MC, V. Closed late Oct.–early May. $–$$*

Old Faithful Snow Lodge. This nonde-script brown motel-style building was the only lodging damaged by the 1988 fires; as a result, its Western cabins are the park's newest. A small lobby with a modern stone fireplace is heavily used in winter (this is one of only two park lodgings open). *Off Old Faithful Bypass Rd., next to visitor center. 31 lodge rooms, 1 with bath; 34 cabins. Facilities: restaurant, gift shop. AE, D, DC, MC, V. Closed mid-Oct.–mid-Dec. and mid-Mar.–mid-May. $–$$*

Roosevelt Lodge. Another budget choice that surpasses more expensive park options, this lodgepole-log lodge, with rustic sleeping accommodations in nearby cabins, was built in 1920. For most of the accommodations, people need to take their own sleeping bags or other bedding. Its long, log-rail front porch lined with rocking chairs is a favorite hangout of tired hikers and horseback riders. Inside, half of the single big room features a sitting area with a large fireplace, rockers, and pine tables; the other half is a restaurant. *At Tower–Roosevelt Junction on Grand Loop Rd. 80 cabins, 8 with bath. Facilities: restaurant, bar, horseback riding, gift shop. AE, D, DC, MC, V. Closed early Sept.–early June. $–$$*

Old Faithful Lodge. Not to be confused with the Snow Lodge, this budget choice is actually nicer than some of the park's mid-range options. Built in 1927, the lodge itself boasts a lodgepole log-and-panel combination exterior and interior. The lobby has a giant (although infrequently used) stone fireplace, wood wildlife carvings by regional artists, rustic pine furniture, and a commanding view of Old Faithful. Lodging is in cabins nearby. *At far end of Old Faithful Bypass Rd. 132 cabins, 83 with bath. Facilities: cafeteria, 2 snack bars, gift shop. AE, D, DC, MC, V. Closed mid-Sept.–mid-May. $*

NEAR THE PARK **Lone Mountain Guest Ranch.** At the foot of the awesome Spanish Peaks and near the Big Sky resort village, some 40 mi north of the West entrance, this is one of the Northern Rockies' premier guest ranches, and it is open year-round. Luxurious log cabins each have a wood stove, front porch with rocking chairs, pine beds, and thick wool blankets to ward off chilly nights. Activities center around horseback riding. Although the ranch will sometimes accept two- or three-night bookings, one-week stays are standard. *Off Big Sky Rd. at U.S. 191, Box 160069, Big Sky, MT 59716, tel. 406/995–4644. 23 cabins. Facilities: restaurant, bar, hot tub, MC, V. $$$–$$$$*

Cody Guest Houses. The closest thing to condominiums you'll find in Cody, these variously sized guest houses are a great choice for families and groups. The Victorian guest house has lace curtains, antique furniture, and ornate decorations. The Trimmer Western Lodge has traditional western decor and a fireplace. *1401 Rumsey Ave. Cody, WY 82414, tel. 307/587–6000, fax 307/587–8048. 3-bedroom house, 4-bedroom lodge, 1-bedroom cottage, executive suite. AE, D, MC, V. $$–$$$*

Gallatin Gateway Inn. Restored and reopened in 1987, this two-story neoclassical Spanish-style hotel 12 mi south of Bozeman was built by the Chicago–Milwaukee Railroad for Yellowstone-bound passengers in 1927. An elaborate facade of rounded, stucco-framed windows gives way to a large checkerboard-tile lobby and a huge lounge/ballroom with mahogany ceiling beams. An entire wall of arched windows and a walk-in fireplace, topped by an original railroad clock, make this hotel nearly as compelling as the historic hostelries within the park. Rooms have been repainted white and stripped of any distinguishing character, but the bathrooms retain their original brass fixtures. Outside there is a fly-fishing casting pond. *Hwy. 191, Box 376, Gallatin Gateway, MT 59730, tel. 406/763–4672. 35 rooms. Facilities: restaurant, 2 bars, pool, hot tub, tennis court, concierge. AE, D, MC, V. $$–$$$*

Huntley Lodge. Actually a full-service hotel in a ski resort 56 mi north of the west entrance, this modern building has a long sleek lobby, slate and pine walls, and spacious modern rooms. Some rooms have three queen beds, one in a loft area, and all have apartment-size refrigerators and wet bars. There are usually vacancies in summer. Guests can take advantage of the nearby tennis court and 18-hole golf course. *Mountain Village at end of Big Sky Rd., off U.S. 191, Box 1, Big Sky, MT 59716, tel. 406/995–4211 or 800/548–4486; 800/824–7767 in MT. 204 rooms. Facilities: 2 restaurants, bar, pool, 2 outdoor hot tubs, health club, concierge, convention center. AE, D, DC, MC, V. $$–$$$*

Irma Hotel. Open year-round, this pine-and-sandstone hotel in downtown Cody was built by legendary Indian scout and Wild West showman Buffalo Bill Cody in 1902 and named after his daughter. The hotel is decorated with mounted buffalo, moose, and bighorn sheep heads; its pièce de résistance is a long cherrywood bar in the saloon, a gift from Queen Victoria. Renovated motel-style rooms still contain some original Victorian furniture, washbowls, and Western art. Ask for a room in the old hotel itself, rather than in the annex. *1192 Sheridan Ave., Cody, WY 82414, tel. 307/587–4221, fax ext. 21. 40 rooms. Facilities: restaurant, bar. AE, D, DC, MC, V. $$–$$$*

Chico Hot Springs Resort. This white-frame property dates from 1900 and is a well-established favorite with locals, who come to soak in its naturally heated mineral pool. Accommodations range from lodge rooms with antique ranch pine furniture and some brass beds to modern motel units, cabins, and chalets. Only the lodge rooms offer the full Chico experience. The lobby, with its big-game heads and antique piano, exudes informality. *2 mi east of U.S. 89, 35 mi north of north entrance (follow signs on U.S. 89), Pray, MT 59065, tel. 406/333–4933 or 800/468–9232, fax 406/333–4694. 82 rooms, 25 with bath; 5 cabins; 5 chalets. Facilities: 2 restaurants, 2 bars, pool, hot tub. D, MC, V. $–$$$*

Pahaska Teepee Resort. Buffalo Bill Cody built his hunting lodge here in the Sho-

shone National Forest in 1901; it's now a National Historic Site. The resort's main log building, decorated with big-game heads, is complemented by a lively saloon. Guests stay in small, basic log cabins, which do not have TVs, phones, or air-conditioning but are heated in winter. This is one of a half dozen lodges along the road to the east entrance, and the closest one to the park. In winter, Pahaska grooms a network of cross-country ski trails and rents skis and snowmobiles. *183 Yellowstone Hwy., Cody, WY 84214, tel. 307/527–7701 or 800/628–7791, fax 307/527–4019. 52 cabins. Facilities: restaurant, bar, hot tub, horseback riding, cross-country skiing, snowmobiling. AE, MC, V. Closed Nov. and Apr. $$*

Lockhart Bed and Breakfast Inn. Once the home of western author Caroline Lockhart, this freshly renovated 1890 Victorian on the west side of Cody is furnished with antiques and serves an all-you-can-eat country breakfast. Smoking is not allowed. Outside there are five RV hookups. *109 W. Yellowstone Ave., U.S. 14-16-20, Cody, WY 82414, tel. 307/587–6074 or 800/377–7255. 7 rooms with bath in inn, 6 rooms with bath in motel, 1 family cabin. D, MC, V. $–$$*

Sportsman's High. Near downtown West Yellowstone, this bed-and-breakfast has antiques-filled rooms and a wraparound porch with an outdoor hot tub. No smoking is allowed. *750 Deer St., West Yellowstone, MT 59758, tel. 406/646–7865, fax 406/646–9434. 5 rooms with bath. AE, MC, V. $–$$*

CAMPING

Yellowstone has 11 National Park Service–operated campgrounds and one RV park operated by Amfac Parks and Resorts. It also has about 300 designated backcountry campsites, most with food-storage poles. Camping in anything other than a designated campsite within Yellowstone is strictly prohibited, but if you can't find a site in the park there are dozens to choose from in the surrounding area. Besides the commercial campgrounds near every town and city outside the park, there are more than four dozen National Forest Service campgrounds set off roads that pass through the nearby Shoshone, Gallatin, Custer, and Targhee national forests.

INSIDE THE PARK All park-service campgrounds have combination tent-trailer sites. Only Amfac Parks and Resorts' Fishing Bridge RV Park has hookups. Reservations are accepted at Bridge Bay, Canyon, Fishing Bridge, Grant Village, and Madison campgrounds; call Amfac Parks and Resorts (tel. 307/344–7311). Prices vary from $10 to $25. From late June to mid-August, all park campgrounds may fill by noon. Pets are not allowed in the backcountry, but they may stay at roadside campgrounds as long as they are on leashes.

Group camping is possible for groups with a designated leader from youth or educational organizations, at Madison, Grant, and Bridge Bay campgrounds from late May through September. Groups may reserve sites in advance for no more than seven days. For further information contact Amfac Parks and Resorts (*see* Visitor Information, *above*).

With 427 sites set back from Yellowstone Lake in a wooded grove 3 mi southwest of Lake Village, **Bridge Bay** is the largest park campground. It has flush toilets, hot water, drinking water, fire grates, a disposal station, a ranger station, and a public phone. Guests take advantage of a marina, rental boats, fishing, campfire talks, and guided walks—but don't expect solitude. Hot showers ($1.50) and a laundry are 4 mi away at Fishing Bridge. The campground is open from late May to mid-September.

The 272-site **Canyon** campground is .25 mi east of Canyon Village, near a laundromat and the visitor center. Facilities include hot showers ($1.50), flush toilets, hot water, drinking water, fire grates, a disposal station, a ranger station, and a public phone. The campground is accessible to Canyon's many short trails, which makes it a hit with families. It's open from early June to early September.

Fishing Bridge RV Park, at Fishing Bridge Junction, is the only full RV facility in the park, with 340 sites. Because of bear activity, only hard-sided units are allowed here. Trailers must be under 40 ft, with no canvas; sites are mostly gravel. Liquid propane is available, and there are laundry facilities nearby. The campground has flush toilets, drinking water, hot water, pay showers ($3.25), a disposal station, a ranger station, and a public phone. Although Fishing Bridge is on Yellowstone Lake, there is no boat access here. The campground is open from mid-May to mid-September.

Grant Village is the second-largest campground, with 411 tent-trailer sites, flush toilets, drinking water, showers ($1.50), fire grates, disposal station, ranger station, and public phone. Near the lake, it has a boat launch but no dock. Maximum trailer size is 45 ft. Try for a site to the right of the far end of the campground road for the best lake views. Grant Village is open from late June to early October.

About 8 mi south of Mammoth near Swan Lake Flats, **Indian Creek** is a creekside campground and a prime wildlife-viewing area. It has 75 combination sites (maximum trailer size 45 ft), with pit toilets, fire grates, and drinking water. Indian Creek is open from early June to mid-September.

Lewis Lake is the park's nicest midsize campground for views and quiet, set somewhat away from the main tourism action, off the South Entrance Road. It has fewer amenities than Mammoth, but it's the only campground besides huge Bridge Bay and Grant Village with a boat launch. Try for a site to the right of the campground loop road for the best lake views. Lewis Lake has 85 tent-trailer sites, with pit toilets, drinking water, fire grates, and a ranger station. It's open from mid-June to early November.

About the size of Canyon campground but with 278 combination sites (maximum trailer size 45 ft), **Madison** is quieter and a little more rugged. Sites near the river are nicest. There are flush toilets, drinking

YELLOWSTONE CAMPGROUNDS

Campground	Total number of sites	Sites suitable for RVs	Number of hookups	Drive to sites	Hike to sites	Flush toilets	Pit/chemical toilets	Drinking water	Showers	Fire grates	Swimming	Boat access	Playground	Disposal station	Ranger station	Public telephone	Reservation possible	Daily fee per site	Dates open
Bridge Bay	427	427	0	•		•		•		•		•		•	•	•	•*	$14.50	late May–mid-Sept.
Canyon	272	272	0	•		•		•	•	•				•	•	•	•	$14.50	early June–early Sept.
Fishing Bridge RV Park	340	340	346	•		•		•	•					•	•	•	•	$25	mid-May–mid-Sept.
Grant Village	411	411	0	•		•		•	•	•		•		•	•	•	•	$14.50	late June–early Oct.
Indian Creek	75	75	0	•			•	•							•			$10	early May–mid-Sept.
Lewis Lake	85	85	0	•			•	•			•							$10	mid-June–early Nov.
Madison	278	278	0	•		•		•		•				•	•	•	•	$14.50	early May–late Sept.
Mammoth Hot Springs	85	85	0	•		•		•		•					•	•		$12	year-round
Norris	116	116	0	•				•							•	•		$12	mid-May–late Sept.
Pebble Creek	32	32	0	•			•	•		•					•	•		$10	early June–late Sept.
Slough Creek	29	29	0	•			•	•		•								$10	late May–early Nov.
Tower Fall	32	32	0	•			•	•		•								$10	mid-May–mid-Sept.

*June to Labor Day only.

water, a ranger station, and a public phone. It's open from early May to early November.

The 85 combination sites at **Mammoth Hot Springs** are on a sagebrush hillside that often attracts elk and mule deer. It is more exposed than most campgrounds and gets quite hot on summer days. The Mammoth complex is just above; its amphitheater, where rangers hold evening talks, is nearby. This campground has flush toilets, drinking water, fire grates, a ranger station, and a public phone. Mammoth is open all year.

Norris is a medium-size park campground, with 116 combination sites (maximum trailer size 45 ft) adjoining the Gibbon River; it's a fishermen's favorite. There are flush toilets, drinking water, and a ranger station. Norris is open from mid-May to late September.

Pebble Creek is right off the Northeast Entrance Road, about 12 mi into the park. Though it's not quite as nice as Slough Creek farther down the road, it does have a view of the 10,554-ft peak called the Thunderer. Pebble Creek has 32 combination sites (maximum trailer size 45 ft), with pit toilets, drinking water, and fire grates. It's open from early June until late September.

A small, creekside campground 10 mi northeast of Tower junction, off a spur road, **Slough Creek** is about as far from Yellowstone's beaten path as you can get without actually camping in the backcountry. There are just 29 combination sites, with pit toilets, drinking water, and fire grates. This campground is open from late May to early November.

Three miles southeast of Tower–Roosevelt junction, **Tower Fall** is heavily trafficked and within short hiking distance of the roaring waterfall. It has 32 combination sites (maximum trailer size 25 ft), with pit toilets, drinking water, and fire grates; hot water and flush toilets are at Tower Store rest rooms nearby. There's a ranger station 3 mi north. The campground is open from mid-May to mid-September.

If you plan on camping in Yellowstone's backcountry, you will have to choose one of the 300 marked campsites. Each has a cleared area for a tent and most have food-storage poles. You will need a free permit, which can be picked up at any visitor center or ranger station (*see* Visitor Information, *above*), no more than 48 hours in advance. They are distributed on a first-come, first-served basis.

At **Lower/Midway Geyser Basins,** six of the most accessible backcountry camping sites are short hikes away from the Biscuit, Midway, and Lower geyser basins parking areas. From Biscuit Basin, a trail leads to campsites at Firehole Meadows and Falls. Both are extremely popular. Fairy and Imperial Meadows campsites are just a few miles from the Midway turnoff, and two small campsites are 2 to 3 mi in from the Sentinel Meadows Trailhead at Lower Geyser Basin. This area is open from early June to mid-March.

The north and east shores of the fairly accessible, lovely backcountry **Shoshone Lake** are lined with 12 campsites, accessible by foot, canoe, or both. Pick up permits at Grant Village or South entrance ranger stations. The ranger station at the campground is open year-round.

At the **Upper Geyser Basin,** the Lone Star Geyser area, 2.5 mi southeast of Old Faithful, and Mallard Lake, 3.5 mi to the northeast, have three campsites each. The one right at Lone Star is one of the park's few handicapped-accessible backcountry sites. Both are open year-round.

Yellowstone Lake's east shore has nine backcountry sites, accessible by way of either the Nine Mile Post Trail or Sedge Bay Trail, both of which begin where the east entrance road meets the lake. Some have restrictions on travel away from campsites. Pick up permits at Lake, Bridge Bay, or Grant Village ranger stations. Some of these sites are available year-round.

NEAR THE PARK **Elk Valley Inn** (3256 N. Fork Hwy., Cody, WY 82414, tel. 307/587–

4149) is a medium-size commercial facility 29 mi from the east entrance. Its 70 tent and 70 trailer sites (maximum size 45 ft) cost $12 and up; there are also cabins and motel rooms that range from $29 to $69. All campers have access to paddleboats, trail rides, and fishing on the Shoshone River. The campground also has flush toilets, hot water, showers, drinking water, fire grates, a playground, and a disposal station, as well as an Italian restaurant, a bar, and a great pizza kitchen. Pets on leashes are allowed. The campground is closed from October through May.

Flagg Ranch Village (Box 187, Moran, WY 83013, tel. 307/733–8761 or 800/443–2311) is a sprawling complex 2 mi from the south entrance, with a campground, a motel and cabins, two restaurants, a saloon with satellite TV, a grocery store, gift and tackle shops, a gas station, hot tubs, interdenominational church service, and guided float and horseback trips. There are 75 tent sites ($17) and 75 grassy RV sites with full hookups ($25 per night). Other facilities are flush toilets, hot water, showers, drinking water, a coin laundry, raft access, and a disposal station. Pets are allowed. Liquid propane is sold. Extra-long (45-ft) spaces are scattered through the campground. Flagg Ranch Village is closed from mid-October through mid-December, and from mid-March through mid-May.

The huge **Yellowstone Park KOA** (Box 327, West Yellowstone, MT 59758, tel. 406/646–7606), 6 mi outside the west entrance on U.S. 20, has 25 tent sites and 200 grassy RV sites, many with full hookups (maximum size 60 ft), flush toilets, hot water, showers, drinking water, fire grates, playground, indoor pool, and two disposal stations. RV sites cost between $27 and $33. There are also cabins, a game room, a hot tub, and miniature golf. Barbecue dinners and pancake breakfasts are available from mid-June through early September. Pets are allowed. The KOA is closed from October through mid-May.

Yosemite National Park
California

Updated by Jonathan Leff

s early as 1881, visitors from around the world entered Yosemite from the south near Mariposa, gleefully riding a stagecoach into a tunnel bored through the trunk of a massive sequoia. At the top of the rise to the south of Yosemite Valley, they came upon an incomparable sight—a deep, green canyon with walls of flawless gray granite rising 3,000 ft into the clouds and graceful waterfalls plummeting down from the heights.

Since those early days, crowds have continued to flock to this well-loved park, undeterred by the devastating flood of January 1997, nor by the Ackerson Complex fires of 1996 and the government shutdown of the same year. Though a day-use vehicle reservation system to limit park traffic is in the works, it will most likely take several years.

The park's popularity is easy to understand. In this one compact valley are two of the world's 10 highest waterfalls (Yosemite and Ribbon), the largest single exposed granite rock on earth (El Capitan), and one of the most recognized peaks (Half Dome) in the Americas. And the 7-mi-long, 1-mi-wide Yosemite Valley is only a small slice of the 750,000-acre national park. In Yosemite's southern tip, for example, is the Mariposa Grove of Big Trees. Giant sequoias are the largest trees on earth, towering 20 stories above the forest floor. One branch of the Grizzly Giant is wider in girth than the trunk of many trees in the forest.

Then there's the high country—take Tioga Road as it rises up from the Valley to eleva-tions of 6,000 to 10,000 ft, where an untamed expanse of rolling meadows, pristine forest, hidden lakes, and rocky domes unfolds. Here backpackers usually begin their journeys into Yosemite's wilderness area, which makes up 95% of the park.

A three- to four-hour drive from San Francisco and seven to eight hours from Los Angeles, Yosemite remains one of the most easily accessible and popular of the West's national parks. With more than 840 mi of trails, Yosemite offers its more than 4 million annual visitors countless means of exploration and retreat.

In 1864 Abraham Lincoln took time off from the Civil War to make Yosemite Valley and the Mariposa Grove of Big Trees a state reserve. At the urging of conservationist John Muir and many like him, the area surrounding the Valley and the Grove was designated a national park in 1890 by President Benjamin Harrison. It wasn't until 1906 that the State of California returned Yosemite Valley and the Mariposa Grove to the federal government, which incorporated these areas into Yosemite National Park.

ESSENTIAL INFORMATION

VISITOR INFORMATION For general information, contact the **Yosemite Information Office** (Box 577, Yosemite National Park, CA 95389, tel. 209/372–0200). Dial 209/372–1000 for recorded information on park programs, ski conditions, road conditions, and park-operated hotels. To request mailings, dial 900/454–9673, which costs $1.95 for the first minute (95¢ each additional minute). You can also call the **Tuolumne Meadows Visitor Center** (tel. 209/372–0263), open only in summer; the **Big Oak Flat Information Center** (tel. 209/379–1899), also open only in summer; and the **Wawona Information Center** (tel. 209/375–9501).

Wilderness permits are required for all overnights in Yosemite's backcountry. Permits cost $3 per person and are available at wilderness permit offices in Yosemite Valley, Wawona, and Tuolumne. Reservations for overnight trail use ($3 per person) are accepted by mail or by phone (tel. 209/372–0740), no more than 24 weeks and no less than two weeks in advance. Send your name, address, daytime phone, number of people in your party, trip date, start and ending trailheads, and a brief itinerary to Wilderness Permits, Box 545, Yosemite, 95389. Fifty percent of the capacity for each trailhead is determined by reservation. The balance is available on a first-come, first-served basis at 6 AM on the day prior to your departure. Trailhead quotas, especially for those leaving the Valley, are usually met early, so plan ahead.

FEES Admission to the park is $20 per car for a seven-day pass or $10 per person if you don't arrive in a car. For $40, you can purchase a one-year pass to Yosemite.

PUBLICATIONS A plethora of publications on Yosemite ranges from simple maps to extravagant picture books. You can find these at visitor centers or order by catalog from the **Yosemite Association** (Box 230, El Portal, CA 95318, tel. 209/379–1906).

The official National Park Service handbook to Yosemite is an informative, 143-page guide with color photos. A foldout *Map & Guide to Yosemite Valley* describes trails, bike paths, flora, fauna, and vista points and gives a brief history of the park, with color photos of major landmarks. For those who like driving, the 77-page *Yosemite Road Guide* tells about the history of each road marker in Yosemite. *Yosemite Magazine,* complimentary to all hotel guests, is an excellent source of informa-

tion and includes color photographs. The *Yosemite Guide* newspaper, available free at entrance gates and visitor centers, is an indispensable resource for current activities and operating hours.

GEOLOGY AND TERRAIN Yosemite National Park encompasses 1,170 square mi, from the popular Yosemite Valley, at a 4,000-ft elevation; east to the nearly deserted backcountry, which rises as high as 13,000 ft at the Sierra crest; south to the Mariposa Grove of Big Trees; and north to the Hetch Hetchy Reservoir and the mountain wilderness beyond.

The area that is now the Sierra Nevada and the Central Valley of California was once a vast sea. Sand, silt, and mud eroded from ancient mountain ranges bordering the waters and settled to the sea floor, eventually becoming rock. Geologic forces warped the rock layers, lifting them up and forming a mountain range. Eighty to 250 million years ago, molten rock cooled and crystallized beneath the mountains. Between 10 and 80 million years ago, this cooled rock uplifted and became the Sierra Nevada. The top layers of the original sedimentary rock from the sea bottom eroded away.

Immense ruptures and cracks in the mountain range—in addition to erosion by running water—led to the creation of canyons and valleys. Several million years ago, during the Ice Age, glaciers deepened and widened the canyons. What is now Half Dome was a tower of rock. A vertical joint cracked, forcing a portion of this immense rock to crumble; some of the rubble was partially carried away by glaciers. But when the last major glacier left Yosemite Valley between 10,000 and 15,000 years ago, Half Dome was still not a dome. Although some of Yosemite's domes were helped along by glacial erosion, most were formed by exfoliation. In this process, layers of rock crack apart and fall off, like the layers of an onion, leaving behind a rounded surface.

Geologists believe that for around 10,000 to 15,000 years following the last Ice Age, a lake filled the Valley bottom. The waterfalls that pour into the Valley brought in silt and sediment that eventually transformed the lake into today's level meadow surrounded by pines and oaks.

FLORA AND FAUNA Yosemite is home to approximately 37 types of trees, 1,400 flowering plants, 80 species of mammals, 250 varieties of birds, and 24 different types of amphibians and reptiles.

The most visible animals are the coyote, often seen along valley roads in the evening, and the mule deer, the only kind of deer in Yosemite. These large-eared deer are especially prevalent in the Valley in winter, when snow forces them down from higher elevations. Deer graze the lawns of the historic Wawona Hotel and of the golf course across the road. Remember that these graceful "Bambis" are wild animals with sharp hooves and antlers; do not approach or feed them.

Bighorn sheep are spotted occasionally in Inyo National Forest (to the east of the park), but sightings are infrequent in the park itself. You're most likely to see them at the eastern edge of the park, just off Highway 120 in Lee Vining Canyon.

The American black bear, which often has a brown, cinnamon, or blond coat, is the only species of bear in Yosemite (the California grizzlies were hunted to extinction by the 1920s). Some are active year-round at any time of day or night, but few visitors ever see them. If you encounter a bear, make loud noises, bang pots, and wave your arms to scare the animal away. If it doesn't scare, retreat. Bears will go after coolers (breaking car windows to get at them) and any food, even cans of soda, so be sure all food and cooking utensils are properly stored. When backpacking, you are required to store all your food in bear-proof canisters.

The most commonly seen bird is the blue Steller's jay, which delights visitors along trails, in campgrounds, and around public buildings. Dedicated birders may catch a glimpse of the rare and endangered great gray owl, which makes its home at the mid-elevations (6,000 to 8,000 ft). The golden

eagle is sometimes seen soaring above the Valley. Three known pairs of the endangered peregrine falcon nest in the park and are carefully protected by the park service.

The Mariposa Grove of Big Trees is the most famous of the three sequoia groves in Yosemite. Sequoias naturally grow only along the west slope of the Sierra Nevada between approximately 4,500 and 7,000 ft in elevation. Starting from a seed the size of a rolled oat flake, each of these ancient monuments assumed remarkable proportions in adulthood. You might want to take a rough measure of some of the bases—the Grizzly Giant takes more than 15 people holding hands to form a human chain around its base. Fires, incidentally, are integral to their existence, releasing seeds from the cones and clearing the forest soil for new growth, and are regularly started by the park service under carefully controlled conditions.

In late May the Valley's dogwood trees bloom with white, starlike flowers. Wildflowers, such as black-eyed Susan, bull thistle, cow parsnip, lupine, and meadow goldenrod, peak in June in the Valley and in July at the higher elevations.

WHEN TO GO Without a doubt, summer is Yosemite's most crowded season, especially in the Valley. The weather is warm and dry—with an average 90°F high and 50°F low in the Valley and a 70°F high and 30°F low in Tuolumne Meadows—and many activities are offered, but you will have to contend with traffic jams, noxious tour buses, and fully booked accommodations. This is, however, the only time of year when the Tioga Road into the high country is sure to be open.

In autumn, the waterfalls may not be the torrents of spring and tourist activities are curtailed, but visitors will find crisp fall air, bargains on lodging, and relative solitude—even in the Valley. Daytime temperatures in the Valley remain warm (60°F to 70°F) until November.

Outdoors enthusiasts will enjoy winter, when visitors are few, deer flock to the Valley from the snowed-in higher elevations, and fires warm the restaurants and lounges. Daytime temperatures are mild (40°F to 50°F), but nights are chilly (20°F to 30°F). Snow on the Valley floor is minimal. Cross-country and alpine skiing, as well as free ranger-led snowshoe walks, are available at Yosemite's Badger Pass Ski Area. Many winter visitors come expressly for the annual Vintners' and Chefs' Holidays (*see* Seasonal Events, *below*).

In spring, the mighty waterfalls reach their peak with the snowmelt from the higher elevations. May greets the white dogwood blossoms suspended in the Valley forest. White and pink Western azaleas bloom in late May and early June. The days become warmer, with temperatures ranging from 60°F to 70°F, and nights are crisp at 30°F to 40°F.

Consult Yosemite Area Road and Weather Conditions (tel. 209/372–0200) for current information on temperatures and precipitation.

SEASONAL EVENTS Mid-November to mid-December: **Vintners' Holidays** (tel. 209/253–5641) are held midweek in the grand parlor of the Ahwahnee Hotel. Free seminars by California's most prestigious vintners culminate in an elegant, albeit pricey, banquet dinner. **January**: At **Chefs' Holidays** (tel. 209/454–2020 Holidays Hotline), similar to the Vintners' Holidays, you can enjoy free cooking demonstrations by celebrated chefs. **Early May to late October**: One of Yosemite's best-loved evening activities is Lee Stetson's portrayal of naturalist John Muir in a celebrated one-man show. Performances of *Conversation with a Tramp, John Muir's Stickeen and Other Fellow Mortals,* and *The Spirit of John Muir* are held several days a week, from early May through summer, at the Yosemite Theater. Tickets are $5.

WHAT TO PACK Sierra weather is unpredictable: sunny one day, cold and rainy the next. Bring layered clothing and sturdy rain gear.

GENERAL STORES You can get almost anything you need in Yosemite Valley's stores, but you'll have to pay the price. You may want to stock up on fruits, trail mix, and other nonperishable picnic goods before coming into the park. Many of the Valley stores are open year-round, from 8 to 9 daily during the warmer months and from 9 to 6 during the cooler months (November through April).

The **Village Store** (Yosemite Village, tel. 209/372–1253) is the largest store in the park, with groceries, magazines, books, film, photo processing, clothing, camping supplies, postcards, gifts, and souvenirs.

Nearby is **Degnan's Delicatessen** (Yosemite Village, tel. 209/372–8454), with made-to-order sandwiches, salads, and other health-conscious foods, and **Yosemite Kids** (Yosemite Village, tel. 209/372–8453), a shop with toys and educational games for kids of all ages. The **Ansel Adams Gallery** (Yosemite Village, tel. 209/372–4413) is the most elegant store in the park, with Ansel Adams prints, fine artwork, and top-quality Native American crafts.

At the Ahwahnee Hotel, the Sweet Shop (tel. 209/372–1205) in the lobby sells Ahwahnee-logo merchandise and sundries, while the **Gift Shop** (tel. 209/372–1409) specializes in fine gifts, Native American jewelry, and handicrafts.

At the Yosemite Lodge, the **Gift/Apparel Store** (tel. 209/372–1297) has Yosemite souvenirs, film, and a fair selection of picnic supplies. Also at the lodge, the **Nature Shop** (tel. 209/372–1438) features environmentally themed gifts and souvenirs.

Curry Village has a year-round **Mountain Shop** (tel. 209/372–8396), with rock-climbing and backpacking supplies, and a Gift Shop (tel. 209/372–8391). Wawona has a small year-round grocery store, **Wawona Store** (tel. 209/375–6574), as well as the **Pioneer Gift Shop** (tel. 209/375–6514). Badger Pass Ski Area has a winter-only **Sport Shop** (tel. 209/372–1333), with ski clothing, sunglasses, and sunscreen. Tuolumne Meadows has a summer-only **Grocery Store** (tel. 209/372–8428) and a rock-climbers' **Mountain Shop** (tel. 209/372–8435), also open only in the summer.

Operating hours for all stores vary according to season and are listed in the Yosemite Guide, which is available free at the park entrances and visitor centers.

ARRIVING AND DEPARTING The most convenient way to travel to Yosemite is by car, but once in the Valley you won't need an automobile. An excellent, free shuttle bus serves eastern Yosemite Valley year-round (7 AM–10 PM in summer, 9 AM–10 PM the rest of the year). In winter, a free bus carries skiers from the Valley to Badger Pass. In summer, there is one daily bus to the high country that costs $20 round-trip. This is especially useful for backpackers, who can take the bus up to Tuolumne Meadows, then hike back down into the Valley, avoiding a grueling 4,000-ft climb on foot (*see* Longer Hikes, *below*). For hiker-bus reservations, call 209/372–8441 or ask at any hotel tour desk.

By Bus. VIA Adventures (tel. 209/384–1315 or 800/727–5287) runs buses to Yosemite from Merced ($38 plus entrance fee round-trip, 2½ hours one way) and Fresno ($38 plus entrance fee round-trip, three hours one way). The Greyhound and Amtrak stations and the Fresno and Merced airports are regular stops, but call ahead to let the bus company know when you plan to arrive.

By Car and RV. Yosemite is a three- to four-hour drive from San Francisco and a seven- to eight-hour drive from Los Angeles. From the west, three highways access Yosemite; all intersect with Highway 99, which runs north–south through the Central Valley. Highway 120 is the northernmost and most direct route from San Francisco, but it crosses a longer portion of foothills and rises higher into the mountains, which can be snowy in winter. Highway 140 from Merced allows for more highway driving and is the recommended route in winter. It is the least mountainous route, and chains

are usually not required. Highway 41 from Fresno is the shortest route from Los Angeles and offers the most dramatic first look at Yosemite Valley, just as you emerge from the Wawona Tunnel.

If you're coming from the east, Highway 120, the Tioga Road, will take you over the Sierra crest, past Tuolumne Meadows and down the west slope of the mountains into the Valley. It's scenic, but the mountain driving may be stressful for some, and it's generally closed between November and May due to heavy snow in the upper elevations.

From late fall until early spring, you should carry chains no matter what your approach to Yosemite. They are often mandatory on Sierra roads during snowstorms. Sierra weather is unpredictable and driving can be treacherous. If you get caught in the Valley and need to buy chains there, you'll pay twice the normal price.

For the most up-to-date information on traffic and highway conditions outside the park, consult the CalTrans Highway Information Network (tel. 800/427–7623).

Yosemite Valley is 229 mi from Sequoia National Park, 180 mi from Kings Canyon National Park, and about 300 mi from Death Valley National Monument via the Tioga Pass (open only in summer).

By Plane. If you're coming in from out of state, you will most likely fly into San Francisco or Los Angeles, then drive. An alternative is to fly into Fresno, which is 97 mi southwest of the park. In addition, **United Express Airlines** (tel. 800/241–6522) has less frequent service from San Francisco to Merced. Bus transportation is available from Fresno and Merced to Yosemite (*see* By Bus, *above*); car-rental companies include **Avis** (tel. 800/331–1212), **Budget** (tel. 800/527–0700), **Dollar** (tel. 800/800–4000), and **Hertz** (tel. 800/654–3131).

By Train. Amtrak (tel. 800/872–7245) has train service to Merced, where you can connect with public bus transportation (*see* By Bus, *above*).

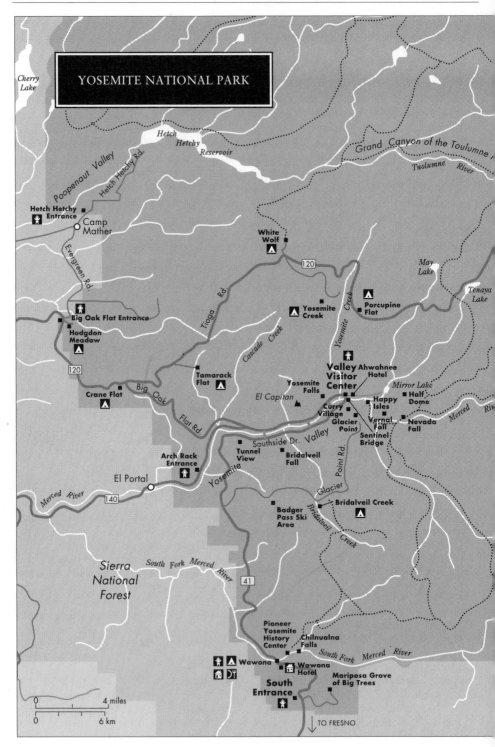

YOSEMITE NATIONAL PARK

Mono
Lake

395

Lee○
Vining

120

Tioga
Pass
Entrance

Tioga Rd.

Visitor Center
ne
ws

Lyell

Pacific Crest Trail

Canyon

Range

Inyo
National
Forest

Grant
Lake

158

Waugh
Lake

Gem
Lake

Thousand
Island
Lake

Garnet
Lake

Sierra
National
Forest

EXPLORING

The magnificent sites of Yosemite Valley are easily accessible by auto or free shuttle bus, with short, handicapped-accessible trails to the bases of the powerful waterfalls. An alternative is to take a guided tour of the highlights (*see* Guided Tours, *below*). If possible, allow time for longer hikes off the well-beaten tourist paths, up the canyons, through the Big Trees, into the high country.

THE BEST IN ONE DAY A woman once asked Carl Sharsmith, longtime Yosemite ranger-naturalist, "What would you do if you had only one day in Yosemite National Park?" "Madam," he replied, "I'd go sit by the Merced River and cry!" One day is enough for a whirlwind tour of the highlights, but it leaves little time for lingering or enjoying the many trails and activities. Still, if that's all the time you have, you'll want to spend most of it in Yosemite Valley.

As you enter the Valley, you may want to orient yourself at the Valley Visitor Center. A brief audiovisual program, available in five languages, suggests an itinerary for those with only one day in the park, and rangers can recommend the best short hikes for the season. But if you're really pressed for time, it's best to stop at the vista points as you come to them. The circle road around the Valley is one way, which means you'll have to return to individual sites you passed on the way to the visitor center.

Your first stop should be the **Bridalveil Fall**. The Ahwahneechee people called this Pohono, or "spirit of the puffing wind," as breezes blow the lacy waterfall sideways along the cliff face. A short paved trail with a slight rise will take you to the base of this graceful 620-ft cascade. The parking lot is about 20 yards up Highway 41 from the Valley road (Southside Drive).

As you head farther into the Valley, **El Capitan** will loom to your left. Turnouts along the road provide unbeatable vistas of this largest single exposed granite rock on earth, rising 3,593 ft—more than 350 stories—

above you. Shadows of clouds set off ever-changing patterns of light on its vertical striations. Those with keen eyes and a pair of binoculars may spot tiny rock climbers as they slowly ascend the vertical surface of "El Cap."

Take a left over Sentinel Bridge and park. Walk to the center of the bridge for the best view of **Half Dome** and its reflection in the Merced River. Photographers take note: This scene is best just before sunset, when the river is still and Half Dome glows with a rosy gold.

Drive back over the bridge and continue on Southside Drive. Hardy hikers may want to go straight to the Curry Village day-use lot, walk to the end of the shuttle-bus road and climb the moderately steep trail to the footbridge overlooking the 317-ft **Vernal Fall** (1.5 mi round-trip; allow 1½ hours). Beyond Vernal Fall, the trail climbs to the 594-ft **Nevada Fall** (*see* Longer Hikes, *below*).

About half a mile after the road crosses the Merced River, take the short side road that dead-ends at the **Ahwahnee Hotel.** Even if you aren't staying in this elegant lodge, it's worth a visit. Reminiscent of a grand hunting lodge, the Ahwahnee has immense common rooms showcasing museum-quality, antique Native American rugs and baskets (*see* Historic Buildings and Sites; Dining; *and* Lodging, *below*).

Back on the main road heading west, follow the signs for **Yosemite Village.** There you'll find gift stores, fast-food restaurants, and, most importantly, the **Valley Visitor Center** (*see* Visitor Information, *above*), which has exhibits on park geology and an excellent selection of books on Yosemite. Behind the center is a small, **re-created Ahwahneechee village.** For more Native American lore, take a quick peek at the **Indian Cultural Museum** next door, where there's an impressive collection of baskets. Both attractions are free.

From here it's a short walk or drive to **Yosemite Falls.** This is the highest waterfall in North America and the fifth highest in

the world. Though it looks like one cascade, Yosemite Falls is actually three waterfalls, a powerful chain of water twice the height of the Empire State Building. From the granite ridge high above you, Upper Fall drops 1,430 ft straight down. The Cascades, or Middle Fall, tumbles over another 675 ft, pouring into the steep 320-ft drop of the Lower Fall. This is an excellent spot to fit in a short hike by following the mile-long loop trail through the forest back to the parking lot (*see* Nature Trails and Short Walks, *below*).

Those with more time in Yosemite should drive up Highway 41 to **Tunnel View.** The parking lots for this vista point are on either side of the road just before the tunnel. Below, tucked into 7 mi of pure inspiration is Yosemite Valley, with Bridalveil Fall on the right, El Capitan on the left, and Half Dome forming the backdrop to this deep, green canyon.

Farther up Highway 41 is the turnoff for the road to **Glacier Point** (open only in summer), which provides another spectacular panorama of Yosemite, taking in the Valley 3,200 ft below, and high country peaks on the horizon (*see* Scenic Drives and Views, *below*).

Highway 41 curves through the mountains south to the **Pioneer Yosemite History Center** (*see* Historic Buildings and Sites, *below*) at Wawona (30 mi; allow 45 minutes). Cross the New England–style covered bridge to this collection of some of Yosemite's first log buildings. The nearby Wawona Hotel (*see* Historic Buildings and Sites; Dining; *and* Lodging, *below*) is a pleasant stop for lunch.

Six miles south is the **Mariposa Grove of Big Trees.** More than 20 giant sequoias are visible from the parking lot, but to get a true feeling for the size of these trees, take the .75-mi walk along the self-guided nature trail to **Grizzly Giant.** This gargantuan tree is 32 ft in diameter, 209 ft tall, and believed to be 2,700 years old.

In the summer, the high country is accessible by driving east out of Yosemite Valley along Highway 120. **Tuolumne Meadows** (55 mi from the Valley) is the most extensive meadow system in the Sierra Nevada. Picnickers and day hikers enjoy the crystalline lakes, rolling fields, and rounded granite domes. Many backpackers begin their journeys from here, but you'll need to get acclimated to the 8,575-ft altitude.

ORIENTATION PROGRAMS For an overview of the beauty, diversity, and history of Yosemite, see the 30-minute audiovisual presentation shown at the Yosemite Valley Visitor Center. The rangers here can tell you about trail conditions, the best hikes in any given season, park activities, and more. Exhibits illustrate the geology and unique natural aspects of the park. The Big Oak Flat Information Station has a slide show.

GUIDED TOURS Tours to fit every schedule and a variety of interests are run by **Yosemite Concession Services Corporation** (5410 E. Home Ave., Fresno, CA 93727, tel. 209/372–1240). Advance reservations are required for all tours except the Valley Floor Tour and the Big Trees Tram Tour (*see below*); tickets may be purchased at tour desks in valley hotels. Tours run from spring through fall, conditions permitting, unless otherwise stated.

The **Valley Floor Tour** is a 26-mi, two-hour tour of the Valley's highlights, with narration on area history, geology, and plant and animal life. It operates all year with open-air trams or enclosed motor coaches, depending on conditions. The price is $17. The **Mariposa Grove Tour** is a $34, six-hour trip from Yosemite Valley to the giant sequoias in Mariposa Grove. A four-hour trip from Yosemite Valley hotels to the vista at **Glacier Point,** 3,214 ft above the Valley, operates approximately from June 1 through Thanksgiving; prices start at $20. For a full-day combination of the Big Trees and Glacier Point tours, with time for lunch at the historic Wawona Hotel, try the **Grand Tour.** It is available from approximately June 1 through Thanksgiving at the price of $44 (lunch not included). The **Big Trees Tram Tour** ($8) is a one-hour, open-air tram tour of the Mariposa Grove of Big Trees. The **Moonlight Tour,** a late-evening version of the Valley Floor Tour, takes place on full-moon nights and the five nights prior, from April through September, depending on weather conditions, for $17.

If you want a full day's outing across Tioga Pass to Mono Lake, opt for the **Tuolumne Meadows Tour.** This is mostly a shuttle bus for hikers and backpackers who want to reach high-country trailheads, but anyone can ride. It operates from July through Labor Day; the price varies with the drop-off point. Round-trip fare to Tuolumne Meadows is $20.

The **Yosemite Association** (Box 230, El Portal, CA 95318, tel. 209/379–1906, fax 209/379–2486) sponsors about 80 in-depth seminars every year: These include lessons on winter ecology and one that turns hiking into an exploration of wildflowers. There are also geology treks and natural-history workshops. Call for a course catalog.

Saddle Trips may continue to leave from Wawona and Tuolumne Meadows (summer only). All saddle and pack animals require guides. Riders must be at least seven years old and 44 inches tall. Reservations are required. Call Yosemite Concession Services (tel. 209/372–1000) for details. **Overnight Cross-country Ski Tours** range from a midweek overnight to Glacier Point ($110) to a six-day Trans-Sierra Expedition ($435), wintertime only. Prices include breakfast, dinner, lodging, guide, and instruction. Photo enthusiasts shouldn't miss the free 1½-hour tours called **Camera Walks** led by professional photographers; they take place Sunday and Monday in summer and from Monday through Thursday in winter. Sign up in advance at hotel desks.

In addition to these commercial tours, park rangers lead several free walks. Check the visitor center or your *Yosemite Guide* for trips and schedules.

SCENIC DRIVES AND VIEWS If you didn't enter Yosemite Valley via **Highway 41 from Fresno,** it's worth the drive up this curvy road just to enjoy the vista from **Tunnel View.** Pull into the parking area on either side of the road immediately before the entrance to the tunnel. This is the most popular view in Yosemite, overlooking the Valley, with El Capitan on the left, Bridalveil Fall on the right, and Half Dome as a backdrop.

From here, you may want to continue through the tunnel and head up to **Glacier Point** (open summer only) for another awe-inspiring view of the Valley. A short walk from the parking lot brings you to the top of a sheer rock cliff, where you can peer straight down at the Valley about 3,200 ft below. Across the Valley, you can see the entire 2,425-ft plummet of Yosemite Falls. Allow about an hour for this 32-mi drive from the Valley.

Highway 41 is also the road from the Valley to the **Mariposa Grove of Big Trees.** If you're planning to include a visit to the giant sequoias, get an early morning start from the Valley. This road winds up through both open and wooded areas, some charred from recent forest fires, and has panoramic views of forested hills. It then curves down to Wawona and back up to the grove.

You may want to stop for lunch at the 1879 **Wawona Hotel,** which has a delightful Victorian-style parlor and dining room (see Historic Buildings and Sights; Dining; and Lodging, below). Nearby, you can explore the **Pioneer Yosemite History Center,** a collection of authentic, century-old buildings that have been relocated here from throughout the park (see Historic Buildings and Sites, below).

In summer, take a drive up through the high country toward Tioga Pass on Tioga Road (a continuation of Highway 120) to the alpine scenery of **Tuolumne Meadows.** Highlights include crystal-blue lakes, grassy meadows, and rounded peaks. Keep a sharp eye out for the neon colors of rock climbers, who seem to defy gravity on the cliffs.

HISTORIC BUILDINGS AND SITES The Yosemite Valley's 1927 **Ahwahnee Hotel,** a stately lodge of granite and concrete beams stained to look like redwood, is a perfect man-made complement to Yosemite's natural majesty. Even if you aren't a guest, take time to visit the immense parlors with their walk-in hearths and priceless, antique Native American rugs and baskets. The dining room is extraordinary, its high ceiling interlaced with massive sugar-pine beams. Guest rooms are expensive and are sometimes reserved up to a year in advance (see Dining and Lodging, below).

The **Wawona Hotel,** in the southern tip of Yosemite National Park, was the park's first lodge, built in 1879. With a whitewashed exterior and wraparound verandas, this is a fine example of Victorian resort architecture—a blend of rusticity and elegance—and is now a National Historic Landmark. The hotel annexes on this estate are also turn-of-the-century, the last built in 1918. Meals and lodging are available here (see Dining and Lodging, below).

Near the Wawona Hotel is the **Pioneer Yosemite History Center,** a collection of Yosemite's first log buildings, relocated here from around the park. A covered bridge that welcomed the park's first tourists leads to a villagelike setting. The late-19th- and early 20th-century buildings include a homesteader's cabin, a blacksmith's shop, a bakery, and a U.S. cavalry headquarters. In summer, costumed docents play the roles of the pioneers. Accessible year-round, the buildings are open from mid-June to Labor Day, Wednesday through Sunday from 9 to 1 and Monday through Tuesday from 2 to 5. Donations are accepted.

NATURE TRAILS AND SHORT WALKS Several short trails will get you out of the car and into the park in quick order. For an excellent map and description of many valley hikes, invest in the colorful *Map & Guide to Yosemite Valley* ($2.50), available at the Yosemite Valley Visitor Center.

Tucked behind the Valley Visitor Center, a short loop trail (about 100 yards) circles through a re-creation of an **Ahwahneechee village** as it might have appeared in 1872,

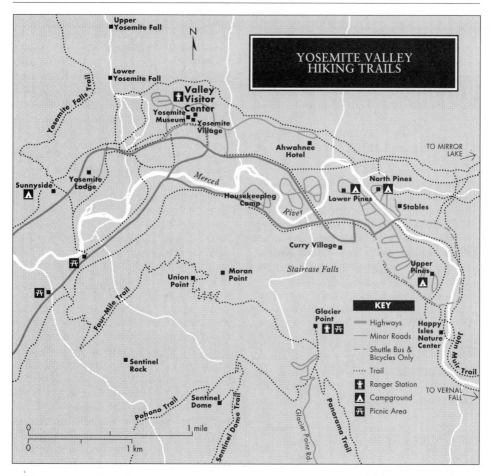

20 years after the Native Americans' first contact with Europeans. Markers explain the lifestyle of Yosemite's first residents. Allow 30 minutes.

A Changing Yosemite is a self-guided nature trail (pick up a pamphlet at the trailhead or at the Valley Visitor Center) that begins about 75 yards in front of the Valley Visitor Center, following the road, then circling through Cook's Meadow. An informative pamphlet explains the continually changing geology of the Valley. Allow at least 45 minutes for this 1-mi paved loop trail, which is wheelchair-accessible.

You can see the dizzying height of **Yosemite Falls** from the parking lot but can only expe-

rience its power by following the .25-mi one-way paved trail to its base. The path leads to a footbridge that crosses the rushing waters below Lower Yosemite Fall; expect to be showered with the mist of the mighty falls. Many return to the parking lot at this point, but if you cross the bridge you'll come to a level, wooded, 1-mi path that winds through the cool forest, meandering several times over creeks via footbridges. In a secluded spot, you'll discover the site of John Muir's cabin, with Yosemite Falls as a backdrop.

You might get wet as you follow the .25-mi trail to the 620-ft **Bridalveil Fall.** The wheelchair-accessible, paved trail follows a rocky creek up to a patio that's often sprayed with the mist of the windblown falls.

A popular, easy 2-mi round-trip leads from Shuttle Bus Stop No. 17 to **Mirror Lake.** But don't expect to find a blue expanse reflecting the surrounding cliffs. In an organic process called succession, Mirror Lake is changing from lake to meadow. In fact, by summer's end, it is often completely dry. Allow one hour for this hike, but if you want to go farther you can continue on the 3-mi **Mirror Lake Loop** for an added hour of pleasant hiking.

For a more strenuous short hike, follow the **John Muir Trail** from Happy Isles (Shuttle Bus Stop No. 16) to a vista of Vernal Fall, with its 317-ft drop. This 1.5-mi round-trip trail is a little steep in places, rising 400 ft altogether, but you'll be rewarded with an outstanding view of Vernal Fall from the footbridge crossing the river. Allow about one hour for this hike. The famous John Muir Trail continues south for 200 mi along the Sierra crest to Mt. Whitney, the highest peak in the contiguous United States (*see* Longer Hikes, *below*).

LONGER HIKES Before heading out on any long hike, it's a good idea to check trail conditions with the rangers. The following trails climb to higher elevations and are closed during winter snows. In warmer seasons, these trails may be muddy and slippery because of their proximity to waterfalls.

The **John Muir Trail,** from Happy Isles to the Vernal Fall vista (*see* Nature Trails and Short Walks, *above*), is the first stretch of a steep but spectacular hike to the top of Vernal Fall. After crossing the river, leave the John Muir Trail for the Mist Trail, which borders the cascading river and its spraying foam. Allow about three hours for the 1,050-ft elevation gain on this 3-mi round-trip hike from Happy Isles.

From the top of Vernal Fall, continue to climb the Mist Trail to the top of **Nevada Fall,** passing the shimmering Emerald Pool on the way. Walk to the brink of this fall (there's a vista point with guardrails) for a dizzying view of the water plummeting 594 ft straight down. (Do not try to edge out over the open rock where the falls begin or

you may be plummeting straight down with them.) From here you can view the panorama of Yosemite's rounded domes. The placid Emerald Pool is an inviting spot for a picnic. Allow six to eight hours for this 7-mi round-trip hike from Happy Isles to the top of Nevada Fall and back. The trail climbs almost 2,000 ft in elevation from Happy Isles.

Ardent and courageous trekkers can continue on the **John Muir Trail** from the top of Nevada Fall to the top of Half Dome. Some visitors attempt this entire 10- to 12-hour, 16.75-mi round-trip trek from Happy Isles in one day. If you're planning to do this, remember that the 4,800-ft elevation gain and the altitude of 8,842 ft will cause shortness of breath. Backpackers can hike to a campground in Little Yosemite Valley near the top of Nevada Fall the first day, then climb to the top of Half Dome and hike out the next day. Wilderness permit reservations are highly recommended at least a month in advance. In any case, wear shoes with excellent traction and gloves. The last pitch up the back of Half Dome is very steep. The only way to climb this sheer rock face is to pull yourself up using the steel cable handrails, which are in place only from late spring to early fall. Those who are squeamish about heights, and even some who aren't, choose not to attempt this last portion of the climb. Those who brave the ascent will be rewarded with an unbeatable view of Yosemite Valley below and the high country beyond.

Steep but rewarding, the **Yosemite Falls Trail** climbs from the Valley to the top of the tallest waterfall in North America. Once you see the 2,425-ft drop of this waterfall from the base and picture yourself on top, you'll know that the trail is for hardy hikers only. A narrow path with a railing leads to the actual brink of Upper Yosemite Fall. The six- to eight-hour hike, with a 2,700-ft elevation gain, is 7.5 mi round-trip from the trailhead at the northwest corner of the Sunnyside campground parking lot (Shuttle Bus Stop No. 8).

There are several options for those who don't want an uphill hump. You can take a bus to Glacier Point ($10), which has one of the Valley's best views, then hike back down from there. **Four-Mile Trail** descends from Glacier Point, zigzagging through forest to the Valley floor, where, with a 1-mi walk, you can catch a free shuttle bus back to your starting point in the Valley. If you decide to hike up the Four-Mile Trail and back down again, allow about six hours for the 9.5-mi round-trip (the trail was lengthened to make it less steep, but its name was not changed), with a 3,220-ft elevation gain.

Another trail starting at Glacier Point is the **Panorama Trail,** which circles 8.5 mi through forest, past the secluded Illilouette Falls to the top of Nevada Fall. There the trail connects with either the Mist Trail or the John Muir Trail to follow first Nevada then Vernal Fall to the Valley floor. Arrange for an early morning bus ride to Glacier Point, and allow a full day for this hike, even though it has an overall 3,200-ft elevation loss.

Another way to enjoy the views without an uphill struggle is to ride the Tuolumne Meadows bus to the high country (available from July through Labor Day), then backpack down to the Valley. You can also take a bus up, enjoy your backpacking trek in the high country, then take the bus back down to your valley starting point. The bus leaves the Valley daily at 8 AM, traveling east on Tioga Road to Lee Vining, then turns around and, after a two-hour stop at Tuolumne Meadows, returns to the Valley at 4 PM. Arrange in advance with the bus driver to be picked up in the high country so that you don't miss the bus. Bus prices vary according to drop-off point. One-way fare to Tuolumne Meadows from the Valley is $13.

In the Wawona area, the **Chilnualna Falls Trail** runs 4 mi one-way to the top of the falls, then leads into the backcountry, connecting with miles of other trails. This is one of the most inspiring and secluded trails, but it is easily accessible off Chilnu-alna Falls Road. Watch for the sign leading to a parking lot to your right, just before the paved road turns to dirt. This hike leads past a tumbling cascade, up through forests, and to a steep ascent, with panoramic vistas at the top. Day hikers should plan on hiking to the waterfall, then returning via the same path.

OTHER ACTIVITIES **Art Workshops.** Pending budget decisons, professional artists may offer free workshops in watercolor, etching, drawing, and other subjects, from early April through early October. In the past, classes have been held outdoors from 10 AM to 2 PM at inspiring spots, depending on the weather. Bring your own materials or purchase the basics for about $10. Register at the **Art Activity Center** (Yosemite Village, tel. 209/372–1442), in the Old Bank Building near the Village Store.

Biking. Yosemite Valley is ideal for biking, especially for families. More than 8 mi of scenic, mostly level bikeways in the Valley provide a safe and pleasant alternative to the relatively narrow roads. Bike rentals, with helmets, are available through the **Lodge Bike Stand** at two locations: Yosemite Lodge (tel. 209/372–1208), which is open year-round, conditions permitting; and Curry Village (tel. 209/372–8319), open during the summer, fall, and spring, weather permitting. Rentals cost $5.25 per hour or $20 per day. These are standard, one-speed bikes with foot brakes. Child-carriers are not available. You'll find a bikeway map on the back of the *Yosemite Guide* and at bike-rental stands. Mountain biking is prohibited on all Yosemite foot and horse trails.

Bird-Watching. Park rangers sometimes lead free bird-watching walks in Yosemite Valley during summer, one day each week (if staffing permits). Binoculars are sometimes available for loan. Several intensive two- to four-day seminars for beginning and intermediate birders are offered April through August by the **Yosemite Association** (Box 230, El Portal, CA 95318, tel. 209/379–1906). Fees range from $120 to $160. More than 200 bird species have been spotted in the park, including the sage sparrow, pygmy owl, blue grouse, and mountain bluebird.

Fishing. The waters in Yosemite are not currently stocked. Trout, mostly brown and rainbow, live here but are not plentiful. Yosemite's stream and river fishing season begins on the last Saturday in April and ends on November 15, but be sure to inquire at a visitor center about exceptions; some waterways are off-limits to anglers at certain times of the year. Fishing licenses (required) cost $26.50 for state residents, and a whopping $71.95 for nonresidents; these are good until December 31 of the year in which they are purchased. Residents and nonresidents may purchase a one-day license for $9.45 at the **Yosemite Village Sport Shop** (tel. 209/372–1286, summer only), between the Village Store and the Old Bank Building, and at the **Wawona Store** (tel. 209/375–6574). For more information, contact the Department of Fish and Game (3211 S St., Sacramento, CA 95816, tel. 916/227–2244).

Horseback Riding. Scenic trail rides range from half days ($45) and full days ($67) to six-day High Sierra saddle trips ($874). Stables are open, in summer only, in **Wawona** (tel. 209/375–6502) and **Tuolumne Meadows** (tel. 209/372–8247). Reservations must be made in person at the hotel tour desks.

Rock Climbing. The **Yosemite Mountaineering School and Guide Service** (tel. 209/372–8344) has lessons and seminars for beginners as well as advanced climbers. The one-day basic lesson ($120 for one person, $85 each for two, $65 each for three or more) includes some bouldering and rappelling and three or four 60-ft climbs. Climbers must be at least 14 years old (12- and 13-year-olds may participate with a parent) and in reasonably good physical condition. Intermediate and advanced classes include instruction in belays, jam-crack techniques, self-rescue, summer snow climbing, and free climbing. Classes run from mid-April through early October. If you are already an experienced climber, ask

at the mountaineer shop in Curry Village what areas are best for your level of skill.

Skating. You can ice-skate from mid-November through mid-March at the outdoor **Curry Village Ice Skating Rink** (Yosemite Village, tel. 209/372–8341). The admission price is $5. Skate rental costs $2.

Skiing. Cross-country and alpine skiing are available at **Badger Pass** in winter. A free shuttle bus carries skiers from Yosemite Valley to the ski area; it takes about 40 minutes. Badger Pass opened in 1934 and is the oldest operating ski area in California. It is a compact area with one base lodge and gentle terrain, factors that make it ideal for families and beginners. Four chairlifts and one surface lift access nine runs. Lift tickets are $28 for one weekend day; $22 for one weekday. Those staying in one of Yosemite's hotels also ski free from Sunday through Thursday between January and March. Alpine and cross-country ski schools and rentals are available. Call 209/372–8444 for cross-country school information, 209/372–1000 for information on downhill ski school and road conditions.

Of Yosemite's 350 mi of skiable cross-country trails and roads, 90 begin at Badger Pass, but you can also ski at Crane Flat and the Mariposa Grove. The Glacier Point Road is not plowed but is groomed in winter. It's a 21-mi round-trip ski from Badger Pass to the vista at Glacier Point. Overnight trans-Sierra ski tours are also available.

Snowshoeing. Park rangers lead free morning snowshoe tours at Badger Pass in winter when the ski area is operating. These two-hour walks include rest stops, during which the ranger explains animal behavior in winter.

Swimming. Several swimming holes with small sandy beaches can be found in mid-summer along the Merced River at the eastern end of Yosemite Valley. Find gentle waters to swim; currents are often stronger than they appear and temperatures are chilling. Do not attempt to swim above or near waterfalls or rapids; fatalities have occurred. Outdoor swimming pools (summer only) are at Curry Village (tel. 209/372–8324) and Yosemite Lodge (tel. 209/372–1250).

CHILDREN'S PROGRAMS The Junior Ranger (ages eight to nine) and Senior Ranger (ages 10 to 12) programs are not as structured as they once were, but ranger-led activities suitable for kids still take place almost every day in summer. Parents may accompany children, but are strongly encouraged to drop them off for the day's activities. After completing a ranger program, children earn a badge. Happy Isles Nature Center Children's Program (ages five to seven) is a free, one-hour, ranger-led program offered in the summer, usually a few days a week; whether or not it will continue in the future depends on ranger availability. There's a less formal Junior Snow Ranger program in the winter.

Children also will enjoy many of the naturalist programs led by park rangers; Wawona's Pioneer Yosemite History Center, with its costumed docents in summer; biking; guided saddle rides; and skiing and ice-skating in winter.

A referral list of baby-sitters who have taken a certification course is available through the Ahwahnee Hotel and the Yosemite Lodge (*see* Lodging, *below*). Advance arrangements are recommended.

EVENING ACTIVITIES In the evenings, ranger talks, slide shows, and documentary films present unique perspectives on Yosemite. Programs vary according to season, but there is usually at least one activity per night in the Valley; schedules and locations are published in the Yosemite Guide. One of the best-loved presentations is Lee Stetson's portrayal of John Muir in *Conversation with a Tramp, John Muir's Stickeen and Other Fellow Mortals,* and *The Spirit of John Muir* (*see* Seasonal Events, *above*). Admission is $5.

Adults can relax with a cocktail at the Yosemite Lodge lounge, with its large-screen television and central fireplace; in

the lounge of the Ahwahnee Hotel; or at the Wawona Hotel, where a ragtime pianist entertains guests on weekends (*see* Lodging, *below*).

DINING

Food served in Yosemite, mostly standard American fare, tends to be overpriced and somewhat dull. It's a good idea to stock up on groceries before you arrive at the park, though basic supplies and picnic fare are available at a number of stores throughout the park. Those on a budget should head for the cafeteria at Yosemite Lodge (open year-round) or the hamburger stand at Curry Village (open spring to fall).

Since nighttime activities are limited, many visitors choose to dine in one of the slower-paced restaurants. The Ahwahnee Hotel, with its magnificent, cavernous dining room, is the park's most elegant choice, and the Wawona Hotel, with its nostalgic, Victorian ambience, is the most romantic. All restaurants in Yosemite are run by Yosemite Concession Services Corporation. The *Yosemite Guide* newspaper, which you will receive as you enter the park, lists the operating hours of restaurants and stores in the park. All restaurants in Yosemite are casual, with the exception of the Ahwahnee, where most dinner patrons wear a sport coat and tie or evening dress.

INSIDE THE PARK **Ahwahnee Dining Room.** This is the most dramatic setting in Yosemite, if not California. In the evening, this massive room, with its floor-to-ceiling windows and soaring, 34-ft-high ceiling supported by immense sugar-pine beams, glows with candlelight. Specialties include poached salmon with peppercorns, roast duckling with caramelized apples and oranges, and prime rib. Most dinner patrons wear jacket and tie or evening dress. *Ahwahnee Hotel, Yosemite Valley, tel. 209/372–1489. Reservations essential. D, MC, V. $$$*

Mountain Room. Choose this restaurant inside the Yosemite Lodge if you're looking for casual fine dining away from the noise and crowds of other Yosemite Valley dining areas but not as formal or expensive as the Ahwahnee. Knicker-clad waiters and a huge glass atrium with stellar views of Yosemite Falls give the Mountain Room a robust atmosphere. The focus is on simply prepared steaks and fish, including sirloin, salmon, and trout. *Yosemite Valley, tel. 209/ 372–1281. Reservations not accepted. D, MC, V. $$*

Wawona Hotel Dining Room. This is a romantic, nostalgic setting dating back to the late 1800s, with pastel tablecloths, tabletop candles in hurricane lamps, and friendly service. Along with the steak, trout, and daily chicken specials, selections include baked sea scallops and grilled polenta. A children's menu and Sunday brunch are also available. *Wawona Hotel, tel. 209/375–6556. D, MC, V. $$*

Degnan's Pasta Place. On the second floor of the large A-frame building that also houses Degnan's Deli and Degnan's Fast Food (*see below*), this is the only sit-down restaurant in Yosemite Village. At lunchtime, you can glimpse Glacier Point and Yosemite Falls from large dormer windows as you enjoy soups, salads, and simple pasta dishes, such as spaghetti bolognese. *Yosemite Village, tel. 209/372–8381. Reservations not accepted. D, MC, V. $*

Garden Terrace. Next to the Mountain Room (*see above*), this large, mostly self-service restaurant accommodates all tastes and budgets with a huge buffet. Among the selections are all kinds of prepared salads (and a salad bar), soups, pastas, vegetarian dishes, and a hot-meat carver. Show up early for dinner or be prepared for a long wait in line in the busy seasons. The restaurant is less crowded at breakfast, when omelets and pancakes dominate. *Yosemite Valley, tel. 209/372–1269. Reservations not accepted. D, MC, V. $*

There are several year-round fast-food options near the Valley Visitor Center. In an alpine-style building with a fireplace, **Degnan's Delicatessen** has sandwiches, salads, and gourmet cheeses, while **Degnan's Fast Food** serves pizza and ice cream. Nearby, the **Village Grill,** open spring to fall, serves hamburgers, croissant sandwiches, and ice cream. Summer-only restaurants are in the **Tuolumne Meadows Lodge** (tel. 209/372–1313) and **White Wolf Lodge** (tel. 209/372–1316).

NEAR THE PARK **Erna's Elderberry House.** Many repeat visitors to Yosemite plan on stopping at this rather formal restaurant on the way to or from the park. Erna's has four dining rooms with a French provincial flair and an outside terrace overlooking the Sierra. Prix-fixe, six-course dinners change nightly but may include truffled goat-cheese soufflé, roast quails filled with green-lentil purée and fresh figs, and caramelized blood oranges with bitter-chocolate ice. *48688 Victoria La., Oakhurst, tel. 209/683–6800. AE, MC, V. No lunch Sat.–Tues.; no dinner Mon. in winter. $$$*

Coffee Express. If you're coming into Yosemite via Highway 120, you'll pass this cozy dinerette. Try the chicken salad with apples and alfalfa sprouts and at least one sliver of irresistible fruit pie. Check out the Iron Door Saloon, one of the oldest operating saloons in California, across the street. *Hwy. 120, Groveland, tel. 209/962–7393. Reservations not accepted. No credit cards. No dinner Sun.–Thurs. $*

PICNIC SPOTS You can find everything you need for a delicious picnic in Yosemite Valley. Try Degnan's Delicatessen (tel. 209/372–8454) for sandwiches and cheeses and the Village Store (tel. 209/372–1253) for all your grocery needs. Ready-made picnic lunches are available through Yosemite hotels with advance notice. There are six picnic areas along the main roads in Yosemite Valley—**Cathedral Beach, Yellow Pine, Sentinel Beach, Church Bowl, El Capitan,** and **Swinging Bridge**—and one just off the main road—**Happy Isles.** All of these areas have picnic tables, rest rooms, and garbage receptacles, but only El Capitan, Sentinel Beach, and Swinging Bridge have grills; only Cathedral Beach and Sentinel Beach have fire rings; and only Happy Isles has drinking water nearby. Outside the Valley, there are picnic areas with tables at **Glacier Point** (rest rooms, garbage receptacles, water), **Mariposa Grove** (rest rooms, garbage receptacles, grills, water nearby), **Wawona** (rest rooms, garbage receptacles, grills, water nearby), **Tenaya Lake** (rest rooms, garbage receptacles, fire rings, some grills), **Glacier Point** (rest rooms, garbage receptacles, water nearby), **Cascades** (rest rooms, garbage receptacles, fire rings), **Yosemite Creek** (rest rooms, garbage receptacles), and **Lembert Dome** (rest rooms, garbage receptacles, fire rings). Many picnickers prefer to hike along one of the many scenic trails and choose an impromptu spot or vista point for a picnic.

LODGING

Lodgings in Yosemite—contrary to media coverage—were not all swept away in the 1997 flood; most of the dramatic footage was of employee housing. Lodging still ranges from the elegant Ahwahnee Hotel to spartan tent-cabins, all exhibiting an air of rusticity complementary to their natural setting. In the Valley, Yosemite Village is the most densely populated area, with several two-story, hotel-style buildings (the rustic cabins you may have once known were all destroyed in the flood and won't return). This area also has the most food, shopping, and restaurant services and is within easy walking distance of Yosemite Falls and the Valley Visitor Center. The Ahwahnee Hotel is in a more secluded, quiet setting, away from the Valley crowds; it is the only hotel in Yosemite with color television, room service, and minibars. Curry Village, another community of wood cabins and tent cabins, is within walking distance of the trails emanating from Happy Isles. In the summer, you can find rustic lodges at Tuolumne Meadows and White Wolf.

Reserve your room or cabin in Yosemite as far in advance as possible. You can make a reservation up to 366 days before your arrival date. The Ahwahnee, Yosemite Lodge, and Wawona Hotel are often sold out on weekends, holiday periods, and all days between May and September within minutes after the reservation office opens. All reservations for lodging in Yosemite are made through **Yosemite Concession Services Corporation** (Central Reservations, 5410 E. Home Ave., Fresno, CA 93727, tel. 209/252–4848).

If you visit anytime from November through March, especially midweek, you'll have a much easier time getting a reservation, and you'll pay a discounted room rate. If you must visit in the busy season and can't get a reservation, try asking for the less popular tent cabins at Curry Village. You may be able to upgrade after you arrive. Call 30 days, 15 days, or seven days in advance of your arrival. Or join a group tour, which often books blocks of rooms in advance. Though risky, you also can put your name on a wait list the day you arrive at Yosemite. Reservations without deposit are held only until 4 PM without a confirmation. If you're very lucky, a room may become available. Otherwise, plan on a long drive (sometimes one to two hours) to the nearest open hotel outside the park.

INSIDE THE PARK **Ahwahnee Hotel.** This grand hotel, with its exterior of granite and concrete painted to look like redwood, is the perfect complement to Yosemite. Now a National Historic Landmark, it has dramatic common areas warmed by walk-in hearths, decorated with Native American rugs and baskets, and graced with views of Yosemite through towering windows. Guest rooms have a Native American motif. *123 rooms. Facilities: restaurant, bar, pool, tennis. D, MC, V. $$$*

Redwoods Guest Cottages. The only lodging in the park not operated by Yosemite Concession Services Corporation, this collection of more than 100 private cabins in the Wawona area is a great alternative to the overcrowded valley. Fully furnished cabins with kitchens range from small, romantic one-bedroom units to bright, resortlike six-bedroom houses with decks overlooking the river. Most have TVs and fireplaces. The property rarely fills up, even in summer, so it's a good choice for last-minute lodging; there's a two-night minimum in the off-season and a three-night minimum in the summer. *Box 2085, Wawona Station, Yosemite National Park, CA 95389, tel. 209/375–6666, fax 209/375–6400. 120 units. D, MC, V. $$–$$$*

Wawona Hotel. An old-fashioned Victorian estate of whitewashed buildings with wrap-around verandas, this circa-1879 National Historic Landmark is in the southern end of Yosemite National Park, near the Mariposa Grove of Big Trees. Rooms reflect their turn-of-the-century origin—most are small and do not have a private bath. The cozy Victorian parlor in the main hotel is fun and romantic, with a fireplace, board games, and a pianist who plays ragtime tunes most evenings. There is a golf course adjacent to the property. *104 rooms. Facilities: restaurant, bar, pool, tennis, horseback riding. D, MC, V. $$–$$$*

Yosemite Lodge. All of the rustic cabins at this facility were damaged in the flood, but with- and without-bath hotel rooms remain. They range from simple motel-style digs to deluxe rooms with balconies overlooking Yosemite Falls or the Merced River. *400 rooms. Facilities: 2 restaurants, bar, cafeteria, pool. D, MC, V. $$*

Curry Village. This is a large community of cabins, tent cabins, and basic hotel rooms in a woodland setting on the eastern end of Yosemite Valley, in the shadow of Glacier Point. The one-room cabins, spartan but adequately furnished, are a lower-cost alternative to Yosemite's hotels. Tent cabins have wood frames and canvas walls and roof. Those without bath share campground-style community showers and toilets. Linen service is provided, but cooking is not allowed in the cabin area. *183 cabins, 427 tent cabins, 18 hotel rooms. Facilities: restaurant, pool, ice-skating. D, MC, V. $–$$*

NEAR THE PARK Additional lodging is available in Yosemite's gateway cities, but the nearest town, El Portal, is still 14 slow mountain mi from the Valley Visitor Center on Highway 140. Farther away on Highway 140 are Midpines, 36 mi from Yosemite Valley, and Mariposa, 43 mi away. To the north on Highway 120, Groveland also has a number of lodging options. South of the park on Highway 41, the tiny town of Fishcamp is about 8 mi from Wawona. Another 14 mi south on Highway 41, the much larger town of Oakhurst has a larger selection of hotels. The **Mariposa Visitors Center** (Box 425, Mariposa, CA 95338, tel. 209/966–2456), covering Mariposa, Midpines, and El Portal, has a free brochure listing all county hotels, motels, bed-and-breakfasts, restaurants, and sights. For hotels in Groveland, ask for the lodging guide from **Tuolumne County Visitors Bureau** (Box 4020, Sonora, CA 95370, tel. 209/533–4420 or 800/446–1333). For a free comprehensive guide to lodging and sightseeing options to the south of Yosemite, including Fishcamp and Oakhurst, contact the **Yosemite Sierra Visitors Bureau** (41729 Hwy. 41, Oakhurst, CA 93644, tel. 209/683–4636 or 209/658–7588).

A number of inns and motels are within a 25-mi (1- to 1½-hour) drive of Yosemite Park. Consider the following: **Cedar Lodge** (9966 Hwy. 140, El Portal, CA 95318, tel. 209/379–2612), 206 rooms; restaurant, indoor and outdoor pools, gift shop; AE, MC, V; $$–$$$. **Berkshire Inn** (19950 Hwy. 120, Groveland, CA 95321, tel. 209/962–6744), 10 rooms; outdoor hot tub, TV in common room, Continental breakfast; D, MC, V; $$–$$$. **Best Western Yosemite Gateway Inn** (40530 Hwy. 41, Oakhurst, CA 93644, tel. 209/683–2378 or 800/545–5462), 118 rooms; heated indoor/outdoor pool, sauna, whirlpools, exercise room; AE, D, DC, MC, V; $$. **Best Western Yosemite Way Station** (4999 Hwy. 140, Box 1989, Mariposa, CA 95338, tel. 209/966–7545 or 800/528–1234), 78 rooms; heated pool, spa, Continental breakfast; AE, D, DC, MC, V; $$. **Shilo Inn** (40644 Hwy. 41, Oakhurst, CA 93644, tel. 209/683–3555 or

800/222–2244), 80 rooms; pool, sauna, whirlpool, steam room, exercise room; AE, D, DC, MC, V; $$. **Comfort Inn** (4994 Bullion St., Box 1989, Mariposa, CA 95338, tel. 209/966–4344 or 800/321–5261), 61 rooms; small pool, whirlpool, gift shop, Continental breakfast; AE, D, DC, MC, V; $$. **Miners Inn** (Rte. 140 at Rte. 49N, Box 1989, Mariposa, CA 95338, tel. 209/742–7777), 67 rooms; pool, whirlpool; AE, D, MC, V. $$–$$$.

CAMPING

Although the 1997 flood knocked out more than 300 Yosemite Valley campsites (two entire campgrounds), the total number of sites in the park should eventually be back up to 1,800. The information here is likely to change somewhat, so call ahead for updated details. At press time, all Valley campgrounds operated on a first-come, first-served basis, though a new reservations system was expected to be in place by spring 1998.

Backpackers can hike to numerous backcountry areas where they can pitch a tent away from the crowds. Wilderness permits are required for overnights in the backcountry; you can get these at wilderness permit offices or by reserving for a $3 fee through the Wilderness Center in advance of your trip (*see* Visitor Information, *above*). When camping in the backcountry, you must be at least 4 mi from any developed area and at least 1 mi from roads and trailheads. Fires are permitted only in existing fire rings at specified elevations; ask a ranger before you head out. Collecting firewood is no longer permitted in Yosemite Valley, nor at elevations over 9,600 ft. "Down and dead" firewood may be collected elsewhere in the park, or you may purchase wood in Yosemite Valley, Wawona, Crane Flat, White Wolf, or Tuolumne Meadows.

Maximum RV length at Valley campgrounds is 40 ft; outside the Valley, it's 35 ft. There are no hookups in the park, but liquid propane gas is available at the service stations. You'll find disposal stations in Yosemite Valley and Wawona, and, in summer only, in Tuolumne Meadows. Generators are permitted sparingly and only from 7 AM to 7 PM. Gravel and dirt RV sites are available in all park campgrounds except the walk-in campgrounds. Larger sites are generally given to big RVs. Tamarack Flat and Yosemite Creek are accessible only by an access road that is not recommended for large RVs or trailers.

Yosemite Valley campgrounds lie along the Merced River on the relatively flat valley floor, at an elevation of about 4,000 ft. They are in forested areas, with pines, oaks, and incense cedars. Campgrounds in the Valley are well maintained but crowded, especially in summer. Lack of undergrowth between tent sites means there's not much privacy. Showers are available for a nominal fee at Curry Village and at valley swimming pools in season.

The **North Pines** campground (85 sites, flush toilets, drinking water, fire grates, swimming, ranger station, public phone, laundry and showers nearby) is in the Valley. North Pines is open all year; sites cost $15 per night.

Upper Pines (238 sites, flush toilets, drinking water, fire grates, swimming, disposal station, ranger station, public phone) is the only valley campground to allow pets. It is open from April to November; sites cost $15 per night. The Valley's **Lower Pines** (60 sites, flush toilets, drinking water, fire grates, swimming, ranger station, public phone) is open from March through October; sites cost $15 per night. Both have laundry and showers nearby.

Sunnyside Walk-in (35 sites, flush toilets, drinking water, fire grates, ranger station, public phone, showers nearby) is the only valley campground available on a first-come, first-served basis and the only one west of Yosemite Lodge. It is a favorite for rock climbers and solo campers, so it fills quickly and is typically sold out by 9 AM every day from spring through fall. Sunny-

YOSEMITE NATIONAL PARK

*per person. **showers nearby.

YOSEMITE CAMPGROUNDS

	Tuolumne Meadows	Porcupine Flat	Yosemite Creek	White Wolf	Tamarack Flat	Crane Flat	Hodgdon Meadow	Bridalveil Creek	Wawona	Sunnyside Walk-in	Lower Pines	Upper Pines	North Pines
	OUTSIDE YOSEMITE VALLEY									INSIDE YOSEMITE VALLEY			
Total number of sites	314	52	75	87	52	166	105	110	100	35	80	238	85
Sites suitable for RVs	314	52	0	87	0	166	105	110	100	0	80	238	85
Number of hookups	0	0	0	0	0	0	0	0	0	0	0	0	0
Drive to sites	•	•	•	•	•	•	•	•	•		•	•	•
Hike to sites										•			
Flush toilets	•			•		•	•	•	•	•	•	•	•
Pit/chemical toilets		•	•		•								
Drinking water	•			•		•	•	•	•	•	•	•	•
Showers										•**	•**	•**	•**
Fire grates	•	•	•	•	•	•	•	•	•	•	•	•	•
Swimming									•	•	•	•	•
Boat access													
Playground													
Disposal station	•								•			•	
Ranger station	•								•	•	•	•	•
Public telephone	•		•	•		•	•	•	•	•	•	•	•
Reservation required	•					•	•				•	•	•
Daily fee per site	$12	$6	$6	$10	$6	$12	$12	$10	$10	$3*	$15	$15	$15
Dates open	mid-June–Sept.	July–early Sept.	July–early Sept.	July–early Sept.	July–early Sept.	June–Oct.	year-round	June–Sept.	year-round	year-round	year-round	Apr.–Nov.	April–Oct.

side is open year-round; sites cost $3 per person per night.

In the southwestern section of the park, near the Mariposa Grove of Tall Trees, there are 100 sites along the river at **Wawona** (flush toilets, drinking water, fire grates, swimming, disposal station, ranger station, public phone). At an elevation of about 4,000 ft, these are open year-round and cost $15 per night.

On Glacier Point Road, past the Badger Pass Ski Area, there is a campground at **Bridalveil Creek** (110 sites, flush toilets, drinking water, fire grates, public phone). It sits higher than 7,000 ft, in an area forested with lodgepole pines, and can be quite brisk in the fall. It is open from June to September; sites cost $10 per night.

Hodgdon Meadow (105 sites, flush toilets, drinking water, fire grates, ranger station, public phone) is on the park's western boundary, near the Big Oak Flat Entrance. At an elevation of about 4,900 ft, it has vegetation similar to that in the Valley, but there is no river and no development here. It is open year-round; sites cost $15 per night.

At 6,200 ft, the **Crane Flat** campground (166 sites, flush toilets, drinking water, fire grates, public phone) is also on the western boundary, south of Hodgdon Meadow, off Big Oak Flat Road. It is just 17 mi from the Valley but far from the Valley's bustle. A small grove of sequoias is nearby. Crane Flat is open from June to October; sites cost $15 per night.

A rough spur road off the western end of Tioga Road brings you to **Tamarack Flat** (52 sites, pit toilets, fire grates), which is in a forested area with lodgepole pines, red firs, and some cedars. This is a more primitive campground, without water, and accommodates only small RVs. It is open from July to early September; sites cost $6 per night.

In the high country (8,000 ft), off Tioga Road, is **White Wolf** (87 sites, flush toilets, drinking water, fire grates, public phone), situated among lodgepole pines. It is open from July to early September, and sites cost $10 per night. Farther east on Tioga Road, a dirt spur road leads to **Yosemite Creek** (75 sites, pit toilets, fire grates, public phone), which is open from July to early September and charges $6 per site per night. Yosemite Creek is not suitable for large RVs.

The primitive **Porcupine Flat** campground (52 sites, pit toilets, fire grates) is at 8,100 ft. It's on Tioga Road, at about the center of the park, and is open from July to early September; sites cost $6 per night.

The most developed high-country campground is at **Tuolumne Meadows** (314 sites, flush toilets, drinking water, fire grates, disposal station, ranger station, public phone). The campground is in a wooded area just south of a subalpine meadow, and it affords easy access to high peaks with spectacular views. Campers here can use the showers at the Tuolumne Meadows Lodge (only at certain strictly regulated times). Tuolumne is open from mid-June to September. Half the sites can be reserved in advance through Destinet (*see above*). Sites cost $15 per night.

NEAR THE PARK If you arrive on a summer holiday weekend and can't find a place to pitch your tent, you'll be glad to know the U.S. Forest Service operates a number of campgrounds in the Inyo, Sierra, and Stanislaus national forests surrounding the park. For information on camping along Highway 41, call the Sierra National Forest **Oakhurst Ranger Station** (43060 Hwy. 41, Oakhurst, CA 93644, tel. 209/683–4665). The Sierra National Forest **Mariposa Ranger Station** (5158 Hwy. 140, Mariposa, CA 95338, tel. 209/966–3638) distributes information on campgrounds along Highway 140. To camp along Highway 120 west of the park, call the Stanislaus National Forest **Groveland Ranger Station** (24545 Hwy. 120, Groveland, CA 95321, tel. 209/962–7825). For information on sites along Highway 120 east of Yosemite, call the Inyo National Forest **Mono Basin Visitor Center and Ranger Station** (U.S. 395, .25 mi north of Lee Vining, Box 429, Lee Vining, CA 93541, tel. 760/647–3044).

Zion National Park
Utah

By Tom Wharton

n 1863 a Mormon settler named Isaac Behunin moved to southern Utah and built himself a cabin in the heart of this great canyon. Having fled religious persecution, Behunin called his new home Little Zion; it was, he felt, the promised land, a place of refuge and peace.

Today, Behunin's sanctuary is Utah's most developed and busiest national park, with more than 2.5 million annual visitors crowding its lodge and two large campgrounds. Close to a major interstate that connects Las Vegas with Salt Lake City, the park is easy to reach, and its 30 mi of paved roads and easy hiking trails make it a pleasure to explore.

Still, don't be fooled into thinking that Zion is too tame for a national park. Anyone who ventures away from the canyon roads will discover rugged trails, sandstone walls reaching 2,000 ft or more into the sky, and a fascinating and complex desert ecology.

The Virgin River, a muddy little stream that can turn into a violent red torrent during the spring runoff or after a summer thunderstorm, is shaping Zion's mighty canyons. Under a bright sky, a hiker in Zion National Park can enter a side canyon barely 20 ft across and be sandwiched between towering sandstone walls, which are washed in shades of crimson, vermilion, tan, and orange, and often stained with dark patches of carbon residue.

The names given to Zion's mountains and canyons reflect the awe with which early visitors greeted them. When first declared a national monument in 1909, the park was called Mukuntuweap, a name given to it by the local Native American Paiute people. The Mormons, however, pressured President Wilson into naming it Zion; Mukuntuweap became Zion National Monument in 1908 and, subsequently, Zion National Park in 1919. Many of the other place-names in the park—Kolob Canyons and Mt. Moroni, for example—are taken from Mormon theology. (Kolob is the star closest to God's residence, and Moroni is a principal figure in the Book of Mormon.) It was a Methodist minister, Frederick Vining Fisher, passing through Zion on a day trip in 1916, who gave the park some of its most evocative names: Angels Landing, the Great White Throne, and the Three Patriarchs.

To learn about local culture and get a feel for small-town life in rural Utah, visit the hamlet of Springdale, at the park's south entrance. Although a few garish motel signs mar an otherwise attractive setting, the town possesses a charm not often seen in gateway communities to national parks. Small shops, simple restaurants, and old pioneer homes dot the landscape.

ESSENTIAL INFORMATION

VISITOR INFORMATION Contact Superintendent, **Zion National Park**, Springdale, UT 84767-1099, tel. 435/772–3256. If you plan on camping in the backcountry or hiking through the Narrows, you must have a backcountry permit, which you can pick up at either the Zion Canyon Visitor Center, near the park's south entrance, or the Kolob

Canyons Visitor Center, in the northwest corner of the park just off I–15 at Exit 40. In winter, the visitor centers open at 8 and close at 5, but hours are extended until as late as 8 during the busy summer months.

FEES A seven-day entrance pass to the park for a passenger vehicle costs $10. Entry for pedestrians and bicyclists is $5 per week. A $10 fee is charged to escort oversize RVs wider than 7 ft 10 inches or higher than 11 ft 4 inches through the long, narrow tunnel on the Zion–Mt. Carmel Highway (Route 9).

PUBLICATIONS The **Zion Natural History Association** (Springdale, UT 84767, tel. 800/635–3959) sells a wide variety of maps and guides at its bookstores in both visitor centers. A list of publications is available, and credit-card orders are accepted by phone.

The best general guidebook to the park is J. L. Crawford's *Zion National Park, Towers of Stone.* The free brochures and park guides given out at park entrances outline the major hikes, but visitors seeking a more detailed description of the trails should consider buying *Hiking in Zion National Park, The Trails,* by Bob Lineback; and *Exploring the Backcountry of Zion National Park, Off-Trail Routes,* by Thomas Brereton and James Dunaway. Hikers may also want to purchase the waterproof, tear-resistant *Trails Illustrated Topo Map of Zion National Park.* Four different videos produced by the Zion Natural History Association present park highlights.

GEOLOGY AND TERRAIN The proclamation President Taft signed in 1909 setting aside Zion Canyon as a national monument justifies its preservation by stating that it is an "extraordinary example of canyon erosion." Zion is indeed a virtual experiment in geology—a powerful testament to the abrasive effects of wind and water on a landscape. About 13 million years ago, the Virgin River and its tributaries began carving out all the canyons of Zion park and sculpting the steep cliffs that today rise 2,000 ft from the Zion Canyon floor.

But the story of Zion goes back much further in time—as far back as 280 million years. Sandstone, shale, and limestone sedimentary layers can be seen on the cliffs. At the bottom is the Moenkopi layer of the early Triassic period, and as your eyes skim up the rock face you will see Shinarump, Chinle, Moenave, Kayenta, Navajo, Temple Cap, Carmel, and Dakota, the most recent layer, which was laid down in the Cretaceous period. It is Navajo sandstone—the remains of ancient sand dunes—that dominates the scenery. These layers are held together by calcium carbonate and iron oxide; the iron oxide causes the red color.

Those expecting to find a bleak desert landscape will be astounded by Zion's brilliant palette and odd geologic formations. The cliffs range from white and pastels to tan, orange, and vibrant crimson. The 147,035-acre park comprises areas of rock that can resemble fairy-tale castles and goblins. Part of the fun of visiting Zion is challenging your vocabulary to find the right words to describe this fanciful world.

Kolob Arch, one of the world's largest natural arches (310 ft), is here at Zion. In the hanging gardens of Weeping Rock, water seeps out of the sandstone allowing wildflowers, moss, and ferns to grow. On the eastern edge of the park is a huge petrified sand dune, aptly named Checkerboard Mesa for the grid that is etched onto its surface. The grid's horizontal lines are remnants of the rock's original sedimentation; the vertical lines are shallow cracks resulting from weathering—freezing, thawing, and heating—as well as expansion and water.

The displays in the visitor center and signs near turnoffs and trailheads explain Zion geology in great detail, but those with a special interest should buy Wayne Hamilton's *The Sculpturing of Zion,* available at the visitor center.

FLORA AND FAUNA Zion National Park has a greatly varied terrain and elevation; the park ranges from Mojave desert to subalpine forest. At times it resembles a huge, red rock garden, with a variety of plants and flowers, and ponderosa pines that seem to grow right out of the hard rock. Zion is especially colorful in the fall and spring, when wildflowers bloom. In winter, the remaining brown oak leaves, practically the same color as the canyon walls, cling to the trees, and after a rainstorm, droplets of water form on the exposed branches of leafless trees. Cottonwood trees grow along the banks of the Virgin River, providing picnickers on the canyon bottom with shade from the scorching summer heat.

Red rocks, greenery, and purple, red, and yellow wildflowers make the hanging gardens one of the most interesting areas to see in the spring and summer months. Golden and cliff columbine, scarlet monkeyflower, and maidenhair fern hang from the sides of the sandstone cliffs along the Riverside Walk (*see* Nature Trails and Short Walks, *below*). The lush growth makes this part of Zion seem more like a tropical rain forest than a desert.

Typical desert plants do, however, thrive in Zion. Yuccas, buffalo berry, hedgehog cactus, and prickly pear are prevalent in the dry exposed areas of the park.

Call the Red Butte Gardens and Arboretum of Utah's "wildflower hot line" (tel. 801/ 581–4747) from April to late September for a recording that tells you which flowers are blooming in Zion and throughout the state. Once you reach the park, use the Zion Natural History Association's *Wildflowers of Zion National Park* to identify the specimens you find.

Along with the wildflowers, there is an abundance of wildlife. Expect to see mule deer in the main Zion Canyon, especially in the late fall and winter months, when leaves drop from the cottonwood trees and the canyon bottoms and meadows are more exposed. Although mountain lions roam the park, you could spend a lifetime here without ever seeing one of these shy, elusive cats. Small lizards are often spotted sunning themselves on the hot sandstone along the trails, and squirrels are common. Some 270 different birds have been identi-

fied here. You may also find birds as large as golden eagles and as small as canyon wrens or Gambel's quail, as well as roadrunners.

WHEN TO GO As is the case in many of Utah's national parks, spring and fall are the best times to visit Zion. Temperatures are moderate, and the crowds are smaller. Adding to the park's already colorful setting are wildflowers, which reach their peak in May, and the autumn leaves of maple, cottonwood, aspen, ash, and oak, which hit their peak in late October and early November.

Summer is high season at Zion, and with the greening of the meadows comes congestion at the visitor centers and main parking lots, as well as on the more popular trails. If you're driving the Zion–Mt. Carmel Highway, prepare for delays near the long tunnel as rangers block off traffic to escort large RVs through. Although the climate is dry, temperatures can top 105°F in summer, and thunderstorms and flash floods are common. On the bright side, there is nothing quite like being in Zion right after a summer thunderstorm, when waterfalls are ubiquitous. Summer also brings a greater choice of interpretive and evening programs.

Relatively mild winter temperatures make Zion a pleasant place for a December sojourn and the easiest Utah park to visit year-round. In winter, park roads are regularly plowed, and they remain open all year, as do Zion Lodge and the Watchman campground. Check with rangers before going hiking in the winter. Some trails become extremely slick and icy, and snow can block trails at higher elevations.

Temperatures in all areas of Zion may fluctuate greatly within the course of a single day, but typically, it is warm at the bottom of the canyon and much cooler at the top. Even in July, however, a hike through the waters of the Narrows can be a chilling experience, and in February the temperature often rises to 60°F only a few days after a winter storm. January highs can range from 39°F to 60°F, lows from 0°F to 27°F. In April, highs are between 62°F and 80°F, lows 37°F and 59°F. The highs for July run from 93°F to 103°F, and lows are fairly constant, between 64°F and 73°F. In October, highs range from 70°F to 88°F and lows from 42°F to 62°F.

SEASONAL EVENTS **Thursday to Saturday after Labor Day:** The **Southern Utah Folklife Festival** (tel. 435/772–3410), held annually in Springdale, adjacent to Zion, is a commemoration of Native American and early Mormon settler life, with displays of foods and crafts, stories from local residents, horse-drawn wagon rides, and square dances. **June 23 to August 30:** The **Utah Shakespearean Festival** (tel. 435/586–7880) at Southern Utah University in Cedar City (59 mi north of Zion), includes three Shakespeare productions each summer, as well as three modern plays. Performances are in three theaters, including an outdoor replica of the Globe Theatre. There are matinees and evening performances; tickets are usually available the day of the show, but reservations are suggested.

WHAT TO PACK If you plan to hike the Zion Narrows, which involves wading through the deep waters of the Virgin River, bring a walking staff, waterproof bags to protect your equipment, and an old pair of hiking boots or sneakers that you don't mind getting wet. Flash floods can make this hike extremely hazardous; be sure to check the weather forecast. On the steeper trails, good hiking boots are recommended—Zion's sheer cliffs can be dangerous.

The desert sun is brutal during summer. Bring water on all hikes and wear wide-brim hats and sunblock. Rain gear is useful even in summer, when sudden thunderstorms and flash floods occur.

GENERAL STORES The markets in and around Zion National Park are small convenience stores that also carry curios and souvenirs. The store nearest the park is in Springdale: the **Canyon Supermarket** (652 Zion Park Blvd., tel. 435/772–3402), open from 9 to 6 in winter and 8 AM to 10 PM in

summer. **Zion Park Market** (855 Zion Park Blvd., tel. 435/772–3251) is open from 9 to 6 in winter and from 8 to 9:30 in summer. **Zion Canyon Campground Store** (962 Zion Park Blvd., tel. 435/772–3237) is open from 8 to 6:30 in winter and from 8 AM to 9 PM in summer. **Zican** (no phone), 2 mi from the park's east entrance, is open from 8 to 6.

ARRIVING AND DEPARTING Most visitors arrive in Zion via car or tour bus. Airports and bus stations in Cedar City and St. George are 62 and 42 mi, respectively, from the park. There are three main entrances to Zion National Park: the south and east entrances, which are linked by Route 9 (Zion–Mt. Carmel Highway), and the less-used Kolob Canyons entrance, at Exit 40 on Interstate 15, in the northwest corner of the park.

By Bus. Greyhound Lines (tel. 801/355–9579 or 800/231–2222) goes from Salt Lake City and Las Vegas to St. George and Cedar City, where you'll need to rent a car or take a taxi or limo (see By Car and RV, below). You can also arrange for a bus tour (see Guided Tours, below).

By Car and RV. Interstate 15 (I–15) runs from Salt Lake City, northeast of Zion, to Las Vegas, to the southwest, and connects to Zion's Kolob Canyons Road. The park's south and east entrances are on Route 9, which branches off I–15 near St. George. A more scenic, although slower, alternative from Salt Lake City to the east and south entrances is U.S. 89, which also links Zion to Bryce Canyon National Park and the Grand Canyon.

Expect a 5½-hour, 309-mi drive from Salt Lake City to Zion; a 2½-hour, 119-mi drive from the Grand Canyon's North Rim; a five-hour, 253-mi drive from the South Rim; a three-hour, 158-mi drive from Las Vegas; and about a two-hour, 86-mi drive from Bryce Canyon National Park.

You can measure the length of your RV at the south and east entrances. RVs wider than 7 ft 10 inches, higher than 11 ft 4 inches, or longer than 40 ft (50 ft including a trailer) require an escort through the narrow tunnel on Route 9, the only road that bisects the park. The $10 escort fee can be paid at either park entrance and is good for two trips for the same vehicle over a seven-day period. In summer, no appointment is needed. Rangers are stationed at both tunnel entrances from 8 AM until 8 PM to coordinate the escort. In the off-season, escorts must be arranged either in advance at the south or east entrances or through the visitor center (tel. 435/772–3256).

RVs longer than 21 ft may not enter or park at the Weeping Rock parking area at any time, or at the Temple of Sinawava parking lot, at the end of the Zion Canyon, from 9 to 5. Passengers may be dropped off at a designated area at Temple of Sinawava. A shuttle service between Zion Lodge, where parking is allowed, and the Temple of Sinawava takes 50 minutes and costs $2.95 round-trip. Check with the lodge for additional tour options.

You can rent a car in St. George from **Avis** (St. George Municipal Airport, tel. 435/634–3940), **Budget** (1275 N. Highland Dr., tel. 435/673–6825), **Dollar Rent-A-Car** (1175 S. 150 E, tel. 435/628–6549), and **National** (St. George Municipal Airport, tel. 435/673–5098).

Cedar City car rentals include **Avis** (Sky West, tel. 435/586–3033) and **National** (Municipal Airport, tel. 435/586–7059).

To rent a car in Las Vegas or Salt Lake City, call **Hertz** (tel. 800/654–3131), **Avis** (tel. 800/331–1212), or any other major rental agency.

By Plane. SkyWest Airlines (Delta Connection, tel. 800/453–9417) has regular flights from Salt Lake City and Las Vegas to St. George (43 mi from Zion) and Cedar City (60 mi from Zion). Rental cars and limousine services are available in both cities, but St. George has more agencies (*see* By Car and RV, *above*). You can also arrange to take a tour bus from Salt Lake City to the park (*see* Guided Tours, *below*).

EXPLORING

Although most people only view the wonder of Zion from the windows of their car as they drive the mere 30 mi of road that cross the park, Zion is a place for walkers. Hiking trails are many, ranging from flat, paved half-mile walks to strenuous eight-hour climbs and multiday backpacking excursions. If you are seeking southern Utah's famed white-water rafting, mountain biking, or four-wheel-drive adventures, head east to Canyonlands National Park.

There are two distinct sections at Zion: the Zion Canyon area in the south, which contains some of the park's most spectacular scenery and receives the great majority of its visitors, and the Kolob Canyons region in the north, which attracts people who put a premium on solitude. You could conceivably see the southern sector in two or three hours by driving the 7 mi up the Zion Canyon Scenic Drive, stopping at a few major turnouts, then backtracking to Route 9 and heading out of the park—but you're better off taking your time and getting out of your car.

Plan on spending at least two or three days in Zion. Take the one-hour horseback ride from the lodge, schedule a half day in the remote Kolob Canyons, strap on a backpack, and sleep under the backcountry stars.

THE BEST IN ONE DAY There is much to see in the Four Corners area of Utah, Colorado, Arizona, and New Mexico, and travelers often try to fit in as many parks as they can in a short amount of time. Those with only one day to spend in Zion should eat breakfast at the Zion Lodge in the early morning. In summer you can sit out on the patio overlooking the canyon and watch the sun rise and the colors change. You'll have to backtrack 3.5 mi to reach the Zion Canyon Visitor Center, near the park's south entrance, but it is the best place to get oriented. Its short orientation video and small museum are informative introductions to the park.

The 7-mi Zion Canyon Scenic Drive, from the Zion Canyon Visitor Center to the Temple of Sinawava, ranks as one of the premier drives in Utah (*see* Scenic Drives and Views, *below*). At the Temple of Sinawava, change into your hiking shoes and head out on the Riverside Walk. The 2-mi, two-hour round-trip course passes through the hanging gardens. After this hike return to the Zion Canyon Scenic Drive and travel south for 1.5 mi, until you reach the trailhead for the easy .5-mi round-trip walk out to Weeping Rock, one of Zion's many unusual geological formations. (For details on both hikes, *see* Nature Trails and Short Walks, *below.*)

The Grotto picnic area, 1 mi farther south, is just the spot for an impromptu canyon picnic. Across from Zion Lodge, .5 mi south of the Grotto, take the 1.25-mi trail to Emerald Pools (*see* Nature Trails and Short Walks, *below*). Watching the waterfall here is refreshing on a hot summer's day, although swimming is prohibited.

Finish off your afternoon by driving east for 11 mi along the Zion–Mt. Carmel Highway past the Checkerboard Mesa to the park's east entrance (*see* Scenic Drives and Views, *below*). Photo opportunities abound as the light of dusk plays over the canyons. Backtrack to the south entrance and exit the park; dinner or a drink in Springdale will help you wind down.

ORIENTATION PROGRAMS Don't miss the Zion Canyon Visitor Center's 15-minute orientation video, which highlights many of the park's premier attractions.

GUIDED TOURS At least three guide services offer individualized tours to Zion National Park: **Passage to Utah** (Box 520883, Salt Lake City, UT 842152, tel. 801/281–4523); **Utah Escapades** (Park City, UT 84060, tel. 800/268–8824, fax 801/649–9948); and **Wild Hare Expeditions** (Box 750194, Torrey, UT 84775, tel. 888/304–4273, fax 801/425–3999). The last concentrates on the Capitol Reef National Park area, although personalized tours to Zion can be arranged upon request.

The National Park Service organizes daily hikes through the park except during the off-season. Check at the visitor centers for times and places. There are also guided tours on horseback, and a few bicycle touring companies lead trips into Zion (*see* Other Activities, *below*). **Zion Park Lodge** (tel. 435/586–3157) runs open-air tram tours daily in the summer. Reservations and information are available at the lodge.

SCENIC DRIVES AND VIEWS The best times to take a drive through Zion National Park are at sunrise and sunset, when the low light accentuates the colors of the surrounding cliffs. There are only four drives in Zion, one of which ventures outside the bounds of the park.

The 13-mi round-trip route of **Zion Canyon Scenic Drive** will put you in the heart of the upper canyon. It begins 1 mi north of the south entrance and ends at the Temple of Sinawava parking area. Several pullouts along the way are ideal for picture-taking. Satisfying short walks are the easy Riverside Walk, which starts at the Temple of Sinawava, and the Weeping Rock Trail, which you can pick up along the scenic drive, 1.5 mi south of Sinawava.

The segment of Route 9 that passes through the park is called the **Zion–Mt. Carmel Highway.** It climbs from the bottom of the canyon at the south entrance, 13 mi up winding switchbacks and through tunnels carved out of the rock, passing the petrified sand dunes of the Checkerboard Mesa before reaching the east entrance. This is the road that connects Zion to Bryce Canyon and the Grand Canyon; it is particularly popular with kids, who love the tunnels. The Canyon Overlook Trail (*see* Nature Trails and Short Walks, *below*), just east of the long tunnel, is one of the most attractive hikes off this road. Those driving oversize RVs must follow special regulations on this drive (*see* Arriving and Departing, *above*).

There are two drives in more remote areas of Zion: the 11-mi round-trip journey along **Kolob Canyons Road,** from the Kolob Canyons Visitor Center to the Kolob Canyons

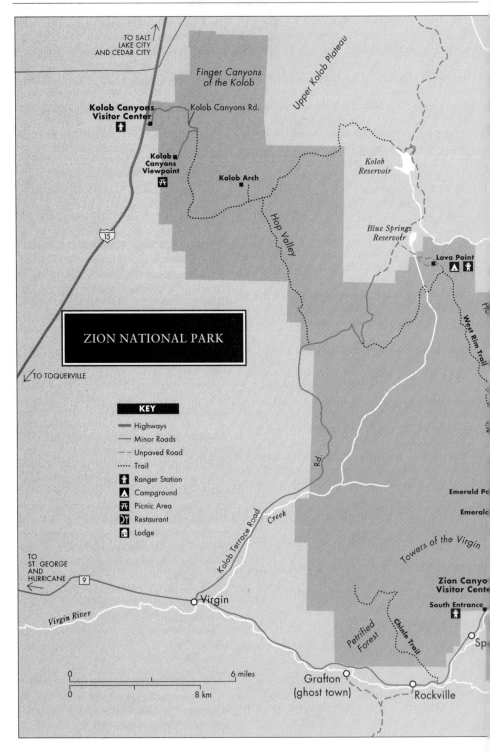

ZION NATIONAL PARK

KEY

Highways
Minor Roads
Unpaved Road
Trail
Ranger Station
Campground
Picnic Area
Restaurant
Lodge

TO SALT
LAKE CITY
AND CEDAR CITY

*Finger Canyons
of the Kolob*

Upper Kolob Plateau

**Kolob Canyons
Visitor Center**

Kolob Canyons Rd.

**Kolob
Canyons
Viewpoint**

Kolob Arch

*Kolob
Reservoir*

*Blue Springs
Reservoir*

Hop Valley

Lava Point

West Rim Trail

TO TOQUERVILLE

TO
ST. GEORGE
AND
HURRICANE

9

Virgin River

Virgin

Kolob Terrace Road

Creek

Rd.

Emerald Pe

Emeral

Towers of the Virgin

**Zion Canyo
Visitor Cente**

SOUTH ENTRANCE

*Petrified
Forest*

Chinle Trail

Sp

Grafton
(ghost town)

Rockville

0   6 miles
0   8 km

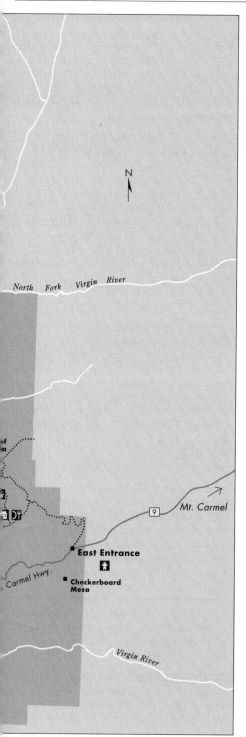

Viewpoint, and the 50-mi round-trip drive from the town of Virgin north along the **Kolob Terrace Road** (closed in winter) to Lava Point and Kolob Reservoir. Kolob Canyons Road climbs more than 1,000 ft in 5 mi and ends at a viewpoint from which you can look out at the narrow finger canyons below. The latter route runs along the western edge of the park, passing farmhouses and bright green fields that form a striking contrast with the red slickrock. A good way to escape the crowds, this drive allows you to enjoy spectacular views from the top of Kolob Canyon without having to take a long hike.

HISTORIC BUILDINGS AND SITES A few examples of Mormon architecture can be found in such tiny towns as Toquerville, Rockville, and Springdale on the outskirts of Zion National Park, but the only truly historic building within the park is the **Zion Lodge**— and it has been rebuilt. The Union Pacific Railroad constructed the first Zion Lodge in 1925; some of the old cabins still in use date back to that time. A 1966 fire during a renovation project completely destroyed the lodge. Rebuilt in 1967, it was rehabilitated in 1986 in keeping with the original design by architect Stanley Underwood (lodges at Bryce Canyon and Yosemite were also designed by Underwood). The lodge is open year-round and has a restaurant, snack bar, curio shop, and auditorium (*see* Lodging, *below*).

NATURE TRAILS AND SHORT WALKS The easiest trails at Zion are in many cases the most interesting. This is especially true of the 1.25-mi round-trip hike to the **Lower Emerald Pool,** where three waterfalls cascade off the red cliffs. Another mile up a difficult incline will take you to the larger **Upper Emerald Pool,** which is at the base of several 1,000-ft sheer sandstone cliffs. The lower pool is accessible by wheelchair, but some assistance may be needed on the last part of the trail.

To see just how imposing Zion Canyon can be, park your car at the Temple of Sinawava and take the easy, relatively flat 2-mi round-trip **Riverside Walk.** This is an especially beautiful route in spring and summer, when colorful wildflowers hang from the canyon walls. It will take about 90 minutes to complete the walk, but the way is shaded and the Virgin River keeps it cool. Interpretive signs tell the natural history of the canyon. The trail is wheelchair-accessible, although some assistance may be needed higher up in the canyon.

The .5-mi round-trip **Weeping Rock Trail,** in Zion Canyon, leads to a spring that issues from a rock and creates hanging gardens in spring and summer. The 1-mi round-trip **Canyon Overlook Trail** begins just east of the long tunnel on the Zion–Mt. Carmel Highway and ends at a viewpoint overlooking lower Zion Canyon, Pine Creek Canyon, and the Zion–Mt. Carmel Highway switchbacks.

LONGER HIKES Perhaps the most famous trail in the park is the 16-mi (one-way) path through the **Zion Narrows,** an aptly named slit of a canyon that acts as a funnel for the icy waters of the Virgin River. If you're hiking all day from the Chamberlain Ranch through the Narrows, a $5 day use permit is required. Because of the danger of flash flooding, you must get a permit from the visitor center the afternoon before making this long trip. Since the area has been overused, the park now issues only 80 permits for those hiking the entire length of the Narrows. It can take two days to cover the 16 mi, although strong hikers can make it in 12 hours. Those who spend the night must camp in one of the 12 group sites. Most people, however, simply hike in from the Temple of Sinawava for a mile or two and then come back (no permit is required to do this). Some hikers start outside the park and hike their way in. Before setting out, check at the visitor center for information on current trail and weather conditions. Flash floods in this canyon have resulted in fatalities; you are responsible for your own safety.

Another challenging hike is the 5-mi round-trip climb to **Angels Landing,** a large

ridge on the west side of Zion Canyon (you can see it from the road below). Plan on four hours for this strenuous hike, which starts at the Grotto Picnic Area and climbs 1,488 ft. The last half mile follows a vertiginous ridge with a drop-off of 1,500 ft. In places where the trail gets narrow, handgrip chains are provided.

The trail to Angels Landing stems off the popular **West Rim Trail,** which is 26.5 mi round-trip. This trail begins at the Grotto Picnic Area and ends at Lava Point, a 3,593-ft climb that takes at least 20 hours to negotiate. Hikers should plan on spending the night in the primitive campsite at Lava Point before heading back to the Grotto. If you only have time to hike part way, you will still be rewarded with views of some fine slickrock canyons not visible from the road.

The 8-mi round trip to Observation Point leads to a spectacular panoramic view of the valley below. Beginning at the Weeping Rock parking lot, the trail climbs 2,148 ft in a series of paved switchbacks cut into the rock. It passes through a twisting canyon so narrow the sky is often hidden from view. A side trip worth exploring is the **Hidden Canyon Trail,** which originates at the Weeping Rock parking lot and travels 2 mi round-trip through a pretty little canyon, ending at a small natural arch.

Venture into the more remote Kolob Canyons area in the northwest corner of the park and consider spending a day making the 14-mi round-trip journey to **Kolob Arch,** which, with a 310-ft span, is one of the world's largest freestanding arches. This trek begins at Lee Pass, on the Kolob Canyons Road, and involves a 699-ft descent into the canyon (that's an ascent on the return). Plan on hiking for 10 hours or, better yet, backpack and spend the night. There is a good, year-round spring at the bottom of the canyon.

OTHER ACTIVITIES **Back-Road Driving.** There are good all-terrain vehicle play areas in the nearby town of Hurricane, but none in Zion. For more information contact the Bureau of Land Management Cedar City District (176 E. D. L. Sargent Dr., Cedar City, UT 84720, tel. 435/586–2401).

Biking. Zion is not a great place to cycle, since bicycles are limited to paved roads, which tend to be narrow and congested. One exception is the 2-mi-long paved bike path, the **Pa'rus Trail,** which runs along lower Zion Canyon. No bikes are allowed on any hiking trails or in the 1-mi Zion–Mt. Carmel tunnel. Since bicycles must be transported through the tunnel, cyclists should check at the entrance station or call ahead to make arrangements. Bicycle rentals are not available in the park, but you'll find them in Springdale at **Bike Zion** (1458 Zion Park Blvd., Springdale, UT 84767, tel. 800/475–4576). Rental costs are $23 per day, $17 for a half day. Write to park headquarters (*see* Visitor Information, *above*) for a free brochure on bicycling in Zion.

Cycling aficionados will find some excellent mountain biking trails outside Zion. Companies operating tours that cover trails outside the park, occasionally passing through the park, are **Backcountry Bicycle Tours** (Box 4029, Bozeman, MT 59772, tel. 406/586–3556) and **Backroads Bicycle Touring, Inc.** (801 Cedar St., Berkeley, CA 94710, tel. 800/245–3874).

Bird-Watching. More than 270 bird species have been identified in Zion National Park, including American dippers, black-headed grosbeaks, American kestrels, turkey vultures, canyon wrens, roadrunners, and even golden eagles. Rarer species are nesting peregrine falcons, Mexican spotted owls, and pygmy nuthatches. You will see the largest variety of birds in May and June. Good places to look for them are near the sewage lagoons or in the cemetery in Springdale, along the Virgin River, and on the uplands, near such plateaus as Checkerboard Mesa and Lava Point. Ask a park naturalist at the visitor center for a bird list.

Boating and Tubing. There is no boating inside the park, but you can put in at Quail Creek Reservoir (tel. 435/635–9412), 30 mi from the park. Rentals are not available.

Despite the danger, which can be considerable during the high-water spring season, many people take inner tubes down the Virgin River. Tubers are restricted to the lower 1.5 mi of the river. The access point is the South Campground amphitheater. Concessionaires operating from a trailer parked outside the park's south entrance rent tubes for $5 a day, from 10 to 7 between late spring and Labor Day weekend. Bike Zion (*see* Biking, *above*) rents tubes for $3 a day.

Fishing. Fishing is limited inside the park, but Kolob Reservoir, roughly 5 mi north of Lava Point and accessible only by dirt road, provides good trout angling. Largemouth bass and trout are found in Quail Creek Reservoir. A Utah fishing license is required both inside and outside the park; you can buy one in local grocery and outdoor stores or from the Division of Wildlife Resources in Cedar City (622 N. Main St., 84720, tel. 435/879–2378). A license, good from the date of purchase to the end of the calendar year, costs $47.50 for nonresidents and $18 for residents; a five-day license costs $15, and a one-day license $5. A $5.25 conservation license, available at the above-mentioned stores, must also be purchased.

Flightseeing. Make reservations at least two days in advance to fly over the park with **Cedar City Air Service** (2281 W. Kitty Hawk Dr., Box 458, Cedar City, UT 84720, tel. 435/586–3881). During summer, early-morning or late-evening flights are best, since midday rides tend to be bumpy and uncomfortable when it's warm outside. In 25 minutes you'll fly from Cedar City over Kolob and Zion canyons and back, a trip that costs $46 per person (a 35-minute look at the same area costs $65). There is a two-person minimum on all flights.

Horseback Riding. Those bothered by elevations and heat should try exploring Zion on horseback. Guided rides along several picturesque trails are available from **Bryce–Zion–Grand Canyon Trail Rides** (tel. 435/772–3810 in season, 435/679–8665 off-season), near the Zion Lodge. One-hour ($15) and three-hour ($37) rides are offered from mid-March through October along the Virgin River and the Sand Bench Trail. No experience is necessary, but children must be at least five years old. Make advance reservations.

Rock Climbing. Rangers recommend Zion's cliffs for experienced rock climbers only, since sandstone is more difficult to negotiate than granite. No permits are required unless you plan to spend the night. You should, however, check with the rangers to find out if there are restrictions on any routes; many climbing areas are closed in spring and summer to protect nesting peregrine falcons. Fall and spring are ideal times to climb; summers are often too hot. For free literature, stop in at the visitor centers or write to park headquarters (*see* Visitor Information, *above*). You must provide your own climbing equipment.

Snowmobiling. Snowmobiles are permitted only on unplowed roads, which are few in Zion, but there are good routes just outside the park. Contact the Utah Division of Parks and Recreation (1636 W. North Temple St., Salt Lake City, UT 84116, tel. 801/538–7220) for snowmobiling information.

Snowshoeing and Ski Touring. Some snowshoeing and cross-country skiing is available on the higher plateau areas of the park; Wildcat Canyon and the upper West Rim Trail have the best conditions. Bring your own equipment, as there are no rental shops in the area.

Swimming. Although a few visitors wade in the Virgin River or more remote streams, swimming at Zion is limited. Some motels in Mt. Carmel and Springdale have pools, but no public facilities exist. The Pah Tempe Hot Springs (tel. 435/635–2879), near La Verkin (27 mi from Zion), and Quail Creek Reservoir are your best bets for a swim in the area.

CHILDREN'S PROGRAMS The Zion Nature Center's **Junior Ranger Program** (tel. 435/772–0165), for kids six to 12 years old,

ranks among the best children's programs in all the national parks. The center is within walking distance of both campgrounds and operates from June through Labor Day, with registration each morning and afternoon. Rangers offer instruction on such topics as wildlife protection and conservation. There is a $3 fee per child.

EVENING ACTIVITIES Evening programs at Zion's campgrounds vary from year to year, often including slide shows, night hikes, and historical vignettes. Other evening entertainment can be had at **O. C. Tanner Amphitheater** (tel. 435/652–7994), a block outside the park's south entrance, where you'll find concerts, slide shows, and ethnic dances. "The Grand Circle," a multimedia show depicting national parks in the area, is presented nightly from May 13 to September 9 on a huge screen. For the finale, the cliffs of Zion are illuminated. Tickets to this hour-long show cost $4 and may be purchased at the door. A Cinemax theater (tel. 435/772–2400) features an entertaining but historically inaccurate show about the Zion area, beginning on the hour daily, 365 days a year. Tickets cost $7.

DINING

Dining around Zion tends to be a down-home American affair. The restaurants in this corner of Utah are neither fancy nor expensive, but the food they prepare is wholesome, filling, and definitely Western. Expect barbecue and a lot of red meat, plus occasional vegetarian selections. The Zion Lodge is the only restaurant inside the park; most of the other good ones are in Springdale, near the south entrance. Most of these have picture windows and patios with canyon views that allow visitors to enjoy the scenery from outside the park.

INSIDE THE PARK **Zion Lodge.** The quintessence of Western family dining, this is one of the classier places to eat in the area. A wall of windows overlooks the maws of the great canyon, a wood-beam ceiling and historic photos lend the room the requisite pioneer atmosphere, and white tablecloths and candles add a formal touch. As busy as it is, the restaurant continues to serve high-quality food, its specialties being steak, prime rib, Utah trout, and pasta. In summer, consider a table on the patio. Other than a small snack bar nearby, this is the only dining area inside the park. *Zion National Park, tel. 425/772–3213. AE, DC, MC, V. $$*

NEAR THE PARK **Switchback Cafe at Zion Park Inn.** This ranks among the classiest restaurants in the Zion area. Guests sit at their tables in a dining room with vaulted ceilings and watch while cooks prepare their meals. Dinners include a good vegetarian menu, sandwiches, pizza, and some interesting Southwest-style dishes. Smoothies are a specialty. This place can be crowded at times. *1149 S. Zion Park Blvd., Springdale, UT 84767, tel. 435/772–3777. AE, D, MC, V. $$$*

Flanigans. The Santa Fe pastels here create a soothing, intimate atmosphere. With its southwestern decor and walls covered with photographs of Utah, this is one of the more refined restaurants in Springdale. The menu varies seasonally, but fresh salmon and Utah trout are regulars. A sidewalk café with a juice bar has nice views of nearby Zion Canyon. *428 Zion Park Blvd., Springdale, tel. 435/772–3244. AE, D, DC, MC, V. Closed occasionally in Dec. $$–$$$*

Bit and Spur. Though it's a bit on the pricey side, this extremely popular Springdale place is one of the best Mexican restaurants in Utah. In addition to standard Mexican dishes, expect such offbeat entrées as rabbit *pollo relleno* with goat cheese. Live rock and country-western music on selected weekends make the atmosphere lively. *1212 Zion Park Blvd., Springdale, tel. 435/772–3498. MC, V. No lunch. Closed 2 wks in Dec. $$*

Bumbleberry Inn. One mile south of the park boundary, this family restaurant is known far and wide for its patented bumbleberry pie. What's a bumbleberry? The waitress will be more than happy to tell you. The inn is also known for its country-fried steaks, chicken, and spaghetti. No alcohol is served or allowed on the premises. *897 Zion Park Blvd., Springdale, tel. 435/772–3224. AE, D, MC, V. Closed Sun. $$*

Log House Restaurant. There's a nice atmosphere at this restaurant, which has open picture windows looking out over the canyon. It has a copper roof and is constructed of massive logs salvaged from the Yellowstone fire, and there's an indoor waterfall and Native American decor. Meals are fairly standard—meat and potatoes, plus a pasta of the day. *2400 Zion Park Blvd., Springdale, tel. 435/772–3000. Reservations not accepted. AE, DC, MC, V. $$*

Pioneer Lodge and Restaurant. Basic American food—meat and potatoes, trout, halibut, pasta—comes with a full salad bar and homemade rolls. An old fireplace and heavy wood beams add a rustic touch. Don't miss the homemade ice-cream pie. *828 Zion Park Blvd., Springdale, tel. 435/772–3009. AE, D, MC, V. Closed Dec.–Mar. $–$$*

Zion Pizza and Noodle Company. You can eat inside or on the porch of this old church, which has been transformed into a pizza and pasta restaurant. Each night brings a different pasta special, but calzones and pizzas are always on the menu. There's an art gallery downstairs and a bookstore next door, so you can shop when you're through with dinner. *868 Zion Park Blvd., Springdale, tel. 435/772–3815. No credit cards. $*

PICNIC SPOTS Of the two picnic spots inside the park, the **Grotto Picnic Area** is the largest and most developed. In the heart of Zion Canyon not far from the lodge, this area is equipped with fire grates, picnic tables, water, rest rooms, and even grass. The other, a small primitive area with tables and pit toilets, is at the end of the Kolob Canyons Road, in the northwest corner of the park. Picnic supplies are available at the small general stores in Springdale or just outside the east entrance. The best place to pick up supplies in the Kolob Canyons area is in Cedar City.

LODGING

Finding a room or campsite in summer or during holiday weekends isn't easy, even in Cedar City or St. George. Plan to arrive early in the day or make reservations well in advance. The most convenient places to stay outside the park are in Springdale, just outside the south entrance, or in neighboring Rockville. Both border the park, which means you can enjoy Zion scenery even though you're staying in town.

Those looking for an authentic brush with rural Utah should consider staying at a bed-and-breakfast, where fluffy towels and good home cooking make you feel as though you're visiting friends. Alternatively, if a swimming pool or hot tub beckon after a day of hiking, a motel in Springdale might be your ticket.

INSIDE THE PARK **Zion Lodge.** The motel-like units and cabins of this property, the only lodging within the park, are booked every night in summer and early fall. The 1920s lodge burned in 1966 but was quickly rebuilt that year, and its exterior was restored to resemble the original. Stone columns hold up the large terrace off the dining room, which was rebuilt using native timber. The modern motel units are spacious, and all have porches or private balconies that open onto splendid canyon views. The 40 private cabins are more rustic, but all have large stone fireplaces (gas-burning) and porches. These are more desirable than the motel units, even though they cost more. The noticeable absence of TV forces guests into the great outdoors. Reservations should be made well in advance, although in winter, rooms can usually be booked on arrival. *Zion National Park, Box 400, Cedar City, UT 84720, tel. 435/586–7686 for reservations, 435/772–3213 for reception, fax 435/586–3157 or 801/586–3157. 121 rooms and cabins. Facilities: restaurant. AE, DC, MC, V. $$–$$$*

NEAR THE PARK **Harvest House Bed-and-Breakfast.** Barbara and Steven Cooper came to Zion for a visit and just couldn't leave. Barbara, the former co-owner and head chef of the Boston-based Harvest Catering Company, delights visitors with fresh homemade pastries, preserves, and other treats. The pioneer-style house has a big front porch, a hot tub with views of Zion Canyon, a koy pond, and four individually decorated rooms displaying the work of local photographers. *29 Canyon View Dr., Box 125, Springdale, UT 84767, tel. 435/772–3880. 4 rooms. Facilities: hot tub. MC, V. $$$*

Zion Park Inn. This is one of the newest properties in Springdale and also one of the most elegant, with balconies overlooking the Virgin River. There are views of Zion Canyon from the well-landscaped swimming pool. The lobby, with its fine artwork and open windows, is a good place to enjoy a few quiet moments. *1215 Zion Park Blvd., Springdale, UT 84767, tel. 435/772–3200 or 800/934–7275, fax 435/772–2449. 120 rooms. Facilities: pool, hot tub. AE, D, DC, MC, V. $$$*

Best Western Driftwood Lodge. On well-manicured grounds, this standard motel has a nicely landscaped swimming pool. *1515 Zion Park Blvd., Box 98, Springdale, UT 84767, tel. 435/772–3702. 47 rooms with bath. Facilities: pool, hot tub. AE, D, DC, MC, V. $$–$$$*

Cliffrose Lodge and Gardens. A quarter mile from the park's south entrance, surrounded by botanical gardens and acres of lawn and trees, this hotel guarantees a quiet night's sleep. Rooms are spacious, with balconies that look out on Zion Canyon and Watchman Mountain. *281 Zion Park Blvd., Springdale, UT 84767, tel. 435/772–3234 or 800/243–8824, fax 435/772–3900. 36 rooms with bath. Facilities: pool. AE, D, MC, V. $$–$$$*

O'Toole's Under the Eaves Guest House. Built in 1935 of sandstone blocks cut from the canyon walls, this antiques-filled B&B has served at various times as the Springdale post office, school, and library. New owners have refinished the hardwood floors and painted the interior walls. A full breakfast often includes homemade muffins and quiche. *980 Zion Park Blvd., Box 29, Springdale, UT 84767, tel. 435/772–3457, fax 435/ 772–3324. 6 rooms, 4 with bath. MC, V. $$–$$$*

Thunderbird Best Western. This has just what you would expect from a Best Western: clean, comfortable rooms and friendly service. Some rooms have views of the nearby golf course. *U.S. 89 and Rte. 9, Mt. Carmel Junction, Box 36, UT 84755, tel. 435/648–2203 or 800/528–1234. 61 rooms. Facilities: pool, hot tub. AE, D, DC, MC, V. $$–$$$*

Canyon Ranch Motel. With both cottages and motel rooms along a paved road back from the highway, this is a great place for families. Many visitors choose rooms with kitchenettes. There are lawn swings on a central grassy area, and shade trees and picnic tables. The location, just .5 mi from the park, cuts driving time substantially. *668 Zion Park Blvd., Box 175, Springdale, UT 84767, tel. 435/772–3357, fax 435/772– 3057. 21 units. Facilities: pool, hot tub. D, MC, V. $$*

Flanigans. Kelly-green carpets and pastel southwestern furnishings contribute to the appeal of this property, which resembles a big log cabin from the outside. Tranquil paths lead to the pool area. *428 Zion Park Blvd., Box 100, Springdale, UT 84767, tel. 435/772–3244 or 800/765–7787, fax 435/ 772–3396. 36 rooms with bath. Facilities: pool. AE, D, DC, MC, V. $$*

Handcart House Bed-and-Breakfast. This stucco home, filled with antiques, was built in the Mormon pioneer style in honor of the owners' ancestors, who pulled handcarts across the country. The generous breakfast is served with a local prickly-pear jelly. *244 W. Main St., Box 146, Rockville, UT 84763, tel. 435/772–3867, fax 435/772– 3165. 4 rooms. AE, MC, V. $$*

Pioneer Lodge. A mile from the park entrance, this large, Western-style motel has wood-trim railings and a restaurant with old wagon wheels hanging above the front doors. *838 Zion Park Blvd., Box 480, Springdale, UT 84767, tel. 435/772–3233. 44 rooms. Facilities: pool, hot tub. AE, D, MC, V. $$*

Zion Canyon Campground Cabins. These cabins are on the grounds of a private RV park, near the Virgin River—a great place to be on a hot summer day. Two people can sleep in each cabin, and one family unit accommodates four. *479 Zion Park Blvd., Box 99, Springdale, UT 84767, tel. 435/ 772–3237. 12 cabins. Facilities: pizzeria, recreation room, coin laundry. MC, V. $$*

Zion Park Motel. Set in the center of downtown Springdale, this motel has its own adjacent general market. It's convenient to everything, but a bit on the bland side. *855 Zion Park Blvd., Box 365, Springdale, UT 84767, tel. 435/772–3251. 23 rooms. Facilities: pool, coin laundry. AE, D, MC, V. $$*

Blue House Bed-and-Breakfast. Here you can watch sunrise break over the jagged sentinels at the entrance to Zion or contemplate an orchard framed by red cliffs. The blue frame house with white trim is decorated with plush carpets, floral bedspreads, wicker, and oak. The ample breakfast, complete with homemade preserves, makes a night here a steal. *125 E. Main St., Box 176, Rockville, UT 84763, tel. 435/772–3912. 3 rooms, 1 with bath. MC, V. $–$$*

CAMPING

INSIDE THE PARK In high season, Zion's two large campgrounds, the 140-site **South Campground** and the 229-site **Watchman,** fill almost every night. These facilities near the park's south entrance resemble those in other national parks, with spacious sites and well-maintained rest rooms with cold running water. Both campgrounds have flush toilets, drinking water, fire grates, a disposal station, and a public phone. Although both areas have sites that are large enough for RVs, neither has hookups or showers. Only Watchman is open year-round; South Campground is open from

ZION CAMPGROUNDS

	INSIDE THE PARK			NEAR THE PARK				
	South	Watchman	Lava Point	Coral Pink Sand Dunes State Park	Snow Canyon State Park	Zion Canyon	East Zion RV Park	Bryce/Zion KOA
Total number of sites	140	229	6	22	36	150	15	81
Sites suitable for RVs	140	140	6	22	36	100	15	59
Number of hookups	0	0	0	0	14	100	15	19
Drive to sites	•	•	•	•	•	•	•	•
Hike to sites								
Flush toilets	•	•		•	•	•	•	•
Pit/chemical toilets			•					
Drinking water	•	•		•	•	•	•	•
Showers				•	•	•		•
Fire grates	•	•	•		•	•		
Swimming						•		•
Boat access								
Playground				•	•	•		•
Disposal station	•	•		•	•	•	•	•
Ranger station				•	•			
Public telephone	•	•			•	•	•	•
Reservation possible			•*	•*	•	•	•	•
Daily fee per site	$10	$10	free	$11	$11–$15	$15–$19	$12	$15–$18.50
Dates open	mid-Apr.–Sept.	year-round	early June–mid-Oct.	year-round	year-round	year-round	Mar.–Nov.	early May–mid-Oct.

*Reservation fee charged.

mid-April to mid-September. These campgrounds are set beneath cottonwood trees near the Virgin River; the best sites are closest to the river and farthest from the road. Both charge $10 per site per night.

The only other campground in the park is the small, primitive **Lava Point,** a free campground with six sites for tents or RVs. These sites have fire grates, but there is no water at Lava Point. It is off the beaten track, on the northern edge of the park, so before you head out, ask at the visitor center if space is available. Lava Point is open from early June to mid-October. Reservations are not accepted for any park campground.

NEAR THE PARK Some of the best camping facilities, especially for tenters, are in the nearby **Coral Pink Sand Dunes State Park** (tel. 435/874–2408). The 22-site campground here tends to be less crowded than those at Zion. Coral Pink's campground has flush toilets, hot showers, drinking water, fire grates, a disposal station, and a ranger station. It is open year-round. All sites cost $11 but there are no hookups. The one group site at Coral Pink does have electricity and can accommodate up to 40 people or five vehicles (call ahead to inquire about the availability of this site). Be aware that 80% of Coral Pink's visitors come to use their off-road vehicles (ATVs and dune buggies) on the 5-mi stretch of sand dunes. Evening quiet hours are strictly enforced, however, so families can still enjoy a good night's sleep. Coral Pink is roughly 10 mi south of Mt. Carmel Junction on U.S. 89 (25 mi from Zion) and a natural place to stop during a journey between Zion and the Grand Canyon's North Rim.

Sixty miles southwest of Zion, on the way to Las Vegas and Death Valley, is **Snow Canyon State Park** (tel. 435/628–2255), which has a 36-site campground set in striking sandstone coves, surrounded by juniper trees. This campground also has flush toilets, hot showers, drinking water, fire grates, a disposal station, a ranger station, and a public phone. It is open year-round. There

are 14 electricity and water hookups for RVs as well as a playground. Tent sites cost $11 and RV sites cost $15 per night.

Reservations are recommended at all Utah state parks, especially in summer. Call 800/322–3770 weekdays from 8 to 5, or write to the Utah Department of Natural Resources (1636 W. North Temple St., Suite 116, Salt Lake City, UT 84116). There is a reservation service charge of $5 per site in addition to the camp fee.

Several good private facilities near the park have RV hookups. The closest is the **Zion Canyon Campground** (Box 99, Springdale, UT 84767, tel. 435/772–3237), about a half mile south of the south entrance and open year-round. This campground has 106 sites, 100 of which are gravel, with full hookups. It is surrounded on three sides by the park's rock formations, and many of the sites are on the river. Facilities include flush toilets, showers, drinking water, fire grates, a disposal station, a public phone, a laundry room, a playground, a game room, and a restaurant. There is swimming in the Virgin River. A site with a hookup costs $19 for two people; without a hookup it's $15 for two. Reservations are requested by mail one month in advance.

In Mt. Carmel Junction, 15 mi east of the east entrance, at the junction of Route 9 and U.S. 89, the 15-site **East Zion RV Park** (tel. 435/648–2326) is little more than a gravel parking lot at the junction of two busy roads. There are, however, a golf course and two restaurants across the street. Sites cost $12 per night, and reservations, though generally not necessary, can be made by phone. It's closed from December through February.

Those headed to or from Bryce Canyon National Park might want to stop at the **Bryce/Zion KOA,** on U.S. 89, about 50 mi from both Bryce and Zion and 90 minutes from the Grand Canyon. This secluded campground is set amid juniper and oak trees at the base of majestic pink cliffs. It has 59 RV sites (30 water/electric and 19 full hookups) and 22 tent sites as well as two large group sites that can each accommodate up to 40 people. There are flush toilets, hot showers, drinking water, fire grates, a disposal station, and a public phone here. Laundry facilities and a general store are convenient additions, and the playground, swimming pool, hiking trails, and guided horse tours will keep campers busy. The KOA is closed from October 15 to May 1. Sites cost $15 to $18.50 and should be reserved in advance. Contact Glendale KOA, Box 186, Glendale, UT 84729, tel. 435/648–2490.

Huge campgrounds and trailer parks in the towns of Hurricane (29 mi away) and St. George (43 mi away) cater primarily to the area's growing retirement community. Some have golf courses and most have swimming pools. Since they tend to attract "snowbirds," summer rates here generally range from $9 to $11 for two people, while full hookups cost as much as $20. These campgrounds almost always have space available.